PRAISE FOR
PATTON AT THE BATTLE OF THE BULGE

"In *Patton at the Battle of the Bulge*, Leo Barron captures the fiery general's commanding presence and the pivotal commitment of his Third Army tanks to relieve the embattled crossroads town of Bastogne. Painstakingly researched and highly readable, the latest work by Barron is a significant contribution to the analysis of the great commander, the endurance of his great army, and the resounding American victory in the great battle."

—Michael E. Haskew, author of *West Point 1915: Eisenhower, Bradley, and the Class the Stars Fell On*

"Patton's battlefield successes were many, but his counterattack to relieve the encircled defenders of Bastogne ranks among his highest achievements. In *Patton at the Battle of the Bulge*, Leo Barron masterfully describes the vigor and sheer determination of Patton's drive. His narrative serves as a perfect complement to *No Silent Night*, his previous book, which described in great fashion the defense of Bastogne. Together, the two volumes not only preserve the history of famed units such as the 4th Armored Division and 101st Airborne, but they cast fresh light on aspects of the battle not detailed in other accounts."

—Don M. Fox, author of *Patton's Vanguard: The United States Army Fourth Armored Division*

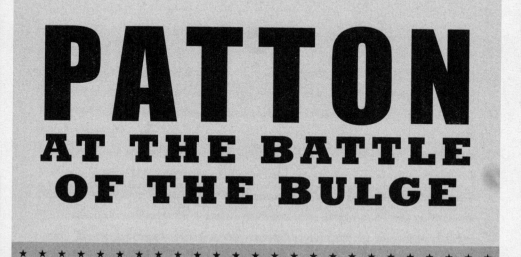

PATTON
AT THE BATTLE
OF THE BULGE

HOW THE GENERAL'S TANKS
TURNED THE TIDE AT BASTOGNE

LEO BARRON

NAL
CALIBER

NAL CALIBER
Published by New American Library,
an imprint of Penguin Random House LLC
375 Hudson Street, New York, New York 10014

This book is a publication of New American Library.
Previously published in an NAL Caliber hardcover edition.

First NAL Caliber Trade Paperback Printing, November 2015

Copyright © Leo Barron, 2014
Maps by Chris Erichsen

For more information about Penguin Random House, visit penguinrandomhouse.com.

NAL CALIBER TRADE PAPERBACK ISBN: 978-0-451-46788-1

THE LIBRARY OF CONGRESS HAS CATALOGED THE HARDCOVER EDITION OF THIS TITLE AS FOLLOWS:

Barron, Leo.
Patton at the Battle of the Bulge: how the general's tanks turned the tide at Bastogne/Leo Barron.
p.   cm.
ISBN 978-0-451-46787-4
1. Ardennes, Battle of the, 1944–1945.   2. Patton, George S. (George Smith), 1885–1945—
Military leadership.   3. World War, 1939–1945—Campaigns—Belgium—Bastogne.   I.Title.
D756.5.A7B258   2014   2014019906
940.54'219348—dc23

Printed in the United States of America
1   3   5   7   9   10   8   6   4   2

Set in Adobe Garamond Pro   •   Designed by Elke Sigal

Penguin
Random
House

CONTENTS

★ ★ ★ ★ ★

Preface		*vii*
Prologue	"MOVE ALL NIGHT!"	*1*
Chapter 1	THE GERMAN PLAN	*9*
Chapter 2	THE AMERICAN RESPONSE	*42*
Chapter 3	FIRST CONTACT	*76*
Chapter 4	CHAUMONT	*111*
Chapter 5	FLATZBOURHOF	*143*
Chapter 6	WARNACH	*176*
Chapter 7	BIGONVILLE	*203*
Chapter 8	TINTANGE	*236*
Chapter 9	CHAUMONT II	*262*
Chapter 10	ASSENOIS	*278*
Epilogue		*324*
Works Cited		*333*
Endnotes		*365*
Index		*411*

PREFACE

★　★　★　★

The Battle of the Bulge, fought between December 16, 1944, and January 25, 1945, was the bloodiest month in the United States Army's history. The U.S. Army in Europe sustained 77,726 casualties in December, and incurred a further 69,119 casualties in January. In December, 15,333 soldiers and airmen lost their lives, and January was not much better: An additional 12,190 soldiers and airmen perished. In total, in those two months our country sustained 146,845 casualties, and of those, 27,523 were deaths. Most of those occurred in that forty-day period when Germany and the United States were locked in the largest battle of the Western Front.

In contrast, in July 1863, the month of Gettysburg and Vicksburg, our country, both North and South, suffered 120,426 casualties combined. In fifty-one days, from May through June 1864, when the battles of the Wilderness, Spotsylvania Courthouse, and Cold Harbor raged, the butcher's bill was 146,046 casualties. The only other bloodletting that came close to the Bulge's total was during the forty-seven days of the Meuse-Argonne Offensive in October and November 1918, when the U.S. Army Expeditionary Force lost 122,063 men, and of those, 26,277 were deaths.

In short, the Battle of the Bulge was truly a national sacrifice, on par with the battles of Gettysburg and the Meuse-Argonne. Citizens of Belgium and Luxembourg still remember our sacrifice and annually commemorate the events of those dark days. Yet many of our own students know little about the Bulge. Their lack of historical appreciation is the number one reason why I chose this subject.

Yet it is not the only reason. The Bulge and the Siege of Bastogne are also compelling stories. When Don Cygan and I decided to publish *No Silent Night:*

The Christmas Battle for Bastogne, I already had planned to write the sequel, because the story about Bastogne is a two-part saga. The most popular is the account about the 101st Airborne Division and its epic defense of the city. However, every story about a besieged force usually has two armies involved: the besieged and the forces sent to relieve them. Now is the time to tell the tale of Patton's 4th Armored Division and their race to relieve the paratroopers and glider men of the 101st.

Like *No Silent Night*, *Patton at the Battle of the Bulge* provides a German viewpoint to contrast with the American perspective. This story follows several German soldiers who fought with the 5th Fallschirmjäger Division. Contrary to popular myth, not all German soldiers were monsters. In this book are several examples where German soldiers showed remarkable kindness and mercy toward their sworn enemies, the American army. Sadly, there are also examples of brutality, where German soldiers executed innocent Belgian civilians.

True, Belgian civilians did perish as a result of American bombs, but those bombs were not meant for the hapless civilians hiding in houses and huddling in cellars. Surgical strikes did not exist in 1944 and 1945, because bombings were far less accurate in World War II than they are today. My research revealed several incidents where Allied aircraft even strafed and bombed *American* tanks instead of German panzers. In the cloud of war, good intentions did not always result in accurate targeting. On the other hand, the Germans did intend to execute civilians.

Furthermore, this work provides a civilian point of view. For those living in the path of these armies, the days around Christmas were harrowing ones. In many cases, they exhibited as much amazing courage and selfless sacrifice as the soldiers and tankers who fought among them. This book is also a story about them.

In addition, I dramatize the German operational briefings, turning them into dialogues. I know some purists might balk at that technique, but I want to present an enthralling story, not a dry account. The words in the briefings are almost entirely verbatim from the sources. In many instances, all I added were quotation marks.

Patton at the Battle of the Bulge, like all good books, was a collaborative effort. I made use of several German and local accounts, for which I would like to thank Roland Gaul, who provided them, including several valuable video interviews and letters; Guy Ries and his website on Bigonville. Jürg Herzig also gave me the lengthy account of Conrad Klemment, which proved indispensable in this story. I would like to thank Ivan Steenkiste, who was crucial in supplying me with information about the battles around Chaumont. His website is a treasure trove of information.

On the American side, I would like to offer my gratitude to several individuals. Jamie Leach, the son of Jimmie Leach, was an excellent resource in regard to his father. His father's 37th Tank Battalion radio logs, complete with notations, were a wealth of information. Rochelle Dwight gave me great material on her father, William Dwight. She still sends me hilarious daily e-mails that make me laugh. I would like to thank Robert T. Murrell, an 80th Infantry Division veteran, who helped me find information on the 318th Infantry Regiment. Andrew Adkins, the archivist for the 80th Infantry Division website, was hugely instrumental in assisting me with personnel records and personal stories from the 318th. I would like to extend my thanks to Chris Bucholtz and Lynn Gamma, who helped me with finding records concerning the 362nd Fighter Group. I would like to thank Doris Davis, an executive officer for the Veterans of the Battle of the Bulge Association. Without her help, I would have never been able to contact countless veterans and their families.

Most important are the veterans and their families who provided me their accounts via questionnaires, letters, or interviews. The following accounts were invaluable to the story of the 4th Armored Division and their support elements: Roscoe M. Mulvey Jr., Armand Poirier, Bob Shaw, Jim Sanders, William Leaphart, Howard Lipscomb, Irving Heath, George Whitten, Robert Calvert, Matteo Damiano, Michael George, Eugene Wright, John P. Tvrdovsky, the family of Jack Holmes, Albert Gaydos and the Gaydos family, and Raymond Green. A special thanks goes out to Irving Heath, who provided me his personal photo album from the war. In addition to Irving Heath, another special thanks goes out to Robert Riley's family, especially his daughter, Linda Riggs, who provided me several written accounts about his wartime experiences. Of course, one of the most valuable interviews was with retired brigadier general Albin F. Irzyk. I spent several hours speaking with him about his experiences. His memory was as sharp as a tack, and it was a wonderful experience providing him with information on the Germans who fought his unit at Chaumont. His autobiography was also an amazing source of information about the 4th Armored Division.

In addition to veterans' interviews, several researchers and archivists also supported me in this endeavor. I would like to thank Dieter Stenger, who once again translated dozens of German documents into English. I would like to thank Susan Strange and Tim Frank, who spent innumerable hours poring over documents in the National Archives at College Park, Maryland. Without them, I would not have had thousands of valuable primary sources to examine. William Murray was my researcher at the Army Historical Education Center and helped me with the Oscar W. Koch collection, which was essential to the 4th Armored Division story. Megan Harris was my contact at the Library of Congress's Veterans Oral History Project. Her assistance was instrumental in my success. Javier Tome, a specialist on the 653rd Schwere Panzerjäger Battalion, sent to me some interesting information on the whereabouts of the 653rd, and his contribution helped me answer the question of who attacked Major Albin Irzyk on December 23 in Chaumont.

I would be remiss if I did not mention Don M. Fox, author of *Patton's Vanguard: The United States Army Fourth Armored Division*. A good historian always builds on the work of other great historians. Don's book was my introduction to the 4th Armored Division. Though I had known about the 4th Armored, it was always in a supporting role to the 101st. After reading Don's book, I realized how special the 4th Armored Division truly was, and I decided to start where he left off. Furthermore, his personal input helped me clear up several issues. His work was first-rate, and it still is the seminal book on the 4th Armored's impact in the Second World War.

I would like to thank my agent, George Bick. His excellent advice pointed me in the right direction, and he is a superb sounding board for ideas. I would also like to thank Talia Platz, my editor, who offered me another chance at NAL Caliber. I hope you do not regret it! I cannot forget Brent Howard, who was my second editor at NAL. Thank you for your title ideas. I owe a debt of gratitude to General Dynamics and the U.S. Army Intelligence Center, which continue to employ me as an instructor at the Military Intelligence Officer Transition Course. Thank you for indulging my research pursuits and allowing me to use the same data from my books to teach future military intelligence officers in the United States Army.

Last, I would like to thank my wonderful wife, Caulyne. No man is an island, and without her support, none of this would have happened. She is the rock in our marriage, and she is my better half.[1]

PROLOGUE

"MOVE ALL NIGHT!"

★ ★ ★ ★ ★

Lead Platoon, Dog Company,
8th Tank Battalion, 4th Armored Division,
Southern Outskirts of Chaumont, Belgium

Private Bruce Fenchel knew Christmas was canceled the moment his first sergeant had barged into his room more than ninety-six hours before and announced, "Pack your duffel bags and get ready to roll. One man go to the kitchen and take any food you can get."

Fenchel had been writing a letter to his mother when the sergeant broke the news, and a collective moan arose from the men. *So much for R & R,* thought Fenchel. Unmoved, the sergeant continued to bark out orders. "The rest of you put the machine guns back on your tanks and gas them and be ready to roll in two hours. The Germans have broken through our line in Bastogne, and Eisenhower has ordered General Patton's 4th Armored to immediately head north."

Twenty-year-old Fenchel could not believe it. His unit, the 8th Tank Battalion, part of the 4th Armored Division, had been locked in combat for months. Now, after more than eighty days on the line, the Eight Ballers were taking a much-needed break. Unfortunately, the Germans had other plans for the hol-

★ I ★

idays. Instead of relaxing for Christmas, Fenchel and the rest of his division were driving back into battle.

Two years before, Bruce Donald Fenchel thought he was joining the Army Air Force. At his induction center at Camp Dodge, Des Moines, Iowa, he had taken several tests and passed all with flying colors. To his surprise, he learned that instead he was going to Fort Knox, Kentucky, where he would learn to drive a tank. Initially crestfallen, he remembered that his induction center company commander had suggested that he apply to Officer Candidate School and become an infantry officer. Fenchel knew that an infantry officer had a short life span. Tanks seemed a whole lot safer than being a bullet catcher—a foot soldier. He decided against the move, and was off to Fort Knox.[1]

Now, Fenchel's 8th Tank Battalion was under the command of a promising young officer, Major Albin F. Irzyk, who like Fenchel was also in his twenties. Irzyk did not waste much time. Receiving the order to move out, he had pushed his battalion onto the roads early on the morning of December 19. All day and night Fenchel and battalion rolled northward from their staging area at Domnom-lès-Dieuze in Lorraine, France, all the way into Belgium. By the morning of the twenty-third, they had reached a point several kilometers south of the village of Chaumont.

The 8th Tank Battalion was part of a larger force known as Combat Command B of the 4th Armored Division. A U.S. Armored Division had three combat commands: A, B, and R (Reserve). Each was a combined arms team that usually was comprised of a tank battalion, an armored infantry battalion, a self-propelled artillery battalion, an assortment of engineers, motorized cavalry (jeeps), and other support units. In addition, each command would further divide its force into task forces, cross-loading various infantry units with armor units. Therefore, 8th Tank Battalion had infantry and tanks as it wound its way north to Bastogne that early morning. Their mission: Get to Bastogne and relieve the 101st Airborne Division before the Germans crushed the beleaguered paratroopers.[2]

Despite the importance of the task ahead, Fenchel simply wanted to stay warm and get some sleep. After clearing the town of Burnon during the previous afternoon, the young tank driver had assumed his unit would establish a perimeter for the night and continue their advance the following morning. He was wrong.

At 1834 hours, the orders came down from Combat Command B Headquarters over the radio: "Push onto Checkpoint Forty-four all night."

A radio operator from another unit asked higher headquarters to confirm the order. It took them only seven minutes to reply: "We are moving on CP Forty-four all night. On foot if necessary." Everyone now knew the command was probably coming from the top man himself—Lieutenant General George S. Patton.[3]

Patton, the commander of the U.S. Third Army, sensed that the road to Bastogne was open. His army's spearhead was the 4th Armored Division, and leading the 4th was CCB. At the forefront of Patton's entire army was Private Fenchel in his little Stuart tank. So far, the 4th had met only determined resistance near Martelange, several kilometers southeast of Fenchel's current position.[4]

During World War II, armored units rarely conducted operations during hours of limited visibility. Unlike today, troopers back then did not have night-vision goggles. They drove their vehicles almost bumper-to-bumper, their eyes fixed on the slivers of light in front of them emanating from the partially covered headlights. These covered lights, known as "cat's eyes," barely gave off enough light for a man to see, and if he fell too far behind, he would lose sight of the vehicle in front of him.

Major Irzyk, deciding that the more maneuverable Stuarts and jeeps might be better suited to driving at night than the heavier and slower Shermans, ordered a platoon of jeeps from Baker Troop, 25th Cavalry Squadron, followed by a platoon of light tanks from Dog Company, to take the lead. Around 2300 hours, after they had completed their refueling, his battalion resumed their progress northward. It was slow going. Coupled with a lack of sleep, Fenchel had a hard time staying focused on the vehicle in front of him. At one point, he lost sight of the cat's eyes. When he found them again, it was too late, and his tank crashed into the rear of another tank in his platoon. Luckily, no one was hurt and neither vehicle was damaged.[5]

Finally, after several hours they reached a point about a kilometer and a half south of Chaumont. The top of the sun was barely over the eastern horizon, illuminating the shapes of the woods and open fields that bordered the road. During the night, Fenchel's column had received intermittent small-arms fire, but nothing serious. Still, tanks were fickle creatures that demanded constant upkeep. Several Stuarts pulled off the road and their crews began routine maintenance while cavalry troopers in their jeeps scouted ahead to provide security.

Suddenly, at around 0845 hours, Germans from the 5th Fallschirmjäger Division opened up with machine guns and Panzerfausts from the woods that lined both sides of the road, catching the column in a deadly cross fire. From along a ridge in the distance, StuG self-propelled assault guns flashed, followed by a deafening crack. Almost instantly, an American jeep exploded, killing all the occupants. The burning vehicle cast an eerie, flickering shadow across the pearl-white snow as it rolled to a stop by a tree.[6] The Germans turned their barrage to another jeep, which also burst into flame.

Fenchel recalled that "most of the men were out of their tanks, and then it—just as day broke—it just appeared that that whole ridge was moving toward us, and that whole ridge was just column after column of German tanks."

Several American Stuart tanks opened up with their machine guns, directing most of their fire toward a piece of high ground several hundred meters north of the Lambay Chênet Woods, which bordered the road to the east. Meanwhile, Irzyk ordered the M5 Stuart light tanks to flush out the German defenders and prevent the enemy from bottling up the column on the road. The drivers pushed hard on their control sticks and the tanks lurched forward onto the hardened fields separating the road and the wood line.[7]

The ferocity of the German ambush dashed Irzyk's hope that the 4th Armored Division would roll to Bastogne with little difficulty. As he received initial reports of casualties, the major knew that he had an arduous fight on his hands. But he had no other options. The paratroopers of the 101st Airborne Division were low on supplies. The 4th simply had to break through. It was a race to see who would reach Bastogne first—German panzers or American Shermans. "Patton's Best" was the unofficial name for the division, and now Patton wanted them to prove it—again.[8]

4TH ARMORED DIVISON: MAJOR GENERAL GAFFEY

★

25th Cavalry Squadron (Mechanized)*: Lieutenant Colonel Goodall
24th Armored Engineer Battalion*: Major Hatch
704th Tank Destroyer Battalion (M18 Hellcats)*: Major Kimsey
489th Antiaircraft Artillery Battalion*: Lieutenant Colonel Murphy

---

COMBAT COMMAND A
Brigadier General Earnest

35th Tank Battalion:
Lieutenant Colonel Oden

  A Company (MED):
  First Lieutenant Barrett

  B Company (MED)**:
  Captain Boller
  First Lieutenant Kingsley

  C Company (MED):
  Captain Berky

  D Company (LIGHT):
  Captain Ridley

51st Armored Infantry Battalion:
Major Alanis

  A Company:
  Unknown

  B Company:
  First Lieutenant Belden

  C Company**:
  Captain Rankin
  First Lieutenant Green

66th Armored Field Artillery BN:
Lieutenant Colonel Wallace

1st Battalion, 318th Infantry***:
Major Connaughton

  A Company:
  First Lieutenant Goerke

  B Company:
  Captain McAllister

  C Company:
  First Lieutenant Santner

COMBAT COMMAND B:
Brigadier General Dager

8th Tank Battalion:
Major Irzyk

  A Company (MED):
  First Lieutenant Kieley

  B Company (MED):
  First Lieutenant Fishler

  C Company (MED):
  First Lieutenant Stephenson

  D Company (LIGHT):
  First Lieutenant Erdnann

10th Armored Infantry Battalion:
Major Cohen

  A Company:
  First Lieutenant Gniot

  B Company:
  First Lieutenant Lange

  C Company:
  Unknown

22nd Armored Field Artillery BN:
Lieutenant Colonel Peterson

2nd Battalion, 318th Infantry***:
Lieutenant Colonel Gardner

  E Company:
  Captain Kirkman

  F Company:
  First Lieutenant Singleton

  G Company:
  Captain Stalling

COMBAT COMMAND RESERVE
Colonel Blanchard

37th Tank Battalion:
Lieutenant Colonel Abrams

  A Company (MED):
  First Lieutenant Whitehill

  B Company (MED):
  Captain Leach

  C Company (MED)**:
  Captain Trover
  First Lieutenant Boggess

  D Company (LIGHT):
  First Lieutenant Donahue

53rd Armored Infantry Battalion:
Lieutenant Colonel Jaques

  A Company:
  First Lieutenant Kutak

  B Company:
  Unknown

  C Company:
  First Lieutenant Smith

94th Armored Field Artillery BN:
Major Parker

---

*The companies/batteries from these units were routinely split up amongst the various combat commands throughout the Bulge campaign, while others remained in a general support role under the division headquarters. Hence, I only included the major maneuver and fire support units under their respective combat command. This was basically the order of battle for December 22 to 26, 1944. The 704th Tank Destroyer and 489th AAA Battalions were not part of the 4th Armored Division, but were attached to the 4th Armored so often that they were treated as part of the division. I also did not include the Headquarters and Headquarters Companies (HHC) and Service companies on this list. Though both HHCs and Service companies were pivotal, due to spacing issues, I chose not to include them on this list.

**Two names for one command slot indicate that the first commander was either wounded, killed, or relieved. Sadly, this was common in WWII.

***The two battalions of the 318th Infantry were from the 80th Infantry Division. They were attached to the 4th Armored Division on December 24, 1944.

Additional Division Support Units as of December 21, 1944:

144th Armored Signal Company	444th Quartermaster Truck Company (Corps)
126th Armored Maintenance Battalion	3804th Quartermaster Truck Company (Corps)
46th Medical Battalion, Armored	1st Platoon 16th Field Hospital (Corps)
253rd Armored Field Artillery Battalion (Corps)	995th Engineer Bridge Company (Corp
274th Armored Field Artillery Battalion (Corps)	

5TH FALLSCHIRMJÄGER DIVISON: COLONEL HEILMANN
★

5th Fallschirmjäger Pioneer Battalion*: Major Mertins
5th Fallschirmjäger Mortar Battalion*: Major Gerres
5th Fallschirmjäger Panzerjäger Battalion*: Unknown
5th Fallschirmjäger Artillery Regiment*: Colonel Bernd Wintzer

---

13TH FALLSCHIRMJÄGER REGIMENT
Major Wahl

1st Fallschirmjäger Battalion:
Unknown

  1st Company : Unknown

  2nd Company: Unknown

  3rd Company: Unknown

  4th Company**: Unknown

2nd Fallschirmjäger Battalion:
Captain Metzler

  5th Company: Unknown

  6th Company:
  First Lieutenant Koch

  7th Company:
  First Lieutenant Petrikat

  8th Company**:
  First Lieutenant Saxe

3rd Fallschirmjäger Battalion:
Major Frank

  9th Company : Unknown

  10th Company: Unknown

  11th Company:
  Second Lieutenant Rang

  12th Company**: Unknown

13th Company***:
Unknown

14th Company****:
Unknown

14TH FALLSCHIRMJÄGER REGIMENT
Colonel Schimmel

1st Fallschirmjäger Battalion:
Captain Kroll

  1st Company :
  Second Lieutenant Wenden

  2nd Company:
  Unknown

  3rd Company:
  Second Lieutenant Loebel

  4th Company**:
  Second Lieutenant Raube

2nd Fallschirmjäger Battalion:
Unknown

  5th Company: Unknown

  6th Company: Unknown

  7th Company:
  Second Lieutenant Schmidt

  8th Company**:
  First Lieutenant Groten

3rd Fallschirmjäger Battalion:
Major Ebel

  9th Company :
  First Lieutenant Ehrich

  10th Company: Unknown

  11th Company:
  Second Lieutenant Schwarz

  12th Company**: Unknown

13th Company***:
Unknown

14th Company****:
Second Lieutenant Fessell

15TH FALLSCHIRMJÄGER REGIMENT
Colonel Gröschke

1st Fallschirmjäger Battalion:
Captain Berneike

  1st Company: Unknown

  2nd Company:
  Second Lieutenant Baukowitz

  3rd Company: Unknown

  4th Company**: Unknown

2nd Fallschirmjäger Battalion:
Captain Kitze

  5th Company: Unknown

  6th Company: Unknown

  7th Company:
  Second Lieutenant Stuebe

  8th Company**: Unknown

3rd Fallschirmjäger Battalion:
Captain Heide

  9th Company :
  First Lieutenant Bertram

  10th Company: Unknown

  11th Company: Unknown

  12th Company**:
  Second Lieutenant Peischer

13th Company***: Unknown

14th Company****: Unknown

---

* The companies/batteries from these units were routinely split up amongst the various regimental commands throughout the Bulge campaign, while others remained in a general support role under the division headquarters. Hence, I only included the major maneuver and fire support units under their respective command. This chart represents the 5th Fallschirmjäger Division at 100% strength, which was not the reality in December 1944. Its artillery regiment was not ready, and therefore the 5th FJ Division had to receive its fire support from the corps. In addition, it did not have most of its antitank battalion assets. As a result, it would receive its antitank support from the 11th Assault Brigade. Finally, some of the infantry battalions did not have all of their infantry companies. Not depicted are 5th Fallschirmjäger Signal Battalion and 5th Fallschirmjäger Medical Company.

**The 4th, 8th, and 12th companies were the heavy weapons companies for 1st, 2nd, and 3rd battalions, respectively.

***13th Company was the mortar and infantry gun company for the regiment.

****14th Company was the antitank company for the regiment.

PATTON'S THIRD ARMY AND MILLIKIN'S III CORPS AT THE BEGINNING OF THE BASTOGNE CAMPAIGN

★

III CORPS:	**VIII CORPS:**	**XII CORPS:**	**XX CORPS:**
Major General Millikin	Major General Middleton	Major General Eddy	Major General Walker

4th Armored Division:
Major General Gaffey

26th Infantry Division:
Major General Paul

80th Infantry Division
Major General McBride

CHAPTER 1

THE GERMAN PLAN

| NOVEMBER 6 TO DECEMBER 15, 1944 |

★ ★ ★ ★ ★

"The last chance in a Game of Hazard."

—*Oberst Ludwig Heilmann, Commander of the 5th FJ Division*

Monday, November 6

South of Krefeld, Germany

Headquarters, Army Group B

Death was never far from the mind of Oberst (Colonel) Rudolph-Christoph Freiherr von Gersdorff. With every summons he received to visit some headquarters for a top-secret meeting, he wondered whether the Gestapo had discovered who he really was—a conspirator, a traitor. Yet von Gersdorff *knew* who he was—in his mind, he was a hero. Germany was under the control of a madman, and that madman branded anyone a traitor who dared to question his authority. More than a year ago, von Gersdorff had done more than just question Adolf Hitler—he had tried to kill the Führer on March 21, 1943. In a half-cocked operation, von Gersdorff had planned to blow himself up while standing next to Hitler, using limpet mines at a Berlin captured-weapons exhibition. He had hidden the mines in his coat pockets, planning to hug Hitler seconds before the mines detonated. Unfortunately, as if divine providence or the devil had whispered in Hitler's ear to keep moving, the Führer rushed through the exhibition before von Gersdorff could reach him. Frustrated, von Gersdorff disarmed the mines in a nearby toilet.

Undeterred, the officer from Silesia tried again, joining the plot known as Operation Valkyrie, which led to the July 20, 1944, assassination attempt. When the plot failed and Hitler miraculously survived, the Gestapo ruthlessly rounded up anyone suspected of involvement and summarily executed scores of men like Count Claus von Stauffenberg, who had planted the bomb. Mere suspicion was usually enough to put anyone in front of a firing squad. Yet no one had accused von Gersdorff, despite his deep involvement in both bomb plots.

It had been several months since the last attempt on Hitler's life, and von Gersdorff was now en route to a meeting at Army Group B Headquarters—still alive and still serving the devil. He shook his head and stared out the window of the car. The view outside did little to assuage his fears and disgust. The once bustling city of Krefeld was now a graveyard. The smashed buildings resembled stalagmites, jutting up from the earth, while overhead, the dreary sky kept up a steady torrent of cold rain. Three months after von Gersdorff's botched suicide bombing attempt, British Lancasters and Halifaxes laid waste to the city by dropping more than two thousand tons of bombs. The venerable old town, which had existed since the Middle Ages and survived several wars, perished under the wrath of the RAF.[1]

Von Gersdorff gritted his teeth. Though he blamed Churchill for the bombing, to this proud Silesian, Hitler also shared much of the responsibility for Krefeld's destruction. Hitler had wanted war, and now, with the war clearly lost, the German government should have been seeking peace terms. Instead, Hitler refused to discuss the possibility, and so the interminable fighting continued, and more cities like Krefeld became mass graves.

Von Gersdorff, like many other senior German officers, wondered when the war would end, but continued to do his duty. He had resigned himself to the horror. At least he had tried to stop Hitler, which was more than he could say for many of his fellow officers. Instead of lying in a shallow grave, though, like his fellow conspirators, von Gersdorff was now a colonel and the chief of staff for the Seventh Army. In 1939, he had been a mere captain, and he owed his meteoric rise through the ranks to his skills, but also to attrition. The crucible of war quickly determined which officers were warriors, and which were worthless.

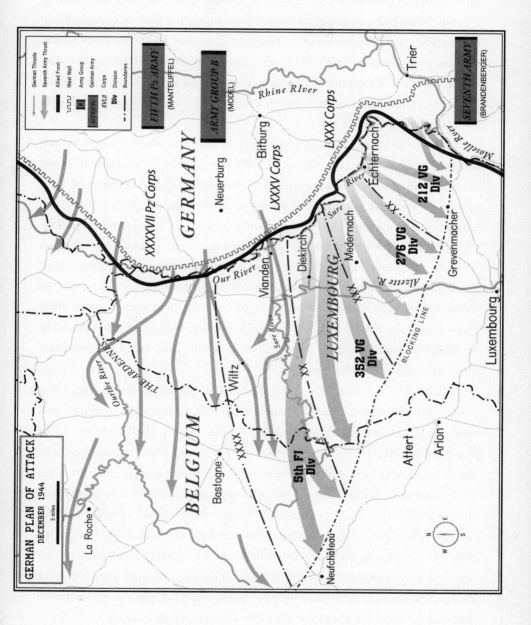

GERMAN PLAN OF ATTACK
DECEMBER 1944

5 miles

German Thrusts
Seventh Army Thrust
Allied Front
West Wall
Army Group
German Army
Corps
Division
Boundaries

XVITH Pz
XVLII
Div

FIFTH Pz ARMY
(MANTEUFFEL)

ARMY GROUP B
(MODEL)

SEVENTH ARMY
(BRANDENBERGER)

GERMANY

Rhine River

Moselle River

Trier

XXXXVII Pz Corps

Neuerburg

Bitburg

LXXXV Corps

LXXX Corps

Echternach

Sure River

212 VG
Div

276 VG
Div

Grevenmacher

Medernach

Alzette R.

Diekirch

Vianden

Our River

Sure River

LUXEMBOURG

352 VG
Div

BLOCKING LINE

Luxembourg

Wiltz

THE ARDENNES

Ourthe River

BELGIUM

Bastogne

5th FJ
Div

Attert

Arlon

La Roche

Neufchâteau

N
E
W
S

Born in 1905 in the town of Lubin, Silesia, the intrepid colonel was only a year shy of forty, but the war had aged him beyond his years. His full head of thick, dark hair had thinned so that it now almost resembled a shaved mohawk.

His father had also served in the army, attaining the rank of major general. Rudolph was too young to serve in the First World War, but he still managed to secure a cadet commission in 1923, when commissions in the Reichswehr were scarce. He reached the rank of lieutenant in 1926 and served in the 7th Cavalry Regiment. Throughout most of the interwar years, von Gersdorff remained in various cavalry units.

In 1938, he attended the War Academy in Berlin to become a general staff officer, and when the war broke out in 1939 he was a captain on the staff of the Fourteenth Army. For the next couple of years he bounced around, serving in various general staff jobs, while simultaneously climbing the ranks. In 1941, he joined the staff of Army Group Center, thanks to General Henning von Tresckow, who introduced him to others who shared his animosity toward Hitler. For two years the conspirators planned, before von Gersdorff conducted his failed suicide bomb attempt. Nine months later he attended the general staff school in Döberitz for future general officers. Upon his completion, he returned to the Western Front and served as the chief of staff for the LXXXVII Corps when the Allies landed in Normandy. By now he was an *Oberst* (colonel), and his hard work had earned him the respect of his peers and superiors.

On July 27, 1944, he became the chief of staff for the Seventh Army. It was not an auspicious start. The U.S. Army's Operation Cobra had begun only two days earlier, and it was the breakout the German army's High Command had feared since D-day. Despite his best efforts, the Allies punched through von Gersdorff's Seventh Army and within several weeks had almost completely surrounded it. Now was the time for escape. Through the perseverance and courage of many officers and soldiers like von Gersdorff, the Seventh survived—barely—and retreated eastward to reach the safety of the Siegfried Line. In recognition of his skills, the German High Command awarded von Gersdorff the Knight's Cross on August 26. The irony probably was not lost on Rudolph. On the day he received his medal for his service to the Third Reich, most of his fellow conspirators were dead and buried, while the German people were feting him as a hero.[2]

Now the war was in its fifth year, and no one could see how it could end well for Germany. Still, he had a duty to his men and to his commander, General Erich Brandenberger, who had ordered him to attend a secret meeting at Army Group B Headquarters, south of Krefeld. When Rudolph arrived, the soldiers standing guard at the front entrance snapped a salute and quickly ushered him inside. It did not take long for the others to arrive, and soon von Gersdorff was with several other army chiefs of staff. First was SS-Brigadeführer Fritz Kraemer, who was a Waffen SS officer and the chief of staff for the SS Sixth Panzer Army. Next to him was Lieutenant General Alfred Gause, the chief of staff of the Fifth Panzer Army. Like Gersdorff, they probably wondered why they were there.[3]

Finally, the door to the room swung open, and General Hans Krebs entered. They exchanged the customary salutations, befitting the ranks of senior officers. *General der Infanterie* Hans Krebs was only few years older than von Gersdorff, and he had held the position of chief of staff of Army Group B since the previous September. A dedicated soldier, he was, like von Gersdorff, a holder of the Knight's Cross.[4]

After several minutes of small talk, Krebs turned to business. "Gentlemen, I must require you to sign an oath swearing absolute secrecy for what I'm about to tell you."

Von Gersdorff could only guess that the other officers were mildly insulted. All had sworn oaths before, and to ask them to swear another seemed like over-kill, especially at this point in the war. Still, they did as they were told and signed. When they were finished, Krebs handed each a message in an envelope. Von Gersdorff opened his and read the coded message to himself. The opening sentence caused his jaw to drop.

"The German war potential enables us," the message read, "by summoning all our powers of organization and by straining every nerve, to form an offensive force by rehabilitating and completely reconstituting the twelve panzer and *panzergrenadier* divisions at present employed on the Western Front, as well as some twenty *volksgrenadier* divisions and two airborne divisions. With the aid of these forces, the last that Germany is able to collect, the Führer intends to mount a decisive offensive. Since such an organization would offer no prospect of a decisive success on the vast Eastern Front, and since a similar operation could not be of decisive strategic significance, he has resolved to unleash his attack from the West Wall. The success of this operation will depend fundamentally upon the degree of surprise achieved. Therefore, the time and place for this offensive will be such as to completely deceive the enemy. Considering the situation, the terrain, and the weather, the enemy will be least likely to expect such an attack shortly before Christmas, from the Eifel, and against a front only thinly held by him. The objective of the offensive will be Antwerp, in order to rob the Allies of this very important supply port and to drive a wedge between the British and the American forces. After achieving the objective, we will annihilate the British and American forces then surrounded in the area of Aachen–Liège—north of Brussels. In the air, the operation will be supported by several thousand of the best and most modern German fighters, which will secure—at least temporarily—supremacy in the air. The most important factor will be first—SURPRISE, and next—SPEED!"[5]

Before von Gersdorff could digest what he had just read, General Krebs presented them with their maps, each stenciled with the respective objectives for each of the three armies. Von Gersdorff unrolled his map while Krebs briefed them on a summary of the concept of the operations.

At the beginning Krebs cautioned the staff officers, "At this time, gentlemen, only your commanding officer, you, your Ia [Operations] officer, and one officer of your choosing can be privy to this operation."

The men nodded their consent, and Krebs continued. Since the SS Sixth Panzer Army was the decisive operation, Krebs outlined its mission first. Then he went over the scheme of maneuver for the Fifth Panzer Army. Finally, he started to brief them on the Seventh Army's objectives, using the map to guide von Gersdorff.

"Oberst von Gersdorff," Krebs began, "the primary mission of your army is the protection of the southern flank of the strong panzer forces of the Fifth Panzer Army." As he spoke, Krebs's finger traced a line that originated at the town of Bastogne and then went to Namur. From there, the line continued westward to Brussels and finally terminated at Antwerp.

"To defend this flank," Krebs continued, "your army will advance to this approximate line." He pointed at several towns on the map. "The line starts in Givet, and then extends eastward to Libramont, on to Martelange, then Mersch, and ends in Wasserbillig."

The *oberst* could see that the task for his army was a daunting one, but he said nothing as Krebs carried on with his brief. The general listed what the Seventh Army would have for this operation. "For the accomplishment of this mission, Army Group B will assign to the Seventh Army the following: three corps staffs, six infantry divisions, one *panzergrenadier* division, several *volks* artillery corps, several battalions of army [Heeres] artillery, two *volks* projector brigades, several artillery brigades to include assault guns, one engineer brigade, one Organization Todt brigade, and six bridging columns."

Krebs concluded his presentation. "Preparations for the offensive will be completed by the end of November. Army Group Headquarters will decide when to reveal the operation to the corps and division staffs, as well the other members of the army staff."

Von Gersdorff accepted the task on behalf of his commander. He did not have a choice. On paper it was a mighty force, but he knew that what existed on paper did not necessarily exist in reality. Krebs probably would not have listened to his doubts anyway.[6]

With that, General Krebs left the room. As the other chiefs of staff gathered their maps and orders as they prepared to leave, von Gersdorff quickly went over the plan in his head. The Herculean task bordered on the impossible. First, the Seventh Army was a shadow of its former self, because the withdrawal from France wrecked the entire army. Some divisions reached the West Wall with only a hundred combat troops, while some of the panzer divisions had only one tank each. In one particular case, the LXXXIV Corps made it to the West Wall with only one working artillery piece. Oberkommando der Wehrmacht (German Army Command, or OKW) would have to rebuild almost entire divisions from scratch. In addition, someone would have to train these replacement soldiers, since many were from the Luftwaffe or Kriegsmarine and, as airmen and seamen, had little experience handling weapons and fighting as infantry. These men would make up the majority of these reconstituted units.

Furthermore, the Allies were not idling along the frontier, allowing the Germans to recover. Instead, the American First Army was hitting hard the area around Aachen, an operation that had continued well into October. General George S. Patton's Third Army was also on the move, having raced across France and slammed into the retreating Army Group G in the Moselle region. To even a civilian, the objectives for the U.S. Twelfth Army Group were obvious. Beyond

Aachen lay the Ruhr river basin, and beyond the Moselle lay the Saar region. Both were the industrial centers of the Reich. Without them, the Nazi war machine would grind to a halt. If the Allies seized the two regions, the war would end in weeks, regardless of Hitler's maniacal plans. As a result, the Allies had focused their combat power in those two sectors, which left a huge gap between them in the Ardennes region, opposite the Eifel.

It was this part of the plan that had merit. German military intelligence had correctly deduced that the Allies, specifically the Americans, were weak in the Ardennes, since it seemed unlikely to them that Germans were going to mount a major offensive from the Eifel. As von Gersdorff knew from experience, the Eifel was unsuitable for major offensive combat operations, especially in the late fall and early winter. Its narrow roads and deep gullies were a nightmare for armored and motorized units, and with the fall rains and winter snows, everything would be roadbound. Therefore, the Americans had left only four divisions to defend it, and those divisions were either green or recovering from the slaughterhouse of the Hürtgen Forest campaign.

Von Gersdorff understood Hitler's reasoning for an attack in the west. Three armies, with a quarter of a million men, would enjoy some tactical success in the east, but the Russians would grind it down like they had done many a German army. Moreover, the Eastern Front was a vast, endless steppe, and strategic objectives were few and far between. To the south, an attack in Italy would do little to relieve the threat to Germany's vital frontiers, especially its industrial region along the Rhine River. On the other hand, Antwerp was only a couple hours by car from the West Wall, and if the Germans captured the port, it would set back the Allied plans by months. In addition, as in May 1940, when the German army trapped a good portion of the French army in Belgium, they could repeat the feat, except the victim this time would be the Americans and the British. Still, it was a long shot, but Hitler wanted to gamble. To von Gersdorff, the Führer would not allow Germany to die a slow death in a war of attrition. No, he wanted to try one last time with a surprise winter offensive. The stakes were high, and the risks were even greater. Despite the odds, Hitler wanted to go down fighting.

The German High Command had made a huge assumption about American intentions. According to their strategic assessment, OKW believed that the Americans would react to the German surprise attack by massing their combat power to prevent a German assault across the Meuse River. Hence, the operation required that the panzer armies reach the Meuse before the Americans could establish a viable defense. The idea that the Americans would instead strike at the flanks of the bulge was something that OKW did not consider. To von Gersdorff, this seemed shortsighted. He was right.[7]

Wednesday, November 29
Seventh Army Headquarters, Camp Falke
Six Kilometers East of Bad Münstereifel, Germany

After several weeks of harried staff work, Oberstleutnant (Lieutenant Colonel) Werner Voigt-Ruscheweyh, the Ia, or operations officer, of the Seventh Army, had finished the initial plan for the winter offensive. Now it was time to conduct a map exercise with the various subordinate corps commanders. As such, Oberst von Gersdorff had summoned them to the Seventh Army Headquarters, east of Bad Münstereifel.

Bad Münstereifel provided a fitting backdrop for the staff exercise. Like many other towns in Rhine-Westphalia, Bad Münstereifel could trace its lineage back to the Middle Ages. Many of its half-timber-framed homes tucked along its narrow cobblestone streets were several hundred years old, while surrounding the town was an impressive stone wall built in the thirteenth and fourteenth centuries. The wall builders, the counts of Jülich, had also built themselves a citadel, which overlooked the town like a sentinel. The quintessential Rhineland town had so far escaped the ravages of war. If the corps commanders, who had gathered together for their exercise, failed in their mission, though, then this quaint town would fall. Even worse, it might end up like Krefeld—a shell, a municipal mausoleum. Von Gersdorff hoped that would not happen, but he had his doubts.[8]

However, he had a meeting to run, and so he put his doubts behind him. All the senior commanders were present, including each of the three corps commanders, General Erich Brandenberger, von Gersdorff's boss and commander of the Seventh Army, and Field Marshal Walter Model, commander of Army Group B and Brandenberger's direct superior. General Brandenberger was older, and his drawn face looked like the American cartoon dog Droopy, his cheeks seeming to dangle slightly over his jaw. He was almost bald, and what little hair he had was shaved, leaving a dark pepper-colored patch at the top of his head. He wore wire-rimmed glasses. Despite his strange appearance, his mind, which years of war had honed like a finely tuned machine, was sharp.

Brandenberger's meritorious career spanned four decades. Born in 1892, he had joined the army in 1911. He fought with distinction in the First World War, serving with the Royal Bavarian Artillery, and for his bravery on the battlefield he was awarded the Iron Cross. During the interwar years, he continued to serve in the artillery as he climbed up the ranks. When the Second World War began, he was the chief of staff of the XXIII Corps, and he participated in the invasion of France in May 1940. The German High Command, rewarding Brandenberger's talents, appointed him the commander of the 8th Panzer Division, which he led during the invasion of Russia that summer. In recognition of his achievements, Adolf Hitler awarded him the Knight's Cross in July 1941. His career did not plateau there. In August of 1943, after reaching the rank of *general der artillerie* (somewhat equivalent to the rank of full general in the U.S. Army), he assumed command of the XXIX Corps. In this role, he continued to earn the praise of his contemporaries on the Eastern Front. Finally, he took over the Seventh Army on August 31, 1944. At the time, the Seventh Army was in tatters, but he managed to nurse it back to health so that it was ready for the Ardennes offensive.[9]

Brandenberger had brought his three corps commanders with him. The first was Dr. Franz Beyer, commander of the LXXX Army Corps. Next to him was General Baptist Knieß, the commander of the LXXXV Army Corps. Knieß was a stocky man who looked more like a fat German baker than a German general. Knieß was seven years older than Brandenberger, and like Brandenberger, he served in World War I, but as an infantry officer. In addition, like his commander, he too earned the Iron Cross in the Great War. After the trenches, he continued to serve as an officer in the Reichswehr. When World War II broke out, he was the commander of the 215th Infantry Division, and he served as its commander for several years through several campaigns, mostly on the Eastern Front. In July 1944, he assumed command of the LXXXV Corps, after having attained the rank of *general der infanterie*, and as the commander of LXXXV Corps, he would lead the initial main effort of the Seventh Army.[10]

The last of the three corps commanders was General der Kavallerie Edwin Graf von Rothkirch und Trach. Rothkirch, born in 1888, bore some resemblance to Hollywood actor Fred Astaire, but unlike Astaire, Rothkirch was an officer in the Royal Prussian Army who had also earned the Iron Cross in the trenches of the First World War. He remained in the cavalry during the interwar years. At the beginning of the Second World War, Rothkirch served in a variety of staff posts before he finally took command of the 330th Infantry Division on the Eastern Front in early January 1942, which he led successfully for several months. In November of 1944, after Hitler promoted him to *general der kavallerie*, Rothkirch became the commander of the newly formed LIII Corps. By the end of November, Rothkirch had only a corps staff and support elements; he did not have a single division or regiment under his direct command. In short, he was a corps commander in name only, but he rightly assumed that would change soon.[11]

Soon the men all huddled around a large map table replete with blocks depicting units and objectives. The Seventh Army operations staff, seeing that everyone was ready, began the brief.

"Gentlemen," one staff officer came forward and announced, as he pointed to the map, "four *volksgrenadier* divisions controlled by two corps will lead the attack. The LXXXV Infantry Corps will be on the right [north], and LXXX Infantry Corps will be on the left [south]. Both will attack abreast in the sector between the towns of Vianden, Wallendorf, and Echternach. They will smash through the enemy front, destroying him in the process. The LXXXV Infantry Corps' immediate objective will be the ridge line and the road from Diekirch to Hosingen." The staff officer, reading from his notes, indicated the location on the map, using a wooden pointer.

When he saw that everyone had found the spot, he continued. "This corps will take this objective before the end of the first day of the attack, and it will continue to advance straight westward, committing—if necessary—its advance reserves in order to seize the crossings over the Clerf and Sauer."

General Baptist Knieß, the thickset commander of the LXXXV Corps, looked closely at the map. He could see the terrain around the Our River was severely restrictive. Steep banks, combined with a fast-moving and swollen river, would make the crossing a difficult proposition. Fortunately, the opponent he faced on the opposite side of the river was a tired one. German intelligence had detected the U.S. Army's 28th Infantry Division, which had recently arrived in the area and was refitting after the bloodbath that was the Hürtgen Forest.

German patrols had reported little activity along the Our River to indicate that the American division was either completely neglecting security (which it was not) or was too spread out (which it was). Either way, Knieß did not expect much resistance from the Americans as his corps tried to cross the Our.[12]

The operations officer continued, tracing another line along the map. "Gentlemen, the 25th Panzergrenadier Division initially will be in the army reserve and behind the right wing following the first day of the attack. It will then be moved across the tank bridge set up in the meantime at Wallendorf. Afterward, this division will push straight ahead through Ettelbruck, to Harlange, and then south of Saint-Hubert, continuing in a westerly direction. It is essential that it maintain contact with the left flank of Fifth Panzer Army and to protect, by aggressive action, the southern flank in the sector of Gedinne and Neufchâteau."

As the men took notes, the briefer glanced over at Count Rothkirch and said, "At this time, the staff of LIII Corps will be placed in operational control of the right wing. The divisions of LXXXV Corps will then go on the defensive, en masse, along the approximate line of Neufchâteau, to Martelange, and finally to Mersch. This will be done so that tactical centers of gravity can be established in accordance with the enemy situation and the anticipated enemy movements along the roads leading north and northeast." Rothkirch acknowledged the briefer, silently nodding.[13]

The officer leaned over and tapped the map with his pointer. "Next, advance elements will push forward rapidly to the Semois sector to reconnoiter the area. In addition, they must deny the crossing sites to the enemy, and to stop, or at least delay, the enemy advance."

He looked up at the audience. "Most important is this: The Seventh Army main effort will definitely be assigned to the right corps [LXXXV and then the LIII Corps]. We will augment this effort with the attachment of two *volks* projector brigades, two *volks* artillery corps, one artillery brigade, which will have self-propelled assault guns, and one heavy tank destroyer battalion. Furthermore, the left corps (LXXX Infantry Corps) will attack with two *volksgrenadier* divisions across the Sauer in the Wallendorf–Echternach sector and then, turning soon thereafter to the south and the southwest, will quickly seize the known enemy artillery area in the vicinity of Medernach, Christnach, and Alt Trier. Then it will conduct a mobile defense along the Wasserbillig–Mersch line, and send strong advance elements into the area north of Luxembourg."

With that, the first portion of the map exercise was complete. Thanks to Werner Voigt-Ruscheweyh's operations staff, everyone in the room had a clear understanding of the upcoming mission. Still, not everyone was satisfied, and many started to discuss various details of the plan. Should the assault start during the hours of darkness? Many in the room felt this was the worst course of action. Their troops were too inexperienced for a nighttime attack, which required the highest degree of training.

The officers debated the type of artillery bombardment that would precede the attack, proposing a short barrage, since they did not have a lot of intelligence on actual American targets. Most of the rounds would likely land in virgin forests and open fields, and not on American positions. Field Marshal Model approved.

The officers proceeded to other topics like the river crossings, the suppression of enemy artillery positions, and the need for an army-level reserve. To Brandenberger, however, the most pressing issue was Patton. While Field Marshal Model and the staff at Army Group B concluded that the American army would strike the Germans at the tip of the bulge, not at the flanks, Brandenberger disagreed. He later wrote:

> Seventh Army, in contrast to this, was firmly convinced that the German operation would evoke a speedy reaction from the enemy. Since it was highly probable that the Franco-Belgian area contained no large reserve, the possibility had to be considered that all available enemy troops in the area of Metz and perhaps also in the sector opposite Army Group G would be brought up for *offensive* action against the southern flank of the attacking German armies. And for that, the roads leading north through Luxembourg and Arlon would be considered first. Seventh Army estimated that strong enemy forces would arrive in [the] Arlon area north of Luxembourg not earlier than the fourth day of the attacks. The fact that these forces would probably be commanded by General Patton (who, in the Battle of France, had given proof of his extraordinary skill in armored warfare, which he conducted according to the fundamental

German conception) made it quite likely that the enemy would direct a heavy punch against the deep flank of the German forces scheduled to be in the vicinity of Bastogne.

To ensure that Patton would not destroy his army, Brandenberger requested more fuel, more ammunition, more artillery, and most of all, more antitank weapons. The response from his superiors was discouraging. Von Gersdorff noted that Brandenberger's "requests were answered with vague promises that a number of units would be placed behind the left wing of the attack as army group, High Command West (OB West) or Wehrmacht reserves and that, consequently, these would be available for temporary use at least, in the southern zone of the attack. The requests of Seventh Army for ample supplies of ammunition, as well as adequate supplies of other equipment, unfortunately remained unheeded."[14]

This lack of support would prove costly to the Seventh Army. At least, thought von Gersdorff, they had a *panzergrenadier* division to lead the main effort. Unfortunately, the Seventh Army was about to lose its much-anticipated *panzergrenadier* division. With the offensive only two weeks away, Army Group G, the southern neighbor to Army Group B, had placed an emergency request for support to stop Patton around the city of Metz, and OKW responded by sending the same *panzergrenadier* division to the south. Its replacement, a reconstituted *fallschirmjäger* division, was not what the Seventh Army needed. To face Patton's Third Army, all they had were four infantry divisions, and none of them had panzers. The only antitank armor support came from a brigade of StuG self-propelled assault guns. It was not enough. For many of the seamen and airmen turned soldiers, this would be their first experience with the horrors of war. They would quickly learn that combat was a harsh teacher, and Patton one of its best students.[15]

Sometime Between December 1 and 10
Area of Operations of 352nd Volksgrenadier Division
Near Roth, Germany, Along the Banks of the Our River

The Our River, near the town of Roth, was a winding snake that twisted its way through the steep, wooded hills. It was this reason that made the Our so defensible. Though it was not wide, its fast-moving current and sheer banks made any crossing treacherous. In early December, it was even more perilous, as autumn rains turned the swollen banks to muddy quicksand.

The German sentries manning the defenses along the West Wall cared little for the pastoral scenery of the Our River. They were tired of war, and sentry duty was dreadfully boring. Early December's weather added to the misery. The temperature hovered above freezing, while drizzly rain saturated their clothes. A soldier would spend most of his shift shivering, looking for excuses to stand underneath a roof.

From across the river the Americans would occasionally send patrols to capture some hapless German to interrogate for intelligence on troop movements, morale, etc. The *landsers* that patrolled the roads near the Our had to be alert. Since November, the sentries had strict orders to prevent units from scouting along the riverbanks. They did not know why, but that was the order, so no one was allowed in the restricted area between the West Wall and the river. It was strictly *verboten*.

Yet tonight, an old-looking private appeared before the sentries, requesting permission to approach the river. The sentries asked for his papers. To their surprise, his documents allowed him to do just that. Asking no more questions, they sent the old private on his way. Within minutes, he vanished in the mist. They probably thought Germany was scraping the bottom of the manpower barrel if it was enlisting middle-aged *gefreiters*.

This *gefreiter*, who bore a striking resemblance to Shemp Howard of the Three Stooges, but with a little more heft, was not a private in the Wehrmacht, but an *oberst* in the Luftwaffe, though not a pilot. He was a *fallschirmjäger* (paratrooper) and the division commander of the 5th Fallschirmjäger Division. His name was Ludwig Heilmann, and he was strolling along the Our River because he was conducting his own reconnaissance. He could not order his men to do this, because his men could not know what he knew—that Germany was preparing to launch a major offensive. To ensure that surprise was complete and total, General Heilmann was the only person in his entire division of more than sixteen thousand men who had knowledge of the impending attack. Heilmann had a job to do, yet he did not want to arouse suspicion, so he donned a *gefreiter*'s uniform and sauntered down to the river alone. If the sentries had seen a Luftwaffe general in the restricted areas, they might have started talking to their comrades in the mess halls, and then who knows what would have happened next. No, Heilmann needed to do it alone, and so here he was, clambering over the slippery rocks and mossy undergrowth that littered the riverbanks, looking for indicators of enemy activity and assessing the terrain.[16]

Ludwig Heilmann was no stranger to important and dangerous missions. At the age of forty-one, he had already seen a great deal of combat. Unlike his senior officers, Ludwig was too young for the First World War. He joined the Reichswehr in 1921, and his first unit was the 21st Infantry Regiment. By 1935, he attained the rank of captain, and was a company commander in the 91st Infantry Regiment when the war broke out in 1939. He participated in the Polish Campaign and in the invasion of France and the Low Countries the following year.

The infantry, though, was not enough excitement for Ludwig, and so he volunteered to join the ranks of the *fallschirmjägers* in November 1940. He soon had his fill of danger and excitement, for in May 1941, he jumped into Crete. On account of his bravery and leadership in the battle for Catania, he was awarded the Knight's Cross. Later that year, he led his unit in the battles around Leningrad. At the end of 1942, the Luftwaffe promoted him to *oberstleutnant* (lieutenant colonel), and he took command of the 3rd Fallschirmjäger Regiment. The following year, he led the 3rd Fallschirmjäger in Sicily and throughout the rest of the Italian Campaign, including Monte Cassino, where he earned the Oak Leaves and Swords for his Knight's Cross. In recognition of his abilities, the Luftwaffe appointed him to command the 5th Fallschirmjäger Division in September 1944, and he was later promoted to *generalmajor* on December 1, 1944 (though he did not learn of the promotion until the twenty-third).[17]

Heilmann's 5th Fallschirmjäger Division was a relatively new unit, having entered the Luftwaffe order of battle in March 1944. When the Allies invaded at Normandy in June, OKW moved the 5th Fallschirmjäger Division to Saint-Lô, where it saw intense combat. By the end of July, the division was wrecked, and only its remnants escaped the Falaise pocket in August. Throughout the fall, the 5th underwent reconstitution, as Heilmann took control of the division.[18]

Unfortunately, Heilmann's division was not much of a fighting force at this point in the war. The division was lacking vital equipment like some of its heavy mortars and antitank guns. True, unlike many of the Wehrmacht units by the fall of 1944, the 5th Fallschirmjäger Division was practically at full strength. On paper, it had twenty thousand men, but four thousand of those were at Trier, undergoing training. Still, sixteen thousand men was a significant force, considering the typical *volksgrenadier* division had only around eleven thousand soldiers. In addition, he had a proper table of organization with three *fallschirmjäger* regiments, an artillery regiment, a pioneer battalion, an antitank battalion, an antiaircraft battalion, a mortar battalion, and attached to the division was the 11th Assault Gun Brigade to provide some mobile striking power for Heilmann.

Despite these impressive statistics, Heilmann knew his division was capable of only defensive operations. The next operation was to be a full-blown offensive. The reason for Heilmann's low estimation was the division's level of individual and collective training. Most of the soldiers were young, under twenty years of age, and most were former Luftwaffe aircrew mechanics and staff. They had received little infantry training, and many barely knew how to shoot a rifle. The commanders and noncommissioned officers were also former Luftwaffe staff officers. It was a clear case of the blind leading the blind. This issue extended all the way up to the regimental commanders. One, the commander of the 14th Fallschirmjäger Regiment, had no infantry experience at all. Oberst (Colonel) Arno Schimmel, the commanding officer of the 14th, was a technical adviser to the German air ministry, a far cry from leading *fallschirmjägers* into battle.

Unlike the 14th, which had an *oberst* as a commander, the commander for the 13th Fallschirmjäger Regiment was Major Goswin Wahl. The 13th also had a dearth of trained soldiers. According to Oberleutnant Rudolf Petrikat, the commander of 7th Company, 13th Fallschirmjäger Regiment, some of the men had fired their rifle only twice at the range, while some hadn't fired a rifle at all. Petrikat, though, had some experience as an infantryman in Crete, and he passed it on to his men the best he could in the limited amount of time he had to prepare his company. As for the other companies in his regiment, Petrikat was not confident in their tactical skills.[19]

Sadly, the division's problems were deeper than a lack of proper training and essential equipment. Many of these senior officers and NCOs had little taste for war. They had spent most of the war in the occupied territories, living a pampered life on the various airfields. For many of the senior NCOs, the war was lost, and the idea to sacrifice themselves in combat seemed like suicide this late in the conflict. Luckily, unlike their leaders, the younger enlisted *fallschirmjägers* were eager to prove themselves in combat.

Heilmann soon discovered, however, that the problems were worse than he thought. While relaxing in the occupied territories, the division staff had concocted a lucrative profiteering scheme. According to Heilmann, everyone on the staff was involved in the nefarious plot. When the general ended the criminal enterprise, he lost the support of his division staff. Thus, he had a staff he did not trust, and the majority of his commanders were not even infantrymen.

In addition to the graft and corruption, the 5th Fallschirmjäger did not have enough artillery. To augment the division, Seventh Army would allocate three battalions of artillery from its order of battle. Generalmajor Paul Riedel, the artillery commander of the Seventh Army, did this because he believed that the two battalions of artillery organic to the 5th Fallschirmjäger had no mobility, and more important, the *fallschirmjäger* artillerymen had received little training.[20]

Not everything, though, was bad. According to Heilmann, his 15th Fallschirmjäger Regiment was a veteran unit. Its commander, Oberst Kurt Gröschke, had led the regiment since the previous July. The regiment had spent five weeks around Bremen, Germany, and Haarlem, Holland, training the new recruits, who were mainly Luftwaffe technicians. The reconstituted regiment arrived at Bitburg on December 10. Unlike many other units, the 15th Fallschirmjäger Regiment still had many seasoned junior and noncommissioned officers who had survived the fighting in France. Furthermore, it had a proper table of organization and equipment. Each rifle squad had the requisite two light machine guns and each squad leader was armed with an MP-40. Sprinkled throughout the rifle companies were automatic rifles like the Fallschirmjägergewehr 42. Each line company had two *panzerschrecks* and the heavy weapons company had several heavy machine guns mounted on tripods and four 8cm mortars.

The 5th Fallschirmjäger Pioneer Battalion, under the command of Major Gerhard Martin, was fully trained and ready for combat. The attached 11th Assault Gun Brigade had twenty assault guns (most likely StuG IIIs). These three units would form the backbone of Heilmann's offensive combat power.[21]

Heilmann was not the only one who was less than thrilled with the 5th Fallschirmjäger Division leading the attack for the Seventh Army. When he learned that the 5th Fallschirmjäger would replace the 25th Panzergrenadier Division, Brandenberger was furious. He jumped the chain of command and complained directly to General Alfred Jodl, the chief of the operations staff of the Armed Forces High Command, but Jodl told him to make do with what he had.[22]

Von Gersdorff, Brandenberger's chief of staff, had come to the same conclusions as his boss. He rated Heilmann as an outstanding division commander, but, like Heilmann, graded most of the regimental commanders as poor. On the other hand, the morale of the younger enlisted *fallschirmjägers* did impress the senior commanders, and the division was lavishly equipped with *panzerfausts* and other antitank weapons. In the end, von Gersdorff concluded in his final evaluation that the 5th had "limited fighting qualities, because of defective training, unqualified commanders and limited mobility."[23]

A division of *limited fighting qualities* was now the main effort for the entire Seventh Army, and its mission was a difficult one. On the first day of the offensive, Heilmann's units had to penetrate the enemy defenses around Wahlhausen, Putscheid, Nachtmanderscheid, Vianden, and Walsdorf. From there, it needed to advance along an axis from Saint-Hubert, to Neufchâteau, on to Mellier, and through Attert. Next, the division's chief purpose was to protect the southern flank of the Fifth Panzer Army, which would be advancing simultaneously to the Meuse River, via Bastogne.[24]

Despite his misgivings, Heilmann scrambled down to the Our River to reconnoiter his crossing points and objectives. He quickly observed that the terrain was excellent for infantry. The thick vales and countless hollows along the eastern banks of the Our River would provide cover and concealment for the infantry assembly areas. On the other hand, few trafficable roads existed, and those that did exist turned into muddy bogs when it rained, which was often this time of year. Hence, moving the towed artillery pieces would be problematic, since they required all-weather roads.

The river itself was a formidable obstacle. With its steep banks, fast current, and up to two-meter depth, the river provided the enemy with terrain that a much smaller force could effectively defend. As General Heilmann knelt down near the river's edge, he stared upward and saw the massive gothic fortress of Vianden towering over the valley like a hawk perched atop a crag, searching for prey. He suddenly realized the prey would be his German *fallschirmjägers*, attempting to cross the river. The intimidating castle, built between the eleventh and fourteenth centuries, had been the seat of the Vianden counts for several hundred years. Its thick walls and arched gables would provide the American defenders excellent cover from small-arms fire and artillery barrages.[25]

Heilmann knew that the Americans had placed few if any forces along the river's edge. Other than an occasional stray rifle shot and errant artillery round, there was little enemy activity along the river itself. From his own intelligence reports, he knew that the American artillery would conduct harassing fire at night, targeting the villages and crossroads, but that was the extent of their operations in this sector. From the same reports, he knew the unit that occupied the positions across the river was not interested in conducting significant offensive operations like raids and ambushes. The 28th Infantry Division was still licking its wounds from the Hürtgen Forest.

Heilmann had seen enough. He stood up, wiped the caked mud and dried leaves from his knees, and started to walk back to the traffic control point. Later that day, when he made it to his command post, a pillbox northeast of Vianden, he pulled out some maps and jotted down some notes. The lack of enemy activity and the current intelligence picture told him that the enemy probably had ceded much of the west bank of the Our River—in effect, turning the ground around the Our into a veritable no-man's-land. The American main line of resistance was likely farther back on higher ground. Heilmann took his pencil and traced a line from Wahlhausen to Putscheid. From there, the line continued to Nachtmanderscheid and on to Walsdorf.

"That's it," he said to himself, tapping the pencil on the map.

Judging the terrain and relying on his own experience, the *fallschirmjäger* general assessed that the Americans were defending the sector with a battalion. In addition, the Americans likely had established listening and observation posts in the castle fortress of Vianden while buttressing those positions with some light artillery. Now he had to devise a plan.

To help himself think, Heilmann scribbled some more notes. After several minutes, he developed a basic concept of operations. First, his division's best chance for success was attacking during hours of darkness. Poor visibility almost always favored the attacker. The American battle positions that overlooked the valley probably had predesignated target reference points with clear fields of fire. The less time the Germans spent out in the open and exposed, the better their chance for success. The early morning hours would give them that required concealment.

However, conducting a night assault was an operation fraught with risk, so Heilmann would rely on his best units to lead the attack. Once they had achieved a sizable penetration, the other units, which were not as well trained, would push through behind them to secure the flanks and rear. The lead units, meanwhile, would advance westward while bypassing centers of resistance. Heilmann estimated that the Americans were occupying strongpoints in the villages and manning roadblocks along the major routes. His *fallschirmjägers* would use the forests as their highways to get around the American defenses. It was a simple plan, but it was the only one that would have any chance of success.[26]

Wednesday, December 13
Sülm, Germany
Headquarters, 5th Fallschirmjäger Division

Oberst Ludwig Heilmann, the commander of the 5th Fallschirmjäger, stood outside the makeshift headquarters as he waited for his overall boss, General Erich Brandenberger, the commander of the Seventh Army, to arrive. The air was crisp, and he thought he could see flurries. Sülm was located in the South Eifel, in the region known as the Rhineland-Palatinate. A small town with fewer than several hundred inhabitants, it was surrounded by rolling hills and spindly forests. The picturesque Kyll River served as the town's eastern boundary, while to the north was the larger town of Bitburg. Sülm had existed for more than a thousand years, but thanks to its small size, it had escaped the attention of Allied bombers. If the Allies knew about this meeting, then Sülm would become very significant, thought Heilmann.

As he watched the general's retinue arrive, Heilmann wondered whether his army commander had the same misgivings about the upcoming operation as he did. After the war, Heilmann wrote, "I prepared the attack in such a way as I thought it to be the duty of a soldier, though I did not believe in a victory of Germany over its enemies . . . [in] a long time."[27]

Two days before, on December 11, Heilmann, along with his corps commander General Baptist Knieß, had attended a conference with more than a dozen other commanders to see Hitler himself at the Führer's headquarters in Ziegenberg to discuss the upcoming Ardennes operation. For the first time, Heilmann saw how sick Hitler had become. "He entered the conference room with slow steps and immediately sat down at the table," Heilmann remembered. "Shrunk, with hanging shoulders and lusterless eyes, waxy faced, the Highest Warlord sat in front of his Generals. . . ."

Heilmann's final impression of the meeting left little doubt as to the importance of the next major operation: "this offensive would stake everything on one throw of the dice; the last chance in a game of hazard." Unfortunately, Heilmann did not think there was much chance of success. The Americans had rigged the game in their favor. [28]

When Brandenberger stepped out of the staff car, Heilmann saluted his superior officer and then led him and his aides inside the headquarters to the map room, where Heilmann's own staff and subordinate commanders were waiting. Heilmann announced that the commander of the Seventh Army had arrived, and everyone stood at attention. Brandenberger nodded and ordered them to take their seats so that the briefing could begin.

Heilmann was the first to speak. "Sir, welcome to our map exercise. You probably know most of the men here, but I will introduce them to you just in case."

The commander of the 5th Fallschirmjäger Division presented to Brandenberger each senior staff officer and regimental commander of his division. After he finished with the staff, Heilmann then started with his subordinate commanders. The first was Oberst Kurt Gröschke, commanding officer of the 15th Fallschirmjäger Regiment, and Heilmann's most experienced commander. Gröschke had commanded the regiment since July, and unlike his contemporaries in the other regiments, who were former Luftwaffe staff officers, Gröschke was a real *fallschirmjäger*. With his slicked-back hair and defined jaw, the veteran officer looked a lot like Albert Speer, the Minister of Armaments and War and Production. Born in 1907 in Berlin, Gröschke was commissioned a lieutenant in the Luftwaffe in 1934 and joined the fledging *fallschirmjäger* corps at the end of 1935. When the war broke out, he was a company commander in the 1st Fallschirmjäger Regiment, and jumped into the Netherlands at Dordrecht in May 1940. The next year, he jumped again into Crete as part of Operation Merkur in May 1941. By 1942, he was a battalion commander, serving in Russia, and twelve months later he was fighting in Italy against the Americans, where he earned the German Cross in Gold. His career continued to rise, and in June 1944, he was in Normandy, where he earned the Knight's Cross on June 9. In recognition of his abilities, the Luftwaffe promoted him, and he assumed command of the 15th Fallschirmjäger Regiment in July. Fortunately, unlike many of his comrades, he escaped the Falaise pocket. The 15th Fallschirmjäger had already seen a great deal of combat, fighting with the 17th SS Panzergrenadier Division, and ceased to exist by the beginning of August due to severe losses fighting in Normandy. Despite this, Gröschke rebuilt much of the regiment by the fall.[29]

Heilmann's other veteran commander was Major Gerhard Martin, the commander of the 5th Fallschirmjäger Pioneer Battalion. Martin was not even twenty-five years old, but he had more combat experience than many of his senior commanders. The rest of the senior officers from the other regiments were novices at ground combat, since many of them were former Luftwaffe airfield staff officers, and Heilmann probably thought that General Brandenberger would not know them anyway because of that fact.[30]

The commanding officer of the 5th Fallschirmjäger Division then directed everyone's attention to the map table in the center of the large room so that he could continue with the map exercise. "Gentlemen," he announced to let everyone know he was starting. In response, several men edged closer to the table to get a better look.

When the shuffling ended, he resumed. "The 5th Fallschirmjäger Division attacks the enemy from an assembly position behind the West Wall in the hilly terrain west of the Our River. From there, it will break through the enemy position with point of the main effort directed at Vianden, and then it will advance as far west as Wiltz. As the offensive proceeds, the division will reach the general line of Sibret, Vaux-lez-Rosières, and Martelange." To orient everyone, Heilmann then would tap on the map with his pointer as he read off the name of each location.

After that, Heilmann mapped out the axis of advance for the follow-on forces. "Next, elements with sufficient combat power will advance as far west as Neufchâteau, Mellier, [and] Attert, as well as Saint-Hubert and Libramont. The division then protects, using a mobile defense, the southern flank of the Fifth Panzer Army, which is advancing with its left wing via Bastogne." He paused to let the information sink in.

Heilmann then glanced over at Oberst Gröschke. "Kurt," he began, "the 15th Fallschirmjäger, your regiment, will attack at Roth and then cross the Our to take possession of the heights at Vianden. From there, you will reach the Wiltz sector by continuing your assault. Your initial objective is to keep open the crossings at Bourscheid. Your next objective is Martelange."

Oberst Arno Schimmel, the commander of the 14th Fallschirmjäger Regiment, was next in line. "Arno," Heilmann said, looking over at the Luftwaffe officer, "the 14th crosses the Our River at Stolzembourg. Next, it will break through the enemy positions at Putscheid. Once you've accomplished that, your regiment will continue westward and take possession of the Wiltz crossings, which are west of Hohscheid. It is crucial that you keep those crossings open."

Schimmel nodded and replied, "Yes, sir."

Heilmann then stared back at the group. "Gentlemen, the 5th Pioneer Battalion will ferry the assault companies across the Our by pneumatic pontoons, build a ferry at Bauler, and reach the Wiltz River with its main forces and ferrying material via Hohscheid. All this will happen on the first day of the attack. Is that understood, Major Martin?"

Major Martin quickly responded, "Understood, sir."

"In addition to this, the following units will move into the assembly area in the vicinity of Sinspelt, Oberweis, and Obergegen so that they can start marching via the town of Roth as soon as the bridge will be ready. Those units are: the 5th Pioneer Battalion, Advance Detachment 15, and Sturmgeschütz Brigade 11." Heilmann then circled the area on the map with his pointer.

He continued his brief. "They must reach the Wiltz crossings between Bourscheid and Hohscheid. After they reconsolidate, they will advance via Nothum, Doncols, and Sibret toward Saint-Hubert. Then they will reconnoiter as soon as possible as far as to the line Vaux-lez-Rosières and Martelange. To ensure effective command and control, Advance Detachment 15 is subordinated to the commander of Sturmgeschütz Brigade 11."

Hauptmann (Captain) Höllander, the commander of the 11th Sturmgeschütz Brigade, nodded, acknowledging the order.[31]

Someone then asked, "Sir, what constitutes an advance detachment?"

Heilmann answered, "Good question. According to the LXXXV Corps' order, the division must form two advance detachments. Each detachment will consist of the following. . . ." Heilmann then pulled out a sheet of paper and read from it. "It will have one rifle battalion, which is reinforced by an engineer platoon. In addition, it will have one heavy machine gun platoon and one light flak platoon. Moreover, each regiment must furnish an assault company with one combat engineer unit, a mine locating unit, and antitank units."

After everyone finished writing down the composition of the advance detachments, Heilmann looked over at Oberst Bernd Wintzer, the commander of the 5th Fallschirmjäger Artillery Regiment, and said, "At the beginning of the attack, we will execute a sudden concentration of fire on the villages occupied by the enemy. Next, during the attack, our artillery will suppress the artillery of the enemy and identify objectives. Moreover, the main effort for our artillery fire is Fouren [Fouhren]. To ensure continuous support, one light field howitzer battalion must be prepared to change position, so that it can cross the river by ferry at Stolzembourg and can support the attack of the 14th Fallschirmjäger Regiment."

Following Heilmann's brief on the specific tasks to his subordinate units, the conversation turned to other pressing items. First, the main road that led to the crossing site near Roth had an almost insurmountable obstacle: a bomb crater. Until someone filled in the gaping hole, no vehicle traffic would cross the Our River. Unfortunately for the Germans, they would have to fill the crater on the day of the attack, because any effort prior to X-day would immediately tip off the American observers that something was afoot on the German side of the river. The solution was to construct a ferry the day of the attack, but Heilmann concluded that his men would be without the support of the larger-caliber weapons until the crater was gone, and that would not likely happen until after the first day of operations.

The various commanders and staff officers then reviewed the plan for the assembly of the troops and equipment. General Heilmann once again started off the discussion. "Gentlemen, on the night before X-day [the day of the attack], the regiments will move without their vehicles into the assigned assembly areas behind the 'West Wall.' Then they will establish communications with the 5th Fallschirmjäger Engineer Battalion, which will assign to each unit a designated guide who is responsible for leading each regiment and battalion through our minefields."

Heilmann tapped his watch, as if reminding them of an upcoming appointment. "This is important," he said. "Military police will control all the roads, but they will allow army pioneers to pass through the traffic. At approximately 0300 hours all troops must be ready to jump off. From 0400 hours onward there will be freedom of movement for the reconnaissance patrols. At X-hour [time of the attack] the division assault companies will cross the Our River and establish a bridgehead. Combat patrols of the engineer battalion will then occupy Vianden. Furthermore, the positions of the artillery and heavy weapons are the immediate objectives of the regiments."

Most of the men present nodded in silence. Heilmann slammed his hand on the map table and declared, "The main thing is to gain the Wiltz crossings intact on the first day. We must bypass the villages and detour around any islands of resistance. Roads are to be avoided. Advance Detachment 15 will quickly travel from the Wiltz sector to Sibret and Vaux-lez-Rosières. From there it will move without its assault guns to Saint-Hubert and make contact with the Fifth Panzer Army. Meanwhile, the main body of the division will form into ranks along the line of Vaux-lez-Rosières to Martelange for defense. The 13th Fallschirmjäger Regiment, under my control, will follow behind the 15th Regiment and clear up any remaining pockets of resistance."

With that, Heilmann ended the map exercise. He wondered whether he'd stressed enough the importance of bypassing pockets of resistance. The goal was to reach Vaux-lez-Rosières and Martelange to establish a strong enough defense for the counterattack that Heilmann predicted would surely come. The more time they wasted mopping up resistance in the tiny villages that dotted this region of the Ardennes, the less time they would have for digging foxholes and preparing fields of fire for Patton's tanks.

Luckily, Heilmann had altered the plan somewhat. His corps commander wanted him to spread his forces out equally, but the seasoned *fallschirmjäger* believed that was a recipe for failure. He had seen how well that tactic had worked in Russia, especially at Stalingrad, where the forces on the flanks were too weak, and the Russians easily swept them aside as they closed the noose around the trapped German Sixth Army. No, Heilmann was going to mass his combat power where his forces butted up against the Fifth Panzer Army along his northern flank. To his south, he would establish a disruption zone, using a screen line of smaller forces that would delay the Americans and buy time for his main effort. He knew his superiors would not approve of his change, and so he kept mum on the subject. It was all he could do, and as the staff filed out of the map room, Heilmann hoped he had prepared them enough for the frosty hell that was sure to come.

Alone with his thoughts, Heilmann glanced over the map one last time and wondered whether his adversaries could sense the impending steel blizzard over the horizon. Surprise was everything. Without it, the German offensive would surely fail. Unfortunately for Heilmann and the men of the Seventh Army, there was one intelligence officer on the American side who had started to piece together the mosaic that was the *Wacht am Rhein* (Watch on the Rhine).[32]

Thursday, December 14
Molitor Barracks, Nancy, France
Headquarters, U.S. Third Army

Everyone in the U.S. Twelfth Army G-2 Intelligence Section thought the Germans were defeated. In fact, Brigadier General Edwin L. Sibert, the G-2 of the Twelfth Army, had published a memorandum on December 12, 1944, in which one of his staff concluded, "It is now certain that the attrition is steadily sapping the strength of the German forces on the Western Front and that the crust of defenses is thinner, more brittle and more vulnerable than it appears on our G-2 maps or to troops in the line." The memo concluded, "All of the enemy's major capabilities, therefore, depend on the balance between the rate of attrition imposed by the Allied offensives and the rate of infantry reinforcements. The balance at present is in favor of the Allies. With continued Allied pressure in the South [Saar region] and in the North [Ruhr region] the breaking point may develop suddenly and without warning."[33]

The officer reading the document took off his horn-rimmed glasses and rubbed his bald head, while looking at the maps on his desk. With his horseshoe-ringed hair and razor-thin mustache, he looked more like a small-town banker than a colonel in the U.S. Army. Despite his mild appearance, Colonel Oscar W. Koch was far from harmless. As the senior intelligence officer in General George

S. Patton's vaunted Third Army, he was one of the reasons for Patton's string of successes throughout the war in Europe and the Mediterranean. Koch had an innate ability to understand the enemy, and as the war progressed, so did his skills. Patton and his staff developed plans based on Koch's assessments, and most of the time Koch was right. Hence Patton won most of his battles, leading to a whirlwind campaign through France that was already the stuff of legend.

Like many of the senior officers in the Second World War, Koch had served during the lean interwar years. At the age of eighteen, Koch joined the army in 1915 as a member of the Light Horse Squadron, later known as A Troop, 1st Wisconsin Cavalry. He did not have to wait long to see action, participating in the Punitive Expedition into Mexico in 1916 under General John J. "Black Jack" Pershing. When the United States entered World War I, the army decided to commission him a second lieutenant when he turned twenty-one. After the war, he became an instructor at the U.S. Army Cavalry School, and later, while serving at Fort Riley, Kansas, he met his future boss, George Patton. His first job in World War II was as Patton's chief of staff for Task Force Blackstone during the invasion of Morocco. Patton recognized his talents, and from then on, Koch worked for Patton.[34]

Since February 1944, Koch had served as the G-2 for Patton's Third Army, which arrived on the continent in midsummer of that year. Since then, he had learned how to analyze and organize intelligence better than most officers on both sides of the front. It was this conviction that was telling him that his senior intelligence counterpart, General Sibert, was wrong. The Germans were not near the breaking point. In fact, the opposite was true—the Germans were getting ready to launch a large spoiling attack and maybe even a counteroffensive.

Earlier that day, Third Army's XII Corps had detained a German soldier who boasted that Hitler had ordered a counteroffensive, and the Germans would attack in the next couple of weeks. The Waffen SS *panzergrenadier* from the 17th SS Panzergrenadier Division had been carrying a verbal message when he had been captured: "Last night's message ordering your retreat was false. Everyone is to hold and prepare for a counterattack that is in the making."[35]

By itself, the message could have been the bluster of a Waffen SS zealot. However, as Koch looked over his notes from the past few weeks, the communication was one of many alarming indicators. The chief issue was the number of uncommitted panzer divisions. According to Koch's estimates, the Germans had amassed eight panzer divisions behind the line: the 1st SS Panzer, 2nd SS Panzer, 9th SS Panzer, 10th SS Panzer, 12th SS Panzer, 2nd Panzer, 116th Panzer, and the Panzer Lehr Division. With all of these, the Germans now had an offensive capability. Three *fallschirmjäger* divisions and three infantry divisions were also refitting behind the front. The question was what Hitler planned to do with these panzers and paratroopers. The most dangerous course of action was a large-scale counteroffensive to disrupt the offensives in the area around Aachen, using the SS panzer divisions, or another attack along the boundary between the Third and First U.S. Armies in Luxembourg, using the 2nd and Panzer Lehr divisions. Still, eight panzer divisions was a significant amount of combat power, and some of them, like the 2nd, had been off the line for more than a month. As a result, unlike many other divisions, the Wehrmacht likely had refitted these units with new equipment and replacements. Now Koch had this prisoner of war claiming a counteroffensive was in the offing.[36]

The G-2 colonel had alerted Patton to his initial suspicions on December 9. In a meeting, Koch outlined the buildup of German forces opposite the U.S. First Army's VIII Corps, the unit directly north of the Third Army. Even though the German concentration was not opposite the Third Army's area of operations, it was in their own area of interest because, by Koch's estimation, a German attack there would threaten their flank.

Koch warned Patton and the rest of his staff that VIII Corps' front was weak. At the time, the corps had three infantry divisions and one armored division, which was not at full strength. Arrayed against them were four enemy infantry divisions, while behind those were two panzer divisions and another three infantry divisions. Even worse was the amount of ground the VIII Corps had to defend— nearly eighty miles of thick forest and deep gullies. Major General Troy Middleton, the commander of VIII Corps, could not concentrate his forces anywhere along that line. If the Germans went on the offensive, they would attack a weak spot in the Allied lines and likely break through. Additionally, bad weather had grounded Allied airpower for most of the autumn months, allowing the Luftwaffe to rebuild its squadrons and train new pilots. Hence the Luftwaffe, in theory, could support ground offensive operations if the need arose.

Bolstered with these facts, Koch concluded his briefing, saying, "The enemy has an approximate two-to-one numerical advantage in the area, offset to some extent by low combat efficiency of poorly trained and inexperienced units. His buildup has been gradual and highly secret. A successful diversionary attack, even of a limited nature, would have a great psychological effect—a 'shot in the arm' for Germany and Japan."

Patton sensed his intelligence officer was right again, despite the estimates and claims from his higher headquarters that the Wehrmacht was on its last legs. Still, he reasoned, Koch's theory was still only a theory. Planning would continue for Third Army's eventual operation to seize the city of Frankfurt, but he ordered Koch and the rest of his staff to prepare for a contingency operation to stop a German offensive in VIII Corps' area of operation.

With the briefing over, Patton stood up and said, "We'll be in a position to meet whatever happens."[37]

Now Koch was growing more convinced that the contingency plan that Patton had ordered on the ninth was about to become *the* plan. Koch did not know it at the time, but he was not the only one with misgivings. His northern counterpart in the U.S. First Army, Colonel Benjamin "Monk" Dickson, also was having doubts. In his "G-2 Estimate Number 27," dated December 10, 1944, Dickson wrote, "It is plain that his [Hitler's] strategy in defense of the Reich is based on the exhaustion of our offensive to be followed by an all-out counterattack with armor, between the Roer and the Erft, supported by every weapon he can bring up to bear." In addition, Dickson reported that the morale of recently captured German soldiers had "achieved a new high." In fact, as evidence of this new development, German prisoners of war were attempting to escape and rejoin their comrades, something that Dickson had not seen in a while, and thereby contradicting the U.S. Twelfth Army Group's assessment that the German army was a beaten and vanquished foe. Even more worrisome was the report of a Colonel Otto Skorzeny seeking to recruit German soldiers who could speak American English. Dickson concluded that the Germans were planning sabotage and other missions behind Allied lines that would be part of a much larger offensive. He assessed that Field Marshal Gerd von Rundstedt would launch this strike once the Allied forces crossed the Roer River.[38]

Dickson grew even more alarmed that day when he learned that the 28th Infantry Division had picked up a Luxembourg civilian who had reported seeing bridging equipment on the German side of the Our River, indicating possible offensive operations. To Dickson, that was the final straw.

"It's the Ardennes!" he reportedly exclaimed to a stunned First Army staff and their commander, General Courtney Hodges.

Unfortunately, according to Lieutenant General Omar Bradley, the commander of the U.S. Twelfth Army Group, Dickson had cried wolf too many times. Bradley described Dickson as "often a pessimist and an alarmist. Had I gone on guard every time Dickson, or any other G-2, called wolf, we would never have taken many of the riskier moves that hastened the end of the war."[39]

Hodges turned a deaf ear to the intelligence officer's warning. He ordered Dickson to go on leave to Paris, which he did. As he departed, Dickson probably felt like Cassandra, the daughter of Priam, the king of Troy. Apollo had blessed her with the gift of prophecy, but when she refused his lustful advances, the vengeful god cursed her so that no one would ever believe her predictions, even though they were true. As a result, none of the Trojans believed her when she warned them about the Trojan horse.[40]

Luckily, Koch had more credibility with his boss, General Patton, than Dickson did with his. The Third Army G-2 looked back at his reports and maps. Maybe he was wrong. Nearly a hundred kilometers from the front lines, maybe he was too far away from the action to understand what was going on. Third Army headquarters were in the old Molitor Barracks, which the French army had built after their disastrous defeat at the hands of the Prussian army in 1871. Before World War I, the city of Nancy was near the frontier, since the Germans had annexed Alsace and much of Lorraine. As result, the French had built a string of forts and barracks to defend the region. The Caserne Molitor was one of those barracks. To add some national flair, the French builders had designed the barracks to resemble châteaus, with their winter white walls and maroon-tiled roofs. Now, these château-style barracks were the home to Third Army staff, who had set up telephone switchboards, meeting rooms, and map rooms for the various staff sections.[41]

On one map were the locations of the German units opposite Third Army. From north to south were the 416th, 19th, and 719th Infantry (Volksgrenadier) divisions, then the 21st Panzer Division, followed by the 55th, 347th, and 36th Infantry (Volksgrenadier) divisions. South of the 36th was the 17th SS Panzergrenadier Division, followed by the 11th Panzer Division. In total, the Third Army faced nine divisions: two panzer divisions, one *panzergrenadier* division, and six infantry divisions. Arrayed against VIII Corps were the 18th, 26th, 212th, 352nd, 560th, 62nd, and 362nd Infantry (Volksgrenadier) divisions. In addition to the infantry divisions, the Germans had positioned the 2nd Panzer and 130th (Panzer Lehr) divisions behind the line—a total of nine divisions, too. In short, Third Army, which had two corps on the line, faced the same amount of German combat power as VIII Corps—a unit half the size of Third Army. To Koch, then, the Germans had more than enough combat power to punch a hole through VIII Corps. The question now was when and where, and according to the German prisoner of war, the "when" was in the next two weeks. Unfortunately for Koch and the American army, though, the prisoner of war was slightly misinformed, because Hitler planned to attack VIII Corps and the rest of the First Army in less than forty-eight hours.

On the German side of the lines, men were girding themselves for battle, while most of the American soldiers were writing Christmas letters to family back home, unaware of the impending hell that Hitler was about to unleash upon them.[42]

2200 Hours, Friday, December 15
Oberstedem, South of Bitburg, Germany
9th Company, III Battalion, 15th Fallschirmjäger Regiment,
5th Fallschirmjägers Division

"Every unit commander, down to the company level, shall have the full authority and jurisdiction of a military court! After giving his own considerations, he shall be authorized to order and carry out a death sentence!" the officer announced to the assembled *fallschirmjägers*. The solitary man, standing before the mob of soldiers, looked like a king's herald, decreeing a new, draconian policy.

With those words, Feldwebel (Sergeant) Conrad Klemment knew the impending operation would be desperate and dangerous. He stared at the faces of the men around him when they heard the news that they were going into combat. Though he was new to the unit, he was not green. He had seen action in Russia, and had been wounded near the Don River in August 1942, where another soldier had pulled him out of the water before Klemment drowned. Now he was going into combat again. He listened in as the officer continued reading off the new rules of engagement.

"Notice shall be given: U.S. prisoners of war shall not have personal belongings removed. We must anticipate that some of us will become prisoners of war and will fall into the hands of the Americans. If our enemies find private American property on our *fallschirmjägers*, the Americans shall accuse them of robbery and they will shoot them!" Klemment noticed that the crowd stirred when they heard this; their mumblings were a signal to the officer that they acknowledged the order, but they did not like it.

The officer then waited for the murmurs to die down. Finally he added, "If you are wounded in battle, you will be left to your own devices." To Klemment, the meaning of the last statement was clear: They could not afford to slow down to care for the wounded. Forward momentum was paramount. It was all or nothing.

After the briefing, the men filed by a distribution point to receive their allotment of ammunition. When they were through drawing supplies and dropping off extraneous personal belongings, the *fallschirmjägers* headed out into the cold, dark evening. By midnight, the men reached a road that led west toward the American lines. Clogging the road were all sorts of men and beasts. Unlike the American army, which was almost completely motorized, the German army still relied heavily on horse-drawn transport. Klemment and his company trudged along beside animals pulling wagons stuffed with ammunition, food, and other goods. Motorcycles, cars, and trucks rolled down the center of the road. Artillery boomed like distant thunder. Klemment recalled the sound after the war. "For those of us that were new [in the unit], it represented a small taste of what we could expect later."[43]

A collision of epic proportions was only hours away. Klemment's 5th Fallschirmjäger Division would play the key role in the defense of the southern flank of the German counteroffensive. Its adversary would be Patton's Third Army. Leading the way would be the 4th Armored Division. In several days, those two divisions would meet on the fields of Belgium to decide the fate of Hitler's winter gamble.

CHAPTER 2

THE AMERICAN RESPONSE

★ ★ ★ ★ ★

"But what the hell, we'll still be killing Krauts."
—*Lieutenant General George S. Patton*

Saturday, December 16
Luxembourg and Southern Belgium
Area of Operations, 5th Fallschirmjäger Division, LXXXV Corps,
German Seventh Army

A round 0530 in the morning, the east bank of the Our River exploded as hundreds of artillery fired into the sky. Seconds later, the west bank of the Our disappeared under a hail of steel as thousands of shells came screaming down back to earth. Hitler's offensive had begun.

For ten minutes, German artillery pounded away at suspected American troop assembly areas and artillery batteries. The night sky was blasted with searchlights to blind the American defenders while providing illumination for the assault teams as they crossed the river. Huddled in rubber boats, intrepid German soldiers pulled themselves across, using tow ropes and other improvised flotation devices, while salvo after salvo of high-explosive rounds roared over their heads. Within minutes, the first troops had crossed and were scampering up the steep riverbanks. By 0820 hours, the German army had more than a thousand men on the west side of the river.

The initial success of the river crossings indicated to the German Seventh Army staff that they had surprised the American defenders throughout much of the sector. Now it was time to exploit this advantage. General Baptist Knieß, the commander of the LXXXV Corps who controlled the northern flank of the Seventh Army's axis of advance, which was the Seventh Army's main effort, ordered his two divisions, the 5th Fallschirmjäger Division and the 352nd Volksgrenadier Division, forward. The 5th Fallschirmjäger, under the commander of Oberst Ludwig Heilmann, was the decisive operation for the Corps, and in fact, the decisive operation for the army. As outlined in the operations order, the 5th's axis of advance was along the northern flank of the corps, and leading the way for the division were two of its regiments: the 14th and 15th Fallschirmjäger regiments. Along the northern approach was the 14th Fallschirmjäger Regiment, while to the south was Conrad Klemment's 15th Fallschirmjäger Regiment.

The 14th Fallschirmjäger Regiment enjoyed some early successes. Seizing the vaunted fortress at Vianden with minimal effort and few casualties, it moved westward, establishing a bridgehead that was several kilometers deep. By that afternoon, the troops had reached Putscheid. They were lucky—the entire regiment faced only F Company of the 109th Infantry Regiment, 28th Infantry Division. Instead of assaulting head-on, the Germans bypassed the American unit and exploited the seam to the north between the 110th Infantry and 109th Infantry, which the Americans had left undefended.

After the initial shock, however, the American army reacted. To slow down the German advance, 2nd Battalion shifted its reserve, G Company, to secure the southern flank of F Company by establishing a battle position northeast of Brandenbourg. Yet the Americans were quickly running out of thumbs to plug all the holes in the dike. Lieutenant Colonel James E. Rudder, commander of the 109th Infantry Regiment, authorized a portion of his regimental reserve to block the Germans from advancing farther west from Brandenbourg. To accomplish this, C Company from 1st Battalion rolled out and recaptured Brandenbourg at 2230 hours. 2nd Battalion's northern flank was secure, but barely. Its southern flank was a different story.

There, the 15th Fallschirmjäger Regiment ran into E Company of the 109th Infantry near the town of Fouhren. Instead of bypassing it, the 15th tried to seize the village with overwhelming force. Initially, the American defenders gave the

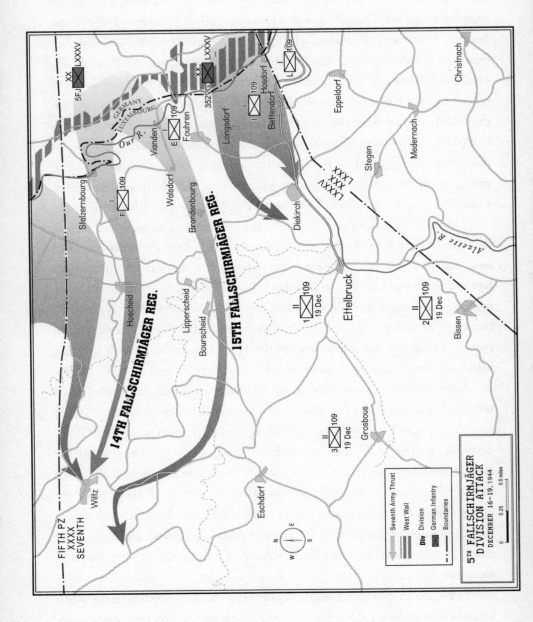

5TH FALLSCHIRMJÄGER
DIVISION ATTACK
DECEMBER 16–19, 1944

Seventh Army Thrust
West Wall
Div Division
German Infantry
Boundaries

0   0.25   0.5 miles

14TH FALLSCHIRMJÄGER REG.
15TH FALLSCHIRMJÄGER REG.

FIFTH PZ
XXXX
SEVENTH

fallschirmjägers a bloody nose, and they failed to take the town. As a result, American forward observers could call for artillery and rain down a steel tempest on the projected bridge site at Roth until the Germans captured Fouhren. In response, units like Conrad Klemment's 3rd Battalion of the 15th Fallschirmjäger began to infiltrate to the south of E Company vis-à-vis the village of Longsdorf, exploiting another seam between E Company and I Company. By 1425 hours, the Germans had cut off landline communication between E Company and 2nd Battalion. Company E's seemingly last message was grim—they were taking heavy mortar fire and facing an entire battalion of Germans. Time was running out. Colonel Rudder ordered Company A with one platoon of tanks to reestablish contact with E Company. Unfortunately, the *fallschirmjägers* blunted the rescue mission south of Longsdorf before it could reach the beleaguered men of E Company. Miraculously, E Company managed to survive the night.

Despite this success, the friction of war started to disrupt the German plans. Without armored vehicles and towed antitank guns, the German forces on the west bank would be sitting ducks against American tanks. To ensure that the lightly armed *fallschirmjägers* had that support, the engineers needed to erect a bridge near Roth at the earliest possible time so that the German army could send the self-propelled assault guns across to buttress the tiny bridgehead. Unfortunately, the narrow roads and steep banks delayed the arrival of the bridging equipment so that the engineers could not complete the temporary bridges until the next day. Luckily for the *fallschirmjägers*, the Americans could not exploit the German vulnerability.[1]

1100–2200 Hours, Saturday, December 16
North of Ettelbruck, Luxembourg
9th Company, 3rd Battalion, 15th Fallschirmjäger Regiment

Feldwebel Conrad Klemment sighed. He was still alive, and for that he was thankful. Since crossing the Our River early that morning, his unit, 9th Company, had made incredible progress. Bypassing several pockets of American resistance, they were now south of Ettelbruck and heading west. They had advanced several kilometers after only five hours, and so far they had not encountered a single American soldier.

As Klemment crossed an open field with the rest of his company, the ground behind them erupted. It was artillery, and no one knew where the next salvo would land. The well-trained *fallschirmjägers* dispersed and sprinted toward the western wood line that could serve as concealment along the edge of the field. Meanwhile, rounds screamed overhead and crashed around them. After what seemed like hours, Klemment reached the wood line and noticed a lone American soldier, roughly three hundred meters away, standing next to a jeep at the corner of the hollow. Klemment raised his rifle and opened fire. The first few cracks convinced the American that he was no longer welcome. He jumped into the jeep and drove off. Within seconds, the artillery ceased.

Once the company had consolidated and reorganized, the company commander, Oberleutnant Bertram, signaled them deeper into the woods. After several hours they reached another clearing. Klemment noticed the plowed fields and a group of farmhouses on the far side of the field. Since it was almost dark, Bertram decided to cross the open field instead of skirting it. They had already traversed several open areas with little trouble.

It was a bad idea. As they moved out, a hidden machine gun opened up, causing the men to hit the dirt while bullets zinged and zipped over their helmets. Klemment thought the machine gun sounded like an MG 42 and wondered whether another German unit had accidentally opened fire on them. Someone else had the same idea. Pulling out a flag emblazoned with the swastika, a group of *fallschirmjägers* began to wave it in the air. The machine gunners directed their fire at the flag wavers.

That was it. "Fire at will!" someone yelled.

German machine guns showered the farmhouse walls with lead. Despite their suppressive fire, Klemment could see that the Americans still had the advantage. He detected one gun position approximately nine hundred meters away, which the enemy had protected with sandbags and concealed beneath branches. The Germans, out in the open, realized that they were dead if they remained where they were, lying in the field like stationary targets on a rifle range. Eventually a bullet would find them. Klemment and his comrades crawled back to the cover and concealment of the wood line.

The leaders of the company gathered to decide what to do next. The 1st

Platoon leader suggested that they try to flank the enemy positions under the cover of darkness and assault it from the nearby northern woods. Bertram agreed and sketched his plan on the ground. It would be a pincer movement with 1st and 3rd platoons as the pincers. Flamethrowers in each platoon would destroy any bunkers they might encounter. Everyone nodded in agreement. As night fell, the company edged its way forward to an attack position five hundred meters behind the Americans.

As the *fallschirmjägers* began the final push toward the enemy, Klemment's senses were heightened. He could hear the snapping of twigs, and was sure that the Americans could hear them approaching. He could see the blackened horizontal lines of roofs beyond the spindly shadows of the pine trees. As planned, the men spread out as they left the tree line, their weapons pointed forward and ready to fire.

It did not matter.

Thunk-thunk-thunk echoed in the night. Tracers streaked by Klemment, and he heard the swishing of a flamethrower as flammable jelly spewed toward the suspected gun crew. Almost instantly the jelly ignited, but it overshot the American bunker, spraying fire behind it.

"The machine gun redirected its fire against the flamethrower," Klemment described. "Locked in combat to the death, the flamethrower released a flame while the enemy machine gun raked fire across the area occupied by the Oberjägergruppe. The burning jelly spread out between our position and the house, which blinded our view. A single round struck the ammunition can in front of me, which caused the can to fly back and hit my helmet."

He dived to the ground while bullets pelted the dirt around him. He crawled out of the direct line of fire and back toward the tree line. Meanwhile, 1st and 2nd platoons pressed their attack. American machine gun fire started to peter out and then stop.

The *fallschirmjägers* had finally turned the tide. "Two shadowy figures approached me from the farm [and] wanted to pass by me on the side," Klemment remembered. "It appeared they were carrying something heavy. I waited with a raised rifle for the most opportune moment to fire. At the last moment I recognized against the moonlight a third person, a severally wounded soldier between the two. He was almost unable to walk. With both arms he supported himself on the shoulders of his comrades, while his head hung down in pain. I could not fire and allowed them to escape in the dark."

Klemment was a soldier, not a murderer. The retreating American soldiers were helping a wounded comrade, and he recalled when he had been wounded and stuck in no-man's-land in Russia in 1942. Another soldier had helped him escape, and for whatever reason, the Russians allowed them to live. He decided to return the favor and let the Americans get away.

The *fallschirmjägers* proceeded to clear the farmhouse, searching for any other American soldiers. By all accounts, it was a victory for 9th Company. They had captured thirty-five Americans along with all their supplies. Regrettably, it was not without cost. Five Germans were dead, and eight were wounded, including their 3rd Platoon leader. Klemment's friend Feldwebel Franzke now assumed command of 3rd Platoon.

After treating the wounded and collecting the dead, Bertram ordered the company to move out. They were already behind schedule; it was now 2200 hours, and Klemment hadn't slept in nearly forty hours. To make matters worse, Bertram ordered the wounded to be left behind. A local farmer would have to take care of them. The tired men grabbed their rifles and resumed their trek westward. Klemment felt as if he were under a dreamlike trance, where the line between sleep and consciousness had blurred.[2]

Sunday, December 17
Luxembourg and Southern Belgium
Area of Operations, 5th Fallschirmjäger Division,
LXXXV Corps, German Seventh Army

Elements of the 15th Fallschirmjäger Regiment renewed their assault on the center and southern flank of 2nd Battalion of the 109th Infantry. After a lengthy artillery barrage, the *fallschirmjägers* threw themselves at G and E companies, respectively, but once again the plucky American GIs fought back and held their positions. Colonel Rudder, sensing an opportunity, ordered Company A and some tanks from the 707th Tank Battalion to relieve the besieged E Company in

Fouhren. This time it was the Germans who held the line. After a bitter battle, the *fallschirmjägers* retained control of Longsdorf and Tandel, thereby preventing A Company from reaching the defenders of Fouhren. Elsewhere, after a bitter fire-fight, the regimental antitank company captured twenty-five German soldiers, and the company commander estimated that his men had inflicted more than 150 casualties between the towns of Diekirch and Bettendorf.

Along the northern flank of 2nd Battalion, F Company kept fighting, but the situation had grown desperate. German soldiers from the 14th Fallschirmjäger Regiment had outflanked their positions and were now operating in the rear, where they captured the F Company kitchen section. As a result, Rudder ordered the regimental support area kitchens to withdraw to Ettelbruck. The Germans, though, sustained casualties, as F Company bazooka men reportedly knocked out several German vehicles.

Luckily, Rudder had reestablished contact with E Company in Fouhren at around 1000 hours that morning via radio. As they were short on ammunition and food, their situation was critical. They needed artillery support to keep back the German horde. Rudder told them he would try to help, and ordered B Company and four tanks to break through the cordon and resupply the unit. As in the previous attempts, though, B Company failed to reach Fouhren. The men of Easy Company would have to wait until the next morning, when B Company would try again. The Germans had other ideas.[3]

Evening, Sunday, December 17
Bunker Near Vianden, Luxembourg
Headquarters, 5th Fallschirmjäger Division,
LXXXV Corps, German Seventh Army

Inside the concrete bunker that served as his division command post, Oberst Ludwig Heilmann reviewed his notes from the previous day and checked them against the map that his staff had laid out on a table. Earlier that day, he had visited the temporary headquarters of Oberst Arno Schimmel, commander of the 14th Fallschirmjäger Regiment, which was in the town of Putscheid. Schimmel, a former Luftwaffe staff officer, had lost control of his regiment. The 14th had crossed the Our River the morning of December 16 and proceeded to lose all cohesion. Men were scattered like seeds in the wind. Several groups retreated back across the river. Even worse, Schimmel's staff had lost its nerve, "seized with a panic," Heilmann wrote. "Attacks of the enemy towards Vianden were reported. Later on we received the message that tanks were approaching Putscheid." Luckily, the 14th Fallschirmjäger had ferried an artillery battery, and with it, they blunted the American armored assault, using the howitzers in the direct-fire mode.

Furthermore, several daring assault gun crews had managed to navigate their Sturmgeschütz IIIs over the Our River, using a weir as a temporary bridge. Thus Heilmann now had armored vehicles on this side of the Our. It was not a permanent solution, but it was better than nothing. Heilmann ordered these few assault guns to drive toward Walsdorf and Nachtmanderscheid to buttress the infantry there. Instructing Schimmel to reorganize his scattered troops, he ordered them to push westward to seize crossing sites over the Wiltz River.

Satisfied with these arrangements, Heilmann returned to his command post. Fortunately, the news from his other regiment, the 15th Fallschirmjäger, under the command of Oberst Kurt Gröschke, was much better. The 15th was a seasoned unit with experienced officers. Though one of its battalions had run into trouble at Fouhren, another battalion had captured a bridge over the Wiltz River near Bourscheid and was continuing to advance westward. To solve the problem at Fouhren, General Knieß had ordered Heilmann to deploy his reserve regiment, the 13th Fallschirmjäger, to seize Fouhren once and for all. To ensure its capture, the LXXXV Corps even added the 914th Volksgrenadier Regiment from the 352nd Volksgrenadier Division to provide even more combat power. The American E Company of 109th Infantry, which had been facing one battalion up till now, would soon face two regiments. To Heilmann, the fall of Fouhren seemed assured.

He traced his fingers northward on the map to the villages of Consthum and Holzthum. He needed Schimmel's green troops to push westward and seize another crossing point over the Wiltz River between those villages and Bourscheid. If they failed, the northern flank of the 15th Fallschirmjäger would be exposed. If they succeeded, his division would have penetrated the American line of resistance. At that point, it would be a race. For the time first in two days, Heilmann was confident. His division might accomplish its impossible mission after all.[4]

1030 Hours, Monday, December 18
Approaching Forward HQ, U.S. Twelfth Army Group,
Luxembourg City, Luxembourg .
Command Group, U.S. Third Army

Colonel Oscar Koch quickly recalled the events of the last forty-eight hours as he braved the elements in an open jeep, racing north to Luxembourg City. The weather was cold and drizzly, and the overcast sky prevented the Army Air Force from flying. Undoubtedly the weather was helping the Germans immensely. Koch had seen it coming, and now the Allied High Command had to react on the fly.

Fortunately, Koch's staff was one of the best in the army, and they had already summarized the previous week's activities in the "Annex 3 to G-2 Periodic Report No. 190," which they had published that morning before he left. The first sentence, thought Koch, said it all: "The long awaited German counteroffensive exploded on 16 December." Koch probably wondered who, besides himself, had "awaited" this offensive. Few had seen it coming, and now everyone was scrambling to stop it. According to initial reports, Field Marshal Gerhard von Rundstedt had thrown at least five panzer divisions and a slew of infantry divisions, including the reconstituted *fallschirmjäger* divisions like the 5th Fallschirmjäger, at the U.S. First Army. If Germany succeeded, the counteroffensive would disrupt and even defeat the various other Allied thrusts, including his own Third Army's operation to seize the Saar region in the coming days.[5]

Lieutenant General Omar N. Bradley, commander of the U.S. Twelfth Army Group and Patton's boss, had ordered Patton to meet with him at his forward command post, known as EAGLE TAC, in Luxembourg City. Bradley wanted Patton to bring his key staff personnel along: namely Colonel Koch, the G-3, and the G-4. Koch sensed that Third Army's big Saar operation was about to be put on hold, which would likely anger his boss. Patton had been waiting since September to invade Germany, and everything was ready—until the Germans decided to stage an offensive of their own.

For Patton, leading a victorious army in war was the culmination of a lifelong dream. It was in his blood. His grandfather, George S. Patton I, was a colonel in the Confederate Army and graduate of the Viriginia Military Institute. In 1864, he was killed during the Third Battle of Winchester while serving as the commander of the 22nd Virginia Infantry Regiment. George S. Patton Jr. grew up in southern California when the area was still the frontier. Patton Jr. also attended VMI. A year after graduation, he returned to southern California, where he met and married Ruth Wilson.

George S. Patton III was born on November 11, 1885, in San Gabriel, California. At an early age, Patton imagined he would be a great warrior, following in the footsteps of his ancestors. Like his father and grandfather before him, Patton attended VMI, but craved a commission in the Regular Army, which only the Military Academy at West Point could guarantee. After one year at VMI, he transferred to West Point. He earned his commission in 1909, and his first duty station was Fort Sheridan, Illinois, serving as a second lieutenant in the 15th Cavalry Regiment.

The next few years were a whirlwind for Patton. On May 26, 1910, he married Beatrice Ayer. Two years later he participated in the Summer Olympics in Stockholm, Sweden. The next year he was at Fort Riley, Kansas, teaching swordsmanship for cavalry troopers. In 1915, Patton was ordered to Fort Bliss, Texas.

In 1916, Patton finally went to war. While he was at Fort Bliss, General John J. Pershing identified the young officer as someone with talent. Around the same time, President Woodrow Wilson selected Pershing as the commander of a punitive expedition to catch Pancho Villa, who had raided the town of Columbus, New Mexico. Impressed with Patton's tactical skills and determination, Pershing selected him as his aide for the expedition. Though the expedition ultimately failed to catch the Mexican guerrilla, it was a boon for Patton's career. Pershing promoted him to captain, and asked him to lead his headquarters troop.

The United States' entrance into the First World War in 1917 meant that Patton's wartime experience was just beginning. Patton, then a cavalry trooper, foresaw the tank as the new cavalry, and became the commander of the young United States Tank Corps. As commander, he developed the army's tank tactics and doctrine while training the new force. In September 1918, he successfully led a brigade of tanks at the Battle of Meuse-Argonne, earning the Distinguished Service Medal for his efforts. After World War I, Patton's career stalled, like many other officers'. Congress refused to spend money on tanks, and Patton returned to the cavalry. Yet Patton continued to study and develop tank doctrine.

Germany's invasion of Poland in 1939 was a turning point. The speed and efficiency of the German panzers stunned the world, and within weeks, Poland surrendered. World War II had begun. Patton's career was reinvigorated by Germany's success on the battlefield. Congress appointed him to command the newly formed 2nd Armored Division in April 1941, and he was promoted to the rank of major general. That summer and fall, Patton led the 2nd Armored Division through several large-scale maneuvers. It was here that he learned how to manage armored formations during complex offensive and defensive operations. With the Japanese bombing of Pearl Harbor that December and Hitler's declaration of war on the United States, once again, Patton was going to war.

His first major combat command was in November 1942, leading the Western Task Force in the invasion of North Africa as part of Operation Torch. His soldiers quickly defeated the Vichy French forces in Morocco, but Patton's success in Morocco was only the beginning. On March 6, 1943, Field Marshal Erwin Rommel's Afrika Korps crushed the U.S. Army's II Corps at the Battle of Kasserine Pass. As a result, General Eisenhower sacked its commander, Major General Lloyd Fredendall, and replaced him with the newly promoted Lieutenant General Patton. Patton did not disappoint. Only two weeks later, Patton led the corps to its first major victory against the Afrika Korps at the Battle of El Guettar. As a reward for this success, Eisenhower chose him to lead the U.S. Seventh Army as part of Operation Husky—the invasion of Sicily.

On the evening of July 9, 1943, Allied paratroopers parachuted into Sicily. A seaborne invasion followed early on the morning of the tenth. Though scattered, Patton's airborne forces from the 505th Parachute Infantry Regiment disrupted Axis operations behind the beaches while his 1st Infantry Division and the Rangers repulsed several armored counterattacks. By July 11, Patton had a secured the beachhead. In less than two weeks, Patton's divisions captured Palermo and all of western Sicily, bagging more than fifty thousand Italian soldiers while losing fewer than three hundred of his own. It was a huge success for Patton and an even greater success for the U.S. Army, which had been at war for fewer than twenty months.

Yet Patton had almost singlehandedly sidelined his own career. On two separate occasions, Patton slapped soldiers who were recovering from battle fatigue in army hospitals on Sicily. Believing that battle fatigue was not a sickness, he claimed the uninjured men were cowards. Within days, rumors about the incidents began to circulate among the soldiers of the Seventh Army. Eisenhower knew he had to do something or he would lose his most talented field general. He ordered Patton to apologize to the two soldiers and to publicly apologize to the divisions of the Seventh Army.

Initially, Eisenhower thought that he had dodged a bullet. The supreme commander even asked reporters not to publish the facts surrounding the incident. Despite Eisenhower's best efforts to suppress the story, word reached the American public in November 1943, when Drew Pearson, a newspaper columnist, reported the incidents on a radio show. It was a disaster for Patton's image. Soon reporters and congressmen were calling for the general's head.

Ike felt the slapping incident as though it were a crushing military defeat. To save Patton's career, he sent a report to the secretary of war, Henry L. Stimson, arguing that Patton was irreplaceable. Cooler heads prevailed and Patton was saved. Still, the slapping incident was an indicator to Eisenhower that Patton was not suitable for anything higher than an army command. As a result, he chose General Omar Bradley, Patton's subordinate, to assume command of the U.S. First Army and, eventually, the U.S. Twelfth Army Group. In effect, Bradley leapfrogged over Patton to become the senior American ground commander for the Normandy invasion. Eisenhower felt Bradley had the right temperament for the job. In contrast, Patton tended to be a hothead and was his own worst enemy.

Patton was still Eisenhower's best field general, and Ike knew it. When the time came, Patton would receive another command. "Old Blood and Guts" was sent to England to wait for the next opportunity. For the first few months of 1944, Patton languished in Great Britain. His main role was acting commander of the fictitious First United States Army Group. This make-believe army group was part of a massive deception operation meant to fool Hitler into thinking the Allied landings would be at Pas-de-Calais, France, and not Normandy. The deception worked. When the Allied invasion landed on June 6, Hitler and his generals were caught flatfooted.

As Allied soldiers stormed ashore and secured the lodgment along the Cotentin Peninsula, Patton was already preparing for his next assignment—command of the U.S. Third Army. On August 1, Bradley and Eisenhower activated the Third as part of Operation Cobra, the breakout force from Normandy. Patton's army, like a racehorse, jumped out of the starting gate, and was rolling across France within days. His tanks were too fast for the Germans, and each time they attempted to establish a blocking position, Patton's men either bypassed it or steamrolled over it.

By September 1, 1944, Patton was within a few hours of the German border. His tanks had sped across France, shattering German units and stunning German generals, who suddenly realized that he was their chief threat along the Western Front. But Patton's stampede had ended: The Allies had run out of gas. The speed of the advance had been as much a surprise to Eisenhower and his staff as it had been to the Germans. The planners had not foreseen such a huge consumption of fuel. In fact, they calculated that they would reach only the Seine River within three months of the invasion. Patton's men had far surpassed that goal and were waiting along the banks of the Moselle, a short drive to the Rhine itself.

The operational pause caused by the supply shortage allowed the Germans to regroup, and in mid-September, they counterattacked Patton's spearheads near the town of Arracourt. For more than two weeks, Patton's tanks battled the German panzers and, in the end, emerged victorious. The Germans lost hundreds of irreplaceable panzers, a steep price to pay for the Americans' short delay of only a few weeks. The next few months were a time of logistical famine for Patton's army. As a consequence, he began to stockpile his supplies for a major push scheduled for the nineteenth of December. His ambitious goal was to bounce over the Rhine and seize the town of Frankfurt. The German offensive that began on December 16 was about to thwart his grand scheme, and he was heading to his boss's headquarters to discuss the change of plans.[6]

After more than an hour of driving, Patton's small convoy of jeeps arrived in Luxembourg City. For several minutes the convoy wound its way through narrow and winding streets, finally reaching a large pie-shaped square near the center of the capital. Bordering the southern edge of the square were two crescent-shaped buildings, flanked with two stubby towers. The jeeps pulled up to the main entrance, and Patton's entourage stepped out. An MP stood at the door and checked their identification papers. Once he verified everyone's credentials, he saluted and waved them inside, where General Bradley was waiting. Prior to the war, the massive stone edifice had been the headquarters of the Luxembourg State Railway. Now it served as the headquarters of the largest U.S. Army formation in history.

Patton and his staff marched straight to the operations room and reported to

Bradley, who stood next to a large map. All the units in the Twelfth Army Group were indicated on the map, as well as the known enemy units. Patton could see that the penetration was far worse than he had originally imagined.

When Bradley had arrived at EAGLE TAC the day before, he, too, was shocked when he saw all the enemy advancements. He asked his chief of staff, Major General Leven Cooper Allen, "Pardon my French, Lev, but just where in hell has this sonuvabitch gotten all his strength?" By that point, Twelfth Army Group had confirmed that the Germans had fourteen divisions in the bulge.

Bradley could now inform Patton that the shoulders were holding. The 7th Armored Division had disrupted the Nazi juggernaut by occupying the vital road net of St. Vith, denying its use to the panzers, while farther south, the 10th Armored Division had bolstered the 4th Infantry Division, locking down the southern shoulder. The problem was the center. "By the following morning, December 18," Bradley later wrote, "the center of our line in the Ardennes had been crushed. . . . Manteuffel's panzers had smashed through the 28th Division to overrun Middleton's reserves and head for Bastogne almost midway between the city of Luxembourg and Liège. To the north the of the unlucky 28th, two regiments of the 106th had already been encircled in position [The two regiments would later surrender]."

Bradley, with authorization of the Allied Supreme Commander, General Dwight D. Eisenhower, had already deployed the 101st Airborne and Combat Command B of the 10th Armored Division to hold Bastogne. In fact, the 10th Armored had been part of Third Army, and Patton had been reluctant to release it to Bradley because he had earmarked it for the Saar Offensive. Patton could see now that he was wrong. First Army needed all the help they could get.

Bradley briefed his fiery subordinate on his idea, using the map to describe his plan. It was simple: Hold Bastogne and limit von Rundstedt's ability to supply his troops. Meanwhile, brace the northern and southern shoulders, thereby forcing "the enemy to funnel his strength due west into the Ardennes where the terrain would sponge it up."

Patton told Bradley what he could do: "I can halt the attack of the 4th Armored and concentrate it near Longwy, starting at midnight." Bradley nodded while Patton continued. "The 80th Division can be removed from the line, and it can start for Luxembourg in the morning. The 26th Division, even though it has four thousand green replacements from headquarters units, can be alerted to move in twenty-four hours."

The Twelfth Army Group commander liked what he heard, and outlined a basic plan for Patton's Third Army. "While First Army rolled with the German's Bulge offensive on the north," Bradley described, "Third Army would slash into its underbelly by wheeling up from the Saar."

Bradley recounted that Patton was not thrilled to postpone his Saar offensive, but he remarked, "But what the hell, we'll still be killing Krauts."

The two commanders worked out some basic details before Patton left for Nancy. As they walked out of EAGLE TAC, Bradley assured him, "We won't commit any more of your stuff than we have to. I want to save it for a whale of a blow when we hit back—and we're going to hit this bastard hard." Patton smiled when he heard Bradley's comments. Now he had to drive back to his headquarters and inform his staff that they had some planning to do.[7]

Late Afternoon to 2300 Hours, Monday, December 18
Molitor Barracks, Nancy, France
Headquarters, U.S. Third Army

Patton's convoy arrived in Nancy early in the evening. The previous day, he had alerted Major General John Millikin, commander of III Corps, that he and his unit might be heading north as part of a new operation. As Patton thought about his discussion with Bradley, it was obvious that III Corps' idea would now become the plan.

At 2300 hours, Patton received a call from Bradley. General Eisenhower wanted to see him, Bradley, and General Jacob L. Devers at EAGLE MAIN in Verdun, France, the following morning at 1100 hours. Patton acknowledged the order and hung up the phone. Knowing that a major shift in Allied operations was in the offing, he directed his own staff to meet him at 0800 the next morning. It would not give them a lot of time to plan, but he knew that his staff could do it.

Colonel Koch's team immediately went to work, researching the various issues. They assessed that there were three avenues of approach from south to north. The first one originated in Arlon, moved north to Bastogne, and then on to

Liège. The second one started in Luxembourg City, wound north to St. Vith, and on to Malmedy. Finally, the third also began in Luxembourg City, snaked its way northward to Echternach, and on to Prüm.

The terrain would be mixed. South of the Sauer River, the undulating hills and numerous secondary roads were favorable to motorized and mechanized movement. However, north of the Sauer and closer to the Our River, forests and numerous creeks severely restricted such traffic. Koch determined that the best axis of advance would be from Arlon to Bastogne and from there to St. Vith. Satisfied, he decided to issue his report at the staff meeting the next morning.

Elsewhere, men and machines had started to stir. At midnight, less than an hour after Patton spoke with Bradley, Major General Millikin's III Corps Headquarters received its initial warning order that they were going to link up with First Army. Millikin's staff immediately packed up and left Metz for Luxembourg City at 0930 hours the following morning. In that span of time, Millikin had to exchange one division and a cavalry group for another two divisions. III Corps now comprised the 80th and 26th Infantry Divisions, and the 4th Armored Division. To ensure that Third Army knew what was happening, Millikin issued a situation report at 1200 hours on December 19, while Patton was attending his meeting in Verdun, that all three divisions were northbound. The race for Bastogne was on.[8]

1100 Hours, Tuesday, December 19
Verdun, France
EAGLE MAIN Headquarters, U.S. Twelfth Army Group

General Eisenhower had called this meeting to discuss what to do about the Bulge. In addition to Patton and Bradley, Ike had asked General Jacob L. Devers, commander of the Sixth Army group, to attend. Also in attendance were several Brits, including Deputy Supreme Commander Air Marshal Arthur Tedder, Ike's second in command and one of the Royal Air Force's best commanders. Each of the senior generals brought several key staff members to assist them with planning.

The American generals were well acquainted. Bradley and Eisenhower had been classmates at West Point, where both earned their commissions in 1915. Patton and Devers were West Point graduates of the class of 1909. Furthermore,

Patton had met Eisenhower in 1918, while serving at Camp Colt, Pennsylvania. Both men had become early advocates of the tank, which spurred their developing friendship.

The meeting room was Spartan, the only source of heat one potbellied stove. The cold atmosphere epitomized the bleak attitude that some of the staff exhibited.

Patton later wrote that Brigadier General Kenneth Strong, Eisenhower's G-2, "gave a picture of the situation which was far from happy."

Eisenhower sensed the gloom and said, "The present situation is to be regarded as one of opportunity for us and not of disaster. There will be only cheerful faces at this conference table."

Patton, picking up on Eisenhower's positive attitude, replied, "Hell, let's have the guts to let the sons of bitches go all the way to Paris. Then we'll really cut 'em up and chew 'em up."

Patton's infectious swagger instantly lightened the mood. Ike smiled. Of course, despite Patton's idea, he did not want the German army to cross the Meuse River. To prevent this, Eisenhower outlined his intent to his subordinates. His plan was simple: Cut the Bulge off from both the northern and southern end. He did not have a force to the north capable of counterattacking the German Sixth Panzer Army. To create one, Ike concluded that he would have to shorten the line so that he could pull units out and prepare them for a counterattack, and such an operation would take time. Luckily, the northern shoulder, though pressed, was holding.

Meanwhile, as General Strong had pointed out to the group, the southern part of the Bulge was the problem. There the Germans had achieved a penetration, and their panzers were already rolling west, surrounding Bastogne and heading to the Meuse. The Allies did not have time to build up a reserve. They needed to attack as soon as possible.

Fortunately, Patton's Third Army *was* in position to strike northward. "How soon will you be able to go, George?" Bradley asked his subordinate.

Patton's answer stunned many in the room. "Forty-eight hours."

According to Patton, his statement "created a ripple of excitement. Some people thought I was boasting and others seemed to be pleased."

After the war, Bradley wrote:

George estimated 48 hours; any other commander would have held his breath and believed himself taking a chance on 98. Now totally reconciled to an indefinite postponement of his Saar offensive, George was itching to start the counterattack. He lighted a fresh cigar and pointed to the Bulge where it pierced the thin blue lines on our war map. "Brad," he exclaimed, "this time the Kraut's stuck his head in a meat grinder." With a turn of his fist he added, "And this time I've got hold of the handle."

Patton explained his basic plan to Eisenhower and the group. He promised that he could attack with a corps of three divisions, and they would strike the German flank as early as December 22. The corps would be Millikin's III Corps, and the three divisions would be the 26th and 80th Infantry divisions, and the 4th Armored Division. If Eisenhower wanted a stronger counterattack force, it would take time to assemble it, and Patton argued that he would lose the element of surprise. In short, hitting the German salient with three divisions sooner was better than hitting the Germans with six divisions later. Patton's reasoning convinced Eisenhower, and he agreed to Patton's plan.

However, Ike warned Patton that he wanted a sledgehammer to hit the German flank, not a pinprick. "I personally cautioned him against a piecemeal attack," Ike later wrote, "and gave directions that the advance was to be methodical and sure." He, Patton, and Bradley quickly agreed that Patton should attack no earlier than December 22, but no later than the twenty-third.

Now the generals had only to work out the details. Dever's Sixth Army Group would extend their forces northward to relieve Patton's Third Army south of Saarlouis (Saurlautern). In addition, Devers would assume control of several of Third Army's units, including the 87th Infantry Division. Since Patton would assume command of Middleton's VIII Corps as he approached Bastogne, Patton's Third Army would be larger than before the Bulge. Moreover, with Dever's Sixth Army Group securing Third Army's southern flank, Patton could now focus solely on relieving Bastogne. Satisfied with their plan, the generals ended the meeting and left to communicate their orders to their respective staff sections.

The war council had been brief, only a few hours; yet those hours were crucial. "The directive issued at Verdun on December 19," Eisenhower later wrote, "established the outline of the plan for counteraction on the southern flank and was not thereafter varied."

Patton called his chief of staff, Brigadier General Hobart R. Gay. Since his staff had already worked out the various plans, to execute the operation he needed only to issue the brevity code: NICKEL. When Gay heard it, he knew the axis of advance would roll to Bastogne via Arlon, and leading the way would be the 4th Armored Division.[9]

0815 to 1200 Hours, Tuesday, December 19
Arlon, Belgium
G-2 Section, 4th Armored Division[10]

While Patton's staff met and finalized the plans for the upcoming operation, the 4th Armored Division's G-2 section had already arrived in Arlon and started to analyze the new enemy forces. Lieutenant Colonel Harry E. Brown, the G-2, directed his men to switch their focus from the Moselle region to Bastogne after he received the change-of-mission warning order. By noon, G-2 was tracking the battle's progress in VIII Corps' sector. The radio operators, logging the messages, could sense it was going to be a tough fight ahead.

The first report set the tone. An operator read the message aloud while another soldier inserted pins on a map, indicating the location of likely enemy forces. The penetration resembled a bulge. Farthest to the north, the Americans were holding on to the vital hub of St. Vith, yet the Germans had almost surrounded it, and their panzer forces had seized the town of Recht to the northwest. In the center of the bulge, VIII Corps still held Wiltz, but German panzers were coming fast. Even worse, intelligence reports indicated that several German divisions were in the immediate area, including the Panzer Lehr and 2nd Panzer divisions, the 26th Volksgrenadier Division, and the 5th Parachute (Fallschirmjäger) Division. Closest to Arlon was the southern flank, where several German divisions were attempting to capture the town of Echternach. The Americans still held the town, but its outcome was bleak. American forces had identified four German divisions nearby.

While staffers logged and analyzed incoming reports, the fighting continued.

The town of Dahl, Luxembourg, fell to German forces at 1130 hours. Simultaneously, German panzers struck American forces east of Bastogne near the town of Bras. The news didn't improve as noon approached. Units of the 9th Armored Division, fighting hard near St. Vith, reported they were now "surrounded." When the radio operator finished reading off the report, the soldier updating the map could see that it would be a tough slog if the 4th Armored Division was heading north.[11]

The 4th Armored Division had earned a well-deserved reputation for speed and efficiency. The Germans called them "Roosevelt's Highest Paid Butchers." By the end of the war, the 4th Armored Division had become "synonymous" with Patton's Third Army. Though it served at times under four different corps commanders, it spent 280 of its 281 days in combat as part of the Third.[12]

By December 1944, the division had seen a great deal of combat. In August it had led the way through France when Patton's army broke out at the end of Operation Cobra. Like a sprinter, it shot out of the starting block and almost beat the Germans back to the West Wall. In September, the division defeated elements of the Fifth Panzer Army in one of the largest tank battles on the Western Front near the French town of Arracourt. During the wet autumn months, the division bludgeoned its way forward before crossing the Saar River on November 23. In early December, elements of the 4th were fighting to break through the Maginot Line. Now Patton was calling on the division again to lead the way to relieve the 101st Airborne at Bastogne.[13]

Despite its stellar record, not everything was well. Two senior commanders had been on the job for only two weeks. Brigadier General Herbert L. Earnest had assumed command of Combat Command A on December 4. The previous commander, Colonel William P. Withers, had been a disaster. Withers had taken over on November 17, but within three weeks had managed to alienate most of his subordinates and superiors. He had to go, and when Earnest arrived, Withers assumed the role of the assistant commander, which was not even an authorized position. Earnest, though new to the job, was a solid performer, and would lead CCA for the next two months before he took over command of the 90th Infantry Division.[14]

Breaking in a combat commander during a major operation like the Bulge would have been a challenge, but the 4th Armored was also breaking in a new division commander. Major General John S. Wood, who had led the division since June 18, 1942, was relieved of command on December 2. The official reason was fatigue, but historian Don M. Fox believes that Wood had run afoul of his then corps commander, Major General Manton Eddy. The two men had butted heads several times in the months leading up to his relief, but the performance of Colonel Wither's CCA in the last weeks of November might have been the final straw for Eddy, who asked Patton to sack the popular officer.

The new division commander was Major General Hugh J. Gaffey, who had been Patton's chief of staff before taking command of the 4th. Prior, Gaffey had been the commander of the 2nd Armored Division, which he led during the campaign on Sicily in 1943. Though he was new to the 4th Armored Division, Gaffey was not new to division command. Luckily, Gaffey had a seasoned Combat Command B commander in Brigadier General Holmes E. Dager, who had commanded Combat Command B throughout all of its major combat operations. Gaffey also had Colonel Wendell Blanchard, who had been on the job since September, to lead Combat Command Reserve, Hence, two out of the three combat commanders were proven performers. In the coming weeks, Gaffey was going to need all three to prove themselves in combat.[15]

0100 to 0125 Hours, Tuesday, December 19, to Wednesday, December 20
Through France, Across Southern Belgium, and into Luxembourg
Combat Command A, 4th Armored Division

While the generals deliberated, the soldiers of the 4th Armored Division were rolling out and driving to Belgium and Luxembourg. One tanker from Baker Company, 35th Tank Battalion, recalled, "The silence was unnatural. No one talking. No messages coming over the radio." For many tank drivers, the greatest danger was boredom, because boredom led to drowsiness.

Another danger was bad weather. Rain coupled with temperatures hovering around freezing turned the road surface to ice. Vehicles slid off the highway and into ditches. Despite their tracks, even tanks fell victim to the ice. Fortunately, tank crews had perfected a drill in response to these common accidents. One driver explained: "You'd get started toward the ditch and you couldn't stop it and you'd just end up in the ditch. Another tank would come along and hook up a cable to it, these one-inch cables, and help that one back on the road and get going again, and that's the way the column went."

Even with accidents, CCA encountered little trouble. Passing through Vigny, France, American forces stopped in Trieux, France, at 1630 hours to refuel and rest the drivers. Around 1915 hours, everyone was back in their vehicles and driving north, and at 0125 hours, many units reached their destination, which were towns like Clemency, Luxembourg, and other villages along the Belgian-French-Luxembourg border. General Earnest was pleased. His combat command had traveled more than a hundred miles in less than twenty-four hours.[16]

0945 to 1900 Hours, Wednesday, December 20
Vaux-lez-Rosières, Belgium
Combat Command B, 4th Armored Division

Combat Command B had spent much of the previous day on the road, driving more than 160 miles through France to Belgium. The main body had left Cutting, France, at 0030 hours on the morning of the nineteenth and arrived in Vaux-lez-Rosières, Belgium, at 2000 hours on the same day. They encountered no German forces. Even more amazing, CCB had only one set of military maps, and General Dager was the one who carried them.

Major Albin F. Irzyk, commander of the 8th Tank Battalion, described how Dager navigated his entire command: "I was guided and directed by General Dager in a variety of ways: he radioed instructions from his jeep; his staff relayed radio messages; he rode alongside to shout directions at me in my turret; and at tricky intersections, he personally dismounted to point the way." After they arrived in Belgium, Dager ordered the units to send out patrols and the rest of CCB to bed down for the night.

Around 0945 hours on December 20, Dager received word to dispatch a task force to Bastogne as soon as possible. Major General Troy Middleton, commander of VIII Corps, had sent a message to CCB informing them that the German army had cut off units from the 101st Airborne near the town of Mande Saint-Étienne, west of Bastogne. Though panzer divisions had not completely surrounded Bastogne yet, Middleton felt that the 101st did not have enough combat power on hand to repel a major armored thrust. Thus, he ordered CCB to cobble together a task force to send into the city.

At the time, confusion reigned. Did CCB belong to VIII Corps or did it belong to III Corps? Regardless, Dager had argued his case with Middleton, asking the corps commander to wait until Major General Hugh Gaffey arrived before he committed any additional forces to Bastogne. Dager's request fell on deaf ears. Middleton wanted more combat power in Bastogne, and so Dager instructed his subordinate, Major Irzyk, to create the task force, which would have one medium tank company from his own battalion, one infantry company from the 10th Armored Infantry Battalion, and one battery of 105mm self-propelled howitzers from the 22nd Armored Field Artillery Battalion. The commander of the task force was Irzyk's own executive officer, Captain Bert P. Ezell.

The makeshift task force set out for Bastogne along the Neufchâteau–Bastogne highway. The trip was short and without incident. After informing Irzyk that he had arrived safely, Ezell reported to Colonel William Roberts, commander of Combat Command B's 10th Armored Division, whose tanks and armored infantry were sharing the battle space with the 101st Airborne.

Meanwhile, the 4th Armored Division headquarters, shortly after it heard about Task Force Ezell, ordered Irzyk to recall it and send it to Nives to rejoin the division. When Irzyk radioed his executive officer, his driver answered and told him that Ezell was already in a meeting with Colonel Roberts.

Irzyk did not have time to wait. "Get him!" he barked.

Minutes later, Ezell got on the handset, and Irzyk told him about the change in plan. Understandably, Ezell was reluctant to tell Roberts about the new mission, but orders were orders. Within an hour, Task Force Ezell was back on the road and heading south. The privates and sergeants, driving the tanks and sitting in back of the half-tracks, probably thought the generals who concocted this scheme were disorganized idiots. Their sentiment was justified.

Fortunately, the gods of war were smiling on the itinerant task force. As they rumbled down the lonely highway, the tankers and infantrymen passed an army truck wedged into a roadside ditch. Stopping to investigate, they discovered the driver was dead. Irzyk remembered that the "top of his head had been blown off above the eyes, apparently by an armor-piercing round."

Farther down the highway, they found muddy tracks that bisected the road and led west toward the Meuse River. The tankers knew that the tread marks did not come from American tanks. More than likely, a unit of German Panthers had crossed the highway only minutes before Ezell's men had arrived. Moving on, Ezell came across two battalions of abandoned towed artillery, some of the engines still running. Not a single American soldier remained. Realizing he could not leave all this operable artillery behind, Ezell ordered his men to hook up the guns and tow them back to Nives.

At 1400 hours, III Corps resumed control of the 4th Armored, and by 1900 hours, Irzyk reported that everyone had returned from their seven-hour odyssey. In short, Ezell needed only a couple of hours to drive to Bastogne on December 20. When the rest of 4th Armored tried to reach the city on the twenty-second, it would take the division five days.[17]

1900 Hours, Wednesday, December 20
Around Flatzbourhof and Bigonville, Luxembourg

"Don't leave the house!" a voice shouted out from the darkness.

Sophie-Lion Lutgen stopped in her tracks. The authoritarian tone told her in an instant who had returned to Bigonville.

"We live on the other side of the street," she pleaded. She had gone to her shed to milk her family's cows with her sister.

"Starting a half-hour ago you may not go out, or we'll shoot."

Sophie pushed her sister back inside the shed. The Germans had returned. She was not surprised. For days, she had known something was wrong. On December 17, American soldiers in and around Bigonville had started seeming anxious. Gone was the infectious American bravado. Traffic increased as American trucks rolled through, traveling to and from the front. That night, the news on the radio reported, "The Germans have crossed the border at Echternach and Vianden."

The next morning, citizens started to pack as more news arrived from the front. The dreaded Hun was returning, and rumors spread that the Germans were near Wiltz. On December 19, the situation worsened. That day she wrote in her diary:

> Already early in the morning it's swarming with refugees outside. Open vans, pulled by one or two horses, with old people, women and children, with suitcases and baskets, are rattling hurriedly down the streets. People on foot laboriously pull their fully-loaded handcarts behind them. They have to travel on the shoulders, because the streets belong to the cars, the motorcycles, and the tractors. . . . Oh, this excitement, this fear! Where do all these frantic people want to go? They don't know themselves; just "farther on," always "farther on."

Sophie and her family made preparations to depart. That afternoon, refugees shuffling through the village informed them that the Germans had taken Arsdorf and Bauschleiden. Their packing continued into the early morning, and by 0300 hours, they decided to sleep before setting out.

When the sun dawned the morning of the twentieth, emptiness had replaced the hustle and bustle of the previous forty-eight hours on Bigonville's streets. Sophie's family decided to stay, yet they urged her brother to leave. The Germans frowned upon military-age males, and either deported them to work in the German war industry or forced them to enlist in the German army. Any young man remaining in town would likely be suspected of working with the resistance and executed without a trial. Sophie's brother agreed, and that afternoon he left on his bike.

For several hours, Sophie and her sister remained stuck in the shed with the cows, trying to keep warm. Suddenly they heard a pounding on the door. Sophie glanced at her sister uneasily, but knew she had to make sure. She opened the door.

The barrel of a rifle was the first thing she saw. "Are there Americans here?" a voice demanded. Two German soldiers held lamps outside the door.

She shook her head and replied, "No."

Convinced she was telling the truth, the *fallschirmjägers* grunted and departed. Several minutes later they returned. This time they asked for coffee. Sophie smiled and agreed, but she told them that to provide them with coffee, she needed to return to her house across the street. Both men nodded and showed her and her sister back to their house, where Sophie brewed them hot coffee and offered them food.

Within minutes, their brusque exterior was gone, and the satisfied Germans entertained Sophie and her family with tales of their adventures. She soon learned that the two men were searching for American soldiers. They would knock on a door, and if no one answered, they would break it down. The *fallschirmjägers* found an abundance of food inside the homes they had ransacked, which they promptly stole, since the German supply system had failed to feed them.

When they were finished eating, they bade Sophie farewell and thanked her family for the hospitality. After they left, Sophie heard a noncommissioned officer or officer yell at the two soldiers, accusing them of leaving their posts. She remained in her house the rest of the evening, wondering what the next morning would bring. More important, she wondered whether the Americans would ever return.[18]

Wednesday, December 20
Luxembourg City, Luxembourg
Tactical Command Post Headquarters, U.S. Third Army

While Sophie pondered her family's fate, General Patton's staff issued the order that would answer her question. As per Eisenhower's discussion in Verdun, Third Army would shift its axis of advance from an easterly direction to a northern one. Patton's task to Third Army was direct: "destroy the enemy on its front and [be] prepared to change direction to the northeast and seize crossings of the Rhine River."

Patton's decisive operation would be General Millikin's III Corps. As planned, he assigned three divisions to III Corps: the 26th and 80th infantry divisions, and the 4th Armored Division. Even though Patton could not task the 4th Armored directly, since that was Millikin's job, everyone understood that the 4th Armored was the main effort in the corps' scheme of maneuver. Like Third Army, III Corps' task was: "Attack north in zone on army order in the direction of St. Vith . . . and destroy the enemy on its front."

To protect its southern flank, XII Corps would assume a supporting role, at-

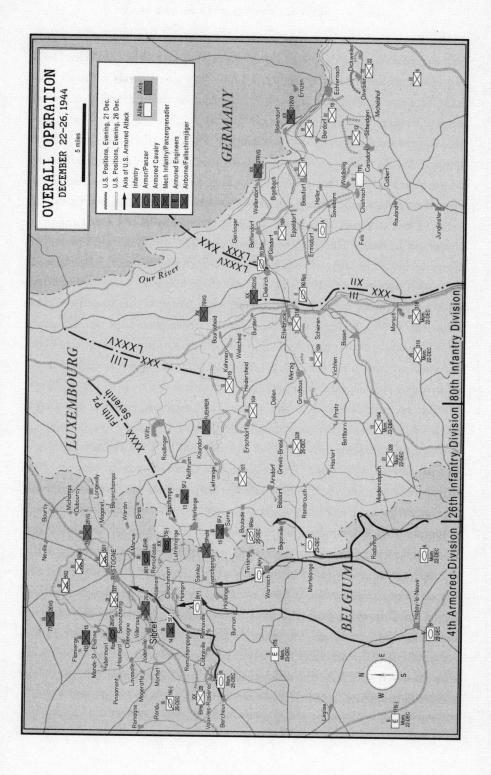

U.S. Positions, Evening, 21 Dec.
U.S. Positions, Evening, 26 Dec.
Axis of U.S. Armored Attack

Infantry
Armor/Panzer
Armored Cavalry
Mech Infantry/Panzergrenadier
Armored Engineers
Airborne/Fallschirmjäger

Allies   Axis

GERMANY

LUXEMBOURG

BELGIUM

Our River

Fifth Pz.
Seventh

4th Armored Division | 26th Infantry Division | 80th Infantry Division tacking German forces to the north, while maintaining control of the west bank of the Moselle River. Plus, it would conduct probing attacks to determine the location and strength of German bridgeheads along the Sauer and Our rivers. Last, XII Corps had to be prepared to attack and penetrate the Siegfried Line near the town of Bitburg.

Farther south was XX Corps, which had been under the command of Major General Walton Walker in all the major operations since D-day. Unlike the other corps, its mission was defensive, and it had the task to defend the Saarlautern bridgehead, while maintaining contact with the U.S. Seventh Army farther south.

The newest addition to Patton's Third Army was VIII Corps, under the command of Major General Troy Middleton. The dog-faced soldiers of VIII Corps had one key task: to keep fighting and be ready to resume the offensive. The main division in VIII Corps was the 101st Airborne, surrounded in Bastogne. Though the German XXXXVII Panzer Corps had encircled the paratroopers, the "Screaming Eagles" were far from beleaguered. In fact, they were tying down several German units that could have served a more offensive role elsewhere in the Bulge. Meanwhile, the 28th Infantry Division, defending the area around Neufchâteau, would be the link between VIII Corps and III Corps. The panzers had bloodied the 28th Infantry in Luxembourg at the beginning of the offensive, but the soldiers from Pennsylvania had delayed the German offensive so that Patton's army could get into position. Now it was payback time.

To provide air support, Patton could call on the strategic bombers of the Eighth Air Force and the medium bombers of the Ninth Air Force. In addition, Patton would have seven fighter-bomber groups, one tactical reconnaissance group, and one night-fighter squadron from the XIX Tactical Air Command. Coupled with the four army corps on the ground, it was an awesome assemblage of combat power.

However, airpower was useless without fair weather. In fact, lousy flying weather had hamstrung his Third Army for several weeks. Unlike his divisions, Patton had no control over the daily forecast, but he knew who did. On December 8, he met with the Third Army chaplain, Father James H. O'Neill, and asked him to write a prayer for good weather. According to Father O'Neill, Patton was a deeply religious man.

During the meeting, he told the chaplain:

I am a strong believer in Prayer. There are three ways that men get what they want; by planning, by working, and by Praying. Any great military operation takes careful planning, or thinking. Then you must have well-trained troops to carry it out; that's working. But between the plan and the operation there is always an unknown. That unknown spells defeat or victory, success or failure. It is the reaction of the actors to the ordeal when it actually comes. Some people call that getting the breaks; I call it God. God has His part, or margin in everything. That's where prayer comes in. Up to now, in the Third Army, God has been very good to us. We have never retreated; we have suffered no defeats, no famine, no epidemics. This is because a lot of people back home are praying for us. We were lucky in Africa, in Sicily, and in Italy. Simply because people prayed. But we have to pray for ourselves, too. A good soldier is not made merely by making him think and work. There is something in every soldier that goes deeper than thinking or working—it's his "guts." It is something that he has built in there; it is a world of truth and power that is higher than himself. Great living is not all output of thought and work. A man has to have intake as well. I don't know what you call it, but I call it Religion, Prayer, or God.

As instructed, Father O'Neill wrote the prayer, and Third Army's adjutant general, Colonel Robert S. Cummings, published and distributed it to the troops. The prayer was as follows: "Almighty and most merciful Father, we humbly beseech Thee, of Thy great goodness, to restrain those immoderate rains with which we have had to contend. Grant us fair weather for Battle. Graciously hearken to us as soldiers who call upon Thee that, armed with Thy power, we may advance from victory to victory, and crush the oppression and wickedness of our enemies and establish Thy justice among men and nations. Amen."

Despite the prayer, the weather was still awful, and thus, much of American airpower remained grounded. God had not yet answered Patton's prayers. That would change in a few days, and once again, Patton would be the main act on the big stage.[19]

After 1600 Hours, Thursday, December 21

Udange, Belgium

Headquarters, Combat Command A, 4th Armored Division

Udange was a quiet farming town where long barns lined the main road, while watching over the village center was the Church of Saint-Servais. On the afternoon of the twenty-first, however, the town was bustling with activity. The hamlet was now the location of Combat Command A's temporary headquarters. In one of the buildings, Brigadier General Herbert L. Earnest read over the latest field order from his boss, General Gaffey. Some of the news was good. The 4th Armored Division commander had selected Earnest's combat command to advance down the main axis of the Martelange–Bastogne highway and seize the key city. In addition, CCA would have the 35th Tank Battalion and the 51st Armored Infantry Battalion as its two main maneuver units. Plus, the 66th and the 274th Armored Field Artillery battalions would provide artillery support, while Able Company of the 24th Engineers would add mobility assets to the team. To deal with the panzers, General Earnest would have Able Company of the 704th Tank Destroyer Battalion. It was a lethal package of combat power.[20]

Though Earnest had been on the job for only a couple of weeks, Gaffey had chosen him to lead the main effort. The new commander was not naive, though. Earnest knew that he could thank his subordinates for his unit's important role in the upcoming operation. Lieutenant Colonel Delk Oden, the commander of the 35th Tank Battalion, had been with the division since the beginning, and prior to commanding the 35th, he had been the commander of the 704th Tank Destroyer Battalion. Commanding the armored infantry battalion was Major Dan C. Alanis. Alanis had assumed command of the 51st Armored Infantry Battalion on December 1, but, like Oden, he had been in the division since almost the beginning. He had served as the 51st's S-3 operations officer before taking command of the 704th Tank Destroyer Battalion. Hence, Earnest had two experienced officers who would lead his task forces into the next battle.[21]

Gaffey had another reason to pick CCA over the other combat commands: It had the highest number of serviceable tanks. According to the division's logistics officer, Lieutenant Colonel Bernard C. Knestrick, CCA's 35th Tank Battalion would have forty-two M4 Sherman medium tanks and seventeen M5 Stuart light tanks as of 1810 hours on the twenty-second. To put it in perspective, 37th Tank Battalion had only twenty-nine Shermans and thirteen Stuart light tanks on the same day. In addition, though CCB's 8th Tank Battalion also had a large number of tanks, according to Major Morris Abrams, the assistant G-4, those tanks were nearing the end of their service life. Brigadier General Holmes E. Dager, the commander of CCB, and Colonel Clay Olbon later claimed, "In fact, the tanks were literally falling apart and the original number of twenty-eight was reduced to eighteen prior to action in this period, due solely to need of repair." Therefore, the main effort went CCA.[22]

Earnest glanced at the map in front of him. Gaffey's mission to CCA was straightforward: "to move from its present position during [the] night . . . to an attack position north of Arlon. Attack on order at H-hour to overcome and destroy enemy in zone. Maintain contact with 26 Infantry Division on [the] right."[23]

After reading the mission statement, the commander of CCA traced the route his forces would take to reach Bastogne. The main road was a first-class highway, but along the route, Earnest could see the woods and villages astride it where the Germans would set up battle positions to block and disrupt his advance. Fortunately, with the exception of Martelange, there were no towns he had to drive through to reach Bastogne.

CCA was the spearhead for the entire corps. To the west, Gaffey ordered CCB, under the command of General Dager, to secure CCA's western flank. Thus, Gaffey would have two combat commands advancing northward, while Combat Command Reserve would provide additional support wherever he needed it. To the east and in the middle of the corps' area of operations, General Millikin had ordered the 26th Infantry Division to clear enemy forces while providing flank security to the 4th Armored and 80th Infantry divisions, respectively. Finally, in the east and along the Our River, the 80th Infantry Division would destroy any enemy forces while securing the western flank of the U.S. Army's XII Corps. Instead of concentrating his combat power at a narrow point, Millikin had decided to overwhelm the German southern flank by assaulting it along its entire front.[24]

Earnest knew he would have a fight on his hands. He paused to look at the town of Martelange on his map. It would be a great spot for the Germans to establish a battle position, because the main highway crossed the Sauer River at that location. While the Sauer was not a wide river, its steep banks were severely restrictive, thereby requiring tanks to use bridges to cross over it. In fact, the 4th Armored G-2 reported that approximately fifty Germany infantry and one panzer were in Martelange as of 1610 hours that afternoon. In addition, forward elements had already captured several German soldiers from the 14th Fallschirmjäger Regiment of the 5th Fallschirmjäger Division. That was a problem. *Fallschirmjägers* tended to be better soldiers than regular infantry. Moreover, it did not help CCA's mission that U.S. engineers were still cratering the roads along his route. Corps was trying to stop them, but as of 1600 hours the engineers from the 299th Combat Engineer Battalion had not received the order to cease demolitions. Thus the craters, which were there to block the panzers, instead were going to block his Sherman tanks. It was not an auspicious start.[25]

The new commander of CCA wanted to do things by the book. He knew that his contemporaries in CCB and CCR could issue orders over the radio and that would be enough for their respective subordinates. Since the other combat commanders had been in charge for several months, their subordinates knew their overall intent. They would not need to see things in writing. Earnest did not have that luxury of shared experiences with his task force commanders, and therefore he chose to produce a written field order for his officers.

He would divide CCA into two task forces. Task Force Oden, under the command of Lieutenant Colonel Delk Oden, would form the eastern column and would have the majority of the armor, while Task Force Alanis, under the command of Major Dan C. Alanis, would have the bulk of the infantry in the western column. Both forces were already forming up in their assembly areas, with TF Oden in Wolwelange and TF Alanis in Toernich. Also, Able Troop of the 25th Cavalry Squadron by this time had departed and was screening to the north between Arlon and the Sauer River. Each task force had one self-propelled artillery battalion in direct support, while the majority of engineering assets and Hellcat tank destroyers were with TF Alanis.

Earnest then dictated his intent to the operations section, which was typing up the order while he spoke. Both task forces would attack. Neither would remain in reserve. TF Alanis, after assembling that afternoon in Toernich, would then ". . . move to attack [an] assembly area north of Arlon on Combat Command order after dark. Then, it would attack north, crossing Phase Line 'Red' at H-hour."

Meanwhile, TF Oden, after assembling in Wolwelange, would ". . . move to attack assembly area north of Arlon on Combat Command order after dark and then consolidate outpost forces into the Task Force while there; then attack north, crossing Phase Line 'Red' at H-hour." As for Earnest and his command post, initially they would travel north to Arlon that night and set up in a monastery there with the division headquarters. The next morning, his command post would then move to the town of Quatre Vents, Belgium, which was south of Metzert. Finally, the main axis of advance would be the Arlon-to-Bastogne highway. Satisfied with the new field order, Earnest instructed his operations section to issue it to Alanis and Oden. Likewise, he would also send a courtesy copy to his boss, General Gaffey. It was early evening when the couriers left the command post to distribute the order. In less than twenty-four hours, Earnest's soldiers and tankers would be locked in combat with the 5th Fallschirmjäger Division.[26]

CHAPTER 3

FIRST CONTACT

| DECEMBER 22, 1944 |

★ ★ ★ ★ ★

"In this operation we must be the utmost ruthless."
—*Lieutenant General George S. Patton*

Early Morning to 1000 hours, Friday, December 22
Near Losange (Approximately 1 kilometer West of
Lutrebois in the Au Calvaire Woods), Belgium
Headquarters Element, 5th Fallschirmjäger Division

Oberst Heilmann looked out the window of his command car and noticed that it was snowing. The bare, leafless trees looked as if the clouds had dumped powdered sugar over the forest while slathering white chocolate frosting on the evergreen branches. If not for the war, he would have enjoyed staying there for a while to watch the snowfall, but he had to attend to more pressing matters.

After several minutes, another staff car drove up. Heilmann looked at his watch. The time was 1000 hours. The snow was coming down so hard now that Heilmann could barely make out anything in the wood line beyond them. The doors of both automobiles opened and several men stepped out, including the commander of the 5th Fallschirmjäger Division. Heilmann saluted first. The other man quickly replied with one of his own. The man Heilmann saluted was his new corps commander, General der Kavallerie Edwin Graf von Rothkirch und Trach.

Both men had much to discuss. Von Rothkirch commanded the LIII Infantry Corps. As a result of the *fallschirmjägers'* success over the past few days, General Erich Brandenberger, the commander of the Seventh Army, decided it was time for LIII Corps to take over the northern shoulder of the Seventh Army's area of operations. As a result, von Rothkirch assumed control of the 5th Fallschirmjäger Division. General Baptist Kniess would continue to command the LXXXV Corps, but his area of operations would extend farther south, as opposed to north and west, which now belonged to LIII Corps' area of operations.

For von Rothkirch, the decision started a chain reaction of activity. After Wiltz fell to the 5th Fallschirmjäger Division on December 20, Seventh Army headquarters activated LIII Corps, which had conducted its battle handoff at noon on the twenty-first. Brandenberger's initial orders to von Rothkirch were concise: "Further rapid advance towards the West. Send vanguard elements to Saint-Hubert and Libramont. Protect southern flank [of Fifth Panzer Army]." With orders in hand, the commander of LIII Corps got to work.

Von Rothkirch's first order of business was the establishment of his corps headquarters and a tour of the battlefield. He selected Dahl, several kilometers southeast of Wiltz, and by 1500 hours on the twenty-first, his corps command post was up and running. The corps commander spent most of the day in his car. Traffic jams—due to poor transportation management, narrow roads, and, of course, the American army—slowed his progress. Still, he saw enough to know that his chief problem lay to the south and not to the west. To the west, the American army had vanished, but to the south, his forces were already engaging elements of an unknown force in the vicinity of Martelange. Moreover, he did not know whether these American forces were stragglers from the decimated 28th Infantry Division, or worse, if they were part of a new American force coming up from Arlon. Thus, he decided to set out for Martelange on the morning of the twenty-second to find the answers.

Early that next morning, von Rothkirch found Oberst Kurt Gröschke, the commander of the 15th Fallschirmjäger Regiment, near Martelange. Gröschke verified the LIII Corps commander's assessment of the southern flank. His *fallschirmjägers* were reporting enemy activity south of Martelange. Von Rothkirch mentally recorded the valuable intelligence and then departed to find the commander of the 14th Fallschirmjäger Regiment, Oberst Arno Schimmel.

Oberst Schimmel was farther west of Martelange, and the corps commander located him later that morning. Fortunately, Schimmel's issues were more command-and-control focused than enemy focused. His regiment lacked experienced officers and soldiers. Therefore, as result of the unit's rapid advance, the regiment, in von Rothkirch's account, ". . . was scattered over a wide area." It would take time to reconsolidate and organize the units. Time, though, was running out.

Now it was 1000 hours, and von Rothkirch wanted to discuss the mission of the 5th Fallschirmjäger Division with its commander, Oberst Ludwig Heilmann. Both men chose to use a map to outline their issues and recommendations. Heilmann spoke first.

"Sir, my intention is to advance toward Libramont, as planned, but I'm concerned with the unsettled situation at Martelange," he reported to his boss, as he circled the areas on the map with his finger.

The count then recalled what he had seen earlier when he visited Oberst Gröschke. Finally, he responded. "General Heilmann," he began, pointing to Martelange on the map, "discontinue your advance to the west for now. Defend Martelange and the rest of the Sauer River sector. In addition, you need to regroup and reestablish the links between all of your units. I cannot stress enough the importance of Martelange."

Heilmann, hearing the change of mission, affirmed the new order. "Yes, sir." The division commander then looked up from the map and asked, "One other thing, sir. Yesterday, I asked General Knieß about the status of the 13th Fallschirmjäger Regiment, which is not under my control right now. I need it back so that I can secure my southern flank. He told me he would look into it."

The count agreed with Heilmann's request and answered, "I will contact Seventh Army Headquarters and see if we can bring up your missing regiment." Both commanders knew that the 5th Fallschirmjäger was too spread out. With his 13th Regiment under the control of the 352nd Volksgrenadier Division, Heilmann had to defend a battle space more than twenty kilometers in length with only two regiments. At this point in the battle, Heilmann's division could not form an adequate defense against a strong push.

Heilmann, though, had to do something until reinforcements arrived. The LIII Corps would soon receive the Führer-Begleit-Brigade from the OKW Reserve, but that unit would not reach the battle space until Christmas, at the earliest. Thus, Heilmann had to block the American counterattack alone. The *fallschirm-jäger* commander quickly reviewed the options in his head. Major Gerhard Martin's pioneers from the 5th Fallschirmjäger Pioneer Battalion had already started blowing bridges along the likely avenues of approach from Martelange. (Ironically, the American engineers had blown most of the bridges already.) Other than that, there was little the division commander could do.

Oberst Gröschke, the commander of the 15th Fallschirmjäger Regiment, had even less flexibility than his division commander. He ordered Hauptmann Heide, the commander of his 3rd Battalion, to defend Martelange. Heide had too much ground to defend with his limited combat power. His battalion normally would have had three rifle companies, but his 11th Company, which was motorized, had remained in the rear. Thus, he had only two infantry companies, and so he selected his 10th Company for the mission. The rest of his 3rd Battalion was spread out. 9th Company was defending Bigonville and Flatzbourhof, while his 12th Company, which was the heavy weapons company, was in Bigonville under the command of a Leutnant Peischer. Meanwhile, Heide had established his command post west of Martelange, in the village of Bodange.

In short, the division commander, Ludwig Heilmann, had yielded the initiative to the enemy. He had no choice. Unfortunately for him and his division, the Americans would never give it back.[1]

0500 to 0830 Hours, Friday, December 22
Along the Arlon–Bastogne Highway, Belgium/Luxembourg Border
D Company, 35th Tank Battalion (TF Oden), CCA

Combat Command A moved out around 0500 hours the next morning. As planned, Task Force Oden advanced, in column, along the eastern flank, while Task Force Alanis, the western column, drove north along the Arlon–Bastogne Highway. Both columns were in blackout, and since the sun didn't rise until 0834 hours, movement was slow. In addition to the impenetrable darkness, the weather patterns of northwest Europe had stirred up a blinding snowstorm.

Sergeant Albert Gaydos, a loader on an M4 Sherman tank, described the snow as "big flakes the size of silver dollars." Gaydos was a part of an artillery forward observer crew from the 66th Armored Field Artillery Battalion that drove a Sherman so it could keep up with the tankers. With him were several other individuals, including First Lieutenant Raymond L. Romig, the tank commander and the attached forward observer for D Company, 35th Tank Battalion. Gaydos's brother, Paul, also served in the same battalion, though the staff normally assigned them to different tank companies. Still, for Albert, having his brother serve in the same battalion was a bonus.

The day before, the officers had drawn straws to see whose Sherman would lead the way for Task Force Oden. Albert lost when his lieutenant drew the short one. Captain John S. Ridley, commander of D Company, grabbed Lieutenant Romig and issued him the company's approach-march plan for the next day, pointing to a green line on a map. That was the next objective. No one knew where the Germans were, but they were somewhere between them and that green line, Romig was told. The lieutenant returned to Gaydos and the rest of his crew to brief them on the plan. Most of the men swore when they got the news.

Gaydos hated traveling with Dog Company, and with good reason: In a tank battalion, D Company was the light company. Instead of Shermans with their short-barreled 75mm guns, D Company drove M5 Stuart tanks, whose 37mm gun, against a panzer, had the same effectiveness as a spitball. When a commander paired a Sherman with a group of Stuarts, the Germans would target the Sherman first, since they had little to fear from the light tanks. This was the situation that Albert faced as they moved out the next morning. His tank was the only Sherman in a platoon of five Stuarts. To Albert, they were now a big, fat target.

The first few hours of the drive were tense, but uneventful. Gaydos could sense the Germans somewhere up ahead in the swirling blizzard, and two local men confirmed his suspicions when they informed Gaydos and his crew that a German patrol had used the same road several hours prior. Lieutenant Romig reported the information back to Captain Ridley, who, unperturbed, ordered them to push onward.

Around 0835 hours, just as the sun peeked over the eastern horizon, Gaydos's tank lurched to a halt. In front of Task Force Oden lay the remnants of a bridge. The American 299th Engineers had done their job too well, blasting the span so that no one could cross it. The lead element of Task Force Oden was approximately 2.5 kilometers south of the village of Holtz. The news was not much better in front of Task Force Alanis, where there was a gaping crater that effectively blocked the main highway between Arlon and Martelange. For the next few precious hours, Combat Command A had to wait.

0835 to 1200 Hours, Friday, December 22
Quatre Vents, Belgium (South of Metzert)
Forward Command Post, CCA

Brigadier General Herbert L. Earnest was the radio's prisoner—he could not step away from it for fear of missing an important message from one of his units. Both task force Oden and Alanis were stuck, thanks to the excellent work of the U.S. Army combat engineers. Instead of blocking a German advance, the combat engineers had disrupted the U.S. Army's main counterattack.

Earnest scanned the map and did some quick figuring in his head. He grabbed one of his staff officers and told him to radio a message to both columns. Earnest could see that a two-pronged attack would not work. The best solution was the simplest: Combine the two columns into one. To do this, he ordered Oden and Alanis to rendezvous at a road junction along the main highway. For Oden, part of the column would have to backtrack and then travel westward over secondary roads. Meanwhile, Alanis's engineers would have to bridge the crater. Whoever reached the road junction first would assume the lead element in the column. However, both task forces would remain intact with their original task organization. Around 0930 hours, CCA's forward command post radioed the change of mission to Alanis and Oden.

Meanwhile, as the two task force commanders coordinated the change in movement, Able Troop of the 25th Cavalry Squadron continued to screen forward of the main body. Between 1000 and 1045 hours, the command post radio operator scribbled a message into the log.

"A Troop, 25th Cavalry reports eight enemy [soldiers] dug in at grid coordinate P601390." Another soldier then took the report and identified the location on the map with a pin. He read the grid. It was near Flatzbourhof, Luxembourg.

Several minutes later, Able Troop sent up another report. This time it was six infantry near Perlé, Belgium. To the staff soldiers, these first reports were indicators of the German screen line. The location of the Wehrmach's main body, though, was still a mystery.

The Germans intended to keep it that way. At 1100 hours, firefights broke out near Flatzbourhof, as Able Troop reported engaging dug-in infantry near that location. After a few minutes, the cavalry troops clarified their initial report and changed it to ". . . received considerable small-arms fire from along a hill to the southwest at 1050 hours." The analyst then plotted the grid on the map. The hill was a wooded rise that overlooked an intersection of secondary roads north of Flatzbourhof. At 1135 hours, the troopers added that the number of enemy was unknown. To the staff of Combat Command A, they had discovered the first line of the German defense. It was time to attack.

Fortunately, Task Force Alanis had bridged the crater that was stymieing its forward progress, and as a result, it reached the designated road junction first. Thus, as per the instructions, Major Alanis ordered his forces to continue northward. They were the vanguard now. Ahead of them was the 5th Fallschirmjäger Division's main line of resistance, and task forces Oden and Alanis had to find a way to penetrate it. The *fallschirmjägers*, though, had other ideas.[2]

1200 to 1330 Hours, Friday, December 22
South of Martelange, Belgium
Task Force Alanis, Combat Command A, 4th Armored Division

Technician Fourth Grade James R. Donaldson was exhausted, but as the driver of an M4 Sherman moving through enemy territory, he must resist sleep.

His tank commander, Captain Vincent J. Boller, was the commanding officer for B Company, 35th Tank Battalion. Boller and Donaldson had been with the division since the beginning. Donaldson liked Boller and said of him after the war, "The best officer I knew was Captain Boller."

However, as with many officers who had served too long on the line, the war was starting to fray the man's nerves. Donaldson commented that after the fighting in the Saar Valley that November, Boller's personality had changed. "He was no longer the nice gentleman," Donaldson remembered. "His temper was getting short. He would get on my back for some of the silliest reasons."[3]

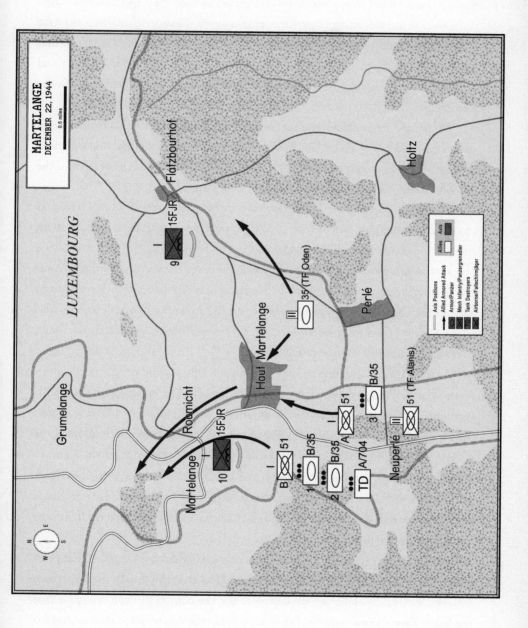

MARTELANGE
DECEMBER 22, 1944

0.5 miles

LUXEMBOURG

Flatzbourhof

Holtz

9 | 15 FJR

35 (TF Oden)

Haut Martelange

Perlé

Grumelange

Roumicht

Martelange

10 | 15 FJR

B | 51

1 | B/35

2 | B/35

TD | A/704

A | 51

3 | B/35

51 (TF Alanis)

Neuperlé

Allies Axis

Axis Positions

Allied Armored Attack

Armor/Panzer

Mech Infantry/Panzergrenadier

Tank Destroyers

Airborne/Fallschirmjäger

Donaldson recalled how Boller reacted when they found out they were ordered north to Bastogne. Most of the soldiers and junior officers had assumed the 4th Armored would take a much-needed break, as both men and machines were worn-out. When Boller departed for a meeting with his superior officers, his men thought he would return with good news. Instead, Hitler decided to spoil their Christmas.

"Where are we going, Captain? Back to Paris?" one soldier asked when Boller returned.

Donaldson remembered the rage in Boller's eyes as he hurled his helmet at the wall. "Paris, hell," he said. "Get packed. We are leaving at dawn. We will head north to Belgium and rescue the 101st Airborne Division, who are trapped in the city of Bastogne about a hundred and fifty miles from here."

Bastogne? Where in the hell is that? most of the men wondered. "The mood changed," Donaldson later wrote. "No one spoke a word. Everyone went about the task of getting everything packed."

Donaldson had slept only a couple of hours over the last several days. It was not all bad. He had enjoyed a night in a château near Arlon, but they were up early and on the road the next morning. After several hours and countless stops and starts, they reached their next objective. In front of them, nestled in the Sauer River valley, was the town of Martelange.

To many of the tank drivers, like Donaldson, all the small northern European towns were beginning to look the same. Martelange was no exception. Rolling hills surrounded it on all sides, while the winding Sauer River acted as the northern border of the town. As in most European villages, a single church dominated the skyline. The Church of St. Martin, built in 1899, was designed in the Romanesque style and topped with a single spire. Bricklayers had walled it with ash-gray stones and lined the corners with auburn-stained bricks. To help the townspeople with their workdays, the builders installed clocks in the tower faces. It was an impressive edifice for such a small town.

Many soldiers, though, probably wondered whether the Germans had positioned artillery spotters or snipers in the tower. If so, then the church would become a target. The main objective, though, was not the church but the bridges across the Sauer River. They were the key terrain, and that was why Donaldson and his company were there.

At midday, the column halted, and Captain Boller hopped out of the tank to attend a meeting with his current commander, Major Dan Alanis, who had devised a plan to seize and occupy the town. For Alanis, the key was infantry. Tanks, like Donaldson's Sherman, would be in the supporting role. First, Able Troop, 25th Cavalry, earlier had reported receiving heavy machine gun fire from the west side of town. Without infantry, towns were bad places for tanks. An individual *fallschirmjäger* with a *panzerfaust* could sneak up and pop off a shot and kill a tank with ease.

As a consequence, TF Alanis would have to flush out the enemy infantry lying in ambush somewhere on the west side of Martelange. To do this, Alanis assigned each of his two infantry companies' objectives. Able Company would seize the area of town east of the Bastogne–Arlon highway, while Baker Company, the main effort, would clear and occupy the western portion of the town. Most important, Baker Company would then seize the bridges over the Sauer. Furthermore, Baker Company, 35th Tank Battalion, would provide two platoons of tanks to support the infantry of Baker Company, 51st Infantry Battalion. In addition, Task Force Oden would establish a support-by-fire position on the high ground southeast of town. From there, it could dominate Martelange with direct fire.

The various company commanders and other officers glanced at their maps to make sure they didn't have any other questions. A few wanted clarifications, but for the most part everyone understood their roles. At 1330 hours, the infantry of A Company, 51st Infantry Battalion, stepped off. Patton's counterattack had begun.[4]

Early Afternoon, Friday, December 22
Near Flatzbourhof, Luxembourg
9th Company, 3rd Battalion, 15th Fallschirmjäger Regiment,
5th Fallschirmjäger Division

Feldwebel Conrad Klemment was kicking himself. He should have dug a little deeper than he had. He had arrived with his company the day before at a small patch of woods overlooking a railroad that passed through the hamlet of Flatzbourhof. Immediately, the officers had ordered them to start digging foxholes. The first few attempts with shovels quickly dispirited the men. The ground was hard from frost, and the soil was chalky. They could not jam their shovel blades deep enough into the dirt. Instead, they had to chip and scratch away at the surface, as if their shovels were steel nails. To add to their woes, they had only a few pickaxes, which would have made their jobs easier if they had had more. What should have been a network of foxholes with interlocking fields of fire was instead a few shallow pits.

"Many objected to the fact that they had to dig their own fighting holes even deeper," Klemment later admitted. "They believed a flat protective depression sufficed. Several did not pay close attention to camouflage, in terms of the view from the front as well as the view from above."

The men needed more time to dig, but just before noon, time ran out. According to Klemment, they observed thirty to forty tanks to the south. The men hurriedly camouflaged their pathetic holes with branches, twigs, and whatever else they could scrounge in the few minutes left.

Luckily, they had more than just a few *panzerfausts* with which to blunt the oncoming American onslaught. Oberst Kurt Gröschke, the regimental commander, had allocated five of the precious Sturmgeschütz assault guns from the 11th Assault Gun Brigade. In addition to the assault guns, the *fallschirmjägers* had commandeered a Sherman tank near Wiltz. In accordance with the laws of war, they had painted a Balkan cross on it to signify that it was now property of the Reich. Still, thought Klemment, five assault guns and a captured tank would not be enough to stop an entire column of Shermans, but that was all they had to throw at the Americans.[5]

Early Afternoon, Friday, December 22
Flatzbourhof, Luxembourg

Paul Kettel watched as three strange cars approached from the town of Holtz, each looking like someone had flipped over a rowboat and attached six wheels where the oars would go. Atop each keel was a rotating turret. They were M8 Greyhounds, the lightly armored reconnaissance vehicles from the 25th Cavalry Reconnaissance Squadron. Mounting a 37mm gun, the Greyhound was designed to scout for the enemy, but not fight them in pitched battles. It had neither the firepower nor the armor to fight other tanks.

Fortunately, the young Luxembourger could see the huge white star painted on the front glacis of the vehicles, so he knew they were Americans. When the reconnaissance platoon reached Flatzbourhof, it passed the Wolters' house, who were the Kettels' neighbors, and then moved into a sheltered courtyard. There, the M8s could hide behind the buildings, and for several minutes the vehicles loitered at that location.

One of the best tactics for reconnaissance units was to draw enemy fire, which troopers would use to identify the locations of enemy weapons. It was a dangerous game; troopers were gambling that the first shots would not be on target. Now the reconnaissance crews decided to drive farther into the village. They knew the Germans were near, but they had to draw them out. The troopers edged their vehicles into the street like children peeking around a corner in a game of hide-and-go-seek. Then the drivers gunned the accelerators, the vehicles lurching and then racing down the street.

Machine gun fire echoed off the walls of the nearby buildings as tracers skipped across the pavement like flat, rounded pebbles over a still pond. Scared but curious, Kettel looked to see where the tracers were emanating from and saw the German fighting position atop a hill, which the locals called the Flatzbour-knippchen. Undeterred, the Americans replied with lead, opening fire on the hill with their 37mm cannons and .50-caliber machine guns. Meanwhile, the three Greyhounds closed in on Paul Kettel's own home.

Paul and his family did not have a cellar, like many of the houses in Flatzbourhof did. Their only recourse was to hide behind one of the walls and hope that the bricks would stop the bullets. Paul's father quickly realized that was not a viable plan. The Germans had started to fire on the house itself, assuming Americans were behind it. Yet the reconnaissance troopers had completed their mission. They knew the main location of the German troops, and now they withdrew back to their headquarters to report what they had seen. By now the house had become a magnet for all the German weapons in the area. Paul Kettel later claimed that a tank round hit his home, decimating a sizable amount of masonry. That was enough for Paul's father, who urged his family to run through a nearby field to escape the onslaught.

For several long minutes the Germans continued to pelt the hapless structure. Finally the firing subsided. Paul's father poked his head into the air, and, realizing that the fighting had stopped, he led his children back home. As they got closer to their destination, Paul saw a group of German soldiers milling outside his house. Paul's father raised his hands high in the air, as if he were a captured prisoner of war.

Paul vividly remembered what happened next. "One of them said that my father was a spy, and that he should be shot on the spot. They had even found an American jacket which the Americans had left behind. Thank God, another German soldier prevented the evil deed and said, 'Leave these people alone; they have nothing to do with this.'"

Fearing that there would be more fighting, Mr. Kettel decided to leave Flatzbourhof. Hitching his horse and wagon, the family left for Bigonville later that day. Along the route, Paul saw a German soldier guarding a man who was digging next to the road. "Later we heard that a man from Wiltz had been shot there," Paul remembered. The hole was to be his grave.[6]

1330 to 2000 Hours, Friday, December 22
Martelange, Belgium
Task Force Alanis, Combat Command A, 4th Armored Division

Farther to the west in Martelange, the battle escalated from probing actions to full-on assaults. The men of A Company, 51st Armored Infantry Battalion, stepped off from their assault positions. Instead of their riding in their M3 half-tracks, the Able Company commander decided that the best way to seize their objective was on foot. Compared to the regular two-and-a-half-ton trucks, the M3 half-track was an excellent mobility asset, with its ability to drive off-road. As an armored platform, however, it was lacking. With its open top and thin side armor, the M3 was a dangerous liability in an urban fight, so the soldiers walked to their objective, the east side of Martelange.

Much of the eastern side was officially in Luxembourg as a result of a map error that occurred when the politicians drew the borders in 1839. For the men approaching the cluster of buildings that afternoon, borders meant little. The most important terrain feature in Able Company's area of operations was a railroad track that paralleled the highway as it wound its way northward into the main part of town. At the center of Able Company's objective was a T-shaped intersection, which was the key terrain. The Americans seized the intersection and declared their sector of Martelange clear of the enemy at 1430 hours. No one had seen a single German.

For Baker Company, 51st Armored Infantry Battalion, it would be a different story. Baker's GIs piggybacked into town on Captain Boller's Shermans. Boller had designated his 1st and 2nd platoons as troop carriers, while his 3rd Platoon, which was not carrying any men, would act as the reserve, trailing behind Able Company.

Wanting to overwhelm the German defenders, Major Alanis needed to ensure that his forces advanced with a contiguous front so that both companies attacked abreast. He ordered the Baker Company tankers to move out at the same time as the Able Company infantrymen. As the muddied ground had started to freeze, making it trafficable, the tankers opted to skirt the highway along its west side, using the open fields as their road. With 1st Platoon, B Company, 35th Tank Battalion, leading the way, ten tanks rolled over the fields like lumbering track-wheeled elephants. They had to maintain a slow speed, since each one was transporting a section of infantry.

Each infantryman kept his rifle at the ready, his eyes scanning for Germans with *panzerfausts*. For some, it was their first taste of combat, while for others it was another fateful roll of life's dice. Everything depended on getting the first shot, because whoever fired first was usually the victor. A little after 1400 hours, 1st Platoon edged past the first row of buildings. No one saw anything yet.

Around 1430 hours, Baker Company's luck ran out. As the lead tank approached the first major intersection, a massive fusillade of machine guns, rifles, and *panzerfausts* erupted, emanating from the houses northwest of the intersection. Infantry jumped off the tanks and scattered toward whatever cover they could find, while the tankers struggled to return fire. Despite the initial burst, not a single infantryman fell dead; nor were any of the tanks damaged. It would be a costly mistake for the Germans.

Fortunately, it didn't take long for the tankers and infantrymen to regain their composure. Within seconds M1 Garands were popping off, while M2 .50-caliber machine guns chugged away at the German defenders. Neither side, though, could gain fire superiority. 1st Platoon radioed back to Captain Boller, telling him they were stuck. For several hours both sides traded shots, with neither side backing down.

At 1700 hours, the company commander of Baker Company, 51st Infantry, reported, "Platoon Baker Fifty-one, pinned down on the slope west of the highway by heavy machine gun fire from houses at grid P 567386." The terse but clear message told Boller and Alanis everything they needed to know: They were not going to punch their way through. To solve this tactical problem, the two officers decided to flank the intersection from the west. Fortuitously, 2nd Platoon, B Company, 35th Tank Battalion, was not decisively engaged. Therefore, Boller ordered it to carry out the assault.

Around 1800 hours, tanks rolled out with a platoon from B Company, 51st Infantry. Their immediate objective was the Church of St. Martin in the center of town. The German defenders did not see them coming. By now the sun had set, and darkness shrouded the attackers. As a consequence, American forces quickly overwhelmed the *fallschirmjägers'* battle position north of the intersection. Within minutes, 75mm guns blasted away with high-explosive rounds, while .30- and .50-caliber machine guns peppered several vehicles near the church square. Suddenly the vehicles exploded. By 2000 hours, the Americans had destroyed the first battle position and were in control of much of Martelange. Ironically, the smoldering vehicles were captured American jeeps and two trucks, which the *fallschirmjägers* had commandeered near Wiltz. The Balkan crosses the Germans had painted on them had led to their demise at the hands of their former owners.

Despite the success, Major Alanis knew they were far from finished. A German position along the northern bank of the river still dominated the crossing points. The soldiers of Task Force Alanis would have to neutralize that position before they could attempt a crossing of the Sauer River. Moreover, they still had not reached the river. Between their current positions and the Sauer was another row of businesses and homes. They would have to clear them before they captured the bridges. In short, the fighting would continue through the night.

Captain Boller, waiting outside of town, was not in the best spot to control his platoons, so he ordered Donaldson to roll into Martelange. Donaldson eased the sticks forward. In the darkness, all he could see were the houses and stores that lined the main street in front of him. After several minutes, Donaldson found a spot in front of what looked like an apartment. He stopped the tank, the crew jumped out, and Donaldson walked to the front of the vehicle, where they kept their rations attached to the hull. Suddenly bullets pinged around him. He dived behind his Sherman and tried to see where it was coming from. Apparently Donaldson's tank had provoked some Germans dug in along the high ground across the river. Knowing that the tank could soon attract heavier fire, the driver and his crew quickly decided that the apartment was the best hiding place and dashed inside. For much of the night, the Germans kept up a steady harassing fire to remind the Americans that they were watching them. In the end, it was not enough to keep James Donaldson awake. He passed out immediately after he finished his guard shift. When he awoke the next morning, the Germans were gone.[7]

1330 to 2000 Hours, Friday, December 22
Near Flatzbourhof, Luxembourg
9th Company, 3rd Battalion, 15th Fallschirmjäger Regiment,
5th Fallschirmjäger Division

Conrad Klemment watched as a column of American tanks moved like a metallic centipede, inching its way northward. The Americans seemed to have overwhelming combat power. "I was amazed that despite the numerical superiority of American tanks that the Americans never launched a direct armored assault," he later wrote.

Klemment didn't know it, but a direct assault was not the mission of Task Force Oden and the troopers of Able Troop, 25th Cavalry. Lieutenant Colonel Delk Oden had no intention of becoming decisively engaged. His mission was to provide direct fire support for Task Force Alanis. To do this, his tankers would occupy a piece of high ground to the southeast of Martelange, near the village of Wolwelange. Oden ordered Able Company, with its thirteen tanks, to provide the main base of fire. Able Company's position was atop a slight rise that overlooked Wolwelange, and this vital high ground allowed the Able Company tankers to engage with direct fire any part of Martelange. Oden assigned Charlie Company as the reserve, since it had only eight tanks. Meanwhile, Able Troop, 25th Cavalry, screened the eastern flank of the division, using direct fire to fix the German forces around Klemment's position so that they couldn't provide any reinforcements westward to 10th Company. In effect, Combat Command A had isolated the defenders in Martelange.

To Klemment, though, the American attack on his company battle position did not seem like an economy of force. Not long after 1300 hours, the American tanks opened up. Since Colonel Oden did not seek a general engagement, the American tankers and cavalry troopers didn't close with the dug-in *fallschirmjägers*. Klemment described the engagement in his memoirs:

> From the safety of our position, it was very interesting to watch the battle develop, some 400 meters away within the lower terrain along the row of houses. At the same time, [enemy] machine gun fire from the houses began to whip through our position. . . . In the distance we observed German tanks engaged in the eastern sections of [Bigonville] moving forward and then withdrawing. . . . American projectiles flew close over our heads. Did they aim too high? With curiosity I looked in the direction from where the projectiles came. North of our position, projectiles landed at the end of a farm field. However, there was nothing to see on top of the snow cover. Further back and to the right I heard the crack of a heavy anti-tank gun firing. . . . More projectiles impacted nearby.

Klemment did his best to keep his head down. As the company headquarters section leader, he was in charge of two machine gun teams and a messenger, but there was little he could do at such a great distance.

While Klemment hunkered down in his foxhole, an 8cm mortar section, located in the southern section of Bigonville, opened fire at the Americans near Wolwelange and Martelange. One mortarman, Horst Lange, wrote, "An advance party had selected a position for our four 80mm mortars. It was a rather good-sized garden which was located at the southernmost end of the main street. Coming from the center of town, just to the right of the garden, was a small house in which a couple of guys from the mortar squad had set up quarters." Now Lange and the others started to hang rounds into their tubes to support their comrades in Martelange. Lange's mortar section was part of 12th Company of 3rd Battalion, 15th Fallschirmjäger Regiment.[8]

Later that afternoon, a forward artillery observer and a radio operator joined

Klemment's team. Earlier, the *fallschirmjägers* had positioned a battery of 10.5cm howitzers in the town of Bigonville. Now the forward observer went to work, calling up fire missions on the American forces near Wolwelange. Klemment wrote, "At will, German artillery rounds from the battery in [Bigonville] howled overhead and landed among American assembly areas."

The artillery battery was 7th Battery, 3rd Battalion, of the 408th Volks Artillerie Corps. The German army had formed the unit in Vienna back in October in preparation for the winter offensive. It was a mixture of German and captured Russian artillery pieces. 3rd Battalion had three batteries, each with six 10.5cm towed howitzers. The division commander wanted 3rd Battalion to provide artillery support directly to 15th Fallschirmjäger Regiment, and Oberst Gröschke decided that 7th Battery would support Klemment's 3rd Battalion. Unfortunately, 7th Battery had only four of its alloted six tubes, since it didn't have enough motor transport to move all six guns. Still, it was better than nothing, thought Klemment.

The constant back-and-forth fire continued into the night. The Germans thought they were scoring hits, and Klemment even said, "The Americans sustained high losses. The heavy antitank gun played a significant role in creating these losses." In fact, Able Company of the 35th Tank Battalion recorded only one tank lost, despite all the lead in the air. Not long after sunset, the German armor withdrew to Bigonville, traveling along a sunken road to conceal their movement.

For the *fallschirmjägers* of 9th Company, the battle had resulted in four wounded and one dead. Klemment recalled that the dead *fallschirmjäger* had a twin brother, writing, "That evening I saw a group of soldiers depart for night guard duty. Among them I saw the twin brother who had a blank look on his face. At the same time, I gathered together the wounded that were capable of walking and brought them to [Bigonville]. Among them, I noticed one younger soldier with a bandage on his head, which resembled a turban. His helmet dangled at his elbow; he looked as if someone split his head open with an ax. A bullet from a heavy machine gun cut his helmet open from front to back. The steel edges of the helmet bent downward and cut open the soldier's head."

The young *feldwebel* knew the fighting was far from over. Throughout the night, as both sides shot at each other, Klemment watched the tracers crisscross in the black sky. He wondered what the morning would bring. In a few hours, he would have his answer.

The *fallschirmjägers* had attracted too much attention. Cavalry troopers from Able Troop had reported significant enemy activity around Bigonville the previous evening. At 1635 hours, a soldier from Combat Command A radioed back to 4th Armored Division, "Had report [that] Bigonville had quite a bit of stuff—four kilometers northeast, two kilometers east of Bigonville. [I say again] quite a bit of stuff—secondary road carrying a lot of traffic going west."[9]

Morning to Early Afternoon, Friday, December 22
Between Menufontaine and Burnon, Belgium
Combat Command B, 4th Armored Division

While Combat Command A was pushing north along the Bastogne–Arlon highway, Combat Command B was also heading north toward Bastogne, via secondary roads. Unlike CCA's two separate axes of advance, General Dager had chosen to proceed along one route. Hence, even though Dager had two maneuver battalions—the 8th Tank Battalion and the 10th Armored Infantry Battalion—it was only one column driving north. In these situations, the tank battalion commander, regardless of rank, was the commander on the ground. Therefore, Major Albin F. Irzyk was the de facto senior task force officer, while Major Harold Cohen, the infantry battalion commander, was second in command of the task force.

Many senior officers of Combat Command B were seasoned veterans, starting with the commander. Brigadier General Holmes E. Dager was born in 1893 in Asbury Park, New Jersey. Even before war broke out in Europe in 1914, Dager was serving in the New Jersey National Guard as an infantryman, and by 1916 he had earned a commission as a second lieutenant. In 1917, he joined the Regular Army and went off to war in 1918, serving with the 51st Infantry. Like Patton, he saw combat in France, and participated in battles around the Vosges Mountains and in the Meuse-Argonne Offensive. By the end of the war, he had attained the rank of major and was even in command of a battalion. Not only was he a good officer, he was a courageous one, and the government awarded him the Silver Star in recognition of his bravery.

Dager remained in the army during the hard slog of the interwar years, attending various schools like the Infantry Officer Advanced Course at Fort Benning, Georgia, and the Command and General Staff College at Fort Leavenworth. He eventually served as an instructor at these schools. When he was not furthering his military education, he served in a variety of roles from company to regimental commander.

After the attack on Pearl Harbor in December 1941, the army selected him to command Combat Command B of the 4th Armored Division. By this time, Dager had achieved the rank of brigadier general. He left for Pine Camp, New York, in early 1942, and helped guide his division through all the rigorous training exercises so that by the summer of 1944, the 4th Armored Division was ready for combat.

When many divisions first entered into combat in Europe and the Pacific, the army brass realized that some of the division and regimental commanders who were good trainers were not necessarily good commanders in battle. Luckily for CCB, Dager could do both, and he led his men throughout all the campaigns from Operation Cobra to the Battle of the Bulge. Dager's best attribute, though, was his subordinates. In December 1944, he had an excellent infantry commander and a precocious tank commander under his tutelage.

Major Harold Cohen, the commander of the 10th Armored Infantry Battalion, had served in that capacity for only two weeks. His predecessor, Lieutenant Colonel Art West, had strayed too close to the front lines during a battle. On December 1, while attempting to observe his unit's advance near the French town of Mackwiller, West was wounded, forcing his evacuation to the rear. Despite this loss, his unit still accomplished their mission, and Major Cohen assumed command. The next day Cohen led the unit back into combat.

Cohen epitomized the American success story. Born in 1916, in Woodruff, South Carolina, he spent his formative years in nearby Spartanburg. The son of Russian Jewish immigrants, Cohen's father, Max, was a successful local businessman who insisted that Harold enlist in 1941 at the age of twenty-five. His drill sergeants recognized officer material, and within a few months, Harold earned his commission through Officer Candidate School.

Unlike Cohen, Major Albin F. Irzyk planned on a career as an officer and joined the army before the war, earning his commission through Reserve Officer

Training Corps at Massachusetts State College in Amherst (which later became the University of Massachusetts). His first unit was the 3rd U.S. Cavalry Regiment located in Fort Myer, Virginia, which he joined in July of 1940 as a second lieutenant. For nearly two years Al's career was predictable, and by the late spring of 1942, he was promoted to first lieutenant. In August, the army transferred him to the 4th Armored Division, where he was assigned to the 35th Armored Regiment under the command of Colonel Hayden A. Sears. It did not take long for Colonel Sears to make an assessment of Irzyk, and he told Al that he would be a major within a year. As it turned out, Sears's prediction came true.

When the 4th Armored Division arrived in France in the summer of 1944, Al Irzyk was the S-3 for the 8th Tank Battalion, organizing and running battalion operations during several battles. According to Irzyk, it was a great primer for command. On December 3, 1944, General Dager asked to see Irzyk, and when the young officer arrived, Dager said, "Tom Churchill [the outgoing commander] has not been able to move the battalion the way I would like him to, so I've had him reassigned to Reserve Command. General Wood and I would like you to take over the battalion right now. Continue the day's operations." Without any ceremony or fanfare, Major Albin Irzyk was the commander of the 8th Tank Battalion. In only four years, he had risen from a second lieutenant to a major in charge of a battalion. The race to Bastogne would be his greatest challenge.[10]

0530 to 1245 Hours, Friday, December 22
Crossing Point at the Sauer River, Burnon, Belgium
3rd Platoon, B Troop, 25th Cavalry Squadron,
Combat Command B, 4th Armored Division

Private John J. DiBattista was not worried about the challenges of command. What worried him was whether or not there were Germans hiding in the wood line up ahead. While the nineteen-year-old soldier had trained as a tanker, somehow he ended up in a cavalry troop, manning a machine gun on the back of a jeep. Serving in an armored division, DiBattista had no armor. The only protection he could count on was a windshield and a helmet.

DiBattista and his section had moved out around 0530 hours that morning amid blinding snow with a mission to scout ahead of the main body and find the enemy. Initially, the only soldiers they found were survivors from the 101st Airborne, 326th Engineers, "soaking wet from heavy wet snow. Heavy beards. No helmets. They were so wet that the GI overcoats looked black. . . . They had been cut-off from their unit in the earlier fighting." DiBattista's section sergeant told the bedraggled paratroopers that if they continued south they would find the rest of the column, and the men shuffled off to safety. This event repeated itself several times, as the scout section found more and more survivors from various units.

Finally, a little after 1200 hours, the cavalry troopers passed through Menufontaine. Beyond lay the Sauer River, the first major obstacle along the way to Bastogne. As they crested the ridge, the troopers could see the Sauer, and overlooking the river, opposite Menufontaine, was Burnon. A road linked the two towns, crossing the Sauer over a stone bridge. The bridge, though, was gone. In its place were scattered stones, and guarding the site were ten enemy soldiers, using a captured American truck. Immediately the troopers radioed reports to their commander, Captain Fred Sklar, who, in turn, relayed the information to Combat Command B. It was now 1245 hours. B Troop had found the enemy.

Several minutes later, the enemy found B Troop. Suddenly a hill east of Burnon started to blink and flash, and 3rd Platoon was under fire as the incoming bullets pelted the snow around them. The men dived behind whatever cover they could find. Soon, DiBattista heard the cries for a medic, and he later learned that his platoon leader had been hit. The wounded lieutenant never returned.

Despite the heavy fire, someone managed to radio higher headquarters around 1300 hours. A radio operator back at the CCB command post scribbled the message as it came over the airwaves. "Undetermined number of enemy infantry dug in from grid coordinates Five One Zero Four Five Five to Five One Niner Four Five Four. And from grid coordinates Five Two Five Four Five Two Break . . . to grid coordinates Five Three Five Four Four Niner. Break. Have received small-arms fire from Burnon." Analysts identified the location on a map. The first position was on a spur known as Hill 450, while the other enemy location was east of there and across a draw, between the village of Strainchamps and Le Parque woods.

Meanwhile, DiBattista and the rest of 3rd Platoon fell back into Menufontaine, their mission accomplished. Now it was time for the main body to come up and seize the bridgehead. DiBattista and his fellow soldiers found a house in which to stay warm, where a woman offered to cook them some food. Across the river, a German self-propelled assault gun moved into position and began lobbing shells over the house. The shells screamed over the river and exploded nearby. The woman, though, continued to bake, as if the booming and crashing shells were simply claps of thunder and lightning. Finally, a Sherman tank rolled up and silenced the bothersome German assault gun with rounds out of its own 75mm gun. The 8th Tank Battalion and the rest of CCB had arrived.[11]

1345 to 1420 Hours, Friday, December 22
Crossing Point at the Sauer River, Burnon, Belgium
8th Tank Battalion, Combat Command B, 4th Armored Division

Major Albin Irzyk was not an engineer, but he even knew that whoever had blown up the bridge between Menufontaine and Burnon had done a bang-up job. The steep banks and swift current precluded any fording operations. Irzyk shook his head. "This was a shocker, because at the rate we were going we thought we would be in Bastogne the next day," he remembered.

The frustrated major had to wait. He called up the 24th Engineers on the radio and requested a treadway bridge that the cavalry troop had estimated would need to be twenty-five feet. By now, the German defenders knew this was a full-scale attack, and were responding with small-arms fire and artillery, using the crossing site as a target. The bridging operation would be a contested crossing—one of the riskiest operations in land warfare.

Irzyk, though, was no novice. He needed to silence the German battle positions around Hill 450. To do that, he would call on his own artillery, and by this time in the war, the American army had a lot more firepower and ammunition to expend than did the Germans. He ordered his Able Company tankers to establish support-by-fire positions on the southern side of the river. One platoon of tanks moved down to the forward slope of Hill 470, southwest of the crossing, while another platoon occupied a battle position at the bridge site. Within minutes, they were pouring .50-caliber rounds and 75mm high-explosive shells on the German positions. Unfortunately for the harried *fallschirmjägers*, that was only the beginning.[12]

1346 to 1620 Hours, Friday, December 22

Just South of Fauvillers, Belgium

Headquarters, 22nd Armored Field Artillery Battalion, 4th Armored Division

"Oasis [Call sign for 22nd AFA] . . . Request Fire Mission. Concentration One Zero Four . . . Enemy infantry dug in," a voice squawked over the radio net. Operators jotted down the numbers and sent the fire mission down to the gun line. The cannon cockers at all three gun batteries confirmed the grids, and within sixty seconds the howitzers were booming. In less than twenty minutes, forty-two rounds of high explosive had been expended.

At 1405 hours, the same voice over the radio reported, "Oasis . . . infantry running on road . . . cannot observe any further. Mission complete." The gun line fell silent.

This was not first fire mission of the day for the 22nd Armored Field Artillery Battalion. Indeed, the redlegs (army jargon for artillery soldiers) already had fired more than 175 rounds for four separate fire missions. Most of the missions were in support of Baker Troop, 25th Cavalry, which was locked in combat with enemy infantry near Strainchamps.

The 22nd was a typical self-propelled artillery battalion, with three batteries, each with six tubes. The tubes were 105mm howitzers mounted on the M7 HMC, or Howitzer Motor Carriage. The M7, or "Priest" as they were known, was built on an M3 or M4 chassis. Its gun was the M2A1 howitzer, with a maximum range of more than eleven thousand meters. Since the M7 was a tracked vehicle, this provided the task force commander a potent amount of mobile field artillery support, and, thanks to the overwhelming output of American industry, each armored division had three fully equipped armored field artillery battalions. Thus, in theory, each combat command could have an armored field artillery battalion in direct support.

In addition, the corps staff normally would augment the armored divisions with general support howitzer battalions. In this case, Combat Command B also could call on the 253rd Armored Field Artillery Battalion and the 776th Field Artillery Battalion for support. Moreover, the 776th had the towed M1A1 155mm howitzers. The "Long Toms," as they were known, had a maximum range of more than twenty-three thousand meters, which gave the U.S. Army an unmatched advantage in long-range firepower. In short, in addition to the eighteen tubes in the 22nd Armored Field Artillery, Major Irzyk could call on another eighteen from the 253rd and an additional eighteen from the 776th, for a total of 54 tubes. Needless to say, when the call went out for more artillery, the normal response resulted in a devastating hail of explosives.

Sensing that the momentum had shifted, at 1515 hours Major Irzyk ordered the first infantry across the river to secure a lodgment on the opposite banks. Two platoons from Charlie Company, 10th Armored Infantry Battalion, answered the call and negotiated the river. By 1530 hours, the first soldiers were almost across. Meanwhile, Irzyk continued to request artillery support to suppress the German defenders while his engineers built the treadway bridge.

Back at the 22nd's Fire Direction Center, another voice on the radio broke through the static. "Oasis . . . Fire Mission . . . Concentration One Zero Four . . . Grid Coordinates Fiver One Niner Break Four Six One. Break. One platoon of enemy infantry. Over."

Three minutes later, at 1533 hours, the gun line roared as all three batteries fired. Within seconds, the rounds pounded the high ground north of Burnon. At the bridge site, the German fire noticeably slackened, and American soldiers continued to pour across the river.

Artillery was not completely responsible for the successful crossing. In one incident, a mortarman by the name of Technical Sergeant Roscoe V. Albertson destroyed a German machine gun team. As bullets pelted the ground around him, Albertson carefully adjusted the dials on his mortar tube after firing each round, as if on a training exercise, until one finally hit the target. Apparently his deadly aim was too much for the Germans who survived his mortar strike—sixteen of them surrendered to him immediately afterward. For his coolness under fire, the army awarded him a Silver Star.

Finally, after one more fire mission at 1630 hours, the forward observers determined that they could no longer fire on Burnon, since the infantry had advanced to its outskirts. To Irzyk and his men, the bridgehead was now secure, and it was only a matter of time before they could roll tanks across.[13]

1605 to 2000 Hours, Friday, December 22
Girls' Normal School, Arlon, Belgium
Headquarters, III Corps

The staff of III Corps had been operating like a machine for the last fifty-five hours. They had arrived at Arlon around 1100 hours on December 20 and had kept up a frantic pace: issuing field orders to the various subordinate divisions, amending them with fragmentary orders, while updating and maintaining situational awareness for their commander, Major General John Millikin. Then, at 1605 hours, General Patton arrived to spur the men even more. Everyone wanted to look good for the boss's boss, and the soldiers enjoyed seeing Patton. For Millikin and Major General Hugh Gaffey, though, Patton's visit was probably a distraction they did not need in the middle of waging a battle.

Like all good officers, the Third Army commander wanted to see how his subordinates were performing in their first major engagement. Though Gaffey had seen combat in other positions, this was the first time that he and Millikin were in combat as commanders of their respective units. Patton, unsure how either man would work out, wanted them on a tight leash.

This was Millikin's time in the spotlight. The son of an Indiana barber, Millikin earned his commission from West Point in 1910, and was posted to the 5th Cavalry in Hawaii. When the United States entered World War I, he became the executive officer for the U.S. Army General Staff College in Langres, France. After the war, he attended the Command and General Staff College and the Army War College, and continued his army career in the cavalry, serving in such places as Fort Riley, Kansas.

As a new war broke out all over Europe, Millikin jumped up the ranks. In April 1940, he assumed command of the 6th Cavalry Regiment at Fort Oglethorpe, Georgia, as a full bird colonel. After a short stint, the army promoted him to brigadier general and selected him to command the 1st Cavalry Brigade at Fort Bliss, Texas, in October 1940. His meteoric rise continued unabated. In April 1941, after receiving glowing praise as a brigade commander, he took over the newly formed 2nd Cavalry Division at Camp Funston, Kansas, and in July the army promoted him to major general. He remained in command of the 2nd

Cavalry until August 1942, when the army transferred him to Hawaii to command the 33rd Infantry Division.

In the late summer of 1943, Lieutenant General Lesley McNair, the commander of U.S. Army Ground Forces, selected Millikin to command the newly formed III Corps. Initially, III Corps dealt only with training and evaluating units. However, after several months, Millikin and III Corps had impressed McNair, who recommended that they deploy to Europe. In September 1944, III Corps left for France, and in October, Third Army assumed control of Millikin's headquarters. In short, other than a few weeks outside of Metz in December 1944, General Millikin had never led his corps in combat. In fact, he had not led anything or anyone in any battle. His first real test would be the Bulge. Patton was worried that his subordinate might not be up to the task.

To ensure that his commanders were meeting his intent, Patton constantly monitored their progress. When he felt they were venturing off the path, he would guide them back with reminders. Ironically, by micromanaging, Patton was violating his own dicta. "This habit of commanding too far down, I believe, is inculcated at schools and at maneuvers," he wrote. "Actually, a General should command one echelon down, and know the position of units that were two echelons down. For example, an Army Commander should command corps, and show on his battle map the locations of corps and divisions, but he should not command the division." In this case, Patton would order combat commands, which were *three* levels down from his echelon.

Patton's meddling started early on in the attack. At 1050 hours the morning of December 22, Patton called the III Corps headquarters and spoke with Colonel James Holden Phillips, III Corps' chief of staff. The general wanted to know how things were going. Phillips reported that the attack was proceeding according to plan. The only notable resistance encountered so far was in Combat Command A's sector, in Martelange. Patton told Phillips "that we drive like hell. That we keep on attacking tonight. That [Patton] feels that this is their last struggle and we have an opportunity of winning the war." Phillips hung up the phone wondering what the men would think about the new order. In 1944, armor units did not conduct attacks at night.

Now all three commanders—Patton, Millikin, and Gaffey—were present for the late-afternoon meeting. Patton wanted updates. After Millikin briefed him on the progress of his three divisions, Patton provided strict instructions to his two subordinates.

Looking at both Gaffey and Millikin, Patton slapped his gloves in his palm like a whip and declared, "No gasoline will be captured. It will be destroyed by us in case capture appears imminent. No ordnance equipment will be captured by the enemy. They will be destroyed. This includes vehicles. No units must be surprised. Necessary security measures will be taken by all commanders. This means that field officers must be gotten up in the line. In case we have to withdraw, roads will be doubly barricaded. Let the tanks through, drop the rear barricade and then shoot them."

The Third Army commander glanced over at Gaffey. "Lead off with tanks, artillery, tank destroyers, and engineers. Keep main body of infantry back. When Jumbo tanks are available put them in the lead. A good formation is a company of medium tanks, a platoon of light tanks, two platoons of medium tanks, artillery, and engineers. Start all envelopments one or one and one half mile back. The envelopment should always be at about right angles. Do not make close envelopments. In this operation we must be the utmost ruthless [sic]. Make all tanks fire." As he spoke, Patton demonstrated the envelopment with his hands as if he were directing aircraft on a runway. Meanwhile, Gaffey and Millikin nodded and occasionally said, "Yes, sir."

Patton and his commanders were confident they could reach Bastogne that night or the following morning. Yet Gaffey's units were not providing him an accurate picture of the battlefield. Major T. J. Sharpe had reported Combat Command B would complete their bridge as early as 1625 hours at Martelange. Yet CCB wasn't at Martelange. CCA was at Martelange, and CCB's bridging operation was near the town of Burnon. Hence, Gaffey—and therefore Millikin and Patton—were under the mistaken impression that A *and* B would both cross the Sauer River that night. For this reason, in Patton's mind, it made sense for both units to push on through the night to reach Bastogne. In the end, only CCB would complete its bridge over the Sauer near Burnon around 1718 hours. CCA would not complete its bridge until midday the next day—nearly twenty hours after the proposed completion time. As a result, instead of two mutually supporting combat commands advancing into enemy territory, CCB would be on its own the next day.

Satisfied that Millikin and Gaffey understood his intent, Patton left them to work out the details for the next day's operations. To continue the attack through the evening, Gaffey had to alert his commanders. At 1834 hours, CCB received word they would continue operations through the night, and by 1945 hours, both A and B would know about the change in plan.

Millikin and Gaffey had other problems. Earlier that day, the commander of the 4th Armored Division had received disturbing reports of heavy enemy activity near Bigonville, which was the eastern flank of his division's area of operations. In addition, the 26th Infantry Division had captured a German soldier near Arsdorf who reported seeing "considerable infantry of the Führer Brigade . . . and forty to fifty 'Tiger' tanks, which had orders to begin a counterattack on 23 or 24 December." Furthermore, a gap had appeared between the 4th Armored and the 26th Infantry.

To Millikin and Gaffey, the decision seemed simple: Plug the hole with Gaffey's Combat Command Reserve, which had been trailing behind CCA. Gaffey knew that deploying the reserve would deny him any more flexibility, because all of his forces would be in the fight. It was a risky scheme, but both commanders decided it was the best choice. At around 2000 hours that evening, Gaffey issued the order to Colonel Wendell Blanchard. Now the *fallschirmjägers* of 9th Company would face all of Combat Command Reserve the following day.[14]

2000 to 2315 Hours, Friday, December 22
Quatre Vents, Belgium (South of Metzert)
Headquarters, Combat Command Reserve

Colonel Wendell Blanchard looked at his watch. He did not have a lot of time to plan. His Combat Command Reserve was rarely deployed as a tactical maneuver element. Usually the units in CCR would rotate in and out with other units in Combat Command A or B, depending on which unit needed to rest and refit. Now, due to the exposed eastern flank of the division, Gaffey had ordered Blanchard's reserve to secure the flank by seizing Bigonville. If the Germans were there in strength, they could easily strike the exposed flank of General Earnest's CCA, advancing north from Martelange. Moreover, if the German prisoner of war was accurate in his claim, then another force of panzers was in Arsdorf, only four kilometers east of Bigonville. Gaffey had to lock down his eastern flank before the Germans attacked.

Compared to his division commander, Blanchard was a veteran at his job. He had assumed command of CCR in September and participated in the autumn battles in Lorraine. Born in Massachusetts in 1902, Blanchard earned an appointment to West Point and graduated in 1924. He then married Marcella Palmer, whose father was retired brigadier general Bruce Palmer Sr.

Blanchard had two seasoned battalion commanders on his team, both of whom were lieutenant colonels. George L. Jaques had commanded the 53rd Armored Infantry Battalion since its inception. Blanchard's tank commander was the already legendary Lieutenant Colonel Creighton W. Abrams, who had led the 37th Tank Battalion during the Battle of Arracourt, one of the largest tank clashes on the Western Front. Patton allegedly said of Abrams, "I'm supposed to be the best tank commander in the army, but I have one peer—Abe Abrams."

With these two racehorses in his stable, Blanchard decided that a verbal order over the radio would suffice. As long as the commanders understood his intent and time line, he would not need to tell them how to do their jobs. He grabbed Major Thomas G. Churchill, his S-3 operations officer, and together, standing over a map, they formulated a basic plan for next day's attack.

At 2315 hours, the plan was complete. An operations officer, probably Churchill, picked up the radio and issued a commander's call. He waited a few moments so that each commander acknowledged his message. When they had done so, he began his transmission. "Reserve Command moves at 0600 hours via initial point, the road junction at grid coordinates Six . . . Zero . . . Seven . . . Two . . . Fiver . . . Eight. I say again, Six . . . Zero . . . Seven . . . Two . . . Fiver . . . Eight. Proceed through Attert, Rodenhoff, Nevperie, Perlé, Holtz, and then Flatzbonville [Flatzbourhof]." He keyed the handset and waited to make sure the commanders could write it all down.

After a moment, he continued. "Recon Platoon from 37th Tank Battalion to precede the advance guard. Mission will be to reconnoiter route, especially Holtz and Flatzbourhof, and then meet elements at Perlé."

He paused and then resumed. "Order of march will be: Recon Platoon, 37th

Tank Battalion, followed by advance guard, which will be one company from the 37th and one company from the 53rd Armored Infantry. Main body will be the headquarters, Reserve Command, the rest of the 37th Tank Battalion followed by the remainder of the 53rd Armored Infantry, and then the medical unit."

As Churchill briefed, he referred back to his map to make sure he was providing the correct coordinates and locations. "Also, a platoon from the 704th Tank Destroyer will dismount in the vicinity of Holtz. Next, the reconnaissance platoon will rendezvous at the initial point at 0500 with a mine-detector unit from the 24th Engineers, which will be attached to the company from the 37th in the advance guard. Finally, the 177th Field Artillery Battalion will be given road clearance to move from Bonnert, then Tontelange, on to Grendel, in order to position its batteries south of Nothomb. This will start after the 53rd clears the initial point at approximately 0730 hours. Acknowledge."

For several minutes, the command net was busy as each commander back briefed the mission or asked questions to confirm the order. By midnight, everyone understood his role in the overall plan. In the next few hours, Combat Command Reserve would move out and join the others in the race to Bastogne. Meanwhile, as Combat Command A struggled to cross the Sauer River, Combat Command B was already across it, and as a result it was the farthest north of any 4th Armored Division unit. Unless the Germans blocked it, CCB was poised to reach Bastogne in the next twenty-four hours.[15]

2130 to 2300 Hours, Friday, December 22
Menufontaine, Belgium
3rd Platoon, Baker Troop, 25th Cavalry, CCB, 4th Armored Division

Private DiBattista did not always mind waiting. To the nineteen-year-old trooper, waiting meant staying alive longer. Since that afternoon, DiBattista and a few other troopers of 3rd Platoon had taken shelter in a hayloft while engineers constructed a bridge over the Sauer River. With the job complete at 1745 hours, Charlie Company, 10th Armored Infantry, and Baker Company, 8th Tank Battalion, headed across the river, cleared Burnon, and established a battle position along the high ground north of town. Meanwhile, the engineers set about clearing a minefield left behind by the Germans, while Major Irzyk ordered his support units to bring forward more gasoline and ammunition. All this movement took time, and to DiBattista, that meant more time to rest.

Yet DiBattista knew he was pressing his luck by relaxing in a hayloft. Incoming artillery shells tended to detonate on roofs or top floors. Most of his fellow troopers were sheltered on the first floors of nearby buildings, which offered more protection. Luckily, the Germany artillery on the twenty-second tended to be inaccurate and intermittent. Deciding the risk was worth it, he and some comrades had spread out their wool blankets on the crunchy, prickly hay and lain down to fall asleep.

Sometime later, a soldier climbed up the ladder and shouted, "Mount up!"

The men moaned. For DiBattista, an order to move out was the worst way to wake up. He was wrong. DiBattista then described what happened next:

> I was the last to leave the loft. Half way down I heard the shell coming, but this time it sounded different. It was not going over us. It hit the roof of the barn and exploded in the hayloft. I found myself lying on the cobblestone. I stumbled into the house where my section was. For a few moments, I could not talk. My friends examined me with a flashlight to see if I was wounded. I came around. Sergeant Mayforth ordered Sims to see what happened. Sims came back and said the shell blew off the top of the barn and demolished the hayloft.

Despite the ringing in his ears, DiBattista's sergeant deemed him fit for duty. They hopped on their jeeps and waited for the order to move out. Fortunately, since they were on point last time, 1st Platoon would now assume the vanguard position. Because of a simple rotation system, fate would spare DiBattista's life. Sadly, the troopers from 1st Platoon would not be that lucky.[16]

Late Evening, Friday, December 22
Girls' Normal School, Arlon, Belgium
G-2 Section, Headquarters, III Corps

As the day drew to a close, III Corps' intelligence section had started to develop a picture from the various puzzle pieces collected over the last thirty-six hours. In front of Combat Command B was the 14th Fallschirmjäger Regiment. Thanks to interrogations of four prisoners, G-2 now knew that the enemy regiment's 3rd Battalion had established a battle position in the vicinity of Burnon. Indeed, the majority of the battalion, including the 10th, 11th, and 12th companies, were around that location. What was troublesome was the combat strength of the battalion. The prisoners revealed that their own 12th Company was almost at full strength with 120 men, as well as its full complement of eight heavy machine guns and anywhere from six to eight 120mm mortars. If the other companies had maintained the same operational effectiveness as the 12th, Combat Command B would be in for a fight.

It was almost midnight, and Combat Command B was in Burnon. Up till this point, Combat Command B had moved farther than any unit in III Corps. If Combat Command B was already in Burnon, then according to the prisoners of war, it should have run into the 3rd Battalion of the 14th Fallschirmjäger Regiment. Other than reports of intermittent small-arms fire and harassment artillery, 8th Tank and 10th Armored Infantry battalions had cleared Burnon and reported no significant enemy forces. Indeed, 10th Armored Infantry had radioed in to Combat Command B that they had outposted the town around 1800 hours that evening. If 3rd Battalion of the 14th Fallschirmjäger Regiment was not in Burnon, then where was it?[17]

Late Night to 2300 Hours, Friday, December 22, 1944
Between Burnon and Fauvillers, Belgium

That night, Irzyk ordered his fuel trucks to come up and refuel all the tanks. To protect the trucks along unsecured roads from Fauvillers to Burnon, he ordered some of the light tanks to travel with the fuelers and ammunition trucks. His tank column was still gassing up when it received word to keep driving through the night.

Technician Fifth Grade Raymond E. Green, a fuel-truck driver for the 8th Tank Battalion, recalled some of those nightly fuel runs, dodging 88s over muddy roads while barreling toward his next destination. A mechanic before the war, Green had removed the governor on his speedometer, making his two-and-a-half-ton truck much faster than the others. Many times, Green would claim, the extra speed saved his life when he drove along darkened roads late at night to supply the tanks around Bastogne.

Yet sometimes speed was not enough. During one late-night supply run, he spotted strange activity down the road. Knowing he could not outrun it, he yelled to his assistant driver, "Get up on that damn gun! There's something ahead of us!"

His assistant driver jumped up to the gun and opened fire. According to Green, no one shot back at him, and so he kept on driving. He did not have time to wonder whether it had been friend or foe. His tankers needed gas and ammunition, and it was his job to deliver it to them. Thanks to the efforts of soldiers like Raymond Green, 8th Tank Battalion and the rest of Combat Command B were ready to move out at 2300 hours. Their next destination was Bastogne. Alas, they had to drive through the tiny village of Chaumont to reach it.[18]

Just After Midnight, Saturday, December 23, 1944
Chaumont, Belgium

The local Belgian civilians knew where the *fallschirmjägers* were hiding. After American artillery blasted the area around Hill 450, the German troops realized they were overmatched and withdrew north to Chaumont. Instead of digging foxholes outside of town, the cold, exhausted *fallschirmjägers* opted to hide inside the homes of villagers.

Maria Gustin Lozet was a young woman when the German offensive began. The first German soldiers had passed through Chaumont on the evening of Wednesday, December 20, wanting food and drink and demanding to know where the American soldiers were located. The next day, more Germans passed through, but this time they were in tracked vehicles and captured American trucks. Villagers wondered whether the Americans would ever return. That afternoon, two German *feldwebels* showed up and asked to stay in Maria's home.

It was late on the night of the twenty-second when the *fallschirmjägers* arrived. They wore different uniforms than the regular German *landsers*. "They occupied all the parts of the house," Maria recalled, "and brought straw to lie everywhere. They were all seventeen to twenty years old."

A little after midnight, a nearby explosion rocked Maria's house. With their home occupied by *fallschirmjägers*, her parents decided to leave, so they packed up the family and escaped to Maria's uncle's house. When they reached Uncle Edward's home, they discovered that the entire extended family had the same idea. Thirty-four people, including thirteen refugees from the village of Marvie, were all squeezed inside the house. Maria's uncle provided her a mattress and she slept the rest of the night. Outside, both armies prepared for the morning's battle.[19]

CHAPTER 4

CHAUMONT

| DECEMBER 23, 1944 |

★ ★ ★ ★ ★

"I want Bastogne by 1350."
—*Lieutenant General George S. Patton*

0230 Hours, Saturday, December 23
Headquarters, Combat Command B, 4th Armored Division
Habay-la-Vieille, Belgium

For the first few hours, Major Albin Irzyk's column inched forward with no issues. Then the Germans struck. The scratchy voice on the radio was succinct. "Column moving. Engaged in firefight at point one kilometer north of checkpoint 57."

An analyst plotted the point on the map as the voice continued. "Small-arms and bazooka fire from woods on both sides of the road. Tanks proceeding."

A soldier handed the radio operator a message that he needed to transmit to G-3 at the division headquarters in Arlon. The operator read the message and shook his head.

He keyed the handset. "Olympic Three [4th Armored Division Operations] . . . This is Oboe [CCB]."

"Go ahead, Oboe," a voice replied through the static.

The radio operator resumed. "Lieutenant Marshall, the S-2 for the 8th Tank Battalion, was captured two kilometers east of checkpoint 49 at around 2030 hours with orders for this evening. Break . . . He had the checkpoint list and other data. G-2 was also notified."

It was worse than that. First Lieutenant William J. Marshall had the passwords for the next four days and the unit locations for the previous day. Now the Germans had them.[1]

Early Morning, Saturday, December 23
14th Fallschirmjäger Regiment, 5th Fallschirmjäger Division
Chaumont, Belgium

Waiting for Combat Command B around Chaumont were at least two reinforced battalions of *fallschirmjägers*. Oberst Ludwig Heilmann had ordered the 14th Fallschirmjäger Regiment, under the command of Oberst Arno Schimmel, to defend the area, though it was too large for a contiguous and in-depth defense. Schimmel instead chose to defend certain key points.

Schimmel chose his 2nd Battalion to thwart the U.S. advance along the Burnon–Chaumont axis. 8th Company, under the command of an Oberleutnant Groten, would block the main road between Burnon and Chaumont. 8th Company was a weapons company, and each of the *fallschirmjäger* infantry battalions had three infantry companies and one heavy-weapons company.

Yet despite its designation as a weapons company, the 8th was lacking most of its heavy weapons. It usually possessed eight MG 42 machine guns, mounted on tripods, and four 8cm mortars. According to one prisoner, the 8th had started with only five heavy-machine guns, but thanks to attrition it had dropped down to three. It had no additional mortars. Indeed, the same prisoner claimed it was no longer a heavy weapons company but a rifle company. As a rifle company, however, it was a poor substitute, since it only had seventy to eighty men.

Those remaining men were not in the best shape, suffering from frostbite and trench foot. As a result of their dwindling numbers, Groten decided that the best terrain for his company's platoon battle positions would be on the western wood line of the Lambay–Chênet woods, east of the Burnon–Chaumont Road, and atop Hill 500, which was west of the Burnon–Chaumont Road. In addition, he would send out a small screen element to an outpost position northeast of Burnon

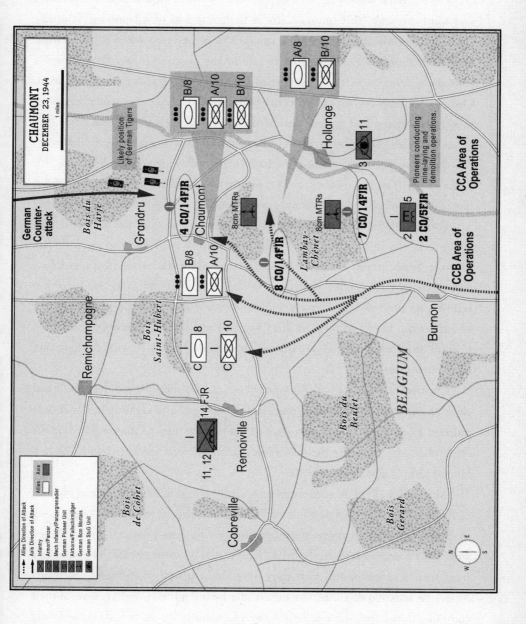

CHAUMONT
DECEMBER 23, 1944

1 miles

Allies

- •••• Allies Direction of Attack
- Axis Direction of Attack
- Infantry
- Armor/Panzer
- Mech Infantry/Panzergrenadier
- German Pioneer Unit
- Airborne/Fallschirmjäger
- German 8cm Mortars
- German StuG Unit

Axis

German Counter-attack

Likely position of German Tigers

A/8   B/10

B/8   A/10   B/10

Hollange

3 | 11

Pioneers conducting mine-laying and demolition operations.

CCA Area of Operations

Bois du Harje

Grandru

4 CO/14FJR   Chaumont

8cm MTRs

8 CO/14FJR

Lambay-Chênet   8cm MTRs

7 CO/14FJR

2 | 5

2 CO/5FJR

2 | 8

CCB Area of Operations

Remichampagne

Bois Saint-Hubert

B/8   A/10

C | 8   C | 10

Bois du Beulet

BELGIUM

Burnon

14 FJR

11, 12   Removille

Bois de Cohet

Cobreville

Bois Gérard

N E S W

to provide early warning. Meanwhile, he would establish his command post in Hollange. It was all Groten had to stop Major Irzyk's column.

On the back side of the Lambay–Chênet woods and oriented to the south and southeast was 7th Company, under the command of a Leutnant Schmidt. 7th Company also had the combat strength of eighty men when it had arrived in the Chaumont area. According to one of the prisoners, the rifle companies started the offensive with an average combat strength of about a hundred men. On paper, they were supposed to have around 170. Typically, a *fallschirmjäger* infantry company had a great deal of firepower, each company with three platoons, and each platoon with six MG 42 or 34 machine guns on a bipod. Moreover, the company headquarters section had three 8cm mortars. Luckily, the 7th Company still had its organic 8cm mortars, which Schmidt had positioned on two hills behind the Lambay–Chênet woods and west of the village of Hollange.

Fortunately for Oberst Schimmel, 2nd Battalion was not the only unit near Chaumont. To the west of the Chaumont–Burnon road was the town of Remoiville, headquarters of Major Ferdinand Ebel's 3rd Battalion. Ebel's battalion had arrived in Remoiville the night of the twenty-second after conducting a fighting withdrawal from Burnon. He had two *fallschirmjäger* companies: the 9th and the 11th. Ebel had ordered 9th Company to establish a strongpoint in the town of Nives while 11th Company was situated in Remoiville with the battalion command post.

Luckily for Ebel, his 12th Company was intact. A heavy-weapons unit, it had eight operational MG 42s on tripods and between six and eight operational 8cm mortars. Ebel split it up into two places. One platoon was in Cobreville, while the other platoons, including the 8cm mortar platoon, were colocated with the battalion headquarters in Remoiville.

Meanwhile, Ebel decided to manage the impending battle in a cozy château in Remoiville, opting for comfort while his men suffered in the cold. According to several captured prisoners, the *fallschirmjägers* were starving, which, combined with their commander's tactlessness, caused morale to plummet. They did not trust their leadership, and now they were facing a well-trained and motivated American armored division. The men of the 14th Regiment, unlike some of their comrades in the 15th, were *fallschirmjägers* in name only; many had received only four weeks of infantry training before the Ardennes Offensive. Sadly, their prospects for success against Combat Command B were grim.

Morale was not the only major issue. According to its table of organization and equipment, each *fallschirmjäger* regiment was authorized three 75mm Pak 40 towed antitank guns for the entire regiment, yet the 14th Regiment had none. Instead, the antitank company, which the Germans numbered as the 14th Company, only had *panzerschrecks*. According to a prisoner, each platoon had between thirty and forty men, and at full strength the company would have possessed fifty-four *panzerschrecks*. Furthermore, one of its platoons, 2nd Platoon, had the mission to secure the rear echelon area around Chaumont.

To replace the missing Pak 40 guns, Oberst Heilmann allocated an additional platoon from the division's antitank battalion consisting of thirty-six soldiers with six *panzerschrecks* and numerous *panzerfausts*. The *panzerschreck* was a much-improved copy of the U.S. Army's bazooka, with an effective range of 130 meters.

Finally, each regiment had one mortar company, and the main mortar system for a *fallschirmjäger* mortar company was the 12cm mortar. This company would have nine total mortars when it was at full strength. The 12cm Granatwerfer had a range of six thousand meters, and sometimes the regimental commander would divide the company into three platoons so that each maneuver battalion would have one platoon of 12cm Granatwerfers supporting it.

Inside the village of Chaumont was 4th Company from 1st Battalion, and the 1st Battalion headquarters. 4th Company was the heavy-weapons company for 1st Battalion and was under the command of a Leutnant Raube, who had established his command post inside Chaumont. Like 8th Company, Raube's weapons company lacked heavy weapons, with only two heavy machine guns and no mortar tubes. Its strength had dwindled to only fifty-two men. Beside Raube's company, Major Ebel had placed 3rd Battalion's support elements in Chaumont, including the battalion kitchen. In summary, Chaumont had a kitchen and a worn-down weapons company to secure the rear area behind 2nd and 3rd battalions.

To make up for the lack of long-range antitank guns, Heilmann allocated to each regiment a battery of StuGs from the 11th Assault Brigade. The StuGs, with their 7.5cm long-barreled guns, were the equal of the American Sherman tank. As evidence, the StuG III could penetrate the hull armor of the Sherman M4A2 at thirty-five hundred meters, while a Sherman M4A2 would need to close to three thousand meters to penetrate the side armor of a StuG III. The closest StuG unit was 3rd Battery, which was laagering in the village of Hollange—only three kilometers away. Moreover, each assault-gun battery was authorized ten assault guns when it was at full strength. One prisoner later claimed that 3rd Battery had twelve StuGs. Hence, the 14th Fallschirmjäger Regiment had some teeth with which to bite Irzyk's approaching column.

For additional artillery support, Schimmel could call on one battalion from the 408th Volks Artillery Corps, which had set up its headquarters nearby in Sainlez. The battalion had three batteries of the towed 7.5cm Feldkanone 40 field cannon, and each battery had six guns. The gun had a range of more than eleven thousand meters. Still, compared to the American artillery, it was a poor challenger, since most of the American artillery were self-propelled 105mm or towed 155mm howitzers, both of which had a longer range and a bigger bang than their German counterparts.

Additionally, Oberst Heilmann had ordered the 5th Fallschirmjäger Pioneer Battalion to disrupt the American advance by laying minefields and blowing bridges. In 2nd Battalion's sector, 2nd Company was conducting the demolition operations along the Burnon–Chaumont axis.

To the pioneers, the American artillery was ubiquitous. Roads and intersections were danger areas, and the Americans, if they suspected any enemy activity, would pulverize these spots with a prodigious amount of artillery. To conceal their positions from American artillery spotters circling over the battlefield in L-4 Piper Cub airplanes, the Germans dug foxholes along the edge of the wood lines. It was all they could do.

Gerhard Martin, the pioneer battalion commander, described his men's experiences: "Over the course of time, everyone assumed a degree of tenacity from the combat, artillery explosions, and attacks by enemy aircraft, the cold, and the starvation. Remarkably, the combat preparedness, camaraderie, and combat spirit were neither compromised nor diminished." They would need that camaraderie in the days to come.[2]

0845 Hours, Saturday, December 23
1.5 Kilometers South of Chaumont, Belgium
Forward Element of Combat Command B, 4th Armored Division

The morning sun was balancing on the eastern horizon when Major Albin Irzyk heard the radio call in his command tank, indicating that German forces had sprung an ambush on the column's lead elements. Within minutes, reports began to filter back that his task force had suffered casualties, and he sensed that trouble was up ahead in Chaumont.

Major Irzyk had experienced a rough evening. At 2030 hours the previous night, he had dispatched his liaison officer, Lieutenant Marshall, to Combat Command B Headquarters with the "mission, checklist, attack order, composition of troops, [and] times." Marshall, driving in a jeep with another soldier, made a wrong turn and headed toward the village of Bodange, which the Germans still controlled. The *fallschirmjägers* there captured him, but the other soldier escaped and reported what had happened. Unfortunately, no one knew whether Marshall had destroyed the classified documents before the Germans caught him. For Irzyk, though, it was too late to change direction now, and so his column plowed ahead.

Irzyk's lead element was a combined-arms task force. A platoon of jeeps was followed by a platoon of light tanks, trailed by a platoon of mediums. Usually the mediums, with better firepower and armor, were up front, but since it was nighttime, the jeeps and Stuarts seemed to be the better choice, because they were more nimble than the lumbering Shermans. Second Lieutenant James E. Bennett, the cavalry platoon leader, cross-leveled the force even further so that the lead element was his jeep platoon, Private Bruce Fenchel's light tank, and three medium tanks. Safely ensconced farther back in the column, Irzyk wondered whether his decision had been the best one.[3]

0845 to 0924 Hours, Saturday, December 23
Lead Platoon, Dog Company, 8th Tank Battalion, 4th Armored Division
Southern Outskirts of Chaumont, Belgium

To Major Irzyk, the trouble was still only on the radio, but for Bruce Fenchel it was all around him. Sixty years later, the memory of that fateful day still remained fresh in his mind:

> The machine gun fire and their big guns were just completely covering us, sweeping the field with fire. I managed to crawl into my driver's seat with machine gun bullets ricocheting off my tank. All of a sudden I was being covered with blood. I looked up and saw my tank commander hanging almost down to my hatch. I knew instantly he was dead, because he had been shot in the face. Two of our crew never even got inside the tank. Tanks were being hit and exploding all around me. My only salvation was to get out of that tank. When I jumped I felt no legs under me because my feet were frozen. I stumbled to the back of the tank for protection from machine gun fire. That instant a German 88 [7.5cm] shell hit the tank, drove completely through the one gas tank, and past my head. The fifty-gallon tank of gas exploded into flames. I tore off my coat and started to stumble away from the tank. Machine gun bullets were grazing past my legs, piercing the snow and throwing dirt into my eyes. My only hope was to return to the burning tank for cover. As I approached it the other fifty-gallon gas tank exploded and the tank was a ball of fire. While [I was] in the process of stumbling away from the rear of the tank and flames, everything went blank. A high-explosive shell landed beside me, and the concussion catapulted me into the air. When I hit the ground I was momentarily knocked out. When I came to, I thought I had lost my legs, because everywhere I looked there was blood on the snow. I pulled myself to a drainage ditch beside the road, which had become a bumper-to-bumper colossal frenzied mess of vehicles ranging from jeeps, artillery, ambulances, tanks, and half-tracks in full retreat from the German onslaught.

Fenchel was the only survivor of this tank crew. The cavalry troopers riding in jeeps fared even worse. Many were dead, including their platoon leader, Lieutenant Bennett. Tracers and shrapnel filled the air as *fallschirmjägers* from 8th Company let loose with *panzerfausts* and machine guns. StuGs were pouring lethal lead into the tanks and jeeps. The self-propelled assault-gun platoon had occupied an ideal firing position on Hill 480, northeast of the Lambay–Chênet Woods, and was hitting the American column from the southeast while the *fallschirmjägers* unloaded on them at a closer range east from the Lambay–Chênet Woods. Another platoon from the 8th Fallschirmjäger blasted them from Hill 500 to the west of the column, catching the Americans' lead elements in a blistering cross fire.

The medium tanks tried to push forward, but it was fruitless. Second Lieutenant Robert H. Day, the light tank platoon leader, was wounded in one attempt. Finally someone made the decision to withdraw the lead element. The next hour was blurry bedlam for Fenchel. As he lay in a ditch, he saw a fuel truck struggling to escape the firestorm with the rest of the column. Crammed inside were four men. Fenchel waved. Luckily, the driver spotted him and shouted, "We can't get you in the cab, but we will hold you against the truck!" Flushed with adrenaline, Fenchel got up and jumped onto the fueler, and two of the cab occupants grabbed onto him.

"I was vomiting all the way," Fenchel recalled, "and my hands were starting to freeze till I had lost feeling in them. I yelled to drop me in front of any house. The driver slowed down and they released me. I crawled to the door and, pounding on the door, I shouted, 'Americano, Americano.' The door opened and the family literally dragged me inside and upstairs to the attic."

The family provided the wounded Fenchel with blankets. Later that day they offered him food, but the young private could not keep anything down, so he declined. Lying there in the attic, he wondered when the Germans would return. He knew the penalty for hiding an American soldier was severe, and the family's bravery was not lost on him. Now the only thing Fenchel wanted was to survive Christmas.[4]

0924 to 1025 Hours, Saturday, December 23
Fire Direction Center, 22nd Armored Field Artillery Battalion,
Combat Command B
Burnon, Belgium

The violent riposte south of town had opened Major Irzyk's eyes. Chaumont would require a deliberate attack, but first he needed to suppress the Germans so that he could extricate his column and reorganize it for the next assault. The sun was up and his artillery observers could see their targets. The 22nd Armored Field Artillery had already conducted one fire mission on the German StuGs on Hill 480. Now Irzyk needed it to lay down a barrage of death on the German positions.

At 0924 hours, the Oasis Fire Direction Center received the call from 8th Tank Battalion. "Oasis . . . Request fire mission . . . concentration one zero eight . . . grid coordinates: fiver one three niner . . . break . . . four niner four four. Target is enemy infantry . . . over."

The radio operator jotted down the coordinates and repeated the message. "This is Oasis. Concentration one zero eight. Grid coordinates are: fiver one three niner . . . break . . . four niner four four. Target is enemy infantry. Is that correct?"

The voice answered over the radio. "Roger."

The radio operator handed the paper to another man, who sent the mission down to the batteries. Within a minute, the redlegs of Able and Charlie batteries were readying their gun tubes for action, and within two minutes, both batteries were firing downrange. For the German infantry on the other end, it was a traumatic experience. Most of the artillery rounds that detonated were standard high-explosive, but one round was white phosphorus. The Americans would use Willie Pete, as it was known, against infantry concentrations in dug-in positions or as smoke to mark targets or to conceal movement. If the burning embers did not kill the German *fallschirmjägers*, then inhaling WP would, as it burned the lining of the lungs. By 0953 hours, the fire mission was complete.

Meanwhile, flying above the fray in an L-4 Piper Cub, First Lieutenant Robert E. Pearson had a bird's-eye view of the battlefield and could direct a more accurate fire mission onto the German positions. At 0928 hours, he spotted an enemy position near the road that connected the villages of Grandrue and

Hollange. Requesting another fire mission, at 0930 hours the first rounds were outbound. Within several minutes the area disappeared as another eleven high-explosive rounds and one WP round detonated atop the enemy position.

The Germans refused to yield, and returned fire with their own artillery. At 1025 hours, the cannon cockers of Charlie Battery detected the unmistakable whistling of an incoming round. The men dived for cover in ditches or behind their vehicles. The first explosion was off, but not by much. One look at the crater told the redlegs that a 12cm Granatwerfer was lobbing rounds at them. The next few were not far behind.

Private Guy Fortney, a medic attached to the mortar platoon of the 10th Armored Infantry Battalion, remembered how effective the German counterbattery fire was during the Bastogne campaign. "We'd shoot those mortars and it seemed like immediately before we could get out of there we'd have returning fire from their artillery," he recalled. "I guess they could follow the trajectory."[5]

1100 Hours, Saturday, December 23
Girls' Normal School, Arlon, Belgium
Headquarters, III Corps

Colonel James Holden Phillips was a busy man as the chief of staff for III Corps. That morning all of III Corps' divisions had barreled headlong into the Germans' main line of defense south of Bastogne, and already the units were reporting that the Germans had slowed the corps' forward momentum. Now he had to deal with Lucky 6, the radio call sign for General George Patton. The Third Army commander was on the phone, and he wanted to know how the operation was progressing.

Patton was not thrilled after Phillips recounted the morning's events. "The going wasn't so good yesterday," the general replied. "I am unhappy about it. I want to emphasize that this is a ground battle and they must move forward. Get them to bypass towns and get forward. I want a definite report at 1315 today on the situation. I want Bastogne by 1350. I have to give it to my boss at that time. Get those boys going. Tell Millikin to get them going if he has to go down to the frontline platoon and move them."

"Yes, sir," was Phillips's reply, and Patton hung up the phone.

Now, Colonel Phillips had to radio General Gaffey and tell him to keep pressing his men. Unfortunately for Gaffey, the Germans had their own plan, too, and it did not end with an American victory.[6]

Late Morning, Saturday, December 23
Losange, Belgium
Headquarters, 5th Fallschirmjäger Division

Oberst Heilmann figured he needed a decent building for his division headquarters, and the château at Losange was perfect for his staff. As it turned out, the staff of the Panzer Lehr Division also found the château to be an excellent site for their headquarters. With a high, multigabled roof and four stories, it was one of the tallest buildings in the area. Painted in pearl white and built of stone, the residence stood out amid the towering pines like a porcelain centerpiece wreathed in evergreen woods. The locals called the building the Diamond Castle.

Heilmann's staff chose one room for the main operations center, setting up a map table where Heilmann read over the first reports of enemy activity along his division's southern boundary. The plan was simple: Hold on as long as he could until armored reinforcements arrived. However, the first reports from Martelange were not encouraging, and he realized that the clock had run out on the Wehrmacht.

Oberst Kurt Gröschke, commander of the 15th Fallschirmjäger Regiment, had radioed earlier that morning that the Americans had struck Martelange before he had established his defenses there. Several units had reported a significant increase in American artillery strikes, a further indicator that the U.S. Army's counterattack had begun. As he feared, Heilmann would later learn that day through Allied prisoners that his men were facing Patton's 4th Armored Division.

Heilmann glanced at the pins on the map that marked the locations of his subordinate units. The next course of action was obvious. His division had reached most of its objectives, and now it was time to switch over to the defense along his entire front. Unfortunately, he could not defend it all. The 13th Fallschirmjäger Regiment had not yet arrived in force, and he did not have the self-propelled assault guns required to stop an armored attack.

"The soldiers were now pretty near exhausted during the attack on account of [the] strain, and most of them had no idea of a battle of matériel. . . ." he later recounted. "On account of my combat experience in Italy it was quite obvious to me that the 5th Fallschirmjäger Division would not stand through tough defensive combat."

Heilmann decided to focus his decisive operation along the Martelange–Bastogne highway. He would set up several strongpoints on both sides of the road, and he allocated the lion's share of his assault guns to that sector, which belonged to the 15th Fallschirmjäger Regiment. In addition, he would insert the 13th Fallschirmjäger Regiment around the villages of Tintange, Boulaide, and Surré, which were all east of the highway. To provide fire support, each regiment would have one battalion of artillery.

Heilmann soon discovered that just because an artillery battalion backed up each regiment did not mean each regiment had adequate indirect fire support. His logistics officer informed him that each gun could fire only seven rounds daily.

Traffic jams were clogging the supply routes more than American bombs, and as result, no one was receiving enough food, parts, petrol, and, most important, ammunition. According to Heilmann, the main disruption point was the bridge over the Our River at Roth. The narrow, muddy roads around the bridge had turned into quicksand for the trucks, and only tractors could negotiate portions of the road. The Germans did not have a lot of tracked vehicles, and thus moving supplies became a significant problem for the Wehrmacht.

Likewise, the German army lacked motor vehicles in general. As a consequence, the 5th Fallschirmjäger Division's organic artillery could not keep pace with the infantry units. To Heilmann's chagrin, only one battalion of the division's artillery had manged to reach the regiment it ostensibly supported. Therefore, Seventh Army had to augment the division with several general support artillery battalions from the various *volks* artillery corps that were part of the army's task organization.

Heilmann knew the supply problem would only worsen if the weather improved, and when he looked out the window that morning, his heart sank—it was sunny, with hardly a cloud in the sky. The U.S. Army Air Force, grounded by bad weather for the last week, would be aloft today, and forcing German supply convoys to move only at night to avoid the ever-present American fighter-bombers, known to the Germans as the "jabos."

Just then, a staff clerk handed him a telegram. Heilmann opened it and read it. To his surprise, Hitler and Reichsmarschall Hermann Goering had promoted him to the rank of *generalmajor* because of his division's stellar performance thus far in the Ardennes Offensive. He whispered some of the telegram's words to himself: "It was of greatest importance that the Division advance to the last breath . . . in order to conquer the most important sectors." He hoped that the coming combat trial would not require that everyone in the division would have to breathe their last breath to accomplish their mission, but he also knew that some would have to die. Frustrated, he stuffed the telegram into his pocket. He would rather have a battalion of panzers than a piece of paper and a promotion.[7]

1100 to 1145 Hours, Saturday, December 23, 1944
8th Tank Battalion, 4th Armored Division
Southern Outskirts of Chaumont, Belgium

Before he crafted a plan, Major Irzyk needed to see the objective. He approached Chaumont from the south, and from the ridgeline, he could see that it would be a risky operation. According to Irzyk:

> It would be dangerous and even foolhardy to continue advancing in column on a narrow front and to move aggressively down into town. Chaumont, in addition to having just the one road, presented other problems. It sat on low ground much like being in the bottom of a saucer. To advance into town, the forces would be going downhill rather sharply. Once committed, there was only one way to go—down and through the town. There was no right, left or back up. Once through the town the road gradually rose again to Grandrue. The ground to the left of the town was higher and wide open. To the right (east) of the town, there was a long, prominent ridge running parallel, with trees on the slopes between the ridge and the town.

Irzyk knew that a radio call would not suffice for this operation. He needed to gather the key players together, in person, and disseminate the plan directly to his subordinates. In addition, he needed more than a few platoons of tanks to conduct the operation. His plan would require all of the 10th Armored Infantry Battalion and all of the 8th Tank Battalion. Thus decided, he issued the radio call, and within minutes all the commanders and operations officers arrived at his command tank.

With map in hand, Irzyk pointed to each objective as he provided a task and purpose for each company task force. First, Irzyk glanced over at Major Harold Cohen, the commander of the 10th Armored Infantry, and told him he wanted two infantry platoons to go with the two tank platoons from his Able Company. They would occupy the high ground southwest of Chaumont, and from there, Irzyk wanted them to provide direct fire support into the town. Able Company, 8th Tank Battalion, was under the command of First Lieutenant Leonard H. Kieley from Massachusetts. Cohen nodded and replied that he would have Baker Company provide the two infantry platoons.

Irzyk continued, staring at First Lieutenant Paul H. Stephenson, a Bronze Star recipient from Wisconsin, and his Charlie Company commander. He told Stephenson he wanted the 10th's Charlie Company and Stephenson's Charlie Company to skirt along the ridge that ran west of Chaumont. Then, his finger stopped on a spur northwest of Chaumont, he informed Stephenson that he wanted them to secure that piece of high ground.

For the decisive operation, Irzyk ordered three infantry platoons and two tank platoons from his Baker Company to roll in and seize the town. Baker Company, 8th Tank Battalion, was under the command of First Lieutenant Bennet Fishler, who had replaced Captain Thornton B. McGlamery. Major Cohen added that he could provide two infantry platoons from his Able Company and one platoon from his Baker Company.

Irzyk tapped his map with his finger and responded that he wanted one more infantry platoon and one platoon of tanks from his Baker Company to occupy this hill at grid 515490. From there, they would provide an additional support-by-fire position as the tanks rolled into Chaumont. Cohen peered at the map and decided that the platoon would be from his Able Company. With that resolved, Irzyk's meeting was over.

Within minutes, the commanders had returned to their units to conduct troop-leading procedures. In the meantime, Irzyk wished he had more tanks. He later described his battalion having "horribly understrength companies." Since leaving France, the Eight Ballers, as they called themselves, had lost several tanks due to mechanical breakdowns. As a result, Able Company had only six working medium tanks, while Charlie Company had seven. Meanwhile, Baker Company had the most with nine, which was why it was spearheading the main effort. The tanks were crucial to the plan, because the infantry would be riding on them. The half-tracks were great for moving troops across the battlefield, but they were woefully lacking in armored protection. Therefore, each tank would carry six to seven men. Two platoons from Able Company, 10th Armored Infantry, would piggyback on the tanks from Baker Company, 8th Tank Battalion, while the one platoon from Baker Company would be dismounted and act as the trail force, providing rear security for the column.

According to Matteo Damiano, a private in Charlie Company, 10th Armored Infantry Battalion, the infantrymen who rode on the tanks had a simple but crucial job. "We were the eyes and ears for the tanks," he said. "When we went into the cities and towns, we would walk alongside the tank, protecting them from an enemy who'd be in a ditch somewhere alongside the road with a bazooka, who wanted to blow the tank up."

Infantry was not the only supporting weapon in Irzyk's toolbox that late morning. He then looked at his watch. It was almost 1145 hours. The artillery he requested was about to bring down fire on Chaumont as if it were Sodom.[8]

1145 to 1241 Hours, Saturday, December 23, 1944
Fire Direction Center, 22nd Armored Field Artillery Battalion,
Combat Command B Burnon, Belgium

"Fire!" shouted dozens of cannon cockers as they yanked the lanyards on their howitzers. Instantly cracks of lightning thundered across Burnon, and the ground shook as three battalions of artillery roared.

Major Irzyk had coordinated with the 776th Field Artillery, the 22nd and the 253rd Armored Field Artillery battalions, to saturate Chaumont prior to the main ground assault. The mighty artillery boomed at 1145 hours, and their first target was on the northwest side of Chaumont. Suddenly the town disappeared as geysers of flame and dirt shot up into the air. For the Germans huddled in buildings inside Chaumont, it was hell as shrapnel whistled and screamed among the buildings, ricocheting like pinballs at supersonic velocity. For several interminable minutes, Chaumont trembled.

Then the storm shifted to the Bois–Saint-Hubert woods northwest of the town. For twenty minutes, the area was a maelstrom as artillery shells exploded among the trees, turning the trunks and branches into deadly splinters. Finally the two general support battalions fell silent, but the 22nd Armored Field Artillery continued to conduct fire missions. By 1300 hours, its four batteries had expended more than 280 rounds of high explosive.

In the skies above, P-47 Thunderbolt fighter-bombers provided close air support, hammering Chaumont and the woods due east of the village. The planes downed two German FW-190 fighters that had attempted to penetrate the air cordon over the battlefield, and the 8th Tank Battalion reported seeing the aircraft crash around 1215 hours.

A great deal of the air support came from the 362nd Fighter Group, which routinely conducted missions for Patton's Third Army. Colonel Joe Laughlin had assumed command in August, following the loss of its first commander. Colonel Morton Magoffin had bailed out over France after his plane sustained flak damage. (Magoffin later escaped with the help of a nurse.) Since then, Laughlin had led his three fighter squadrons (377th, 378th, and 379th) with skill and courage.

December 23 was the first day since almost the beginning of the Ardennes Offensive that 362nd Fighter Group could conduct close air-support missions. Unfortunately for the German Army, the twenty-third was only the beginning. The 4th Armored Division would call on the 362nd over the next few days, with devastating results. [9]

1200 Hours to Midafternoon, Saturday, December 23
Menufontaine, Belgium
253rd Armored Field Artillery Battalion

German artillery had not been idle during the American barrage. Mortars had targeted the U.S. general support batteries several kilometers behind the front lines. Like the 22nd Armored Field Artillery, the 253rd was conducting fire missions for Combat Command B. A general support battalion under Third Army, it had attached to III Corps and the 4th Armored Division on December 19.

The men of the 253rd had already sustained several casualties even before reaching Belgium, when one of their M7 tracked howitzers rolled over during the long drive northward. Three men had died, and the rest of the crew members were injured. Despite the loss, the unit continued to support the tankers and soldiers of Combat Command B. The gun crews had been up all night as Irzyk's men fought to open the road between Burnon and Chaumont. The Germans knew who they were, and when the column halted for several hours, they harassed the 253rd with mortar fire. One mortar round scored a hit, injuring a mess sergeant.

Finally, on the morning of the twenty-third, outside Menufontaine the howitzer batteries lined up to conduct fire missions for Irzyk's attack on Chaumont. The main targets were Chaumont and Grandrue. Around 1200, the batteries opened fire. Soon after, Baker and Charlie batteries shifted some of their fire toward the high ground east of Chaumont. Around noon, a pair of Me-109s flew over the gun line. Despite the presence of American fighters, the 109s dived and strafed the howitzers. Luckily no one was injured, and one report even claimed it was the 253rd that shot down the pair of German fighters.

Soon after the gun line belched fire, the Germans responded with their own counterbattery, and the area around Menufontaine burst with exploding shells and ricocheting shrapnel. The Germans pasted the area with Nebelwerfer rockets, mortar rounds, and 10.5cm towed howitzer shells, whose batteries were located north of Hollange. Unlike the 109s, the counterbattery drew blood, wounding six men. The road to Bastogne was no longer a highway. Now, thanks to the Germans, it had become a gauntlet.[10]

1200 to 1600 Hours, Saturday, December 23
8th Tank Battalion and 10th Armored Infantry
Battalion Column, 4th Armored Division
Southern Outskirts of Chaumont, Belgium

As his artillery opened fire, Major Irzyk issued the command, and the various company task forces started to roll out to their respective objectives from their assault positions. Almost immediately things started to go awry. As they headed toward the high ground east of Bois–Saint-Hubert, five tanks from First Lieutenant Paul Stephenson's Charlie Company got bogged down in a stream hidden by recent snowfall. The soft, waterlogged ground trapped the Sherman tanks as if they were metal mammoths in white-frosted tar pits.

Luckily, Able Company was still moving. Irzyk wanted the Able Company tankers to "keep abreast of B Company and I [Irzyk] felt that A Co . . . would be flank protection for B Company if their lead elements kept abreast of B Company's lead elements."

For Baker Company, the fighting was fierce inside the village. As GIs searched house-to-house for German soldiers, enemy machine gun teams on the outskirts of Chaumont attempted to pick them off. Simultaneously, German StuGs near Hollange resumed fire on Lieutenant Fishler's Baker Company. Yet the Shermans of Baker and Able managed to suppress the few German assault guns, allowing the infantry to push forward toward the center of town.

Corporal Tony Giallanza was one of the tank drivers who participated in the attack on Chaumont. Giallanza described how the tankers would fire on both sides of the road to suppress the German machine guns. The lead tank would fire to the right, while the second tank would fire to the left, and the column would continue this pattern until the last vehicle. Initially, it worked. Then, as Giallanza drove down the hill into the center of Chaumont, an antitank round slammed into his Sherman. The crew, sensing they were goners if they remained in their tank, immediately evacuated the doomed vehicle. Right after the last crewman jumped off the tank, another round hit it, causing it to explode.

Giallanza later wrote, "We ran up the hill so fast that if there was a record for running up that hill we broke all records. We were lucky that the Germans kept their heads down."

Meanwhile, the two platoons from Able Company, 10th Armored Infantry, had the unenviable task of rooting out German *fallschirmjägers* from inside the homes of Chaumont. In one instance, a pesky machine gun crew had suppressed Staff Sergeant Lumpkin Glenn's platoon, halting their advance. Undeterred, Glenn crept up to the house and tossed a few grenades inside, forcing the machine gun crew to withdraw. Elsewhere, when leaders fell, others stepped up. Technical Sergeant Paul F. Price assumed command after his platoon leader was wounded.

Instead of waiting for reinforcements and orders, Price continued the assault. Despite the efforts of Glenn and Price, Able Company could not take Chaumont on its own.

After an hour, Irzyk ordered more reinforcements into the town. A platoon from Baker Company, 10th Armored Infantry, and an additional tank platoon from Charlie Company entered the fray. It was not enough. By 1600 hours, the commander of 8th Tank Battalion ordered Damiano's platoon from Charlie Company, 10th Armored Infantry, to enter the tempest for the final push.

West of there, Dog and Easy troops of the 25th Cavalry Squadron were harassing German forces that were attempting to reinforce their beleaguered comrades in Chaumont. D Troop had established their screen line around 0810 hours that morning, and their mission was to secure the western flank of the entire 4th Armored Division by establishing overwatch positions that could observe the towns of Remoiville, Cobreville, and Nives. After the battle for Chaumont kicked off, the troopers started to see German forces assembling around Nives and Remoiville, ostensibly for a counterattack. In response, the troopers from Dog and Easy opened fire and destroyed one towed antitank gun, a truck, and an estimated forty enemy personnel. Thanks to them, those forces failed to reach Chaumont in time.

A little after 1600 hours, the Sherman tanks finally reached the northern end of Chaumont, where the road hooked northeast as it snaked its way to Grandrue. Years later, Major Irzyk recalled that moment of satisfaction. "We got to the far end of Chaumont, and we felt that Chaumont now was ours."

He was wrong.[11]

Noon to 1230 Hours, Saturday, December 23
26th Volksgrenadier Division Headquarters
Hompré, Belgium

Oberst Heinz Kokott was the commander of the 26th Volksgrenadier Division, and his unit shared a boundary with the 5th Fallschirmjäger Division to the south. Like the 5th Fallschirmjäger, the 26th Volksgrenadier had a nearly impossible mission. Kokott's division had to seize Bastogne so that the other panzer divisions in the XXXXVII Panzer Corps could roll westward to the Meuse

River. The *volksgrenadiers* were undermanned and underequipped for such a task. Originally, Kokott's mission was to invest the town, but now higher head-quarters wanted it in German hands, because, like a rock plopped into a pond, the besieged town was disrupting German logistics, since the slow-moving supply trains had to circle far to the north to bypass it before heading west to the panzer divisions.

Born in 1900, Kokott had been in the service since 1918, when he joined the army as an infantryman. He spent the next fourteen years with the 7th Infantry Regiment. In 1934, he attained the rank of *hauptmann*, and became the company commander for an infantry training battalion. He missed out on the Polish Campaign when the war broke out in 1939, but the lack of combat service did not preclude him from taking command of the 2nd Battalion of the 196th Infantry Regiment, which was part of the 68th Infantry Division.

Finally, after several decades, he commanded troops in combat. In 1940, he led his battalion through the campaigns in France in May and June, and again in Russia in 1941 as part of Army Group South. In December 1941, he took over the 178th Infantry Regiment, which was part of the 76th Infantry Division. His service was short-lived. In June of 1942, the Wehrmacht transferred him to command the 337th Infantry Regiment, which he led until January of 1943, when he was wounded in combat. For his sacrifice, the Wehrmacht awarded him the Knight's Cross, and he spent the next couple of months recovering in a hospital. Afterward, he was the commandant of the cadet school in Beverlo, Belgium.

In July 1944, the Wehrmacht selected him to command the 1135th Grenadier Brigade, part of Army Group North in Russia. In August, the army disbanded the brigade, and its cadre became the staff for the 291st Infantry Division. Kokott, on the other hand, became the division commander of the 26th Volksgrenadier Division, which had been reconstituting in Poznań, Poland. In November, the division left the Eastern Front for the Eifel region of Germany to prepare for the Ardennes Offensive.

His division had so far performed well in the offensive. After securing crossing sites across the Our River, his men moved steadily westward. In the process, they wrecked the 110th U.S. Infantry Regiment and encircled the town of Bastogne, trapping the 101st Airborne.

Though the XXXXVII Panzer Corps had augmented his division with the

901st Panzergrenadier Regiment from the Panzer Lehr Division, he still lacked the combat power to seize Bastogne. Inside Bastogne was an entire airborne division and one combat command of tanks. In addition, the Americans had tank destroyers and a never-ending supply of artillery. In short, Kokott knew he did not have the requisite three-to-one ratio for an attack against a dug-in opponent.

Even worse, cloud cover that had grounded the U.S. Army Air Force had faded away and the dreaded "jabos" were back, plying their deadly trade as Thunderbolts rained hellfire on the German supply columns and troop concentrations farther to the east. Meanwhile, along the far-west end of the Bastogne perimeter, Kokott's 26th Reconnaissance Battalion, together with several attached panzers from the 2nd Panzer Division, had initiated their attack on Flamierge, Flamizoulle, and Mande Saint-Étienne. The initial reports, fortunately, were positive, as the commander, Major Rolf Kunkel of the 26th Reconnaissance Battalion, reported that they had captured Flamierge.

Then chaos hit. Around 1200 hours Kokott first heard the commotion emanating from outside his headquarters. "Toward noon there appeared on the division command post at Hompré at first singly, but then in droves, men of the 5th Parachute Infantry Division," remembered Kokott. "They were coming from the forward lines and were moving on to the east. Barely an officer was in sight." Disturbed by what he saw, Kokott asked one of the *fallschirmjägers* what was wrong.

The nameless man replied, "The enemy has broken through! He moved to the north with tanks and has captured Chaumont!"

Suddenly the siege of Bastogne mattered little to Kokott. His southern flank was gone. Now, instead of contending with a besieged group of paratroopers, he had to deal with an American armored unit of unknown strength. Kokott shook his head, swearing to himself. He had little in the way of tanks. His only armored force in the immediate area belonged to the 901st Panzergrenadier Regiment, which had two companies of panzers. Moreover, it was preparing for an attack that was to take place that night. He then looked to the south toward Chaumont, realizing that American tanks could be rolling up the road in minutes.

Before he could gather his wits, another crisis arose. A supply column of horse-drawn carts, approaching from the west, stampeded through the town, invoking bedlam. "The vehicles became entangled with those coming from the east," Kokott remarked, "[and] blocked the road." It did not take long for some American pilots to notice the massive target in and around Hompré.

Within minutes, a series of popping and chugging sounds drowned out the neighing horses and shouting men. Instinctively, Kokott shot a glance to a nearby antiaircraft battery and saw that the flak guns had opened fire. It was too late. The commander later wrote, "Enemy fighter bombers swooped down on Hompré and pushed their thrusts of fire into the fluctuating and congested mass."

The culprits were eight P-47 Thunderbolts from the 514th Fighter Squadron of the 406th Fighter Group. Originally they had been escorting a flight of thirty-six C-47 Skytrains heading north to Bastogne to air-drop supplies to the trapped paratroopers. When the fighter pilots discovered the traffic jam below, they decided to attack. After receiving permission, the American aviators dived in, guns blazing. One pilot reported seeing a column of twenty trucks heading west between Hompré and Sibret, some towing artillery while others towed staff cars. The hungry predators spared no one. The jabos made six passes. When the last plane pulled out, twelve vehicles were on fire, and another eight were damaged.

"Houses caught on fire," Kokott remembered, "vehicles were burning, wounded men were lying in the streets, [and] horses that had been hit were kicking about."

The division commander heard a low, droning sound above him. He gazed upward, and through the creamy black smoke, he saw a line of airplanes that stretched across the heavens. Bundles tumbled out of the planes by the hundreds and soon parachutes filled the entire the sky.

A voice cried out, "Enemy parachutists [are] jumping and landing in our rear!"

Bastogne now had to wait. Kokott needed to shore up his rear area before he could contemplate tackling the 101st Airborne Division again. As he watched the stream of men pass by him, he quickly decided the best course of action would be to organize the demoralized and frightened stragglers from the 5th Fallschirm-jäger Division. In reality, he had no other viable option. His own division was already overstretched. The best he could do was to fortify Hompré with his division staff and the stragglers from the 5th Fallschirmjäger and then support them with the flak batteries, which he could utilize in a ground-fire mode.

More important, Kokott had to find a way to blunt the American column approaching his headquarters from Chaumont at that moment. With the help of his staff, he rounded up some pioneers with demolition equipment, some grenadiers from the division combat school, and an artillery liaison detachment, and sent them southward to Grandrue and Remichampagne. To bolster them, he needed armor to destroy the American tanks. For once, fortune smiled on him. As his staff gathered the blocking force of pioneers and artillerymen, four Tiger I tanks lumbered into Hompré.

Weighing in at fifty-eight metric tons, the massive metal juggernauts were one of the deadliest in Hitler's arsenal. With ten centimeters of frontal armor and eight centimeters on the sides, the Tiger I was impervious to most Allied guns. Its feared 8.8cm KwK 36/L56 cannon could penetrate the frontal armor on an M4 Sherman at eighteen hundred meters and the flank armor at thirty-five hundred meters. The typical Sherman with a 75mm gun had to close to within a hundred meters to penetrate the flank armor on a Tiger, and even at point-blank range a Sherman could not penetrate the German tank's frontal armor. However, the M4A4, with the longer-barreled 76mm gun, had a better chance, but it still needed to close to within seven hundred meters for a frontal shot and eighteen hundred meters for a flank shot. In short, the Tiger could outshoot almost any Allied tank on the Western Front. On the other hand, these giants were slow, with a top speed of forty-five kilometers per hour.

Still, Kokott did not foresee a battle of maneuver near Chaumont. The dense vegetation and sloping hills precluded that possibility. Hence, if the Tigers were in the right location, they could pick off the American tanks before the Shermans could close in and return fire. Even then, a 76mm or 75mm round would most likely bounce off the Tiger's armor like a tennis ball at normal combat ranges. Convinced that he now had a viable plan, Kokott hailed the crew and ordered them south to blunt the American advance.

A scratch force of Tiger tanks and a smattering of infantry was all Kokott had to throw at Irzyk's armored column rolling northward from Chaumont. Kokott later remarked, "The action of the 5th Fallschirmjäger Division was of vital concern to me. I was facing Bastogne. The American 4th Armored Division's drive north threatened my rear. It is an uncomfortable feeling to have someone launching a drive toward your rear, so, boundary or not, 5th Fallschirmjäger Division was of constant concern to me. The situation was not aided by my knowledge that 5th Fallschirmjäger Division was a very poor division. I feared the U.S. 4th Armored Division. I knew it was a 'crack' division."

Facing that crack division was a division that was cracking. Behind the 5th Fallschirmjager was the 39th Fusilier (Volksgrenadier) Regiment, which was under the command of Oberstleutnant Walter Kaufmann. With only two battalions of infantry, the 39th had received few replacements to make up for the losses sustained during the previous week of heavy combat. Each rifle company was now down forty to fifty men, giving the battalions approximately 300 to 350 riflemen. In total, the entire regiment, according to Kokott, had an effective strength of eight to nine hundred men (this number also included support staff in addition to the riflemen).

Kokott watched the Tigers plod southward toward Chaumont like giant sauropods, wheezing and clanking as they moved. Hope was all he had left. Even if a miracle did happen and the Tigers blunted the 4th Armored Division, Kokott estimated that the line would likely break by the twenty-fifth. General der Panzertruppe Hasso von Manteuffel, the commander of the Fifth Panzer Army, and therefore Kokott's overall commander, later told him in a phone call not worry about his rear areas. Regardless, it was up to the Tigers now.[12]

1600 to 1620 Hours, Saturday, December 23
378th Fighter Squadron, 362nd Fighter Group
In the skies above Burnon, Belgium

First Lieutenant Richard D. Law scanned the skies in front of him. As the leader of Blue Flight, Law and his men were part of a mission to provide close air support for the American forces around Bastogne. His flight of four planes had taken off from Étain, France, at 1430 hours, and now they soared over the target area after escorting a long line of C-47 transports to Bastogne. The entire strike package was sixteen Thunderbolts loaded with a variety of munitions, including five-hundred-pound general-purpose bombs, 260-pound fragmentation bombs, and containers of a new weapon called napalm. Law was a pilot in the 378th Fighter Squadron, which was one of the three squadrons in the 362nd Fighter Group. Poor weather had left them sitting on their butts for several days, dawdling, while their comrades on the ground were dying. Now, with visibility out to four miles, it was payback time.

Within minutes of arriving over Burnon, they found worthwhile prey. The pilots spotted a column of vehicles snaking its way along a road. Law determined that the majority were tanks and medium trucks and gave the signal to attack. Seconds later, the four P-47 Thunderbolts lined up and dived on the hapless column.

German infantry and tankers hated P-47s. Mounting eight .50-caliber machine guns, the fighters could deliver a lethal fusillade that could destroy most vehicles with a short burst, and its bombs or rockets could knock out any tank. There was little a man on the ground could do to stop a flight of P-47s from decimating a column of trucks and panzers. The only defense the German convoys had was to load up on machine guns and travel with self-propelled antiaircraft guns.

Law made some quick calculations as he pushed down on his stick. With his flight carrying three fragmentation bombs, he could dole out a great deal of punishment. For several minutes, the Thunderbolts dived and weaved over the column like seagulls hunting for fish. The planes made three passes over the convoy, and left several vehicles blazing.

As they were pulling out of the last pass, Law received a call from "Street Cleaner," the name for Second Lieutenant William B. Foster's plane. Foster informed Law that his propellers had started to sputter. For several minutes, the group flew south toward home. Then Foster alerted Law that he was losing power and he would have to ditch the plane. Both pilots looked for a suitable spot to crash-land the aircraft and found one near grid square 5046, which happened to be Burnon. Foster banked his plane and landed the aircraft on its belly. Flying above the damaged Thunderbolt, Law watched it skid to a stop, and to his great relief he saw Foster pop open the canopy and jump out, waving to Law as he flew overhead. Foster, as trained, then scurried off to the nearby wood line to avoid capture.

Despite their efforts to help the 4th Armored Division, Blue Flight failed to see the column of panzers heading south toward Chaumont. This was the column Blue should have attacked. Unfortunately for Combat Command B, the Thunderbolts hit the wrong column.[13]

1630 to 1720 Hours, Saturday, December 23
8th Tank Battalion and 10th Armored Infantry Battalion Column,
4th Armored Division
Chaumont, Belgium

Major Albin Irzyk was convinced that Chaumont was finally under American control. For several hours, his soldiers and tankers had wrestled with the German defenders, scraping and clawing for possession of the town. The *fallschirmjägers* who had remained to fight the Americans had contested every inch, as if they were defending their own homes. Unbeknownst to them and the Americans, they had bought time in exchange for their lives. Now it was the Germans' turn to strike back.

With the fortunes of war finally on their side, the Germans struck the American forces at the worst time. Irzyk's tanks and Cohen's infantry were finishing up an assault, and as a result, the men were tired and disorganized. They had not established any prepared fighting positions, and were not ready for a massive counterstroke.

Moreover, though the soldiers and tankers of Combat Command B now owned Chaumont, they did not control the high ground to the northeast and northwest. As a result, the German Tiger tanks had perfect attack-by-fire positions, which their tank commanders exploited.

The German infantry rode in on the tanks and dismounted as they approached the village. Reports varied as to the size of the German force. Some claimed that the Wehrmacht assaulted with twenty-two tanks and around five hundred infantry. In reality, the number of panzers was far less. There were at least four Tiger tanks and probably several StuGs from 3rd Battery, 11th Fallschirmjäger Sturmgeschütz Brigade. However, the number likely did not exceed ten armored vehicles. As for the number of German infantry, it was enough to overwhelm several exhausted armored infantry companies, so the estimate of five hundred infantry might have been accurate.

Major Irzyk was on the radio, communicating with his company commanders when the first 8.8cm rounds hit. "It was the frightening, demoralizing, intimidating, unreal sounds, screeches, and screams of high velocity tank gun rounds hitting, crashing, exploding, and ricocheting all around them," he later wrote. "It shook, staggered, numbed, alarmed and unnerved the men."

Private Matteo Damiano recalled that the attack caught everyone off guard. His platoon had just reinforced the other infantry companies when Tiger tanks opened fire on the M4 Shermans from Baker Company. "First thing you know," he said, "boom, boom, boom, counterattack!" He continued. "I see everybody running back [and] I'm running back with them alongside the colonel [Major Cohen]."

The German attack was so sudden that Cohen immediately decided that establishing a defense would be futile. Sherman tanks were blowing up around him as their ammunition cooked off like popcorn, and thus a withdrawal seemed the better choice. He ordered the men to fall back, while yelling, "Counterattack!"

Damiano did not need the encouragement. He could see that Chaumont was lost, and with the rest of his battalion he scrambled toward safety south of town. He almost did not make it. A high-velocity round from an 88 zipped by him, detonating nearby. The concussion tossed him into the air like a discarded toy. Luckily, Damiano escaped unharmed, but he spoke with an uncontrollable stutter for the next few days as result of the shell shock.

Not everyone was as lucky as Damiano. Everywhere it was pandemonium, but despite the hellish madness, some soldiers refused to panic. Staff Sergeant Charles W. Bennett, a soldier from Able Company, 10th Armored Infantry, rushed through the tempest of lead and fire to rescue a wounded tank crew. Braving the pinging bullets, and after crawling a hundred yards, he jumped inside the tank and managed to drive it back to friendly lines. Later, the army awarded him the Silver Star.

Staff Sergeant Stanley M. Kosiek, who had assumed command of his platoon on December 3, acted like a veteran lieutenant and led his platoon out of the hell that was Chaumont. Nearby, Technical Sergeant Samuel K. English carried a wounded comrade nearly twenty-five yards across an open area, while artillery and mortars burst around him. For his heroic actions, the army awarded him the Bronze Star.

During the chaotic retreat, Private First Class James M. Carey discovered an abandoned German ambulance, which he used to ferry casualties to the battalion aid station. German artillery rounds plastered the area as he navigated the narrow village streets. Once would have been noteworthy, but Carey went back two more times to rescue his comrades. For his heroism, the army awarded him the Silver Star.

It got worse once the soldiers reached the outskirts of Chaumont. South of the village, the terrain was wide-open as it sloped upward. Second Lieutenant William P. Patton, in an effort to save his men, tried to find a way out and exposed himself to machine gun fire as he scrambled up the hill. The daring officer from West Virginia failed to save himself. For his bravery, the army awarded him a posthumous Silver Star.

Another Able Company officer, First Lieutenant Charles C. Gniot, decided to cover the withdrawal of his remaining troops. Grabbing a Browning automatic rifle (BAR), Gniot opened fire on the assaulting Germans while the rest of his company ran to safety. Sadly, for his courageous action, he paid with his life. The army ensured that his bravery would not go unnoticed, posthumously awarding him the Distinguished Service Cross.

In the meantime, the Tiger tanks perched on the northeast ridge rained carnage on the 8th Tank Battalion. Lieutenant Fishler's Baker Company, stuck along the narrow village roads like proverbial sitting ducks, bore the brunt of the onslaught. Worse, the 88s on the Tigers outranged the stubby American 75mm guns. Within minutes, Baker Company ceased to exist as a fighting force.

Southeast of town, First Lieutenant Leonard Kieley's Able Company was the only force capable of resisting. Kieley's tankers had occupied a support-by-fire position earlier to provide covering fire for the assaulting Baker Company. Now his tanks were attempting to lay down a barrage of fire so that everyone else could escape from the hell storm inside Chaumont. Unfortunately, it was the only resistance the Americans could offer. Since the fighting was so chaotic, no one could discern where the front lines were. As a result, forward observers could not call in artillery support for fear of hitting American soldiers.

Meanwhile, Major Irzyk had his own problems. As he watched the Tiger tanks shred his battalion, he quickly realized that his own Sherman would be a target soon. Checking to see whether he could turn around his command tank, he assessed that the roads were too constricted. Backward was the only option. He ordered his driver to crank the gearshifts into reverse. Simultaneously, the gunner and the loader were loading and firing as fast as they could. Replying to the driver's movements, the thirty-five-ton vehicle lurched backward and bolted to the rear as if shot from a crossbow.

After several anxious minutes, they reached the edge of the town. Now the battalion commander decided to rotate the turret, because he needed to see where he was going, even though he would be sacrificing firepower for mobility and control. In those few seconds, Irzyk believed it was a worthwhile trade-off. He whipped the turret around as his tank climbed up the twisty, winding road. The tank was still in reverse, but since he could see better, it was easier for him to direct the driver. As a result, the tank was accelerating as it ascended the hill.

Irzyk and his crew thought they had escaped. Behind him lay the blazing ruins of Chaumont. He described what happened next:

There was a low, loud, deafening, earsplitting sound, followed by a terrible, horrible, powerful, frightening blow. The tank was shoved violently forward. It was as though the tank had been hit in the back by a huge sledgehammer, and picked up and thrown forward by a superhuman hand. The three in the turret were tossed and bounced like rag dolls. Stunned and dazed, they quickly untangled themselves and got back on their feet. This was not easy. While on the turret floor, they had been part of the clutter and utter chaos in the tank. The large, heavy tank gun rounds, which had been clamped upright, were now strewn like huge matchsticks on the turret floor. Every single item in the tank had been tossed about and pitched hither, thither, and yon. It was as if a giant hand had grabbed everything in the turret and tossed it violently about. Not a single item was anywhere near its original resting place. The inside of the tank looked as though a bunch of tables at a rummage sale had been picked up and upended.

The crew looked at one another, wondering what had just happened. Irzyk was the first to recover from the dazed stupor that had dulled their senses like alcohol.

"Keep moving!" he shouted.

Fortunately, no one seemed injured. The driver pushed the throttle and got the tank moving again. Searching for hull damage, Irzyk turned around and glanced at the rear of the turret, seeing a glimmer of sunlight shining through the armor. Apparently an 8.8cm round had grazed the tank turret, cracking it open, but instead of penetrating the armor, it ricocheted like a golf ball, bouncing off a tree trunk. Even though it was glancing blow, it was enough to knock the tank back several feet while jostling everyone in the turret like pinballs.

Finally they reached a concealed position southeast of town. The last few minutes had made Irzyk and his crew believers in a higher power. Irzyk looked down at his right hand. He was wearing a mitten that he described as "soggy with blood." He decided to leave the glove on his hand, since it would help the blood clot. Despite the wound, he was grateful that it was the only casualty in his crew.

Taking stock of his battalion, he learned to his horror how badly the Germans had licked them. He had lost eleven medium tanks in Chaumont. Fishler's Baker Company incurred most of those losses. When the final tally was complete, seven M4 Shermans, one M4 Sherman (76mm gun), three M4A3E2 Shermans, one light tank, one jeep, and two M18 Hellcat Tank Destroyers were smoldering hulks. Later on, Irzyk's battalion would recover seven of the medium tanks, but the others were a total loss. Baker Company now had no operating medium tanks, while Able and Charlie companies could barely field a platoon of tanks each. Moreover, Baker had lost a platoon leader, First Lieutenant William K. Blackmer, a twenty-six-year-old from Michigan.

Major Harold Cohen's 10th Armored Infantry Battalion also sustained serious losses. A platoon from Baker Company had suffered five causalities, but for Able Company the attack was a bloodletting, with the loss of all of its officers and more than sixty-five casualties.

With so few tanks available, Irzyk had to be creative when he positioned his forces for the night. Everyone was assigned to secure part of the perimeter, including his light tanks under the command of First Lieutenant Roy G. Erdmann and the attached cavalry troop under the command of Captain Fred Sklar. To keep the Germans occupied, Irzyk requested the 22nd Armored Field Artillery Battalion to conduct harassment and interdiction fires, which it did for most of the evening. It was all he could do, and for years he wondered why the Germans did not exploit their advantage. Decades later he learned that the Germans had never intended to advance beyond Chaumont. They were content with blocking the American advance along the Burnon-Chaumont-Grandrue-Clochimont-

Assenois–Bastogne axis. Indeed, the Germans could not sustain a major attack along that avenue of approach anyway.

That night, Irzyk decided to report to Brigadier General Holmes Dager in person. In Combat Command B's after-action report, Irzyk claimed "that [the] fighting and counterattack at Chaumont was the heaviest ever encountered by his unit. Attack consisted of 22 enemy tanks moving on right and left flanks and from the north. Our infantry, dug in by the tanks, fought magnificently, not withdrawing until every round of ammunition was expended."

The tanks of Combat Command B had penetrated deep into the German defense zone, but the Tiger tanks had stopped them cold. It would be several days before Holmes Dager's force could resume their advance, because both Irzyk and Cohen had to find replacements for their lost tanks and dead infantrymen. Cohen's companies were so short of trigger pullers that the 80th Infantry Division would lend them an entire battalion of infantry to augment Combat Command B. For now, though, the 5th Fallschirmjäger Division had bought itself time in the western sector of its area of operations. As result, it could concentrate its combat power elsewhere: namely against Combat Command Reserve and Combat Command A.[14]

CHAPTER 5

FLATZBOURHOF

| DECEMBER 23, 1944 |

★ ★ ★ ★ ★

"We can do nothing. The Americans are coming from every direction!"
—*Unknown German* Fallschirmjäger *from 15th Fallschirmjäger Regiment*

0005 to 1120 Hours, Saturday, December 23
Combat Command Reserve Column, 4th Armored Division
South of Flatzbourhof, Luxembourg

To the east of Combat Command B, where the 4th Armored Division's boundary butted up against the 26th Infantry Division, the soldiers and tankers of Combat Command Reserve were prepping for battle. The men of the 37th Tank Battalion were dog-tired. For their commanders it was even worse, since they'd had to attend various meetings the previous night after the men had bedded down. This early morning was no exception. A little after midnight, Lieutenant Colonel Creighton Abrams summoned all the company commanders for a meeting at his tent in Meix-le-Tige. Measuring only nine by twelve feet, the command tent was a tight squeeze for the officers. Nearby sat the half-tracks for the S-2 and the S-3 sections, while the men of Headquarters Company provided local security.

Colonel Abrams started off with a recent intelligence report that indicated that a force of thirty to forty panzers was threatening the eastern flank of the 4th Armored Division. In response to this report from the 26th Infantry Division, the

4th Armored Division had ordered Combat Command Reserve to secure the eastern flank. The objective was the small town of Bigonville.

Abrams outlined the plan. Leading the column would be Baker Company of the 37th Tank Battalion, followed by Baker Company from the 53rd Armored Infantry. The rest of Combat Command Reserve would follow behind the two lead companies. Using a map, Abrams traced the route, which led north to Perlé, then east to Holtz, and finally north again to Flatzbourhof and on to Bigonville. After briefing them on the order of movement, Abrams instructed the battalion reconnaissance platoon to move out ahead of the main force at 0500 hours. After they completed their route reconnaissance, the platoon leader would send back a messenger to the main body and report the conditions of the road. Meanwhile, the main body would form up, and would consist of the battalion headquarters, Headquarters Company, and Able and Charlie companies.

Once the column reached the area south of Flatzbourhof, the two Baker companies would clear the woods east of Flatzbourhof and establish a blocking position on the road that led east to Arsdorf. Meanwhile, the column would set up their mortars to provide suppressive fires on Bigonville and down the draw east of town. The 94th Armored Field Artillery Battalion would serve as direct support for Combat Command Reserve.

Like the rest of the 4th Armored Division, the 37th Tank Battalion was short on tanks, with eighteen 75mm Shermans, six more with the 76mm gun, and five more with the 105mm howitzer variant. To put it in perspective, a tank battalion at full strength would have fifty-three M4 tanks (a mix of 75mm and 76mm versions) and six Shermans fitted with the 105mm howitzer. For this mission, Abrams would not even have Dog Company—his light tanks—because they were guarding the Combat Command Reserve headquarters. As a result, he was short twenty-nine medium tanks, and he had no light tanks.

The shortages, though, did not deter Abrams, who had already established himself as one of the premier tank battalion commanders in the European Theater of Operations. Born in 1914 in Springfield, Massachusetts, Creighton William Abrams graduated from West Point in 1936 as a second lieutenant. His first duty assignment was with the 1st Cavalry Division, and in that same year, he married Julia Berthe Harvey. He remained a lieutenant until 1940, when the army granted him a temporary promotion to captain. It was in 1940 that Abrams saw how

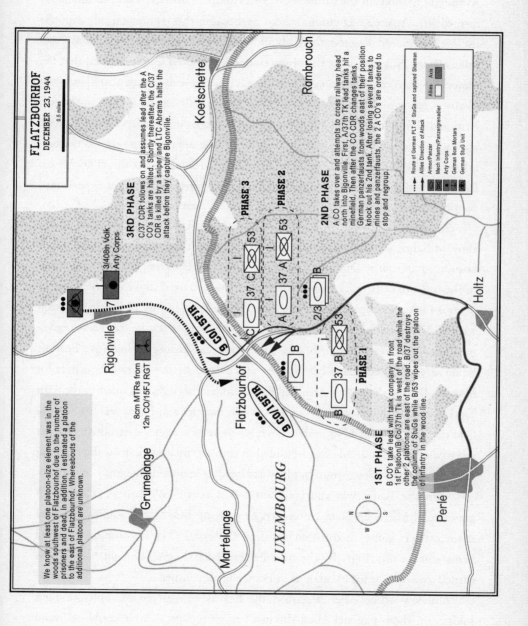

FLATZBOURHOF
DECEMBER 23, 1944

0.5 miles

We know at least one platoon-size element was in the woods southwest of Flatzbourhof due to the number of prisoners and dead. In addition, I estimated a platoon to the east of Flatzbourhof. Whereabouts of the additional platoon are unknown.

3RD PHASE

C/37 CDR follows on and assumes lead after the A CO's tanks are halted. Shortly thereafter, the C/37 CDR is killed by a sniper and LTC Abrams halts the attack before they capture Bigonville.

2ND PHASE

A CO takes over and attempts to cross railway head north into Bigonville. First, A/37th TK lead tanks hit a minefield. Then after the CO CDR changes tanks, German panzerfausts from woods east of their position knock out his 2nd tank. After losing several tanks to mines and panzerfausts, the 2 A CO's are ordered to stop and regroup.

1ST PHASE

B CO's take lead with tank company in front 1st Platoon/B.Co/3/7th Tk is west of the road while the other 2 platoons are east of the road. B/37 destroys the column of StuGs while B/53 wipes out the platoon of infantry in the wood line.

Martelange

Grumelange

Rigonville

8cm MTRs from
12th CO/15FJ RGT

Koetschette

Rambrouch

3/408th Volk
Arty Corps

7

LUXEMBOURG

Flatzbourhof

9 CO/1/5FJR

9 CO/1/5FJR

B

C 37 C 53

A 37 A 53

2/3 B

PHASE 3

PHASE 2

B 37 B 53

PHASE 1

Holtz

Perlé

Route of German PLT of StuGs and captured Sherman

Allies Direction of Attack

Allies   Axis

Armor/Panzer

Mech Infantry/Panzergrenadier

Arty Corps

German 8cm Mortars

German StuG Unit

N
W   E
S

successful the German panzers were in France, and he decided to join the armored corps, where his first job was as a tank company commander in the 1st Armored Division. In the summer of 1941, Abrams transferred over to the newly formed 4th Armored Division, where he became the regimental adjutant for the 37th Armored Regiment. In March 1943, he became the regimental executive officer. Not long after the promotion, the Armored Corps decided that the armor division's organizational structure was too unwieldy, so the army-level staff planners reorganized most of the existing armored divisions, including the 4th Armored. The 37th Armored Regiment disappeared, but the 37th Tank Battalion took its place, and Abrams was appointed the new commander. He led the battalion during Operation Cobra and the battles around Arracourt. Though his battalion had the fewest tanks in the division, Abrams was the most experienced commander, and one of General Gaffey's greatest weapons.

Abrams was not the only star in his battalion. His executive officer, Major Edward Bautz, was young for his rank. Born in 1920 in Union City, New Jersey, he grew up in nearby Dumont. He attended Rutgers University, where he enlisted in the Reserve Officer Training Corps. Bautz was drafted into the service before the war broke out, reporting to Pine Camp, New York, in July 1941. His first unit was the 37th Armored Regiment, and one of the first officers he met was the regimental adjutant, Creighton Abrams. In the two years before deploying to Europe, Bautz served as a company commander and eventually the operations officer for his unit. By this time, 37th Armored Regiment had been downgraded to the 37th Tank Battalion, but Abrams was now the commander and Bautz was his S-3. He held that position until November 1944, when he took over the executive officer's job when the previous one was wounded in combat. By now Bautz was a major at the young age of twenty-four, but he was already a seasoned veteran.

Opposite Bautz was the battalion S-3, Captain William A. Dwight. A graduate of Michigan State University, he grew up near Grand Rapids, and like many officers had earned his commission through ROTC, becoming a second lieutenant on July 1941. By the time he reached Bastogne, Dwight had already earned a Silver Star for his actions in France in September.

A fellow officer later described the S-3 as a "courageous, up-front tank soldier, in whom Colonel Abe [Abrams] had great faith . . . He could be found everywhere—especially where needed."

Dwight, Bautz, and Abrams were supported by other promising young company commanders. Heading Able Company was twenty-one-year-old John Arthur Whitehill, who was only a second lieutenant. Thanks to attrition, it was not uncommon to see lieutenants in command of companies this late in the war.

Baker Company was led by Captain James H. Leach. Like Whitehill and the others, Leach was only several years out of high school. Born in Houston, he decided to join the Texas National Guard at the youthful age of sixteen in 1938. By the fall of 1944, he had led his Baker Company tankers across France and at the Battle of Arracourt. He was more experienced than most of his older contemporaries in other divisions.

Rounding out the battalion task force was Charlie Company's Captain Charles U. Trover. Hailing from Illinois, Trover was a recipient of the Bronze Star. Prior to commanding Charlie, Captain Trover had commanded Dog Troop in the 25th Cavalry Reconnaissance Squadron. He had led the troop well during the fighting around Lorraine in September, and as a reward, the G-1 transferred him to a company command in the 37th Tank Battalion.

Abrams had three young but experienced company commanders to spearhead his attack. In addition, Lieutenant Colonel George Jaques would provide the infantry from his 53rd Armored Infantry Battalion.

Major Bautz was confident that the two precocious lieutenant colonels would accomplish the mission. On the other hand, he was not too sure of Colonel Wendell Blanchard, the commander of Combat Command Reserve. After the war, Bautz commented, "this guy [Blanchard] was a real pain, an incompetent, really. So, what would happen is, the artillery and infantry battalion commander, whatever, [had] come to our command post, Colonel Abe, and they said, 'Okay, what are we going to do now?' So, they got a general mission, and then they decided what to do."

For the first few hours, nothing occurred that shook Bautz's confidence in his leaders. Not long after 0800, Leach linked up with the reconnaissance platoon guides. His forward momentum, though, was short-lived after the tanks passed the village of LaFolie, just south of Martelange. Once again, nature had thwarted them. The hills were too steep and the roads too icy, slowing down Leach's progress, much to Abrams's chagrin. This stop-and-go dance continued for the next couple of hours. For the men in the half-tracks and tanks, it felt like they were riding along on a massive accordion, expanding and shrinking as they traveled on the frozen trails and highways.

By midmorning, the tankers and armored infantrymen were approaching Flatzbourhof. At 1005 hours, Bautz radioed back to headquarters. "Met no enemy yet. Have seen fresh tracks of one enemy tank. Some of our people are in that area."

At 1010 hours, an unidentified voice on the radio reported, "Smoke up [in the] woods to right."

The men started to glance eastward at the snow-covered trees that lined the road, looking for the smoke. They were now only a few kilometers south of Flatzbourhof. Everyone sensed the enemy was close.

At 1100 hours, another voice over the command net reported, "Enemy activity: Fiver . . . Niner . . . Eight . . . Three . . . Niner . . . Eight."

Men scrambled for their maps, hurriedly plotting the grid. The location was in a coppice that crowned a spur overlooking Flatzbourhof from the north. Some of them probably wondered whether they were in fact German soldiers.

At 1120 hours, they got their answer. Colonel Abrams heard some explosions, and he called Bautz on the radio. "How are things going?"

Bautz replied, "Arty and mortar [fire] coming from [the] north."

Now all three combat commands of the 4th Armored Division were locked in combat. For General Gaffey, there was no turning back. He had committed everyone and everything to the fight.[1]

1120 to 1130 Hours, Saturday, December 23
9th Company, 3rd Battalion, 15th Fallschirmjäger Regiment
Flatzbourhof, Luxembourg

Klemment admired his new camouflage. In the winter, his original Splittermuster camouflage was not the best clothing for concealment because the forest-shaded, jagged shapes tended to stand out against the pearl-tinted snow. Fortunately, someone in his unit had commandeered some white bedding, and now they were all wearing sheets and pillowcases, blending into the white background like ghosts. Klemment thought the camouflage would protect him. He was wrong.

The young *feldwebel* recalled what happened next: "Soon we received orders to defend the strongpoint at all costs with *panzerfausts*. For most of us, except for myself, this was our first close-quarter tank battle. Every group in the company had at least one or two *panzerfausts*. Our company actually had several more than authorized by the table of equipment or allowance."

The 9th Company was not alone. The StuGs had returned to the *fallschirm-jägers'* strongpoint in the woods southwest of Flatzbourhof with a captured American tank. According to Horst Lange's account, four to five assault guns and the captured tank were waiting there in ambush for the unsuspecting tanks in Abrams's column.

Around 1130 hours, a Piper Cub buzzed over Klemment and the 9th Company's strongpoint. Lange, in nearby Bigonville, had named the Piper Cubs "Lame Ducks," yet he noted that the planes were far more terrifying than the jabos because they meant American artillery. Despite the danger, Lange's mortars opened fire on the American column. Time and again, the crews hung the mortar rounds over the gaping tubes as if they were offering a sacrifice to Mars. For the Americans on the receiving end, Lange's mortars were deadly accurate, and the incoming shells sent anyone who was in the open scurrying for cover.[2]

1130 to 1147 Hours, Saturday, December 23
Combat Command Reserve Column, 4th Armored Division
South of Flatzbourhof, Luxembourg

Unbeknownst to Lange and Klemment, the observer in the Piper Cub radioed back to the 37th Tank Battalion: "Enemy infantry going in woods with white capes near town of checkpoint 52 [Flatzbourhof]. Could we put some artillery there? They're firing direct fire in there."

A voice replied, "Put artillery north [of] Grid 40 . . . west of town in [the] woods."

Eight minutes later, Captain William Dwight, the S-3, called over to Bautz on the radio. "How about getting arty in woods? [I see] infantry in small groups."

Bautz called back, "Use what you have. Air reports an enemy command post at Flatzbourhof."

Dwight quickly responded, "Enemy [is] wearing white capes."

The S-3 realized he had to force the issue. If he failed, the attack would lose momentum and bog down. Resolved to act, he summoned Captain Leach, the Baker Company commander, to the radio, ordering, "Use the infantry you have up there." The implied task for Leach was to assault the woods with both his tanks and the other Baker Company infantry.

Farther back in the column, Lieutenant Colonel George Jaques, the commander of the 53rd Armored Infantry, sensed it would be a hard-hitting fight. From his location, he could see that the German *fallschirmjägers* were using the railroad bed that bisected the north–south road as a natural redoubt. In addition, the wood line behind their fighting positions provided them excellent concealment from the air. Jaques quickly surmised that clearing the woods of German infantry would require artillery and, more important, infantry. Likewise, the fighting would probably devolve into hand-to-hand combat. This time his men would have to fix bayonets to finish the job.[3]

1151 to 1214 Hours, Saturday, December 23
Baker Company, 37th Tank Battalion, 4th Armored Division
South of Flatzbourhof, Luxembourg

Captain James Leach heard Captain Dwight's voice squawk over the command net: "Cooke reports one Sherman and one SP coming from the north toward our positions. They are getting in position to take them under fire."

Leach, riding in his tank "Blockbuster," scanned the northern horizon. They had already heard reports of the Germans using captured vehicles, so it did not surprise the veteran company commander that the Krauts had chosen to use a Sherman against its former owners. Captain Thomas J. Cooke, the senior liaison officer from the 94th Armored Field Artillery Battalion, was the one who was in constant contact with the forward observers in the Piper Cubs, buzzing above them. Initially he did not see the German armor. He needed more information.

Leach's commander, Colonel Abrams, was thinking the same thing, and he piped in on the command net, "3 [Captain Dwight], get the plane to watch vehicles for you." The time now was 1200 hours.

As he approached the intersection, the Baker Company commander arrayed his three platoons thusly: 1st Platoon was on his left flank (west of the road), and

2nd and 3rd platoons were on his right flank (east of the road). Meanwhile, Leach was traveling with his right flank, which was his main effort. Leach wondered who would see whom first.

In armored warfare, whoever saw their adversary first usually won the firefight. Sometime between 1200 and 1205 hours, the Germans drew first blood. Leach's left flank was under the command of Staff Sergeant John Fitzpatrick, who was the acting platoon leader for 1st Platoon. Fitzpatrick had taken over the platoon after First Lieutenant William F. Goble was injured earlier that month, at the Battle of Singling, France. Fitzpatrick, like most tank commanders, was standing in his turret, revealing his head and shoulders so that he could see the whole battlefield. When a tank commander buttoned up during a battle, he sacrificed situational awareness for his own safety. Hence, most tank commanders preferred to ride with their turret hatches open and their bodies exposed. This time the staff sergeant paid the consequences for his actions.

A German riflemen or a machine gunner managed to acquire a good sight and opened fire, wounding Fitzpatrick with a bullet through his cheeks. The quick-thinking sergeant grabbed a bandage and shoved it into his mouth to stanch the bleeding, then wrapped the bandage straps around his head. Though he lost some teeth, Fitzpatrick survived. His comrades were not as lucky.

From his position, Fitzpatrick could see that most of the German fire was emanating from a clump of spruce trees northwest of Flatzbourhof. He ordered one of his tank commanders, Sergeant John H. Park, to drive his tank toward the clump of trees, while Fitzpatrick and the other tanks in 1st Platoon would provide a base of fire. Park then edged his tank forward, using a country lane that crossed over the railroad embankment. As his tank approached the copse, Park suddenly fell back into the turret and on top of his crew.

Herman Coffy, one of the gunners in Park's tank, grabbed his lifeless body and noticed the hole above Park's right eye. It was obvious to Coffy that Park was dead—a victim of a German sniper. Despite the loss of his leader, Coffy coolly nudged Park's body aside and assumed control of the tank. He ordered Russell Holland, the driver, to reverse the Sherman back over the embankment when a StuG laid its gun on Coffy's retreating tank and opened fire. A supersonic round then shrieked through the cold air before slamming into the Sherman, setting it ablaze. Coffy scrambled out of the turret, while the Holland escaped through the driver's hatch. Private Edward H. Clark, the gunner, did not. He was consumed in the fire.

At 1205 hours, Captain Dwight, who probably saw Park's tank get hit, called Leach on the radio. "Have you any information on the left flank?"

A moment later Dwight had his answer, and Leach heard the S-3 warn Colonel Abrams via the command net with a terse message: "Two pieces [of] armor. Fiver Niner Six . . . Three Niner Fiver. By plane."

Leach grabbed his map and looked for the coordinates. The location was a crossroads a few hundred meters north of Flatzbourhof. Looking northward, he saw a Sherman tank emblazoned with a Balkan cross and behind it the two StuGs. Corporal John Yaremchuk, the gunner, slewed the gun onto the target. Unlike most of the Shermans in his company, Leach's tank mounted a 76mm long-barreled gun, which the engineers had designed specifically to kill other tanks.

By now Leach was behind the rail bed, using it as cover and concealment. Seeing his opponents rolling down the road, the commander ordered his driver to edge the behemoth forward so that the tank would be in a hull defilade position. In a hull defilade position, the tank commander would expose only the turret, thereby making the tank harder to hit.

Satisfied, Leach ordered Yaremchuk to open fire. Much to Leach's chagrin, the first shell was too low, bouncing off the railroad track and zipping harmlessly into the cold air. Leach ordered Technician Grade Four Kenneth B. Jeffries to load another round into the breech.

Not wanting to repeat the first miss, Leach told his driver, "Push up a little bit."

Seconds later, Yaremchuk fired and missed again as the round ricocheted off of the second rail.

"Push it up further," shouted Leach, who was probably wondering why the Germans had not fired at his own tank.

Like machines, the crew repeated the loading process, and Yaremchuk raised the gun once more. This time he hit the target. The captured Sherman exploded as the 76mm round ripped through the hull. In quick succession, Yaremchuk and Leach acquired the two StuGs that were trailing the Sherman and destroyed both of them. The battle was only minutes old, but both sides already had sustained losses.

Leach later refused to take credit for the kills. According to his tactics, he wanted to mass his company's fires on each target so that if the first round missed or failed to neutralize the enemy, then the second or third round would finish the job. He was adamant that his company team had killed the three armored vehicles. Regardless, the two StuGs and one captured Sherman were no longer a threat.

By 1210 hours, Captain Dwight informed his boss, Creighton Abrams, of the fate of Park's vehicle: "One tank hit by direct fire."

Dwight then called Leach and said, "Give me direction [of fire] that hit the tank." Dwight needed to know whether the assault guns the observer saw north of the intersection were the same ones that had destroyed one of Leach's tanks. If not, there were more German StuGs, and that was a problem.[4]

1220 Hours, Saturday, December 23
9th Company, 3rd Battalion, 15th Fallschirmjäger Regiment
Flatzbourhof, Luxembourg

Feldwebel Conrad Klemment knew the answer to Captain Dwight's question. As they were preparing for the inevitable American assault, another sergeant told him to look to the southeast. Klemment could see thick, inky black smoke billowing into the sky. The sergeant told him that the Americans had destroyed two of their armored vehicles. Klemment probably wondered how long the other three would remain to defend his strongpoint.[5]

1221 to 1240 Hours, Saturday, December 23
Combat Command Reserve Column, 4th Armored Division
South of Flatzbourhof, Luxembourg

Meanwhile, Captain Dwight was trying to run a battle when he glanced down the road from his tank. What he saw disturbed him, and he called Colonel Abrams on the command net, "Doughs are moving to the rear too much." Soldiers were hurrying past his tank like children returning from recess. ("Doughboy" was a term the tankers used to describe the infantrymen.)

He asked one of the soldiers what was going on.

The GI replied with an air of certainty, "My CO told us to take off."

Dwight could see that the attack was disintegrating. The infantrymen were marching in the wrong direction, but he seriously doubted that any of the company commanders had told them to fall back to the rear. Either the soldier was lying or it was a breakdown in communication as a result of the natural friction of war.

The S-3 decided to update Abrams about the retreating soldiers. "GI said his CO told him to take off. They are streaming past me."

While Dwight radioed reports, his gunner had found the StuGs that had fired on Leach's tanks. He opened fire. The round hit the target, but nothing happened, so the loader rammed another shell into the breech and gave the signal that the gun was ready. The gunner looked through the periscope and fired again. This time the armored vehicle began to smoke.

Dwight called Leach on the command net. "I'm pecking away at one on the hill. Is that one you knocked out?"

Leach replied, "It's smoking. It was knocked out." The Baker Company commander added, "There's a half-track beyond that tank. I believe it to be knocked out."

Dwight responded, clicking the handset, "I'll get air on that half-track."

Dwight searched for the German vehicle through the clouds of smoke. Around 1230 hours, he spotted something and picked up his handset to report it on the command net so that everyone would hear about it. "There are two more tanks north of this point."

In the meantime, the cannon cockers of the 94th Armored Field Artillery Battalion closed the breeches on all of their tubes. Seconds later, the command to open fire was given and the entire battalion responded as eighteen guns thundered. The rounds traveled over Dwight and the rest of Combat Command Reserve and crashed into the earth, the wood line disappearing as high-explosive shells pounded the German positions. The deluge continued until 1530 hours. In one concentration alone, Baker Battery fired more than 130 rounds of high explosive. For the American soldiers, it was a morale boost.

Soon, Dwight informed Major Bautz, the executive officer, "Doughboys on our left are moving up again, but ones on the right are not." Dwight knew Colonel Abrams and Colonel Jaques would fix the soldiers on the right soon. He sighed. Thanks to the king of battle, the artillery, the attack was back on track.[6]

1100 to 1240 hours, Saturday, December 23
Bigonville, Luxembourg

Joseph Thomas was only nine years old. The day before, his parents had heard the skirmishing between the 25th Cavalry Squadron and Klemment's *fallschirmjägers*, and believed that to remain aboveground would invite certain death. They decided to retreat with their children to a nearby neighbor's cellar. "This cellar had a strong foundation wall," Thomas remembered, "and was located behind the main house and therefore not exposed to direct fire. All the same, fear was everywhere in that cellar."

Twenty to thirty people were huddled in the dank room, shivering from cold and fear. Outside, a lone German *fallschirmjäger* was perched in a nearby walnut tree, and he opened fire at a low-flying American aircraft "like a madman," hoping that one bullet might bring down the plane.

Without warning, either a bomb or an artillery shell detonated near the house, showering the area with shrapnel while the concussion wave shook the building like an earthquake. "The building shuddered, a chapel was destroyed, and also the young German was no more," Thomas recalled. "We, on the other hand, prayed for our lives, and those people who had learned how to say their beads muttered over their rosaries and tried to calm the children."

Earlier that morning, Nicholas Molitor had watched a German *leutnant*, who was the platoon leader for the StuG platoon, exhort his men prior to the battle: "*Denn das schönste Weihnachtsgeschenk, dass wir dem Deutschen Volk, der Heimat, machen können, das sind wir durch unseren siegreichen Vormarsch jetzt im Begriffe zu tun. Sieg Heil!* [The best Christmas present for the folks at home, the German people, would be our victorious advance! *Sieg Heil!*]" he shouted. Finished with his speech, the young *leutnant* folded up his map, which he had laid across the front of his vehicle, and then climbed aboard the StuG. Minutes later the platoon rumbled southward. Not long after the battle started, Captain Leach killed the *leutnant* when his 76mm shell hit the platoon leader's StuG.

Molitor recalled that the heavy shelling began around 1230 hours. Like most villagers, he scrambled down into the closest cellar to wait out the attack. "Over there you can hear the barking machine guns," he remembered. "The dance begins. For many it will be the dance of death . . . villagers squeeze themselves into the cellars. They pray the rosary, and they believe that their last hour had struck."

With the villagers were dozens of German *fallschirmjägers*, hoping to survive the tempest. The wide-eyed German boys were expecting reinforcements from the Grossdeutschland Panzer Division, because they knew that their light weapons would be almost useless against American tanks. Some officer probably had told them that help was on the way, trying to keep their spirits up. The reality was far worse. The Americans, as Molitor observed, had won the race. When the Americans did attack, the *fallschirmjägers* would be alone.

Paul Kettel, a resident of nearby Flatzbourhof, wrote that when the American barrage started, "All hell broke loose in Bigonville." Running for his life, Kettel and his family grabbed what they could and hid in someone's basement. It was a short stay. American artillery sparked a fire outside, and soon the house was in flames. The Kettels rushed upstairs and scrambled to another residence, where they stayed for much of the battle.

At one point, a German *fallschirmjäger* stumbled into the cellar, looking "half-starved." Devouring a pot of lard he had discovered in the kitchen above, he blurted, "We can do nothing. The Americans are coming from every direction!" He was right. The Americans were coming.[7]

1230 to 1300 Hours, Saturday, December 23
9th Company, 3rd Battalion, 15th Fallschirmjäger Regiment
Flatzbourhof, Luxembourg

For Conrad Klemment, the billowing smoke from the destroyed StuG heralded the beginning of the American attack. From his position, the *feldwebel* watched the American tanks push forward, as if they were steamrollers with nothing in front of them. At the far end of the company strongpoint, a forward observer attached to Klemment's company screamed into his handset, begging for artillery. The battery of 10.5cm howitzers located near Bigonville answered the call.

Despite the additional support, Klemment knew artillery would not stop the tanks. They needed more StuGs. Unfortunately, his company had only *panzerschrecks* and *panzerfausts* at their strongpoint, and none of those were at Klemment's fighting position. Amidst the thunderstorm of blasting high-explosive shells, the *fallschirmjägers* at Conrad's location debated how to stop the Shermans with the weapons they had. While the scared men discussed their options, the veteran Klemment quickly realized that his soldiers had received scant antitank instruction as part of their basic training when they had joined the *fallschirmjäger* ranks. It was an alarming development, since an armor assault was already upon them.

Klemment offered his own ideas to the group. "I knew the tracks were the most vulnerable," he recalled. "A steel rod placed within the tracks could disable a tank, as well as smearing closed the vision blocks." Alas, he had no steel rods, nor any way to smear the driver's vision blocks. Then it happened.

"I heard the rumbling sound of the tanks as they neared us," he said. The Americans had arrived.[8]

1240 to 1330 Hours, Saturday, December 23
Combat Command Reserve Column, 4th Armored Division
South of Flatzbourhof, Luxembourg

Dwight glanced at the wood line from the turret of his tank. From his location he could see the German infantry, and he grabbed his radio handset to call for a fire mission.

Thanks to the development of the FM radio, the American army had the best tactical communication system in the world. No one could compete with them on the battlefield—not even the vaunted German army. Combining the SCR-300 radio at the company and battalion level with its platoon counterpart, the SCR-536 walkie-talkie (AM frequency band), forward observers attached to the infantry and tank battalions could call upon artillery fire and unleash it anywhere on the battlefield. For the German army, the American advantage in artillery seemed insurmountable, and with this advantage, Captain Dwight unleashed a massive artillery barrage on the German defenders.

Amid the cacophony of bangs and booms, Dwight received another call on the receiver. It was Captain James Leach. He reported that the artillery was clearly affecting the German forces. "Enemy personnel moving back toward the town. Snipers are active on our left," he said over the scratchy static.

Clicking the handset, he asked for Major Bautz, the executive officer. "What about smoke on [the] edge of woods to help D, B get up there?" he requested. [He must have forgotten that Dog Company was not there.]

"We are preparing to fire on that position," Bautz assured him.

Dwight could see that not everyone was evacuating the woods—some were returning. "Quite a few men with capes are running into woods, about twenty to twenty-five," he said over the command net. The caped Germans did not know what was coming, but Captain Dwight did. "We are about to fire there. Let us know effect," he asked Bautz.

Dwight then alerted Leach to the next fire mission. "I can see a bunch of white people in that woods. We are bringing fire on them."

Leach responded seconds later, "That's very good."

At 1247 hours, another unknown voice on the command net added, "The coordinates on that woods is Fiver . . . Niner . . . Fiver . . . Three . . . Niner . . . Zero. Infantry is this side of the railroad."

Dwight peered through the smoke. Like ants scrambling towards an anthill, the Baker Company infantry from the 53rd Armored Infantry Battalion were inching toward the rail bed. Once over, they would be on top of the German positions.

Several minutes later, Dwight called Leach again on the SCR-300 radio. "Is it possible to get by that vehicle up there?" From his vantage point, Dwight was likely looking at one of the smoldering German self-propelled assault guns that Leach had knocked out.

Leach replied, "I don't know." The Baker Company commander then reminded Dwight, "There's an SP and a half-track after that."

Dwight was about to acknowledge Leach's message when Major Bautz hailed him on the radio again. "Did you see that round?" he asked, referring to the last artillery barrage. Bautz needed to know whether it was on target.

Dwight scanned the area around the woods, and spotted smoke lingering where the rounds had impacted. After calculating the distances, he responded, "Short one hundred, right two hundred. Another round to the right."

Dwight waited three minutes while, several kilometers behind him, the cannon cockers of the 94th Armored Field Artillery Battalion and the 177th Field Artillery Battalion adjusted their guns. Finally, Bautz warned, "On the way." Seconds later, Dwight heard the unmistakable sound of outgoing artillery as an orchestra of howitzers boomed.

The ground exploded again, and Dwight saw German soldiers scurrying and scrambling like a horde of headless chickens, searching for cover from the steel rain. He nodded. "That's good," he informed Bautz. "That's making them move."

With the next barrage, the impact areas were in a different location, as if they were drifting in the wind. Dwight then picked up the handset and called Bautz. "Artillery too short," he said. The S-3 did some quick figuring in his head as he squinted at the target area. "Increase range two hundred yards."

Leach broke in over the intermittent static. "They [German infantry] are leaving the woods."

Dwight waited to see whether the next barrage was on target. Within seconds, geysers of dirt and snow, shrouded in smoke, erupted along the wood line. Dwight clicked in. "Good. Increase two hundred more."

Another salvo crashed into the woods, cracking the air like lightning. To Dwight and Leach, the scene reminded them of thunderclouds, except these flashing clouds were on the ground. With adrenaline pumping through his body, Dwight encouraged the listeners on the command net. "That was a good one," he said, referring back to the artillery barrage.

At 1303 hours, Bautz alerted Dwight, "On the way."

Dwight looked northward at the wood line, waiting to see the next volley. The detonations wreaked havoc, and he watched as the shell-shocked Germans exited the woods and staggered toward Flatzbourhof. "Enemy heading back toward town," he reported to Bautz.

Bautz probably did not hear Dwight's report, because he asked, "Do you see anything?"

The S-3 smirked and replied, "No, most of them have left the woods."

A moment later, Dwight heard Bautz over the command net request Lieutenant John A. Whitehill and Captain Charles U. Trover (Able and Charlie company commanders, respectively) to report to Colonel Abrams at the command post. Bautz wanted them to bring the infantry company commanders that were colocated with them. Dwight could sense that the CO wanted to push ahead with the plan. Baker

Company had seized the assault position and now it was time for Able and Charlie to finish the job and seize the wood line and eventually Bigonville.

Meanwhile, Baker Company infantry from the 53rd Armored Infantry Battalion had started to clean up the small copse west of Flatzbourhof. Several tanks from Leach's company provided direct fire support as the GIs cleared out foxhole after foxhole. In his after-action report, Lieutenant Colonel George Jaques claimed that his grunts killed thirty Germans while capturing an additional fifteen more. For the Germans, it was hell. They had endured a never-ending cyclone of artillery fire, and now they were grappling with grizzled infantry from the 4th Armored Division, who had decided to close in with the bayonet. It was no contest.

At 1330 hours, an unidentified voice reported, "On the CO's order, Able and Charlie and infantry move out to assault Bigonville."

Dwight nodded his head. The next phase of the battle was about to begin.[9]

1240 to 1330 Hours, Saturday, December 23
9th Company, 3rd Battalion, 15th Fallschirmjäger Regiment
Flatzbourhof, Luxembourg

Fortunately for Klemment, when the American Baker Company infantry assaulted his strongpoint, he was located on the far eastern end, and thus was spared. His comrades were not as fortunate. He heard what happened from the few survivors who managed to escape:

When the Americans broke into our position they did not take any prisoners. Or did it only appear that way? Machine guns and tanks tracks solved this problem (POWs) far easier, until the *panzerfausts* brought an end to the melee. The tanks that followed stopped immediately and left behind the smoking hulks. Only one tank remained; at the southeast tip of the strongpoint the tank overran an MG nest and turned back and forth with the tracks and thereby flattened evenly the ground. The fighting holes were not deep enough to offer protection in the hard ground.

Somehow, the 9th Company's forward observer avoided capture and hid in the cellar of a nearby farm. From there he continued to radio in fire missions. In the meantime, the Sherman tank that had crushed the machine gun position beneath its treads remained at the southeast corner of the woods, while its turret faced northeast at Bigonville. In the distance, artillery continued to pound the town.

For Oberleutnant Bertram, commander of the 9th Company, his options were dwindling fast. He had lost an entire platoon defending the copse. Predicting that the next American attack would be a flanking assault from the east, he ordered Klemment's company headquarters section, with the MG 42 machine gun team, to move to a position two hundred meters north of the main intersection. From there, the machine gun team could provide suppressive fire down the road. Klemment looked at the location before he moved and noticed a snow-powdered hedgerow. It would serve as their only cover and concealment. Behind the hedge was what Klemment called a "shallow depression," the only spot that provided protection. It was better than nothing, but it was not a deep foxhole, thought the *feldwebel*.

Satisfied with the fighting position, Klemment grabbed his section and the machine gun team, and they dashed across the open ground. Thanks to their white camouflage, no one saw them at first, and they reached their new location safely. The machine gun team set up their gun and waited. Overhead, the Piper Cub droned on like a fly that would not leave, no matter how many times someone swatted at it. Klemment wondered when the spying eyes of the air observer finally would see them, but so far their uniforms had concealed them.

From their position, Conrad Klemment had decent fields of fire. He described it in his account:

> The clear and open white terrain in front of us descended slightly. A road fronted by trees passed across our view at a distance of approximately 600 meters. A railroad track ran behind and parallel to the road. To the left we had observation onto the outskirts of Bondorf. To our right, our field of observation was restricted by the higher elevated strongpoint surrounded by low-growing shrubbery. A road leading southeast ran in front of the strongpoint for about 150 meters before it disappeared behind a large hedgerow, where the earlier MG nest was grinded into the ground. This is where the American tank now sat. That was our new and special field of observation.

Despite the new spot, Klemment still felt powerless. Though they were in a defensible position, the initiative remained with the Americans, and so the *feld-webel* and the rest of 9th Company had to wait for the next blow to fall.[10]

1330 to 1540 Hours, Saturday, December 23
Able Company, 37th Tank Battalion, 4th Armored Division
South of Flatzbourhof, Luxembourg

Second Lieutenant John Whitehill got the orders from his boss, Lieutenant Colonel Abrams, and hopped back onto his tank. He knew Leach's company had already suffered some casualties, and he knew that German StuGs were out there and maybe some captured American tanks, too. But that was all he knew. However, Abrams wanted to push ahead, despite the unknown dangers that were lurking in Bigonville. Whitehill couldn't blame him. They were sitting ducks if they remained stationary in the low ground south of town. Therefore he girded himself for combat and climbed inside his tank. A natural leader, Whitehill decided that his tank would take the lead as they passed through Leach's formation. His crew probably wasn't thrilled with the prospect, but they went ahead anyway.

As his tank lurched forward, Whitehill grabbed his radio to listen to the chatter on the command net. The first transmission he heard was between Major Bautz and Captain Dwight. Like him, Bautz was concerned with the whereabouts of additional German armor, and requested from Dwight, "Have plane check and see if these two tanks are still near that crossroads."

Dwight answered a second later. "Plane can't see tanks, but there's an SP and personnel in the town. [We] are taking them under fire."

Hearing this, Whitehill made a mental note of the two StuGs, which were commonly called SPs over the radio.

Then, at 1402 hours, Abrams called him directly over the command net. "The two enemy tanks reported to you are gone." Whitehill acknowledged his commander's transmission, hoping Abrams was right. He wondered whether his colleagues were counting the tanks as the SPs or vice versa. Double counting was normal in the heat of battle, but it made battle tracking a nightmare.

Several minutes later, as Whitehill was briefing his own company over the radio, Captain Dwight received additional intelligence from the Piper Cub flying above the battlefield, which he reported to Bautz: "There are at least 2 SPs in that town . . . one by the church . . . one painted white."

Bautz quickly confirmed the report with the Able Company commander. "Did you get that last message?"

Whitehill responded, "Yes." The company commander then stood up in his turret and looked for the church to see whether he could find the lurking StuG in Bigonville.

At 1420 hours, Colonel Abrams ordered, "Move out on mission." Then Whitehill heard Abrams say to Captain Trover over the radio, "Whitehill's moving out. You follow [him]."

By now, Whitehill had his tank moving. He could hear the gurgling roar of the engines as his vehicle passed through Leach's lines. His intermediate objective was the railroad crossing several hundred meters away. The crossing bisected a road that was part of a four-way intersection, and several buildings flanked the road on either side.

Dwight cautioned him over the radio, "As you come up this hill in the woods there is infantry and in town two or three SP guns."

Heeding the S-3's warning, Whitehill scanned the woods after warning his gunner. A moment later, he listened to the S-3 instruct Captain Trover on the next phase of the attack: "As Whitehill goes over, the doughboys on the left ought to stick their nose over hill and help them out. I'm going to put HE in [the] woods when the infantry moves up."

An earsplitting explosion rocked Whitehill's tank, jolting it to an abrupt halt. For several seconds, he could hear nothing but a sharp ringing, as if an amplified tuning fork were being held next to his ears. Finally the noise faded enough so that he could hear what was around him. He ducked down into his tank to see whether everyone was okay. Only his driver had sustained minor wounds. Everyone else was unharmed. Whitehill pulled himself up through the commander's hatch to check the damage on the outside of the tank. From where he stood, he could see bits of track near the left side of his Sherman, lying uselessly in the snow. He did not know whether it was a mine or tank round that had caused the damage, and so he called his wingman, Staff Sergeant Herman Walling, who was trailing behind him in another tank. Walling told him it was a mine.

Meanwhile, voices on the command net demanded answers. Dwight called

Whitehill at 1430 hours. "What was that puff of smoke?" he asked the Able Company commander.

Whitehill replied, "My left track [was] knocked off."

The young lieutenant was still trying to make sense of things when the S-3 called him again and told him, "You'd better get on another vehicle."

His head still throbbing from the blast, Whitehill scampered off his tank and examined the damage. The explosion had "removed a three to four foot long section of track, one bogey wheel and caved in the bottom of the tank injuring the tank driver," he wrote. Though he was no mechanic, he knew his tank would require a tow, so he ran toward Sergeant Walling's Sherman and assumed command of his vehicle. Walling was ordered to take control of the stricken tank and accompany Whitehill's former crew back to the rear.

Despite the loss of a tank, Able Company was still in business. Whitehill quickly donned the headset and heard Leach inform Dwight, "Cook just saw a couple of trucks move into the edge of town."

The lieutenant surveyed the area, knowing a minefield of unknown size lay hidden in front of him. Deep snow prevented him from seeing any mines, though he assessed that they were on and near the north–south road on which he was driving. He instructed his driver to pull away from the road and skirt the area by following the fence line that led northeast to the railroad and Bigonville, the rest of his company trailing in a line formation. Meanwhile, engineers approached the minefield and began to clear the route, while a tank recovery vehicle from Able Company drove up alongside the damaged M4 to tow it back to the rear.

Not everyone successfully avoided the minefield. Nearby, First Lieutenant Donald E. Guild, the forward observer for the 94th Armored Field Artillery, blew off his tank's bogey wheel and damaged some of his tracks. Luckily, the explosion failed to wound any of the crew, but the loss of Guild's Sherman meant that the 94th had no tanks for their forward observers.

At 1535 hours, as Whitehill positioned his company north of the railroad, he heard a voice over the command net report to Abrams, "Just north of where the tanks were knocked out is a concrete house and Jerries are running from the woods into [the] house." As the lieutenant looked to see where the German soldiers were running, three successive projectiles slammed into his tank's turret. Once again, his head was buzzing. He glanced down and noticed three marks on the turret where the rounds hit. Fortunately, none of them penetrated the armor. As trained, his crew reported their status. His loader had banged-up ribs, while his driver was holding his arm. While none were seriously injured, Whitehill assessed that they were temporarily unfit for combat.

Farther back, Colonel Abrams saw what had happened and ordered Captain Trover, the Charlie Company commander, to continue with the mission. "Whitehill received bazooka fire from [the] woods," he told Trover. "We will take [the] woods under fire and you will proceed into town."

Whitehill still had a mission to accomplish. Ordering his shaken-up crew to head back to the rear, Whitehill checked the battle-worthiness of his vehicle. When he sat in the driver seat and gunned the engine, he was pleasantly surprised to discover that the tank was still operable. He drove it back to the rear and reunited it with its former crew.

While Whitehill was away, another second lieutenant, Robert Gilson, led the company. Gilson had arrived at Able Company only three weeks before the Bulge, and his tenure as commander now was brief—his tank suffered a direct fire hit, wounding him. This left Whitehill as the only remaining officer in the entire unit, which had an authorized strength of five officers. When he returned from the rear, Whitehill realized that command tanks had become magnets for German antitank gunners, and decided to proceed on foot. If he needed to use a radio, he figured he would use the one on Staff Sergeant Ralph Rowland's tank, hitching a ride on the back while transmitting any messages. Whitehill needed all his tanks in the fight, and he did not want to lose one so that he could have a comfortable seat. For the Germans facing Whitehill, comfort was the farthest thing from their minds.[11]

1330 to 1540 Hours, Saturday, December 23
9th Company, 3rd Battalion, 15th Fallschirmjäger Regiment
Flatzbourhof, Luxembourg

Crack! The sharp echo startled the men in Conrad Klemment's section. It sounded to Klemment like a German Pak 40 7.5cm towed antitank gun. He could not see the weapon, but he was sure it was located somewhere on the edge of Flatzbourhof, firing away at the Sherman tanks.

The Americans heard it, too, and their tanks started to move, spitting fire and smoke. Klemment watched as Whitehill's Able Company rolled forward from the western outskirts of the town. The tank drivers seemed to be aware of the Pak location, and to avoid it, they drove northwest slightly before turning back to the northeast, like small planes avoiding thunderheads.

It was to no avail. Klemment observed an explosion and saw the first tank stagger and come to a halt, like a locomotive derailing. He thought it was a *panzerfaust*, but he was likely looking at Whitehill's tank, which a mine had disabled. He then watched Sergeant Walling's M4 tank approach the stricken commander's track. By now, *panzerfaust* rockets were zipping through the air like Roman candles. Within twenty minutes, Klemment spotted Guild's FO tank strike a mine, and then he saw Whitehill's other command tank sustain several hits from *panzerfausts*. To Klemment, these successive losses blunted Able Company's momentum.

Able may have been out of action, but Captain Trover's Charlie Company had started to push through Able's formations, heading north toward Bigonville. The surviving *fallschirmjägers* could see that the jig was up. At 1500 hours, the lone artillery observer reported that his radio was losing power. When Klemment tried to confirm this report, no one answered. Another tank approached from the southeast of Klemment's position. Within minutes he knew his position would be untenable.

Klemment watched in awe as a *fallschirmjäger*, assigned as a runner, ran the gauntlet of pinging bullets and bursting shrapnel, heading toward their postion. When the runner reached their cover, he summoned Conrad back to the company command post, and told the huddled men that an American tank was now northeast of their location, and behind them. Using the hedgerow that lined the road for cover, Klemment and his section crept back to the company headquarters. When they reached the road, they found an opening in the hedgerow. Seeing the road and knowing that an American tank was lying in ambush somewhere to the north, Klemment decided to send each man through the gap and across the road one at a time. He ordered the machine gun team to race across first. The two teenagers took deep breaths and took off like sprinters. An instant after they dived safely into the ditch that lined the road, an unseen machine gun ripped off a burst, pelting the macadamized surface. Conrad could discern from the report that it was an American machine gun.

Now it was the *feldwebel*'s turn to dash across. He remembered the incident years later:

Soon thereafter, I began to cross the road. Immediately, MG fire erupted and struck around me. A voice in my head told me: "Do not take another step!" I fell down in the middle of the road facing the tank and played dead. I lay two hundred meters away from the enemy on a silver platter for target practice! I could hear the nerve-racking whistling of bullets flying past me. My one thought: Hopefully they will not hit me. I could hear one of our machine gunners say, "Now they got Klemment, too!" Thinking I was hit, the tank machine gunner fired at the farm. Immediately I jumped up and within several bounds I made it to safety. The two machine gunners looked at me with disbelief. Then I realized how close I managed to escape death.

Several minutes later, they reached a farm, where they found their commander huddled in the cellar with several other German soldiers. Klemment reported to Oberleutnant Bertram the presence of the American tank blocking the northern intersection. By now everyone knew that the soldiers and tankers of the 4th Armored Division had almost surrounded the *fallschirmjägers* of 9th Company. The only escape route was an open field north of their current position. Unfortunately, since it was a wide-open meadow, the Americans could observe anyone trying to flee and pick them off at will.

While Bertram and Klemment discussed their options, the medic reminded them that they had four severely wounded soldiers who needed medical attention. The medic suggested that he place them on a two-wheeled cart and, using his Red Cross badge as cover, he would pull the cart back to Bigonville and bring the wounded to the aid station there. Bertram shook his head. The fighting had been bitter, and no one was taking prisoners. He told the medic to come up with a better idea.

The medic argued, "I know the Americans from Monte Cassino and Normandy. They acknowledge the Red Cross."

Klemment recalled that the medic had attended a Catholic seminary before the war, but had not yet taken his holy orders when the war broke out. Luckily, he was drafted into the medical corps, and so his service did not violate his pacifist conscience. Years later, the *feldwebel* still remembered the medical orderly as a good and honest man. Now the intrepid caregiver was placing his faith in cloth brassards and painted red crosses as if they were invulnerable armor. Despite his efforts, the medic's commander couldn't dissuade him from seeking medical help for those wounded under his charge. Thus, Klemment and Bertram helped the medic push the cart onto the road. The time was 1530 hours.

By now, they could see the M4 Sherman tank perched at the crossroads north of their position. As the medic turned the cart onto the road, disaster struck. "The closest tank fired at the sad bunch," Klemment wrote. "The medic sank to the ground and the cart full of several wounded tipped over in the hail of bullets. We were all gripped with grief. The Geneva Convention did not apply to us; we were all wanted dead."

A frenzied rage gripped the company commander and the remaining *feldwebel*. Klemment recalled the fury he felt. "I became determined that I would cause as much damage to the enemy if I were to die here."[12]

1540 to 2230 Hours, Saturday, December 23
Thunderbolt, Command Post for 37th Tank Battalion, CCR, 4th Armored Division
South of Flatzbourhof, Luxembourg

Lieutenant Colonel Creighton Abrams watched the battle unfold from his tank, "Thunderbolt." He knew from the last report that the Germans were scampering from the woods into the nearby houses. Though two of his companies had sustained some losses, he had one more company to deploy. Therefore, he had ordered Captain Trover, the Charlie Company commander, to follow on and assume the advance from Lieutenant Whitehill's Able Company.

At 1543 hours, Trover called Colonel Abrams on the radio: "Will have to swing to [the] left of Whitehill. Can't get down [the] draw." The colonel glanced at his map. Sure enough, there was a creek that snaked its way to the northeast.

Two minutes later, Abrams called Leach. He needed Baker Company to act as a support-by-fire position for Trover's Charlie Company. "Take town under fire with anything you have in position," he instructed Leach.

Several minutes later, the M4 tanks of Baker Company opened fire on Bigonville, the crack of their 75mm and 76mm guns reverberating over the undulating ground. Then Abrams heard only silence on the radio. He had expected status updates from Captain Trover, but there was nothing from Charlie Company. At 1630, mines and direct fire were still hounding the assault, and as a result, the Americans had not reached Bigonville.

Finally Abrams found out why Trover was not on the radio. A platoon sergeant from Charlie Company walked up to Abrams's tank, where the battalion commander and Captain Leach were having an impromptu face-to-face. The sergeant informed them that a sniper had killed Captain Trover while he was standing up in his turret. For Abrams, that was the final blow. He decided to call off the attack until the follow morning. He had lost a good commander, and Lieutenant Whitehill had experienced too many close calls while losing two tanks. Furthermore, the sun was setting, and Abrams did not feel comfortable pressing the attack through the night, when friendly fire probably would kill as many of his men as the Germans. He already had designated an assembly area in a draw several hundred meters southwest of Flatzbourhof for the rest of his battalion. For the line companies, he ordered them to remain where they were for the night and then resume the attack on Bigonville in the morning.

Later, Abrams and Jaques reported their losses to Reserve Command. Around 2035 hours, the commander of the 37th Tank Battalion calculated that the Germans had suffered around 150 casualties defending Flatzbourhof. Furthermore, Abrams' tanks had knocked out at least one, if not two StuGs and one captured Sherman tank. On the other hand, Abrams' battalion had sustained thirteen casualties, including several killed in action. Moreover, he had sixteen M4 Shermans (75mm variants) ready for combat, which was down from the previous day's eighteen. Abrams knew that in twenty-four hours his maintenance teams would work miracles and repair several of those tanks, but he was far from operating at peak strength.

At 2230 hours, Lieutenant Colonel George Jaques radioed in his losses. Since he was an infantry battalion commander, his losses were far higher than Abrams's. Able Company had sustained fifteen casualties, while Charlie Company fared a little better with only thirteen. Baker Company, locked in combat since midmorning, suffered the most, with thirty-one casualties. Though some were only lightly wounded, Jaques knew that some of his men would never walk again.[13]

1600 Hours to Midnight, Saturday, December 23
9th Company, 3rd Battalion, 15th Fallschirmjäger Regiment
Flatzbourhof, Luxembourg

Across no-man's-land, Feldwebel Conrad Klemment tried to squeeze himself under his helmet like a turtle hiding in its shell as another American artillery barrage hammered away at the survivors of 9th Company. He wondered whether they were the only German soldiers left on the battlefield. After the fire lifted, he gazed out over the fields and observed six tanks clinking and clanking toward their position like lumbering monsters. Nearby were the two tanks that had occupied a position at the southeast corner of the recently abandoned strongpoint. Suddenly the *feldwebel* heard a whooshing sound as a *fallschirmjäger* opened fire with a *panzerfaust*. Seconds later, another one rocketed from its tube. From where he was crouching, Klemment swore that the pair of rockets hit the two lead tanks in the group of six. The vehicles rolled to a stop, and the remaining tanks halted. The attack had ended for now.

The section leader sighed. They would survive for at least another hour. But the company had shot all their *panzerfausts* and were now without any significant antitank capability. Klemment shook his head. Resistance, at this point, would be in vain.

Finally a voice rose in the fading light of the day. "The company shall attempt a breakout during the night!"

The battle was over for 9th Company, and now survival was the mission. Oberleutnant Bertram decided that breaking out of the encirclement in one large group would only lead to capture. Instead, he proposed that a smaller group of eleven men under the command of Feldwebel Franzke would lead the way and find a path to infiltrate through the American lines. The objective was Bigonville, still controlled by the 3rd Battalion. Though they had lost radio contact with their battalion headquarters, Bertram believed that Bigonville still remained under German control. The company commander informed Klemment that he would travel with Franzke's group.

At 1700 hours, the group prepared to move out, gathering any remaining ammunition while Bertram checked to see whether the way was clear from the farm gate. While they waited for the command to leave, the group could make out the lifeless bodies of the dead medic and his charges. Klemment wrote what happened next:

> On command, we all jumped across the road and into the lower-lying field, which was protected from observation by the hedgerow along the road embankment leading to [Bigonville]. In a tactical single file we quickly ascended north across the slight rising field but soon were exposed from the embankment. Tank fire erupted and chased us leapfrogging away. A simple 100 meters became very long. In a depression in the field we escaped the fire from the tank, but an observer aircraft spotted us from above. Our objective was to reach the high bushes at the edge of the field that stood some 300 meters away. Separated by distance and with our weapons at the ready we kneeled in the snow. Our camouflage shirts would need to help us. Luckily, many dark earth spots were exposed through thin snow cover, considering we were not completely in white. We were not spotted. The aerial spotter circled and shifted to the south until eventually the aircraft landed and disappeared out of sight. We then continued toward the bushes at the edge of the field and entered a low-lying valley filled with groups of trees and bush works.

For several hours, the undaunted group crept over fields and across roads. Darkness fell, affording them some concealment from the prying American Piper Cubs. They finally reached Bigonville around 2300 hours, and after several minutes of searching, they found the battalion command post in a house on the west side of town.

When they entered the main room, Klemment saw another *feldwebel* from the 9th Company, and he asked him, "Where are you coming from? We lost radio contact with you around 1500 hours." Like Klemment, the other soldier from the 9th had managed to survive the hellish ordeal of the past few days.

As the clock struck midnight, Oberleutnant Bertram with the remaining survivors of 9th Company staggered into the battalion headquarters like half-dead zombies. The fortunate few *fallschirmjägers* soon found a place to sleep in a neighboring residence, where, to escape the threat of American artillery, they holed up in the basement. There, senior *feldwebels* conducted roll call to determine who had made it back to Bigonville. "When no response was heard," Klemment wrote, "the name was called a second and third time. The question then came if anyone knew the whereabouts of the person named. The fate of the individual was revealed with the least amount of words. It appeared as if the reporting person reluctantly recalled the fate of the dead."

The survivors tried to piece together what had happened that day. According to Klemment, most of the fighting had occurred in the southern and western portions of the strongpoint. The combat had been costly. Twenty-four hours ago, the company had had ninety men. Now, thanks to the Americans, they had only thirty *fallschirmjägers* left to fight the next day's battle. What had once been a company was now no more than a weakened platoon. Not a single *fallschirmjäger* who had carried a *panzerfaust* had survived. Klemment realized that his continued existence was the result of their selfless sacrifice.

For Oberleutnant Bertram, the only silver lining was a break from the fighting. Due to his company's catastrophic losses, it would return to the rear and wait for replacements before it would go into battle again. Bertram knew his commander would honor that agreement, but he was not sure the Americans would. The young *leutnant* would soon learn that his concerns were well-founded.[14]

Late Evening, Saturday, December 23
No-man's-land between American and German Lines
Flatzbourhof, Luxembourg

While the men from Combat Command Reserve prepared for the morrow's attack on Bigonville, the German wounded were dying. Trapped in the woods and near the crossroads, they had survived the maelstrom, but due to their weakened condition, they failed to reach German lines. For the American soldiers, huddling in frozen foxholes and frigid tanks, the haunting cries were too much to bear. First Lieutenant Jack Holmes, an officer in the 37th Tank Battalion, recalled that horrible night:

> Many were crying out for their mothers. Colonel Abrams had told us not to leave our position, so there was nothing we could do except listen. It

was then that I realized those poor boys out there dying in the snow were not very different from us. They were just ordinary soldiers serving their country. They weren't the monsters we thought they were. They stopped screaming a couple of hours before dawn, so we thought their people had rescued them. At dawn, we moved over the battlefield, and they were all dead. Those who hadn't died from their wounds had died from the cold.

Unfortunately for the Germans, they had yet to pay the butcher's bill in full. Generalmajor Ludwig Heilmann, Commander of the 5th Fallschirmjäger Division, knew he had to commit more men to Bigonville if he wanted to hold it. Moreover, the price for Bigonville would be expensive, and the currency would be more German blood.[15]

Late Evening, Saturday, December 23
Charlie Company, 188th Engineers, (Attached) 4th Armored Division
East of Flatzbourhof, Luxembourg

Sergeant Bruce Burdett had a job to do. He was a squad leader in Charlie Company, 188th Engineers. As a combat engineer, his job consisted of clearing and emplacing minefields, blowing and building bridges, and clearing and emplacing roadblocks. It did not usually include screening operations, which was the job of the cavalry squadrons. Tonight, however, his commander tasked his squad to do just that—to screen the flank of the 4th Armored Division. His unit, the 188th Engineers, was a support unit that was routinely attached to divisions to provide additional engineer support. In this case, Third Army attached them to the 4th Armored Division.

Indeed, his small squad of eight men was supporting Combat Command Reserve, which had conducted a deliberate attack earlier that day near the hamlet of Flatzbourhof. Now CCR wanted his squad to drive east of Flatzbourhof and establish a screening position to prevent German units from striking the flank of Combat Command Reserve. Thus, after nightfall, his squad hopped in their jeeps and started to drive northward. Their destination was between the towns of Flatzbourhof and Koetschette. The area to which they were headed was heavily wooded, and since they were driving in blackout conditions, it was even darker. Fortunately, it was a half-moon that night, so they had some illumination as the squad navigated the twisting and winding roads.

What bothered Burdett even more was the lack of information. No one knew where the Germans might be. No one knew whether the Germans were still in Koetschette; nor did anyone know whether the Germans were still in Bigonville, which was north of their destination. At least his superiors told him that if someone approached from Koetschette they were likely the enemy. That was all the information they had when they set out that night. The lack of information would cost them.

After they passed through the forward trace of Captain Leach's Baker Company, they reached the intersection at Flatzbourhof. Instead of heading north to Bigonville, they turned right and headed east toward Koetschette. Several minutes later, they reached a spot about three hundred yards east of the intersection, where they emplaced around fifteen mines and rigged the trees with nitro starch. If someone did attempt to breach the minefield, the engineers would detonate the explosives on the trees, causing them to fall across the road, further blocking the highway. After they had completed the task, Lieutenant Harmon, the platoon leader, ordered most of Burdett's squad to remain at the roadblock and provide overwatch. The squad had few weapons, including rifles, some grenades, two bazookas, one of which was malfunctioning, and several rockets. Moreover, they had neither machine guns nor a radio. Burdett was not optimistic about his squad's chances if the Germans did show up, and since he lacked any communication equipment, his men would have no way to alert others nor call for reinforcement. Orders were orders, though, and he told his men to guard the obstacle.

With his task complete, he now had to escort his platoon leader back to the company headquarters. After informing Combat Command Reserve about his squad's location, he would return to his squad on foot and remain with them for the night. Satisfied with the plan, his platoon leader jumped into his jeep and led the small convoy, while Burdett trailed behind in his truck. Burdett watched his lieutenant's jeep surge ahead and disappear into the darkness.

A terrific explosion shattered the stillness of the night. Burdett soon reached the wreckage of his lieutenant's jeep, lying on its side, its wheels still spinning. An unseen mine had been the culprit. While the driver had suffered only a few scratches, the lieutenant had lost part of his heel, but at least he was going home alive.

The lack of information had almost killed Burdett and his squad—they had driven through the same minefield that had wreaked havoc on Lieutenant White-hill's tank earlier that afternoon. By a stroke of fate, Burdett's men had passed through the minefield without incident when they had initially driven out to their roadblock, but on the return trip their luck had run out. Burdett was now without a platoon leader.

After securing medical attention for Lieutenant Harmon, Burdett returned to his roadblock, where he remained for the duration of the night. Fortunately, the Germans did not attack them. However, they did watch a firefight break out behind them in Flatzbourhof. He described it in his account he wrote after the war:

> . . . some flares went up back at the Flatzbourhof area. Immediately we heard the sounds of an intense fire fight, and saw tracers arcing off in all directions. The shooting, which included some heavy weapons fire, was all directly behind us, and we had no idea what it meant, either for CCR or for our little blocking force. The firing lasted perhaps five or ten minutes, then gradually died down and stopped, though something continued to burn, flaring up fitfully during the rest of the night.[16]

At Burdett's position, no one knew what the morning would bring. Farther to the west, though, the fighting had been raging all day and all night.

CHAPTER 6

WARNACH

| DECEMBER 23 TO 24, 1944 |

★ ★ ★ ★ ★

"The general impression was that we could just cut our way through."
—*Lieutenant Colonel Hal C. Pattison, Executive Officer for Combat Command A*

0300 to 1430 Hours, Saturday, December 23
Forward Command Post, Combat Command A, 4th Armored Division
Near Martelange, Belgium

While Combat Command B and Combat Command Reserve slugged it out with the 5th Fallschirmjäger Division, Brigadier General Herbert L. Earnest's forces remained south of the Sauer River, waiting for the engineers of Baker Company, 188th Combat Engineer Battalion, to erect a bridge since 0300 hours that morning.

Fortunately, thanks to an oversight on the part of the Germans, they did not have to clear the northern bank before the engineers started working. For some unknown reason, when the survivors of the 15th Fallschirmjäger Regiment withdrew from Martelange, they chose not to establish a battle position along the ridge that dominated the northern skyline. Instead, they withdrew their forces almost all the way to Warnach. Even worse, they had failed to complete the demolition of the Radelange bridge that crossed the Sauer River west of the main N4 highway. As a result, infantry could walk across the Sauer, and by 0500 hours, Able Company, 51st Armored Infantry Battalion, had occupied the northern ridge. Therefore, the engineers could commence their operation with little fear of a German attack.

By 1100 hours, Able Company had reported minimal German activity north of Martelange. The soldiers had seen possible German observer posts and heard some vehicle movement west of their positions. Later, they saw some small-arms fire in the woods northeast of them, but that was all. The *fallschirmjägers* did not test their defenses; nor did they attempt to flank them. To men of the Able Company, the Germans seemed to have lost their will to fight.

Despite the lack of German activity, the engineers discovered that the Sauer River itself was their greatest enemy that morning. Though it was not a wide river at that point, the Sauer had steep, treacherous banks, and the soldiers could not use a pontoon or treadway bridge to cross it. Instead, they had to build a bailey bridge, which took more time. It was not until 1430 hours before they had completed their task. By then, General Earnest had only a few hours of daylight left, but that did not deter him. Soon after the engineers had completed their bridge, the tankers of Task Force Oden drove over it and headed north toward Bastogne.

In spite of this setback, Lieutenant Colonel Hal C. Pattison, the executive officer for Combat Command A, said, "The general impression was that we could just cut our way through. Perhaps we could have with tanks alone, but they would have been cut off without supplies and nothing would have been gained."

Unbeknownst to the officers and men of Combat Command A, the Germans had not withdrawn completely. An entire battalion was waiting for the Americans, and like Combat Command B and Combat Command Reserve, Earnest's men were about to find themselves fighting for their lives within a few hours.[1]

1430 Hours, Saturday, December 23
2nd Battalion, 15th Fallschirmjäger Regiment
Warnach, Belgium

Waiting for Task Force Oden was 2nd Battalion of the 15th Fallschirmjäger Regiment. Earlier, Generalmajor Ludwig Heilmann, the commander of the 5th Fallschirmjäger Division, had ordered Oberst Kurt Gröschke, the commander of the 15th Fallschirmjäger Regiment, to block the Bastogne–Arlon Highway, since it was the most likely avenue of approach for American forces advancing from the

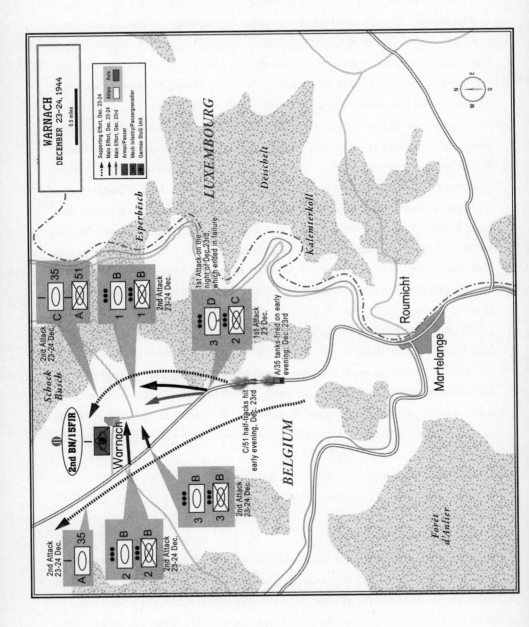

WARNACH
DECEMBER 23–24, 1944

0.5 miles

Supporting Effort, Dec. 23–24
Main Effort, Dec. 23–24
Main Effort, Dec. 23rd
Armor/Panzer
Mech Infantry/Panzergrenadier
German StuG Unit

Allies
Axis

LUXEMBOURG

Esperbësch

Deiscbelt

Kalemterkoll

Roumicht

Martelange

BELGIUM

Forêt
d'Anlier

Schock
Busch

2nd BN/15FIR

Warnach

35   C
       A   51
2nd Attack
23–24 Dec.

B   1
B   1
2nd Attack
23–24 Dec.

D   3
C   2
1st Attack
23 Dec.

1st Attack on the
night of Dec. 23rd,
which ended in failure

A/35 tanks fired on early
evening, Dec. 23rd

C/51 half-tracks hit
early evening, Dec. 23rd

B   3
B   3
2nd Attack
23–24 Dec.

35   A
2nd Attack
23–24 Dec.

B   2
B   2
2nd Attack
23–24 Dec.

N
W   E
S

south. Therefore, Gröschke had allocated far more combat power here than else-where, and thus it was the one area where the American forces marginally out-numbered the German defenders. Warnach was one of the areas that Gröschke chose to defend in depth, and so he positioned his entire 2nd Battalion there.

2nd Battalion had three rifle companies and one heavy weapons company, composed of recently transferred Luftwaffe technicians and antiaircraft crews, many between the ages of eighteen and twenty-two. Fortunately for the incoming airmen, its core group of NCOs and officers were survivors from the campaigns in Normandy. The commander was a Hauptmann Alfred Kitze. Furthermore, its weapons company had a section of 20mm towed antiaircraft guns in addition to its usual complement of two heavy machine gun platoons, and four 8cm mortars.

The young *fallschirmjägers* had fought well at the beginning of the offensive. They had crossed the Our River near Goebelsmuehle, Luxembourg, where they had encountered scant resistance. Their first major battle was south of Wiltz, Lux-embourg, where they had defeated the American forces and captured more than 120 enemy soldiers. Commandeering more than fifty American vehicles, they put them to good use, transporting their men and moving supplies. To adhere to the Geneva Convention, they concealed the white stars with mud and dirt, since paint was unavailable.

Since their victory near Wiltz, though, the *fallschirmjägers'* morale had de-clined. Despite the boon of capturing the dozens of American trucks and cars, their rear-echelon units had failed to supply them with additional food, and many of the infantrymen were "living off the land," stealing from local farmers and looting the bodies of the fallen. In short, the men were growing weak with hunger, and their esprit de corps was deteriorating. This was their condition when the 4th Armored Division arrived on the early evening of the twenty-third. It was likely Hauptmann Alfred Kitze knew someone was coming, since stragglers from 10th Company had escaped from Martelange and retreated to Warnach.

Despite the early warning, his chances for a victory were still in doubt. In ad-dition to his battalion, there was a battery of StuG self-propelled assault guns, but that was it. Fortunately, since he was the defender, he chose the terrain. Warnach was to the east of the main Bastogne–Arlon highway, but between the highway and the village, it was wide-open terrain, providing his battalion excellent fields of fire for their few antitank guns. Hence, though Warnach was not on the N4, it dominated it, and therefore the Americans would have to seize Warnach to open the road.

More important, once the Americans were inside Warnach, their advantages in artillery and air support would be of little use, since the distances between attacker and defender would be in meters, not in kilometers. To prevent friendly fire, the Americans would have to curtail their artillery and air support. Furthermore, Kitze's *fallschirmjägers* could then use their *panzerschrecks* and *panzerfausts* to neutralize the American advantage in armor. Finally, house-to-house fighting tended to exhaust the attacker, and it took more time. Time was Kitze's ultimate goal. In short, he could not possibly hold Warnach against a determined American assault, but if he delayed the Americans long enough, then they might not reach Bastogne in time to relieve it.[2]

1430 to 1645 Hours, Saturday, December 23
Lead Elements of Task Force Oden (35th Tank Battalion), CCA,
4th Armored Division South of Warnach, Belgium

Lieutenant Colonel Delk Oden kept looking north, toward Bastogne. His column had crossed back into Belgium, and he sensed the Germans were somewhere up ahead of him. Leading his column were elements of Able Troop, 25th Cavalry. For the first hour, they encountered little enemy activity other than a few desultory rounds of artillery that landed harmlessly in Martelange. Then, at 1600 hours, as the jeeps from Able Troop crossed over the crest of the hill, where the road bent, the Germans opened fire, forcing the cavalry troopers to withdraw back below the crest.

Wondering what was wrong, a lieutenant from 3rd Platoon, Able Company, 35th Tank Battalion, then got off his tank and marched up to talk with the cavalry troopers. After receiving their input, the lieutenant next decided to see the German position for himself, proceeding on foot as his tank followed behind him. As he walked along the bend in the road, skylining himself along the crest, the German machine gun team made him pay for his curiosity. Regrettably, he was not the only one to fall victim—the deadly crew also ambushed several infantrymen riding on the lead tanks. Moreover, the Germans also had positioned a 2cm antiaircraft gun and were using it in a direct-fire mode. The enemy had zeroed in on the road bend, since it was a natural choke point, and now the *fallschirm-jägers* were prepared to wipe out any vehicle that emerged around the bend and crested the hill.

Oden realized that he could move more of his force if he split them into three columns, so he shifted Able Company farther to the west onto the fields. With the meadows frozen solid and caked in snow, the tanks could easily drive across. The armor column would push north, but parallel to the N4. Meanwhile, Charlie Company, 51st Armored Infantry, would continue to drive alongside them, using the highway. In the middle, but trailing behind Able Company, would be the light tanks of Captain Ridley's Dog Company. To beef up Dog Company, Colonel Oden had attached all six Sherman 105mm assault tanks to it. Hence, Ridley had, in effect, four platoons of tanks under his command: three light tank platoons and one assault tank platoon.

To ensure maximum firepower coverage to the front, Ridley's platoons would travel behind Able Company but closer to the road, so that the armor column would appear staggered from the air. Hence, they could open fire to their front without fear of hitting Able Company, which also would be moving parallel to the road, but farther west of them. Satisfied with the arrangement, the three columns pushed ahead: Able Company in the west, Dog Company in the center, and the GIs from Charlie Company in the east.

As for the German ambush team, the obvious answer was artillery. It would have been foolish for the American column to roll into a presighted kill zone. Thanks to the wounded lieutenant, they now knew where the Germans were and pounded them with artillery for thirty minutes. By 1645 hours, it was over. When they cleared the area, the attached infantry discovered one destroyed antitank gun and captured around sixty German soldiers. In retaliation, a *panzerschreck* crew destroyed one tank from Able Company.

Thinking the worst was behind them, the soldiers and tankers of Task Force Oden continued to push ahead. By now, everyone knew they were going to drive through the night to reach Bastogne. The infantrymen and tankers hoped that the howitzers had silenced the German opposition. In fact, for many of them, huddled in the back of their open-topped half-tracks, the plunging temperatures and piercing wind seemed far worse than the German army. They were mistaken.[3]

1700 to 2015 Hours, Saturday, December 23

2nd Platoon, C Company (51st Armored Infantry), 3rd Platoon,

D Company (35th Tank)

Warnach, Belgium

Meanwhile, soldiers at another German battle position waited for the right time to unleash their coiled fury. They had seen what had happened to the first ambush team and decided that half-tracks were a better target, since one shot would likely destroy the vehicle and potentially kill most of the infantry riding along in the back. Minutes after the artillery lifted, they saw their targets: the first two Charlie Company half-tracks, loaded with infantry.

First Lieutenant Walter E. Green, the Charlie Company commander, watched in horror as a tracer round zipped across over the open field and slammed into one of the half-tracks with tremendous force. Before anyone could respond, another half-track exploded.

Captain John Ridley, commander of Dog Company, ordered his attached assault guns to open fire on Warnach, and the six Shermans wheeled around and let loose with their 105mm howitzers to suppress the German gunners. General Earnest was near the front of the column and saw what had happened. To Earnest, the second German strike on his column was enough. His blood was up, and he ordered Colonel Oden to fix the problem—and fixing the problem meant clearing Warnach.

Sergeant Albert Gaydos was one of the first to know about Earnest's order. Gaydos was waiting inside his tank with his lieutenant, Raymond Romig, who was the forward observer for Dog Company, 35th Tank Battalion. As the forward observer, Romig was privy to the chatter on the battalion command net. On the radio, Colonel Oden kept asking for status reports from Captain Ridley, the Dog Company commander.

Soon after the commanders realized that the German defenders had wiped out the two platoons, Oden squawked on the radio, "Take your light tanks and go into that town and see what's in it."

"I am too light . . . how about we send in some of our big stuff?" Captain Ridley pleaded, referring to the medium tanks.

Colonel Oden refused to hear it. "I don't give a damn; we have to get to Bastogne!"

Several minutes later, Oden piped up again and ordered, "Put someone from the infantry on the microphone."

For a few minutes, the net was silent. Finally, Gaydos heard a voice. Oden asked, "Son, what is your rank"?

"I'm a private," he answered.

Gaydos could hear Oden's tone switch from that of an irate commander to an eager coach. "Consider yourself a sergeant . . . how about you taking a patrol into that town?" he asked the promoted soldier.

The battalion commander then directed his attention toward Lieutenant Romig. "Forward Observer," he began, "I want you to fire into Warnach as I am sending in a patrol . . . make it easier for them!"

Romig replied, "Five volleys okay?"

Oden answered, "Fine, eighteen guns, each gun five rounds!"

Several minutes later, the M7 howitzers from the 66th Armored Field Artillery boomed, and within seconds, outgoing rounds screamed over their heads before impacting inside Warnach. It was a short barrage, and Romig soon lifted it to allow the patrol to reach the town unmolested. For a while, nothing happened. Finally the voice from the patrol leader broke the radio silence to report.

Oden was impatient. "What did you find, son?"

The new sergeant replied, "We saw no Krauts, but did retake one of our own six-by-six trucks with two Krauts in it . . . but no others."[4]

Oden did not think the force in Warnach was large enough to warrant a full-scale deliberate attack as they had done with Martelange. Assessing that whatever was there was probably the same size as the first ambush team, he ordered Captain Ridley and First Lieutenant Green to create a small task force to clear out the village. Ridley gave up his 3rd Platoon while Green offered up his 2nd Platoon to accomplish the mission. It would be a costly calculation, and one Oden would later regret.

Edward Rapp, a tank gunner in 3rd Platoon, Dog Company, had seen the first two half-tracks burn up, and then the column halted. By now it was dark, but thanks to the half-moon's light and its reflection off of the virgin snow, he could see far into the distance. Soon he spotted a solitary figure approaching his tank. Suddenly a German artillery round detonated nearby, hurtling the figure into a nearby snowdrift. Miraculously, the man stood up and continued to walk toward his tank. He staggered and stumbled up to the side of Rapp's Stuart and told him that Captain Ridley wanted 3rd Platoon to go into Warnach with a platoon of infantry from another company.

Rapp noticed the soldier was holding his stomach with one hand. He had been hit by shrapnel from the artillery round. Realizing they could not leave him there, Rapp and the rest of his crew pulled him onto the tank and told him to hold on. Though they did not have a medic at their location, they could drive him to one. Sergeant William Lucas, Rapp's tank commander, ordered Ford Gurrell, the driver, to move "cross-country" and link up with the rest of 3rd Platoon and the waiting infantry. When they arrived, the infantrymen lifted the wounded soldier off the tank and carried him to the medics. Rapp never found out what happened to the wounded man, but remembered the runner's dedication to his mission.

Meanwhile, the two platoon leaders argued about how to conduct the attack while the tankers and the infantrymen waited to move out. Staff Sergeant Gaynor Caldwell was another tank commander in 3rd Platoon. He was there when General Earnest ordered Colonel Oden to seize Warnach. To Caldwell, the mission was a bad idea. The M5 Stuart was designed to find the enemy and then wait for the medium tanks to destroy them. Now Oden was using them as if they were medium tanks.

Furthermore, U.S. armored doctrine frowned upon the use of tanks in a night attack, because it negated the advantages that tankers had over infantry: namely, long-range fires. Now, even with the moonlight, the tank crews might not see their target until they were within a few hundred meters of each other, and that meant an intrepid *fallschirmjäger* with a *panzerschreck* might get a shot off before the gunner could see him. Despite these disadvantages, Oden ordered the two platoons to press on ahead into Warnach.

By now, it was almost 2000 hours. The tanks of 3rd Platoon maintained a slow rate of speed so the infantry could keep up as they approached the village from the rear. For the infantry, slogging through the deep snowdrifts, it was an exhausting experience, like marching through wet sand.

To provide some illumination, Rapp opened fire on a haystack with his 37mm peashooter. Using an HE round, Rapp figured it would ignite the straw and create a flaming bonfire to light up the surrounding area. Instead the haystack exploded, as if the Germans had hid gasoline or ammunition underneath it. W. King Pound, Staff Sergeant Caldwell's gunner, had the same idea but with a twist. He aimed at the thatched roofs with his coaxial machine gun to achieve the same illumination effect. Unbeknownst to them, the patrol had failed. The Germans were in Warnach, and thanks to the tracers from 3rd Platoon's light tanks, their gun crews now had an aiming point.

Hidden among the stone farmhouses and bales of hay were several StuG III self-propelled assault guns. Hearing the gurgling and rumbling engines on the Stuart tanks reverberating over the frosted plateau, the German gunners waited patiently; then, seeing the tracers and the muzzle flashes on the light tanks, they turned the StuGs, aimed, and opened fire.

Pound heard Caldwell scream over the sound of the chugging coaxial machine gun, "We've been hit!"

So consumed was he in his search for targets, Pound never felt the impact from the 7.5cm round that had sliced through his tank. He scrambled out of the turret and jumped off the stricken Stuart. As he scampered away, he realized he had left his weapons back inside the tank. He dropped down in the snow for cover.

Caldwell, his tank commander, saw Pound and crawled over to shout in his ear, "Go back to the tank; you left the turret hanging over the driver's and bog-gunner's hatches and they can't get out and he's been hit!"

It was a design flaw found in American tanks. Unfortunately, it was a flaw that cost the lives of countless tankers who would die a horrible death as the fires inside their vehicles consumed them while their buddies, who had escaped the burning traps, looked on helplessly, watching as their friends perished.

For Pound, he had no choice. Braving the hail of bullets, he jumped up, ran back to his tank, and realigned the turret so that the remaining crew members could escape. Hearing the turret move, Gene Hyden struggled to pull himself out of the driver's hatch. Pound could tell that Hyden was wounded, and he pulled him out of the hatch the rest of the way. When they stepped off the tank, Hyden crumpled, and Pound noticed that the driver's foot was covered in blood. He lifted Hyden onto his back and started to jog toward the highway and friendly lines.

To avoid detection, Pound set out for the tree line, which would provide them some concealment. Once there, he continued toward the highway, lugging the wounded Hyden on his back. The sound of a motor loomed behind him, and, fearing it was Germans, the two men flattened down and waited until the mysterious vehicle drove past their location. After several minutes, Pound lifted Hyden back up and resumed his slog—until he heard another vehicle.

At first, Pound thought it was a Sherman tank; then Hyden whispered in his ear, "Hell, that's not ours; that's one of theirs!"

They dropped to the ground, and even in the darkness, Pound thought he saw a German armored half-track. Several German soldiers accompanied the vehicle, scanning the area, searching for Americans. Pound later recalled, "I had a hand grenade and could have thrown it, but on figuring the odds quickly, decided against it."

After several tense minutes, the Germans moved on, leaving Pound and Hyden behind in the woods. Once again, Pound boosted Hyden onto his back and plodded toward the highway off in the distance. Eventually, Hyden's weight was too much, and Pound's knees buckled. Hyden slipped off Pound's back and slid onto a snowbank. Pound could not take another step with Hyden on his back. Both of them lay there, exhausted.

Nearby, Rapp's tank staggered and stopped. Ford Gurrell, his driver, jammed the throttle and yelled that he couldn't restart the engine. Like Pound, neither Gurrell nor Rapp realized that the Germans had gutted the engine with an AP round, forcing the Stuart to roll to a halt. Lucas shouted out that their tank had been hit. Rapp could hear the pinging from machine gun bullets ricocheting off of the outside armor on his turret, reminding him of hailstones bouncing off the hood of a car.

A stationary tank was a dead duck, thought Rapp, and so he bailed out, with Lucas right behind him. The two tankers hurried behind a nearby snow-covered privet hedge, hoping it would provide some cover and concealment from German gunners. Rapp quickly realized that he had forgotten to center his tank turret, trapping Gurrell and his bog gunner, Marcelle Noll, inside. Rapp remembered:

Instinctively, I ran back to the tank, climbed into the turret and centered the turret, enabling them to raise their hatches and jump out and join us behind the near privet hedge. It seemed that from all directions of the homes around us, we were receiving only small-arm[s] fire. Bullets seemed to "whisper" as they hit the snow. We could see two of our other tanks knocked out nearby and could hear men calling for medics.

Panting and wheezing from his fearless dash, Rapp spotted some infantrymen who were emplacing their machine gun. Rapp asked, "Hey, fellas, we're tankers and not accustomed to being caught out in the open without our tank . . . what do you fellas do in a case like this?"

"We were never in a case like this!" one of them shot back. The young tanker could see the agitation and terror in the gunner's face, and he backed away.

Despite the fusillade of German bullets whizzing through the air, an unknown infantryman braved the maelstrom, climbed aboard Rapp's stricken tank, got behind the commander's .30-caliber machine gun mounted on the turret, and opened fire on the Germans hiding in the houses. From behind the hedge, Rapp watched in awe as the man continued to fire, tracers flying by him like supersonic lightning bugs. The soldier kept kept up the stream of lead until he expended all of his ammunition. He had suppressed the German fire long enough that the Americans caught in the open were able to crawl to safety. Rapp believed that the man's action saved the lives of many tankers and infantrymen.

Meanwhile, the stranded tankers' best option was to remain behind the hedge and let the infantry fight it out until someone needed them. Periodically, one of them would pop his head over the hedge to see what was happening and get his bearings. At one point, Marcelle Noll peered over the bush—and collapsed. Rapp wrote:

He seemed to be shot somewhere in the upper torso. He lay on his back muttering in shock. There was so little that we could do for him. Like all tankers, Noll was wearing "long john" winter underwear, uniform, sweater, tanker jacket, and overalls. We tried but could not get to his wound in the positions we were in and in fear to raise our bodies any higher. We urged him to try and crawl with us, for now word had gotten around to get back to the highway. Noll could not be of any help to us when we tried carrying him in our slouched positions. Regretfully, we had to leave him.

Rapp, Lucas, and Gurrell continued on toward the highway, but within minutes, the chaos around them resulted in their tiny band splitting up.

Rapp heard the familiar thumping sound of mortars as he ran. He ducked, but it was too late. A mortar round detonated almost on top of him and sent him flying through the air before he landed on his butt. He felt his lip, and saw blood on his fingertips. "Between my lower lip and teeth," he wrote, "there was a tiny pinhead of a shell fragment, which I quickly spit out when I became aware of it."

Rapp promptly recovered his wits and resumed his trek toward the Bastogne–Arlon highway. Not long after surviving the mortar impact, Rapp found another member of his platoon, whom he recognized but did not know. The two of them continued back toward the N4 when they discovered Eugene Hyden, Pound's driver, "lying in the snow with what seemed to be a bleeding lower part of one of his legs." Both of them lifted Eugene up and carried him the rest of the way, bringing him to a basement where the medics were treating the wounded. After Rapp dropped Hyden off, he stepped outside and located Gurrell and Lucas, who had minor wounds. Pound also managed to return to friendly lines later that evening. Two weeks later, Pound, Gurrell, and Lucas all received a Purple Heart for wounds sustained that night outside of Warnach.

Not all of the soldiers who participated in the first attack on Warnach were so lucky. Sadly, Gurrell, Lucas, and Rapp later learned after the war that Noll had died, and was buried in the American cemetery in Hamm, Luxembourg. In the end, the tally for the disastrous Warnach mission was high: Four light tanks destroyed, and most of 2nd Platoon, Charlie Company, 51st Armored Infantry, were either dead or missing.[5]

While the men of 2nd Platoon, Charlie Company, and 3rd Platoon, Dog Company, suffered and died, the rest of the men of Combat Command A were trying to keep warm. They could see the distant tracers from the firefight, but few knew what was happening inside Warnach. Private Robert Calvert, an infantryman in 1st Platoon, Charlie Company, 51st Armored Infantry, wrote in his journal, "Tanks that could still move formed a defensive circle—much as one might do with a covered wagon train. We infantry had no blankets, for the attack was scheduled to last all night. No one dared fall asleep; all you could do was to keep moving. The most overworked joke of the night, from our days training in the south, was 'Get those men out of the hot sun.'"[6]

2030 Hours to Early Morning, Saturday, December 23,
to Sunday, December 24 Baker Company,
35th Tank Battalion, CCA South of Warnach, Belgium

Most soldiers thought the tankers had it a lot easier than the doughboys, who had to stay out in the cold. Technician Fourth Grade James R. Donaldson, a tank driver in Baker Company, 35th Tank Battalion, disagreed. He realized earlier that autumn that it got plenty cold in a tank. Even worse was waiting in a frigid, stationary tank, which was like sitting in a meat locker. Now they had been stuck on the side of a hill for several hours awaiting their next mission. To keep himself occupied, Donaldson was tapping tunes on his toes with a ball-peen hammer as if they were bars on a xylophone.

His tank commander was Captain Vincent Boller, who also was the commander of Baker Company. Boller, though, had become ill, and had hopped in a jeep and driven toward the rear of the column to find the medics. Meanwhile, Donaldson was listening to the command net while his boss was away. For the past several hours, a battle had been raging up ahead in Warnach, and Donaldson could tell by the amount of chatter that the fighting was not going well.

When he heard Colonel Oden call for Captain Boller over the radio, Donaldson informed the battalion commander of Boller's condition. For Oden, it was inexcusable for a company commander to leave his tank during a battle, even if he was sick. Without a second thought, Oden fired the missing company commander over the radio, and asked for First Lieutenant John "Buck" Kingsley. Not only was Kingsley the new commander of Baker Company, he also had his first combat mission. He would have little time to plan—Colonel Oden wanted Warnach that night.

2030 Hours to Early Morning, Saturday, December 23, to Sunday, December 24

Baker Company, 51st Armored Infantry Battalion, CCA

South of Warnach, Belgium

Howard Peterson had spent the last few hours wondering how he ended up in this strange place. Only days before, he had been gliderman in the 325th Glider Infantry Regiment, part of the 82nd Airborne Division, recovering in Reims, France, after the Market Garden operation in Holland. Four days later he was in Arlon, Belgium, and in another unit in an entirely different division.

The 4th Armored Division had fewer infantry than an airborne or infantry division. Therefore, it always needed replacements, and as a consequence Howard Peterson was a new infantryman in Baker Company, 51st Armored Infantry. He knew no one, and now he and his unit were stuck on a road somewhere in Belgium, trying to reach some town named Bastogne.

It was a new experience for him. Instead of walking over fields or cruising along in a glider, Peterson was hanging off the back of a Sherman tank. He quickly learned that to keep from tumbling off, he had to rotate his hands. One hand always had to grip something on the tank, but in the biting cold he could hold on for only so long before that hand went numb, at which point he would grab on with his warm hand. It was a constant back-and-forth to keep his blood circulating.

Periodically, he would check his kit to make sure he still had everything. Possessions tended to disappear or fall off during a combat movement. To keep warm, he wore a pair of long johns beneath his pants and shirt, plus two pairs of socks, with another pair shoved underneath his armpits to stay warm and dry. Every pocket and crevice on his body was jammed with extra food and ammunition, from K rations to grenades. Like most GIs, Peterson was armed with what he called his "good old M1" semiautomatic rifle. In addition to the standard combat load, he also strapped across his back two more bandoliers, crammed full with more ammo clips. Finally, in case there were panzers, he carried three bazooka rockets for the bazooka gunner. Unlike his new comrades, Peterson still sported the jump boots he had been issued as a gliderman. To him it was mark of distinction. He was more than a grunt—he was a gliderman.

Jolting him back to his senses, Peterson's platoon of four tanks veered west off the highway. Since Peterson was on the lead tank, his tank commander ordered him and the other infantrymen riding along on the back to jump off and check out some nearby shapes. He approached the shadowy figures with his rifle at the ready, thinking they were German infantry, but the GIs discovered much to their relief that the mysterious men were actually fence posts. Peterson remembered how scared he was and recalled how the fear caused "another laundry problem."

Before Peterson could regain his composure, the tanks started to roll out, and he climbed back aboard his own vehicle. "One of the other tanks broke through a barbed wire fence and a strand of barbed wire slapped a G.I. across the face," he later wrote, "turning his face into raw hamburger. A G.I., wearing an unbuttoned overcoat, jumped off his tank and when the coat tails billowed out behind him they caught in the tracks and sucked his legs into the bogie wheels of the tank."

Peterson's tank lurched and stopped, and another Sherman's machine gun opened fire on a haystack next to a barn, two hundred meters in front. For more than a minute, .30- and .50-caliber tracers ripped through the curtain of darkness. Hidden underneath the haystack was a German armored vehicle. When two AP rounds hit it, the vehicle started to smoke and pop like logs smoldering in a fireplace.

Peterson's tank then lunged forward again and stopped. The private could hear the engine struggle as the tracks spun helplessly. He looked down and saw that his Sherman had lodged itself in a streambed hidden by the dense snow. Peterson and the other GIs decided it was time to go, and they jumped off the tank. The squad leaders and platoon sergeants then collected the soldiers and herded them back toward the road. Peterson counted around twenty-six men in his platoon, milling about like penguins. For a while, they waited for their next order. The leaders then told them they were marching toward Warnach, which was east of their present location.

0001 to 0400 Hours, Sunday, December 24
Headquarters, 35th Tank Battalion, CCA
South of Warnach, Belgium

Colonel Oden had learned his lesson. No more hasty attacks, thought the task force commander. The plan to seize and clear Warnach would be a classic double envelopment with an inner and outer encirclement. For the wider cordon, Colonel Oden would use Charlie Company and Able Company from his own tank battalion. Several platoons of infantry from Able Company, 51st Armored Infantry, then would move out with Charlie Company, 35th Tank Battalion, to attack the western edge of the Schock Busch forest, which was northeast of Warnach. Meanwhile, the medium tanks of Able Company would push north toward Strainchamps and secure the western leg of the cordon.

Both of these operations, though, were supporting efforts for the decisive operation, which was the two Baker companies. The Baker Company infantry would ride on the back of the Baker Company medium tanks and surround Warnach from both sides. To accomplish this, they would approach the town with two platoons forward and one platoon trailing behind them. Then 3rd Platoon would penetrate Warnach from the south while 2nd Platoon would sweep into Warnach from the west. Finally, 1st Platoon, the trail platoon, would pass the town on the eastern side and then swing back and attack any surviving Germans from the northeast side of Warnach.

Oden was going to throw everything at Warnach, because he intended to crush the German forces defending the village. According to the 51st Armored Infantry Journal, the column would attack Warnach from the west and south sometime between 0430 and 0530 hours. Because it was December, sunrise was still several hours away, so it was still dark.

0405 Hours, Sunday, December 24
Girls' Normal School, Arlon, Belgium
Headquarters, III Corps

Major R. W. Harrison, the assistant S-3 for III Corps, was the watch officer that morning when he received the radio report from Captain Stedman Seay, his counterpart in the 4th Armored Division. The news was bad. As of 0405 hours, 4th Armored Division was stuck.

The previous day had started well. Combat Command B had advanced as far as Chaumont. Indeed, at 1440 hours, 4th Armored Division's G-3 Section had reported that CCB had cleared the town. Meanwhile, Combat Command Reserve was inching its way toward Bigonville, but they were making progress. Last,

Combat Command A had just completed its bridge at Martelange and was moving north toward Bastogne.

Then the wheels fell off. First the Germans counterattacked at Chaumont. III Corps' deepest penetration toward Bastogne ended with a crushing reversal. General Holmes Dager's losses were high. CCB had lost more than a dozen tanks and several tank destroyers. Chaumont was not the only disappointment. At 2045 hours the previous night, Major Harrison had learned that CCR's attack sputtered to a stop and, despite earlier reports, had not captured Bigonville. Olympic 3, which was the call sign for 4th Armored Division's G-3 Section, tried to reassure him by telling him that CCR would try again later that morning. Finally, General Herbert Earnest's CCA was struggling to get past Warnach thanks to some antitank guns and artillery.

It did not help that Third Army wanted updates constantly. In fact, the Third Army G-3, Colonel Halley G. Maddox, had called III Corps around 2120 hours to ask that III Corps inform the Third Army the moment any element of 4th Armored Division linked up with any element from the 101st Airborne, who were still trapped inside Bastogne. Harrison then glanced at the map. The distance between the closest unit of the 4th Armored Division and Bastogne was about twelve kilometers. To some staff officer at Third Army headquarters, the distance might seem negligible, but to the grunt on the ground, a lot of Germans were in those twelve kilometers.

Harrison looked at his watch. At daybreak, both Combat Command A and Combat Command Reserve would resume their attacks. Hopefully, thought the major, Christmas Eve would bring better luck to the 4th Armored Division.[7]

0430 to 0530 Hours, Sunday, December 24
Baker Company, 51st Armored Infantry, CCA
Warnach, Belgium

Finally, Peterson's platoon and the rest of the two Baker companies moved out. First Lieutenant Daniel Belden, 51st Armored Infantry, and First Lieutenant John Kingsley, 35th Tank, who were the two Baker company commanders, spent several hours assembling their forces and disseminating their plans before they moved out from their final assault positions several hours after midnight. As

Peterson and the others trudged up the road, he saw something. "A little way up ahead was an American 2½ ton truck nose down in the ditch and it had a big red Nazi flag with a black swastika on it across the front of the radiator. We had to climb the road embankment to get around the rear of the truck and as I passed by the cab of the truck I could see another good Kraut sitting behind the wheel with the top of his head blown off." It was a macabre sight, causing some of them to gawk as they marched by the derelict vehicle, and they probably wondered who the man was.

The sudden *rat-a-tat-tat* of machine guns and the *boom-boom* of tank cannons interrupted their viewing. Up ahead, three Shermans had encircled a farmhouse. An infantrymen walked up to them and asked one of the tank commanders why they were firing at the house. The tanker claimed that a sniper was inside, and had already shot three soldiers. Satisfied, the soldiers kept marching while the tankers blasted away at the farm. Within minutes, the high-explosive rounds from the Sherman tanks reduced it to bits of brick and smashed stones.

Eventually the tanks caught up with Peterson and the rest of the infantry. Despite their size and the noise, Peterson was glad the tanks were close—they kept him warm, because the exhaust from the radiator was an excellent heat source.

Unbeknownst to Peterson, a German StuG, hiding in an orchard, had drawn a bead on the Sherman closest to Peterson. Confident they had the tank lined up in their sights, the crew of the StuG opened fire.

The Sherman exploded. The StuG rocked backward again, firing another round. Amid the smoke and flames, Peterson saw a pair of soldiers dive into a ditch and try to assemble a folding bazooka so that they could fire it at the StuG. They struggled with the tube, but they could not get it to work.

Finally, one of them exclaimed in fear and frustration, "Let's get out of here!" The pair got up and scurried away, hoping the crew of the StuG hadn't seen them.

Peterson started to run back to the Arlon–Bastogne highway. Along the way, he found a pair of tankers, one of whom was badly wounded. Together, Peterson and the unharmed man carried the injured soldier to a medic. Afterward Peterson came across his squad, who were huddled by a barn with some German prisoners of war. There they waited for several hours until dawn.

0530 to 0605 Hours, Sunday, December 24
1st Platoon, Baker Company, 35th Tank Battalion, CCA
Northeast of Warnach, Belgium

In the meantime, 1st Platoon, Baker Company, 35th Tank Battalion, swung past Warnach and headed north. Private First Class Robert E. Riley was a gunner in one of the 1st Platoon tanks. He grew up in Kansas City, Missouri, where he worked at the Fruehauf Trailer Company. Unlike some of the other tankers, Riley had been a replacement, and the army had assigned him to the 4th Armored Division in late summer of 1944, after the Allies had liberated Paris. Riley had been an infantryman prior to his time in the 4th. His original military occupational specialty was tank gunner, but after a rollover accident where his tank driver had died during a training exercise, the G-1 transferred Riley to the infantry.

When Riley arrived at his new division, he soon learned that the life span of an armored infantryman in the 4th Armored was rather short, and he submitted a request for transfer to one of the tank battalions, since they also needed trained tankers. Riley figured his chances at survival were better behind several tons of steel. His request was approved, and soon he was a tank gunner again. Now it was the morning of December 24. He and his tank commander, Sergeant John T. Foster, were the only experienced crewmen left in their Sherman. The loader, the driver, and the assistant gunner were all new replacements.

As they rolled northward, Riley's Sherman was the lead tank, and as the gunner, Riley was required to be scouting ahead by peering through his gun sight, which magnified distant objects. Riley and Foster could barely see a thing in the inky blackness, so Sergeant Foster grabbed his radio and requested permission to fire a white phosphorus round to illuminate the area. After several seconds, Foster tapped Riley on the shoulder and told him to fire one WP round. As the loader rammed a shell into the breech, the gunner from Missouri scanned for targets and found a haystack. He adjusted his aim and fired the round. Like a flaming arrow landing on a thatch roof, the haystack burst into flame, and the whole area was awash in light.

Foster looked through his own periscope and spied two vehicles lurking behind a nearby barn. Even with the burning haystack, Foster could not discern what type of vehicles they were, and so he sought a second opinion.

"D-d-do th-th-they look like fr-fr-friendly TDs?" he stammered. According to Riley's postwar interview, Foster suffered from a speech disorder, which caused him to stutter when he spoke.

Riley then looked at the vehicles to confirm Foster's assumption. He replied, "Yeah, they look like TDs."

Despite Riley's assessment, Foster remained unconvinced, and radioed his platoon leader to see whether any American tanks were ahead of them. The answer was definitive: No American tanks were north of Warnach. The sudden truth socked them in the jaw, but before they could digest the information, the enemy vehicles started to approach them like two hoodlums advancing toward their victim. The armored vehicles were most likely two StuGs from 2nd Battery, 11th Sturmgeschütz Brigade. Since they carried assault guns, the tank had a limited traverse of only twenty-four degrees, which meant that the crews had to turn the entire vehicle and lock its tracks before they could engage and fire at a target that was outside of that twenty-four-degree arc. For Foster, it was the final telltale sign when the StuGs locked their tracks so that they could get into a proper firing position.

"Th-th-they're Hiney t-t-tanks!" he yelled.

Despite the rumbling tank engine, everyone heard Foster, including the loader, who shoved another round into the breech. When Riley heard the thunk of the breech closing, he popped the main gun pedal with his boot, firing the gun. In response, the cannon belched fire while the Sherman rocked backward. According to Riley, one of the StuGs fired simultaneously, and within seconds both vehicles shuddered as their respective 75mm shells ripped through each other, splicing wires and chewing up metal.

Luckily for the crew of the Sherman, the 75mm StuG armor-piercing round slammed into the rear of the tank, where the engine was. Instead of ripping through flesh and bone, the round detonated and set fire to the engine assembly. Though slightly wounded, the crew had precious seconds to clamber out of the dying tank before the fire reached the ammunition stowage. When Riley hit the ground, he instinctively hunched over, because he sensed the Germans would gun down his crew as they attempted to escape. Then the tankers dashed back to

Warnach, using ditches and hedgerows for cover and concealment. Later, Foster, the driver, and the bog gunner received Purple Hearts. For them, the race to Bastogne was over.[8]

0605 to 1000 Hours, Sunday, December 24
2nd Platoon, Baker Company, 35th Tank Battalion, CCA
Warnach, Belgium

Second Lieutenant Joe V. Horton, the 2nd Platoon leader, rolled forward in his command tank and knocked out one German armored vehicle almost immediately upon entering Warnach from the west. Minutes later, a German *panzerschreck* crew returned the favor and shot three rockets into Horton's tank, destroying it. Luckily, Horton and his crew bailed out, and despite the close call, Horton ordered his four remaining tanks in his platoon to continue the attack. He divided his platoon in two, with a section on either side of the east–west road that led directly into Warnach.

Despite the loss of his tank, the young lieutenant from Arizona decided he would lead the attack as an infantryman. By 0735 hours, his platoon and 3rd Platoon had cleared two-thirds of Warnach and had reached the Church of St. Anthony in the center of town. First Lieutenant Daniel Belden, the Baker Company infantry commander, reported their progress to Major Dan Alanis, the 51st Armored Infantry Battalion commander. In the meantime, Horton kept advancing, and ten minutes later his tank platoon and the rest of the infantry had cornered the German defenders into a pocket on the north side of Warnach. They estimated thirty German infantry and one German armored vehicle remained.

The trapped *fallschirmjägers* were in no mood to surrender, though, and the volume of fire told Kingsley and Belden that the last phase in the fight for Warnach would be bloody if they continued to push north. Together they decided to soften up the northern half of Warnach with artillery. Colonel Oden agreed, and at 0900 hours, the infantry and armor pulled back from the area around St. Anthony so that they would not be targets of their own artillery barrage.

Once they were far enough away, Oden ordered the artillery to blast the area. The cannon cockers of the 66th Armored Field Artillery Battalion obliged him, and opened fire with eighteen 105mm howitzers. For almost an hour, the artillery pounded the area. Finally, around 1000 hours, the infantry and armor resumed their attack. Horton's dogged persistence had paid off, and for his bravery, the army awarded the Silver Star to Second Lieutenant Horton on January 16, 1945.

1000 to 1715 Hours, Sunday, December 24
Baker Company, 51st Armored Infantry, CCA
Warnach, Belgium

Private Howard Peterson, the infantryman from Baker Company, 51st Armored Infantry, had spent the last few hours trying to catch some sleep in a barn. It was a lost cause. His squad leader then roused him and the rest of the group for one more try at taking Warnach. Within a few minutes, they stepped out on the road, heading east. Peterson was in action again. Their squad approached a tank, and popping out of the turret of the metal monster was a lieutenant who was asking for volunteers. Peterson labeled him a "ninety-day-wonder Louie."

Much to Peterson's surprise, this lieutenant wanted someone to man the .50-caliber machine gun on the tank and "rake the roadside and 'scare the hell' out of the Germans." To Peterson, the plan was dubious at best, and so he did not volunteer for the job. Someone else did, and the brave soldier opened fire with the M2 machine gun, spraying the roadside. After one hundred rounds, the gun jammed.

Flummoxed, the platoon leader then waved the infantry forward. As they rounded a corner, Peterson and the other infantry discovered a Kettenkrad in the middle of the street. The Kettenkrad was a Wehrmacht motorcycle hybrid. To Peterson, it was a centaur. The front looked like a motorcycle while the back looked like a tractor. Seeing the abandoned vehicle, the lieutenant ordered his driver to go in reverse, and in response, the Sherman tank rolled backward. The tanker lieutenant then told Peterson's squad leader that he was going to blast the Kettenkrad with his main gun, because the platoon leader believed that the Germans might have booby-trapped the derelict cycle. The sergeant nodded and urged his squad to fall back as instructed. Satisfied that everyone was safe, the gunner on the Sherman then lowered the 75mm barrel onto the target and opened fire. The Kettenkrad exploded, showering the street with bits of metal and rubber.

Seconds later, a tracer sliced through the platoon leader's tank, setting it ablaze. Hidden among the buildings was another StuG. It had waited for the tank to fire at the Kettenkrad so its crew would not have time to reload the main gun before the StuG blasted it with its own long-barreled 7.5cm killer. The ruse worked. Unfortunately for the German assault gun crew, they had failed to notice the other two Sherman tanks that were loitering nearby. The American tankers saw the other Sherman brew up, and in reply, they swung their turrets toward the StuG. In less than a minute, they scored several hits on the StuG, and, Peterson remarked, ". . . blew the German S.P. gun to perdition."

The StuG's destruction broke the will of the German defenders who were hiding in the nearby buildings and trees. In his postwar account, Peterson described the attempted escape of one pair:

Suddenly somebody yelled and two Krauts broke out of a copse of trees about 200 yards further down the road, where it [a German soldier] took a half dozen steps and then retreated to the safety of the trees. The other one ran along the fence for about 200 feet, calmly climbed over the fence just as you or I might do it today, and started to run up the road. Another 20–25 feet and he would have been safe, but all of a sudden he went about ten feet in the air, came down face first and never moved. When the two German soldiers broke out of the trees, we all started to fire at them—M1's, Thompsons, BAR's, carbines, grease guns, and maybe a couple of .45's, too.

The Germans were on the run. Officers and sergeants sensed it was time to push the soldiers to finish the job and clear Warnach once and for all. Wanting to keep the momentum going, an officer saw Peterson and ordered him and a pair of nearby infantry soldiers to clear out a nearby farmhouse. Apparently Peterson was the only one left in the group who had grenades, which were essential in clearing out buildings.

When they approached the farmhouse door, Peterson tried to pull the pin on one of his grenades. He fumbled with it for a few seconds, and then realized that his fingers were too numb from the cold to grasp the ring. Instead, he flung it to one of the other soldiers, who managed to pull the pesky pin. With the safety ring pulled, the soldier threw the grenade, and the spoon popped off, arming it. To

Peterson's horror, the grenade then careened off the side of the entryway and back into the yard.

The soldier who tossed it shouted, "I missed the door!"

Peterson dived behind a pile of garbage, hoping the trash would protect him from the shrapnel. After an eternity, the grenade detonated, and fortunately no one was hurt. The ad hoc three-man team then rushed into the building. Peterson was the second man in, and all three opened fire in different directions. Peterson expended his whole clip in front of him while the number one man, who also carried a Garand, shot all eight rounds into a room that was to the left. Meanwhile, the number three man, a Thompson submachine gunner, cleaned out the stairway to the right. Satisfied that the building was clear, the men stood there, ". . . just like the Three Stooges."

Before they could celebrate, a Sherman tank rolled up and its crew opened fire on the same farmhouse with their machine guns. For several harrowing minutes, the Sherman poured round after round into the house. Fortune, though, was smiling on Peterson, and not a single round hit him or the other two infantrymen. Finally the Sherman left, leaving the three infantrymen behind, pissed off but alive.[9]

By midafternoon, the fighting for Warnach was over. Combat Command A declared Warnach officially cleared at 1715 hours. The Germans had refused to yield Warnach even after the tankers and infantrymen of CCA had kicked them out, and the survivors conducted a counterattack from the woods northeast of Warnach. Using artillery, the American forces easily thwarted their attempts and remained in control of the town.

Meanwhile, as the two Baker companies slugged it out in Warnach, the rest of CCA was far from idle. Charlie Company, 35th Tank Battalion, and Able Company, 51st Armored Infantry Battalion, as planned, had advanced to a line just south of the Strainchamps–Tintange road, clearing much of the Bois de Melch woods of enemy forces, while isolating the northwestern portion of Warnach. In the west, Able Company and the rest of Dog Company, including the six Sherman 105mm assault guns, from the 35th Tank Battalion pushed north toward Strainchamps. Assisting them were the two remaining platoons from C Company, 51st Armored Infantry.

They were not the only American forces. Eight P-47s from the 377th Fighter Squadron had taken off from Étain, France, at 1330 hours, and were now over the battlefield. Loren W. Herway was the commanding officer of the 377th, and this was his third time in command of the squadron. "Beagle," who was the ground controller for Combat Command A, vectored the pilots toward the Bois de Moriéval just to the east of Strainchamps. The Thunderbolts then pounded the woods with general-purpose five-hundred-pound bombs, and even napalm. Although the pilots could not see the effects of their handiwork, the ground controller reported "good results." By nightfall, American forces had advanced to the Strainchamps–Tintange road on both sides of the Bastogne–Arlon highway.

The losses on the German side were severe. Over the next two days, the Corps G-2 detention cages processed 116 enlisted soldiers from 2nd Battalion, 15th Fallschirmjäger Regiment. The S-2 section from the 51st Armored Infantry reported that they had found an additional 160 German bodies, and the medics treated another 140 German casualties. In short, 2nd Battalion of the 15th Fallschirmjäger Regiment was no longer a viable fighting force. Its survivors probably numbered no more than a hundred men.

Besides the destruction of 2nd Battalion, 15th Fallschirmjäger, CCA also captured *fallschirmjägers* from the 13th Fallschirmjäger Regiment. In fact, the Corps G-2 cages processed twenty-three soldiers from 3rd Battalion, 13th Fallschirmjäger Regiment. Most of them were *fallschirmjägers* from 10th Company. In the coming days, CCA would see more of the 13th.

In terms of equipment, the 2nd Battery, 11th Assault Brigade, lost at least one if not two or three StuG IIIs. 2nd Battalion, 15th Fallschirmjäger, lost most of its mortars and towed Pak 40 antitank guns. The *fallschirmjägers* had been using mostly captured American equipment, and some of it CCA had recovered intact. However, the one captured M8 Greyhound did not survive the fight for Warnach.

American losses were light compared to the Germans'. 51st Armored Infantry sustained sixty-eight casualties, including eight enlisted men killed and four wounded officers. Many of those casualties came from 2nd Platoon, Charlie Company, which the Germans had wiped out the previous evening. Also, the Germans had captured three soldiers of that platoon, but later they were freed when the rest of the 51st Armored Infantry seized the town of Warnach.

In regard to equipment, the losses for CCA were not as bad. Dog Company had lost four light tanks the previous night, and Charlie Company, 51st Armored Infantry, had lost two half-tracks before that. Though the Germans had damaged several M4 Sherman tanks during the battle for Warnach, the Americans recovered and repaired most of them, so that by 1800 hours on the twenty-fourth, 35th Tank Battalion had more medium tanks than they had the previous evening.

Despite the American victory, the Germans had stalled CCA's advance for twenty-four crucial hours. Those were hours they paid for in blood. In Combat Command A's official history, Brigadier General Herbert L. Earnest described the defenders of Warnach thusly: "This enemy was fanatical, tenacious, and daring and continued to be. He could not be pinned down during a night fight and at 0600 24 December our troops were ordered to break off the fight and go into a protected assembly area to the south and west of the town." More important, Earnest realized that the presence of another German unit, namely the *fallschirmjägers* from the 13th Fallschirmjäger Regiment, indicated that his command had defeated one unit, only to have the German army replace it with another one. Thus, CCA's battle was far from over. They had taken Warnach, but now they had to capture the hamlet of Tintange.[10]

CHAPTER 7

BIGONVILLE

| DECEMBER 24, 1944 |

★ ★ ★ ★ ★

"And tomorrow is Christmas. . . ."

—*Sophie-Lion Lutgen, resident of Bigonville*

Early Morning, Sunday, December 24
Command Post, 37th Tank Battalion, 4th Armored Division
South of Bigonville, Luxembourg

The tankers and soldiers of Combat Command Reserve had wanted to seize Bigonville the night before, but thanks to a spirited German defense, they had to wait until the following morning to complete the mission.

Lieutenant Colonel Creighton Abrams, the commander of the 37th Tank Battalion, gathered his company commanders together early that morning to issue his operations order. According to Captain William A. Dwight, the Battalion S-3 officer, Abrams preferred oral instructions because he disliked the standard five-paragraph operations order. As a result, other than the task and purpose of an operation, the subordinate officers were left to devise their own plans.

At the beginning of the assault, Abrams wanted the 94th Armored Field Artillery Battalion to suppress enemy forces to the north and east of Bigonville. In addition, he wanted the artillery to harass reported German howitzer batteries located in and around Bilsdorf and Arsdorf. Captain Thomas J. Cooke, the liaison officer from the 94th Armored Field Artillery, nodded to acknowledge that he understood the 94th's upcoming mission.

Abrams then looked over at his tank commanders. First Lieutenant Charles P. Boggess had assumed command of Charlie Company after the death of Captain Trover. Boggess had been the executive officer for Charlie Company, and so he knew his way around the company. Boggess was older than most lieutenants. Born in 1912, he grew up in Illinois, and he enlisted in 1942. As a civilian, Boggess worked as an undertaker and was married. Despite the sudden assumption of command, Abrams was confident in Boggess. Still, since he was new to the job, he would not lead the attack. Instead, Charlie Company would provide flank security to the east.

In fact, General Gaffey still was concerned that the reported German panzer force around Arsdorf would strike the division's vulnerable eastern flank, and so Abrams decided to secure that flank using Charlie Company. Referencing his map, Abrams then pointed to a draw that was southeast of Bigonville. To Abrams, that draw was the most likely axis of advance for a German panzer counterattack. Therefore, he ordered Boggess to secure that area by occupying a position that would provide flank security to his main effort.

For the main effort, Abrams chose Second Lieutenant John A. Whitehill's Able Company to lead the operation. Whitehill's dogged determination the previous day had impressed Abrams, and as a result, Whitehill's company of tanks, coupled with Able Company, 53rd Armored Infantry, would attack Bigonville from the south. Whitehill sensed it would be a tough fight, but he was ready for the opportunity.

Finally, Captain James Leach's Baker Company would secure the left flank of the main effort by attacking Bigonville from the southwest. Lieutenant Colonel George L. Jaques, the commander of the 53rd Armored Infantry, would augment Leach's company with infantry from his C Company. The two company task forces then would assault Bigonville around eight o'clock that morning. Even though Leach was the senior company commander, his company had taken point the previous day and had sustained some losses. Thus, Abrams decided to give his company a break. Furthermore, Whitehill had more tanks.

Jaques had the same problem. His Baker Company would remain in reserve, because they had sustained more than thirty casualties during the attack on

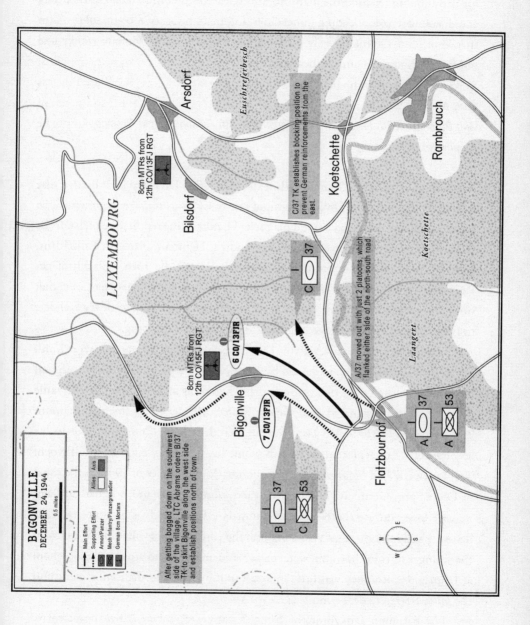

BIGONVILLE
DECEMBER 24, 1944

0.5 miles

Main Effort

Supporting Effort

Armor/Panzer

Mech Infantry/Panzergrenadier

German 8cm Mortars

Allies

Axis

LUXEMBOURG

Arsdorf

Euschtreferbesch

Bilsdorf

8cm MTRs from
12th CO/13FJ RGT

Koetschette

Rambrouch

C/37 TK establishes blocking position to
prevent German reinforcements from the
east.

C | 37

Koetschette

8cm MTRs from
12th CO/15FJ RGT

6 CO/13FIR

A/37 moved out with just 2 platoons, which
flanked either side of the north-south road.

Laaangert

Bigonville

7 CO/13FIR

A | 37

A | 53

After getting bogged down on the southwest
side of the village, LTC Abrams orders B/37
TK to skirt Bigonville along the west side
and establish positions north of town.

Flatzbourhof

B | 37

C | 53

N
W   E
S

Flatzbourhof on the twenty-third. That meant Abrams had three medium tank companies and two infantry companies involved in the operation. Satisfied that his battalion understood the plan, Abrams released his commanders so that they could conduct troop-leading procedures for their respective companies. As it turned out, the Germans knew the Americans were coming. Moreover, they had reinforced Bigonville during the night.[1]

Early Morning, Sunday, December 24
2nd Battalion, 13th Fallschirmjäger Regiment, 5th Fallschirmjäger Division
Bigonville, Luxembourg

For several days, the German 5th Fallschirmjäger Division had battled the American 4th Armored Division without one of its *fallschirmjäger* regiments, like a boxer with one hand tied behind his back. Thanks to the repeated requests of the recently promoted division commander, Ludwig Heilmann, the 5th Fallschirmjäger Division started to receive reinforcements from the 13th Fallschirmjäger Regiment on the twenty-third. In Bigonville, the reinforcements were essential, since 9th Company, 15th Fallschirmjäger Regiment, had less than thirty men left to fight. In fact, they were heading back to the rear that morning.

The acting commander of the 13th Fallschirmjäger, Major Goswin Wahl, selected his 2nd Battalion to defend Bigonville. 2nd Battalion was Wahl's original battalion, and he could not command his battalion and regiment at the same time. Hence he designated Hauptmann Walter Metzler to assume command of 2nd Battalion. Meltzer had been the commander of 6th Company prior to his "promotion." His replacement for 6th Company was Oberleutnant Adolf Koch. The Luftwaffe had organized the battalion back in October of 1944 in the town of Oldenburg, Germany. Like many other *fallschirmjäger* units, it had suffered massive losses during the Normandy campaign. Fortunately, a group of veterans had survived, and these survivors became the core of the new battalion. Many of the younger recruits, however, were former students who had attended pilot school at Leipzig. Hence, they had little infantry training prior to their enlistment into the *fallschirmjäger* corps.

The battalion arrived at the front in early December. After the offensive started, it crossed the Our River into Luxembourg near the town of Bettel on the seventeenth. For several days, it participated in the battles around Fouhren. Once Fouhren had fallen, the regiment headed west to rejoin its division. Like the other *fallschirmjäger* battalions, it had three line companies and one heavy-weapons company. Each line company had three platoons. According to Oberleutnant Rudolf Petrikat, who was the commander of 7th Company, the *fallschirmjägers* in his company had more than the usual allotment of submachine guns. However, because it was a *fallschirmjäger* unit, the companies had little in the way of transport. As a result, when the supply system broke down, the companies and the battalion were unable to support the soldiers with ammunition or food. By the twenty-fourth, the men had not eaten anything substantial for days, and it was affecting morale.

Moreover, Petrikat had a low opinion of the acting battalion commander. According to Petrikat, Hauptmann Metzler had been a transfer from a flak battalion. Hence he had little experience in ground combat, unlike his predecessor, Major Wahl. Moreover, Petrikat said, "Metzler was also a fine commander but he was clueless." Unfortunately, he would be Petrikat's leader during a crucial battle.

Hauptmann Metzler decided to concentrate the majority of his combat power inside Bigonville. Therefore, he placed both 7th and 6th companies inside the town. To mitigate the Allied advantages in heavy weaponry, the battalion commander believed that the best defense was a knife fight, so his *fallschirmjägers* would battle from inside the homes and farms of Bigonville, thereby forcing the American infantry to clear each room. Metzler's goal was to make it costly and time-consuming for the Americans. Finally, in addition to his own *fallschirmjägers*, Metzler would have some stragglers from the 9th and 10th companies, 15th Fallschirmjäger Regiment, who had somehow survived the previous forty-eight hours and had escaped to reach Bigonville.

For heavy-weapons support, 8th Company, under the command of an Oberleutnant Saxe, would remain in Arsdorf, where it could provide mortar support with its 8cm mortars. In addition, 2nd Battalion had one section of 12cm mortars from the regiment's heavy-mortar company. Furthermore, each of the two line companies would have four MG 42s mounted on tripods from 8th Company's heavy machine gun platoons. Alas, unlike some of the *fallschirmjäger* units, Metzler's battalion did not have a lot of *panzerfausts* and *panzerschrecks*. In fact, captured U.S. bazookas provided most of his antitank capability.

Heilmann and Wahl knew that his battalion lacked the power to stop Combat Command Reserve. Therefore, the mortar platoon from 12th Company of the 15th Fallschirmjäger Regiment would remain in Bigonville. This would add an additional four 8cm mortars to Metzler's force. Hence, mortarman Horst Lange would remain in Bigonville, too. Also, the eight tripod-mounted MG 42s from 12th Company would also stay there, which meant that the Germans would have a total of sixteen heavy machine guns with which to defend the town. They had two captured American single-barrel 40mm towed antiaircraft guns, which they could use in the direct-fire role. On the other hand, Metzler had no more StuGs, because Leach and the other tankers had destroyed most of them in the earlier fight for Flatzbourhof.

Besides the mortars, the 2nd Battalion would still have a battery of 10.5cm howitzers for indirect fire support. Since the Americans were so close, the cannon cockers of 7th Battery of the 408th Volks Artillery Corps had withdrawn from Bigonville and reestablished their positions between the towns of Baschleiden and Boulaide, Luxembourg, which were several kilometers north of Bigonville. Nevertheless, because of the persistent supply shortages, the battery was running low on ammunition.

Late on the twenty-third, the inexperienced Metzler had chosen the town of Bodange as his battalion command post. That was a mistake. Bodange was several kilometers west of Bigonville, and when Combat Command A assaulted Warnach the same night, it cut the ground line of communication between the battalion headquarters and three of its companies. Luckily for 2nd Battalion, Metzler was in Bigonville when this occurred, so he was still in command of his forces. As planned, 2nd Battalion had company. 3rd Battalion, from the 13th Fallschirmjäger Regiment, had set up their command post in Boulaide, a few kilometers north of Bigonville and behind German lines.

Before Metzler left for Bigonville, Major Goswin Wahl, the acting commander of the 13th Fallschirmjäger Regiment and Metzler's boss, had warned him what they were up against. "The unit [2nd Battalion] is facing a crack panzer unit, the 4th U.S. Armored Division." Hearing this from his regimental commander, Metzler wondered whether his men even had a chance.

In total, it was not a fair fight between the Americans and the Germans. 2nd Battalion had two intact infantry companies and two heavy-weapons companies to stop the Americans, who had two infantry companies and three tank companies. In terms of artillery, Metzler had one battery, while Abrams could call on at least six batteries, and three of those batteries were 155mm "Long Toms." Finally, Abrams had the 362nd Fighter Group, with three squadrons of P-47s. Metzler had no answer for that. The only significant advantage for Metzler was that he controlled the high ground.[2]

0600 Hours to Midmorning, Sunday, December 24
Remnants of 9th Company, 3rd Battalion, 15th Fallschirmjäger Regiment
Bigonville, Luxembourg

Feldwebel Conrad Klemment awoke at 0600 hours to find himself still in his nightmare. At least he was leaving it behind this morning. Oberleutnant Bertram collected the few survivors from 9th Company and issued his final directive—they were heading back to the rear. The men breathed a sigh of relief.

Yet thanks to the American artillery, the journey would be fraught with danger. Already, 155mm Long Tom batteries were pounding the area. Klemment, having lived through countless barrages, could tell that their adversaries were using a different type of shell that morning. In fact, the Battle of the Bulge was the first time the U.S. armies used the proximity-fused artillery shell named POZIT.

The proximity-fused shell was the latest in U.S. technology, developed originally as an antiaircraft weapon. American antiaircraft gunners had used it against the low-flying V-1 rockets with success. The shell would send out a radio signal, and when close enough to the target, it would detonate. The weapon was effective, since it did not have to hit an aircraft to damage or destroy it, increasing the likelihood of shooting down the target.

In a ground role, the radio signal would cause the round to detonate at a predetermined height, creating an airburst. An airburst was much more effective than a ground detonation. Shrapnel from a ground burst went in only one direction—upward. Lying on the ground offered a good chance of survival for a ground detonation, but offered no protection against an airburst, because the explosion would scatter the shrapnel in every direction. In a letter to General Leven Campbell, chief of ordnance, General Patton later wrote:

The new shell with the funny fuze [sic] is devastating. The other night we caught a German battalion, which was trying to get across the Sauer River, with a battalion concentration and killed by actual count 702. I think that when all armies get this shell we will have to devise some new method of warfare. I am glad that you all thought of it first.

Unfortunately for Klemment and his comrades, the gunners of the 177th Field Artillery Battalion had decided to utilize the new POZIT fused shells that morning. Oberleutnant Bertram determined that his group's survival hinged on operating in smaller sections. Therefore, he divided up the company into squads of six. They were to dash outside and "leapfrog" from building to building while there was a lull between detonations.

Klemment could see the reluctance on the men's faces as Bertram explained, but they had no other choice. If they stayed, the impending American attack would delay their departure, or worse, they would end up dead or prisoners of war. Bertram chose Klemment as the leader for the second group. After the first group left, Klemment led his section out into the street. Several minutes later, both groups rendezvoused near Bigonville's main intersection. The shelling had left them dumbfounded and shell-shocked.

Despite the stupor, Klemment realized they had to keep moving. He estimated that the rounds exploded every ten seconds. If the artillery caught them out in the open, it would kill or maim them instantly. The only cover was behind stone buildings or manure piles. While they debated, Klemment could hear the boom of artillery, then the whistle of the incoming round. A short span of time, but predictable. Klemment decided that was the best time to run.

"I ordered three men to proceed ahead on the right side and three on the left side of the road," he wrote. "The first group wanted to see how well my plan worked. Once the shrapnel from the last projectile fell to the ground, the first group took off. They repeated the same one house after another."

When Klemment's group reached the last house, he stumbled. He wrote:

I became entangled in a cable from a shot-up street light post and fell to the ground. A single second seemed like an eternity. Thoughts of electrical shock flashed through my head. Frantically I attempted to free my leg while I heard the sound of incoming projectiles. With one determined effort I managed to free myself from the cable and then I jumped into the small gaps between the wall of the house and the pile of manure. As I fell to the ground I heard the explosion but the manure protected me from the shrapnel.

Klemment got up and scampered to the next building. After several minutes, he counted the members of his group. All were there, panting and wheezing but alive and unharmed. When they reached the edge of Bigonville, they were outside the American artillery's beaten zone and could walk without fear of incoming shells. They hiked for an hour before they reached the Sauer River. There they met a group of pioneers who were prepping the bridge for demolition. The pioneers pointed them toward the millhouse where the 9th Company had intended to rendezvous. Inside the mill, they met another *fallschirmjäger* who was acting as a liaison. Seeing Klemment's bedraggled section, the stranger asked what had happened to the rest of 9th Company, and Klemment told him that the company had split up.

The last hour had been exhausting for Klemment. He staggered into a room, sat down, and crashed. He was thankful that he was still alive and had escaped the hell of Bigonville.[3]

0800 to 0823 Hours, Sunday, December 24
37th Tank Battalion, 4th Armored Division
South of Bigonville, Luxembourg

Not long after 0800 hours, the infantry and tank companies of Combat Command Reserve commenced their final assault on Bigonville. As planned, the 94th Armored Field Artillery Battalion unleashed a tremendous barrage that landed on the reported German positions in and around Bigonville. To provide concealment, the 94th also blanketed the area with smoke. Yet Lieutenant Colonel Creighton Abrams could barely see the smoke that was supposed to hide them as their tanks approached their attack positions. By 0816 hours, he ordered his batteries to cease the useless smoking operation.

Simultaneously, Second Lieutenant John A. Whitehill, company commander for Able Company, 37th Tank Battalion, pushed north directly into town. His unit was down to only nine tanks, and he was commanding two platoons instead of the usual three. On his left flank was Staff Sergeant Ralph Rowland's platoon, with four tanks, moving up the west side of the north–south road so that it could tie in with Captain James Leach's Baker Company, which was farther west. Meanwhile, on the right flank, moving north was Staff Sergeant F. Woods and his platoon of four tanks. Woods's platoon was the first to reach the edge of the village at approximately 0821 hours. German defenders welcomed him with mortars and machine guns. Occasionally a *panzerfaust* or bazooka rocket would zip through the air.

Farther back, Captain John T. McMahon, the battalion's senior intelligence officer, called Whitehill over the FM radio and asked, "Have you run into anything?" McMahon was trying to figure out where the Germans were so that he could help the S-3, Captain Dwight, direct the battalion's assets. Abrams had selected McMahon to act as a liaison between the two Able companies and his command element. Abrams trusted McMahon, who was not your typical desk-riding staff officer. As evidence, the native from Maryland had earned the Silver Star for his bravery on August 7, 1944, in Hennebont, France.[4]

0830 to 0849 Hours, Sunday, December 24
Baker Company, 37th Tank Battalion, 4th Armored Division
West Side of Bigonville, Luxembourg

While Whitehill struggled to move north into the village, Leach's two platoons had penetrated Bigonville from the southwest side of town. The *fallschirmjägers* watched as Leach's seven tanks drove past them. To suppress the *fallschirmjägers'* fighting positions, Leach ordered the tankers to open fire on the houses, and .30- and .50-caliber tracers ripped into the masonry.

Despite the steel storm, the Germans fought back. A sniper squeezed off a round and an American tank commander slumped over the side of the turret. Staff Sergeant Walter P. Kaplin had replaced Staff Sergeant John Fitzpatrick less than twenty-four hours ago. The bullet killed him instantly. The luckless crew secured his body inside the turret and pressed eastward. Despite the loss, Leach's company of seven tanks continued to roll forward, but they were too sluggish for Abrams.

At 0825 hours, Abrams called Leach and said, "Let's move in there. Move in."

Leach put down the radio handset and watched the battle unfold. So far it was slow. The grunts from Charlie Company, 53rd Armored Infantry, were not aggressive enough. Realizing that he needed to maintain the offensive tempo, Leach yelled at the infantry to spur them into the buildings. They were not his soldiers, but he needed them to attack, because without them their division would never take the town.

Neither Abrams nor his staff was satisfied with the operation's progress. At 0833 hours, Leach heard McMahon's voice on the radio. Apparently McMahon was still waiting to hear from Whitehill, and he squawked again. "Move out," he said to the Able Company commander.

Colonel Abrams did not need the radio to know what was going on. He could see that all of his tanks were creeping forward, but the accompanying infantry were lagging behind. Abrams called Lieutenant Colonel George Jaques over the radio and growled, "Have him [Jaques] report to me. I want to show him what his troops are doing."

Meanwhile, Leach continued through the narrow streets along the southwest edge of Bigonville. Germans were everywhere, and he urged the infantry to clear out each room in each building. Suddenly Leach collapsed. An unseen German rifleman had shot him in the head.

"The bullet went into the helmet . . ." Leach later said, "and cut the sweatband off of my head . . . and knocked me out. So I passed out and fell into the turret floor. They [his crew] jokingly said, 'Captain, get your butt back into the turret; you got work to do.'"

The bullet wound had as much effect on Leach as a mosquito bite. Leach pulled himself up and continued to lead his forces through the west side of Bigonville. At 0840 hours, he radioed Abrams, "Lot of sniping."

Seconds later, Abrams responded, "Hold right there."

Abrams, needing to regain momentum, decided to alter his plan. Instead of pushing Leach through the southwest side of town, he would order him to envelop the town by occupying the high ground north of Bigonville. In effect, he would trap the Germans. At the same time, Whitehill would continue his advance from the south, pushing the retreating Germans toward Leach's blocking position. Hopefully the Germans would surrender instead of attempting a bloody breakout.

At 0849 hours, Abrams called Leach and told him the plan. "Move west and pick up some infantry," he ordered.[5]

0901 to 0929 Hours, Sunday, December 24
Able Company, 37th Tank Battalion, 4th Armored Division
South Side of Bigonville, Luxembourg

Whitehill was also struggling with a timid infantry. By 0901 hours he still was not gaining any traction. McMahon relayed a message to Abrams, informing him of Whitehill's plight. "Infantry won't move. Platoon went into first building and won't move."

For several minutes, McMahon hounded Whitehill. From his position farther back in the column, he could see the infantry as if they were milling about on a playground. At 0910 hours, he called Whitehill again. "Move your left flank up even."

Abrams was unsatisfied with Whitehill's progress. Fifteen minutes after McMahon called him, Abrams asked the Able Company commander, "What is your situation?"

Whitehill replied, "Infantry slowly catching up."

Three minutes later, Abrams informed McMahon and Whitehill of the altered plan. "I'm going to send Leach onto the high ground north of town, skirting the town. Have Whitehill leave a few vehicles on this side of town for cover." Whitehill acknowledged the message. Meanwhile, he was trying to fight a battle.

Farther to the west, Captain Leach's Baker Company started to roll northward to envelop the Germans in Bigonville.[6]

0931 to 1000 Hours, Sunday, December 24
Baker Company, 37th Tank Battalion, 4th Armored Division
West Side of Bigonville, Luxembourg

At 0931 hours, Captain Dwight called Leach to hear a progress report. "Do you have that platoon skirting the town?" he asked Leach.

Bastogne was a vital road hub in southeastern Belgium, and it became decisive terrain in the Battle of the Bulge. Hence, the paratroopers of 101st Airborne Division refused to surrender it to the Germans. In response, the German army surrounded the town and laid siege to it. General Patton knew he had to relieve the 101st if he wanted to win the battle, and he ordered the 4th Armored Division to relieve the paratroopers trapped inside the cordon. ★ *Courtesy of the Don F. Pratt Museum, Fort Campbell, Kentucky*

Lieutenant General George S. Patton (*right*) speaks to the defenders of Bastogne: Brigadier General Anthony C. McAuliffe, Commander of the 101st Airborne Division (*left*), and Lieutenant Colonel Steve A. Chappuis (*center*), Commander of the 502nd Parachute Infantry Regiment. ★ *Courtesy of the Don F. Pratt Museum, Fort Campbell, Kentucky*

The standard M4 Sherman was the mainstay of most tank battalions in the U.S Army. This particular Sherman is in McAuliffe Square in the center of Bastogne. Though the markings in this photo indicate the tank was part of the 4th Armored Division, it was originally part of the 11th Armored Division, which also fought around Bastogne. ★ *Courtesy of the Don F. Pratt Museum, Fort Campbell, Kentucky*

The M3 half-track was the primary transport for U.S. soldiers in armored divisions. The half-track here was from the 35th Tank Battalion and was most likely some type of headquarters vehicle, judging by the number of antennae. ★ *Courtesy of Matt Tuccillo*

This Sherman is an M4A3, fitted with a long-barreled 76mm gun. Most tank platoons had at least one of these vehicles. This tank, from the 4th Armored Division, is seen near the N4 highway south of Bastogne. Unlike the stubby 75mm on earlier Shermans, the long-barreled 76mm could penetrate almost 100mm of armor from as far as a thousand meters away. Unfortunately, a German panzer crew could easily distinguish this Sherman from other Shermans, due to the muzzle break on the end of its barrel, making it the first tank the panzers needed to knock out in a fight. ★ *Courtesy of U.S. Army Heritage and Education Center, U.S. Army Signal Corps WWII photograph collection*

A tank platoon from the 35th Tank Battalion outside of Bastogne. Most of the Shermans pictured here were armed with the stubby 75mm gun, which was excellent against infantry and bunkers, but performed poorly against German panzers. ★ *Courtesy of Battlefield Historian website*

The staff of the 4th Armored Division prior to Operation Cobra. Major General John S. Wood (*center*) was still commander then. By the time of the Bulge, he had been replaced by Major General Hugh J. Gaffey. However, many of the staff were still in the division. Lieutenant Colonel Harry E. Brown (*second from left*) was still the division's G-2. Meanwhile, Colonel Wendall Blanchard (*to the right of Wood*) had moved up from deputy chief of staff to commander of Combat Command Reserve. Lieutenant Colonel John B. Sullivan (*second from right*) was still the G-3 for the division at the time of the Battle of the Bulge.

★   *Courtesy of the National Archives Annex at College Park, Maryland*

Snowfall began on December 22 and continued throughout much of the fighting around Bastogne. Here, soldiers from the 51st Armored Infantry Battalion patrol a section of woods near Bastogne. Many soldiers improvised and used confiscated white bedsheets as camouflage. It appears these soldiers, though, are wearing regulation parkas.   ★   *Courtesy of U.S. Army Heritage and Education Center, U.S. Army Signal Corps WWII photograph collection*

Sergeant Albert Gaydos was part of a forward observer team attached to the 35th Tank Battalion. His tank was one of the lead tanks for Combat Command A as it drove north toward Martelange. He later saw action outside of the town of Warnach on December 23–24, 1944. His brother, Paul, served in the same unit, and later died during the fighting around Bastogne. ★ *Courtesy of Albert Gaydos's family*

4th Armored Division trucks drive past the corpses of American soldiers on a road near Chaumont, Belgium. These men were from 1st Platoon, B Troop, 25th Cavalry Squadron. They were ambushed by soldiers from the 14th Fallschirmjäger Regiment, who were defending Chaumont on the morning of December 23.

★ *Courtesy of U.S. Army Heritage and Education Center, U.S. Army Signal Corps WWII photograph collection*

Bruce Donald Fenchel, a driver on a M5 Stuart Tank in D Company, 8th Tank Battalion, seen here at Fort Knox, Kentucky, at tank school during the summer of 1943.

★　*Courtesy of the Veterans Oral History Project*

This jeep from 1st Platoon, B Troop, 25th Cavalry Squadron was destroyed in an ambush on the morning of December 23 outside of Chaumont. The town fell to Combat Command B late that afternoon, but the Germans counterattacked with a platoon of Tiger tanks and drove out the Americans.

★　*Courtesy of Battlefield Historian website*

A view from inside Chaumont, looking to the northeast at a ridgeline. German tiger tanks counterattacked from this ridgeline, knocking out eleven American tanks inside Chaumont.

★ *Courtesy of the author*

The officers of the 37th Tank Battalion pose in England, May 1944. Lieutenant Colonel Creighton Abrams is seated in the bottom row, directly in the middle. William A. Dwight (*bottom row, third from left*) would later become the S-3. Directly to the right of Dwight is Edward Bautz, who would become the executive officer of the battalion during the relief of Bastogne. James H. Leach (*middle row, second from left*) would command B Company and earn the Distinguished Service Cross for his actions around Bigonville. Walter Wrolson (*back row, fourth from right*) was one of only two officers left in C Company when they pushed into Bastogne on December 26. Richard Donahue (*back row, eighth from right*) would command D Company during the relief of Bastogne. Many of the other officers did not survive the war.

★ *Courtesy of Rochelle Dwight, daughter of William A. Dwight*

James H. Leach, seated on top of the cannon, poses in a photo taken in England, when he was still a platoon leader. Leach eventually took command of B Company, 37th Tank Battalion, and was promoted to captain. During the fight for Bigonville, he was wounded twice. For his bravery, the Army awarded him the Distinguished Service Cross.

★ *Courtesy of Jamie Leach, son of James H. Leach*

"Blockbuster III," Captain James H. Leach's tank during the fighting around Bastogne. Tankers typically gave their tanks colorful names. Leach's crew knocked out two StuGs and a captured Sherman tank near the town of Flatzbourhof, Luxembourg, on December 23. ★ *Courtesy of Jamie Leach, son of James H. Leach*

Hobart Drew, Captain James Leach's driver in his command tank, "Blockbuster."

★   *Courtesy of Battlefield Historian website*

Captain William A. Dwight was the S-3 for the 37th Tank Battalion. He was awarded the Silver Star for his actions outside of Assenois, Belgium, on December 26. Notice the tanker helmet, which was modeled off of the football helmets of the time.

★   *Courtesy of the Rochelle Dwight, daughter of William A. Dwight*

Lieutenant Colonel Delk M. Oden (*left*) was the commander of the 35th Tank Battalion. Captain James K. Tanner is on the right. Brigadier General Herbert L. Earnest selected Oden to be a task force commander for the attack on Martelange. Later, Oden led his battalion in the battles around Warnach.

★   *Courtesy of Irving M. Heath*

Captain John Ridley (*right*), the company commander for D Company, 35th Tank Battalion, with Captain L. J. Ryan (*center*), the battalion S-3. D Company was the light tank (M5 Stuart) company for Combat Command A during the operations around Bastogne.   ★   *Courtesy of Irving M. Heath*

Second Lieutenant Irving M. Heath photographed this knocked-out StuG III somewhere between Bastogne and Arlon along the N4 highway, which linked the two towns. The StuG was most likely from the 11th Assault Gun Brigade, attached to the 5th Fallschirmjäger Division during the Bulge Offensive. Tanks from Heath's unit, the 35th Tank Battalion, destroyed several StuGs like this one outside the town of Warnach.

★   *Courtesy of Irving M. Heath*

The 35th Tank Battalion lost several tanks in the fight for Warnach. Irving Heath photographed this tank, knocked out by an antitank gun while on the way to Bastogne.   ★   *Courtesy of Irving M. Heath*

Soldiers watch C-47s fly over Bastogne. The planes were the workhorse of the U.S. Army Air Corps Troop Carrier Command. Air resupply started to arrive on December 23. It was this sight that prompted Lieutenant Colonel Creighton Abrams, the commander of the 37th Tank Battalion, to race into Bastogne, ending the siege on December 26. ★ *Courtesy of the Don F. Pratt Museum, Fort Campbell, Kentucky*

This is what First Lieutenant Charles P. Boggess first saw when he rolled into Assenois from the south. Assenois was the last line of defense for the German army, surrounding Bastogne. Once Boggess was through the town, he would be only several hundred meters from the American lines, defending Bastogne. German soldiers from the 39th Volksgrenadier Regiment defending Bastogne had other ideas. ★ *Courtesy of the author*

The Cobra King crew—First Lieutenant Charles Boggess, Corporal Milton Dickerman, and privates James G. Murphy, Hubert Smith, and Harold Hafner—pose for a celebratory photo in the vicinity of Bastogne shortly after the tankers led the armor and infantry column that liberated the city. ★ *U.S. Army*

M5 Stuart tanks escort a convoy of trucks heading toward Bastogne on December 27. At the time, this was the only route into Bastogne, so the Stuart tanks, which were most likely from the 37th Tank Battalion, provided protection to the convoys since the corridor was still narrow and German forces flanked it on both sides. The soldiers watching from the side of the road were also from the 4th Armored Division.

★ *Courtesy of the National Archives Annex at College Park, Maryland*

Soldiers from the 10th Armored Infantry Battalion, part of Combat Command B, pose somewhere between Bastogne and the Bois Bechu. After Combat Command Reserve penetrated the German cordon near Assenois on December 26, CCB had the task to secure CCR's eastern flank, which included the town of Salvacourt. This photo was taken on December 27. ★ *Courtesy of the National Archives Annex at College Park, Maryland*

A soldier from the 53rd Armored Infantry Battalion, 4th Armored Division escorts a group of German POWs. In the winter of 1944–45, the harsh weather was an enemy for both sides.

★ *Courtesy of the National Archives Annex at College Park, Maryland*

The final resting place of a German soldier in a patch of woods, east of Bastogne. For many Germans, this was the fate that awaited them when they battled against the 4th Armored Division. The helmet indicates that this soldier was a *fallschirmjäger* who most likely was a member of the 5th Fallschirmjäger Division.

★   *Courtesy of the National Archives Annex at College Park, Maryland*

An MP from the 4th Armored Division herds a group of German POWs past a half-track on December 27. Most of the prisoners were from the 104th Panzergrenadier Regiment or some element of the 26th Volksgrenadier Division.

★   *Courtesy of the National Archives Annex at College Park, Maryland*

Soldiers from the 37th Tank Battalion escort their prisoner, General der Kavallerie Edwin Graf von Rothkirch und Trach, the commander of LIII Corps during the Siege of Bastogne. Rothkirch's corps had assumed control of the 5th Fallschirmjäger Division after it had reached the town of Martelange. Despite his best efforts, Rothkirch could not provide the necessary reinforcements to stop Patton's Third Army.

★   *Courtesy of U.S. Army Heritage and Education Center, U.S. Army Signal Corps WWII photograph collection*

General Jacob L. Devers presents the Presidential Unit Citation to the 4th Armored Division on June 14, 1945, near Landshut, Germany. Standing behind him was Major General William M. Hoge, who had assumed command of the 4th Armored Division from Major General Hugh J. Gaffey. The Presidential Unit Citation is the highest award a unit can receive. The 4th Armored Division earned it when it broke through the German cordon at Bastogne.   ★   *Courtesy of U.S. Army Heritage and Education Center, U.S. Army Signal Corps WWII photograph collection*

Colonel James H. Leach (*left*) and Brigadier General Albin F. Irzyk (*right*) pose together on September 18, 2009, in Lunéville, France, during a commemoration of the sixthy-fifth anniversary of the 4th Armored Division's liberation of Lunéville. Both men were instrumental in the 4th Armored Division's relief of Bastogne. Much of eastern France and Belgium remember the men who liberated them and treat them as heroes when they visit the battlefields.   ★   *Courtesy of Ivan Steenkiste*

Leach answered, "Yes."

Seconds later the wounded commander spotted a group of twenty *fallschirm-jägers* leaving the village. Before he could swing his guns around, the group raced between his tanks and disappeared into a gulley.

Realizing that he could not ignore the dismounted enemy infantry, Leach ordered Staff Sergeant Max V. Morphew to go after them with his own tank while Leach continued northward. Unfortunately for Morphew, the gulley was severely restrictive terrain, and his Sherman could not negotiate the narrow ravine. The *fallschirmjägers* made good their escape. After the war, Leach learned that the leader of the group was Oberleutnant Rudolf Petrikat, the commander of 7th Company. When the two officers met after the war, they became friends.

Several minutes after Petrikat's daring dash, Dwight called Leach again for more information. "Where are you located now?"

"West side of town," Leach shot back. The Baker Company commander was trying to orchestrate a battle. He understood that the S-3 needed to know what was going on, but sometimes the pestering probably was annoying. His head was throbbing from the sniper's bullet, adding to his already foul mood.

Finally Dwight told him, "Turn around." Leach turned around and saw another tank. It was Captain Dwight. Abrams earlier had ordered him to link up with Leach to facilitate command and control, and that was why he wanted to know where Leach was. Like McMahon, Dwight now was acting as a liaison between Leach's group and Colonel Abrams.

Dwight then picked up his radio and informed Colonel Abrams, "We are on the north [side] of town now."

Suddenly Leach felt a stinging in his right arm, and he winced. After several seconds, he glanced over and saw some torn bits of clothing. Without a second thought, he grabbed his radio and called Dwight. "I just got hit in the arm," he said. The wound was minor, and Leach continued to lead his company.

For Dwight, it was another close call. They could ill afford to lose another company commander. It was 1000 hours, and the battle for Bigonville was far from over.[7]

1002 to 1025 Hours, Sunday, December 24
Able Company, 37th Tank Battalion, 4th Armored Division
South Side of Bigonville, Luxembourg

For the first couple of hours of the attack, Whitehill likely felt that Abrams was measuring Staff Sergeant Woods's platoon's progress in inches. To spur his acting platoon leader, Whitehill pushed ahead in his own tank to lead the assault.

Then he heard the droning sound of aircraft above, and instinctively he looked up and saw a flight of four P-47 Thunderbolts. His heart jumped. Four "Jugs," as they were known, could rip the heart out of the German defenses. Within moments, however, he realized that the Jugs were not interested in the Germans. Without warning they dived toward the earth, and Whitehill could see the wings flashing and blinking as the eight .50-caliber machine guns opened up on Baker Company's location northwest of town. Whitehill gasped as the planes struck like eagles diving on their prey. It was over in seconds.

Suddenly, amid the self-inflicted carnage, McMahon called the harried Able Company commander on the radio. "How are you doing?" Clearly McMahon did not know that the Thunderbolts had strafed and bombed their own tanks.

Exasperated, Whitehill picked up his handset and responded, "Moving along as fast as we can. It is getting hot. Snipers are getting hot. Our planes fired on us." The P-47s were most likely from the 362nd Fighter Group, which had been providing direct support that day for III Corps. In fact, one of their squadrons, 377th Fighter Squadron, mentioned a mission south of Bastogne in their daily logs.

37th Tank Battalion was lucky. The Thunderbolts originally were carrying five-hundred-pound general-purpose bombs, fragmentation bombs, and napalm. Fortunately, the pilots had already dropped that ordnance near the town of Bavigne, six kilometers northeast of Bigonville, where they had encountered nearly forty motor trucks and even some type of armored vehicle. According to the pilots in their after-action report, they had destroyed thirty of the trucks and a house. As a result, they could only strafe Abrams tankers.[8]

At 1010 hours, Whitehill heard Colonel Abrams's chime in and ask Captain Dwight, "Did they do any damage up there [meaning planes]? I used two red flares; I guess they recognized us."

Leach later surmised that his isolated company blocking position was the reason behind the potential fratricide attack. Furthermore, some of Leach's Shermans were facing south toward the rest of CCR, as if they were preparing to fire on Whitehill's tanks. With the rest of CCR south of Bigonville, including the tanks, artillery, and all the support trucks, his lone company would have seemed out of place for a fast-moving Thunderbolt pilot—despite the fact that his tanks had the correct markings.

Fortunately, as a smiling Leach recalled in an interview, "They didn't hit a thing." Nonetheless, it was a close call.

Whitehill sighed and resumed his advance. For several minutes the Able Company commander prodded the reluctant doughboys. Finally he radioed McMahon and exclaimed, as if he were throwing up his arms in disgust, "I cannot get the infantry moving to clear out the bazookas."

Captain McMahon then suggested, "See if you can send some of your vehicles down side roads."

Whitehill clicked on his handset and replied, "The streets are [too] narrow." From his turret, the commander could see that some of the streets would become death traps for his tanks. He did not relish the idea of pushing his Shermans through the village, whose streets would have been alleys in some American cities.

Seconds later, the Able Company commander listened as McMahon relayed Whitehill's situation to Colonel Abrams. He said, "Whitehill can't go any further without infantry. The CO [Whitehill] is there. Anyway I can't get infantry up there." For almost an hour now, infantry had been congregating at McMahon's location near the outskirts of Bigonville.

Abrams then suggested, "Use concrete fuse." Concrete-fused shells were bunker busters. They would penetrate bunkers and detonate after they had passed through the concrete walls and into the crew spaces. Against machine gun nests they were lethal. Thus Abrams believed the shells would have the same impact on German troops hunkered down in Luxembourg's stone houses.

In his postwar personal account, Whitehill wrote what happened next:

These comments [McMahon's and Abrams's] motivated me so the barn was set afire with a grenade to chase the enemy away so we could move forward without being under fire by Panzerfaust shells. During the above time frame a sniper was firing at me as I stood in the turret. His shells were flaking paint from the turret in my eyes as I peered out of the open hatch. I was saving tank ammunition and tried to silence the sniper with machine gun fire with my sub machine gun and as I raised my hand out of the hatch area he wounded me in the right hand. This wound was to be my third wound of four that I received during WW II. After being hit in the hand we laid the tank gun on the sniper area position and with a round of 75 MM HE cleared the street and proceeded through the village.

Whitehill's tactics started to work, and the infantry began to gain some ground within the town. At 1025 hours, McMahon radioed him again for a status update. "How are you coming now?" he asked.

This time the lucky lieutenant had good news. "We are moving behind the buildings. I finally got the infantry to move."[9]

Midmorning, Sunday, December 24
Bigonville, Luxembourg

For the citizens of Bigonville, the morning was a flurry of fire and steel. In one instance, Sophie Lion-Lutgen, a resident of the town, recalled how the shelling began in the early-morning darkness, and continued unabated for most of the morning. To combat the darkness of the cellar, she and the rest of her family lit their last candles. She remembered the desperation everyone felt. In her postwar account, she wrote, "[W]e're getting close to the end. Our nerves are stretched to the breaking point. Courage threatens to leave us. Even if we come out of here alive, the whole house and the whole village will lie in rubble and ashes."

Sophie and her family were not alone in the cellar. Cowering like frightened dogs in a thunderstorm were several German soldiers. Outside, the artillery crashed and boomed. Meanwhile, Sophie could make out the ripping sound of the *fallschirmjäger* machine guns, but soon another American artillery round would explode nearby, silencing the guns for a while. Then the machine guns would resume firing until another shell landed. This process repeated itself over and over again until they heard strange clicking noises outside. By now it was past

1000 hours. The German soldiers huddled with the Lion-Lutgen family assured them that the clicking sounds were American soldiers communicating with one another.

Then the family members' noses started to twitch and sting. "The barn is on fire!" one of them finally shouted.

To calm the family's nerves, one of the *fallschirmjägers* bounded upstairs to check to see whether the barn was in fact on fire. Seconds later he returned—the barn was not in flames. Much of the town was, however, and smoke filled the streets. Sophie wondered whether it was only a matter of time before the fiery holocaust reached their home. For now, all they could do was wait.[10]

0900 to 1000 Hours, Sunday, December 24
12th Company, 3rd Battalion, 15th Fallschirmjäger attached to
13th Fallschirmjäger Regiment
Bigonville, Luxembourg

Unlike many of his terrified comrades, Horst Lange slept through much of the shelling, since he was not on shift and had not slept for days. He had left his mortar tubes not long after the shelling started at 0300 hours that morning and passed out in a nearby house. Since his company was the heavy-weapons company for 3rd Battalion, many of them had survived the battles of the last week, because they rarely were locked in direct contact with the American forces, unlike the riflemen in the three line companies. As a result, the division commander had attached Lange's intact company to the newly arrived 2nd Battalion, 13th Fallschirmjäger Regiment, to provide that battalion more indirect fire support.

As a consequence of that decision, Lange's 12th Company remained in Bigonville. For Lange and his fellow mortarmen, their luck ran out that morning. At 0900 hours, Lange's superiors rousted him and his friend from their slumber and ordered them to return to their mortar emplacements near the cemetery. Braving the exploding shells, they stepped out after eating a tiny breakfast. Almost immediately they ran into one of their fellow squad members, who was stumbling back toward the house. He had suffered a terrible facial wound, and his nose was a bloody mess. Seeing this, Lange and his friend decide to avoid using the open streets. Instead they climbed over the walls and sneaked through the backyard gardens like they were rabbits. The tactic worked for a few minutes.

Then Lange saw several American soldiers exit one of the farmhouses. The sudden appearance of Amis had opened his eyes ("Amis" was a German term for Americans). Lange next spotted some Sherman tanks rumbling along a nearby street. Even worse, the American infantry had seen him. Lange and his friend knew resistance was useless, and running was out of the question. Thus, both of them threw up their arms, indicating their surrender.

The American soldiers approached and proceeded to search the *fallschirmjägers*. In seconds the GIs tossed through their pockets and left Lange with only a handkerchief. Then they forced the two German captives to wait with their hands locked behind their heads before escorting them to a stable.

One of the captors told Lange and his friend he was from Chicago. Lange replied in English, "I am from Hamburg." As a token of mercy, the American infantryman then offered him a cigarette.

A few minutes later, another American soldier marched into the stable and asked Lange some questions. Lange, whose English was rudimentary, did not understand the interrogator, and therefore did not answer the questions. As a result, the interrogator perceived Lange's silence as passive resistance and decided to soften him up. In quick succession, he punched the *fallschirmjäger* in the face with a right and then a left hook. Lange remained silent. Realizing that Lange was a dead end, the frustrated interrogator stomped out of the stable. Soon other captured *fallschirmjägers* joined Lange in the shed. To the mortarman, the Germans had lost the battle for Bigonville. For him and his comrades, the war was over.[11]

1129 to 1234 Hours, Sunday, December 24
Able Company, 37th Tank Battalion, 4th Armored Division
Approaching the Center of Bigonville, Luxembourg

By 1129 hours, Second Lieutenant Whitehill's company had reached the church in the center of town.

For the tankers of Able Company, it had been a tough slog. Though some of the enemy had surrendered, many continued to fight. The *fallschirmjägers* had turned every stone house into a fortress and every cellar into a bunker, forcing the

American infantry to clear every room. Typically an infantryman would sneak up to a doorway and toss a grenade inside. Once it exploded, the squad would rush in and shoot whoever was left standing. It was a thorough tactic, but it took time. Meanwhile, German soldiers with *panzerfausts* and captured bazookas would try their luck at one of Whitehill's tanks. Fortunately for Able Company, the German gunners so far had missed, but everyone knew it was only a matter of time before one of the gunners scored a hit.

Whitehill radioed Captain McMahon to let him know his company's progress. "Passing the church now. Still bazooka men around. Don't see our infantry," he reported. McMahon quickly replied, "Only infantry I see are the ones going back."

Whitehill grimaced. For several minutes he pushed ahead. City fights were brutal on an attacking unit, chewing up men and time. Frustrated, he finally called McMahon. "Progressing along. Need more infantry." The tank commander knew it was a long shot. He had been asking for more infantry all morning, and McMahon had little to offer the beleaguered officer.

McMahon confirmed Whitehill's assumption. "You'll have to just use what you got," the S-2 told him over the static.

Whitehill kicked the inside of his turret and clicked his handset. "It will be a slow process," he predicted.

McMahon's response was almost patronizing, as if Whitehill had been firing confetti at the defenders. "Use HE on those buildings," he suggested. Realizing he was on his own, Whitehill put down his handset. His only option was to lower his head and keep attacking the enemy. Eventually the German defenses would break.

Elsewhere, the battalion's progress was better. Baker Company had established a blocking position on Hill 490, north of Bigonville. It had been costly for the leadership, because Leach had lost his executive officer, First Lieutenant Rob Cook. Cook had sustained an injury to his chest, and when he left to find a medic he got lost. Wandering through the town, he stumbled upon some *fallschirmjägers* from 6th Company, 13th Fallschirmjäger Regiment, who captured him. Despite the loss, Leach continued to maintain control of his company's battle position. Thanks to Baker Company, the escape route to the north now was closed.

A few minutes after 1200 hours, the fighting flared up north of the town center, as Whitehill's forces continued to advance. For the defenders, it was their last, dying gasp. A *fallschirmjäger*, carrying either a *panzerfaust* or a bazooka, saw Staff Sergeant Woods's tank as it clanked down the street and decided it was a worthwhile target. He aimed his weapon and fired. Like a Roman candle, the rocket whooshed out of the tube and slammed into the front bogie wheel, damaging it and the tracks. Wood's tank lurched and stopped. Fortunately, the vehicle was still operable. The damage was mostly cosmetic.

Though farther back in the column, McMahon saw what had happened. "Where did that shell come from?" he shouted into his radio.

As if on cue, machine gun and rifle fire erupted around Whitehill's tanks. The lieutenant replied into his handset, "I don't know but they are playing hell."

McMahon asked, "Could you identify what that was that hit the tank?"

With bullets pinging on his turret and hatch, Whitehill winced every time one ricocheted off his Sherman. Finally he answered, "I think it's bazookas."

Chaos exploded around the S-2 as well. McMahon saw a figure dash into a house, but he was not sure whether he was the enemy or not. Surmising that Whitehill's company had advanced far enough to the north that he might be close enough to Leach's tanks and the attached infantry company, he called Dwight on the radio.

"Do you know of any forward troops in the building in this end of town?" he asked the S-3.

Dwight's voice interrupted the static. "No."

"I just saw a man run into a building," McMahon explained. "I couldn't identify him."

"Probably enemy."

McMahon watched as the infantry darted inside each building. Seconds later he heard grenade explosions and rifles popping. He wondered whether he could devise a better way to clear out the residential redoubts.

He offered an idea to Whitehill. "Fifty-cal will set them [the buildings] on fire as well as incendiary." The S-2 figured that they could smoke out the defenders from their hiding places.

He clicked on his handset again. "Blow holes into the buildings and shoot fifties into the holes. Fire HE into the building. Then cease fire and move on up with the doughs."

On the outskirts of town, McMahon observed several German soldiers near a haystack. They were standing still, which McMahon thought was odd. He wondered whether Dwight saw them, since they were near his position.

He alerted the S-3. "Four or five Germans walked over to that haystack."

Dwight clicked in. "I know; I saw one waving a white flag."

McMahon looked at his watch. It was 1234 hours. The Germans were finally breaking, and the battle for Bigonville was almost over.[12]

1310 to Midafternoon Hours, Sunday, December 24
Remnants of the 15th Fallschirmjäger Regiment
Bigonville, Luxembourg

Josef Schroder was one of the few survivors from the 15th Fallschirmjäger Regiment who had remained in Bigonville. He had spent most of the battle hiding in an abandoned home with three other soldiers. With no ammunition, all they could do was wait out the attack and then try to escape during the night. When the assault began, Schroder and his group ran down into the cellar. It was their home for several hours as the artillery and cannons thundered outside, leveling homes and barns. Schroder later wrote:

> We were sitting huddled under quilts, for want of anything else, which we had found in the house, and were awaiting the outcome, surrounded by potatoes. Suddenly we heard the sound of hobnail boots upstairs. I peeped from under the quilt and caught sight of American paratrooper's boots, familiar from past combat with our brothers from the opposite side. Everything that followed happened in a flash. Two hand grenades exploded in the cellar. The quilts took the fragments. I thought the time had come now to surrender, so I ran to the cellar stairs, yelled "Stop firing" and looked straight down the barrels of American rifles. "Hands up" came the terse answer from above, and so with our hands above our heads the four of us went up the stairs one after the other. It was a frightening moment. But they didn't shoot. At 1:10 p.m. I looked at my watch for the last time. We were only allowed to keep the clothes we were in. Photographs, letters and service record books lay in shreds on the floor, everything else scattered around the room. If we were too slow the sol-

diers helped us along with blows from their rifle butts. Then four of them led us to a street nearby. The place looked like any other where war has been: people dead and wounded, houses destroyed, vehicles and tanks on fire. First-aid attendants and an army chaplain were moving around the scene offering what help they could—both sides, as I observed. Dead animals lay on the road; pigs, cattle, calves, burned with phosphorus, were writhing on the ground.

At a crossroads, Schroder and a companion were separated from their fellow soldiers and escorted by two GIs down a street and into a courtyard. The captured *fallschirmjäger* remembered that the American soldiers spoke to one another in Polish, which he thought was strange. The Americans motioned with their rifles, ordering the captives to stand atop a pile of manure and face the courtyard wall. Schroder recalled the thoughts going through his head:

We had survived every infernal moment of this war, had lost our freedom at the end but remained alive, only now to be closer to death than ever before. We weren't able to see what they were doing but we could hear what was going on. It seemed they couldn't reach an agreement: one was for; the other appeared to waver. With our faces still to the wall we just couldn't tell for sure. The one thing we knew only too well was the sound of a rifle being reloaded. And when we thought we heard that sound, perhaps we even considered for a split second whether American rifles were fired differently from ours. It is here on the manure heap in Bigonville that my buried memories of the war become vividly alive again. Every detail, every sound, the burned pigs running around, the grey wall in front of me, the stench, all this has come flooding back to me every Christmas Eve since. It has been so for fifty years now, and I expect it will always be so.

Then, from behind him, Schroder heard a voice. "What are you doing there?" The voice rang with authority and told the captives to turn around and step off the manure pile. Schroder followed the order. When he faced about, he saw an

American officer standing before him with a pistol and a hand grenade. At that moment, Schroder knew he was safe. The officer told the *fallschirmjägers* and GIs to walk in front of him, and he led them back to the intersection.

When they returned to the crossroads, Schroder noticed that the Americans had captured dozens more *fallschirmjägers*. The officer grabbed him and led him to a nearby house and ordered him to walk down into the cellar. Schroder heard a baby crying, so he knew it was not an execution. As in many of the homes, the battle had scarred the house, but the cellar had remained intact. Schroder climbed over the rubble and masonry and down the stairs. There he found a woman and child lying on a blanket. The woman, like many Luxembourgers, spoke German. Perhaps that was why the officer took him there, and since Schroder understood basic English, he could act as a translator between the American officer and the Luxembourg mother.

Her pained expression did not need a translation—she was distraught. Schroder knelt down beside her and listened as she told her story. She was not from the town but had come here as a pregnant refugee when the German offensive began. When the Americans attacked Flatzbourhof yesterday, the stress of combat induced her labor. Now she was stuck in a cellar with a battle raging above her head. Even worse, the strain and stress of battle prevented her from breast-feeding. To explain her plight, she even squeezed her breast, but no milk flowed out.

Despite the ringing in his ears from the shelling, Schroder heard a cow mooing. He found a pail and walked upstairs with the American officer. They discovered the cow across the street in an abandoned cowshed. Miraculously, the animal had survived the cataclysm unharmed. Schroder noticed that the udder was bursting with milk, since no one had milked the poor beast for several days.

Schroder wrote in his account:

I took a milking-stool and the bucket and steeled myself. I never forget those first drops of milk. One summer holiday I had tried my hand at milking the neighbor's cow, but this was my professional debut, so to speak. And I found it wasn't that difficult. Sometimes, when you're between the devil and the deep blue sea, the Lord still provides. Back in the cellar the two of us scalded the milk and I unearthed an old dirty milk bottle. The man, who only this morning had been my enemy, looked on, as I did, at this "Ceremony of Milk." And the baby just did what hungry babies do. She drank up what she was given. Totally indifferent to everything around her.

Afterward, the officer led the helpful *fallschirmjäger* back to the group of prisoners at the crossroads. He never knew what happened to the mother, nor the officer who had spared his life, but he never forgot them, even years later, when he penned his account of the battle. At least he would survive the war.[13]

1530 to 1600 Hours, Sunday, December 24
Bigonville, Luxembourg

After the cracking report of rifles and the boom of howitzers had faded, Sophie Lion-Lutgen and the rest of her family decided to leave the safety of the cellar. They left behind two *fallschirmjägers*, who were debating whether to surrender to the Americans or escape the encirclement.

Almost immediately the family encountered American soldiers, "looking fierce, with bearded faces and a mysterious fire in their eyes, weapons leveled," who ordered them back inside. Returning to the cellar, they informed the two German soldiers about the Americans searching all the houses, barns, and basements. One of the young men did not want to surrender. He was not a die-hard Nazi, and knew the war was lost, believing it was near the end. He wanted to be with his family, and if he surrendered, he was afraid the Americans would send him to the United States, where many German prisoners of war ended up.

His comrade then admonished him, "Don't make any trouble for these people! You'll get to know America."

That convinced the other soldier, and they both marched up the stairs. At 1600 hours, Sophie and her family went back outside. By now the American infantry were rounding up scores of German prisoners, and the center of the town was full of them. Within minutes, American soldiers escorted the family to the rear for processing. Meanwhile, Sophie learned that two of her neighbors had perished during the battle. Despite the safety of their cellar, the two women chose to seek solace elsewhere, and during one of the barrages they stormed out into the fields, where bursting shrapnel killed them.

Sophie's beloved village was gone. She wrote:

The street presents a horrifying, wretched spectacle. Everywhere lie dead German soldiers, many terribly mangled. Cows are wandering around loose. One of them drags a piece of wood from the manger behind her on her chain. A few lie dead on the ground. The corner of our house, and our neighbors' as well, have taken hits. Big holes gape in the walls and roofs. The front wall of one house is demolished. Will the riddled and shattered church steeple remain standing? The ground is covered with stones, roof slate, laths, and the trash of war. Torn-up wires hang from the electric poles. Up in the village a house is burning, and the flames flare up eerily in the growing darkness. It still is not completely safe. Shells whistle overhead and gunfire resounds from nearby. The few people who have stayed here appear out in the street again. Everybody is coming face to face with the terrors of the past days. Each person has something bad to report. And nevertheless we are all happy that we have lived through it unhurt. And tomorrow is Christmas. . . .[14]

★ ★ ★ ★ ★

The cost for Bigonville had been severe. According to Guy Ries, a local Bigonville historian, the fighting destroyed thirty-eight homes and six farms, and killed more than one hundred cattle. Artillery shrapnel struck down citizens who ventured outdoors. Unlike the Americans, the Germans killed several civilians intentionally. The occupiers executed Nicholas Conrardy, whom they had forced to dig his own grave. Nicholas Urth, a member of the Luxembourg resistance, was arreseted and beaten before being executed. His body was dumped in a makeshift grave in a nearby garden.

Despite the destruction, the civilians were thankful that the American army had returned. The GIs brought candy, clothes, and food. The generosity of the American army was a lasting, happy memory for children of the survivors. To this day, the citizens of Bigonville commemorate Christmas Eve as the day when the American army liberated them from the German occupiers.

1530 to 1620 Hours, Sunday, December 24
378th Fighter Squadron, 362nd Fighter Group
In the Skies Above Hollange and Chaumont, Belgium

While the battles for Bigonville and Warnach raged, fighter-bombers from the 362nd Fighter Group continued to provide close air support for the units around Bastogne. In fact, the fighter jockeys from Mogin's Maulers, which was their nickname, had already conducted several missions on behalf of III Corps and the 4th Armored Division. Earlier, one of its squadrons, 377th, had bombed targets north of Bigonville, while the 378th bombed and strafed German positions. By late afternoon, the 378th was on its third mission for the day in direct support for III Corps. For this flight, twelve Thunderbolts were flying south of Bastogne and over the towns of Sainlez and Chaumont. Like the previous operations, the Jugs had a mix of general bombs and napalm. Both towns received equal treatment, as the P-47s blasted and strafed several motor trucks hiding among the buildings.

First Lieutenant Donald Stoddard was the Yellow flight leader. He recalled that the weather was almost perfect for flying with no cloud cover and clear visibility for up two miles. When he saw two trucks in Sainlez, he gave the signal and his four aircraft dived down toward the village and dropped their bombs, causing several fires to break out. Then, as Stoddard started to pull up on his stick, he heard Yellow Two, or Second Lieutenant Richard K. Grant, his wingman, tell him that his engine had cut out. He claimed it was mechanical trouble. To Grant it sounded like someone choking as his radial engine sputtered and died. Grant realized he needed lift, so he jettisoned his remaining five-hundred-pound bombs.

Stoddard directed him to turn his wounded plane southward, toward France. He could see that Grant's plane was losing altitude. The ground controller warned him to bail out, since the surrounding area was not suitable for a crash landing. Grant thought otherwise and rode the plane in. With great skill, he glided the stricken Jug underneath a power line and plopped the fighter-bomber atop a hill. Inertia forced the plane down into a creek, where some unseen rocks tore the fuselage apart. Luckily, Grant survived, and Stoddard watched him hop into a jeep that had arrived on the scene several minutes after the crash. Grant was blessed. Flying in support of the 4th Armored Division over the next few days, several other pilots in the 362nd Fighter Group would not be so lucky.[15]

1115 to 2300 Hours, Sunday, December 24
Girls' Normal School, Arlon, Belgium
Headquarters, III Corps

As the battle of Bigonville started to wind down, elsewhere staffs deliberated and generals planned. The race to Bastogne had hit a snag. Many had hoped that the 4th Armored Division would drive into the town after encountering only minimal German resistance. The unexpected rebuff at Chaumont and the fanatic defense of Warnach had dissuaded even the most optimistic officers that the road to Bastogne was open. Indeed, the German forces, despite their lack of airpower and artillery, had stymied the 4th Armored Division.

Therefore, Major General Hugh Gaffey needed assistance. In this case, he needed more foot soldiers. His problem was structural. Lieutenant General Lesley J. McNair, who had been the commander of U.S. Army Ground Forces before his untimely death in July 1944, had designed the armored division to specialize in exploitation and pursuit operations. As a consequence of this decision, most armored divisions had three armored infantry battalions, three tank battalions, and three self-propelled artillery battalions. In contrast, a standard infantry division had nine infantry battalions, and thanks to American industry, each corps typically attached one independent tank battalion and one independent tank destroyer battalion to each of these divisions. In the heady days of August and September 1944, when the German army was retreating pell-mell to the Siegfried Line, these designs sufficed. Infantry divisions led the way when penetration and frontal assaults were required, while the armored divisions conducted most of the mobile operations.

Now the 4th Armored Division was locked in combat with a Wehrmacht that was fighting, and despite Patton's order to avoid villages, Gaffey had to clear the towns to secure the roads. Villages consumed infantry, and because he had only three battalions of infantry to commit to these scraps, the battle for each was bleeding them white. This problem was more acute with combat commands A and B. Warnach and Chaumont had been costly, and the replacement system was not working fast enough to make up for the losses. Thus he needed to find infantry battalions from other units to augment his depleted force.

At 1115 hours, Gaffey phoned Colonel James Holden Phillips, the chief of staff for III Corps. Phillips and his boss, Major General John Millikin, both had agreed to send some troops to Gaffey, but the 4th Armored Division commander was in a hurry. When the staff officer handed Phillips the phone, the colonel knew he had to assuage Gaffey's concerns.

Phillips cut to the chase. He immediately informed Gaffey of the situation. "Sir," he began, "we have trucks loading now and want to turn them over to you at a place called Attert. They should be there at about 1530." Phillips stared at the map to make sure it was the right town.

The unknown staff officer could hear only Phillips's answers as he typed up the memorandum for the record. The colonel continued. "That is as fast as we can get them ready. . . . I don't know how much delay there will be over at Mack's place. . . . I gave them twenty minutes to load—that is what we are hitting for. It is going to be a CT [Combat Team] minus one."

Phillips started to shake his head. Gaffey wanted more artillery, but the chief of staff and the III Corps commander refused to send any more howitzer battalions to the 4th Armored. Phillips explained his reasoning to Gaffey. "I question the artillery because I think you have all you need. I don't know what they are going to send up, to be honest with you, but if it comes along, okay, and if it doesn't, okay. They will be in on that road from the right."

Phillips paused while Gaffey spoke for several minutes. The chief of staff finally added, "On this thing we were talking about up above, Paul [Major General Willard Paul, Commander of the 26th Infantry Division] is going to take the block from the town that Blanchard just took [Bigonville]. We are going to make available a battalion of C engineers—the 188th to go on from where Herb [Combat Command A commander, Herbert L. Earnest] was held up yesterday over to connect with the unit on your right. . . . They are actually going north of where Herb was bothered [Warnach]. You will have to put them in and as soon as you have gotten them in, then anything that you have there can be pulled out. . . .

You see that they block those roads and prepare them for demolitions. Cover them with fire and connect up with Paul at Bigonville."

Phillips's answer satisfied Gaffey, and the chief of staff then hung up the phone. Millikin and Gaffey both agreed that 4th Armored Division had sustained a beating. They needed more troops, and the best place to get them was from the 80th Infantry Division. Major General Horace L. McBride commanded the 80th Division, and it had been fighting the Germans on the far eastern flank of the corps's area of operations. When McBride received the order to detach a regimental combat team, he chose the 1st and 2nd battalions from the 318th Infantry Regiment. Prior to the alert order, the 318th had been slugging it out with the *volksgrenadiers* from the 352nd Volksgrenadier Division, who had been defending the town of Ettelbruck, Luxembourg. Instead of recovering from the bitter contest that was Ettelbruck, the soldiers of the 318th would have to hop on trucks and drive westward to link up with another division. In addition, 1st Battalion lost their battalion commander, Lieutenant Colonel Albert S. Tosi, who was wounded during the fighting on the twenty-third. His replacement was Major George W. Connaughton, who had been the battalion's executive officer. His first mission as the battalion commander would be a harrowing one.

Thirty-five minutes later, Gaffey called III Corps headquarters again. He wanted to update Colonel Phillips on his division's progress, since everyone from Millikin to Patton to Bradley and even Eisenhower wanted to know when the 4th Armored would break through the German cordon surrounding Bastogne to relieve the 101st Airborne. He confirmed with the III Corps chief of staff that Combat Command B had lost at least several tanks at Chaumont on the twenty-third. On the other hand, Combat Command Reserve had captured most of Bigonville, and some elements were already north of the village. However, Combat Command A was still sparring with the Germans near Warnach and had lost four tanks the previous night. Gaffey argued that Patton's order to fight through the night had been a bad idea. As he listened to Gaffey remonstrate, Phillips nodded his head.

Finally, Gaffey alerted Phillips to the German forces on his western flank. He assessed that the Germans had at least three airborne battalions massing there. Moreover, the 4th Armored Division commander argued that it was this force that had been instrumental in Combat Command B's defeat. Unbeknownst to

Phillips, Gaffey was laying the groundwork for a huge shift in forces. Since the 26th Infantry Division was taking over the area around Bigonville, CCR was now free for other commitments. Gaffey concluded that the best place for Colonel Wendell Blanchard's unit was on the western flank of his division, where the German forces supposedly were massing. In short, CCR would now secure the western flank while CCB resumed offensive operations the morning of the twenty-fifth.

In the latter part of the afternoon, around 1605 hours, Gaffey reported that CCB was under attack south of Chaumont. The attacks had started around 1340 hours, when 8th Tank Battalion reported receiving heavy mortar fire on their western flank while simultaneously defending against German infantry, who were attempting to infiltrate their lines on their eastern flank. The skirmish was a brisk one, as two platoons from Baker Troop, 25th Cavalry, engaged the *fallschirm-jägers* along the right flank. B Troop, under the command of Captain Fred Sklar, was there because Combat Command B had lost so many troops and tanks the previous day that the cavalrymen of B Troop were acting as infantry instead of conducting reconnaissance, which was their primary mission. At 1515 hours, Captain Sklar ordered his 2nd Platoon to attack a German position. After two failed attempts, Sklar chose to lead them one last time. Unfortunately, the third attempt also ended in failure, but this time the *fallschirmjägers* wounded and captured Sklar (Sklar later died in a German prisoner of war camp.)

The loss of Sklar and the repeated German attempts to infiltrate U.S. lines further convinced Gaffey that he needed to secure his western flank. To Gaffey, the only option was CCR. Early in the evening, Gaffey alerted Blanchard that CCR was moving out. Lieutenant Colonel Creighton Abrams and the rest of the men from CCR then heard about the new orders at 1910 hours that night. Time was short, because Blanchard told them they would move out at thirty minutes after midnight.

The Division G-3 finally published the official order at 2300 hours. In it, CCR's new mission was to assemble near the town of Neufchâteau, and then attack toward Bastogne along the Bastogne–Neufchâteau highway. In addition, Gaffey wanted CCR ". . . .to destroy any enemy encountered, assist advance of CCB, and protect the left flank of [the] division and corps." To help out CCR,

Gaffey would allocate one cavalry troop from the 25th Cavalry and one battery of 155mm Long Tom howitzers from the 177th Field Artillery Battalion, which meant that CCR would now have eighteen 105mm howitzers and six 155mm howitzers in direct support.

Like a good commander, Gaffey kept pestering his higher headquarters for more assistance. At 2145 hours, while his staff was finishing up the new fragmentary order, he phoned Phillips again. This time it was for CCA. General Herbert Earnest had run into trouble north of Warnach. Instead of withdrawing, the survivors from Warnach had joined other German units to defend the town of Tintange. No matter how hard he tried, Earnest kept finding himself in tussles for towns. To prepare for the attack scheduled in the morning, he would pulverize Tintange with artillery, but he believed that airpower would be even better. Therefore, on behalf of CCA, Gaffey was requesting more close air support from Phillips. He even asked the chief of staff that ". . . he be given high consideration in the allotment of air for a Christmas present."

Gaffey's request was not based on an overestimation of German combat power. His fears were justified. For some, Tintange would be a worse scrap than Warnach.[16]

Afternoon to Christmas Eve, Sunday, December 24
2nd Company, 5th Fallschirmjäger Pioneer Battalion, 5th Fallschirmjäger Division
Liverchamps, Belgium

Meanwhile, it was Christmas Eve. While many in the United States and in Germany were trying their best to celebrate the holidays, soldiers from both countries were slaughtering one another. In some cases, however, both sides stopped to remember the holiday. For one company of pioneers, the evening began with another combat mission. 2nd Company was under the command of Oberleutnant Rolf Greif, who, at the age of thirty-five, was old for a junior officer. In fact, he was ten years older than his battalion commander. Greif received a task to lead his company toward the town of Liverchamps, where his unit would establish a blocking position.

Before they even left Wiltz, though, they sustained casualties. A nearby

American unit had opened fire with several mortars, showering their assembly area. One man, Gefreiter (Corporal) Erwin Friedel, suffered a terrible wound when a piece of shrapnel nearly severed his arm. Only his veins, looking like dangling streamers on a kite, kept his appendage attached to his body. The medic rushed over and, using a knife sterilized with cognac, he sliced the remaining veins, freeing the dead limb from Friedel's shoulder. Greif felt powerless, but to show his admiration for his soldier's stoicism in the face of such agony, he pinned his Iron Cross on Friedel's bloody uniform. That was the last they saw of Friedel, whom they evacuated to the rear area for surgery. Unfortunately, due to the fortunes of war, he never reached the safety of German territory. The Wehrmacht reported him missing, and he was never heard from again.

The other pioneers of 2nd Company wasted little time mourning their wounded comrade. As pioneers, they had received better training than their infantry counterparts. Many of them were veterans. Hence they shook off the shock and moved out to Liverchamps. Later, Oberfeldwebel Günther Buhl, the platoon leader for 3rd Platoon, found a storage shed along the periphery of Liverchamps, which he decided they would use as their shelter that night. They were not alone. Several families also had chosen the building. They were stubborn, and they refused to leave. Hence both sides reached an agreement whereby the civilians slept in one corner of the building.

Leutnant Greif decided to lighten the mood. He ordered Obergefreiter (Senior Lance Corporal) Johann Listl to find a Christmas tree. Happy to oblige, Listl left the shed to cut down a tree. He soon found one and was dragging it back to the shed when several patrolling fighter-bombers pounced on him. He dropped the tree and scurried under a bridge while the P-47s raked the area with .50-caliber slugs. Meanwhile, the civilians and soldiers thought Listl had perished.

To their surprise, Listl returned early in the evening with the tree tucked under his arm. His first words to his commander were, "Now, that was an ordeal." Hearing this, everyone within earshot smiled. Despite the war, the Christmas celebrations would continue.[17]

Christmas Eve to Christmas Morning, Sunday to Monday, December 24 to 25
101st Airborne Division
Bastogne, Belgium

While Listl and the rest of 2nd Company sang Christmas carols to commemorate the evening, the Luftwaffe blasted Bastogne. Ju 88 bombers, flying from air bases in Germany dropped their ordnance in the center of town. Unbeknownst to the bombardiers, one of the targets was a hospital where the soldiers of Combat Command B, 10th Armored Division, were treating their battlefield wounded. Dozens died in the explosion, including a Belgian nurse.

Amidst the carnage, Patton's Third Army radioed VIII Corps and asked them to pass a message on to the 101st Airborne: "Xmas Eve present coming up. Hold on." The acting division commander acknowledged the missive and returned to work. It was good to know, but at the moment he had to deal with more pressing problems.

As it turned out, the bombing was the first act in a multipronged German effort to crush Bastogne. Early Christmas morning, the 115th Panzergrenadier Regiment and the rest of the 26th Volksgrenadier Division attacked the 502nd Parachute Infantry Regiment and 327th Glider Infantry Regiment on the western side of the Bastogne perimeter. The 101st Airborne, together with tank destroyers from the 705th Tank Destroyer Battalion, defeated this latest German attack, but it was a close call.

In fact, at 0915 hours, Christmas morning, Brigadier General Anthony McAuliffe, the acting commander of the 101st Airborne Division, radioed General Gaffey directly and reported, "101st Airborne Division in Bastogne received a counterattack this morning by enemy tanks and infantry from the West. Some of the enemy broke through into the artillery positions. Situation's sticky but the 101st will handle [it]."

The 101st Airborne had bought some time for the 4th Armored Division, but the question remained: Would the tankers and infantrymen of the 4th Armored Division capitalize on the German defeat? The next thirty-six hours would answer that question.[18]

CHAPTER 8

TINTANGE

| DECEMBER 24 TO 25, 1944 |

★ ★ ★ ★ ★

"Compared to this morning, I could not recognize the village."
—*Feldwebel Conrad Klemment, 9th Company, 15th Fallschirmjäger Regiment*

Evening to Morning, Sunday, December 24, to Monday, December 25
Elements of the 5th Fallschirmjäger Heavy-Mortar Battalion,
5th Fallschirmjäger Division
North of Tintange, Belgium

Alfred Worch wondered how he had ended up as a *fallschirmjäger*, fighting the American army near the tiny town of Tintange in Belgium. Drafted in August 1944 at the age of eighteen, he was originally a sailor in the Kriegsmarine, but soon found himself shuffled into the *fallschirmjäger* corps. His first duty station was in Wittstock, Germany, where he learned how to be an infantryman, but received no jump training. From there he traveled to Hude, Germany, near Bremen, for additional instruction, and in November the Luftwaffe sent him to Hillegom, Netherlands, where he began his training on the 12cm mortar system. After only a month of firing, emplacing, and displacing the weapon, Worch officially became a mortarman in the 5th Fallschirmjäger Mortar Battalion, 5th Fallschirmjäger Division.

The heavy-mortar battalion was a distinct unit found only in a German *fallschirmjäger* division. In contrast, U.S. Army infantry, airborne, and armored divisions lacked separate mortar battalions. All divisional mortar units were organic to the infantry and armor battalions. In fact, a division typically had only 60mm or 81mm mortar systems. The U.S. equivalent of the 12cm mortar was the 4.2-inch mortar, which belonged to the chemical battalions at the corps or army level. (In practice, though, the corps usually allocated a company from the chemical mortar battalion to each division.) The *fallschirmjäger* division was the only one that had a separate mortar battalion in the German army. True, the *volksgrenadier* and *panzergrenadier* units had the 12cm mortar system, but they existed only under the infantry regiments. As a result, the *fallschirmjägers* had double the number of mortar tubes, which increased their firepower significantly. Usually the division commander would augment each infantry regiment with one of the three companies from the mortar battalion. Each company had three platoons, and each platoon had four mortar tubes. In Worch's case, his company supported the 15th Fallschirmjäger Regiment.

Worch linked up with the 5th Mortar Battalion near Maßholder, southwest of Bitburg, Germany, in December 1944. Though his company had mortars, they were short of trucks, and his section had to rely on horse-drawn transport, commandeering carts from local farmers to carry the massive tubes. When the offensive kicked off on December 16, they waited twenty-four hours before moving out. To help move the weapons, the crews pressed the farmers into service, and they traveled with the team until they found an abandoned American half-track near the town of Esch-sur-Sûre, Luxembourg. Afterward, they bade good-bye to the helpful civilians and hitched the mortar to the M3 half-track. For several days Worch's team remained in a reserve role, waiting for a fire mission.

On the morning of the twenty-fifth, Worch's section had set up their mortar tube between the village of Tintange and the Surbich River, which was a stream that served as the border between Luxembourg and Belgium. The team chose this spot because it was high ground and overlooked the Surbich to the north and Tintange to the south. For concealment, they selected a spot behind a barn. As a result of their latest firing position, they would participate in the impending battle. Looking back, Worch recalled that fateful morning, and described it as the "first catastrophe." Luckily, his mortar section had company.[1]

Defending Tintange was another battalion from the 15th Fallschirmjäger Regiment. This time it was 1st Battalion, under the command of Hauptmann Rudolf Berneike. Unlike 2nd and 3rd battalions, 1st Battalion was ostensibly motorized. Oberst Kurt Gröschke, the commander of the 15th Fallschirmjäger Regiment, had selected it to be the assault battalion for the regiment. It had formed up in Germany, three kilometers west of Vianden, on December 10. On the sixteenth it had crossed the Our River at Vianden, but due to a lack of vehicles it had to wait until the seventeenth for the rest of its transportation. From there the battalion had traveled through Luxembourg to Hochscheid and then to Wiltz. On the twenty-second, the battalion assaulted the town of Sibret, Belgium, but by then it had sustained serious losses. 4th Company, the weapons company, had incurred many of the casualties during the bitter fighting in Sibret. Despite the casualties, they soldiered on to the next objective.

1st Battalion next assumed the main defensive positions around Tintange on the twenty-fourth, as a result of the losses to its sister 2nd Battalion in Warnach. Like the rest of the *fallschirmjäger* battalions, it had three infantry companies and one weapons company. However, at the time of the attack on Tintange, 1st Company's whereabouts were unknown. In addition to that, Oberst Gröschke attached two heavy-mortar platoons (12cm mortars), an antitank platoon, and one pioneer platoon from the regimental support units to the battalion. A Leutnant Baukowitz was the commanding officer for 2nd Company, while due to losses, 3rd Company was on its fifth company commander since the beginning of the offensive.

Besides the two infantry companies, the weapons company, and the attachments, Major Gerhard Martin, the commander of 5th Fallschirmjäger Pioneer Battalion, had dispatched his 4th Company to secure the roads around Tintange. By the morning of the twenty-fifth, eighty men were left in the company. They had *panzerfausts* and *panzerschrecks* but no heavy machine guns, nor mortars.

Their first commander was Leutnant Hans Prigge, but he had died on the twenty-second when he went to conduct a patrol around the villages of Sibret, Honville, and Liverchamps. A squadron of American P-47s had caught him out in the open, and he ran into a house for cover. Unfortunately, the building was an easier target for the fighter-bombers, which dropped several bombs and obliterated the structure. For the pioneers of 4th Company, Prigge's replacement was Leutnant Heinz Richter. Despite the losses, their morale remained high.

The pioneers' 3rd Platoon, under the leadership of an Oberfeldwebel Meier, set up a roadblock at the intersection of the N4 and the Tintange–Strainchamps road. There the platoon emplaced three light machine guns and, using Teller mines, they laid several minefields, hiding the mines under piles of cow manure. To slow down the U.S. tanks and troops, they even built some abatis and laid them across the main highway. Finally, most of the remaining combat power would hide in the wood line, lying in ambush.

By now, stragglers from other units had started to gather in Tintange and swell Berneike's overall numbers. First to arrive were the survivors from 2nd Battalion who had managed to escape Warnach. Amazingly, 8th Company still had about eighty men left from their original number of 130. Unfortunately, they had few of their heavy weapons, which they had lost in the battle for the village. Next came the remnants of units from 3rd Battalion, like Conrad Klemment's 9th Company, who had infiltrated through American lines to reach the village. Also, small groups of *fallschirmjägers* from 1st and 3rd battalions, 13th Fallschirmjäger Regiment, staggered into the perimeter after they had evaded Combat Command Reserve and the 26th Infantry Division. They had escaped from Bigonville only to reach the illusory safety of Tintange. Last to arrive were the driblets of soldiers from the 14th Fallschirmjäger Regiment who had traveled east to get away from Combat Command B.

By now, LIII Corps and Seventh Army Headquarters both grasped the severity of the situation on their westernmost flank, and as a result they started to shift forces to buttress the 5th Fallschirmjäger Division. General Erich Brandenberger, the commander of Seventh Army, ordered LXXXV Corps to transfer all of its *volks* artillery battalions, save one, to LIII Corps. Included in that transfer was another battalion of 7.5cm towed dual-purpose guns. Unfortunately this battalion would arrive late, since the corps lacked sufficient motor transport to tow the weapons to the western flank. Furthermore, even if they had the transportation assets, American fighter-bombers would have made short work of them if they traveled on the roads during the hours of daylight.

By the evening of the twenty-fourth, the staff at Seventh Army headquarters sensed the tide might have shifted in favor of the Americans. They knew Martelange had fallen. On their maps, the 15th Fallschirmjäger Regiment's front ran from Hollange to Tintange. The only additional combat power they could send was the Führer-Begleit-Brigade, which they transferred to LIII Corps. Other than that, they were powerless to affect the impending battles. Even worse, the replacement battalions could not maintain a steady flow of personnel to the decimated line units. Hence the rifle companies were running out of men. It was only a matter of time before the dam broke. The only question was when.[2]

Evening to Morning, Sunday, December 24, to Monday, December 25
Combat Command A, 4th Armored Division
Warnach, Belgium

While Brigadier General Herbert L. Earnest looked over the reports on Christmas Eve, he realized that Warnach was only one scene in a long play. It would have been obvious to an amateur tactician that Tintange would be the next act. In response, Earnest ordered his staff to craft another field order, like the one they had done before CCA had seized the crossings at Martelange. With the additional battalion from the 318th Infantry, Earnest had a lot of moving parts, and he wanted to make sure everyone understood their roles in the upcoming operation.

The plan was simple. The attack would commence at 0800 hours. CCA's mission was to "attack north at 250800 in zone and link up with friendly troops south of Bastogne." Earnest looked at his map. Bastogne was still twelve kilometers north of his frontline trace, but he was optimistic. To accomplish this operation, in the west, 51st Armored Infantry would clear the enemy in zone, along the N4 highway, while to the east, 1st Battalion, 318th Infantry, would seize the town of Tintange, and then both battalions would continue northward and link up with 101st in Bastogne.

To provide additional support, the CCA commander attached to both infantry battalions a platoon of engineers and a platoon of tank destroyers. In the meantime, the 35th Tank Battalion would wait in a general support role and "exploit" any penetration of the German defenses. Furthermore, Earnest planned a preparatory artillery barrage, and he had two battalions of artillery in direct support and one battalion of 155mm Long Toms in general support. The engineers would clear any minefields, and to secure the eastern flank they would demolish the crossing sites along the Surbich River, which was the boundary between the

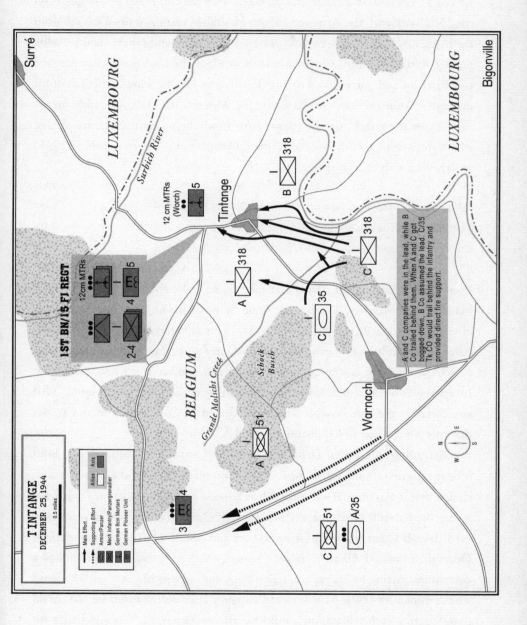

TINTANGE
DECEMBER 25, 1944

0.5 miles

Main Effort
Supporting Effort
Armor/Panzer
Mech Infantry/Panzergrenadier
German 8cm Mortars
German Pioneer Unit

Allies
Axis

Surré

LUXEMBOURG

Surbich River

12 cm MTRs
(Worch)

5

Tintange

B 318

A 318

C 318

C 35

1ST BN/15 FJ REGT

12cm MTRs

5

2-4 4

Grande Molscht Creek

Schock Busch

BELGIUM

A 51

E 4
3

Warnach

C 51

A/35

LUXEMBOURG

Bigonville

A and C companies were in the lead, while B Co trailed behind them. When A and C got bogged down, B Co assumed the lead. C/35 Tk CO would trail behind the infantry and provided direct fire support.

N W E S

26th Infantry and the 4th Armored divisions. With the bridges out, any German units in the 26th Infantry Division's area of operations would not be in position to strike CCA's vulnerable eastern flank. Next, since the two Baker companies from the 35th Tank and 51st Armored Infantry battalions had sustained casualties in the battle for Warnach, they would remain in Warnach and provide rear security. Finally, Earnest's command post would move along the N4 highway between the two battalion task forces like a roving franchise owner checking in on each of his managers. After the hard-fought battle for Warnach, CCA's commander determined that the attacks on the twenty-fifth would be primarily infantry affairs, which was a change from his original plan. Initially not everyone in his command was thrilled with that prospect.[3]

2200 Hours to Morning, Sunday, December 24, to Monday,
December 25 Headquarters, 51st Armored Infantry,
Combat Command A, 4th Armored Division Warnach, Belgium

Even though Major Dan Alanis and Lieutenant Colonel Delk Oden were both battalion commanders, Alanis sensed that he was not Oden's equal. Besides the obvious pay-grade difference, he was right. In an armored division, the tank battalion commander was senior if both an infantry and armored commander were present in the same task force, regardless of rank. However, the relationship between the two commanders was supposed to be cordial and professional. That was certainly the case between Irzyk and Cohen in Combat Command B, but that was not the case in Combat Command A.

According to Captain Dello G. Dayton, a historian who interviewed both officers, the two commanders, especially Alanis, resented each other. Dayton concluded that it was mutual jealousy. When Earnest decided to shift his focus from an armored assault to an infantry one, he kept Oden in charge of the task force, even though Oden was a tank commander and Alanis was the infantry officer. Oden then ordered Alanis to seize Tintange. With only two available infantry companies, Alanis balked at the assignment and argued his case with Earnest. The commander of the 51st Armored Infantry later claimed that he was afraid that "control of his battalion would be almost impossible" in the battle for Tintange, especially when the overall commander would have been Colonel Oden.

The general refused to hear Alanis's pleas, telling his subordinate that "he would do as he was instructed."

The arrival of 1st Battalion of the 318th Infantry solved the problem. Earnest relieved Alanis of his mission to seize Tintange and gave the assignment to 1st Battalion. Instead of Tintange, Alanis had to clear the western sector, but this time he would be his own task force commander. Motivated to succeed, Alanis instructed his small staff to write up a battalion operations order, which his S-3 section had issued to the companies at 2200 hours on the twenty-fourth.

Like CCA's deliberate clearance operation, Task Force Alanis would have two columns advancing north and abreast of each other. In the west was Charlie Company, and in the east was Able Company. In the middle was the N4 highway, which served as a boundary between the two companies. Alanis wanted Charlie Company to clear the town of Strainchamps, and supporting it was one platoon from Able Company, 35th Tank Battalion. This platoon would occupy a support-by-fire position on the high ground northeast of Strainchamps. In addition, each infantry company received one section of tank destroyers, while a platoon of engineers would clear the roads along their respective routes in advance of the attacking infantry. Last, as ordered, Charlie Company, 51st Armored Infantry, would remain behind in Warnach to recuperate and conduct rear security.

To provide better command and control, Major Alanis would move along the N4 highway and between the two columns. In the meantime, his S-3 would shadow Charlie Company in the west, while his executive officer would do the same for Able Company in the east. Satisfied with his plan, Alanis waited for the artillery barrage, which was set to begin at 0800 hours the morning of the twenty-fifth. Farther to the east, the recently arrived 1st Battalion, 318th Infantry, was also going through its troop leading procedures.[4]

0230 to 0700 Hours, Monday, December 25
Headquarters, 1st Battalion, 318th Infantry Regiment,
Attached to 4th Armored Division Tactical Assembly Area,
Eight Hundred Yards Southeast of Warnach, Belgium

Major George W. Connaughton wanted to be a battalion commander, but he had hoped he would assume command when Lieutenant Colonel Albert Tosi transferred to the division staff or took over another regiment. Alas, the Germans had decided to interject themselves in the promotion process near Ettelbruck, Luxembourg, by wounding Tosi. As the executive officer, Connaughton then took over the battalion and continued the attack to seize the town. By midday on the twenty-third, Connaughton could see that the attack had failed to wrest the town from the German defenders, and at 1730 hours on the twenty-third, the 80th Infantry Division's commander, Major General Horace L. McBride, ordered his artillery to level the town so that his forces could safely withdraw. By the morning of the twenty-fourth, Connaughton's battalion had sustained more than a hundred casualties, and most of those losses were in the line companies.

During the attack on Ettelbruck, all the rifle company commanders were either injured or killed. As a result, First Lieutenant Gordon D. Goerke replaced the wounded Captain Otto Schultz in Able Company, while Captain Reid McAllister took over for wounded First Lieutenant John Henry Scanlon in Baker Company. Charlie Company's replacement, First Lieutenant John C. Santner, was permanent since Captain Joseph F. Grady had been killed. First Lieutenant Edward E. Hueske was now the S-3, and together with Major Connaughton, they had to develop a plan to seize the town of Tintange.

The two officers faced a daunting task. Tintange sat atop a hill, and a valley separated Tintange from Warnach and their assembly area. With such severely restrictive terrain, Tintange was an infantry objective, because there were only few avenues of approach that the tanks could use, and the German defenders most likely had those approaches covered with antitank weapons. Plus, the men were dead-tired. They had been fighting nonstop for several days, and instead of resting and recuperating, III Corps had decided to send them and 2nd Battalion to help out the 4th Armored Division.

Moreover, the relief in place at Ettelbruck had not been smooth. After Colonel Lansing McVickar, the 318th Regimental commander, ordered his 3rd Battalion to replace 1st Battalion, the Germans counterattacked as the units were conducting their relief operation, and this delayed the shifting of forces. Finally, by 1900 hours on the twenty-fourth, 1st Battalion left the town of Berg and headed to Martelange by trucks. When they arrived, Connaughton met with General Earnest, who outlined a new mission for 1st Battalion. Meanwhile, Connaughton's soldiers moved out to the assembly area, and at midnight the men finally bedded down to grab some sleep on the cold ground.

While the grunts tried to snatch a few hours of shut-eye, Connaughton and his S-3 had to brief the new company commanders on the upcoming operation. For them, there would be no sleep at all. It was already 0230 hours on the twenty-fifth when the major brought his commanders together to look at the map. Lieutenant Hueske, the S-3, estimated that the battalion would have to move out from the assembly area at approximately 0700 hours in order to reach the line of departure by 0800 hours. Able and Charlie companies would lead the attack, while Baker Company would trail behind them and act as a reserve. The northern boundary for the battalion was the Warnach–Tintange road, while the southern boundary was the Sauer River. The main axis of advance would be along an azimuth of forty-five degrees. To provide additional support, 1st Battalion had eight tanks from Charlie Company, 35th Tank Battalion, under the command of Captain Eugene Berky, and the 66th Armored Field Artillery Battalion would conduct preparatory fires starting at 0800 hours. Also, CCA staff officers claimed they would receive several air sorties of P-47s, too. Connaughton hoped it would be enough to soften up the German defenders.

Connaughton and Hueske explained to the company commanders their individual key tasks. First, Able Company would occupy a piece of high ground, which was several hundred meters southwest of Tintange. From there, First Lieutenant Gordon D. Goerke would lead his company to secure the northwest sector of Tintange and then on to the hill northwest of the village. Meanwhile, First Lieutenant John C. Santner would take Charlie Company and clear out the rest of Tintange. Finally, Baker Company, under the command of Captain Reid McAllister, would push into the valley south of Tintange, and then head north up the valley and link up with Able Company northeast of town. The mission seemed simple enough, but no one had seen the ground. Since they had little time to prepare, they were relying on their maps for their reconnaissance. That planning flaw would cost them in the coming hours.[5]

0100 to 0800 Hours, Monday, December 25
Remnants of 9th Company, 3rd Battalion, 15th Fallschirmjäger Regiment
North of Bigonville, Luxembourg

The remnants of 9th Company had decided to sing that night to buoy their spirits. As his comrades murmured "Silent Night," Feldwebel Conrad Klemment looked on. He did not add his voice to the harmony of their tired voices. Christmas Eve was just another night of combat. His company was now down to only twenty-three men. Earlier that day, they thought they were marching back to the rear, but not long after they had departed the millhouse, a courier on a motorcycle caught up with them and ordered them to return. The news crushed their morale. They all knew that they were heading back into combat. The Wehrmacht needed every man in the upcoming battle, and this included Klemment's company, even though it had only twenty-three men. Like a funeral procession, they had marched back to the millhouse that afternoon, their heads hanging low.

Early Christmas morning, Oberleutnant Bertram summoned Klemment. When Klemment arrived, Bertram opened up his map, and, using a flashlight to illuminate it, he pointed to a village named Tintange as their next objective. Klemment sensed this would be his last objective.

After several hours of sleep, the men awoke around 0600 hours to set out for Tintange. While they gathered their belongings, Klemment noticed that several more *fallschirmjägers* had joined their ragtag group, but he did not recognize them. Oberleutnant Bertram soon lined them up in a column and led them to the Sauer River, which they used as a concealed approach to Tintange. It took only two hours to reach their destination.

When they arrived, Bertram learned that his company would be the reserve. Since they were not on the battle line, the senior commander did not allocate any *panzerfausts* to them. The haggard and unshaven *fallschirmjägers* staggered over to three houses, where they were to remain until the commander called them. As they walked through the village, Klemment noted that it was still relatively un-scathed despite all the fighting. He wondered how long that would last.

Tintange was situated atop a hill, and to the southwest was Warnach, where the American army was waiting. The distance between the two villages was two kilometers, but between them was a deep gorge. A narrow road connected the two towns, but it was steep. Furthermore, if the road had iced over, then it was nearly impassable. Hence Tintange was defensible, key terrain. If the Americans chose to assault the town, Klemment and the other soldiers knew it would be a tough fight. While they walked toward their homes, they wondered when the attack would begin.

The incoming rounds of 105mm artillery answered their question. The men scattered as the shells impacted and exploded. Many rushed into the closest building, which turned out to be an apartment. They searched for the basement, but when they found it, they noticed that the floorboards above the basement had wooden planks, which offered no protection against a penetrating artillery shell. Outside, the American howitzer batteries continued to pound the area. Meanwhile, one of the *fallschirmjägers* noticed a stone barn close to the house. All of them hurried back outside and into the barn, where, to their delight, they found that the ceiling was concrete. Moreover, piles of hay feed lined the walls, as if they were packed sandbags. It was a veritable ready-made bunker. Despite the artillery showering the area outside with shrapnel, the men sat down and waited. They were safe . . . for now.[6]

0700 to 1059 Hours, Monday, December 25
1st Battalion, 318th Infantry Regiment, Attached to 4th Armored Division
West of Tintange, Belgium

When the three infantry companies left their assembly area at 0700 hours, sunrise was more than ninety minutes away. The company commanders hoped that the darkness would provide some concealment for them as they approached the objective. They were mistaken. Before they reached the line of departure, the GIs started to receive small-arms and mortar fire from the direction of Tintange. Even worse, the line of departure was not a stream. Connaughton described the terrain thusly: "The country was badly cut up and very rugged. Over it were low pine trees under which there lay a several-inch mantle of snow. The line of departure, selected by map reconnaissance, which was the Grande Molscht Creek, turned out to be a gorge with steep slopes on either side. The stream itself was not an obstacle, but the slopes certainly were."

As the doughboys attempted to negotiate the sheer sides of the gorge, the

German defenders started to roll their grenades downhill, as if they were rocks in a landslide. Meanwhile, because the precipitous slope could not support tanks, Charlie Company's eight Shermans had to find another way to reach Tintange and their support-by-fire positions. It wasn't until 0830 hours that the infantry from the two assault companies started to cross the Grande Molscht Creek in force. By now the sun was up, and the *fallschirmjägers* could see the infantrymen as they trudged uphill through the deep snow. It was a shooting gallery, and a textbook example of why high ground was so important. The steady staccato of machine gun fire filled the still morning air, and scores of bodies began to fall. By 1059 hours, Combat Command A was reporting to Division G-3 that 1st Battalion was facing stiff opposition. The two assault companies, Able and Charlie, had crossed the creek, but were pinned down along the side of the hill. For now, until the tanks returned, the German machine guns had the advantage.

Despite the danger, one man chose to risk it all. Staff Sergeant William J. Murphy, a squad leader in Charlie Company, realized that the Germans would eventually pick off each of his soldiers unless he did something drastic. As the bullets zipped over his head, he scanned the area, searching for the nearby machine gun nest. After several seconds he found it. Then, lifting a grenade off his belt, he pulled the pin. Suddenly he stood up and charged toward the machine gun team, while urging his men forward. At the last second he hurled the hand grenade at the *fallschirmjägers*, who swung the machine gun toward him. Within a split second, the gunner pulled the trigger and let off a deadly burst of fire, killing Murphy instantly. Despite their final fusillade at the charging squad leader, it was too late. The grenade landed in their foxhole and exploded, wrecking the machine gun and injuring the crew. For his bravery, the army awarded Murphy a posthumous Silver Star.

Farther north along the ridge, Able Company was facing the same dilemma. The storm of lead spewing from the German machine guns had suppressed much of the company, with most of the grunts hugging the ground for dear life. One of the platoon leaders, Second Lieutenant George W. Kane, understood that if they remained glued to the side of the hill they would fail in their mission. Glancing over his right shoulder, he could see the tracers as they skipped across the snow. Every so often one would hit a man, eliciting a cry for help. Kane knew that he had to do something, or it was only a matter of time before the *fallschirmjägers* slew them all. Close by him were two of the platoons. He started to bark orders, trying to boost their flagging confidence. Finally, after several minutes, he pushed himself up and began to lead them up the ridge to their initial objective. His courage paid off, and the two platoons, despite their dwindling numbers, followed behind him. It would take time, but at least they were moving. The army would later award Lieutenant Kane the Silver Star. Unlike Sergeant Murphy, he would be alive for the ceremony.[7]

Midmorning to Early Afternoon, Monday, December 25
Charlie Company, 35th Tank Battalion, CCA, 4th Armored Division
West of Tintange, Belgium

For the first time that he could remember, 3rd Platoon's Private Orie Williams closed the hatches on the turret of his M4. Outside, it was bedlam. Though they had been in some serious scrapes in France, the crew had never seen anything like this. Mortar rounds were falling from the sky like pumice stones from an exploding volcano, and everyone was afraid that one might land right inside the turret. If that happened, the next crew would have to scrape Williams's charred remains from inside the tank like grease on a fryer.

Meanwhile, Captain Eugene Berky, the Charlie Company commander, knew he had to do something. As the intensity of the battle increased, chatter jammed his radio. Unfortunately the banks around Grande Molscht were too sheer, and therefore he could not drive across the creek. The only place he could cross was the bridge, and he knew the Germans had a big, fat target on that. On the other hand, his tanks were idle, and men from the 318th were dying on the ridge south of Tintange. Resolved to act, he ordered his seven tanks to cross the bridge.

The two platoons started to rumble down toward the Grande Molscht. As they began their descent, Private Williams noticed that one of his crew appeared addled and nervous. The rattled tanker was a replacement, and Williams chalked it up to inexperience in combat. It was worse than that. The soldier was claustrophobic. Between the locked-down hatches and the popping and booming of 12cm mortar rounds outside, the tension was too much for the nameless newbie. After they crossed the bridge and started to drive back up the hill, he cracked.

Williams described what happened next in a postwar interview: "[H]e just started screaming, threw the hatch open, jumped out of the tank and was screaming all the way. Every step he was taking, he was just running just as fast as he could. [He] run [sic] back down the way we had come, so we don't ever know— we never heard from him again. We don't know what happened to him, but he just couldn't stand it in there being claustrophobic."

Despite this setback, Williams's tank continued to roll forward. The German mortar crews did score hits on two of the vehicles, but the damage was negligible. Second Lieutenant Harold Madison, 3rd Platoon leader, then pushed his tanks toward the eastern flank to provide support to the beleaguered infantry from the 318th. The fight was far from over, but at least the tanks had arrived on the right side of the Grande Molscht.[8]

Midmorning to 1130 Hours, Monday, December 25
Baker Company, 1st Battalion, 318th Infantry, CCA, 4th Armored Division
West of Tintange, Belgium

Captain Reid McAllister had been the company commander for Baker Company for only twenty-four hours, and he was itching to do something. His unit was in the reserve, behind the two assault companies. However, despite its position in the rear, it was close enough to the German lines that it was sustaining casualties from machine guns, mortars, and one self-propelled gun. He received word that both assault companies were pinned down on the slopes that led to Tintange.

Thinking he could break the deadlock, McAllister requested permission to push through Able and Charlie companies and assume the vanguard. After several minutes, the battalion commander granted his request. McAllister's plan was a basic single envelopment. He would fix the defenders with two of his platoons, and then flank them with his 3rd Platoon. Satisfied with his basic scheme of maneuver, he explained to his platoon leaders his concept of operations, and after the lieutenants passed along the plan, he signaled his company to advance toward Tintange.

Almost immediately, the boys from Baker Company started to take casualties. Private Edward Bredbenner, a rifleman, remembered that the company was already down to fifty-eight men when they stepped off that morning for the assault. As they pushed through the woods, Bredbenner felt something bite him in the ear and neck. He recalled that it was a "burp gun" that hit him, the force of the impact knocking off his helmet. He felt his neck and discovered that the towel he had wrapped around it was torn from a bullet graze. A nearby medic slapped on a bandage and told him to keep fighting.

Like a good soldier, Bredbenner ignored the pain and kept moving forward. Close by were the tanks from Charlie Company, but their presence did not deter the *fallschirmjägers* from turning the dell into a killing ground. The air was full of bullets zipping and whipping through the trees. Occasionally one round would ricochet off of a trunk or a soldier and hit someone else. Above his head, the German artillery shells were shattering and smashing the evergreen pines with tree bursts, spraying wooden shards that were as lethal as the metal bits that had split them.

Finally, one exploded over Bredbenner and a splinter nailed him in the leg, ripping open his thigh. Another medic rushed to his side and quickly poured sulfa powder on the wound and then bandaged it. Luckily the gash did not prevent him from walking, but it was enough for the medic, who ordered him to head back to the rear. Bredbenner nodded his head and started to stagger back toward the battalion aid station. Apparently, when the American infantry pushed over the creek, they had bypassed pockets of German resistance, and many of these fanatical *fallschirmjägers* continued to snipe at the soldiers who were trying to return to the support areas. As a result, stretcher bearers failed to reach many of the seriously wounded men in forward lines. Bredbenner found two other walking wounded, and together they resumed their slog back to the rear. For them, the war was almost over. The rest of Baker Company had to stay put and slug it out with the Germans, and by 1100 hours, the battle for Tintange had reached a stalemate.

At 1130 hours, CCA reported to the division that "318 receiving estimated infantry company counterattack vicinity Tintange."

To Major Connaughton, 1st Battalion and his attached tankers needed some help if they were going to break the back of the German defense. Luckily, help was on the way.[9]

0955 to 1250 Hours, Monday, December 25
Communications Between 3rd Battalion and the 15th Fallschirmjäger Regiment

While 1st Battalion, 318th Infantry, struggled to take Tintange, radio traffic between the 15th Fallschirmjäger Regiment and its 3rd Battalion indicated that the German defenses were beginning to unravel. The U.S. Army's 3254th Signal Service Company, which was attached to VIII Corps, had been intercepting German tactical communication since the start of the German offensive.

At 0955 hours, American signal analysts listened in on one conversation between the two German headquarters. "Twenty-five [U.S.] tanks have attacked the flank of the battalion," the German voice reported. Unbeknownst to the 3254th, CCA's two-pronged attack had begun, and one of the columns was pushing north along the N4 Bastogne–Arlon highway near Hollange.

Several minutes later, the analyst intercepted another transmission to the command post in Harlange. "Reserve for attack not on hand." The translator quickly deciphered the message and handed it over to the analyst.

At 1047 hours, the *fallschirmjäger* regiment finally had an answer for its beleaguered battalion near Hollange. "Change positions. Evacuate casualties. No contact with 2nd Battalion. Haey at T." It didn't take long for the soldier to translate the message. The analyst did not know who or what Haey was, but when he looked at the map, he deduced that the town of Tintange was probably the "T" mentioned in the transmission. By this time, thanks to CCA's attack on the twenty-fourth, 2nd Battalion was shattered, but the staff officers of the 15th Fallschirmjäger Regiment did not know that yet.

Thirteen minutes later, the signal operators picked up another voice message from the regiment to 3rd Battalion. It was terse. "Reorganize and hold positions." The operator jotted down the message for dissemination.

At 1130 hours, the battalion finally replied to regiment, but the news was bleak. "Enemy has taken point 488." Indeed, CCA's western column had rolled past the Strainchamps–Tintange road, which was Point 488 on German military maps.

Regiment immediately responded. "Build strongpoints and hold to the end." The translator probably grimaced when he heard that verbal order. The fatalism was a sign that the German positions were crumbling.

The *fallschirmjäger* regimental radio operator then added, "*Panzerschrecks* are coming. What else do you want?"

There was no reply from 3rd Battalion. Several minutes before noon, the regiment called the battalion again to let them know that the regiment had not forgotten them. "*Panzerschrecks* and reinforcements going to front lines."

An hour later, the signal operators from the 3254th picked up one more message. "Collect your units and stop. 2nd Battalion is in a mess," the German soldier ordered over the command net.

To the American analyst, the German units possibly were retreating, and as a result, the staff at the regimental headquarters was ordering them to consolidate and hold. Moreover, 2nd Battalion was more than a mess. It was a battalion in name only. In reality, the only battalion that still was a viable fighting force was 1st Battalion in Tintange. The U.S. Army Air Force, though, was about to change that fact.[10]

1200 to 1315 hours, Monday, December 25
377th Fighter Squadron, 362nd Fighter Group
Over Tintange, Belgium

Flying over Tintange was a flight of eight P-47s. Loaded for battle, the planes carried sixteen five-hundred-pound general-purpose bombs, eight five-hundred-pound incendiary bombs, and sixteen rockets. They had taken off from their airfield at Étain, France, at 1120 hours, and when they arrived over the battlefield, the ground controller, "Pink Pig," vectored them toward a convoy southwest of Bastogne. For several minutes, the Jugs circled over the reported target area, but they did not find any German convoy.

"Pink Pig" then handed them off to "Beagle," another ground controller. "Beagle" knew CCA was waging a battle for Tintange, and so he radioed the coordinates to the pilots. This time the Thunderbolts hit the jackpot. The P-47s arrived on station at 1200 hours, and almost immediately went to work on the German defenders. For more than an hour, the Jugs dived and strafed the town. When it was over, they had dropped all their bombs and shot all of their rockets, noting that six fires had broken out inside the village. Though they did not observe any secondary explosions, they did see the American infantry reach the outskirts of the town as they pulled away and returned to base. For the Germans below, the arrival of the dreaded jabos was the decisive point in the battle.

The pilots of the 362nd Fighter Group would fly a total of nine missions in support of III Corps on the twenty-fifth, and many of those ended up supporting the men of the 4th Armored Division. Each squadron conducted three missions throughout the day, and the results were devastating for the Wehrmacht. By the end of the day, the pilots of the 377th reported that they had destroyed fifteen motor trucks, one tank, and one bridge. Not to be outdone, the Jug drivers of the 378th added another seventy-three trucks to their total. In addition, they claimed two half-tracks destroyed, six artillery pieces knocked out, a supply dump set ablaze, and six structures flattened. Finally, the 379th fighter jockeys racked up an impressive total, too: twenty-four trucks splattered, three tanks obliterated, and one self-propelled gun annihilated. Plus, one of the pilots scored an aerial kill by shooting down a Bf 109 fighter.[11]

1200 to 1430 Hours, Monday, December 25
Remnants of 9th Company, 3rd Battalion, 15th Fallschirmjäger Regiment
North of Bigonville, Luxembourg

For several hours, the American artillery had pummeled the town of Tintange. Suddenly it stopped. Klemment stepped outside to speak to a guard who was standing on the barn's balcony. Both wondered why the artillery had ceased. Far off in the distance, they detected the droning of radial engines, quickly dashing their hopes that the attack had ended. On the contrary, the U.S. Army Air Force had upped the ante with the introduction of fighter-bombers.

Soon the area around the barn became a killing ground. Klemment noticed that the American aircraft were operating with impunity, and he wished that the *fallschirmjägers* had larger antiaircraft artillery. However, all they had were light machine guns, which were ineffectual against the fast-flying Thunderbolts. Within minutes, American artillery rejoined the fight. Everywhere was death and destruction.

As they huddled inside the barn, Klemment and the survivors of 9th Company were pondering their potential fate when the guard appeared again with a member of the Volkssturm. The Volkssturm were older men and younger boys who were either too old or too young to serve in the regular army, but due to the losses incurred by the Wehrmacht, they were recruited for a variety of subsidiary roles so that military-age males could serve in line units. (By the end of the war, the Volkssturm were also on the front line.) Apparently the air raid had caught the Volkssturm soldier in the village as he was transporting a supply of six *panzerfausts* in a handcart to another unit. Klemment wished he would hand over the *panzerfausts* to them, because he knew the Americans had tanks, and Klemment's unit had nothing in their arsenal to stop the metal monsters. At least, thought Klemment, the six *panzerfausts* would offer them a fighting chance.

Later a messenger arrived and told them that they were withdrawing, and they would leave around dusk. Hearing the news, Klemment and Oberleutnant Bertram realized that the defenses around Tintange were breaking, and it was only a matter of time before the American tanks were driving up and down the village streets. They hoped that they would be long gone before that happened.

During a lull in the firestorm, the Volkssturm soldier then ran out to make sure that the jabos had not blown his cart of *panzerfausts* into tiny bits. Meanwhile, Klemment watched from the barn window a group of *fallschirmjägers* falling back to the east.

He shouted to the last man he saw, a machine gunner, asking him, "What is going on?"

In his memoirs, Klemment then described what happened next:

He [the machine gunner] stopped and turned around. Before he could respond, he suddenly ducked down and ran away. Fighter-bomber aircraft swooped overhead as we cursed the comrade for not telling us what was transpiring. Then a huge explosion hit. The house and barn were struck as if by a giant fist. The cows frantically cried out and pulled at their chains to escape. In my subconscious I could hear hooves kicking the walls and doors. We were terrified, but the ceilings and walls did not give. We were lucky. The bomb that was aimed at our house flew along its flat trajectory too high, over the house, and hit the main road behind us, which was three meters at a higher elevation. Only the explosive cone hit the top of the roof. The old Volkssturm man came running into the house yelling that the attack fighter-aircraft shot up his cart full of Panzerfausts and set them on fire. Again artillery fire began.

Fortunately, that strafing pass was the last one. For a few more minutes, the survivors of 9th Company waited in the barn. Then a series of detonations, in quick succession, rocked the building. Klemment figured it was the *panzerfausts* exploding. Shortly thereafter, a nearby machine gun opened up on some unknown target.

Then the guard reappeared, spluttering to Klemment and the others like a man who had seen the devil, "The Americans have broken through! An American tank is moving forward behind the house right below us!"

Klemment and the rest of the *fallschirmjägers* scrambled to find their weapons. One of them then ran toward the back door and discovered that something had fallen in front of it during the bombing raids, which prevented anyone from opening it from the inside. Even worse, when they tried to squeeze through the few windows, they found that all of them had bars on them like a jailhouse. They were trapped.

Soon Klemment and the others heard the sounds of American English from the front of the barn. Seconds later gunshots rang out, and Klemment noticed tracers zipping by the barn wall. This was it, he thought. The American gangsters would execute him and his comrades inside the barn. Then a voice called out to his group, ordering them to disarm and come out from the back of the building with their hands above their heads. One of the *fallschirmjägers*, who knew some English, acted as an interpreter and translated for the group. All of them looked at one another. Finally, one by one, they started to destroy their weapons. Klemment then took his MG 42, removed the bolt, and tossed it onto a pile of hay.

"Let's go! Come on!" a GI barked, as if the *fallschirmjägers* were unruly convicts.

When the survivors of 9th Company were finished smashing their weapons, they started to file outside through the front door, where the American infantry were waiting. The tired and haggard-looking GIs were not interested in taking lives; they only wanted souvenirs. When they were through searching their defeated foes, the soldiers prodded the *fallschirmjägers* toward another part of town, where they would process them and then send them to a makeshift prison camp near Arlon. Klemment had survived the battle and would return to Germany after the war. At 1430 hours, 1st Battalion was reporting to CCA that the battle for Tintange was over. As for Tintange, Klemment remarked, "Compared to this morning, I could not recognize the village. Eighty percent of the village was in ruins." By choosing to defend from inside the town, the Germans had forced the Americans to level the village to capture it. Sadly, Tintange would not be the last to suffer this fate.[12]

Mid- to Late Afternoon, Monday, December 25
Elements of the 5th Fallschirmjäger Heavy-Mortar Battalion,
5th Fallschirmjäger Division
North of Tintange, Belgium

Mortarman Alfred Worch and the rest of his team had been hanging mortar rounds for much of the day. Initially their targets were Warnach, Sainlez, and the road that linked them, but as the fighting dragged on, Worch adjusted the dial on his mortar tube so that "the firing elevations became steeper and the loads smaller." In simple terms, the higher elevations on the tubes meant the Americans were getting closer and closer. Eventually the Americans would be too close, and Worch's team would have to break down the tubes and withdraw. As morning became afternoon, Worch wondered when that time would come.

Not long after the fighter-bombers ravaged Tintange, the 12cm mortar teams received another fire mission. This time they would have to adjust the dials so that they were firing the guns at maximum elevation. When Worch heard that, he estimated that the American forces were only five hundred meters from his position.

Unbeknownst to Worch, Baker Company, 318th Infantry, together with the tanks from Charlie Company, 35th Tank Battalion, had gained a foothold thanks to the timely air support. Captain McAllister's plan was working. The majority of the German forces were fixated on his two platoons that were mounting a frontal assault. In doing so, they had revealed their locations to 3rd Platoon, which was flanking them from the east.

As a result, 3rd Platoon surprised the German defenders and started to roll up each position, one after the other. They even captured the self-propelled gun

258 ★ PATTON AT THE BATTLE OF THE BULGE

intact. Second Lieutenant Hal C. Mitchell then led his platoon and assaulted one of the machine gun positions that was holding up the rest of the battalion. By fire and maneuver, his men destroyed the machine gun and slew the gunners. He then guided the tanks through the town, and in one case personally shot and killed a *panzerschreck* team.

Suddenly one of the tanks reached the edge of Tintange, and its gunner discovered Worch's mortar team in the distance. It opened fire. Luckily for Worch, the limited cover and the long range were enough to keep them safe, and the first few rounds from the Sherman did little damage. Still, they all knew it was time to depart. Their section leader ordered them to disassemble the 12cm Granatwerfer and establish a new firing position somewhere near the town of Surré, which was several kilometers northeast of their current location. Fortunately they had no ammunition left, so that was one less thing to carry.

Suddenly everything started to go wrong. The baseplate, which affixed the massive tube into the ground like an anchor, was frozen solid in the dirt, as if it had become part of the soil. For a few precious seconds the men chipped away at the ground, trying to free it, but it was like hammering away at bedrock without a pick. It was useless. Finally one of the men grabbed a grenade, pulled the safety, and dropped it on the baseplate. Amazingly, it worked. The resultant explosion was enough to break up the earth around the baseplate, but it was not enough to damage it.

Unfortunately, that was not the only minor disaster. The driver on the captured American half-track yelled out to his comrades that the clutch was not engaging the gears. Hence, the half-track was going nowhere. If they had time, they might have been able to fix it, but time was something they did not have. The Shermans were closing in on them, firing away. Their only option was to pull the mortar themselves.

The six-man section began to haul the ponderous mortar down the side of the hill and toward the Surbich River. Because it didn't have brakes, the men had to make sure the cumbersome contraption didn't pick up speed as they descended. Otherwise inertia would have taken over, and the mortar would have rolled right over them. It was a delicate balance. Finally, after several backbreaking hours, they reached the river and lugged the Granatwerfer across it. For them, the battle for Tintange was over. Survival was all that mattered now.[13]

0800 to 1700 Hours, Monday, December 25
Headquarters, Combat Command A, 4th Armored Division
Somewhere on the Bastogne–Arlon Highway,
Between Warnach and Strainchamps, Belgium

Brigadier General Herbert L. Earnest did not want any foul-ups on Christmas, and so he did everything he could to make sure that the mission would be successful with a minimal amount of casualties. At 0800 hours, the attack began with an artillery bombardment. Earnest soon realized that the heavy fighting would be in Tintange, where the battalion from the 318th ran into a heavily defended German strongpoint atop a mountain.

Fortunately, according to radio reports, the fighting in Task Force Alanis's sector was progressing according to plan. Charlie Company, 51st Armored Infantry, under the command of First Lieutenant Walter E. Green, dispatched a single platoon into Strainchamps, while providing overwatch was a platoon from Able Company, 35th Tank Battalion. The clearance operation was short, and by 0930 hours, Charlie Company reported that Strainchamps was now under American control. Meanwhile, Able Company, 51st Armored Infantry, which was east of the N4, was receiving some mortar fire and small-arms fire as it advanced northward. Eighty minutes later, the tankers from Able Company, 35th Tank Battalion, radioed to CCA that they had reached the Strainchamps–Honville road. In the meantime, Green's Charlie Company discovered a minefield at the intersection of the Tintange–Strainchamps road and the N4. Together with the attached engineers, they were clearing it.

Around noon, General Earnest entertained a guest when General Patton decided to pay him a visit. Like all great generals, Patton enjoyed being with the troops, and throughout the twenty-fifth, his mobile command post was on the move, dropping by to see how the battle was progressing and to boost the morale of the soldiers. Earlier, he had written a Christmas greeting for the troops: "To each officer and soldier in the Third United States Army, I wish a Merry Christmas. I have full confidence in your courage, devotion to duty, and skill in battle. We march in our might to complete victory. May God's blessing rest upon each of you on this Christmas Day."

Technician Grade Five Eric L. Peterson, who drove the S-3 operation's half-track for the 51st Armored Infantry, remembered the visit. He remarked, "I thought it was quite a thrill to see him that close."

While Peterson stood next to him, Patton then faced the troops that were nearby and shouted, "Give 'em hell, boys! Give 'em hell!"

For Peterson and the rest of the GIs, Patton's visit was a boon to morale. The driver later said, "It gave us all a little more pep after that." It impressed Peterson that Patton was willing to face the same dangers and share the same sacrifices as the men. The half-track operator recalled that artillery was still falling when Patton arrived, and that did not deter him from seeing the troops.

Soon after Patton left, at around 1230 hours, Charlie Company, 51st Armored Infantry, reported that they had pushed ahead and were approaching a nameless patch of woods south of the village of Parque. In addition, they had overrun a platoon position of *fallschirmjäger* pioneers, and in the aftermath, the armored infantry had captured several German soldiers. The prisoners later revealed that they were from 4th Company, 5th Fallschirmjäger Pioneer Battalion.

Along the east side of the N4, Able Company, 51st Armored Infantry, stumbled into a German battle position, entrenched along the edge of the Bois de Melch. Instead of wasting precious infantry lives in a costly assault, Captain Ridley's light tanks from Dog Company, 35th Tank Battalion, occupied an attack-by-fire position and opened up with all their machine guns. The fiery fusillade was a scythe that cut down the few German defenders. By 1205 hours, few *fallschirmjägers* remained who were capable of resistance, and Able Company, 51st Infantry, easily captured the battle position. By 1410 hours, the armored infantry from Able had reached their portion of the Strainchamps–Honville road.

By now, General Earnest felt better about the day's operation. After a bloody brawl, Tintange had fallen to Connaughton's 1st Battalion, and by 1430 hours, the 318th was reporting that the Germans had lost the battle for Tintange and were surrendering in large numbers. In the western portion of CCA's area of operations, Task Force Alanis was nearing the town of Hollange, which was only eight kilometers south of the 101st Airborne's perimeter.

This time the Germans were waiting, and they opened fire on the forward elements of Lieutenant Green's Charlie Company at 1630 hours. In response, Green ordered an infantry patrol to reconnoiter the area, and his soldiers came under direct fire at 1700 hours. By then Earnest knew it was too late to conduct a deliberate attack on Hollange. He did not want a repeat of Warnach, where the battle had raged all through the night, but no real progress was made until the following day. Thus, the seizure of Hollange would have to wait until the morning of the twenty-sixth.

Despite the small setback, Combat Command A had performed well. When the final tally was complete at 2205 hours that night, the S-2 section counted more than two hundred prisoners of war. In addition, they estimated that the Germans had sustained an additional three hundred casualties in wounded and killed. Also, CCA had destroyed two heavy mortars, four trucks, and four heavy machine guns. Next, the soldiers of CCA had recaptured one U.S. Army truck, three jeeps, and three half-tracks. In short, Earnest's command had wrecked another *fallschirmjäger* battalion. Generalmajor Ludwig Heilmann, the commander of the 5th Fallschirmjäger Division, was running out of men, and unfortunately for him, the 4th Armored Division was far from finished. The next move would be to the west of CCA. Major General Hugh Gaffey, the division commander, still wanted Chaumont, and he was willing to try again with CCB to take it.[14]

CHAPTER 9

CHAUMONT II

| DECEMBER 25, 1944 |

★ ★ ★ ★ ★

"My men followed boldly and blindly."

—*Second Lieutenant Robert Connor, 1st Platoon, George Company,*
318th Infantry Regiment

2300 Hours to Early Morning, Sunday, December 24, to Monday,
December 25 Headquarters, 8th Tank Battalion,
4th Armored Division Near Burnon, Belgium

Major Albin F. Irzyk was savoring the moment. Several lieutenant colonels and a bevy of majors and captains had turned out to see him conduct a briefing. For the next mission, he would be their commander. At the age of only twenty-seven, he had been selected by Brigadier General Holmes Dager to develop and execute a massive operation involving more than a thousand soldiers. It was an impressive accomplishment for an officer his age and a sign he had earned Dager's trust.

Irzyk would serve as the commander on the ground, leading several battalions besides his own. The newest addition was 2nd Battalion, 318th Infantry Regiment, under the command of Lieutenant Colonel Glenn H. Gardner. Supporting him would be three battalions of artillery: the 22nd and 253rd Armored Field battalions, and 776th Field Artillery Battalion. In conjunction with those units, Irzyk could also call on the 10th Armored Infantry, a company of tank destroyers and engineers, and Baker Troop from the 25th Cavalry.

His mission was simple: Seize Chaumont and continue the advance to Bastogne to link up with the 101st Airborne Division. Irzyk recalled the last time he tried to capture Chaumont. Four German Tigers had given the Eight Ballers a bloody nose, and several of his tanks were abandoned in the town. Worse, the 10th Armored Battalion had suffered horrendous casualties, forcing III Corps to augment Dager's combat command with an additional infantry battalion.

Now Irzyk had to deploy this battalion. Like his own, 2nd Battalion, 318th Infantry, had suffered some losses over the past few days, fighting with 1st Battalion at Ettelbruck. Yet it was in better shape than the 10th Armored Infantry, and therefore would assume the main effort in the upcoming operation.

Irzyk directed the assembled officers' attention to his map. First, Gardner's battalion would conduct a preliminary operation to clear the Lambay-Chênet Woods, which were between Burnon and Chaumont. German ambush teams had ravaged Irzyk's column on the twenty-third from positions inside those woods, and he now wanted it purged of Germans before the rest of his force arrived. To support his grunts, Irzyk would augment the battalion with Lieutenant Leonard Kieley's Able Company's medium tanks.

Once Gardner's soldiers had cleared the woods, the rest of CCB would advance north. In the west, Major Harold Cohen's 10th Armored Infantry would press ahead and occupy the Bois Saint-Hubert Woods, northwest of Chaumont. To assist them, Lieutenant Paul Stephenson's Charlie Company, 8th Tank Battalion, would provide additional direct fire support to Cohen's grunts. Meanwhile, in the east, 2nd Battalion, 318th Infantry, would move ahead and seize Chaumont, while securing the high ground to the northeast. To avoid a replay of the twenty-third, Irzyk decided to deny that key terrain from any potential German counterattack. Next, Irzyk's own Baker Company would act as a reserve, while Lieutenant Roy Erdmann's light tank company would go where Irzyk needed it.

Colonel Gardner listened as Irzyk outlined his plan. Gardner was not an arrogant officer. He understood his role in an armored unit, and he did not mind taking orders from a major. Irzyk clearly had General Dager's confidence, and so the colonel was willing to hear out the young officer. In addition, Irzyk knew the ground. Gardner did not, and he knew the ground was everything in land warfare. When Gardner arrived, he approached Irzyk and said, "I was told to report to you and to be attached to you for the rest of the operation to Bastogne."

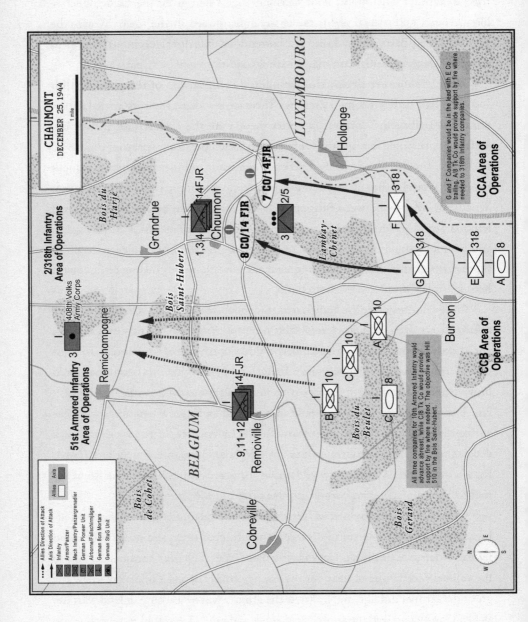

CHAUMONT
DECEMBER 25, 1944

1 mile

LUXEMBOURG

Hollange

G and F Companies would be in the lead with E Co
trailing. A/8 Tk Co would provide support by fire where
needed to 318th Infantry companies.

CCA Area of Operations

7 CO/14 FJR

14 FJR

Chaumont

2/5

8 CO/14 FJR

3

Lambay-Chenet

2/318th Infantry Area of Operations

Bois du Harjé

Grandrue

1,3,4

F | 318

I | 318

E | 318

A | 8

G | 318

51st Armored Infantry Area of Operations 3

408th Volks Army Corps

Remichampagne

Bois Saint-Hubert

BELGIUM

Bois de Cohet

Bois du Beulet

14 FJR

9,11-12

Remoiville

B | 10

C | 10

A | 10

A | 10

C | 8

Burnon

Cobreville

Bois Gerard

CCB Area of Operations

All three companies for 10th Armored Infantry would
advance abreast, while C/8 Tk Co would provide
support by fire where needed. The objective was Hill
510 in the Bois Saint-Hubert.

Allies Direction of Attack
Axis Direction of Attack
Infantry
Armor/Panzer
Mech Infantry/Panzergrenadier
German Pioneer Unit
Airborne/Fallschirmjäger
German 8cm Mortars
German StuG Unit

Allies
Axis

N
W — E
S

Gardner had assumed command of his battalion in October 1944 while it was fighting in the Moselle River region of France. For a battalion commander in the 318th, that was a long time. Since arriving in France in August, the 318th had lost a regimental commander and several battalion commanders. In fact, when he assumed command of 2nd Battalion, Gardner was a senior captain. In less than two months, because of attrition, he was now a lieutenant colonel.

After the meeting ended, Gardner crafted his portion of the plan with his S-3, Captain Prentiss Foreman. It would be a reverse wedge with Captain Ernest M. Stalling's George Company on the western flank and First Lieutenant John R. Singleton's Fox Company on the eastern flank. Trailing behind would be Captain Rex O. Kirkman's Easy Company. For armor support, Gardner had the eight medium tanks from the 8th Tank Battalion.

Gardner's one chief concern was his eastern flank. A narrow creek served as the boundary between him and Combat Command A, which also was advancing simultaneously and was supposed to keep abreast of CCB. However, if CCA got bogged down, then its absence would expose Gardner's eastern flank. That said, he had no ability to influence CCA's outcome, and therefore all he could do was maintain situational awareness on his vulnerable right flank.

Major Harold Cohen, commander of the 10th Armored Infantry, also was conducting troop-leading procedures following Irzyk's briefing. Fortunately, his troops did not have to return to Chaumont. His Able Company had lost all of its officers in that attack, and he did not want to subject his men to another violent street fight. For the Christmas offensive, he would assign each company a separate axis of advance. From west to east it would be Baker Company, then Charlie Company, and finally Able Company. The final objective was Hill 510 in the Bois Saint-Hubert Woods, along its northern edge. From there they could dominate the surrounding area. Though Cohen expected contact, he did not assess that the main German battle positions would be along his axis of advance. Everyone estimated that the German forces would be in Chaumont. However, in case he ran into significant opposition, he had seven tanks from the 8th Tank Battalion to bail him out.

Major Irzyk scheduled the first phase of the operation to commence at approximately 0850 hours, fifteen minutes after sunrise. The next phase, the attack on Chaumont, would not begin until 2nd Battalion had mopped up the Lambay-

Chênet Woods. Prior to the attack on Chaumont, Irzyk planned a massive bombardment using all three battalions of artillery at his disposal. Any German *fallschirmjäger* not in a foxhole or a cellar would be shredded to bits so that Irzyk's tankers and infantry could march into Chaumont and face only halfhearted resistance. As a commander, Irzyk would rather have expended firepower than waste manpower to take an objective.[1]

Late Evening to Early Morning, Sunday, December 24,
to Monday, December 25 Inside Chaumont, Belgium

As the Americans planned their next attack, the German defenders of Chaumont celebrated Christmas. In one home, the *fallschirmjägers* gathered around and drunkenly sang carols.

Upstairs, hidden away, was Private Bruce Fenchel. The last twenty-four hours had been nerve-racking for the young tanker. After 8th Tank Battalion had withdrawn from Chaumont, leaving him behind, the wounded Fenchel had found a family who was willing to hide him in their house. Stowed away up in their attic, he listened as German soldiers intermittently entered downstairs and asked the family questions. When Christmas Eve celebrations commenced, he eavesdropped on their singing. Though he spoke no German, he sensed that some of the songs were about defeating the Americans and throwing them back into the sea. He wondered whether his fellow tankers would return to liberate Chaumont.

Then a minor miracle happened. Fenchel described it in a postwar interview:

> And then all of a sudden, it became very still, and I heard footsteps on the stairs. And I thought, Well, I have seen my last Christmas. Instead, it was a—it was a young girl—I would assume fifteen or sixteen—that opened the attic door, and in her broken English, she said, "We asked the Germans if they would leave the bar so we could celebrate Christmas Eve." And I did go downstairs with her, and I ate Christmas Eve dinner, supper, whatever, with them. It consisted of sweet butter, which is just butter without salt, black bread, and head cheese. And for the younger people that don't know what head cheese is, it is whatever meat they can

salvage off a hog's head, and it is put into a gelatin, and then it's sliced. That was—that was the total dinner. And I even got so bold that I taught them a card game, and we played cards till the wee hours on Christmas morning and then [I went] back up to my attic.

Elsewhere in Chaumont, Lozet-Maria Gustin prayed for an end to the fighting. The battle had cost her family dearly. Her aunt and uncle were injured by an artillery round that had exploded and shattered the wall of their stable. A neighbor had died from artillery shrapnel wounds. When the Germans returned the night of the twenty-third, Gustin remarked that the *fallschirmjägers* were "looking more triumphant than ever." Early Christmas morning, everyone huddled in their cellars or hidden in someone else's attic pondered what would happen next.[2]

Early Morning, Monday, December 25 Headquarters,
14th Fallschirmjäger Regiment,
5th Fallschirmjäger Division Hompré, Belgium

Oberst Arno Schimmel's regiment was dying. After more than ten days of constant combat, the 14th Fallschirmjäger Regiment was a shadow of its former self. On the previous evening, his units were stretched across several kilometers like a rubber band about to snap. 1st Battalion's area of operations extended from the town of Liverchamps to Chaumont, while the vestiges of 2nd Battalion occupied battle positions between Hollange and the Lambay-Chênet Woods. 3rd Battalion, under Major Ferdinand Ebel, was the only force relatively intact, and was defending the villages of Sure Nives, Cobreville, Remoiville, and Vaux-lez-Rosières. Behind them, Schimmel had established his headquarters in the town of Hompré.

In front of American forces in the Lambay-Chênet Woods were two depleted German companies from 2nd Battalion. To buttress these companies were antitank teams from 2nd Company, 5th Antitank Battalion, under the command of Leutnant Thomas. Thomas, even though he was a company commander, was in charge of only one platoon. The other two platoons had remained behind in Holland. 3rd Platoon had thirty-six men, broken down into six *panzerschreck* teams with a large number of disposable *panzerfausts*. To maximize their effectiveness, Thomas had positioned his AT teams in and around the town of Chaumont.

Coupled with the AT teams were several elements from several different units. Leutnant Wenden had established his 1st Company battle position inside Chaumont and in the woods directly east of the town. With Wenden's 1st Company were elements of 3rd and 4th companies, 14th Fallschirmjäger Regiment. To provide additional long-range indirect- and direct-fire capability, the 408th Volks Artillery Corps had positioned a battery of four 7.5cm towed dual-purpose howitzers on the ridge, northwest of Chaumont. From there, the battery could dominate Chaumont and the roads leading into it. For indirect artillery support, he had several howitzer batteries located outside of Assenois. Sadly, the Tiger tanks and StuGs were gone.

Morale had collapsed. For several days the men had had little to eat, because the supply trucks and wagons couldn't reach them. Many were now smoldering wrecks abandoned along the roadsides of southern Belgium and northern Luxembourg. The American fighter-bombers had succeeded in disrupting the German supply chain. In addition, the constant artillery harassment had begun to wear down the German defenders. Many who had survived the fighting on the twenty-third did not want to repeat that hellish experience when the heavens had rained fire on them. In short, it was a mentally broken, hodgepodge force that did not have the necessary combat power nor motivation to stop CCB. Still, they had little choice but to soldier on and fight. On the morning of the twenty-fifth, the *fallschirmjägers* once again cocked their bolts back to the rear on their rifles and closed the feed trays on their machine guns while they waited for the American onslaught.[3]

0850 to 1113 Hours, Monday, December 25
Headquarters Tank, 8th Tank Battalion, CCB, 4th Armored Division
Near the Lambay-Chênet Woods, Belgium

At 0850 hours, Major Albin Irzyk radioed to Combat Command B, "We have jumped off. Arty is all set. Air is working for us. Clearing woods on right flank."

As planned, Captain Stalling's George Company and Lieutenant Singleton's Fox Company stepped off and proceeded to clear the Lambay-Chênet Woods.

George Company's axis of advance was on the western flank, while Fox Company was on the eastern flank. Irzyk was confident that Colonel Gardner's battalion would accomplish the mission. To ensure success, all of the battalion and company commanders had conducted a cursory ground reconnaissance that morning before the attack, which allowed the officers of 2nd Battalion, 318th Infantry, to see their objective up close.

In an interview several weeks after the battle, Colonel Gardner described the intensity of the fighting. "It was difficult to oust the paratroopers out of their foxholes and many were bayoneted while still in them."

Irzyk soon realized that the GIs needed help. Most of the resistance was machine gun and rifle fire, but fortunately not incoming rockets from *panzerfausts* or *panzerschrecks*. Therefore, the commander of 8th Tank Battalion ordered Lieutenant Erdmann to dispatch two platoons of his M5 Stuart light tanks to sweep the woods with their machine guns. The tanks rolled forward and opened fire. Thanks to the withering fusillade from the tanks, the doughs got up and moved forward again.

At 1030 hours, Irzyk received a message from Colonel Gardner: "Right [Fox] company through the woods. Second company [George] 150 yards from the north edge of woods."

That was signal for Albin Irzyk. He then ordered his fire-support officer to initiate the massive barrage they had planned. Able 1-6, the fire support coordinator, rang up the fire direction center at 1045 hours. "Oasis, this is Able 1-6. Fire the following concentrations: One eleven . . . Break . . . One twelve . . . Break . . . One-oh-eight . . . Break . . . One-oh-nine . . . Break . . . One fifteen . . . Break . . . One sixteen . . . Break . . . One seventeen . . . Break . . . One eighteen . . . Over," he said.

The FDC then repeated the transmission to ensure that they had copied the right targets. Able 1-6 then confirmed their fire mission. For several minutes the cannon cockers adjusted their tubes and then loaded up their high-explosive shells. The forward observers had designated the targets on the twenty-third, so they were confident that the barrage would land in the right place.

While the gun bunnies readied their 105mm tubes of destruction, Irzyk got back on the radio and reported to CCB, "Doughs on right flank have cleared the woods. . . . Break . . . We are moving out. . . . Over."

At 1053 hours, he alerted CCB. "Oboe . . . in ten minutes there will be an eighteen-minute arty concentration . . . break . . . after which we will move on to the objective . . . over."

The artillery was ready, and around 1055 hours, the redlegs yanked the lanyards, causing thirty-six howitzers of the 22nd and 253rd Armored Field Artillery battalions to roar. For nearly twenty minutes the gun lines flashed and boomed. Meanwhile, the ground west and northwest of Chaumont vanished underneath a hailstorm of surface lightning and steel splinters. In that span of time, the 22nd Armored Field Artillery alone shot more than three hundred rounds of high-explosive. Despite the lethal rain, it was not enough to deter the German defenders.

1112 to 1124 Hours, Monday, December 25
George Company, 2nd Battalion, 318th Infantry Regiment, Attached to CCB
North of the Lambay-Chênet Woods, Belgium

The three companies from 2nd Battalion, 318th Infantry, left the cover of the Lambay-Chênet Woods at around 1112 hours and began to bound by squad across an open field. Waiting for them at the edge of the wood line opposite were several platoons of dug-in *fallschirmjägers*. Almost immediately the Germans opened fire. Lead stitched the snow, while mortars pounded. In the middle, George Company bore the brunt of the German small-arms blitz.

Second Lieutenant Robert Connor was the 1st Platoon leader, a replacement who joined up with George Company in early November while the division fought its way through eastern France. The night before this attack, Captain Stalling, the company commander, had passed out maps to each platoon leader. Connor was surprised—he had never had a map before an operation. Only commanders had maps, and this was an indication to him that this attack was a big deal. When he had heard that his unit was now an attachment to Combat Command B of the 4th Armored Division, the young lieutenant was leery. He had worked with a tank battalion before this, and his last experience was not a positive one. He remembered that the gutless tankers, sitting behind steel, wanted his infantrymen to move out ahead of them. This made little sense to Connor, since his only piece of armor was his battlefield wits.

According to Connor, the 4th Armored Division "was supposed to be different."

Initially, the coordination between his company and the tankers worked. Before Connor's platoon entered the Lambay-Chênet Woods earlier that morning, Erdmann's light tanks had arrived and sprayed the wood line, allowing Connor's infantry to approach unmolested. After they had cleared the woods, George Company reached the top of a hill just north of the Lambay-Chênet. From there, it was open ground until the next tree line.

Connor hoped that the armor would repeat that task. Instead the light tanks departed, and Lieutenant Kieley's Able Company replaced them with eight Shermans. When Connor met up with Kieley and asked him to move out and lay down some suppressive fire while his men trailed behind, Kieley balked. He told Connor that his tanks were all "shot up"; the officer likely still was smarting from the shellacking the battalion had received on the twenty-third. Instead, Kieley wanted the infantry to clear out the wood line, while his tanks followed. Connor tried to change his mind, but to no avail. Connor requested that Kieley call for artillery, but the tankers refused.

Chastened, Connor stomped back to his platoon to speak with his commander, Captain Stalling. If Connor hoped that his superior would step up and argue his case with Kieley, it was a misplaced aspiration. Looking ahead, Stalling ordered his mortar section leader, Staff Sergeant John J. McNiff, to bombard the likely German positions with the company's 60mm mortars—an ineffective tactic, most likely—and instructed the sergeant to lift fire even before the men moved out. Connor shook his head. If they lifted fire too early, he argued, the Germans just would just return to their guns while the George Company soldiers were out in the open, exposed and vulnerable. Stalling held firm and ordered Connor and McNiff to carry out his orders.

The discussion over, Connor returned to face his men. His platoon would be in the lead. He took one look at his soldiers and realized that he would have to be out front to spur them to move forward. He quickly informed them of the plan and waited for the mortars to open up. For several minutes, the sixties plastered the area. When they stopped, Connor waved his hand forward, and his platoon stepped off. "My men followed boldly and blindly," Connor remembered.

For several hundred meters the doughs bounded ahead, firing and moving as they went. At first the German machine gun fire was inaccurate, but as the Americans approached the halfway mark, the enemy found the range. Suddenly men started to fall. Connor "felt something tear through my left side." He knew he was hit and started to scramble for cover, but it was too late.

"While I was half turned, another shot got me," he continued. "This one went through my neck and felt like I had been hit with a baseball bat. It knocked me down and I couldn't move. I was scared to death. I was paralyzed from the neck wound."

Luckily, the paralysis would be temporary, but at the time Connor did not know that. He was lying on the ground, helpless, as bullets zipped over his head. Fortunately, one of his soldiers found him sprawled on the snow. As the battle raged, the soldier grabbed the lieutenant's rifle and jammed it into the dirt, using the bayonet like a stake. He plopped Connor's helmet on the buttstock as a marker for the medics, who were following behind the company. With that, the soldier left the hapless platoon leader and continued forward. Later, the medics found Connor and evacuated him to a field hospital, where the doctors treated his wounds. For him, the war was over.[4]

1124 Hours, Monday, December 25
Headquarters Tank, 8th Tank Battalion, CCB, 4th Armored Division
Near the Lambay-Chênet Woods, Belgium

Within minutes, Major Irzyk received the news that 2nd Battalion, 318th Infantry, had run into a hornet's nest. He updated CCB at 1124 hours: "Arty concentration still going on. . . . Break . . . People on right moving forward. . . . Break . . . Left unit [Easy Company] 318th Infantry is jumping off for main objective [Chaumont] to southeast of woods towards checkpoint Sixty. . . . Break . . . And southwest [George and Fox companies] bothered by snipers and machine gun nests in open. . . . Break . . . Taking them under with light tanks. . . . Over."

Irzyk looked at the map. The open area between the woods was six hundred meters across. The GIs' olive-drab uniforms made perfect targets against the newly fallen snow, and the men were close enough to the Germans that it would be difficult to call for fire on the *fallschirmjäger* positions. The tankers and infantrymen would have to accomplish the mission without any additional artillery support. Also, the major had no inkling that his Able Company commander had refused to support Gardner's grunts with his tanks. At this point, all Irzyk could do was wait.[5]

1124 to 1245 Hours, Monday, December 25
George Company, 2nd Battalion, 318th Infantry Regiment, Attached to CCB
North of the Lambay-Chênet Woods, Belgium

Blistering fire from the *fallschirmjäger* machine guns had pinned down the men of George Company, their rifles no match for the Germans' weapons. Someone had to find a way to silence the enemy before they wasted every American soldier huddled in the open.

One by one, key individuals took initiative. Lying on his stomach in the snow, Sergeant McNiff noticed on their eastern flank a German machine gun team with an excellent enfilade fire on the rest of the company. McNiff knew someone had to knock out that weapon before the infantry could inch forward toward the next patch of woods. Scanning the ground, he discovered a path that led up to the German foxhole. He crawled toward it, tucking his rifle in his arms while his elbows plowed furrows in the snow.

Finally he reached a spot close to the enemy position. He yanked a grenade off his belt and pulled the safety. Popping off the spoon, which triggered the fuse, he tossed the grenade into the nearby foxhole. Before the gunners could react, the grenade detonated, showering the team with shrapnel. Simultaneously, McNiff stood and opened fire with his Garand, emptying his entire clip into the Germans. Within seconds it was over. Two *fallschirmjägers* lay dead, and the other two quickly raised their hands to surrender. For this act of valor, the army later awarded McNiff the Silver Star.

Sergeant Celestino E. Lucero was a squad leader from New Mexico. Like McNiff, when the bullets started flying, he looked for the offending machine gun team, who were hiding in a nearby draw. When Lucero found them, he ordered his squad to remain behind in cover while he crawled up and knocked it out with hand grenades, destroying the machine gun. Lucero bagged the surviving crew. He later received the Silver Star.

Private First Class William H. South was a BAR gunner from Missouri. An artillery burst sent him flying through the air, and for several seconds he was unconscious. When he recovered his senses, he saw his fellow soldiers hugging the ground, machine gun tracers zipping overhead. His squad was going nowhere. Instead of waiting for orders, South knew what he had to do. Spotting the German machine gun nest, he searched for a route that would provide him defilade from it. He found one on its flank, and started to crawl the one hundred yards to reach it. The machine gun team never saw him coming. When he was close enough, South pulled the trigger on the BAR, and the gun kicked back like a mule, chugging away at the Germans. Instantly two of the defenders crumpled from their wounds and the remaining four threw up their arms. For his initiative, the army awarded South the Bronze Star.

While South, Lucero, and McNiff chose stealth, Private First Class Roscoe S. Putnam used trickery to attack his foes. As Putnam's squad neared the wood line, an MG 42 ripped into them from inside a barn. Putnam turned toward the muzzle blasts and estimated that it was more than a hundred and fifty yards to the machine gun nest. Despite the distance, the intrepid private took off. Within seconds the German gunners drew a bead on him. After only twenty-five yards, Putnam could hear the snapping of bullets as they raced by his ears.

In that moment, Putnam had an idea. He slumped to the ground as if hit. The ruse worked, and the Germans shifted their fire to another target. Putnam caught his breath, then sprang to his feet and took off toward a spot near the barn. The enemy gunners failed to detect the American soldier before he reached cover. In quick succession, he tossed two grenades into the barn. Only a few seconds after the second one exploded, Putnam barged in, firing his Garand until his clip was empty. Despite the flying shrapnel and lead, Putnam did not kill a single German, but the sheer ferocity of his assault stunned the gunners, who were shell-shocked from the grenades. They surrendered. The army later awarded Putnam the Silver Star.

Yet much of George Company remained pinned in the open by German machine guns. Since every *fallschirmjäger* platoon had six MG 42s, the loss of one was not necessarily fatal to a platoon's overall defense. In short, the men of George Company had to knock out more than just a few MG 42s before they could advance.

Private Paul J. Wiedorfer was only twenty-three years old when he joined up with the company as an infantry replacement from Baltimore, Maryland. He got his first glimpse of a dead body while sitting on the back of a truck headed to the front line. It was the corpse of a German soldier sprawled on the side of the road.

Christmas morning, 1944, was a day Wiedorfer would never forget. As the soldiers of the 318th left the safety of the Lambay-Chênet Woods, German machine gunners opened fire. Wiedorfer's platoon hit the dirt. Lieutenant Connor, up front, was one of the first to fall. "When they started to fire," Wiedorfer remembered, "we were bogged down. We had about a company of men or better strung across there. Nobody could move and nobody was moving."

Wiedorfer realized that time was not on their side. Though many of his comrades were behind cover, they were vulnerable to mortar rounds, and it was only a matter of time before the Germans started lobbing them. Lifting his head to search for the Germans, he spotted an enemy machine gun team forty yards away. He jumped up and ran toward it. After several agonizingly long seconds, he slipped on the ice, an accident that probably saved his life—the gunners swung their MG 42 toward Wiedorfer and opened fire. When the shots ceased, Wiedorfer hopped up and sprinted a few more yards. Once he was close enough, he popped the safety off the grenade and tossed it into the foxhole. His aim was perfect.

"I heard a big boom," Wiedorfer remembered, "and I immediately jumped up and followed the grenade right into the hole." Without a second thought, he opened fire on the three Germans, killing them.

Nearby was another machine gun team. Wiedorfer scampered out of the foxhole and charged them, flinging a grenade at their position. The explosion wounded one German, and six others, unharmed, threw up their arms in surrender. Wiedorfer's one-man attack had unhinged a significant portion of the German lines and led to the overall success of the 2nd Battalion operation.[6]

1245 to 1900 Hours, Monday, December 25
Headquarters Tank, 8th Tank Battalion, CCB, 4th Armored Division
Chaumont, Belgium

At 1245 hours, Major Irzyk felt that they had turned the corner, and he reported to Combat Command B, "Unit on right [318th Infantry] situation . . . Doughs are in and almost through woods to 52 Grid Line. South of C-Town [Chaumont] approaching and almost reached road. . . . Break . . . Unit on left [10th Armored Infantry]—unit approaching high ground that was set as their objective. Opposition light . . ."

An hour later, Irzyk radioed more good news: "One platoon's stuff across stream and road east and north of C-Town [Chaumont]. On left, we are still moving north. Doughs are moving in C-Town."

By 1809 hours, the soldiers of the 10th Armored Infantry and 2nd Battalion of the 318th Infantry were collecting prisoners, and at 1900 hours General Dager reported to Division G-3, "C-Town is ours."

For Easy Company, the clearance of Chaumont had been a lengthy process of checking each room in each building. After George Company had reached the Chaumont–Hollange road, it pushed north and established a battle position for the night. To accomplish this follow-on mission, Colonel Gardner attached an additional light machine gun and ten men from Easy Company, who remained inside Chaumont, and three heavy machine guns from the weapons company.

The fighting had been costly. Easy Company had lost nine soldiers during their clearance of Chaumont, while George lost an additional seven in the open area between the Lambay-Chênet and the unnamed patch of woods east of the town. In fact, George Company had only forty-nine men on the rolls, while Fox Company had even fewer, with twenty-nine. The situation for Easy Company was so dire that Colonel Gardner attached twenty-four men from the regiment's Intelligence and Reconnaissance Platoon to Easy Company. He even switched out commanders and appointed the I&R platoon leader, First Lieutenant Edmund A. Wellinghoff, to assume command of Easy Company, relieving Captain Kirkman.

It was not all bad news. On the other hand, 8th Tank Battalion had recovered seven of the lost tanks and repaired them. In addition, CCB reported that they had processed seventy-seven prisoners of war, and estimated that they had inflicted another 260 casualties on the defending German units. They also had destroyed one German Pak 40. In total, CCB had seriously damaged 1st, 3rd, and 4th companies of 1st Battalion, 14th Fallschirmjäger Regiment, and finally wrecked 7th and 8th companies of 2nd Battalion, 14th Fallschirmjäger Regiment. Major Irzyk's plan had worked splendidly, and by all accounts, the men of CCB and the 318th Infantry had won a great victory.[7]

Evening, Monday, December 25
Inside Chaumont, Belgium

Bruce Fenchel kept seeing tanks rumbling up and down the street. They were Sherman tanks, but he also knew that the Germans had commandeered some Shermans earlier, so he was not convinced that the 4th Armored had recaptured Chaumont. He decided to wait until he saw some GIs. After several minutes he started to hear the soldiers, and they were speaking English. That was enough evidence for him, and he descended from the attic and stepped outside.

Amazingly, the first tank he saw as he walked out into the street was an M5 Stuart light tank, and the driver was his old gunner. Somehow his gunner had survived after all. Both recognized each other immediately.

Fenchel remarked as he climbed aboard the tank, "Just give me the Purple Heart. I want to go home."

His former gunner replied, "You're not going anyplace. I'm going up in the turret of this tank, and you're getting into the driver's seat."

Fenchel smirked as he lowered himself into the driver's seat. For the next few weeks the tank had a crew of two, but they survived. In fact, Fenchel, according to the War Department, was dead. A tanker who was driving behind Fenchel's tank reported that he had seen Fenchel die when his tank got hit. Fortunately for Fenchel's parents, the army corrected that report.[8]

Despite CCB's success in recapturing Chaumont, it had not reached Bastogne, which was still eight kilometers north of their position. Moreover, another German unit was moving into the area, and was now between them and the city. That unit was the 104th Panzergrenadier Regiment from the 15th Panzergrenadier Division. The 115th Panzergrenadier, which was the other maneuver unit in that division, already had participated in a major attack that Christmas morning. The 104th, unlike the *fallschirmjäger* regiments that the 4th had faced, was a fresh regiment with armor and a lot of infantry. In a word, 4th Armored Division was running out of time.[9]

CHAPTER 10

ASSENOIS

★ ★ ★ ★ ★

"Glad to see you . . ."

—*First Lieutenant Duane Webster of the 326th Engineers, 101st Airborne Division*

0720 to 0850 Hours, Monday, December 25
Headquarters, CCR, 4th Armored Division
Molinfaing, Belgium

Lieutenant Colonel Creighton Abrams was exhausted. He and his men had been on the road all night, traveling more than thirty kilometers from Bigonville to the area northeast of Neufchâteau. When he arrived at Bercheux, Belgium, early in the morning, he and his staff retired to a quaint country home, gathered around the kitchen table, and for an hour discussed possible plans for the day's operations.

At 0720 hours, Abrams's radio operator informed him that Colonel Wendell Blanchard had requested his presence at Combat Command Reserve's command post in Molinfaing, several kilometers southwest of Bercheux. Abrams stood up from the table and said to the other officers, "I'll go back and see what the orders are going to be."

When Abrams arrived, he saw his friend Lieutenant Colonel George Jaques, commander of the 53rd Armored Infantry Battalion, and Major Robert Parker, commander of the 94th Armored Field Artillery Battalion. Besides them, Colonel

Blanchard was there with his staff. Blanchard did not waste a lot of time with small talk. They had a new mission.

Blanchard's plan was simple. The advance guard, composed of Abrams's light tank company (Dog Company), Baker Company from the 53rd Armored Infantry, and a squad of engineers from Charlie Company, 24th Engineers, would proceed from their current location around Bercheux to the town of Vaux-lez-Rosières. From there they would continue northeast to the village of Petite Rosière. To provide more firepower, Blanchard allocated an additional company minus from the 704th Tank Destroyer Battalion (M-18 Hellcats), which would trail behind the advance guard but ahead of the main body. Once the advance guard had secured Petite Rosière, it would wait until the rest of the main body arrived to relieve them. (A "company minus" meant a company with one less platoon. Companies usually had three platoons. In this case, this company had two platoons since the other platoon had been detached to another unit.)

Then Blanchard wanted CCR to change its axis of advance from northeast to due east. Both A companies and both C companies from 37th Tank and the 53rd Armored Infantry battalions, respectively, would roll eastward from Petite Rosière to the town of Nives. Meanwhile, Dog Company would screen to the north of Petite Rosière to provide early warning and flank protection from any German attack in that direction. The two B companies would remain in the vicinity of Petite Rosière.

If German resistance in Nives was light, then the column would proceed to Cobreville and thence on to Remoiville. Blanchard believed that his lead elements likely would have to reconnoiter the stream between Remoiville and Remichampagne for a suitable crossing site, since the Germans probably would have blown the bridges. Meanwhile, the rest of CCR would wait in a tactical assembly area north of Remoiville. Once the engineers had erected a bridge or the scouts had found a fording site, the main body would resume its advance and head north to Remichampagne. From there, the distance between his column and the front lines of the 101st Airborne Division was only seven to eight kilometers. Then the CCR commander ordered Major Parker, artillery battalion commander, to plan for preparatory fires on the following villages and woods: the hamlets of Nives and Cobreville, and the southern edge of the Bois de Cohet.

With his plan now on the table, Blanchard opened the discussion to hear

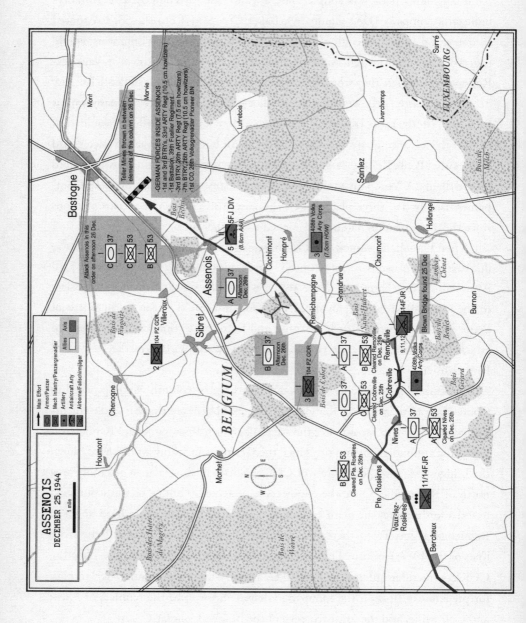

ASSENOIS
DECEMBER 25, 1944

1 mile

N
W E
S

Main Effort
Armor/Panzer
Mech Infantry/Panzergrenadier
Artillery
Antiaircraft Arty
Airborne/Fallschirmjäger

Axis
Allies

GERMAN FORCES INSIDE ASSENOIS
-1st and 3rd BTRYs, 33rd ARTY Regt (10.5 cm howitzers)
-1st Battalion, 39th Fusilier Regiment
-3rd BTRY, 26th ARTY Regt (7.5 cm howitzers)
-7th BTRY, 26th ARTY Regt (10.5 cm howitzers)
-1st CO, 26th Volksgrenadier Pioneer BN

Teller Mines thrown in between
elements of the column on 26 Dec.

Attack Assenois in this
order on afternoon 26 Dec.

C 37
C 53
B 53

A 37
Afternoon
Dec. 26th

5FJ DIV
5 A (8.8cm AAA)

408th Volks
3 Arty Corps
(7.5cm HOW)

BELGIUM

LUXEMBOURG

Bastogne
Mont
Marvie
Lutrebois
Livarchamps
Sainlez
Surré
Bois de
Melch

Bois de
Bretin

Assenois
Sibret
Villeroux
Clochimont
Hompré
Remichampagne
Grandrue
Chaumont
Hollange
Lambay-
Chênet
Burnon

104 PZ GDR
2

B 37
Afternoon
Dec. 26th

104 PZ GDR
3

Bois de
Cobert

C 37
C 53

A 37
B 53
Cleared Cobreville
on Dec. 25th

Cobreville

14FJR
9,11,12

Removille
Cleared Removille
on Dec. 25th

Bois
Saint-Hubert

Blown Bridge found 25 Dec

Bois du
Beulet

Bois de
Geard

408th Volks
1 Arty Corps

A 37
A 53
Cleared Nives
on Dec. 25th

Nives

B 53
Cleared Pte. Rosières
on Dec. 25th

Pte. Rosières

11/14FJR

Vaux-lez-
Rosières

Bercheux

Houmont

Bois de
Fragotte

Chenogne

Morhet

Bois des Hâtes
de Magery

Bois de
Wiave

ideas from his commanders. Colonel Abrams proposed that the infantry clear the towns along the route. He reasoned that if the towns were under complete American control, then the soft-skinned trucks and jeeps could navigate the route without fear of enemy ambushes. Blanchard agreed.

Blanchard instructed his subordinate commanders to use channel twenty on their FM radios, and more important, to alert the 101st Airborne as they neared the Bastogne lines. The call sign for the 101st was its commander's first name, Tony, while CCR's call sign would be "One of Hugh's Boys." It was not a great code, but Blanchard hoped that they would break through to the besieged paratroopers before any German signal intercept unit could decode it. Blanchard looked at his watch. It was now 0850 hours. He looked back at his officers and ordered them to be ready to move out at 1100 hours. The battalion commanders bade their boss farewell and returned to their units.

Blanchard believed that his most important mission was to penetrate the German cordon and reach Bastogne. In fact, according to Captain Stedman Seay, an officer in 4th Armored Division's G-3 Operations Section, "The original plan was to use CCR to the left of CCB to guard against a possible enemy thrust from the northwest. It was anticipated that *CCB* [italics mine] would make first contact with the beleaguered troops in the Bastogne pocket." Apparently Blanchard had decided that the screening operation was secondary. He wanted the bigger prize— Bastogne. The German defenders between CCR and the vital road hub had other ideas.[1]

Morning, Monday, December 25 3rd Battalion,
14th Fallschirmjäger Regiment,
5th Fallschirmjäger Division Remoiville, Belgium

Thanks to American tactical intelligence, Colonel Blanchard and General Gaffey assessed that several German *fallschirmjäger* battalions were west of Chaumont. They were not far off in their assessment. In the vicinity of Remoiville was 3rd Battalion, 14th Fallschirmjäger Regiment, under the command of Major Ferdinand Ebel.

Ebel's largely untouched battalion had escaped Combat Command B's onslaught through Chaumont, and he had established a blocking position around

Remoiville to prevent U.S. forces from utilizing the road that led from there to Remichampagne. To provide early warning, he placed more than a platoon of *fallschirmjägers* from his 11th Company in the towns of Vaux-lez-Rosières and Petite Rosière. In addition, the platoon had a team of three forward observers from the 408th Volks Artillery Corps. The platoon combat security outpost had one *panzerschreck* team to give it an antitank ability. Since it had a radio, its main purpose to was to alert Ebel's command of an impending American attack while disrupting any potential attack with long-range artillery fire. It lacked the combat power, though, to become decisively engaged.

Organic to his battalion, Ebel had two rifle companies and one weapons company (one rifle company, the 10th, had not accompanied the battalion). 9th Company was under the command of an Oberleutnant Ehrich. Originally it had been located near Nives, but most of it had pulled back to Remoiville by the twenty-fifth, while 11th Company was under the command of Leutnant Max Schwarz, and it, too, was defending Remoiville, with the exception of the one platoon in Vaux-lez-Rosières. Moreover, Leutnant Friebe, the battalion's weapons company commander (12th Company), had kept most of the heavy machine guns and 8cm mortars in and around Remoiville. For antitank support, Ebel had several more *panzerschrecks* and *panzerfausts* from the 14th Company, which was the 14th Fallschirmjäger Regiment's antitank company. Finally, Ebel's 11th and 12th companies were near full strength on the morning of the twenty-fifth.

Unlike the unfortunate *fallschirmjägers* in Tintange and Bigonville, 3rd Battalion had two batteries of 7.5cm dual-purpose howitzers (most likely a version of the FK40), which the crews could use in either an indirect-fire role or an antitank role. The batteries were from the eagerly anticipated 1st Battalion, 408th Volks Artillery Corps, which had finally arrived on the battlefield. One battery, 1st Battery, under the command of Leutnant Günther Scholz, had six guns and was located on the forward slope of a spur north of the town of Nives, while 3rd Battery, under the command of Hauptmann Talfel, had only four guns in operation and was in position on the high ground between Grandrue and Remichampagne. In fact, Talfel's battery was the same battery that was buttressing 1st Battalion in Chaumont, because from its current location it could provide long-range fire for both battalions. Since 3rd Battalion had little in the way of large-caliber artillery, the crews were using the 7.5cm howitzers as indirect artillery assets. Luckily, the gun crews had both armor-piercing and high-explosive ammunition on hand. Most important, they were not the only German unit between Bastogne and CCR.[2]

0500 to 0800 Hours, Monday, December 25 1st Battalion,
104th Panzergrenadier Regiment,
15th Panzergrenadier Division Remichampagne, Belgium

As fate would have it, on the morning and afternoon of the twenty-fourth, the advance elements from the 104th Panzergrenadier Regiment had started to roll into the town of Remichampagne, north of Remoiville and directly in the path of CCR. The 104th, unlike the *fallschirmjäger* regiments, was motorized, and thus had more heavy weapons on its table of organization and equipment.

The 104th Panzergrenadier was part of the 15th Panzergrenadier Division. Unlike the adjacent 26th Volksgrenadier Division, which had fought mainly in Russia for most of the war, the 15th had earned its stripes fighting against the Americans and British in Italy around Monte Cassino. After Italy, the regiment left for France in the late summer of 1944 and fought in battles around Lunéville. From there, it traveled to Holland and fought in the area around Venlo until the end of October. Prior to the Bulge, it was refitting north of Aachen.

The 104th had a veteran chain of command. The commander was Oberstleutnant Eberhard Nolte, and the 1st Battalion commander was Hauptmann Ludwig Gross. Many of the junior officers and NCOs were also veterans. In fact, a large portion of the NCOs were walking wounded who had volunteered to return to their regiment instead of languishing in a convalescent unit, safely behind the front lines. Interrogators later commented that the 104th's espirit de corps was high, and the soldiers were "very security-minded because they considered themselves superior to American soldiers. They were all convinced of Germany's ultimate victory."

Since the 104th was a motorized *panzergrenadier* regiment, it had a large assortment of trucks. Indeed, the 104th was comparable to a reinforced American infantry regiment in terms of motor transport, and as a result it had plenty of food and ammunition when it arrived at the front. On the other hand, the 104th had only two motorized infantry battalions, as opposed to their sister regiment, the 115th, which had three.

1st Battalion was the first to arrive. Like most infantry battalions, it had three infantry companies and one weapons company. However, its infantry battalions had 12cm mortars and 2cm antiaircraft guns in its heavy-weapons company. That morning, the line companies had around ninety men each. For command and control, Hauptmann Gross set up his headquarters in Sibret, while Oberstleutnant Nolte established his command post northwest of Hompré.

Ludwig Gross knew the task before him was a daunting one. His commander expected him to keep up the pressure on the 101st Airborne Division still trapped inside Bastogne. Additionally, he wanted 1st Battalion to backstop the *fallschirm-jägers*, since it was clear to the German high command that an armored thrust from the south was imminent. As a result, Gross was attacking in one direction and defending in another. It was not a desirable situation.

Gross's solution was to sandwich his 2nd Company between the Assenois–Bastogne highway and the Sibret–Bastogne railroad. He ordered his 3rd Company, under the command of Leutnant Wilhelm Klouker, to defend the town of Remi-champagne to prevent the U.S. forces from reaching Assenois. He positioned his 1st Company, under the command of Leutnant Kurt Winzker, near the town of Morhet with the task of securing the battalion's western flank. In short, two companies, 1st and 3rd, were in defensive positions, while 2nd Company had an offensive mission.

For artillery coverage, the *panzergrenadiers* of 1st Battalion, 104th Panzer-grenadier Regiment, had two batteries of artillery in direct support. 1st and 3rd batteries of the 33rd Artillery Regiment (Motorized) were both comprised of four 10.5cm towed howitzers, and both batteries were from 1st Battalion, under the command of Major Karl Heinz Teller. To provide effective coverage, Teller set up his two batteries in the vicinity of the village of Assenois. From there he could easily provide indirect-fire assistance across the entire battle space for 1st Battalion, 104th Panzergrenadier Regiment.

Gross's first combat operation started early. Before sunrise, his 2nd Company, as part of the larger division-level operation to capture Bastogne, attacked the high ground north of Assenois. Lacking heavy weapons, 2nd Company moved out. The dug-in paratroopers of 2nd Platoon, Able Company, 326th Airborne Engineers, easily foiled the attack and sustained only a few casualties. Meanwhile, 2nd Company had suffered grievously, with sixteen dead and twelve wounded, including the company commander. By 0800 hours, it was over. The company went into reserve after the debacle later that night at 1800 hours, leaving 1st and 3rd companies on the line to fend for themselves. For 3rd Company, the loss of 2nd Company placed them alone and in a precarious position: behind a *fallschirm-jäger* battalion that was a paper tiger.[3]

Morning, Monday, December 25
1st Battalion, 39th Fusilier Regiment, 26th Volksgrenadier Division
Assenois, Belgium

Behind 3rd Company, 104th Panzergrenadier Regiment, were the tattered remains of the 39th Fusilier (Volksgrenadier) Regiment, under the command of Oberstleutnant Walter Kaufmann. Though it had the honorific title of Fusilier, the 39th was a standard *volksgrenadier* regiment with two battalions with a total of ten companies. Most of the soldiers in the 39th hailed from the city of Mühlheim, which was in the Ruhr region of Germany. Most were transferees from the Kriegsmarine and other services, and had received only eight weeks of infantry training prior to the Ardennes offensive.

As a *volksgrenadier* regiment, the 39th had a slightly different table of organization and equipment. Each *volksgrenadier* infantry squad had only one light machine gun, as opposed to the *fallschirmjäger* squad, which had two. To offset that loss of firepower, the *volksgrenadiers* tended to have more of the new Sturmgewehr 44 assault rifles, which were the progenitors of today's modern assault rifles. It used a thirty-round magazine and could fire both semi- and fully automatic. As a result, several soldiers firing StG 44s could easily suppress a U.S. rifle squad. In fact, the weapon was so deadly, the Russians copied it, and their version is today's ubiquitous AK-47.

The standard *volksgrenadier* company had nine infantry squads, divided into three platoons. Unlike a *panzergrenadier* or *fallschirmjäger* company, the *volksgrenadier* infantry company had no weapons platoon. It had two platoons that primarily were composed of soldiers armed with StG 44s and one platoon with the standard Kar 98 bolt-action rifle.

To augment the line companies with heavier firepower, the *volksgrenadier* battalion had a standard weapons company. The 4th and 8th companies respectively had four platoons each. 1st and 2nd platoons each had four heavy machine guns, mounted on tripods, for a total of eight. The 3rd platoon had four 7.5cm infantry howitzers to provide local indirect-fire support. The 4th platoon was the mortar platoon, and it had six 8cm mortars.

For more firepower, the 13th Company, or the regimental howitzer company, had two platoons, each with four 12cm mortars, and 3rd Platoon, which had four more 7.5cm infantry howitzers. Next, the 14th Company, like the other 14th companies, was the antitank company, but it had only a short-range antitank capability in the form of fifty-four *panzerschrecks*. Thus, if the regiment wanted Pak 40 7.5cm antitank guns, then it had to request them from the division.

Despite this firepower, the 39th Fusilier Regiment was a shadow of its former self. The *volksgrenadier* infantry company, at full strength, had 119 soldiers and officers in total. Indeed, the line companies of 1st Battalion crossed the Our River on the sixteenth with about 110 men each. By the evening of the twenty-fifth, the entire 1st Battalion had a total rifle strength of only 103 enlisted men and three officers. They had lost hundreds of men in the battles for Villeroux and Isle le Pré. As a result, they were woefully understrength. Fortunately, the battalion still had most of its support weapons operating, including the heavy machine guns and mortars. Moreover, many of the veteran NCOs and junior officers were survivors of the Russian campaigns, and Oberstleutnant Kaufmann hoped that they still had some fight left in them. They would need it.

For command and control purposes, Kaufmann decided to occupy the towns. He ordered 1st Battalion to defend the town of Assenois and the area around it, while 2nd Battalion would protect the German flank near Senonchamps. Sadly, the attrition of officers was so acute that 1st Battalion was under the tutelage of an *oberleutnant*, the equivalent of putting a first lieutenant in charge of an entire battalion. 2nd Battalion's situation was not much better. A *hauptmann*—a captain— was its commander. Kaufmann, though, had little choice. He was running out of officers.

The 26th Artillery Regiment, directly supported by the 26th Volksgrenadier Division, had several batteries around Assenois. Like its parent division, the 26th Artillery Regiment had barely survived the fighting on the Eastern Front, and the Wehrmacht reconstituted it with the rest of the division in September 1944 in Poznań, Poland. In terms of composition, the regiment had four battalions of artillery. 1st Battalion had three batteries of 7.5cm dual-purpose howitzers, each with six guns. 2nd and 3rd battalions had two batteries each, and in each battery were six 10.5cm howitzers. The 4th Battalion was the heavy-artillery battalion, and it had two batteries, and each battery had six 15.5cm howitzers.

Oberstleutnant Rabe, the overall commander of the regiment, allocated several batteries of dual-purpose howitzers to the 39th Fusiliers. One was 3rd Battery, under the command of Leutnant Knabe. Following orders, the battery commander positioned his six 7.5cm dual-purpose howitzers on the outskirts of Assenois to serve in an antitank role. For better command and control, Knabe set up his command post nearby in the town of Salvacourt, several hundred meters southeast of Assenois.

7th Battery, which fell under 3rd Battalion, was also in the vicinity of Assenois. The battery had six 10.5cm howitzers. In fact, the 3rd Battalion command post was in Assenois with 7th Battery.

In addition to the howitzers and antitank guns of the 26th Artillery Regiment, Oberst Heinz Kokott had allocated pioneers from the 26th Volks Pioneer Battalion to lay minefields in the Assenois sector. The pioneers had already seen a lot of action, and had been responsible for building the pontoon bridges across the Our River, near Hosingen, at the beginning of the Bulge offensive. Now, under the command of Hauptmann Schweda, 1st Company was allocated to augment the forces around Assenois.

The 1st Company, under the command of Leutnant Ehrig, had three mine-laying platoons and one heavy-weapons platoon. The mine-laying platoons carried Teller antitank mines, but the soldiers were armed only with rifles and submachine guns. The weapons platoon was more lavishly equipped, with two 8cm mortars and two heavy machine guns on tripods. With a strength of nearly a hundred men, Ehrig's company still had a lot of trigger pullers. Ironically, many of the pioneers had been prisoners of war who had volunteered to join the German army in order to leave the stalag prison camps. To lead them were German NCOs and officers. To ensure the best coverage, Ehrig positioned his platoons inside Assenois.

Scattered throughout the area around Assenois were several antiaircraft units. Most likely they belonged to the 5th Fallschirmjäger Flak Battalion, part of the 5th Fallschirmjäger Division. Since the Germans were so fearful of Allied airpower, the Luftwaffe had stuffed the flak battalions with tremendous amounts of firepower—three batteries of FlaK 38, quad 2cm antiaircraft guns. Each battery had six of these monsters, and each gun system, with four barrels, could spew nearly eight hundred rounds per minute over a distance of 5,230 yards. Against roving fighter-bombers they were deadly, and against infantry and soft-skinned vehicles they were even more effective.

For ground units, though, the FlaK 38 was the lesser of two evils. In addition to the three batteries of 2cm AA guns, the battalion had two batteries of the dreaded 88s. In a ground-attack role, the 88s easily outshot any Allied tank, and each battery had six of these tank killers. Even worse, the ground between Assenois and Clochimont was wide-open—ideal for these beasts. The battery commander placed four of them on the southeastern edge of Assenois, watching over the rolling, snow-covered fields like hunters lying in ambush.

In summary, between Combat Command Reserve and the 101st Airborne Division were several German battalions: 3rd Battalion, 14th Fallschirmjäger Regiment, around Remoiville; 3rd Company, 1st Battalion, 104th Panzergrenadier Regiment, around Remichampagne; and 1st Battalion, 39th Fusilier (Volksgrenadier) Regiment, around Assenois. Though many of the German units were understrength, so was CCR. Furthermore, the Germans had many of the open areas covered with 88s or other antitank guns. It was a gauntlet, and on paper the odds were stacked against Colonel Blanchard's CCR.[4]

1100 to 1438 Hours, Monday, December 25
Combat Command Reserve Command Post, 4th Armored Division
Bercheux, Belgium

At 1100 hours, the Combat Command Reserve radio operator received a transmission from 37th Tank Battalion: "We are moving out." The final push had begun.

Northeast of Bercheux, the 37th Tank Battalion's S-2, Captain John T. Mc-Mahon, led the advance guard toward Vaux-lez-Rosières. He commanded the light tanks of Dog Company, plus infantry from Baker Company, 53rd Armored Infantry Battalion, one squad of engineers, and some tank destroyers from Charlie Company, 704th Tank Destroyer Battalion. Thirteen minutes after they had crossed the line of departure, McMahon radioed to CCR, "No resistance in first town [Vaux-lez-Rosières]. We are moving right through." Several soldiers plotted the advance guard's progress on a map.

At 1125 hours, McMahon chimed in again: "Advance elements have gone through second town [Petite Rosière]. Have encountered small-arms fire. Break. Doughs mopping up." The situation did not sound serious. McMahon's forces had found the Germans, but many of the command post staff wondered whether it was a screen line or a battle position. They waited for more information.

As outlined at the morning conference, Dog Company, 37th Tank Battalion, and Charlie Company, 704th Tank Destroyer Battalion, occupied the high ground northeast of Petite Rosière to provide a support-by-fire position, while Baker Company, 53rd Armored Infantry, started to sweep through the town. For several hours the advance guard fought the *fallschirmjägers* from 11th Company, 14th Fallschirmjäger Regiment. By 1200 hours, Colonel Blanchard knew that his soldiers had taken at least fifty prisoners, and at 1320 hours, the radio operator from the 53rd Armored Infantry Battalion reported that the advance guard had cleared all of Petite Rosière. So far German resistance had been negligible and ineffective. Once again a staff clerk plotted the location of the advance guard on the map. According to the agreed plan, the column would now swing east.

The next objective was Nives. This time the column would proceed without the advance guard, which would remain in Petite Rosière to secure the western flank of CCR. Meanwhile, the two Able companies from the 53rd Armored Infantry and the 37th Tank Battalion, respectively, would assume the lead.

Fortunately, the occupation of Nives was uneventful. As the infantry from Able Company, 53rd Armored Infantry, finished off the operation, the two Charlie companies pushed through and continued the advance eastward toward Cobreville. As they approached the next village, First Lieutenant Charles Boggess, who had been the commander of Charlie Company, 37th Tank Battalion, for only forty hours, took over the vanguard. Boggess, deciding to play it safe, dismounted the infantry and proceeded methodically to clear the town while his tanks rumbled through the streets like roving squad cars looking for hoodlums. While his men searched the houses, Boggess reconnoitered the area east of Cobreville on foot.

When he reached the eastern outskirts of the hamlet, he discovered that the Germans had demolished the bridge that linked Cobreville with Remoiville. All that remained was a gaping crater. Boggess returned to his tank and requested a bulldozer, which arrived on the site a few minutes later. As they discussed their options, the driver noticed a stone wall nearby. He figured that if he shoved the stones from the wall into the hole, the debris would easily fill it, thereby allowing vehicles to drive over the crater. Boggess liked the plan, and the bulldozer driver went to work. At 1438 hours, 37th Tank Battalion relayed Boggess's message to CCR over the command net: "Bridge completed. Moving out to continue mission."

1450 to 1700 Hours, Monday, December 25 Able Company,
53rd Armored Infantry Battalion, CCR,
4th Armored Division West of Remoiville, Belgium

At 1450 hours, the radio operator for Reserve Command alerted the troopers of 25th Cavalry: "We are attacking the town two kilometers south of checkpoint seventy-four [Remoiville]. You will have to pull back to safety. Meet us there after the attack."

Nestled along a creek, Remoiville, with ridgelines surrounded it on all sides, was only twelve hundred meters east of Cobreville. More important, the main all-weather road wound its way through it, so CCR could not bypass the town. So far Colonel Blanchard's tankers and infantrymen had clashed only with the forward screen of the German army, but Blanchard knew that the German main line of resistance was somewhere up ahead. In fact, he would find it in Remoiville.

Since the Charlie companies had seized and cleared Cobreville, the operation to take Remoiville fell on the two Able companies from the 53rd Armored Infantry and 37th Tank battalions. The 94th Armored Field Artillery, together with the one battery from the 177th Field Artillery, opened up with a paralyzing barrage. For minutes Remoiville thundered and quaked as several hundred rounds detonated among its buildings, stunning the German defenders and sending them retreating into the cellars.

Simultaneously, Lieutenant Boggess ordered his Charlie Company, 37th Tank Battalion, to roll out and occupy the western spur that overlooked Remoiville. Close behind his tanks were the infantrymen from Charlie Company, 53rd Armored Infantry. When they reached the key terrain, the tanks added their own steel to the maelstrom, shooting high-explosive rounds from their 75mm and 76mm cannons.

Meanwhile, the two Able companies advanced down the main road. As they closed in, the tankers blasted the town with their main guns while the half-track gunners peppered the walls with .30- and .50-caliber slugs. Leading the way was First Lieutenant Frank R. Kutak, the infantry Able Company commander. The Germans could not reply in kind because they were hunkered down in the cellars, praying for the tempest to abate. To ensure that the artillery suppressed the *fallschirmjägers*, the howitzer shells were exploding only several hundred meters in front of the lead tank in the column. It was a dangerous technique, since a short round might crash into the column, resulting in fratricide, but the commanders weighed the risks and deemed that the danger-close artillery suppression was worth it.

They were right. Since the Germans were cowering in the shelters, no one was manning the machine guns nor antitank guns along the western edge of town. As a result, Kutak's infantry half-tracks reached the center of Remoiville unmolested. By then Kutak had requested the artillery to lift, but for the Germans, the cessation was too late. As the *fallschirmjägers* clambered up the steps from the cellars to repel the attackers, American infantry greeted them with hand grenades and lead.

Kutak was fearless, and his men fed off his frenzied zeal. Nothing could quench their fiery malice. Instead of surrendering, some German defenders chose to fight to the death. The GIs obliged them, torching them with flamethrowers. Some *fallschirmjägers* managed to fire a couple of *panzerfausts*, hitting two Shermans. Luckily, the damage was minor. Mortar rounds detonated amongst the half-tracks, but did little to slow down the Americans. Despite sustaining two wounds, Kutak soldiered on, exhorting his men to keep pressing the fight. He refused to shirk behind cover, leading the attack from the front.

By 1700 hours, the American soldiers had broken the German morale, and the *fallschirmjägers* from 3rd Battalion, 14th Fallschirmjäger Regiment, had started to stream out from the smoldering homes and smashed businesses. For the diehards who wanted to continue fighting, time was running out, because Charlie Company, 53rd Armored Infantry, was squeezing the cordon as it cleared the western side of Remoiville. The only way out was north, and few escaped.

The final tally was staggering. In less than two hours, CCR had wrecked an entire battalion of *fallschirmjägers*. Accounts varied, but at least three hundred *fallschirmjägers* surrendered to the GIs, including Major Ferdinand Ebel, the battalion commander. Furthermore, American infantry destroyed four 12cm mortars, dozens of machine guns, and several vehicles. More than fifty German soldiers lay dead, and American medics evacuated more than forty German wounded, for a total of four hundred casualties. In short, CCR had erased 3rd Battalion from the German order of battle. For the German Seventh Army, CCR's attack had ruptured its lines at the worst time.

Few on the German side understood the scale of the disaster. 3rd Company, 104th Panzergrenadier Regiment, under the command of Leutnant Wilhelm Klouker, was the only unit that probably knew what had happened. At 1200 hours, they had passed along the information that the *fallschirmjägers* were under attack near Remoiville, and by 1600 hours, 3rd Company informed the 104th's headquarters that the *fallschirmjägers* had left Remoiville and were streaming north toward the small town of Jodenville. Other than that, no one else knew the fate of Ebel's command. Still, Klouker had only an inkling of what had slammed into the last battalion of *fallschirmjägers*. Unfortunately for him, he would find out what was coming for him and his company the next morning.[5]

Evening, Monday, December 25
Headquarters, XXXXVII Panzer Corps
Château de Roumont, Belgium

As he stared at the map in his operations room, General der Panzertruppen Heinrich Freiherr von Lüttwitz knew the great winter offensive was over. Christmas had been a day of defeats for his corps, and he was a man not used to defeats. He had led the 2nd Panzer Division throughout much of the Normandy campaign, and as a result his star rose while those of many others fell. For his reward, the Wehrmacht promoted him and gave him command of the XXXXVII Panzer Corps. His first operation had been against Patton in the Lorraine region of France, where he did his best against long odds. Despite the lackluster performance of Lüttwitz's corps against Patton's Third Army in September and October 1944, General der Panzertruppen Hasso von Manteuffel selected his unit to be the Fifth Panzer Army's main effort for the winter offensive. Initially, Lüttwitz did not disappoint. His panzers went farther than any corps' armored battalions, and the reconnaissance units of the 2nd Panzer Division almost reached the Meuse River.

Alas, by the evening of the twenty-fifth, the spirit of victory had left his command. The panzers of 2nd Panzer Division had run out of gas, and its advance *kampfgruppe* was isolated and at the mercy of U.S. counterattacks. Even worse, the crestfallen corps commander could not order a retreat, because the German high command was afraid of Hitler's wrath. Instead of withdrawing, 2nd Panzer Division, which was short of food, fuel, and fire, had to attack to reestablish contact with its advance detachment. Even von Lüttwitz's superior, General von Manteuffel, knew this was a fool's hope, but they felt they had no choice but to continue the offensive.

The 26th Volksgrenadier Division's much-anticipated attack to capture Bastogne had ended in failure, weakening Oberst Heinz Kokott's division even further. For Lüttwitz, this signaled the end. Now he was receiving reports from the Seventh Army that an American armored counterattack was approaching from the south and heading toward Bastogne. The corps commander looked at his map. If the American thrust reached Bastogne and continued on to Houffalize, it would have cleaved his corps in two. He realized something had to be done, because he could no longer rely on the Seventh Army to protect his southern flank. Resolved, he requested reinforcements from the Fifth Panzer Army. Unbeknownst to him, he had run out of time. Few people on the German side grasped the tenuous nature of the XXXXVII Panzer Corps's southern flank. When CCR decimated Ebel's *fallschirmjäger* battalion, it had removed the only sizable force between it and the support zone of the 26th Volksgrenadier Division. In short, Lüttwitz had less than twenty-four hours to remedy the situation.[6]

1926 to 0311 Hours, Monday, December 25, to Tuesday, December 26
Headquarters, 101st Airborne Division
Heinz Barracks, Bastogne, Belgium

As a result of the morning victory, morale in the division headquarters of the 101st Airborne was still high. The paratroopers of the 502nd Parachute Infantry Regiment and the glidermen of the 327th Glider Infantry Regiment, together with the tank destroyers of the 705th Tank Destroyer Battalion and the redlegs of the 463rd Parachute Field Artillery Battalion, had smashed the panzers and *panzergrenadiers* from Kokott's recently arrived 115th Panzergrenadier Regiment. Everyone was elated. For several days, the staff had sensed that the Germans were readying themselves for a big push, and the G-2, Lieutenant Colonel Paul A. Danahy, even had predicted that it would come on Christmas morning. It had hung over them like the sword of Damocles. Now, thanks to the brave stand of their soldiers earlier that morning, the sword was gone.

Still, the dawn victory was only part of the story. Everyone wanted to know where Patton was. To figure out where Third Army's tanks were, Brigadier General Anthony C. McAuliffe ordered First Lieutenant Ben Wright, a forward observer, to hop into his L-4 Piper Cub plane and find them.

Wright's tiny aircraft lifted off and flew south of Bastogne. As he circled over the German lines, the young lieutenant observed the activity of the various German units and recorded their locations. When he returned, he reported what he had seen to General McAuliffe.

When McAuliffe began listening to Wright's long-winded report, he shook his head and then interrupted the lieutenant. "Hell, I know that! I want to know where the 4th Armored is."

Fortunately for the staff, their parent headquarters, Third Army, via VIII Corps, was providing them with updates of the 4th Armored Division's progress. At 1926 hours, Third Army headquarters reported that CCA was north of Strainchamps, CCB was north of Chaumont, and CCR was assembling their forces near Massul, Belgium. As it turned out, that report was more than seven hours old by the time it had reached the 101st Airborne. At 2215 hours, General McAuliffe received a radio call from Major General Troy Middleton, the commander of VIII Corps. In a short conversation, Middleton revealed that 4th Armored Division was nearly five thousand yards from the Bastogne perimeter. The closest point was north of Chaumont, where CCB had stopped. The distance between the divisions meant that the 4th Armored Division likely would not reach Bastogne for at least another twenty-four hours.

The news was disheartening for McAuliffe. "We have been let down," he remarked to Fred MacKenzie, the only reporter in Bastogne with the 101st Airborne.

The Screaming Eagles, via VIII Corps, received the next situation report at 0311 hours. According to SITREP 584, as of 1800 hours, CCA had barely moved and was a kilometer north of Strainchamps, but it had finally captured Tintange. On the other hand, CCB still was cleaning out Chaumont. However, CCR was moving, and it had reached Cobreville by midafternoon. Though the soldiers and tankers of CCR had the farthest to travel, by the end of the day they would be the first ones in Bastogne.[7]

0925 to 1345 Hours, Tuesday, December 26
37th Tank Battalion, CCR, 4th Armored Division
South of Remichampagne, Belgium

Lieutenant Colonel Creighton Abrams, standing in his tank, "Thunderbolt VI," looked north toward Remichampagne, his next objective. The previous night, he and Lieutenant Colonel George Jaques, the commander of the 53rd Armored Infantry, had met with their commander, Colonel Wendell Blanchard. The CCR commander verbally issued the order, because it was simple: He wanted CCR to roll northward and seize the town of Sibret, only a few kilometers southwest of Bastogne. According to intelligence reports, Sibret was a German strongpoint, and Blanchard felt that CCR had to take it prior to Bastogne.

Before Abrams could tackle the Germans in Sibret, he needed to deal with them in Remichampagne. Fortunately, he had a plenty of artillery support. At 0925 hours, Abrams listened as the howitzer rounds screamed overhead, and he watched them impact in the Bois de Cohet, west of Remichampagne.

Around 0945 hours, Abrams saw some artillery detonating along the southern edge of Remichampagne. He recalled that most of the artillery was supposed to land in the vicinity of the Bois de Cohet and not inside the village, because the staff of CCR were not sure of the location of Combat Command B's forward elements.

Abrams picked up his radio and called Captain James Leach, the Baker Company Commander. "Is that your arty falling in that town?" he asked.

Leach replied within seconds. "Yes."

Each company had a Sherman tank with a 105mm howitzer mounted in the turret, instead of the normal 75mm or 76mm long gun. It gave the company commander the ability to provide indirect-fire support for his unit. Leach was leading two companies, his company and Baker Company from the 53rd Armored Infantry, because Abrams had assigned him the task of clearing the town of Remichampagne. Leach's axis of advance was over an open field east of the north–south highway that led directly into town. Meanwhile, west of the same highway were the two Charlie companies, under the command of Lieutenant Charles Boggess. Abrams had ordered Boggess to establish a support-by-fire position to the west of town as part of a larger supporting effort.

As Boggess's column neared the edge of the Bois de Cohet, he detected some movement up ahead and radioed Abrams. "Troops observed going into woods."

The colonel glanced at his map and responded, "Those troops must be enemy."

For the German *panzergrenadiers*, the Bois de Cohet was the worst place to hide. While CCR closed in on Remichampagne, an unexpected flight of eight P-47s from the 377th Fighter Squadron arrived overhead and plastered the same area. Each aircraft carried two five-hundred-pound general-purpose bombs. In addition, five of the Jugs were hauling napalm canisters, and another four had rockets nestled under their wings. For nearly fifty minutes, the aircraft laid waste to the Bois de Cohet as they unloaded seven general-purpose bombs and one canister of napalm, leaving the woods in flames. Within minutes, the Bois de Cohet had become the *panzergrenadiers*' funeral pyre.

At 0955 hours, the grunts of Baker Company, 53rd Armored Infantry, reached the edge of Remichampagne. During the next hour they pushed through the hamlet. In the meantime, Leach drove ahead with his tanks and occupied a spot fifteen hundred meters southwest of Clochimont, the next intermediate objective. From there he could interdict any reinforcements from Clochimont or prevent any German survivors from escaping Remichampagne.

Around 1050 hours, CCR received word from Colonel Abrams that the two Baker companies had cleared most of the objective, and CCR then relayed that report to division. Meanwhile, Lieutenant Boggess and the two Charlie companies started to weed out the German *panzergrenadiers* from the Bois de Cohet. Thirty minutes later, the lieutenant spotted trouble west of the woods and on the high ground two kilometers north of Petite Rosière.

He quickly alerted Colonel Abrams: "Report six AT guns at left front."

The six guns were most likely from 1st Battery, 408th Volks Artillery Corps, which had escaped the destruction of 3rd Battalion, 14th Fallschirmjäger Regiment, the previous day. Now, from their current position, they could engage targets moving between Remichampagne and Cobreville. From his present position, Boggess realized that an armored attack from his location would likely result in the destruction of his company, since the German guns probably could outrange him, and therefore destroy his company before he reached them.

Farther back in the main body, Captain William Dwight, the 37th Tank Battalion S-3, looked at the map and reached the same conclusion as Boggess. He called up the Charlie Company commander to get more data on the target.

After several minutes sharing information, Dwight summoned the fire-support officer over the command net. "Get forty-sevens to work this area," he requested. "Two enemy AT guns at four, six, five, five, zero, seven. Infantry dug in from four, six, eight, five, one, two, to grid four, seven, zero, five, zero, niner." The fire-support officer then forwarded the message to CCR.

At 1200 hours, the fire-support officer called First Lieutenant Richard Donahue, the Dog Company commander, and informed him, "Promise air on the target." Donahue quickly acknowledged the message. Like Boggess and Charlie Company, Donahue also had to worry about the same antitank guns that were northwest of his position.

Fifteen minutes later, CCR's radio operator called and told them to stand by.

At 1220 hours, higher headquarters added, "Your air request—you'll get it as soon as it's in the area." Luckily for Combat Command Reserve, air support was coming, and this time it would be a flight from the 379th Fighter Squadron. Ironically, even though the pilots of the 379th had prepped their birds for bombing runs, their best weapon in the impending fight would be their machine guns.

In the meantime, Colonel Abrams needed a status update from his commanders. He sensed that the fight for Remichampagne was over, and he was looking ahead to the next engagement. Over the radio, Abrams asked Captain Leach about his ammunition levels. Leach answered, "Fine, but I'm a little low on HE."

Abrams clicked on his handset and said, "Well, I haven't used A or C Co. yet. I'm going to put A Co. on the left to screen the flank from Sibret." Resolved, Abrams ordered Second Lieutenant John Whitehill, the Able Company commander, to advance his forces through Baker Company and occupy a screen line northwest of Clochimont.

Meanwhile, Abrams linked up with Captain Leach and Baker Company, between Clochimont and Remichampagne. Leach was still waiting for his doughboys to catch up when Abrams arrived. As the 37th Tank Battalion commander's small force rolled up, a group of Germans in a slit trench opened fire. The fight was short, and the defenders scored no hits on Abrams's tiny force, who ordered them to surrender.

As the tankers processed the detainees, Abrams drove forward to Leach's tank, "Blockbuster." He noticed a German gun more than a thousand meters away, north of their position, lobbing rounds at the approaching tanks of Whitehill's Able Company. He ordered Leach "to take care of it," so the Baker Company commander instructed one of his tankers to deal with the pesky gun.

One of the Baker Company tanks started to shift position to acquire a better shot. Abrams was impatient. Embarrassed and amazed, Leach watched as Abrams edged forward in "Thunderbolt VI." "[Abrams] fired one round—it was an AA gun mounted on the back of a vehicle of some sort," Leach wrote. "So he knocked it out. And I recommended him for the DSC right there. After all here's the Colonel—a lot of colonels stay back at the goddamn flagpole but not Abrams. So he knocked that gun out [and] then he pushed A Company on through to screen." Apparently when the single round hit the truck, the gun flew into the air as if a gust of wind had blown it.

By 1345 hours, the German defenders had started to surrender in droves. When the processing was complete, the doughboys from Charlie Company, 53rd Armored Infantry, had captured thirty-three German soldiers. Many of their comrades had not been so lucky. The fight for Remichampagne now was over. The fight for Assenois was about to begin.[8]

0400 to 1200 Hours, Tuesday, December 26
Headquarters, 1st Battalion, 104th Panzergrenadier Regiment,
15th Panzergrenadier Division
Near Fontaine de Burton, Belgium

Unbeknownst to anyone above regimental level, the *panzergrenadiers* from 3rd Company of the 104th Panzergrenadiers had lost the battle. 1st Battalion, under the command of Hauptmann Ludwig Gross, started to receive reports as early as 0400 hours, when Leutnant Winzker's 1st Company claimed to see American tanks leaving Vaux-lez-Rosières, heading north in the direction of Morhet. Ten minutes later the same tanks vanished when they entered the Bois de Wavre forest, southwest of Morhet. It was probably a false report.

On the other hand, the artillery exploding amid the homes of Remichampagne were real. At 0710 hours, Leutnant Wilhelm Klouker, the 3rd Company commander, radioed the battalion command post and reported that American howitzers were engaging targets inside the town and east of it. Back at battalion, Gross wondered if this was the main attack he had feared since the previous day. Five minutes later, he got his answer.

Suddenly tank rounds exploded outside his makeshift command post, setting it ablaze. Gross had to evacuate, and his small staff decided that the tiny settlement of Fontaine de Burton, north of their current location, was the safest spot for a new temporary headquarters. Hauptmann Gross issued the order, and the staff began to scramble and pack as more rounds crashed outside. Little did Gross know, but the main attack was still two hours away. This was only the softening-up period.

Nevertheless, Gross's *panzergrenadiers* counted twenty-six American Sherman tanks south of their current spot. The battalion commander realized that his force of *panzergrenadiers* stood little chance against this American force. Unfortunately, before he could issue any more orders, he lost contact with Klouker's 3rd Company in Remichampagne at approximately 0720 hours. From that point on, Klouker was on his own.

For another hour, American artillery pounded the area, while Abrams's tanks shot up the likely locations of German units with their main guns. At 0830 hours, Leutnant Winzker's 1st Company alerted the battalion that the Americans also were attacking his company, which was north of Vaux-lez-Rosières. Since Gross no longer had contact with 3rd Company, his only option was to wait and see until the Americans showed their hand.

At 1000 hours, Gross received another report from 1st Company. This time it was the feared jabos. This was the same flight that had ravaged the Bois de Cohet forest, and according to Leutnant Winzker, the fighter-bombers also struck the town of Morhet, four kilometers northwest of the Bois de Cohet. Their attack destroyed a mortar position located near the railroad station in the town, resulting in three German casualties.

Winzker's *panzergrenadiers*, refusing to be cowed, fought back. Thirty minutes after the P-47s attacked, a towed antitank gun crew, located with Winzker's company, fired on several tanks. The crew later claimed they destroyed one. Though American records made no mention of losing a tank that morning to antitank gunfire, the tankers were aware of the antitank guns located near Morhet. In fact, it was those guns that probably prompted the request for more air support from Dog Company and Charlie Company, 37th Tank Battalion, respectively.

By 1200 hours, Hauptmann Gross concluded that he would not regain radio or telephone contact with Klouker's 3rd Company. According to his other intact units, the American tanks had reached the area around the Clochimont–Salvacourt road. In reply, he ordered his mortars to open fire and delay the American advance. In the meantime, he allowed his 1st Company to withdraw north of the Morhet–Remichampagne road. Later that evening, after Gross had established his new command post in Fontaine de Burton, he realized that 3rd Company had ceased to exist. In recognition of this new reality, the remnants of his entire battalion consolidated around Sibret and Jodenville. Unfortunately for the Wehrmacht, no one else besides Gross knew the extent of the disaster, because communication between his regiment and the XXXXVII Panzer Corps was non-existent. As a result, Kokott's 26th Volksgrenadier Division was woefully unprepared for the next assault, which would fall on his division, because no one was left between his unit and the tidal wave of tanks from the 4th Armored.[9]

1200 Hours to Midafternoon, Tuesday, December 26
Command Post, 26th Volksgrenadier Division
Givry, Belgium

Oberst Heinz Kokott read through the morning reports, unaware that his southern buffer zone had disintegrated. Still, he sensed something was amiss. It was the last set of radio communiqués that disturbed him the most. Major Kaufmann, the commander of the 39th Fusilier Regiment, had reported fighting to his south in the 5th Fallschirmjäger Division's area of operations. Kokott tried to get more information from XXXXVII Panzer Corps, his higher headquarters, but the corps staff had little to offer other than an assurance that American forces coming from the south would not penetrate the German cordon today.

Meanwhile, the Americans trapped in Bastogne were not idle. At noon, the paratroopers with some tanks attacked near Isle le Pré, in the southwest sector of the German encirclement. Fortunately, the attack achieved little, but it probably indicated to Kokott that the Bastogne garrison was no longer on the defensive. He assessed they had amassed enough supplies from the airdrops to attempt small probing attacks.

Not long after the abortive attack on Isle le Pré, the headquarters staff received another report from the 39th Fusilier Regiment. This time it was more serious than the sounds of battle to its south, because now American artillery was landing inside Sibret and Assenois. Initial reports revealed that the artillery fire was emanating from south of Assenois and not from Bastogne. In short, the American armored forces advancing from Arlon were a lot closer than originally thought.

When Kokott heard this troubling report, he called his corps headquarters on the phone. He asked whether the corps staff had any more information on the status of the 5th Fallschirmjäger Division. The unknown officer replied that the *fallschirmjägers* were "for some time engaged in battle with advancing enemy tanks around Remichampagne. Steps for sealing off the enemy penetration had been initiated, however."

Alas, the German response to parrying the armored thrust was a battalion-size counterattack. Hauptmann Alfred Kitze, the commander of 2nd Battalion, 15th Fallschirmjäger Regiment, had received an order to strike the eastern flank of the American penetration. However, 2nd Battalion was a battalion in name only. The fighting around Warnach had devastated it. At this point, the Germans were reaching for straws, but Kokott had not fully grasped how desperate the 5th Fallschirmjäger Division's condition was. Thanks to tactical signal intercepts, the 4th Armored Division's G-2 section was aware of the proposed counterattack. In short, the Americans knew more about Kokott's southern neighbor than did Kokott.

Still, the *volksgrenadier* commander had an inkling that something was awry, and despite the promises of the unknown staff officer, Kokott knew he had to make arrangements in case the Americans had penetrated his southern zone. He ordered the 39th Regiment and his attached 901st Panzergrenadier Regiment to push out security detachments south of their positions to provide early warning. However, because of his current mission, that was all he could do. On account of the defiant 101st Airborne in Bastogne, he had to commit everything else to the cordon around that infernal city.

For the commander of the 26th Volksgrenadier Division, the situation was daunting but not hopeless. In a postwar interview, he remarked, "Despite the numerous rumors, alarms, and exaggerated reports which, during the afternoon, kept coming in from the southern sector, hope (at least at the division) was not lost that the southern front would remain intact until darkness."

He knew that if the southern defense zone held out until evening, then it was safe until the following morning, because the American army typically had not conducted offensive operations at night or late in the afternoon. Moreover, the anticipated reinforcements from the Führer-Begleit-Brigade would arrive sometime in the evening or early the next morning. Therefore, the newly arrived brigade, with its additional panzers, would be in position to meet the next American attack the following day.

After the war, Kokott recalled his optimism on the twenty-sixth, commenting, "All of these were, of course, only hopes! And they should soon prove themselves fallacies. . . ."[10]

1400 to 1415 Hours, Tuesday, December 26
79th Troop Carrier Squadron, 436th Troop Carrier Group, 9th Air Force
Membury Airfield, England

While Oberst Kokott struggled with his decisions, elsewhere events rapidly were approaching a climax. Back in England, another group of C-47 Skytrains were preparing to take off and head to Bastogne. One of the pilots was Second Lieutenant Bill Leaphart, who had been in England for only ten days. Leaphart had grown up in Montana, where he attended the University of Montana as a cadet in the Army ROTC program. After attending various flight schools from July 1943 to September 1944, the young Bill Leaphart was ready to fly night fighters. Alas, after receiving his commission as a second lieutenant, Leaphart learned that his first unit after flight school was a glider unit. Disappointed, he left for Lubbock, Texas, to learn how to fly the Waco glider. According to Leaphart, his first mission likely would have been an airdrop into Frankfurt, Germany.

Luckily for him, he would have other opportunities to fly before that operation. In early December, he boarded a troopship for Great Britain and arrived in England on the sixteenth of December, the same day the Bulge kicked off. When he arrived at Membury Airfield, his commander did not know what to do with him, since the command needed C-47 pilots and not glider drivers. Thus, for the next ten days, Leaphart got a crash course in how to fly the C-47 plane.

Now it was the twenty-sixth, and Leaphart was going through the preflight checklist. His first mission was to fly over some town in Belgium named Bastogne. Oddly, Leaphart had no idea that it was a combat mission. He assumed it was another training flight. Leaphart's job was to fly over Bastogne, and then his crew would toss "parapacks" out the cabin door. The containers then would float down to the ground, where the paratroopers would collect them.

Leaphart's squadron was not the first to fly over Bastogne that day. The 440th Troop Carrier Group had already flown a major resupply mission. In fact, a glider from the 96th Troop Carrier Squadron had landed in Bastogne around 1400 hours. This glider carried an advanced surgical team, which was crucial, because most of the 101st Airborne surgeons were languishing in a makeshift prisoner-of-war camp after the Germans had overrun the division's field hospital earlier in the siege. On the other hand, the single glider and tow plane had alerted the German antiaircraft gunners on the ground. As a result, they were ready when the large, lumbering transports appeared on the southern horizon.

Lieutenant Leaphart was in one of the groups that was approaching Bastogne. His aircraft was part of a squadron of fifteen Skytrains, and his 440th Troop Carrier Group had four squadrons cruising over Bastogne that afternoon, nearly sixty C-47s. When Leaphart saw the tracers arcing in front of his cockpit, he realized it was a combat mission. Looking north, he watched as the lead plane started to make a wide turn, and then he heard on the radio that the group leader had missed the target. As a result of his mistake, the entire carrier group would have to wheel around and repeat the entire run, giving the German gunners another chance at bagging a Skytrain.

As the herd lined up for the second go-around, the rookie pilot from Montana spied a flock of German fighters in the distance. Fortunately they had other problems, and they left the Skytrains alone. Finally the troop carriers were ready again, and as Leaphart's plane flew toward Bastogne, he noticed colored panels on the ground, indicating the forward trace of the American lines. This time the convoy accomplished its mission, delivering their parapacks on target. Fortunately, despite the ground fire, not a single C-47 from Leaphart's carrier group was lost to antiaircraft artillery, though some of the fuselages looked like Swiss cheese from all the flak. For their unwavering bravery, Leaphart and his fellow pilots later were awarded the Air Medal.[11]

1400 to 1415 Hours, Tuesday, December 26
379th Fighter Squadron, 362nd Fighter Group, 9th Air Force
Two to Three Thousand Feet over Witry, Belgium

Leaphart claimed he saw only a few German fighters. In fact, twenty-five FW-190s had arrived over Bastogne to contest the aerial resupply of the 101st Airborne. Eight Thunderbolts from the 379th Fighter Squadron were responding to a request for close air support from CCR and the 4th Armored Division when the German wolves revealed themselves. Luckily for the sheep, the P-47 shepherds also saw the wolves. Even though the Luftwaffe flight outnumbered them nearly three to one, the eight American pilots were thirsty for aerial combat, and they jettisoned their bombs and dived after the 190s.

First Lieutenant Barton T. Williams, a pilot in the 379th, described what happened next: "We arrived just as a 'gaggle' of about thirty German FW-190s attacked our ground troops. We rolled right in and began shooting them down—whereupon they 'hit the deck' in rapid retreat down small valleys toward the 'Vaterland.'"

Williams slid behind one of the Focke-Wulf 190s and pressed the trigger on his stick. He watched the tracers rip into the fuselage of the German fighter, which caught fire and plunged toward the earth. Williams was far from finished.

The other German pilots were desperately racing toward the illusive safety of German airspace. To avoid the frenzied Yankees, the Luftwaffe aviators tried to hide by flying low in the valleys, like soldiers ducking behind hedges. For many, this tactic proved fruitless.

After Williams downed the first Focke-Wulf, he crested a ridge and found another bandit screaming eastward. He lined up his Jug behind the fleeing plane and he opened fire. The eight M2 machine guns chugged away, and bits of metal flew from the dying 190. Within a few seconds it was all over. The FW-190 started to pop and explode as it hurtled toward the earth.

Second Lieutenant Forrest H. Fegan and First Lieutenant Ralph L. Sallee each downed a pair of German fighters, while First Lieutenant Howard M. Sloan and Second Lieutenant Joseph R. Murphy added one kill each to the overall tally. In total, the Luftwaffe lost eight irreplaceable pilots and aircraft over Bastogne.

It was not without cost. Sloan's aircraft suffered some hits, and he had to bail out. Luckily, he jumped out over American lines, and he promptly returned to his squadron that evening. The American Army Air Force had prevented the Luftwaffe from controlling the skies over southern Belgium. As a result, the weakened Luftwaffe never seriously challenged the American advantage in close air support during the daylight hours over Bastogne. This defeat would cost the German army dearly.

All throughout the day, the 362nd Fighter Group wreaked havoc on the Wehrmacht around Bastogne. In addition to the morning mission that punished the German forces around the Bois de Cohet woods, the 377th Fighter Squadron conducted another close air support mission between 1355 to 1500 hours, in which a flight of eight more Thunderbolts strafed targets around Harlange and Morhet.

In conjunction with the 377th, the 378th Fighter Squadron also conducted several missions in support of the 4th Armored Division. In one particular operation, twelve P-47s laid waste to targets around Sibret between 1300 and 1320 hours. Overall, in addition to the downed FW-190s, the three squadrons of the 362nd Fighter Group destroyed at least two tanks, four 7.5cm howitzer positions, two motor trucks, and three small-caliber antiaircraft guns around the surrounded city. The Germans shot down several Thunderbolts, killing only one pilot, but for the Americans, replacing aircraft at this point in the war was easy. Thus, according to the statisticians, the exchange was a fair trade, since the German Luftwaffe hardly could afford to keep up with the American aviation industry, which was rolling out aircraft by the tens of thousands. Even worse, on account of the fuel shortages that had curtailed its flight training, the Luftwaffe could not replace its pilots, while the Americans, who had no fuel shortages, could.[12]

1200 to 1500 Hours, Tuesday, December 26
Area of Operations, 4th Armored Division
Ten to Twenty Kilometers South of Bastogne, Belgium

As the procession of C-47s thundered overhead, the soldiers of the 4th Armored Division watched in awe. It was a fitting testimony to American might. Hundreds of planes filled the sky, but unlike the fighters, which bounced around helter-skelter, the transports followed a fixed course. The entire airborne motorcade lasted three hours.

Meanwhile, the Germans seemed powerless below. According to observers on the ground, they did see some ground fire, but it was negligible. Few saw any C-47s fall from the sky. According to the flight logs, only one Skytrain failed to return to base. Considering that more than 289 planes and ten gliders participated in the airlift, the loss of only a single aircraft was a resounding success.

Sergeant Eugene Wright, a mechanic in the 4th Armored's 489th Antiaircraft Artillery Battalion, recalled that there were "probably twenty or thirty minutes of them [with] nothing but C-47s going by."

Second Lieutenant Irving M. Heath was a platoon leader in Charlie Company, 35th Tank Battalion, which was outside of Honville, Belgium, that afternoon.

"Then we heard a tremendous noise," he remembered, "and we looked up, and there were C-47 cargo ships. Forty, fifty, maybe fifty-five, [they] were flying low and dropping supplies into Bastogne."

He continued. "It was the most beautiful sight I had ever seen, and I have never seen anything to match because the sky was blue and the parachutes were all different colors: blue, green, orange, purple, [and] red."[13]

1500 to 1610 Hours, Tuesday, December 26
Lead Elements of CCR, 4th Armored Division
In the Vicnity of Clochimont, Belgium

Among the thousands of onlookers who watched the airborne motorcade was Captain William Dwight, the 37th Tank Battalion's S-3. Dwight was located near Remichampagne with the two Charlie companies, and he remembered what he witnessed. He said, "I saw these damn C-47s coming in to drop their colored parachutes for the 101st. They . . . were taking one hell of a beating. We trembled standing there and watching it."

Lieutenant Colonel Creighton Abrams and Lieutenant Colonel George Jaques were farther north, near Clochimont. As he looked on, Abrams finally broke the silence and said to Jaques, "Well, if those fellas can take that, we're going in right now."

Colonel Jaques agreed with Abrams, and the two men quickly began to formulate a course of action. Thanks to the abundance of radios in the U.S. Army, Abrams could delegate and coordinate over the FM net without having to meet with the various players in person. It was one of the biggest reasons why the U.S. Army was so successful in World War II. It could react a lot quicker than its adversaries as a result of its robust communications infrastructure. The one person Abrams failed to call was Colonel Blanchard, the CCR commander.

Lieutenant Colonel Hal Pattison, the executive officer for Combat Command A, knew both Colonel Blanchard and Colonel Abrams. According to Pattison, many, including Abrams, thought Blanchard was timid, and as a result, Abrams did not want to request permission from Blanchard, because he felt that the CCR commander would have denied the request.

Pattison supported Abrams's controversial decision to disobey orders. He later remarked, "Not too many commanders over the course of history have had the courage to make the right decision in the face of wrong orders."

As for Abrams's motivations, Pattison reasoned that "the combat commander [Blanchard] hadn't been anywhere near the action all day long, and he [Abrams] was in a far better position to assess what should and shouldn't be done."

Both Abrams and Jaques agreed that the task of seizing Sibret was beyond their current capabilities. If the Germans were defending Sibret in force, as intelligence indicated, then the weakened condition of both 53rd Armored Infantry and 37th Tank battalions meant success was unlikely. Jaques was short 230 infantrymen, while Abrams had only twenty operating tanks to commit to the operation. Therefore, the two commanders concluded that the axis of advance needed to go through the town of Assenois, which they felt was a better intermediate objective, since Assenois did not sit astride the main highway, and thus the Germans did not consider it the likely avenue of approach for American forces. Because of this, the two officers estimated that Assenois would not be as heavily defended as Sibret. Furthermore, from Assenois, it was about two kilometers to the 101st Airborne's outer perimeter.

At 1511 hours, Abrams grabbed his radio and summoned his S-3, Captain Dwight. "Alert those two companies up there for movement. You are in command. Get everything well in hand, over. It's the push!"

When Captain Dwight and Lieutenant Boggess, C Company commander, arrived at Abrams's location, the Skytrains still were still streaming overhead. Amid the droning of hundreds of radial aircraft engines, Abrams outlined his basic plan. He wanted Dwight to lead the two Charlie companies through Assenois and then on to Bastogne. Trailing behind would be Baker Company, 53rd Armored Infantry. Baker Company had the mission to clear Assenois. Abrams did not want the two Charlie companies to waste time in an urban fight, because he wanted Dwight's column to drive hell-bent for leather through Assenois and keep on going until it made contact with the 101st Airborne. Meanwhile, Whitehill's Able Company would continue to screen between Clochimont and Assenois and along the western flank. Farther back and in reserve would be Leach's Baker Company from the 37th Tank Battalion, and Kutak's Able Company from the 53rd Armored Infantry.

Abrams showed Boggess the route he wanted Charlie Company to take.

Boggess was to lead the column that would penetrate the German lines and reach Bastogne. It was daunting task. Like the other companies, Boggess's unit was understrength, with only nine tanks, two officers, and forty-three enlisted men. The other officer was Second Lieutenant Walter Wrolson. Luckily, Charlie Company had received an M4A3E2 Sherman, which was an up-armored version, which Boggess named "Cobra King." Besides "Cobra King," his eight other tanks were the standard M4A3 and M4A1 models, a mixture of 76mm and 75mm main guns.

Abrams directed Boggess to use the hardball (paved) road that linked Clochimont and Bastogne via Assenois. It was a straight shot. On the other hand, Abrams confessed to Boggess that he had little idea what was waiting for them down that road, since no one had ordered any ground reconnaissance previously along that route. Fortunately, aerial reconnaissance had revealed several possible antitank guns that the Germans had positioned in front of the rail bed that ran southeast of Assenois. Boggess examined the map. Between Clochimont and Assenois, it was wide-open terrain with undulating hills. Boggess realized that the antitank guns would have excellent fields of fire along his axis of advance if the artillery failed to suppress them.

Beyond Assenois, the road ran between two wooded areas. The larger, southeastern forest was called the Bois Bechu. Abrams believed that the woods likely concealed German infantry, since the narrow road corridor between them was only several hundred meters at the widest part. Hence, *volksgrenadiers*, armed with *panzerfausts* and *panzerschrecks*, easily could target a column of tanks while remaining hidden in the wood line. To Abrams, the woods were now targets for the artillery because of this likelihood. Finally, after the road ran through the severely restrictive terrain of the Bois Bechu, it exited into an open area. According to an overlay that an artillery spotter pilot had managed to get out of Bastogne the previous evening, the 101st Airborne's foxhole line was about a kilometer beyond the exit.

With the briefing concluded, Abrams closed the discussion by saying, "Gentlemen, there are no questions."

Boggess agreed. He understood his mission and nodded.

Abrams issued one final order to Boggess and Dwight: "Get to those men in Bastogne." With those parting words, he returned to his tank to finish coordinating the operation.

With a clear task and purpose, the Charlie Company commander left to conduct his own troop-leading procedures. He called his tank commanders together in front of "Cobra King." "As company commander," Boggess later wrote, "I would be in the lead tank (Cobra King) and I would set the speed of the attack—I would fire straight ahead. Lieutenant Wrolson would be in the second tank firing to the right, the following tank to the left—and so on down. Each man was given the route and the objective—each tank was to continue the attack to the last tank, if necessary, and with that we were ready."

Boggess knew he was taking a risk by assuming the vanguard in the column, but the position had several advantages. "Cobra King," with an additional 38mm of armor welded to the hull, on both the front and the flanks, had more protection than the other tanks in his company. Furthermore, the designers had added more than 90mm of steel to the front of the turret. In short, it could take a beating. On the other hand, the extra weight resulted in slower speeds, but that was not a problem, since Boggess was the pacesetter for the column. What's more, as the company commander, Boggess had the best crew. Hubert J. J. Smith was his driver, and Milton Dickerman was the gunner. Harold Hafner was the bog gunner, and James G. Murphy was the loader. Boggess described them as "all battle proven veterans."

While Boggess laid out his plan to his soldiers, Abrams continued to refine his portion of the operation. To succeed, he needed artillery. When he returned to his tank, he immediately called Captain Thomas J. Cooke, his artillery liaison officer, who still was at CCR's main command post in Remoiville. Cooke decided that he needed more help, so he rang up his other commander, Major Robert Parker, the commanding officer for CCR's 94th Armored Field Artillery Battalion.

Both men realized that one battalion of 105mm howitzers and one battery of 155mm Long Toms was not enough combat power to provide the curtain of fire that Abrams needed. Cooke radioed the division fire direction center and requested more tubes. Within minutes of Cooke's request, Major R. H. Meyer, the division artillery's operations officer, informed Cooke that he had one more battalion of 105mm howitzers (253rd Armored Field Artillery) and another battalion of 155mm howitzers (776th Field Artillery) on call. Next, Cooke called the 22nd Armored Field Artillery's fire direction center directly, and the 22nd also agreed to provide its eighteen howitzers for an on-call mission. In less than thirty minutes, Cooke had managed to secure two more battalions of 105mm howitzers and another battalion of 155mm howitzers, for a total of fifty-four 105mm tubes and twenty-four 155mm tubes. Thanks to Cooke's and Parker's coordination, Abrams would have a steamroller of shrapnel rolling in front of his column.

Now that he had the guns, Cooke needed to assign them targets. Luckily, the redlegs of the 94th Armored Field Artillery already had registered their guns around Assenois, and Cooke asked them to pass along their firing data to the other battalions via the division's fire direction center. Cooke decided that each firing battery of the 94th would have separate targets. Able Battery would suppress possible targets in the wood line, northwest of Assenois, while Charlie Battery would hit the Bois Bechu, northeast of Assenois. At the same time, Baker Battery would neutralize the reported antitank guns between the railroad and Assenois–Lune road, southeast of Assenois. The 253rd and 22nd Armored Field Artillery battalions would support the 94th's fire missions as needed. While the 105s pounded the area around Assenois, the 155s from Charlie Battery, 177th Field Artillery, would saturate the center of Assenois. If the 177th needed more steel on target, then its fire direction center could request additional support from the 776th Field Artillery Battalion.

With his work complete, Cooke notified Captain Dwight via the command net at 1545 hours: "Concentration nine [in Assenois]. We can get four units. Three small [the 105mm howitzer battalions] and one big on fifteen minutes' notice [the 155mm howitzer battalion]." In less than hour, Cooke would execute his fire plan.

By now, Able Company, 37th Tank Battalion, already was rolling toward its screen line, northwest of Clochimont. Abrams, standing inside his turret on Thunderbolt VI, called for a status report from Lieutenant Whitehill, the company commander.

Whitehill responded, "I've moved north of town [and] on high ground now."

"Are you meeting any resistance?" Abrams inquired. For two minutes, he heard nothing but static. He radioed Whitehill again, "What are you running into?"

Whitehill finally reported, "Looks like direct fire."

"Can you tell where it is coming from? I'd like to know that," asked Abrams.

When no response came, Abrams realized that Whitehill was busy fighting a battle, and he stopped pestering him. For several minutes, the back-and-forth continued over the command net as all the actors made last-minute adjustments before the final act. Finally, at 1610 hours, Abrams called his S-3 and asked, "Are you ready to go?"

Captain Dwight replied almost immediately, "Yes."

Abrams put down his radio and gestured his hand forward. From his tank at the front of the column, Boggess saw Abrams wave. He ordered Hubert Smith to move out, and the young tanker shifted the transmission into first gear, causing Cobra King to lurch forward. One by one, the tanks of Charlie Company started to roll down the road to Assenois. Interspersed among the column was a single jeep, which carried the forward observer team led by First Lieutenant Ellsworth B. Chamberlin. Trailing behind the tanks were the half-tracks of Charlie Company, 53rd Armored Infantry, under the command of First Lieutenant Dewitt C. Smith.

As the last tank swung in behind the column, a truck arrived and a soldier jumped off the back. His name has been lost to history, but he was a Charlie Company tanker. According to Boggess, the man had been languishing in a hospital for the past several days. Knowing the significance of this attack, he chose to come back to his company and his fellow soldiers. He hopped onto the last tank and squeezed himself inside the turret. Thanks to this dedicated GI, Boggess now had forty-four enlisted tankers under his command, and hopefully he would have the same number when he reached Bastogne. Unbeknownst to Colonel Blanchard, the final attack had begun.[14]

1610 to 1655 Hours, Tuesday, December 26
Charlie Company, 37th Tank Battalion, CCR, 4th Armored Division
Moving North of Clochimont, Belgium

Initially, Boggess did not see any worthwhile targets. Regardless, he opened fire with every machine gun he had, peppering the road in front of him. The other tank commanders followed his lead, unleashing a maelstrom of lead to the left and right of the column. Not wanting to present to the Germans a slow-moving target, Boggess ordered Smith to open up on the throttle, causing the tank to accelerate. Since "Cobra King" would be the slowest vehicle in the column, Boggess believed the other tanks would have little difficulty keeping up with his Sherman.

In the meantime, the command net was buzzing. Almost immediately, at 1615 hours, Boggess heard Captain Leach ping Colonel Abrams about German infantry hiding in buildings toward his front. Moments later, Leach identified a German vehicle with SS markings. Abrams told him to annihilate it with his Sherman assault gun. After several minutes, Abrams demanded information on Sibret, which Whitehill and Able Company were observing to the northwest. Seconds later, Whitehill assuaged his commander's concerns and replied that he did not see any activity inside the town.

During all of this chaos, Boggess continued to plow ahead. Several hundred meters beyond Clochimont, the company commander detected a crater in the road meant to block his movement, but Boggess easily bypassed it.

Despite the din around him, Boggess listened as his commander called the fire support officer over the radio. "Get that ready. Tell Cook," said Abrams. A hurricane of artillery was about to let loose on Assenois.

Farther back, Captain Dwight monitored the net. His tank, "Tonto," was the fourth vehicle in the column. His job was to provide situational awareness to his boss, while maintaining control of the two Charlie companies. This command scheme allowed Boggess to fight the battle without interruptions from his commander. This was Abrams's plan. He wanted his company commanders to have unfettered control of their units during the battle. In the meantime, the S-3 or S-2, depending on the situation, would update him on the situation. For his subordinates, the system worked.

Dwight looked ahead and saw "Cobra King" closing in on Assenois. It was almost time, and so he called Boggess over the radio. "Charlie, make sure your people are ready." The clock read 1630 hours.

A minute later, both Dwight and Boggess heard First Lieutenant John P. Young, from Combat Command B north of Chaumont, radio Colonel Abrams directly. "Our FO [Forward Observer] would like to know where your leading elements are?" he asked.

By now, the danger of fratricide was real, because CCB and CCR were almost

314 ★ PATTON AT THE BATTLE OF THE BULGE

on a collision course as their lead elements advanced north of the Sibret–Hompré road. Abrams reported his position. "We're on the high ground by the crossroads [just south of Clochimont]. Your rear elements protect our supply line."

Four minutes later, Boggess heard his battalion commander call Cooke on the command net. "Can I get a concentration on a minute's notice?"

Cooke shot back, "Yes."

Boggess peered ahead. He estimated that the distance between his tank and the outskirts of Assenois was approximately a thousand meters. Luckily, the Germans had not spotted him yet, and his column had approached the town unmolested. He took a deep breath and summoned his commander on his handset. "Boggess to CO . . . Request number nine concentration." He glanced at his watch: 1635 hours.

Abrams had been waiting for the call, and he quickly relayed it to the CCR fire support officer. "Play it soft and sweet," he remarked. He did not need to clarify the message, because everyone listening in knew what Abrams had meant.

Despite the commander's soothing words, the artillery barrage sounded more like a discordant, untrained orchestra than a jazz quartet. Boggess recalled that "almost immediately, the town seemed to erupt."

A moment later, Boggess requested the artillery to lift, and Abrams adjusted its aim. He ordered the fire support officer, "Raise arty three hundred."

Boggess watched the geysers of dirt as he edged closer to Assenois. Seconds later, another barrage came screaming overhead and it exploded. This time it was even closer. For the German antitank gunners and howitzer crews, the incoming fire was deadly. Along the southern border of Assenois, a 10.5cm howitzer battery and two antitank guns received the brunt of it, and the incoming volleys slaughtered several soldiers who did not find cover in time.

From where he stood, Abrams could see that it was danger-close, and he called the fire support officer again. "Raise arty four hundred more," he instructed.

At the head of the column, Boggess requested the fire to lift again, but he did not account for the rounds that already were in flight. It was too late. As he continued to approach the outskirts of the town, the next volley detonated on top of his column. The first series of explosions hit Lieutenant Chamberlin's jeep, killing the driver instantly and leaving Chamberlin wounded and dazed, lying on the side of the road. Another salvo crashed into the half-tracks of Smith's infantry company. Almost instantly, a half-track blew up. Luckily, most of the infantry were in the process of dismounting when the shells impacted, so the short rounds only caused three casualties.

The chaos led to confusion in the column. Suddenly, Boggess's "Cobra King" pulled ahead, but behind him were only two tanks. Before the Germans realized it, Boggess was through Assenois, yet between his group and Dwight's group was a gap of about three hundred meters. The break was large enough for several German pioneers to dash onto the road and lay twelve Teller antitank mines.

With Dwight was one tank from Boggess's company and a half-track, whose crew had somehow managed to push too far ahead of the infantry in their open-topped vehicle. Farther back in the column, the turmoil confused two Sherman drivers, who lost their way around the winding streets of Assenois, leaving Dwight's ad hoc team to push ahead.

Despite the artillery mishap, the barrage had been effective. Since the rounds were still landing while Boggess was navigating through the winding streets of Assenois, the Germans never managed to get a shot off at his group. Indeed, they were hunkered in the cellars almost the whole time. After Boggess exited Assenois, his group then continued to drive north down the road. Woods flanked him on either side, with the Bois Bechu to his south. Boggess wrote what happened next.

I saw a large pillbox ahead and ordered Dickerman to throw several rounds into it—it was demolished. I saw the enemy in confusion on both sides of the road. Obviously, they were surprised by an entry on this road, as some were standing in a chow line. They fell like dominoes. As we cleared the woods, we came upon a small, open field, where we saw multi-colored parachutes—these had been recently used to drop supplies of food and ammo to the 101st Airborne Div. This meant that we were near the line defending the town. I slowed the tanks down and we cautiously approached what seemed to be a line of foxholes, spaced about fifty feet apart. Out of each hole, a machine gun was leveled at my tank, with a helmeted figure behind each gun. The men of the 101st knew full well that the enemy had been using American uniforms and equipment during the past few weeks and they were taking no chances. I called out to them, "Come on out, this is the Fourth Armored," but no one moved. I called again and again and, finally, an officer emerged from the nearest foxhole and approached the tank. He reached up a hand, and with a smile said, "I'm Lieutenant Webster of the 326th Engineers, 101st Airborne Division. Glad to see you." He was no more glad to see me than I was to see him! As I shook his hand I knew that Company C of the 37th Tank Battalion, Fourth Armored, Third Army had broken through the bulge and that the siege of Bastogne was over.

Almost a thousand meters behind him, Dwight had no idea that Boggess had linked up with the 101st Airborne Division. After his group had left Assenois, he realized he had only three vehicles in his element: a half-track, another tank, and his Sherman, "Tonto." Everyone was still firing their .50- and .30-caliber machine guns, and Dwight sensed that German infantry were lying in ambush in the woods that bordered each side of the road. A terrific explosion rocked the half-track that had pulled ahead of Dwight's tank, and within seconds a fire started inside the stricken M3.

Without hesitation, Dwight jumped off his tank and ran toward the burning vehicle. Several others joined him. By now the Germans were firing back, and Dwight could hear the snapping and cracking of rifle rounds. When he reached the flaming wreck, he soon saw what had caused the blast. Lying on the ground in front of him were eleven Teller mines. Grabbing an unexploded one, he then tossed it into a nearby ditch. Other soldiers followed his example, clearing the road. Meanwhile, men pulled out the wounded from the half-track and bandaged them.

For several agonizing minutes they were exposed as Dwight and the others cleared the mines. To provide cover, the two remaining tank crews laid down suppressive fire on both wood lines, using their machine guns. The tactic worked, and in less than ten minutes they had removed the barrier. Dwight ordered the column to resume its trek northward, and he hopped back onto "Tonto." It was now 1650 hours. For his courage under fire, the army later awarded Captain Dwight the Silver Star.

The S-3 had no idea what happened to Boggess, and so Dwight immediately raised him on the radio. "How are you doing?" Dwight asked the Charlie Company commander.

For several seconds, Dwight heard only static. Finally, at 1653 hours, Boggess replied, "Have reached objective."

The S-3 ordered Boggess with a terse command, "Consolidate."

Two minutes later, Dwight radioed Boggess again and advised, "You have a tank back up here—make him move." The S-3 knew that the road they had opened was more of a gauntlet than a corridor. To make it a viable supply line, they had to clear the Germans completely out of Assenois and the woods that lined the road. To do that they needed infantry, and all they had were tanks, because the infantry was back in Assenois, fighting for their lives against a furious foe.[15]

1640 to 1701 Hours, Tuesday, December 26
Command Post, 53rd Armored Infantry Battalion, CCR,
4th Armored Division Nives, Belgium

At 1640 hours, Colonel Blanchard called Major Edward Bautz, the executive officer for the 37th Tank Battalion, over the radio. "We are going to do it tonight. Get everything together. I want to meet Abe and Jaques at checkpoint seventy-four in about forty-five minutes." Blanchard did not know that Boggess and the rest of CCR were already approaching Bastogne.

Bautz responded, "Can I meet you?"

Blanchard answered, "Yes." Several minutes later, the major arrived. "Now, I want you to pick up everything and move it all into Bastogne," Blanchard told him.

Bautz had not been privy to Abrams's plan, and had not been briefed entirely about what was happening in Assenois. As a result, he tried to dissuade the CCR commander. "Sir, I don't think we want to do that," he argued.

Bautz opened his map and started to point at the various unit locations. "You know, we've been fighting along here. We've got a light tank company over here, on the flank; we've got B Company over here on this flank, and A Company over here, while C Company is in there with the contact."

Blanchard shook his head. "I said to move it in."

The discussion was over, and the major returned to his tank to coordinate with Colonel Abrams over the radio.

Bautz later recounted what had happened when he told Abrams about Blanchard's idea. "I called Colonel Abe, and I explained the situation, and he came back with . . . a quick, quiet answer, you know, 'You do as you suggested. Just bring in the trains of the 101st and the other stuff in the headquarters,' and so, Colonel Blanchard said, 'What was that? What was that up there?' and I said, 'Static, sir, static.'"

On the other end of the radio, Abrams now realized that it was time to tell his boss what was going on in Assenois. At 1650 hours, he found out about the linkup from Boggess, and he relayed it to CCR. "We have contacted unit required," he reported via the fire support officer.

Five minutes later, Blanchard understood Abrams's message. He radioed Bautz, who was still waiting in his tank outside the command post in Nives. "Find an assembly area for the whole command in the area Abe went to."

At 1700 hours, Blanchard wanted confirmation that Abrams had achieved linkup. "Was that physical contact or Abe personally?"

On behalf of his boss, Bautz clicked on the handset and replied, "Physical contact."

A moment later, the fire support officer transmitted Blanchard's order to Abrams. "Pick an assembly area for the entire command."

CCR had kicked in the door to Bastogne, but could they keep it open?[16]

1701 to 1725 Hours, Tuesday, December 26
Command Post, Thunderbolt VI, 37th Tank Battalion, CCR,
4th Armored Division Between Clochimont and Assenois, Belgium

Abrams probably wished he had not been so glib with his commander about moving in the combat trains and support troops. When he received the order to select an assembly area for CCR, he realized he needed to clarify the situation for Blanchard. He picked up his handset and replied to the fire support officer, "The whole road is ablaze. There's fighting going on."

Abrams needed more information, and he was hoping that Captain Dwight would tell him what was happening beyond Assenois. At 1703 hours, his S-3 chimed in over the command net, "We're here but no infantry. The arty at checkpoint nine was pretty heavy. Met a captain and set up an outer defense for the town, and I'll go ahead and put our people in position. There must have been a tank that got lost back in that town."

The 37th Tank Battalion commander knew his plan had a hiccup. Charlie Company, 53rd Armored Infantry, should have accompanied the tanks, but according to the S-3, they were not there. As he tried to determine what had happened to the infantry, Abrams listened to another conversation over the net. Bautz was relaying his message back to Colonel Blanchard. "The whole place and roads are ablaze," Bautz repeated to the CCR commander. Then he added, "If G-4 brings supplies up to the place we talked about, it will be best."

Captain Dwight hailed Abrams over the radio, warning, "At the edge of the woods, there's Teller mines on the ground. I got a couple of tanks through. I think it's okay now."

Abrams was relieved that beyond the Bois Bechu it was a clear road, but Assenois, on the other hand, was still a cauldron. It would not matter whether the tanks reached Bastogne if the infantry failed to clear out Assenois and the road behind them. At 1725 hours, Abrams radioed the fire support officer and ordered him to transmit another message back to Colonel Blanchard. Even though Abrams was not the CCR commander, he knew what needed to be done, and he had to convince Blanchard to do it. Moreover, if Lieutenant Smith's infantry from Charlie Company could not defeat the German defenders in Assenois, he would need to send in Baker Company to finish the job. "Everyone should attack," he said to Blanchard. "Get off their high horse. Have everyone attack, [including] CCB." Abrams laid down the handset and waited to hear more news about the fight for Assenois. The next hour would determine the success or failure of the entire operation. The decisive moment in the battle had come.[17]

1635 to 1755 Hours, Tuesday, December 26
Charlie Company, 53rd Armored Infantry Battalion, CCR,
4th Armored Division Assenois, Belgium

Shivering in the back of a half-track, Private Howard V. Lipscomb listened as artillery rounds whistled overhead. Assenois was in chaos. As half-tracks entered the town, Lipscomb remembered that "Germans were running everywhere after the artillery started up." He stood and opened fire with his Garand at the scampering *volksgrenadiers*.

Even for the veterans, the fight for Assenois was a hellish one. Roscoe M. Mulvey was a mortar section sergeant in Charlie Company, and his team hauled around the platoon's 60mm mortar in the back of their M3. Though it was their primary weapon, they rarely used it in combat. During their trek through Assenois, most of Mulvey's team were plugging away with their Garands while he fired the .50-caliber machine gun mounted on the half-track.

By World War II standards, Mulvey was an old veteran at twenty-one. As a private, the Pittsburgh native had survived his first battles in the Normandy hedgerow country in July and participated in the dash across France in August. He had fought in the Battle of Arracourt the following September. By December, Mulvey had been promoted to sergeant and placed in charge of the mortar section. By experience and by fate, he had outlived many of his comrades. With the exception of the battalion commander, his first sergeant, and some of the staff, few soldiers in the 53rd Armored Infantry had more experience than Roscoe Mulvey.

"When the tanks started pulling out, we followed right in behind them," he remembered.

Mulvey recounted the order he received when he hopped in the gunner's turret. "We were just told that we were supposed to fire up on each side of the road. Just to fire ammunition; that's all."

As they approached the town, Mulvey recalled the shelling. "[The commanders] wanted the barrage to continue firing, and it was going right over our heads."

Suddenly one of the half-tracks up ahead flipped up into the air as if a gust of wind had tossed it aside. The explosion killed several of the crew instantly and wounded a few others, including Mulvey's company commander, First Lieutenant DeWitt Smith. Soldiers leaped from the other half-tracks and hit the ground as more shells came screaming in. Their quick dispersal probably saved most of their lives. At the time, Mulvey did not know that it was American artillery that had blasted the hapless vehicle.

James R. Hendrix, a private from Arkansas who was nicknamed "Red" (on account of his red hair), experienced the artillery fire from an even closer vantage point. He had been in the doomed half-track seconds before the shell hit it. "We went over a hill in our half-track," Hendrix remembered, "and an artillery shell hit our track and wiped out our whole squad, but I had jumped out of it, because you can't fight artillery. If you're lucky enough, you can outrun some of it, [and] I was trying to outrun it."

Despite the pandemonium around him, Hendrix kept his cool. Spotting the German artillery positions to the southeast of Assenois, he began to make his way toward the booming guns. When he was closer, he noticed that the tubes were a pair of 8.8cm antiaircraft guns, known to GIs as 88s. They could easily wreak havoc on a column of vehicles.

"I went up over there by myself," Hendrix said. "I could see them through a hedgerow, and I was laying [sic] under their gun—a big 88, and I see our troops had pulled back, to reorganize or something—to get out of the artillery. So I seen them Germans. They're moving around, and I got me a good position. I was yelling and a-hollering for them to surrender."

When the German gunners refused to admit defeat. Hendrix realized he had to motivate them. "One poked his head out of a foxhole," Hendrix recalled, ". . . and I shot him through the neck. I got closer and hit another on the head with the butt of my M1. He had American matches on him. Others came out then with their hands up."

Thirteen German soldiers surrendered to the private. He had single-handedly neutralized a pair of 8.8cm dual-purpose guns. As he was searching the prisoners, the rest of his platoon assaulted his position. Once again he was eating dirt and snow as bullets zipped over his head. Incredibly, he survived the second barrage of rifle fire.

When one of the Charlie Company sergeants realized what was happening, he ordered everyone to cease fire. The sergeant then asked him, "What the hell are you doing here, Red?"

Stunned and bewildered, Hendrix responded, "I don't know. I know the Germans are trying to kill me, but you guys are trying to kill me too."

The freckled kid from Arkansas had dealt a significant blow to the German cause, but his acts of extraordinary courage had only just begun. Thanks to men like him, Charlie Company had cleared most of the area directly to the southeast of Assenois, destroying or capturing most of the German artillery and antitank guns on the near side of the town. However, the grunts still had to seize Assenois itself, and so the tired and cold doughboys hopped back onto their half-tracks and drove into the village. Inside Assenois, the surviving *volksgrenadiers* from the 39th Regiment were waiting for them.

The ride was a terrifying roller coaster for the troops huddled in the backs of half-tracks. As the column started to wind its way through the narrow streets of Assenois, the Germans threw everything at them. *Panzerfaust* rockets zipped through the air like Chinese fireworks, while *volksgrenadiers* tossed hand grenades down from the buildings. Several of the open-topped vehicles were hit, and one of them blocked the road in front of Mulvey's M3. Sergeant Mulvey described what he saw:

> We pulled in behind this tank and one of our vehicles had been knocked out. . . . And it seemed like there was firing coming from the left side of the road, and I swung my .50-caliber around, and I emptied the whole rest of the belt up there . . . all of sudden here comes this tank, [which] whips right past us, and whatever was firing up from that left side of the road must have tried to hit that tank, and a big ball of fire shot right between them. And that man will never know how close he'd come, because he was going faster than the half-tracks were.

Elsewhere, Red Hendrix was trying to stay alive in the back of another half-track as bullets pinged off the side of his vehicle. A German hand grenade dropped into the M3 in front of Hendrix's transport and exploded. The half-track caught fire and rolled to a stop. Without hesitation, the brave soldier from Arkansas jumped over the side of his half-track and rushed to the burning vehicle in front of him. Pulling two wounded soldiers from the wreckage, he laid them down in a nearby ditch. A third man remained trapped in the vehicle. According to Hendrix, "A grenade had exploded between his legs and everybody else got out, but he was hollering for help."

Before he could save the man, two German machine gunners zeroed in on him and the two wounded men in the ditch. Hendrix raised his Garand and opened fire on the gun positions. He emptied clip after clip, hoping to score a hit.

Eventually his marksmanship paid off, and he silenced the two gun teams. Meanwhile, other soldiers arrived and carried the wounded out of harm's way.

Red still had to save the soldier trapped inside the burning half-track. Risking his life, Hendrix returned to the blazing M3. "I tugged at him and got him out on the road, but he was badly burned," he remembered. "I tried to find water to put out the flames but the water cans were full of bullet holes, so I beat out the flames as best I could. He died later."

Despite the dogged determination of the German defenders, Charlie Company's onslaught started to wear them down. When Baker Company, 53rd Armored Infantry, entered the fray, the German defenders realized the game was up and started to surrender. By 1755 hours, most of the fighting was over, and Colonel Abrams declared over the command net for everyone to hear, "Checkpoint nine [Assenois] is clear and secure."

Later that night, tankers and infantry of Combat Command Reserve escorted a convoy of fifty trucks to Bastogne. On the return trip, the trucks carried out scores of seriously wounded paratroopers. Though the Germans still could shell the Assenois corridor, they could not close it. Assenois was a stunning victory for the men of CCR. According to the 53rd Armored Infantry records, the GIs processed around 380 prisoners, and the S-3 estimated that the attack on Assenois killed more than 150 *volksgrenadiers*. American infantry captured five 10.5cm towed howitzer guns and four 8.8cm towed antiaircraft guns while destroying two Mark IV panzers. In return, the Germans knocked out a total of five half-tracks. More important, the siege of Bastogne was over.[18]

EPILOGUE

★ ★ ★ ★ ★

The linkup between the 4th Armored and the 101st Airborne Division in the late afternoon of December 26 signaled the official end of the Siege of Bastogne. East of CCR, Combat Command B, after fighting through the town of Grandrue on the twenty-sixth, reached the southernmost lines of the 101st Airborne on the morning of the twenty-eighth. Combat Command A took one more day, but the 51st Armored Infantry finally made contact with the Screaming Eagles and CCB north of the village of Remoifosse around 1045 hours on the twenty-ninth. Patton had kept his promise.

Despite this tremendous success, the fighting was far from over. Though Hitler realized that his dream of reaching Antwerp and splitting the Allied armies in two was no longer possible, he still wanted to exact revenge on the Allied forces, and thus he chose Bastogne as the target for his wrath. He ordered his generals to sever the tenuous link that the 4th Armored Division had established, and for several more days the battles seesawed back and forth. In the end, despite the introduction of more units, including several Waffen SS divisions, the Wehrmacht could not encircle the town again.

By the beginning of the New Year, even the German commanders on the ground could see they were fighting a battle of diminishing returns and began to clamor for a withdrawal back to the Siegfried Line. Hitler finally acquiesced, and by the end of January, the Battle of the Bulge was over. Hitler's gamble had failed. He had expended his strategic reserve in a bid to halt the Allied advance into western Germany. Now he was powerless to stop any major Allied offensive.

The next blow fell in the East, when Joseph Stalin ordered his Soviet Armies to attack the weakened Wehrmacht along the river Vistula on January 12, 1945.

Since the Wehrmacht no longer had a strategic reserve thanks to the Battle of the Bulge, it did not have the capability to counterattack and destroy any major Soviet penetration. Army Group A was powerless then to stop Marshal Georgy Zhukov's 1st Belorussian Front and Marshal Ivan Konev's 1st Ukrainian Front when they attacked on the morning of January 12. As a result, the German armies on the Eastern Front reeled from the blows, and they retreated hundreds of miles, ceding the rest of Poland to the Russian horde. By the beginning of February, the Soviet armies had reached the river Oder, which was less than an hour's drive from Berlin. Two months later, Zhukov and Konev struck again, and their armies crossed the Oder to take Germany's capital at the end of April, ending the war in Europe.

The race for Bastogne was one of the turning points in the Battle of the Bulge and in World War II. Once General Hugh Gaffey's 4th Armored Division broke through the German cordon, the Germans did not have the necessary combat power to reseal the gap. Bastogne became the stepping-stone for Patton's counter-offensive, which ultimately erased the Bulge and crossed into Germany later that winter.

Many historians have debated why the Ardennes offensive ended in defeat for the German army. Certainly, the inability of the German forces to capture Bastogne was one chief reason, and their inability to halt Patton's advance was another. In fact, many historians and army officers, including former Wehrmacht commanders, argued that the German army was too weak at this point in the war to conduct major offensive operations.

I would propose that even if the German army had been in better shape, it would have lost to the American army. Granted, it would have been an even tougher fight for the GIs. Nevertheless, the German army, even in its heyday in 1941, did not have the command and control capabilities that the American army possessed in late 1944. True, the Germans were the pioneers of blitzkrieg, but the American army perfected it. With the introduction of handheld FM and AM radios, a platoon leader in the U.S. Army could call on artillery from several battalions, thanks to a fire direction center. No matter how many MG 42 machine guns were in a German platoon, they could never compete against the hell storm of American artillery, which dominated the battlefield in 1944 and 1945. A German infantry platoon leader did not have that capability in the offense; nor, in some cases, did his company commander. The result was that every time an American platoon leader or company commander ran into trouble, he would call on the artillery to saturate the German positions. For the lonely *volksgrenadier* or *fallschirmjäger* it must have been demoralizing, because he could do little against the Yankee maelstrom other than hunker down in some foxhole while the heavens dumped molten steel on him.

Moreover, the Wehrmacht never fully motorized its standard infantry divisions. Though the panzer and *panzergrenadier* divisions were mobile, the standard German infantry division did not have an organic motorized capability. Hence the soldiers in that division either marched to the battlefield on foot or hopped on a train. At most, an infantry division in the Wehrmacht could motorize a battalion or two.

On the other hand, infantry divisions in the American army could easily move about the battlefield because of the limitless number of transportation units at the division and corps echelons. For example, a standard U.S. infantry division had almost fifteen hundred vehicles, while the standard *volksgrenadier* division in late 1944 had around four hundred vehicles. Ironically, a *fallschirmjäger* division had, on paper, more than twenty-one hundred vehicles. In contrast, the other divisions in the Wehrmacht's Seventh Army were all *volksgrenadier* divisions, which meant that the Seventh Army staff likely would have allocated any additional motor transport at the corps level and army level to the *volksgrenadier* divisions and not to the 5th Fallschirmjäger Division, since the *volksgrenadier* divisions were woefully short on prime movers. Moreover, the 5th Fallschirmjäger Division was well below its authorized strength in regard to the number of motor transports. In fact, Ludwig Heilmann, its division commander, mentioned this acute shortage in his postwar account.

III Corps exemplified this disparity when it alerted its divisions late in the morning of December 24, and then moved two battalions from the 80th Infantry Division to the 4th Armored Division in less than twelve hours over a distance of approximately thirty kilometers, so that by the evening the 1st and 2nd battalions of the 318th Infantry Regiment were ready to execute attacks the following morning. That was routine for American armies in late 1944. Meanwhile, Erich Brandenberger's Seventh Army had trouble finding the necessary transport to move a single battalion of towed antitank artillery pieces to support his 5th

Fallschirmjäger Division. The result was that the *fallschirmjägers* failed to have enough antitank weapons to blunt the American tank battalions on the twenty-fourth through the twenty-sixth. The resultant lack of transports also led to a breakdown in troop morale, since the Wehrmacht could not feed its troops. Meanwhile, American soldiers were eating turkey for Christmas dinner.

The Americans had an overwhelming advantage in airpower. In early 1943, that was far from a foregone conclusion. The Luftwaffe committed the majority of its fighter squadrons and its best aircraft against the Royal Air Force and the U.S. Eighth and Ninth air forces to contest the airspace of the Greater German Reich. It was a bloody affair, but by the end of 1944 the two Allies were undisputed masters of the skies over Western and Central Europe. As a consequence, the German army could move only during periods of limited visibility. If they did move along the roads in good weather, they did so at their own peril, and in many cases the P-47s of the Ninth Air Force exacted a heavy toll. Burning hulks of German vehicles and rotting carcasses of German horses around Bastogne stood as mute testimony to their effectiveness.

The U.S. Third Army was the one major unit that Hitler's winter offensive did not catch flatfooted. Colonel Oscar W. Koch deserved most of the credit for that. He saw what many others failed to see: a resurgent Wehrmacht preparing for potential offensive operations. As a result of Koch's intelligence assessment, Patton and his staff had developed contingency plans for just such an occasion. Moreover, Patton trusted his staff and allowed them the latitude to come up with solutions. When Patton made the decision to swing his army north, his staff was already ahead of him, alerting subordinate units, etc.

Furthermore, most of Patton's soldiers respected and trusted him. Matteo Damiano, a private in Charlie Company, 10th Armored Infantry Battalion, said, "Patton was a genius." Orie Williams, a tanker in the 35th Tank Battalion, stated, "[Patton] was the best field commander they had and Eisenhower knew it." Technician Fifth Grade Raymond E. Green, a driver in the 8th Tank Battalion, said of Patton and some of his controversial decisions, "I admired him . . . there wasn't a second thought . . . I admired him."

In spite of its shortcomings, the Sherman was a far more reliable tank than its German counterparts. Many of the 4th Armored Division's tanks had engines that supposedly were nearing the end of their operational life. Many had been driven more than a thousand miles on their original engines when General Gaffey required them to move another 130 miles from France to Belgium. Some broke down, but many more managed to complete the trip. For comparison, a U.S. tank battalion normally had a readiness rate of around ninety percent, while a typical German Panther tank battalion had readiness rates of only seventy percent due to mechanical issues and other factors. Therefore, American tank battalions tended to put more tanks on the battlefield than the Germans, even though, on paper, the German panzer battalions were similar in size.

Irving M. Heath, a second lieutenant in Charlie Company, 35th Tank Battalion, provided several more advantages that the American Shermans had over the German panzers. In an interview with the author, he explained U.S. Army tank doctrine. The designers of the Sherman tank wanted an armored vehicle that was the 1940s' manifestation of cavalry. When the horse cavalry disappeared in the late thirties and early forties, armored cars and jeeps replaced it and became the chief scouting vehicles of the U.S. Army. However, cavalry did more than just scouting. Throughout history, generals have used cavalry to disrupt enemy supply lines and rear areas. Moreover, they also have used cavalry to pursue a defeated foe. These were the driving factors behind the design of the Sherman tank.

The M4 was meant to be a balanced vehicle with adequate armor and reliable engines. It had rubber tracks so that it could travel on roads without destroying them, and with several machine guns, including the M2 .50-caliber heavy machine gun, it was better suited to fight infantry than other tanks. The standard M4 had a stubby 75mm cannon, which was devastating against infantry and bunkers but not so much against panzers. In that respect, the Sherman was the opposite of later German armor like the Panther and Tiger, which were better against other tanks but worse against infantry.

Once the infantry divisions had achieved the penetration, the armored divisions would break through and wipe out enemy forces in the rear areas while severing the enemy's supply lines. Since they had tanks with rubber tracks and dependable engines, the U.S. Army tank battalions could travel hundreds of miles without a significant amount of maintenance. That exact situation presented itself in the late summer of 1944, when Patton's Third Army ripped through France. Meanwhile, panzers like a Tiger I needed trains to transport them as close as possible to the battlefield, because their underpowered engines tended to have shorter life spans. Hence, less travel translated into longer engine life.

When German panzers did appear on the battlefield, the generals wanted the tank destroyers to deal with them. Typically each combat command would have one tank destroyer company attached to it, their sole purpose to destroy panzers. Their 76mm or even 90mm cannons, designed to kill tanks but not people, had longer barrels, which translated into a faster muzzle velocity and better penetration power. The 4th Armored Division had M18 Hellcats, and they had the 76mm long-barreled gun, which was adequate against Panthers and Mk IVs. Against Tigers, however, they were at a significant disadvantage. Unfortunately, that was little consolation for Major Irzyk when a platoon of Tigers attacked his battalion at Chaumont. Despite this setback, the majority of the battles the 4th Armored fought were against infantry, and in that respect, the Sherman was a superb weapon.

The 4th Armored Division's level of training for the tank crews and infantry easily surpassed its opponent, the 5th Fallschirmjäger Division. Most of its regiments had mostly transferees from Luftwaffe aircraft mechanic units and staff clerk sections. This was obvious at Bigonville, where the defenders could not stop Combat Command Reserve, even though they displayed a "fanatical" zeal for fighting. In fact, Abrams wondered whether they even had a scheme of maneuver at all. "They seemed to have neither a defense nor a withdrawal planned," he said, As it turned out, most of the defenders in Bigonville were from the 13th Fallschirmjäger Regiment. Bravery, coupled with a lack of tactical skill, usually resulted in poor outcomes for the German defenders.

Only the 15th Fallschirmjäger Regiment had a majority of trained junior officers and NCOs. Despite being outnumbered, the *fallschirmjägers* in the 15th's three battalions fought hard at Tintange, Warnach, Martelange, and Flatzbourhof, disrupting the advance of Combat Command A and Combat Command Reserve. Feldwebel Conrad Klemment's dogged determination was the norm in those units—not the exception. Moreover, the commander, Oberst Kurt Gröschke, was a veteran regimental commander.

In contrast to the 13th and 14th Fallschirmjäger regiments, the battalion commanders in the 4th Armored Division were some of the best in their army, and many would go on to successful army careers. Albin F. Irzyk, commander of the 8th Tank Battalion, would later serve as the commander of the 14th Armored Cavalry Regiment in the early 1960s and retire as a brigadier general. Delk M. Oden, commander of the 35th Tank Battalion, reached the rank of major general and became the commanding officer of U.S. Army Support Command, Vietnam, in the mid-1960s. Creighton Abrams, commander of 37th Tank Battalion, would go even further than his contemporaries. He reached the rank of general and succeeded General William Westmoreland as commander of Military Assistance Command, Vietnam. His last assignment was as chief of staff of the United States Army. The greatest tank in history, the M1A2 tank, is named after him.

Battalion staff officers and company commanders also excelled. Edward Bautz, executive officer for the 37th Tank Battalion, later became the commander of the 25th Infantry Division. He retired as a major general. Jimmie Leach, commander of Baker Company, 37th Tank Battalion, later commanded the 11th Armored Cavalry Regiment in the late 1960s. He retired at the rank of colonel. Captain William Dwight, the 37th Tank Battalion's S-3, retired as a colonel, after commanding 2nd Brigade, 2nd Armored Division in the sixties.

As for the senior commanders in the 4th Armored Division, both Holmes E. Dager and Herbert L. Earnest later would go on to command divisions, and both would retire several years after the war as major generals. Sadly, Major General Hugh J. Gaffey died in a tragic plane crash in 1946. He was serving as the commandant of the Armor School at Fort Knox, Kentucky, at the time of the accident.

In short, the 4th Armored Division was blessed with a special crop of midlevel officers. Many were not even thirty years old at the time of the Battle of the Bulge, but regardless of their youth, they performed like seasoned veterans. Their tactical acumen and quick thinking led directly to the division's success.

In addition to the superb officers, the 4th Armored Division and its attachments from the 80th Infantry Division had two soldiers who earned the Medal of Honor. Paul Wiedorfer and James Hendrix both continued to serve on the front lines, unaware that their senior officers had submitted their names for the medal. In fact, Paul Wiedorfer almost was not alive to receive it. An artillery round detonated near him in February, wounding him, but he survived and was lying in a hospital when he learned that he had received the nation's highest honor. Army officials conducted the award ceremony at his bedside. He admitted in 2008, "To be perfectly honest, I wasn't really sure what the hell [the Medal of Honor] was, because all I was, was some dogface guy in the infantry."

Fortunately, Wiedorfer left the army in 1947 as a master sergeant. He later married and had four children. He spent most of his life working at Baltimore Gas and Electric, retiring in 1981. He passed away in 2011 at the age of ninety.[1]

James Hendrix attended an awards ceremony at the White House in August 1945, where President Harry S. Truman presented him the Medal of Honor. After the war, Hendrix chose to remain in the army. In 1949, he was injured in an airborne jump when his two chutes failed to deploy. Miraculously, despite plummeting nearly a thousand feet, he landed on his back in a freshly plowed field, sustaining only minor injuries.

Hendrix later married, and his wife, Helen, gave birth to four daughters. During that time, "Red" shipped out to fight in the Korean War, and in 1965, after serving twenty-two years and in two wars, Master Sergeant James R. Hendrix retired from the army. He and Helen eventually moved to Davenport, Florida, where he succumbed to cancer in 2002 at the age of seventy-seven.

Wiedorfer and Hendrix were the epitome of the courageous men who fought for Patton's army. The countless tankers, artillerymen, and infantrymen of the 4th Armored and 80th Infantry divisions were the final ingredients in Patton's recipe for victory. Despite the cold and exhaustion, these brave Americans persevered, and without them, victory would have been impossible.[2]

WORKS CITED

★ ★ ★ ★ ★

A.O.K. 7/Ic/AO—Feind Unterlagen, Westen T-312, 75868. Intelligence Report, Captured German Records Microfilmed at Alexandria, Virginia: Wehrmacht, December 1944–February 1945.

Abrams, Creighton W. Recommendation for Award to Captain William Dwight: Oak Leaf cluster to Silver Star for Gallantry in action near Assenois, Belgium, 25 December 1944. Award Recommendation, Department of the Army, January 8, 1945.

Abrams, Creighton W., Edward Bautz, William Dwight, and John A. Whitehill, interview by L. B. Clark. Relief of the Bastogne Pocket Combat Interiew #279 (January 5, 1945).

Abrams, Morris, interview by L. B. Clark. Interview with Major Abrams, Assistant G-4, 4th Armored Division Combat Interview 279 (January 1945).

Alanis, Dan, and Harry Rockefeller, interview by D. G. Dayton. Drive Toward Bastogne—51st Armored Infantry Battalion. Combat Interview #279 (February 16, 1945).

Altenburger, Andreas. "5. Fallschirm-Jäger-Division." Lexikon der Wehrmacht. 2012. http://www.lexikon-der-wehrmacht.de/Gliederungen/ Fallschirmjagerdivisionen/5FJD-R.htm (accessed October 21, 2012).

———. "7. Armee." Lexikon der Wehrmacht. 2012. http://www.lexikon -der-wehrmacht.de/Gliederungen/Armeen/7Armee.htm (accessed October 9, 2012).

———. "Artillerie-Korps (tbew. mot) 408 Volks-Artillerie-Korps (tbew. mot) 408." Lexikon der Wehrmacht. 2012. http://www.lexikon-der-wehrmacht.de/

Gliederungen/VolksArtKorps/VolksArtKorps408.htm (accessed June 12, 2013).

———. "Brandenberger, Erich." Lexikon der Wehrmacht. 2012. http://www .lexikon-der-wehrmacht.de/Personenregister/B/BrandenbergerE-R.htm (accessed October 12, 2012).

———. "Fallschirmjäger-Regiment 13." Lexikon der Wehrmacht. 2012. http:// www.lexikon-der-wehrmacht.de/Gliederungen/Fallschirmjagerregimenter/ FJR13.htm (accessed July 23, 2013).

———. "Fallschirmjäger-Regiment 14." Lexikon der Wehrmacht. 2012. http:// www.lexikon-der-wehrmacht.de/Gliederungen/Fallschirmjagerregimenter/ FJR14.htm (accessed July 23, 2013).

———. "Fallschirmjäger-Regiment 15." Lexikon der Wehrmacht. 2012. http:// www.lexikon-der-wehrmacht.de/Gliederungen/Fallschirmjagerregimenter/ FJR15.htm (accessed October 25, 2012).

———. "Gause, Alfred." Lexikon der Wehrmacht. 2012. http://www.lexikon -der-wehrmacht.de/Personenregister/G/GauseAlfred-R.htm (accessed December 29, 2012).

———. "Generalkommando Knieß LXXXV. Armeekorps z.b.V. (85)." Lexikon der Wehrmacht. 2012. http://www.lexikon-der-wehrmacht.de/Gliederungen/ Korps/LXXXVKorps-R.htm (accessed December 29, 2012).

———. "Graf von Rothkirch und Trach, Edwin." Lexikon der Wehrmacht. 2012. http://www.lexikon-der-wehrmacht.de/Personenregister/R/ RothkirchundTrachEdwinGrafv.htm (accessed October 12, 2012).

———. "Gröschke, Kurt." Lexikon der Wehrmacht. 2012. http://www.lexikon -der-wehrmacht.de/Personenregister/G/GroeschkeK.htm (accessed December 29, 2012).

———. "Heilmann, Ludwig." Lexikon der Wehrmacht. 2012. http://www .lexikon-der-wehrmacht.de/Personenregister/HeilmannL.htm (accessed October 19, 2012).

———. "Knieß, Baptist." Lexikon der Wehrmacht. 2012. http://www.lexikon -der-wehrmacht.de/Personenregister/K/KniessBaptist-R.htm (accessed October 12, 2012).

———. "Krebs, Hans." Lexikon der Wehrmacht. 2012. http://www.lexikon

-der-wehrmacht.de/Personenregister/K/KrebsH-R.htm (accessed December 25, 2012).

———. "Schwere Panzerabteilung 506." Lexikon der Wehrmacht. 2012. http:// www.lexikon-der-wehrmacht.de/Gliederungen/PanzerAbt/PanzerAbt506-R .htm (accessed June 28, 2013).

American Battle Monuments Commission. "Charles U. Trover." Fold3. April 8, 2013. http://www.fold3.com/page/529937148_charles_u_trover/#a-facts (accessed July 8, 2013).

Balsam, Robert. "Ritterkreuzträger Heinz Kokott." Ritterkreuztraeger-1939–45. 2013. http://www.ritterkreuztraeger-1939-45.de/Infanterie/K/Ko/ Kokott-Heinz.htm (accessed June 25, 2013).

———. "Ritterkreuzträger Rudolph-Christoph Freiherr von Gersdorff." Ritterkreuztraeger-1939–45. 2012. http://www.ritterkreuztraeger-1939-45.de/ Infanterie/G/Ge/Gersdorff-Rudolph-Christoph-Freiherr-von.htm (accessed October 5, 2012).

Barron, Leo G., and Don Cygan. *No Silent Night: The Christmas Day Battle for Bastogne*. New York: NAL Hardcover, 2012.

Basaraba, Nicole. "Luxembourg city in . . . Luxembourg." Nicole Basaraba. Writer. Traveler. Communicator. September 5, 2011. http://nicolebasaraba.com/ luxembourg-city-in-luxembourg/ (accessed April 28, 2013).

Bastnagel, Raymond J. After Action Report, 25th Cavalry Reconnaissance Squadron (Mechanized), 1–31 December 1944. After Action Report, College Park, Maryland: Department of the Army, February 6, 1945.

Battiselli, Pier Paolo. *Panzer Divisions 1944–45*. Oxford: Osprey Publishing, 2009.

Battista, John J. Di. "With CC B/4th Armored Division in the Bulge." Battle of the Bulge Memories. December 12, 2002. http://www.battleofthebulgememories .be/stories26/32-battle-of-the-bulge-us-army/157-with-cc-b-4th-armored -division-in-the-bulge.html (accessed May 31, 2013).

Baum, Abraham J., and Harold Cohen. interview by C. Angulo. Relief of Bastogne—10th Armored Infantry Battalion, 4th Armored Division 20–29 December 1944, Combat Interview #279 (January 8, 1945).

Bautz, Edward, interview by Shaun Illingworth and Michael Ojeda. An Interview with Edward Bautz, for the Rutgers Oral History Archives of World War II (October 15, 1999).

Bayerlein, Fritz. *Bayerlein: After Action Reports of the Panzer Lehr Division Commander, From D-Day to the Ruhr.* Atglen, Pennsylvania: Schiffer Military History, 2005.

Bernstein, Melvin. OPREP A, No. D-23B, second of three, for twenty-four hours ending sunset, December 23, 1944. Ninth Fighter Command Field Order No. 145. Operations Report, Maxwell Air Force Base: U.S. Army Air Force, 1944.

———. OPREP A, No. D-24A, first of three, for twenty-four hours ending sunset, December 24, 1944. Ninth Fighter Command Field Order No. 146. Operations Report, Maxwell Air Force Base, Alabama: U.S. Army Air Force, 1944.

———. OPREP A, No. D-24B, second of three, for twenty-four hours ending sunset, December 24, 1944. Ninth Fighter Command Field Order No. 146. Operations Report, Maxwell Air Force Base: U.S. Army Air Force, 1944.

———. OPREP A, No. D-25A, first of three, for twenty-four hours ending sunset, December 25, 1944. Ninth Fighter Command Field Order No. 147. Operations Report, Maxwell Air Force Base: U.S. Army Air Force, 1944.

———. OPREP A, No. D-25B, second of three, for twenty-four hours ending sunset, December 25, 1944. Ninth Fighter Command Field Order No. 147. Operations Report, Maxwell Air Force Base: U.S. Army Air Force, 1944.

———. OPREP A, No. D-25C, last of three, for twenty-four hours ending sunset, December 25, 1944. Ninth Fighter Command Field Order No. 147. Operations Report, Maxwell Air Force Base: U.S. Army Air Force, 1944.

———. OPREP A, No. D-26A, first of three, for twenty-four hours ending sunset, December 26, 1944. Ninth Fighter Command Field Order No. 148. Operations Report, Maxwell Air Force Base, Alabama: U.S. Army Air Force, 1944.

———. OPREP A, No. D-26B, second of three, for twenty-four hours ending sunset, December 26, 1944. Ninth Fighter Command Field Order No. 148. Operations Report, Maxwell Air Force Base, Alabama: U.S. Army Air Force, 1944.

———. OPREP A, No. D-26C, last of three, for twenty-four hours ending sunset, December 26, 1944. Ninth Fighter Command Field Order No. 148. Operations Report, Maxwell Air Force Base, Alabama: U.S. Army Air Force, 1944.

Blanchard, Wendell, interview by C. J. Angulo. Description of Action Relief of Bastogne Combat Interview #279 (January 6, 1945).

Bodenstein, W. Activities during the Americans' Campaign on the Western Front Ardennes 16 December 1944 to 25 January 1945 MS B-032 (April 17, 1946).

Boggess, Charles. "Letter to George Koskimaki. Charles Boggess, Company C, 37th Armored Tank Battalion." 1984.

"Bomber Command's Summary of the Raid on Krefeld, Germany 21/22 June 1943." 429th Squadron, Royal Canadian Air Force. 2010. http://www.429sqn.ca/bcmi21jun43krefeld.htm (accessed October 5, 2012).

Bozzuto, Tom. "MG Bautz Assumes Command of 25th Division." *Tropic Lightning News*. April 6, 1970. http://www.25thida.org/TLN/tln5-14.htm (accessed August 30, 2013).

Bradley, Omar N. *A Soldier's Story*. New York: The Modern Library, 1999.

Bredbenner, Edgar E. "We Never Got to England." Battle of the Bulge Memories. May 1998. http://www.battleofthebulgememories.be/stories26/32-battle-of-the-bulge-us-army/668-we-never-got-to-england.html (accessed September 10, 2013).

Brown, Harry E. Periodic Report No. 116, G-2, 4th Armored Division. G-2 Periodic Report, College Park, Maryland: Department of the Army, December 23, 1944.

———. Periodic Report No. 117, G-2, 4th Armored Division. G-2 Periodic Report, College Park, Maryland: Department of the Army, December 24, 1944.

———. Periodic Report No. 121, G-2, 4th Armored Division. G-2 Periodic Report, College Park, Maryland: Department of the Army, December 27, 1944.

———. Periodic Report No. 122, G-2, 4th Armored Division. G-2 Period Report, College Park, Maryland: Department of the Army, December 28, 1944.

Brown, Stuart H. Oprep A No. D23D (fourth of four missions) for twenty-four hours ending sunset December 23, 1944. Mission No. 292. IX Fighter Command Operations Order No. W51-2. Operations Report, Maxwell AFB, Alabama: Department of the Army, 1944.

Bucholtz, Chris. "Unpublished Manuscript on the 362nd Fighter Group." June 2013.

Bull, Stephen. *World War II Infantry Tactics: Company and Battalion*. Oxford: Osprey Publishing, 2005.

Burdett, Bruce. "Bruce Burdett, 188th Engineers." Bigonville. Edited by Guy Ries.

2010. http://www.bigonville.info/Bigonville_in_World_War_II/Bruce-Burdett
.html (accessed July 25, 2013).

Bush, Reid C. After Action Report, December 1944, 94th Armored Field Artillery
Battalion. After Action Report, College Park, Maryland: Department of the
Army, 1944.

Calvert, Robert. "Battle of the Bulge: Letter to the Author Concerning His Service
with the 51st Armored Infantry Battalion." Garrett Park, Maryland, October
18, 2010.

Carpenter, Lisa. "Bad Münstereifel—a medieval gem." Bad Münstereifel. 2012.
http://www.bad-muenstereifel.de/seiten/kur_erholung/sehenswuerdigkeiten/
hs_Sehenswuerdigkeiten.php (accessed October 8, 2012).

Cercle d'Histoire de Bastogne. "Assenois." In De témoignent civil, Bastogne, Hiver
44–45, 257–61. Bastogne, Belgium: Cercle d'Histoire de Bastogne, 1994.

———. "Chaumont." In De témoignent civil, Bastogne, Hiver 44–45, 269–72.
Bastogne, Belgium: Cercle d'Histoire de Bastogne, 1994.

Chekan, George, ed. "253rd Armored Field Artillery Battalion." *Bulge Bugle*,
Volume XIX, Number 3, August 2000: 7–8.

Churchill, Thomas G. After Action Report for the Period 15 December 1944 to 31
December 1944, Headquarters, Reserve Command, 4th Armored Division.
After Action Report, College Park, Maryland: Department of the Army,
January 18, 1945.

Clark, L. B. Narrative Summary of Combat Command B's part in the Relief of
Bastogne, 20 through 29 December 1944, Combat Interview #279. Narrative
Summary, College Park, Maryland: Department of the Army, 1944.

———. Narrative Summary of Operations of 4th Armored Division in the Relief of
Bastogne, 22–29 December, Combat Interview 279. Narrative Summary,
College Park, Maryland: Department of the Army, 1945.

Cole, Hugh M. *The Ardennes: The Battle of the Bulge.* Washington, D.C.: Office of
the Chief of Military History, Department of the Army, 1965.

"Combat Diary, 506th Schwere Panzer-Abteilung." *In Tigers in Combat: Volume I*,
by Wolfgang Schneider, 267–77. Mechanicsburg, Pennsylvania: Stackpole
Books, 2004.

Commanding General, Third U.S. Army, TAC. Situational Report Number 583

From 250600A to 251200A. Situational Report, College Park, Maryland: Department of the Army, 1944.

———. Situational Report Number 584 from 251200A to 251800A. Situational Report, College Park, Maryland: Department of the Army, 1944.

———. Situational Report Number 585 from 251800A to 252400A. Situational Report, College Park, Maryland: Department of the Army, 1944.

Connaughton, George W., interview by Dello G. Dayton. Actions of 1st Battalion, 318th Infantry Regiment, in the drive toward Bastogne, Belgium, Combat Interview #279 (January 29, 1945).

Connolly, Robert M. General Order Number 100, Headquarters, 4th Armored Division. General Orders, College Park, Maryland: Department of the Army, 18 December 1944.

———. General Order Number 20, Headquarters, 4th Armored Division. General Orders, College Park, Maryland: Department of the Army, August 28, 1944.

———. General Order Number 25, Headquarters, 4th Armored Division. General Orders, College Park, Maryland: Department of the Army, February 6, 1945.

———. General Order Number 4, Headquarters, 4th Armored Division. General Orders, College Park, Maryland: Department of the Army, January 11, 1945.

———. General Order Number 9, Headquarters, 4th Armored Division. General Orders, College Park, Maryland: Department of the Army, January 16, 1945.

———. General Order Number 11, Headquarters, 4th Armored Division. General Orders, College Park, Maryland: Department of the Army, January 18, 1945.

———. General Order Number 16, Headquarters, 4th Armored Division. General Orders, College Park, Maryland: Department of the Army, January 27, 1945.

———. General Order Number 23, Headquarters, 4th Armored Division. General Orders, College Park, Maryland: Department of the Army, February 3, 1945.

———. General Order Number 3, Headquarters, 4th Armored Division. General Orders, College Park, Maryland: Department of the Army, January 9, 1945.

———. General Order Number 77, Headquarters, 4th Armored Division. General Orders, College Park, Maryland: Department of the Army, May 8, 1945.

———. General Order Number 8, Headquarters, 4th Armored Division. General Orders, College Park, Maryland: Department of the Army, January 15, 1945.

Connor, Robert. "Unpublished Memoir." Robert Connor Collection

(AFC/2001/001/10577), Veterans History Project, American Folklife Center, Library of Congress. Compiled by Joel Besson. Washington, D.C.: West Virginia University School of Journalism, October 26, 2011.

Cooke, Thomas J. Coordination of Artillery with the Tank-Infantry Team. Military Monograph, Fort Knox, Kentucky: Instructor Training Division, General Instruction Department, May 6, 1948.

Cowles, Donald H. "A Reconnaissance Troop in Attack." Maneuver Center of Excellence Libraries, Donovan Research Library, Armor School Student Paper. May 5, 1948. www.benning.army.mil/library/content/Virtual/Armorpapers/CowlesDonald H.MAJ.pdf (accessed July 18, 2013).

Crane, William M. "S-3 Journal, 51st Armored Infantry Battalion, December 1944." Combined Arms Research Library Digital Library. December 1944. http://cgsc.contentdm.oclc.org/cdm/singleitem/collection/p4013coll8/id/3769/rec/3 (accessed May 19, 2013).

Dager, Holmes, and Clay Olbon, interview by L. B. Clark and William J. Dunkerley. Relief of Bastogne, Combat Interview #279 (January 7, 1945).

Damiano, Matteo, interview by Leo G. Barron. Interview with Matteo Damiano, C Company, 10th Armored Infantry Battalion (March 15, 2013).

Dayton, Dello G. After Action Report for Unit Citation (51st Armored Infantry Battalion)—Bastogne Combat Interview #279. After Action Report for Unit Citation, College Park, Maryland: Department of the Army, 19 December 1944 to 10 January 1945.

Department of the Army. "Charles C. Gniot, Distinguished Service Cross." Military Times Hall of Valor. May 20, 1945. http://projects.militarytimes.com/citations -medals-awards/recipient.php?recipientid=22166 (accessed July 24, 2013).

———. "Charles U. Trover, Silver Star." Military Times Hall of Valor, 1944. http://projects.militarytimes.com/citations-medals-awards/recipient .php?recipientid=137832 (accessed July 8, 2013).

———. "General Orders 74, James R. Hendrix." Center of Military History, U.S. Army. September 1, 1945. http://www.history.army.mil/html/moh/wwII-g-l .html (accessed October 10, 2013).

———. "James H. Leach, Distinguished Service Cross." Military Times Hall of Valor, 1945. http://militarytimes.com/citations-medals-awards/citation .php?citation=8835 (accessed July 2, 2013).

————. "John A. Whitehill, Distinguished Service Cross." Military Times Hall of Valor, February 17, 1945. http://projects.militarytimes.com/citations-medals -awards/recipient.php?recipientid=22783 (accessed June 30, 2013).

————. "Paul J. Wiedorfer, Medal of Honor citation." Victory Institute. 1945. http://www.victoryinstitute.net/blogs/utb/2000/12/paul-j-wiedorfer-medal-of -honor-citation/ (accessed September 24, 2013).

D'Este, Carlos. *Patton: A Genius for War.* New York: Harper Collins, 1995.

Dickson, Benjamin. G-2 Estimate Number 27, 10 December. Intelligence Estimate, United States Army Heritage and Education Center, Carlisle Barracks, PA: Headquarters, First Army, 1944.

Donaldson, James R. "James R. Donaldson Collection (AFC/2001/001/8147), Veterans History Project, American Folklife Center, Library of Congress." Unpublished, 1993.

Donnelly, Thomas J. 10th Armored Infantry Battalion, 4th Armored Division, After Action Report for 1–31 December 1944. After Action Report, College Park, Maryland: Department of the Army, 1945.

Doyle, Hilary, and Tom Jentz. *Sturmgeschütz III and IV, 1942–1945.* Oxford: Osprey Publishing, 2001.

————. *Tiger I Heavy Tank 1942–1945.* Oxford: Osprey Publishing, 1993.

Dupuy, Trevor N. *Hitler's Last Gamble: The Battle of the Bulge December 1944–January 1945.* New York: Harper Collins Publishers, 1994.

Dwight, Rochelle. "E-mail from Rochelle Dwight, concerning her father's actions." December 15, 2013.

Dwight, William A. "Letter to Professor Harding Ganz." April 11, 1979.

Earnest, Herbert L. Combat Command A, After Action Report, December 1944. After Action Report, College Park, Maryland: Department of the Army, 1945.

————. Field Order #1, Combat Command A, 4th Armored Division. Field Order, College Park, Maryland: Department of the Army, December 21, 1944.

————. Field Order #2, Combat Command A, 4th Armored Division. Field Order, College Park, Maryland: Department of the Army, December 24, 1944.

Edwards, W. B. Message # 42 to Chief of Staff, III Corps, from Counsel 6. Radio Message Receipt, College Park, Maryland: Department of the Army, 1944.

Eisenhower, Dwight D. *Crusade in Europe.* Baltimore: John Hopkins University Press, 1997.

Eisenhower, John S. D. *The Bitter Woods: The Battle of the Bulge.* New York: De Capo Press, 1995.

Ellis, John B. Headquarters, 4th Armored Division, Photo Interpretation Team #56. Photo Interpretation Report Number 41. College Park, Maryland: Department of the Army, 1944.

Ellis, Robert H. After Action Report, 22nd Armored Field Artillery Battalion, December 1944. After Action Report, College Park, Maryland: Department of the Army, January 29, 1945.

Estate of George S. Patton Jr. "Biography of General George S. Patton Jr." The Official Website of General George S. Patton Jr., 2014. www.generalpatton .com/biography/index.html (accessed April 29, 2014).

Fenchel, Bruce Donald. "Bruce Donald Fenchel Collection, (AFC/2001/001/2978), Veterans History Project, American Folklife Center, Library of Congress." Veterans History Project, 2001. http://lcweb2.loc.gov/diglib/vhp/bib/2978 (accessed December 25, 2012).

Fenn, M. J. "Visiting Luxembourg City's 'Place de Metz' and its State Savings Bank building: imposing setting and historical memories." M. J. Fenn Hub Pages. 2013. http://mjfenn.hubpages.com/hub/Visiting-Luxembourg-Citys-Place-de -Metz-and-its-State-Savings-Bank-building-imposing-setting-and-historical -memories (accessed April 26, 2013).

Ferrell, Robert H. "Summary of America's Deadliest Battle: Meuse-Argonne, 1918." University Press of Kansas. 2013. http://www.kansaspress.ku.edu/ferame.html (accessed August 30, 2013).

Fleischman, L. E. After Action Report, 4th Armored Division Artillery, December 1944. After Action Report, College Park, Maryland: Department of the Army, 1944.

Fortney, Guy, interview by Leo Barron. Interview with Guy Fortney Concerning His Service with Headquarters Company, 10th Armored Infantry Battalion during the Battle of the Bulge (August 26, 2012).

Fox, Don M. *Patton's Vanguard: The United States Army Fourth Armored Division.* Jefferson, North Carolina: McFarland & Company, Inc., Publishers, 2003.

Frantzen-Heger, Gaby. "Vianden Castle." Vianden Castle. 2012. http://www .castle-vianden.lu/english/index.html (accessed December 29, 2012).

G-1 Section, 4th Armored Division. Headquarters, 4th Armored Division, G-1

Journal December 1944. G-1 Journal, College Park, Maryland: Department of the Army, 1944.

G-2 Section, 4th Armored Division. G-2 Journal, Headquarters 4th Armored Division, from 181600 December 44 to 191600 December 44. G-2 Journal, College Park, Maryland: Department of the Army, 1944.

———. G-2 Journal, Headquarters 4th Armored Division, from 211600 December 44 to 221600 December 44. G-2 Journal, College Park, Maryland: Department of the Army, 1944.

———. G-2 Journal, Headquarters 4th Armored Division, from 221600 December 44 to 231600 December 44. G-2 Journal, College Park, Maryland: Department of the Army, 1944.

———. G-2 Journal, Headquarters 4th Armored Division, from 231600 December 44 to 241600 December 44. G-2 Journal, College Park, Maryland: Department of the Army, 1944.

———. G-2 Journal, Headquarters 4th Armored Division, from 241600 December 44 to 251600 December 44. G-2 Journal, College Park, Maryland: Department of the Army, 1944.

———. G-2 Journal, Headquarters 4th Armored Division, from 251600 December 44 to 261600 December 44. G-2 Journal, College Park, Maryland: Department of the Army, 1944.

———. G-2 Journal, Headquarters 4th Armored Division, from 261600 December 44 to 271600 December 44. G-2 Journal, College Park, Maryland: Department of the Army, 1944.

G-2 Section, Headquarters, 4th Armored Division. Annex Number 1 to G-2 Periodic Report Number 119. G-2 Periodic Report, College Park, Maryland: Department of the Army, December 26, 1944.

G-2, Twelfth Army Group. "Weekly Intelligence Summary No. 18 for Week ending 092400 December 1944." Combined Arms Research Library Digital Library. December 12, 1944. http://cgsc.contentdm.oclc.org/cdm/singleitem/collection/p4013coll8/id/644/rec/20 (accessed December 24, 2012).

G-3 Section, 28th Infantry Division. G-3 Journal 170001A, December 1944 to 172400 December 1944. Operations Journal, College Park, Maryland: Department of the Army, 1944.

———. G-3 Journal 220001A, December 1944 to 222400 December 1944.

Operations Journal, College Park, Maryland: Department of the Army, 1944.

G-3 Section, III Corps Headquarters. G-3 Journal, HQ, III Corps, from 251200 December 1944 to 261200 December 1944. G-3 Journal, College Park, Maryland: Department of the Army, 1944.

G-4 Section, 4th Armored Division. G-4 Journal, Headquarters, 4th Armored Division, December 1944. G-4 Journal, College Park, Maryland: Department of the Army, 1944.

Gardner, Glenn H., Prentis W. Foreman, and John A. Shuford, interview by Dello G. Dayton. Action of the 2nd Battalion, 318th Regiment, 80th Division in the Bastogne Salient 24–28 December. Combat Interview #279 (January 25, 1945).

Gaul, Roland. *The Battle of the Bulge in Luxembourg: The Southern Flank December 1944–January 1945*, Volume I. Atglen, Pennsylvania: Schiffer Military, 1995.

Gaydos, Albert. "Headquarters Battery, 66th Armored Field Artillery Battalion, 4th Armored Division." *Bulge Bugle*, Volume IX, Number 2, June 1990: 21–22.

———. "Letter to Author About His Service with 66th Armored Field Artillery Battalion." 2013.

Geking, Charles F., and Edward E. Hueske, interview by S. J. Tobin and D. G. Dayton. Interview with Officer 1/318th Infantry—Relief of Bastogne (January 26, 1945).

Gersdorff, Rudolf Christoph Freiherr von, and Erich Brandenberger, interview by W. B. Ross. Seventh Army, MS A-876 (July 6, 1946).

Gersdorff, Rudolf Christoph Freiherr von. Evaluation and Equipment of the Units Attached to the Seventh Army during the Ardennes Offensive MS A-932 (Between 1945 and 1954).

Gersdorff, Rudolf Christoph Freiherr von, interview by H. P. Hudson. Seventh Army in the Ardennes Offensive ETHINT 54 (November 26, 1945).

Gersdorff, Rudolf Christoph Freiherr von, interview by A. Zerbel. The Ardennes Offensive MS A-909 (August 8, 1945).

Giallanza, Tony. "E-mails from Tony Giallanza to Don Fox." April 6, 2002.

Goldstein, Richard. "James R. Hendrix, War Hero, Dies at 77." *New York Times*, November 21, 2002.

Grand Rapids Herald. "Grand Rapids Officer Leads Tanks into Bastogne, Wins Star." January 2, 1945.

Grand Rapids Michigan Press. "Local Man Led Rescue Thrust." January 1, 1945.

Greatest Tank Battles: Race to Bastogne. Directed by Paul Kilback. Performed by James H. Leach. 2010.

Green, Raymond E., interview by Leo Barron. Interview with Raymond E. Green, Concerning His Service with Support Company, 8th Tank Battalion During the Battle of the Bulge (March 28, 2013).

Green, Tobin L. "The Hammelburg Raid Revisited." DTIC Online. July 7, 1994. http://www.dtic.mil/cgi-bin/GetTRDoc?AD=ADA281238 (accessed June 2, 2013).

Greer, Darroch. "Counting Civil War Casualties Week-by-Week, for the Abraham Lincoln Presidential Library and Museum." 2005. http://www.brcweb.com/alplm/BRC_Counting_Casualties.pdf (accessed August 30, 2013).

Grillenberger, Rudolf. January 1945, Monthly Status Report for the 653rd Schwere Panzerjager Abeitlung. Status Report, Freiburg, Germany: Wehrmacht, January 4, 1945.

Harding, Andrew S. "Two Generals Apart: Patton and Eisenhower." Military History Online. 2004. http://www.militaryhistoryonline.com/wwii/articles/twogeneral.aspx (accessed April 30, 2013).

Harley, Jeffrey S. Reading the Enemy's Mail: Origins and Developments of U.S. Army Tactical Radio Intelligence in World War II, European Theater of Operations. Masters Thesis, Fort Leavenworth, Kansas: U.S. Army Command and General Staff College, 1993.

Tifton Gazette. "Harold Cohen—Obituaries for Aug. 16, 2006." August 15, 2006. http://tiftongazette.com/obituaries/x323683351/Obituaries-for-Aug-16-2006/print (accessed June 2, 2013).

Harrison, R. W. Message #38 to Captain Hower, G-3, from Captain Seay, Olympic 3. Radio Message Receipt, College Park, Maryland: Department of the Army, December 23, 1944.

———. Message #44 G-3, Century, from Lucky 3. Radio Message Receipt, College Park, Maryland: Department of the Army, December 23, 1944.

———. Message #6 to Commanding General, III Corps, from Olympic 3. Radio Message Receipt, College Park, Maryland: Department of the Army, December 23, 1944.

———. Message #6 to Commanding General, III Corps, from Olympic,

Lieutenant Colonel Sullivan. Radio Message Receipt, College Park, Maryland: Department of the Army, December 22, 1944.

———. Message #62 to Commanding General, III Corps, from Olympic 3 Capt. Sharpe. Radio Message Receipt, College Park, Maryland: Department of the Army, December 23, 1944.

———. Message #63 to Major Harrison, Century 3, from Captain Seay, Olympic 3. Radio Message Receipt, College Park, Maryland: Department of the Army, December 24, 1944.

———. Message #64 to Major Harrison, G-3 Operations, from Captain Seay, Olympic 3. Radio Message Receipt, College Park, Maryland: Department of the Army, December 24, 1944.

———. Message #66 to Major Harrison, Century 3, from Capt Seay, Olympic 3. Radio Message Receipt, College Park, Maryland: Department of the Army, December 24, 1944.

———. Message #77 to Commanding General, III Corps, from Olympic 3. Radio Message Receipt, College Park, Maryland: Department of the Army, December 23, 1944.

Hays, Robert G., and Oscar W. Koch. *G-2: Intelligence for Patton*. Atglen, Pennsylvania: Schiffer Military History, 1999.

Headquarters Section, 379th Fighter Squadron. "379th Fighter Squadron." In *Mogin's Maulers*, 424–94. Chicago, Illinois: Dan Gianneschi, 1986.

Headquarters, 10th Armored Infantry Battalion. 10th Armored Infantry Battalion, Unit Journal, December 1944. Unit Journal, College Park, Maryland: Department of the Army, 1944.

Headquarters, 10th Armored Infantry Battalion. Unit Diary, 10th Armored Infantry Battalion. Unit Diary, Department of the Army, 1944–1945.

Headquarters, 1st Battalion, 318th Infantry Regiment. "318th Company B, Recommendation for Commendation, 25 December 1944." 80th Division. January 15, 1945. http://www.80thdivision.com/WebArchives/MiscReports .htm (accessed September 10, 2013).

Headquarters, 25th Cavalry Reconnaissance Squadron (Mechanized). 25th Cavalry Reconnaissance Squadron (Mechanized) Unit History—December 1944. Unit History, College Park, Maryland: Department of the Army, 1944.

Headquarters, 362nd Fighter Group. "362nd Group History & Headquarters

Section." In *Mogin's Maulers*, 40–176. Chicago, Illinois: Dan Gianneschi, 1986.

Headquarters, 37th Tank Battalion, 4th Armored Division. S3 Unit Journal, 37th Tank Battalion, December 1944. Unit Journal, Department of the Army, 1944.

Headquarters, 8th Tank Battalion, 4th Armored Division. Unit Journal, December 1944. Unit Journal, College Park, Maryland: Department of the Army, 1944.

Headquarters, Combat Command "A," 4th Armored Division. Headquarters, Combat Command "A," 4th Armored Division, Unit Diary—Period 1–31 December 1944. Unit Diary, College Park, Maryland: Department of the Army, January 18, 1945.

Headquarters, III Corps. G-3 Journal, Headquarters, III Corps, from 181200 December 1944 to 191200 December 1944. G-3 Journal, College Park, Maryland: Department of the Army, 1944.

———. G-3 Journal, Headquarters, III Corps, from 191200 December 1944 to 201200 December 1944. G-3 Journal, College Park, Maryland: Department of the Army, 1944.

———. G-3 Journal, Headquarters, III Corps, from 221200 December 1944 to 231200 December 1944. G-3 Journal, College Park, Maryland: Department of the Army, 1944.

———. Headquarters, III Corps. December 1944, After Action Report. After Action Report, College Park, Maryland: Department of the Army, 1944.

Headquarters, III Corps, Artillery. Period 241100–242300 December, Intelligence Summary. College Park, Maryland: Department of the Army, 1944.

Headquarters, Reserve Command, 4th Armored Division. Reserve Command Journal, December 1944. Daily Journal, College Park. Maryland: Department of the Army, 1944.

Headquarters, Third Army. Frank R. Kutak, Distinguished Service Cross, General Orders Number #33. General Orders, Department of the Army, February 9, 1945.

Headquarters, Third U.S. Army. Third Army Narrative. Fort Leavenworth, Kansas: Department of the Army, 1945.

Heath, Irving M., interview by Leo Barron. Interview with Irving M. Heath to discuss his experiences with C Company, 35th Tank Battalion during the Battle of the Bulge (May 2, 2013).

Heilmann, Ludwig, interview by G. Schneider. 5th Parachute Division (1 December 1944–12 January 1945), MS B-023 (1945–1954).

Heilmann, Ludwig, interview by H. P. Hudson. Evaluation of the 5th Fallschirmjager Division (December 1944) (March 1, 1946).

Hermes, Matthew. Tanker Jimmie Leach. September 27, 2009. http://jimmieleach .us/preface.html (accessed June 30, 2013).

Historical War Militaria Forum. "Gliederung 5. Fallschirmjäger division." Historical War Militaria Forum. July 10, 2012. http://www.historicalwarmilitariaforum. com/18-gliederung-5-fallschirmj-ger-division.html (accessed October 20, 2012).

History Section, European Theater of Operations. "Battalion and Small Unit Study No. 8." Fold3. 1945. http://www.fold3.com/image/291875781/ (accessed July 10, 2013).

Holmes, Jack. Interview with Jack Holmes (n.d.).

Horner, M. G-2 Periodic Report Number 14, from 212000 December to 222000 December, III Corps. G-2 Periodic Report, College Park, Maryland: Department of the Army, 1944.

———. G-2 Periodic Report Number 18, from 252000 December to 262000 December, III Corps. G-2 Periodic Report, College Park, Maryland: Department of the Army, 1944.

———. G-2 Periodic Report Number 19, from 262000 December to 272000 December, III Corps. G-2 Periodic Report, College Park, Maryland: Department of the Army, 1944.

Hower, J. H. Message to Captain Hower, Century 3, from Captain Seay, Olympic 3. Radio Message Receipt, College Park, Maryland: Department of the Army, December 23, 1944.

Hoy, Bonnie. "William Keith Blackmer." Find a Grave. September 21, 2011. www .findagrave.com/cgi-bin/fg.cgi?page=gr&GRid=76873764 (accessed July 22, 2013).

Hunt, Wheeler H. After Action Report, Combat Command B, 4th Armored Division for the Period of 1 to 31 December 1944. After Action Report, College Park, Maryland: Department of the Army, 1944.

———. Combat Command "B" History, 1–31 December 1944, 4th Armored Division. Unit History, College Park, Maryland: Department of the Army, 1944.

Interrogation Prisoner of War Team #60, 134th Infantry Regiment. "1 x Prisoner of
War from 3rd Battalion, 14th Parachute Regiment, 5th Parachute Division."
www.coulthart.com. December 29, 1944. http://www.coulthart.com/134/
ipw-index-44-12.htm (accessed June 6, 2013).

———. "2 x Prisoner of War from 8th Company, 15th Parachute Regiment, 5th
Parachute Division." www.coulhart.com. December 28, 1944. http://www
.coulthart.com/134/ipw-index-44-12.htm (accessed July 26, 2013).

Interrogation Prisoner of War Team, III Corps. Detailed Prisoner of War
Interrogation Report No. 9, Annex No. 3 to G-2 Periodic Report No. 17.
Interrogation Report, College Park, Maryland: Department of the Army,
December 25, 1944.

———. Detailed Prisoner of War Interrogation Summary No. 6, Annex No. 2 to
G-2 Periodic Report Number 15. Daily Interrogation Summary, College Park,
Maryland: Department of the Army, December 23, 1944.

———. Detailed Prisoner of War Interrogation Report No. 10, Annex No. 2 to G-2
Periodic Report No. 18. Interrogation Report, College Park, Maryland:
Department of the Army, December 26, 1944.

———. Detailed Prisoner of War Interrogation Report No. 11, Annex No. 3 to G-2
Periodic Report No. 19. Interrogation Report, College Park, Maryland:
Department of the Army, December 27, 1944.

———. Detailed Prisoner of War Interrogation Report No. 12, Annex No. 2 to G-2
Periodic Report No. 20. Interrogation Report, College Park, Maryland:
Department of the Army, December 28, 1944.

———. Detailed Prisoner of War Interrogation Report No. 6, Annex No. 4 to G-2
Periodic Report No. 14. Interrogation Report, College Park, Maryland:
Department of the Army, December 22, 1944.

———. Detailed Prisoner of War Interrogation Report No. 8, Annex No. 2 to G-2
Periodic Report No. 16. Interrogation Report, College Park, Maryland:
Department of the Army, December 24, 1944.

Irzyk, Albin F. *8th Tank Battalion History—19 October 1944 to 10 February 1945*.
Operational History, College Park, MD: Department of the Army, 1945.

———. "Bastogne: A Fascinating, Obscure Vignette." *Armor: Magazine of Mobile
Warfare*, March–April 1986: 24–28.

———. "Battle for Chaumont, Belgium. December 23, 1944." C.R.I.B.A. June 17,

2006. http://www.criba.be/index.php?option=com_content&view=article&id
=284:battle-for-chaumont-belgium-december-23-1944&catid=1:battle-of-the
-bulge-us-army&Itemid=6 (accessed May 31, 2013).

———. "Firsthand Account 4th Armored Division Spearhead at Bastogne."
History.Net. November 1999. http://www.historynet.com/firsthand-account
-4th-armored-division-spearhead-at-bastogne-november-99-world-war-ii
-feature.htm (accessed September 9, 2013).

Greatest Tank Battles: Race to Bastogne. Directed by Paul Kilback. Performed by
Albin F. Irzyk. 2010.

———. *He Rode up Front for Patton.* Raleigh, North Carolina: Pentland Press Inc.,
1996.

———. Interview by Leo G. Barron. Interview with Albin F. Irzyk (May 29, 2012).

———. Interview with Albin F. Irzyk (June 12, 2012).

Sache, Ivan. "Martelange (Municipality, Province of Luxembourg, Belgium)." Flags
of the World. September 1, 2007. http://www.crwflags.com/fotw/flags/
be-wlxma.html (accessed May 22, 2013).

Trone, J. W. General Orders Number 13, Headquarters, 80th Infantry Division.
General Orders, Department of the Army, January 13, 1945.

———. General Orders Number 16, Headquarters, 80th Infantry Division.
General Orders, Department of the Army, January 16, 1945.

———. General Orders Number 19, Headquarters, 80th Infantry Division. General
Orders, Department of the Army, January 19, 1945.

———. General Orders Number 25, Headquarters, 80th Infantry Division.
General Orders, Department of the Army, January 25, 1945.

———. General Orders Number 33, Headquarters, 80th Infantry Division.
General Orders, Department of the Army, February 2, 1945.

———. General Orders Number 37, Headquarters, 80th Infantry Division. General
Orders, Department of the Army, February 6, 1945.

———. General Orders Number 42, Headquarters, 80th Infantry Division.
General Orders, Department of the Army, February 11, 1945.

"James Hendrix, Medal of Honor, WWII." YouTube. September 27, 2011. http://
www.youtube.com/watch?v=cqfhtReCDuc (accessed October 12, 2013).

Jaques, George L. *History of the 53rd Armored Infantry Battalion in the Battle for the*

Relief of Bastogne, Belgium. College Park, Maryland: Department of the Army, January 8, 1945.

Jaques, George, and Henry Crosby, interview by C. J. Angulo. Description of Action Relief of Bastogne Combat, Interview #279 (January 8, 1945).

Johannis. Inspection Report Damaged Jagdtiger s.Pz.Jg.Abt 653. Inspection Report, Freiburg, Germany: Wehrmacht, 16 January 1945.

Johnson, Reuben H. "After Action Report, December 1944, 53rd Armored Infantry Battalion." Combined Arms Research Library Digital Library. January 1, 1945. https://server16040.contentdm.oclc.org/cdm4/item_viewer.php?CISOROOT=/ p4013coll8&CISOPTR=3772&CISOBOX=1&REC=10 (accessed May 29, 2013).

Johnson, Reuben H. Unit Diary, 53rd Armored Infantry Battalion, 1 December 1944 to 31 December 1944. College Park, Maryland: Department of the Army, 1944.

Kettel, Paul. "Kettels Poli erinnert sich, Mit freundlicher Erlaubnis von Herrn Paul Kettel." Bigonville, 2010. http://www.bigonville.info/Bigonville_in_World _War_II/Paul-Kettel.html (accessed July 10, 2013).

Kimsey, Charles L. "After Action Report, 51st Armored Infantry Battalion, December 1944." Combined Arms Research Library Digital Library, 1944. http://cgsc.contentdm.oclc.org/cdm/singleitem/collection/p4013coll8/id/3769/ rec/3 (accessed May 19, 2013).

King, Fred. "John Arthur Whitehill, Jr." Find a Grave. November 16, 2004. http:// www.findagrave.com/cgi-bin/fg.cgi?page=gr&GRid=9908276 (accessed July 7, 2013).

Kinnard, Harry W. G-3 Report, 101st Airborne Division, Number 7, from 242400 to 252400 December. College Park, Maryland: Department of the Army, 1944.

Klemment, Conrad. "Diary of the 9th Company, III Battalion, 15th Fallschirmjäger Regiment, 5th Fallschirmjäger Division." Translated by Dieter Stenger, n.d.

———. "Unpublished Manuscript: The 9th Company, III Battalion of the Parachute Regiment 15 During the Ardennes Offensive Until 25 December 1944." Translated by Dieter Stenger. Unknown.

Knieß, Baptist, interview by R. E. Merriam. LXXXV Infantry Corps (November–26 December 1944) ETHINT 40 (August 11, 1945).

Knieß, Baptist, interview by G. Hoehne. The Ardennes, 16 December 1944 to 12 January 1945, MS B-030 (May 21, 1946).

Koch, Oscar W. After Action Report, U.S. Third Army, 1 August 1944 to 9 May 1945, Volume II Staff Sections. Intelligence Summary, Department of the Army, December 14, 1944.

———. After Action Report, U.S. Third Army, 1 August 1944 to 9 May 1945, Volume II Staff Sections. Weekly Intelligence Summary, Department of the Army, December 10, 1944.

———. After Action Report, U.S. Third Army, 1 August 1944 to 9 May 1945, Volume II Staff Sections. Intelligence Summary, Department of the Army, December 13, 1944.

———. OB Map to accompany G-2 Periodic Report No. 183, 11 December 1944. Map of Known Enemy Locations, Department of the Army, December 11, 1944.

———. Preliminary Study of the Terrain Area: Liege (K4887)—Arlon (P6222)—Trier (L2129)—Zulpich (P2333). Terrain Analysis Report, Carlisle Barracks, Pennsylvania: Department of the Army, 1944.

———. Significant Enemy Order of Battle Facts in West—Week 10/17 December 1944, Annex No. 3 to G-2 Periodic Report No. 190. G-2 Periodic Report, United States Army Heritage and Education Center, Carlisle Barracks, Pennsylvania: Department of the Army, 1944.

Kokott, Heinz. Ardennes Offensive—Battle of Bastogne MS # B-040. Foreign Military Studies Historical Division, College Park, Maryland: Department of the Army, 1950.

Kokott, Heinz, interview by H. P. Hudson. Breakthrough to Bastogne—ETHINT 44 (November 29, 1945).

Kokott, Heinz. Employment of the 26th Volksgrenadier Division from 16 to 31 December 1944. After Action Report, Captured Records Microfilmed at Alexandria, Virginia: Wehrmacht, January 5, 1945.

Koskimaki, George E. *The Battered Bastards of Bastogne: A Chronicle of the Defense of Bastogne December 19, 1944–January 17, 1945.* Havertown, Pennsylvania: Casemate, 2003.

Koyen, Kenneth. *The Fourth Armored Division: From the Beach to Bavaria.* Munich, Germany: Herder Druck, 1946.

Kulinich, Simon, interview by Adam Schumaker, and Caroline Spellman B. J. Siasoco. Interview with Simon Kulinich (May 22, 2001).

Lange, Horst. "Dezember 1944 Bigonville." Bigonville. Edited by Guy Ries. 2010. http://homepage.mac.com/guyries/page9/page18/page6/page6.html#english (accessed July 5, 2013).

Law, Richard D. "Missing Air Crew Report—William Bert Foster." Fold3. December 29, 1944 (accessed August 1, 2013).

Lay, Homer B. 35th Tank Battalion History, 1–31 December 1944. College Park, Maryland: Department of the Army, 1944.

———. After Action Report, 35th Tank Battalion, December 1944. After Action Report, College Park, Maryland: Department of the Army, 3 January 1945.

Lay, Homer B., and L. J. Ryan, interview by L. B. Clark and William J. Dunkerley. Relief of Bastogne, 35th Tank Battalion of the 4th Armored Division Combat, Interview #279 (January 8, 1945).

Leach, James H., interview by Paul Kilback. Interview with Jimmie Leach (unedited), Breakthrough New Media and Frima Studios in association with History Television, 2009.

———. "Twenty Days in December 1944." *Officer Review*, December 1998: 8–10.

Leach, James, interview by Matt Hermes. Interview with James Leach (January 6, 2007).

Leaphart, Bill, interview by Leo Barron. Questionaire for Bill Leaphart, C-47 Pilot (2013).

Lipscomb, Howard, interview by Leo Barron. Questionaire for Howard Lipscomb, C Company, 53rd Armored Infantry (March 21, 2013).

Lutgen, Sophie-Lion. "Erinnerungen an die folgenschweren Tage der Rundstedtoffensive, Aus meinem Tagebuch von Sophie Lion-Lutgen." Bigonville. Edited by Guy Ries, 2010. http://www.bigonville.info/Bigonville _in_World_War_II/Sophie-LionLutgen.html (accessed July 11, 2013).

Lüttwitz, Heinrich Freiherr von, interview by Alfred Zerbel. The Assignment of the XLVII Panzer Corps in the Ardennes, 1944–1945, MS # A-939 (June 13, 1950).

Luxembourg City Tourist Office. "City History—Origins." Luxembourg—My City. 2013. http://www.lcto.lu/en/rd/13/187/origins-city (accessed April 26, 2013).

MacDonald, Charles B. *A Time for Trumpets: The Untold Story of the Battle of the Bulge.* New York: Perennial, 2002.

MacKenzie, Fred. *The Men of Bastogne.* New York: Ace Books, 1968.

Mantz, Joseph. "Kriegserinnerungen von Jos. Mantz." Bigonville. Edited by Guy Ries. 2010. http://www.bigonville.info/Bigonville_in_World_War_II/Jos-Mantz.html (accessed August 12, 2013).

Marshall, Samuel Lyman Atwood. *Bastogne: The First Eight Days.* Washington D.C.: Center for Military History, Facsimilie Reprint, 1988.

Martin, Gerhard. *Fallschirmpioniere in der Ardennenschlacht 1944–1945, Im Rahmen der 5. Fallschirmjägerdivision.* Preuss, Germany: Verlag K.W. Schutz KG, 1984.

Maxsted, Frederick J., interview by Dello G. Dayton. General Summary 318th Regiment, 80th Division during the period of 18–24 December 1944 (January 26, 1945).

McAlister, H. J. Message No. 25 to CG, III Corps, from CG, 4th Armored Division. Radio Message Receipt, College Park, Maryland: Department of the Army, December 24, 1944.

———. Message No. 52 to Major McAlister, Assistant G-3, III Corps, from 4th Armored Division. Radio Message Receipt, College Park, Maryland: Department of the Army, December 23, 1944.

———. Message No. 54 to Major McAlister, G-3 Sec, III Corps, from OLYMPIC 3. Radio Receipt Message, College Park, Maryland: Department of the Army, December 23, 1944.

McManus, John C. *Alamo in the Ardennes: The Untold Story of the American Soldiers Who Made the Defense of Bastogne Possible.* Hoboken, New Jersey: John Wiley & Sons, Inc., 2007.

Mettlen, Justin. *Patton's Best: The Fourth Armored Division in World War II.* Graduate Student Paper, University of Kansas: Prepared for Dr. Leonard Ortiz, History 696, Seminar in U.S. History, December 17, 2001.

Mewshaw, Harry. Message #4 to 26 Division, General Harkness, from Century 5. Radio Message Receipt, College Park, Maryland: Department of the Army, December 24, 1944.

———. Field Order #1, Headquarters, III Corps, Arlon, Belgium. Field Order, College Park, Maryland: Department of the Army, 1944.

————. G-3 Situation Report No. 44: Period 190600A to 191200 A December 44, Operational Priority to: Commanding General, Third U.S. Army. G-3 Situation Report, College Park, Maryland: Department of the Army, 1944.

————. G-3 Situation Report No. 45: Period 191200A to 191800 A December 44, Operational Priority to: Commanding General, Third U.S. Army. G-3 Situation Report, College Park, Maryland: Department of the Army, 1944.

————. G-3 Situation Report No. 57: Period 221200 to 221800 December 1944, Operational Priority to: Commanding General, Third U.S. Army (TAC)l. Situational Report, College Park, Maryland: Department of the Army, 1944.

————. G-3 Situation Report No. 63: Period 240001A to 240600A December 1944, Headquarters III Corps. Situation Report, College Park, Maryland: Department of the Army, 1944.

————. Message #3 to Hercules 6, from Century 6. Radio Message Receipt, College Park, Maryland: Department of the Army, December 24, 1944.

————. Message #5 to Olympic 6, From Century 5. Radio Message Receipt, College Park, Maryland: Department of the Army, December 24, 1944.

————. Operations Directive No. 1 (Confirmation of Fragmentary Orders). Reference Field Order #1, 21 December 1944. Operations Directive, College Park, Maryland: Department of the Army, 1944.

————. Operations Directive No. 2 (Confirmation of Fragmentary Orders) Reference Field Order #1, 21 December 44, III Corps. Fragmentary Order, College Park, Maryland: Department of the Army, December 24, 1944.

Meyer, R. H., interview by C. J. Angulo. Description of Action Relief of Bastogne, 20 to 29 December 1944, S-3, Division Artillery, Combat Interview #279 (January 7, 1945).

Molitor, Nicholas. "Kriegsgeschehen in Bondorf, Dezember 1944." Bigonville. Edited by Guy Ries. 2010. http://www.bigonville.info/Bigonville_in_World _War_II/Nic-Molitor.html (accessed July 10, 2013).

Moll, Jakob. *Regimentsgeschichte des Infanterie-Füsilier-Regiments 39 für die Zeit von 1936 bis 1945*. Dusseldorf: Selbstverlag, 1968.

Moon, Roy C. "37th Tank Battalion After Action Report." Combined Arms Research Library Digital Library. January 7, 1945 (accessed August 8, 2013).

————. "37th Tank Battalion Diary." Combined Arms Research Library Digital Library. February 11, 1945 (accessed May 29, 2013).

Moora, Bob. "James R. Hendrix." *Stars and Stripes*, Europe, Mediterranean, and North Africa Edition, July 5, 1945.

Mulvey, Roscoe, interview by Leo Barron. Interview with Roscoe Mulvey, C Company, 53rd Armored Infantry Battalion (March 3, 2013).

Murrell, Robert T. *318th Infantry History, European Theater of Operations, 80th "Blue Ridge" Infantry Division*. Lewiston, Pennsylvania: Robert T. Murrell, 1968.

Oden, Delk M. "4th Armored Division—Relief of the 101st Airborne Division." Combined Arms Research Library. 1946–1947. (accessed May 17, 2013).

Oden, Delk M., William J. Peterson, Howard F. Widner, Joseph V. Horton, Harold Madison, Elmore F. Rounsavall, interview by G. A. Harrison. 35th Tank Battalion: Relief of Bastogne, 22–30 December 1944 (February 16–17, 1945).

O'Neill, James H. "The True Story of the Patton Prayer." Pattonhq.com. October 6, 1971. www.pattonhq.com/prayer.html (accessed September 30, 2013).

Parker, Danny S. *Battle of the Bulge: Hitler's Ardennes Offensive, 1944–1945*. Cambridge, Massachusetts: Da Capo Press, 1999.

———. *To Win the Winter Sky: Air War over the Ardennes 1944–1945*. Conshohocken, Pennsylvania: Combined Publishing, 1999.

Parker, Robert, interview by C. J. Angulo. Description of Action of Relief at Bastogne, 94th Armored Field Artillery Battalion (January 7, 1945).

Patterson, Michael Robert. "Holmes Ely Dager." Arlington Cemetery. January 28, 2006. http://www.arlingtoncemetery.net/hedager.htm (accessed June 1, 2013).

———. "Wendell Blanchard." Arlington Cemetery. January 20, 2007. http://www.arlingtoncemetery.net/wendell-blanchard.htm (accessed June 2, 2013).

Pattison, Hal C., interview with Lieutenant Colonel Pattison, Executive Officer, CCA, 4th Armored Division at Command Post, Preish, Combat Interview 279 (January 13, 1945).

Patton, George S. "Conference with General Patton—Attended by General Gaffey and General Millikin." College Park, Maryland: Department of the Army, 1944.

———. *War as I Knew It*. Boston: Houghton Mifflin Company, 1995.

"Paul Wiedorfer, Medal of Honor, WWII." YouTube. September 27, 2011. http://www.youtube.com/watch?v=hpRpXh66CpQ (accessed September 24, 2013).

Pearson, Ralph E. *En Route to the Redoubt: A Soldier's Report as a Regiment Goes to War, A Chronological Account of Some of the Activities of the 318th in Europe.* Chicago: Adams Printing Service, 1957.

Stanchak, Peter J., Thomas B. Castle, Martin G. Jenkins, and Basil Verlangieri. History of the Second Battalion, 318th Infantry Regiment, 80th Division. Department of the Army, 1945.

Peterson, Eric L., interview by Gary Swanson. Eric L. Peterson Collection (AFC/2001/001/9588), Veterans History Project, American Folklife Center, Library of Congress (August 4, 2003).

Peterson, Howard. "Laundry Problems." *Bulge Bugle*, Volume XII, Number 1, February 1993: 20–22.

Petrikat, Rudolf, interview by Roland Gaul. Interview with Leutnant Rudolf Petrikat, 13th Fallschirmjäger Regiment, 5th Fallschirmjäger Division (unknown).

Phillips, James Holden. Memorandum for Record—Phone Conversation Between Colonel Phillips and General Gaffey at 2145. College Park, Maryland: Department of the Army, December 24, 1944.

———. Memorandum for Record, 22 December 1944. College Park, Maryland: Department of the Army, 1944.

———. Memorandum for Record, 23 December 1944, 1100, Phone Call from Patton. College Park, Maryland: Department of the Army, 1944.

———. Memorandum for Record, 24 December 1944. College Park, Maryland: Department of the Army, 1944.

———. Telephone Conversation Between Colonel Phillips, chief of staff this Headquarters [III Corps] and Olympic 6, at 1115, 24th December. College Park, Maryland: Department of the Army, 1944.

Pound, W. King. "D Company, 35th Tank Battalion, 4th Armored Division." *Bulge Bugle*, Volume IX, Number 2, June 1990: 21.

Quarrie, Bruce. *The Ardennes Offensive: First Armee & Seventh Armee, The Southern Sector.* Oxford: Osprey Publishing, 2001.

———. *The Ardennes Offensive: U.S. III & and XII Corps, The Southern Sector.* Oxford: Osprey Publishing, 2001.

Rapp, Edward. "D Company, 35th Tank Battalion, 4th Armored Division." *Bulge Bugle*, Volume IX, Number 2, June 1990: 19–21.

Revell, Scott. "Schwere Panzer Abteilung 506." Defending Arnhem. 2004. http://
www.defendingarnhem.com/schpzabt506.htm (accessed June 28, 2013).

Rickard, John Nelson. *Advance and Destroy: Patton as Commander in the Bulge.*
Lexington, Kentucky: University Press of Kentucky, 2011.

Riedel, Paul. Battle in the Ardennes (16 December 1944 till 25 January 1945). The
activity of the artillery of the 7. Army Supplement to the report of General
Major Freiherr von Gersdorff, at the time Chief of Staff of the 7. Army. MS
B-467 (between 1945 and 1954).

Riedel, Paul, interview by H. Heitman. Fighting in the Ardennes, 16 December to
25 January 1945, Seventh Army Artillery MS B-594 (between 1945 and 1954).

———. Fighting in the Ardennes, 16 December to 25 January 1945, Seventh Army
Artillery MS B-594 (between 1945 and 1954).

Ries, Guy. "Bitter Truth." Bigonville. 2010. http://homepage.mac.com/guyries/
page10/page30/page30.html (accessed August 12, 2013).

"Ritterkreuzträger Rudolf Berneike." Ritterkreuzträger 1939–1945. 2013. http://
www.ritterkreuztraeger-1939-45.de/Luftwaffe/B/Be/Berneike-Rudolf.htm
(accessed August 26, 2013).

Robbins, Jack E. Report on Air Supply to the 101st Airborne Division at Bastogne.
Memorandum for Record, College Park, Maryland: Department of the Army,
January 11, 1945.

Rottman, Gordon L. *World War II Battlefield Communications.* Oxford: Osprey
Publishing, 2010.

Rudder, James E. Unit Report No. 6, 109th Infantry Regiment, 28th Infantry
Division, from 01 December 1944 to 31 December 1944. Unit Journal, College
Park, Maryland: Department of the Army, 1944.

Rueske, Edward E., Thomas L. Murphy, and John Ryan, interview by S. J. Tobin.
Action of 1st Battalion, 318th at Ettelbruck, Luxembourg, and in drive toward
Bastogne, Belgium, December 22–28, 1944 (January 30, 1945).

Rust, Kurt Albert. Der Weg Der 15. Panzergrenadier Division von Sizilien Nach
Wesermunde Teil II. Berlin: Self-Published, 1990.

S-2 Section, 327th Glider Infantry Regiment. Keepsake S-2 Journal Covering Period
18 December to 31 December 1945 (1944). S-2 Journal, College Park,
Maryland: Department of the Army, 1944.

S-2 Section, 51st Armored Infantry Battalion, 4th Armored Division. S-2 Journal, 51st Armored Infantry Battalion, December 1944. Combined Arms Research Library Digital Library, 1944. http://cgsc.contentdm.oclc.org/cdm/singleitem/collection/p4013coll8/id/3769/rec/3 (accessed May 20, 2013).

S-2 Section, 8th Tank Battalion. After Action Report from 19 December 1944 to 15 January 1945, 8th Tank Battalion. College Park, Maryland: Department of the Army, 1945.

S-2 Section, Combat Command Reserve, 4th Armored Division. S-2 Journal, December 1944. College Park, Maryland: Department of the Army, 1944.

S-2 Section, Headquarters, CCB, 4th Armored Division. S-2 Journal, December 1944. College Park, Maryland: Department of the Army, 1944.

S-3 Section, 327th Glider Infantry Regiment. S-3 Periodic Reports for December 1944. College Park, Maryland: Department of the Army, 1944.

S-3 Section, CCB, 4th Armored Division. S-3 Journal, Combat Command B, 4th Armored Division December 1944 Box 12418. College Park, Maryland: Department of the Army, 1944.

"Salute to LTC Harold Cohen on His Receipt of Distinguished Service Cross." C-SPAN Video Library. May 6, 1996. http://www.c-spanvideo.org/appearance/597025033 (accessed June 2, 2013).

Sauvonsmolitor. "Il y a urgence à sauver la Caserne Molitor." Center Blog. December 10, 2007. http://sauvonsmolitor.centerblog.net/ (accessed December 25, 2012).

Sayen, John. *U.S. Army Infantry Divisions, 1944–45.* Oxford: Osprey Publishing, 2007.

Schmidt, Erich, interview by E. Matti. 352nd Volks Grenadier Division (16 December 1944–25 January 1945), MS B-067 (1946).

Schramm, P. E. Preparations for the German Offensive in the Ardennes, September to 16 December 1944, MS A-862. Operational Account, U.S. Army Military History Institute, n.d.

Schrijvers, Peter. *The Unknown Dead: Civilians in the Battle of the Bulge.* Lexington, Kentucky: University Press of Kentucky, 2005.

Schroder, Josef. "Josef Schroder." Bigonville. 2010. http://homepage.mac.com/guyries/page9/page18/page38/page38.html (accessed August 12, 2013).

Seay, Stedman, interview by L. B. Clark. Relief of Bastogne (January 4, 1945).

Shapiro, T. Rees. "Paul J. Wiedorfer, WWII Medal of Honor recipient, dies at 89." *Washington Post*, May 26, 2011.

Sharpe, T. J. Message #15 to Commanding General, III Corps, from Olympic 3. Radio Message Receipt, College Park, Maryland: Department of the Army, December 23, 1944.

Sharpe, T. J. Message #26 to Commanding General, III Corps, from Olympic 3. Radio Message Receipt, College Park, Maryland: Department of the Army, 1944.

Slotnik, Daniel E. "Paul J. Wiedorfer, Hero of the Battle of the Bulge, Dies at 90." *New York Times*, May 30, 2011.

Sorley, Lewis. *Thunderbolt: General Creighton Abrams and the Army of His Time.* New York: Simon and Schuster, 1992.

Spires, Lowell A. Combat History, 4th Armored Division, 17 July 1944 to 9 May 1945. College Park, Maryland: Department of the Army, October 19, 1945.

Stastical and Accounting Branch, Office of the Adjutant General. "Battle Casualties." Army Battle Casualties and Non-Battle Deaths in World War II: Final Report, 7 December 1941 to 31 December 1946. October 1, 1950. http://www.ibiblio.org/hyperwar/USA/ref/Casualties/Casualties-1.html#page45 (accessed August 30, 2013).

Stauber, B. E., interview by L. Clark. Relief of Bastogne—8th Tank Battalion (January 7, 1945).

Steenkiste, Ivan. "Chaumont, Ardennes." May 8, 2005. http://users.skynet.be/wielewaal/Chaumont_english.htm#introductie (accessed June 6, 2013).

———. "E-mail from Ivan." November 28, 2012.

Stoddard, Donald. "Missing Air Crew Report—Richard K. Grant." Folder 3. December 24, 1944 (accessed September 5, 2013).

Sullivan, John B. Field Order #8, 4th Armored Division, 211600A December 1944. College Park, Maryland: Department of the Army, 1944.

———. Operations Instructions Number 13, Headquarters, 4th Armored Division, 242300 December. College Park, Maryland: Department of the Army, 1944.

Summers, Robert R., Lew M. Kelly, Frederick W. Hawksworth, Ian F. Turner, Clovis D. Heard, Elliot C. Cutler, Jr., James T. Kolb, and William W. Gist III.

"Armor at Bastogne: A Research Report Prepared by Committee 4, Armor School." Combined Arms Research Library. May 1949 (accessed May 17, 2013).

Taylor, Jack C. "Missing Air Crew Report—Berry Chandler." Fold3. December 28, 1944 (accessed October 14, 2013).

Third Army Headquarters. "Third Army Radio Intelligence History in Campaign of Western Europe." In *U.S. Army Signals Intelligence in World War II*, edited by James L. Gilbert and John P. Finnegan, 196–210. Washington, D.C.: Center of Military History, U.S. Army, 1993.

Thomas, Joseph. "Joseph Thomas damals 9 Jahre alt." Bigonville. Edited by Guy Ries. 2010. http://www.bigonville.info/Bigonville_in_World_War_II/Jos-Thomas.html (accessed July 10, 2013).

Thompson, Royce L. Employment of VT Fuzes in the Ardennes Campaign, European Theater of Operations: 16 December 1944–January 1945. Historical Study, College Park, Maryland: European Section, Historical Division, Department of the Army, January 10, 1950.

Toland, John. *Battle: The Story of the Bulge.* Lincoln, Nebraska: University of Nebraska Press, 1999.

Tourism Office of Arlon. "Udange." Arlon—Royal Office of Tourism. 2013. http://www.ot-arlon.be/indexc135.html?lg=fpdb/otarlon_en&page1=a-pays.htm&page2=a-a-villes_et_villages.htm&rep=a-pays&rep2=a-a-villes_et_villages&page3=a-a-q-udange.htm (accessed May 12, 2013).

Trach, Edwin Graf von Rothkirch und, interview by W. O. Reiners. Corps Headquarters, LIII Army Corps (8 December 1944 to 21 January 1945), MS #B-029 (April 12, 1946).

Turbiville, G. H. Narrative of 326th Airborne Engineer Battalion Activities from 18 December through 31 December 1944. Narrative History, College Park, Maryland: Department of the Army, March 10, 1945.

Wall-Reddy, Sarah Riggs. "WWII: Through my Grandfather's Eyes (Robert E. Riley)." May 2003.

Walter Noller, Interrogation Prisoner of War Team #68. "Prisoner of War, Interrogation Report, Interrogation of Theodore Nottenkamper, 8th Company, 14th Parachute Regiment." January 3, 1945. http://www.coulthart.com/134/ipw-index-45-1-3.htm (accessed September 24, 2013).

War Department. "Chapter II Organization of Field Forces." Handbook of German Military Forces. March 15, 1945. http://www.ibiblio.org/hyperwar/Germany/HB/HB-2.html (accessed June 6, 2013).

———. "Chapter VII Weapons." Handbook of German Military Forces. March 15, 1945. http://www.ibiblio.org/hyperwar/Germany/HB/HB-7.html (accessed October 26, 2013).

War Diary (Kriegstagebuch), Armee Korps LIII, December 1944 to March 1945, T-314, Roll 1335, 1st Frame 415, 76106. Captured German Records Microfilmed at Alexandria, Virginia: Wehrmacht, 1944–1945.

Warnock, Bill. "The Face of Battle." WWII History, October 2010: 36–45.

Watkins, C. F. Message #2 to Commanding General, III Corps, from Olympic, Chief of Staff. Radio Message Receipt, College Park, Maryland: Department of the Army, 1944.

West, Morris G. "Battalion Journal from 16 December to 22 December 1944, 299th Engineer Combat Battalion." Bigonville, Luxembourg. December 27, 1944. http://homepage.mac.com/guyries/page9/page13/page13.html (accessed May 22, 2013).

Whitehill, John A. "Reports of the liberation of Bondorf, Luxembourg." Bigonville. December 30, 1997. http://www.bigonville.info/Bigonville_in_World_War_II/John-A-Whitehill.html (accessed June 30, 2013).

Williams, Orie, interview by Larry Ordner. Orie Williams Collection (AFC/2001/001/334), Veterans History Project, American Folklife Center, Library of Congress (April 9, 2002).

Winton, Harold R. Corps Commanders of the Bulge: Six American Generals and Victory in the Ardennes. Lawrence, Kansas: University Press of Kansas, 2007.

Worch, Alfred. "Letter to Roland Gaul." June 2007.

World War II Enlistment Records. "Charles P. Boggess, Jr." Fold 3. 2013. http://www.fold3.com/page/90250062_charles_p%20boggess%20jr/details/ (accessed December 3, 2013).

Wright, Ben, interview by George Koskimaki. Interview with Ben Wright (n.d.).

Wright, Eugene, interview by Leo G. Barron. Interview with Eugene Wright, Sergeant in the 489th AAA Bn (March 17, 2013).

Wynendaele, Patricia Matthew. "Diamond Castle." Royalement Blog. September 9,

2011. http://royalementblog.blogspot.com/2011/09/le-chateau-de-losange.html (accessed June 19, 2013).

Young, Charles D. "Mission to Bastogne, 27 December 1944, Part II: Plans and Coordination." U.S. Army Air Force Troop Carrier. September 7, 2013. http://www.usaaftroopcarrier.com/bastogne/Glider%20Mission-2.htm (accessed November 10, 2013).

Zaloga, Steven J. *M3 & M5 Stuart Light Tank, 1940–1945*. Oxford: Osprey Publishing, 1999.

———. *Panther vs. Sherman: Battle of the Bulge, 1944*. Oxford: Osprey Publishing, 2008.

———. *Sherman Medium Tank, 1942–1945*. Oxford: Osprey Publishing, 1993.

———. *U.S. Armored Divisions: European Theater of Operations, 1944–1945*. Oxford: Osprey Publishing, 2004.

———. *U.S. Field Artillery of World War II*. Oxford: Osprey Publishing, 2007.

Zimmer, Ed. "The Story of the 440th Group Carrier Group." *Bulge Bugle*, Volume XIX, Number 1, February 2000: 8–9.

Zweiter-Weltkrieg-Lexikon.de. "Parachute Assault Gun Brigade 11." Zweiter-Weltkrieg-Lexikon.de. 2009. http://www.zweiter-weltkrieg-lexikon.de/index.php/Luftwaffe/Gepanzerte-Verbande-der-Luftwaffe/Fallschirm-Sturmgeschutz-Brigade-11.html&usg=ALkJrhjwmcYvFuR2TYd4zphL VAmUn_Vw9g (accessed December 29, 2012).

END NOTES

★ ★ ★ ★ ★

| PREFACE |

1   (Ferrell, 2013); (Statistical and Accounting Branch, Office of the Adjutant General, 1950, 31–32); (Greer, 2005, 20–38).

PROLOGUE | "MOVE ALL NIGHT!"

1   (Fenchel, 2001); for the specifications of a M3 or M5 Stuart tank see, (Zaloga, M3 & M5 Stuart Light Tank, 1940–1945, 1999, Plate D).

2   (S–2 Section, 1945, 1–2); (Irzyk, 8th Tank Battalion History—19 October 1944 to 10 February 1945, 16–17).

3   (S–3 Section, CCB, 4th Armored Division, 1944).

4   (Irzyk, *He Rode Up Front for Patton,* 1996, 246–247).

5   (Fenchel, 2001); (Stauber, 1945); (Irzyk, *He Rode Up Front for Patton*, 1996, 247); (S–3 Section, CCB, 4th Armored Division, 1944).

6   According to Ivan Steenkiste, a local resident of Chaumont, there is an interesting story behind the tree. He writes, "I was myself who gave it the name of the BEECH TREE. First, when I discovered the tree, I thought it was an OAK TREE and on my first webpage, I called the story 'The OAK TREE OF CHAUMONT.' During a later visit, my wife who knows much more about trees discovered it wasn't an Oak Tree but a BEECH TREE. So, I had to correct my webpage, and from that day on, it was the BEECH TREE OF CHAUMONT. As such, it was taken up in many articles." (Steenkiste, e-mail from Ivan, 2012).

7   (S–3 Section, CCB, 4th Armored Division, 1944); (Fenchel, 2001); (Dager, 1945, 3); (Stauber, 1945, 2); (Baum, 1945, 2).

8   For a good summary of the battles between 4th Armored Division and 5th Fallschirmjäger Division, see Quarrie, *The Ardennes Offensive: First Armee & Seventh Armee, The Southern Sector,* 2001, and Quarrie, *The Ardennes Offensive: U.S. III & and XII Corps, The Southern Sector,* 2001; for an excellent summary of the entire Battle of the Bulge, see Toland, 1999, MacDonald, 2002, J. S. Eisenhower, 1995, Cole, 1965, and Dupuy, 1994; for the story about the 101st Airborne at Bastogne, see the following: (Marshall Facsimilie Reprint, 1988), (Koskimaki, 2003), (Barron, 2012), and (McManus, 2007).

CHAPTER 1 | THE GERMAN PLAN

1   (Bomber Command's summary of the raid on Krefeld, Germany, 21/22 June 1943, 2010).

2   (Robert Balsam, 2012).

3   (Altenburger, Gause, Alfred, 2012).

4   (Altenburger, Krebs, Hans, 2012).

5   (R. C. Gersdorff, 1946, 15–16).

6   (R. C. Gersdorff, 1946, 16–17).

7   (R. C. Gersdorff, The Ardennes Offensive, MS A–909, 1945, 1–5); (R. C. Gersdorff, 1946, 6–8).

8   (Carpenter, 2012).

9   (Altenburger, Brandenberger, Erich, 2012).

10   (Altenburger, Knieß, Baptist, 2012).

11   (Altenburger, Graf von Rothkirch und Trach, Edwin, 2012).

12   (Knieß, The Ardennes, 16 December 1944 to 12 January 1945, MS B–030, 1946, 3); (Knieß, LXXXV Infantry Corps (November–26 December 1944) ETHINT 40, 1945, 2); (Altenburger, Generalkommando Knieß LXXXV. Armeekorps z.b.V. (85.), 2012).

13 (Bodenstein, 1946, 1); (Trach, 1946, 3).

14 (R. C. Gersdorff, 1946, 21–27); (R. C. Gersdorff, 1946, 29–32); (R. C. Gersdorff, Seventh Army in the Ardennes Offensive, ETHINT 54, 1945, 3); Staff of the Seventh Army, see http://www.lexikon-der-wehrmacht.de/Gliederungen/Armeen/7Armee.htm (Altenburger, 7. Armee, 2012); (Schramm, n.d., 163, 189–91).

15 (R. C. Gersdorff, The Ardennes Offensive, MS A–909, 1945, 8).

16 (Heilmann, 5th Parachute Division (1 December 1944–12 January 1945), MS B–023, between 1945–1954, 6–7); (R. C. Gersdorff, Seventh Army in the Ardennes Offensive, ETHINT 54, 1945, 2); (Schmidt, 1946, 1).

17 (Altenburger, Heilmann, Ludwig, 2012).

18 (Altenburger, 5. Fallschirmjäger–Division, 2012).

19 See Altenburger, Fallschirmjäger–Regiment 13, 2012; (Altenburger, Fallschirmjäger–Regiment 14, 2012); (Petrikat, unknown).

20 (Riedel, Fighting in the Ardennes 16 December to 25 January 1945, Seventh Army Artillery, MS B–594, Between 1945 and 1954, 8); (Riedel, Battle in the Ardennes (16 December 1944 till 25 January 1945). The activity of the artillery of the 7. Army Supplement to the report of General Major Freiherr von Gersdorff, at the time Chief of Staff of the 7. Army. MS B-467, between 1945 and 1954, 12–13).

21 (Heilmann, 5th Parachute Division (1 December 1944—12 January 1945), MS B–023, between 1945–1954, 1–2, 3–5); (Heilmann, Evaluation of the 5th Fallschirmjager Division (December 1944), 1946, 1); for a good list of German commanders in the 5th Fallschirmjäger Division, see Historical War Militaria Forum, 2012; (Zweiter-Weltkrieg-Lexikon.de, 2009); (Interrogation Prisoner of War Team, 25 December 1944, 4–5).

22 (R. C. Gersdorff, Seventh Army in the Ardennes Offensive, ETHINT 54, 1945, 2).

23 (R. C. Gersdorff, Evaluation and Equipment of the Units Attached to the Seventh Army During the Ardennes Offensive, MS A-932, between 1945 and 1954, 1).

24   (Heilmann, 5th Parachute Division (1 December 1944–12 January 1945), MS B-023, between 1945–1954, 5–6).

25   (Frantzen–Heger, 2012).

26   (Heilmann, 5th Parachute Division (1 December 1944–12 January 1945), MS B-023, between 1945–1954, 7–10).

27   (Heilmann, 5th Parachute Division (1 December 1944–12 January 1945), MS B-023, between 1945–1954, 19).

28   (Heilmann, 5th Parachute Division (1 December 1944–12 January 1945), MS B-023, between 1945–1954, 12–13, 17).

29   Kurt Gröschke was a seasoned commander for the 15th Fallschirmjäger Regiment. For information on Kurt Gröschke see: http://www.lexikon-der-wehrmacht.de/Personenregister/G/GroeschkeK.htm. (Altenburger, Gröschke, Kurt, 2012); for information on the 15th Fallschirmjäger Regiment, see http://www.lexikon-der-wehrmacht.de/Gliederungen/Fallschirmjagerregimenter/FJR15.htm (Altenburger, Fallschirmjäger–Regiment 15, 2012).

30   For a list of the staff of the 5th Fallschirmjäger, see http://www.historicalwarmilitariaforum.com/18–gliederung–5–fallschirmj–ger–division.html. (Historical War Militaria Forum, 2012).

31   For a decent list of the commanders in the 5th Fallschirmjäger Division, see Gaul, 1995, 39.

32   (Heilmann, 5th Parachute Division (1 December 1944–12 January 1945), MS B-023, between 1945–1954, 10–11, 19–24); (R. C. Gersdorff 1946, 39).

33   (G-2, Twelfth Army Group, 1944, 1).

34   See Hays, 1999, 11.

35   (Koch, After Action Report, U.S. Third Army, 1 August 1944 to 9 May 1945, Volume II, Staff Sections, December 14, 1944, CXVII).

36   (Koch, After Action Report, U.S. Third Army, 1 August 1944 to 9 May 1945, Volume II, Staff Sections, December 10, 1944, CXIV); (Koch, After Action Report, U.S. Third Army, 1 August 1944 to 9 May 1945, Volume II, Staff Sections, December 13, 1944, CXVI).

37   (Hays, 1999, 92–94).

38   (Dickson, 1944, 1–3).

39   (Bradley, 1999, 463–64).

40   See D. S. Parker, *Battle of the Bulge: Hitler's Ardennes Offensive, 1944–1945*, 1999, 44–45.

41   (Sauvonsmolitor, 2007).

42   (Koch, OB Map to accompany G-2 Periodic Report No. 183, 11 December 1944, CXV).

43   (Klemment, "Unpublished Manuscript: The 9th Company, III Battalion of the Parachute Regiment 15, During the Ardennes Offensive until 25 December 1944," unknown).

CHAPTER 2 | THE AMERICAN RESPONSE

1   (Heilmann, 5th Parachute Division (1 December 1944–12 January 1945), MS B-023, between 1945–1954, 26–27); (R. C. Gersdorff, 1946, Volume II, 1–5); (R. C. Gersdorff, The Ardennes Offensive, MS A-909, 1945, 14–15); (Knieß, The Ardennes, 16 December 1944 to 12 January 1945, MS B-030, 1946, 3–4); (Knieß, LXXXV Infantry Corps (November–26 December 1944), ETHINT 40, 1945, 3); (G-3 Section, 28th Infantry Division, 1944); see map at the back of Heilmann's account, which shows the 14th Fallschirm-jäger Regiment to the north and the 15th Fallschirmjäger Regiment to the south. (Heilmann, 5th Parachute Division (1 December 1944—12 January 1945), MS B-023, between 1945–1954); (Klemment, "Unpublished Manu-script: The 9th Company, III Battalion of the Parachute Regiment 15 During the Ardennes Offensive Until 25 December 1944," unknown); Klemment's map clearly shows that it was the 15th Fallschirmjäger Regiment that crossed south of the 14th Fallschirmjäger Regiment on the morning of the sixteenth, contrary to the assertions of von Gersdorff. In addition, the U.S. unit, the 109th Infantry, recorded capturing men from the 15th Fallschirmjäger Reg-iment, but not the 13th, which adds to Klemment's and Heilmann's account (Rudder, 1944).

2   (Klemment, "Unpublished Manuscript: The 9th Company, III Battalion of the

Parachute Regiment 15 During the Ardennes Offensive Until 25 December 1944," unknown).

3   (Rudder, 1944).

4   (Heilmann, 5th Parachute Division (1 December 1944—12 January 1945), MS B-023, between 1945–1954, 27–30); (R. C. Gersdorff, 1946, 12–13, Volume 2); (Schmidt, 1946, 4–5).

5   For a list of identified German divisions facing VIII Corps, see page 4 of Koch, Significant Enemy Order of Battle Facts in West—Week 10/17 December 1944, Annex No. 3 to G-2 Periodic Report No. 190, 1944, 1–4.

6   For a great biography on Patton, see D'Este, 1995; (Estate of George S. Patton Jr,. 2014).

7   (Hays, 1999, 105, 107); (Patton, *War as I Knew It*, 1995, 189–90); (Bradley, 1999, 465–69). For a picture of EAGLE TAC, see Basaraba, 2011; (Luxembourg City Tourist Office, 2013); for a history of the buildings, see M. J. Fenn, 2013).

8   (Patton, *War as I Knew It*, 1995, 189, 190); (D. D. Eisenhower, 1997, 350); (Headquarters, III Corps, 1944); (Mewshaw, G-3 Situation Report No. 44: Period 190600A to 191200A, December 44, Operational Priority to: Commanding General, Third U.S. Army, 1944); (Headquarters, III Corps, 1944); (Koch, Preliminary Study of the Terrain Area: Liège (K4887)—Arlon (P6222)—Trier (L2129)—Zulpich (P2333), 1944).

9   (D. D. Eisenhower, 1997, 350–52); (Patton, *War as I Knew It*, 1995, 190–92); (Bradley, 1999, 470–72); (Mewshaw, G-3 Situation Report No. 45: Period 191200A to 191800A, December 44, Operational Priority to: Commanding General, Third U.S. Army, 1944); (Headquarters, III Corps, 1944); (Harding, 2004); (Rickard, 2011, 99); Rickard's account and analysis of Patton is an excellent source. As Rickard noted, there's some discrepancy as to what time line was promised. In Patton's book *War as I Knew It*, which was heavily edited, according to Rickard, Patton said he would attack on the twenty-second, which corroborates the historical record. Bradley, however, claimed that Patton said "forty-eight hours." In a sense, Patton was already moving. As III Corps records indicate above, Millikin had already received his marching orders and had moved out. In addition, III Corps had issued the warning orders to its units.

Hence the question becomes, What did Patton mean by forty-eight hours? Did he mean he would attack in forty-eight hours, or did he mean he would assume his final assault position at Arlon in forty-eight, which makes more sense? We'll never really know.

10   (G-2 Section, 4th Armored Division, 1944).

11   (G-2 Section, 4th Armored Division, 1944).

12   (Koyen, 1946, 175, 179).

13   For a great historical account of the 4th Armored Division in World War II, read *Patton's Vanguard*, by Don M. Fox (Fox, 2003).

14   Fox's account of the relief MG John Woods can be found in chapter eight of his book (Fox, 2003, 221–32).

15   (Headquarters, Combat Command "A," 4th Armored Division, January 18, 1945, 2); (Spires, October 19, 1945, December 3, 1945); (G-1 Section, 4th Armored Division, 1944).

16   (Crane, December 1944, 3 (31)); (Williams, 2002); (Donaldson, 1993).

17   (Hunt, After Action Report, Combat Command B, 4th Armored Division for the Period of 1 to 31 December 1944, 2 (14)); (S-3 Section, CCB, 4th Armored Division, 1944); (Headquarters, 10th Armored Infantry Battalion, 1944); (Irzyk, Firsthand Account, 4th Armored Division Spearhead at Bastogne, 1999); (Irzyk, "Bastogne: A Fascinating, Obscure Vignette," 1986); (S-3 Section, CCB, 4th Armored Division, 1944).

18   (Lutgen, 2010).

19   (Headquarters, Third U.S. Army, 1945, 172); (O'Neill, 1971).

20   For information on Udange, Belgium, see Tourism Office of Arlon, 2013; (Crane, December 1944, 4); (H. B. Lay, 35th Tank Battalion History, December 1–31, 1944).

21   (Sullivan, Field Order #8, 4th Armored Division, 211600A, December 1944).

22   (G–4 Section, 4th Armored Division, 1944). To understand the code, A=M4 with 75mm gun. B=M4 with 76mm gun. C=M4 with 105mm howitzer. D=M5 with 37mm gun. E=M8 with 75mm howitzer. U=M20 armored car. V=M18

tank destroyer. W=M7 with 105mm howitzer. Y=half-track; (M. Abrams, 1945); (Dager, 1945, 3).

23   (Sullivan, Field Order #8, 4th Armored Division, 211600A, December 1944).

24   (Sullivan, Field Order #8, 4th Armored Division, 211600A, December 1944); (Mewshaw, Field Order #1, Headquarters, III Corps, Arlon, Belgium, 1944, 1–2); (Pattison, 1945); (Clark, Narrative Summary of Operations of 4th Armored Division in the Relief of Bastogne, December 22–29, 1945, Combat Interview 279).

25   (G-2 Section, 4th Armored Division, 1944); (West, 1944).

26   **COMPOSITION OF FORCES [CCA]**

LEFT COLUMN	RIGHT COLUMN
51 Inf (–1 Co.)	35th Tk Bn (–1 Co.)
Co./35	Co./51
A/24 (–1 Plat + 2 Br Trk)	Plat/A24 plus 2 Br Trk.
A/704 (–1 Plat)	Plat/A/704
274 F.A. Bn	66 F.A. Bn.
Medical Support	Medical Support

(Earnest, Field Order #1, Combat Command A, 4th Armored Division, 21 December 1944); (Headquarters, Combat Command "A," 4th Armored Division, 18 January, 1945, 4–5).

CHAPTER 3 | FIRST CONTACT

1   (Heilmann, 5th Parachute Division (1 December 1944–12 January 1945), MS B-023, between 1945–1954, 36–38); (Trach, 1946, 3–5); (Bodenstein, 1946, 1–4); (War Diary (Kriegstagebuch), Armee Korps LIII, December 1944 to March 1945, T–314, Roll 1335, 1st Frame 415, 76106, 1944–1945, 446); (Martin, 1984, 120–28); (R. C. Gersdorff, 1946, Volume 2, 26–31). According to Heilmann, the 13th Regiment was not at Martelange. In fact, the only regiment close to Martelange was the 15th and elements of the 5th Pioneer Battalion. (G-2 Section, 4th Armored Division, 1944); (Klemment, "Diary of the 9th Company, III Battalion, 15th Fallschirmjäger Regiment, 5th

Fallschirmjäger Division," n.d.); (Interrogation Prisoner of War Team, December 25, 1944, 4–5).

2   (Crane, December 1944, 39); (Crane, December 1944, 50); (Kimsey, 1944, 4 (24)); (H. B. Lay, After Action Report, 35th Tank Battalion, December 1944–3 January 1945, 2); (H. B. Lay, 35th Tank Battalion History, December 1–31, 1944, 5); (Oden, 1945, 1); (Oden, 1946–1947, 6–7); (Pattison, 1945); (Robert R. Summers, 1949, 106); see map on Robert R. Summers, 1949, page 109, sketch 7; (G-2 Section, 4th Armored Division, 1944); (Earnest, Combat Command A, After Action Report, December 1944–1945, 3–4); (Headquarters, Combat Command "A," 4th Armored Division, January 18, 1945, 5); (Calvert, 2010); (Gaydos, Letter to author about his service with 66th Armored Field Artillery Battalion, 2013); for list of artillery officers see Fleischman, 1944.

3   (Donaldson, 1993, 29, 39).

4   (Crane, December 1944, 50); (Crane, December 1944, 4 (32)); (S-2 Section, 51st Armored Infantry Battalion, 4th Armored Division, 1944, 10 (69)); see map in Robert R. Summers, 1949, 109 (Sketch 7); (Oden, 1945, 1); (L. R. Lay, 1945, 2); (Donaldson, 1993); (Calvert, 2010, 65); (G-2 Section, 4th Armored Division, 1944); (G-2 Section, 4th Armored Division, 1944); (Ivan Sache, 2007).

5   (Klemment, "Unpublished Manuscript: The 9th Company, III Battalion of the Parachute Regiment 15 During the Ardennes Offensive until 25 December 1944," unknown).

6   (Kettel, 2010).

7   (Crane, December 1944, 50); (Crane, December 1944, 4 (32)); (S-2 Section, 51st Armored Infantry Battalion, 4th Armored Division, 1944, 10 (69)); See map in Robert R. Summers, 1949, 109 (Sketch 7); (Oden, 1945, 1); (L. R. Lay, 1945, 2); (Donaldson, 1993); (Calvert, 2010, 65); (G-2 Section, 4th Armored Division, 1944); (G-2 Section, 4th Armored Division, 1944); (Ivan Sache, 2007).

8   (Lange, 2010).

9   Klemment said he saw the tanks around 1000 hours, but that is impossible, since TF Oden was trying to circumvent the blown bridge at the time. It was

likely closer to noon when TF Oden approached Wolwewange. (Klemment, "Unpublished Manuscript: The 9th Company, III Battalion of the Parachute Regiment 15 During the Ardennes Offensive until 25 December 1944," unknown); (Interrogation, Prisoner of War Team, III Corps, December 26, 1944, 2–4, 7); (Oden, 1945, 1); (L. R. Lay, 1945, 2); (Calvert, 2010, 65); (G-2 Section, 4th Armored Division, 1944); (G-2 Section, 4th Armored Division, 1944); (Oden, 1945, 1).

10   (Michael Robert Patterson, 2006); (Donnelly, 1945, 1); (T. L. Green, 1994, 44); (Harold Cohen—Obituaries for August 16, 2006); for a great speech in conjunction with the award of Cohen's Distinguished Service Cross, see "Salute to LTC Harold Cohen on His Receipt of Distinguished Service Cross," 1996; (Irzyk, *He Rode Up Front for Patton*, 1996, 1–12); (Spires, October 19, 1945); (Irzyk, *He Rode Up Front for Patton*, 1996, 200).

11   (S–3 Section, CCB, 4th Armored Division, 1944); (Battista, 2002).

12   (Headquarters, 10th Armored Infantry Battalion, 1944); (Irzyk, *He Rode Up Front for Patton*, 1996, 244–46); (Irzyk, Battle for Chaumont, Belgium, December 23, 1944, 2006); (Irzyk, Interview with Albin F. Irzyk, 2012); (Irzyk, Interview with Albin F. Irzyk, 2012); (Hunt, After Action Report, Combat Command B, 4th Armored Division for the Period of 1 to 31 December 1944, 1–2); (Hunt, Combat Command "B" History, December 1–31, 1944, 4th Armored Division, 1944, 4); (S-2 Section, Headquarters, CCB, 4th Armored Division, 1944); (Donnelly, 1945); (S-2 Section, 1945, 1); (Irzyk, *8th Tank Battalion History, October 19, 1944–February 10, 1945,* 16–17); (Headquarters, 8th Tank Battalion, 4th Armored Division, December 22, 1944); (Headquarters, 25th Cavalry Reconnaissance Squadron (Mechanized), 1944, 8–9); (Bastnagel, February 6, 1945, 11); (G-2 Section, 4th Armored Division, 1944).

13   (Ellis, January 29, 1945, 12); (Clark, Narrative Summary of Combat Command B's Part in the Relief of Bastogne, 20 through 29 December 1944, Combat Interview #279, 1944, 1–2); (Baum, 1945, 1–2); (Dager, 1945, 3); (Stauber, 1945, 2); (Ellis, January 29, 1945, 2); for the Table of Organization and Equipment for an Armored Field Artillery Battalion, see Zaloga, *U.S. Armored Divisions: European Theater of Operations, 1944–1945,* 2004, 38–40; for performance specifications on the M7 and the 155mm howitzer, see Zaloga, *U.S. Field Ar-*

tillery of World War II, 2007, 15, 24, 41; (Headquarters, 10th Armored Infantry Battalion, 1944–1945).

14 (Patton, "Conference with General Patton—Attended by General Gaffey and General Millikin," 1944); (Headquarters, III Corps, 1944); (Phillips, Memorandum for Record, December 22, 1944); (Mewshaw, G-3 Situation Report No. 57: Period 221200 to 221800, December 1944, Operational Priority to: Commanding General, Third U.S. Army (TAC)l, 1944); (Watkins, 1944); (Harrison, Message #6 to Commanding General, III Corps, From Olympic, Lieutenant Colonel Sullivan, December 22, 1944); (Sharpe, 1944); (Mewshaw, Operations Directive No. 1 (Confirmation of Fragmentary Orders). Reference Field Order 1, December 21, 1944); for a great summary of the meeting and other activities, see Winton, 2007, 44–48, 216–21; also see Rickard, 2011, 154–58; (Headquarters, III Corps, 1944, 8–12); (Patton, *War as I Knew It*, 1995, 147); (Hunt, After Action Report, Combat Command B, 4th Armored Division for the Period of 1 to 31 December 1944); (S-3 Section, CCB, 4th Armored Division, 1944); (Horner, G-2 Periodic Report Number 14, from: 212000 December to: 222000 December, III Corps, 1944, 1); (Edwards, 1944); (Crane, December 1944); (Blanchard, 1945).

15 (Churchill, January 18, 1945, 1–2); (Headquarters, Reserve Command, 4th Armored Division, 1944); (Johnson, Unit Diary, 53rd Armored Infantry Battalion, 1 December 1944 to 31 December 1944); (Johnson, After Action Report, December 1944, 53rd Armored Infantry Battalion, 1945, 9); (G. L. Jaques, January 8, 1945, 1); (Moon, 37th Tank Battalion Diary, 1945); (H. C. Jaques, 1945, 1); (Seay, 1945); (Fox, 2003, 153); for information on Wendell Blanchard see Michael Robert Patterson, 2007.

16 (Battista, 2002); (Headquarters, 10th Armored Infantry Battalion, 1944); (Irzyk, *He Rode Up Front for Patton*, 1996, 245–46).

17 (Horner, G-2 Periodic Report Number 14, from: 212000 December to: 222000 December, III Corps, 1944); (Interrogation, Prisoner of War Team, III Corps, December 22, 1944); (Headquarters, 10th Armored Infantry Battalion, 1944).

18 (Irzyk, "Battle for Chaumont, Belgium," December 23, 1944, 2006); (R. E. Green, 2013); (S-2 Section, 1945, 1).

19 (Cercle d'Histoire de Bastogne, 1994).

CHAPTER 4 | CHAUMONT

1   (S-3 Section, CCB, 4th Armored Division, 1944); (S-2 Section, Headquarters, CCB, 4th Armored Division, 1944); (Irzyk, Interview with Albin F. Irzyk, 2012); (Irzyk, Interview with Albin F. Irzyk, 2012). According to G-2, he was the S-2 for 8th TK BN. According to 8th TK BN, he was an LNO. (G-2 Section, 4th Armored Division, 1944); (Irzyk, 8th Tank Battalion History, October 19, 1944–February 10, 1945, 17–18); (Bastnagel, February 6, 1945, 12).

2   (Interrogation, Prisoner of War Team, III Corps, December 26, 1944, 2–3, 7); (Interrogation, Prisoner of War Team #60, 134th Infantry Regiment, 1944); (G-2 Section, 4th Armored Division, 1944); (G-2 Section, 4th Armored Division, 1944); (Martin, 1984, 51, 122–23); see maps in back of Heilmann, 5th Parachute Division (December 1, 1944–January 12, 1945), MS B-023, between 1945–1954); (H. E. Brown, Periodic Report No. 116, G-2, 4th Armored Division, December 23, 1944, 1); (H. E. Brown, Periodic Report No. 117, G-2, 4th Armored Division, December 24, 1944, 1); for the German OOB for Fallschirmjäger Division, see War Department, 1945; for a great deal of information pertaining directly to the battle of Chaumont, see Steenkiste, Chaumont, Ardennes, 2005; (Interrogation, Prisoner of War Team, III Corps, December 24, 1944, 4); (Interrogation, Prisoner of War Team, III Corps, December 23, 1944, 1); for *panzerschreck* information, see Bull, 2005, 45–46; (S-2 Section, Headquarters, CCB, 4th Armored Division, 1944); "b. Operations of Component Elements: (1) Inf: CCB rpts SA and mortar fire S CHAUMONT (P5149) 232205A." (H. E. Brown, Periodic Report No. 117, G-2, 4th Armored Division, December 24, 1944, 2); (H. E. Brown, Periodic Report No. 116, G-2, 4th Armored Division, December 23, 1944, 2); (Horner, G-2 Periodic Report Number 14, from: 212000 December to: 222000 December, III Corps, 1944, 1); (Interrogation, Prisoner of War Team 25, December 1944, 4); (Riedel, Battle in the Ardennes (16 December 1944 till 25 January 1945), The activity of the artillery of the 7. Army Supplement to the report of General Major Freiherr von Gersdorff, at the time Chief of Staff of the 7. Army. MS B-467 between 1945 and 1954, 14); to find more information on the 408th Volks Artillery Corps see Altenburger, Artillerie-Korps (tbew. Mot 408 Volks-Artillerie-Korps (tbew. Mot) 408, 2012); for information on the Sturmgeschütz III, see Doyle, Sturmgeschütz III, and IV, 1942–1945, 2001, 21; for great information on the

Sherman tank and how it matches up with German tanks, see Zaloga, *Sherman Medium Tank, 1942–1945*, 1993.

3   (S-3 Section, CCB, 4th Armored Division, 1944); (S-2 Section, 1945, 1–2) (Irzyk, 8th Tank Battalion History, October 19, 1944–February 10, 1945, 17); (G–4 Section, 4th Armored Division, 1944); (Headquarters, 10th Armored Infantry Battalion, 1944); (Hunt, Combat Command "B" History, December 1–31, 1944, 4th Armored Division, 1944, 17); (Stauber, 1945, 2–3); (Baum, 1945, 67–68); (Bastnagel, February 6, 1945, 12); (Harrison, Message #77 to Commanding General, III Corps, from Olympic 3, December 23, 1944); (Harrison, Message #62 to Commanding General, III Corps, from Olympic 3, Captain Sharpe, December 23, 1944); (McAlister, Message #54 to Major McAlister, G-3 Sec, III Corps, from Olympic 3, December 23, 1944); (McAlister, Message #52 to Major McAlister, Assistant G-3, III Corps, from 4th Armored Division, December 23, 1944); (G-2 Section, 4th Armored Division, 1944); (S-2 Section, Headquarters, CCB, 4th Armored Division, 1944); (H. E. Brown, Periodic Report No. 117, G-2, 4th Armored Division, December 24, 1944, 2); (H. E. Brown, Periodic Report No. 116, G-2, 4th Armored Division, December 23, 1944, 2); (Interrogation, Prisoner of War Team 25, December 1944, 4).

4   (Fenchel, 2001).

5   (Ellis, January 29, 1945, 13); (Fortney, 2012); (Connolly, General Order Number 100, Headquarters, 4th Armored Division, December 18, 1944).

6   (Phillips, Memorandum for Record, December 23, 1944, 1100 Phone Call from Patton, 1944).

7   (Heilmann, 5th Parachute Division (1 December 1944–12 January 1945), MS B-023 between 1945–1954, 38–42); (R. C. Gersdorff, 1946, 64–69); (Bodenstein, 1946, 4–5); (Trach, 1946, 6–7); (G–2 Section, 4th Armored Division, 1944); (Wynendaele, 2011).

8   (Irzyk, *He Rode Up Front for Patton*, 1996, 247–50); (Stauber, 1945, 2–3); (Irzyk, 8th Tank Battalion History, October 19, 1944–February 10, 1945, 17); (Donnelly, 1945, 3); (Headquarters, 10th Armored Infantry Battalion, 1944); (Baum, 1945, 2–3); (Clark, Narrative Summary of Combat Command B's Part in the

Relief of Bastogne, 20 through 29 December 1944, Combat Interview #279, 1944, 2–3); for the map outlining U.S. positions, see Clark's map at the end of his account (Clark, Narrative Summary of Combat Command B's Part in the Relief of Bastogne, 20 through 29 December 1944, Combat Interview #279, 1944); for the interview of Matteo Damiano, see Damiano, 2013; (Hunt, Combat Command "B" History, December 1–31, 1944, 4th Armored Division, 1944, 4); (Hunt, After Action Report, Combat Command B, 4th Armored Division for the Period of 1 to 31 December 1944 1944, 3); (S–3 Section, CCB, 4th Armored Division, 1944); (G-2 Section, 4th Armored Division, 1944); for a list of artillery officers, see Fleischman, 1944, 13; (Connolly, General Order Number 4, Headquarters, 4th Armored Division, January 11, 1945); (Connolly, General Order Number 8, Headquarters, 4th Armored Division, January 15, 1945); (Connolly, General Order Number 77, Headquarters, 4th Armored Division, May 8, 1945); (Fox, 2003, 266); (Connolly, General Order Number 4, Headquarters, 4th Armored Division, January 11, 1945).

9   (Ellis, January 29, 1945, 13); (D. S. Parker, *To Win the Winter Sky: Air War over the Ardennes, 1944–1945,* 1999, 228); (Bucholtz, 2013).

10   (Chekan, 2000, 7).

11   (Irzyk, *He Rode Up Front for Patton,* 1996, 247–50); (Stauber, 1945, 2–3); (Irzyk, *8th Tank Battalion History—19 October 1944 to 10 February 1945,* 17); (Donnelly, 1945, 3); (Headquarters, 10th Armored Infantry Battalion, 1944); (Baum, 1945, 2–3); (Clark, Narrative Summary of Combat Command B's Part in the Relief of Bastogne, 20 through 29 December 1944, Combat Interview #279, 1944, 2–3); for the map outlining U.S. positions, see Clark's map at the end of his account (Clark, Narrative Summary of Combat Command B's Part in the Relief of Bastogne, 20 through 29 December 1944, Combat Interview #279, 1944); for the interview of Matteo Damiano, see Damiano, 2013; (Hunt, Combat Command "B" History, December 1–31, 1944, 4th Armored Division, 1944, 4); (Hunt, After Action Report, Combat Command B, 4th Armored Division for the Period of 1 to 31 December 1944 1944, 3); (S-3 Section, CCB, 4th Armored Division, 1944); (G-2 Section, 4th Armored Division, 1944); for a list of artillery officers, see Fleischman, 1944, 13; (Headquarters, 25th Cavalry Reconnaissance Squadron (Mechanized), 1944, 9);

(Bastnagel, February 6, 1945, 11); (Irzyk, Interview with Albin F. Irzyk, 2012); for award citations, see Headquarters, 10th Armored Infantry Battalion, 1944–1945; (Giallanza, 2002).

12   (Kokott, Ardennes Offensive—Battle of Bastogne MS #B–040, 1950, 111–12); for information on Heinz Kokott, see Robert Balsam, 2013; (Bayerlein, 2005, 81); (S. H. Brown, 1944); (Kokott, Ardennes Offensive—Battle of Bastogne MS #B–040, 1950, 112–14); the only American or British armor that stood a chance against a Tiger I were the British Fireflys, which were Sherman tanks that mounted the 17-pdr the M36 tank destroyer, which mounted a 90mm gun, and eventually the M26 Pershing, which also mounted a 90mm gun. (Doyle, *Tiger I Heavy Tank, 1942–1945*, 1993, 8, 19); (Altenburger, Schwere Panzerabteilung 506, 2012); (Revell, 2004); (Kokott, Breakthrough to Bastogne, ETHINT 44, 1945, 1–4); by now, the German army had an accurate estimate as to the strength of the various American divisions. I found a document in the German Seventh Army files that depicted the various combat strengths of each type of American division. For instance, the German army's intelligence staff estimated that an American tank battalion had sixty-five medium tanks and eighteen light tanks. They weren't far off. The typical tank battalion in November 1944 had an authorized strength of fifty-nine medium (76mm and 105mm included) and seventeen light tanks. The German army was a hundred percent accurate when it came to assessing the armored field artillery battalions, and were close in estimating the manpower strength of the armored infantry battalions. In short, Kokott knew that an American combat command was a lethal combined arms force. (A.O.K. 7/Ic/AO—Feind Unterlagen, Westen T–312, 75868, December 1944–February 1945, 608–09); the story of the Tiger platoon is an interesting one. Many historians concluded that the four mysterious vehicles were Jagdtigers from the 653rd Heavy Panzer Hunter Battalion. In fact, I thought the same thing, too. However, after much research, I concluded that they were four Tiger tanks. Kokott called them Tigers in ETHINT 44, and he called them *schwere panzer* in his other account, Manuscript B–40. Neither of these terms indicated that he meant to call them Jagdtigers. *Schwere panzer* was a term used by the German army to denote Tiger battalions. The 653rd's monthly status report for January 1945, which dealt with December 1–31, 1944, mentioned nothing about operations in the

Ardennes. It mentioned only a long road movement of 130 kilometers and a lack of success. Additionally, a 653rd Inspection Report mentioned only one contact: "I explained that the Inspector General of Armored Forces had not yet heard anything about good performance and successes of the Jagdtiger. According to Oberleutnant Haberland, Company Commander of the 1. schwere Panzerjäger–Abteilung 653, only a few Jagdtiger have been deployed in the Zweibrucken area—as artillery. One Sherman has been knocked out and one Jagdtiger completely destroyed by an explosion (cause unknown)." This is hardly the success story we would have expected if the Jagdtigers were at Chaumont. On the other hand, there were Tiger Is in the vicinity. According to the 506th Heavy Panzer Battalion Unit Diary, there were fifteen to twenty Tigers in Eschdorf, Luxembourg, on December 22. This was in the Seventh Army's area of operation. Moreover, we have a report from the U.S. 28th Infantry Division, on the evening of the twenty-second, that stated at 1740 there were four Tiger tanks attacking Nives, Belgium (Message No. 102). True, U.S. soldiers were notorious for reporting everything as Tigers. In this case, though, Nives is only five kilometers from Chaumont, and Kokott said he saw his four Tigers around midday on the twenty-third. Next, the only other unit that might have used tanks in the area was the Panzer Lehr Division, but the Panzer Lehr's area of operations did not extend south of the Remichampagne–Morhet road. Thus, though possible, it is unlikely that these were tanks from the Panzer Lehr Division. The 5th Fallschirmjäger, moreover, had no tanks—only self-propelled StuGs. Therefore, since there were no other tanks in the area, these were probably Tigers from Eschdorf. The only counter to this argument is that the unit diary doesn't mention the Chaumont operation. Who knows why? (Schneider, 2004, 274); (G-3 Section, 28th Infantry Division, 1944); (Grillenberger, January 4, 1945); (Johannis, January 16, 1945).

13 (Law, 1944, 1–5); (Bernstein, OPREP A, No. D-23B, second of three, for twenty-four hours ending sunset, December 23, 1944. Ninth Fighter Command Field Order No. 145, 1944); (Headquarters, 362nd Fighter Group, 1986).

14 (Headquarters, 10th Armored Infantry Battalion, December 23, 1944); (Donnelly, 1945, 3); (Baum, 1945, 69–70); (Damiano, 2013); (S-2 Section, 1945, 2); (Irzyk, 8th Tank Battalion History, October 19, 1944–February 10, 1945, 17); (Irzyk, Battle for Chaumont, Belgium, December 23, 1944, 2006); (Irzyk, Greatest Tank Battles: Race to Bastogne, 2010); (S-3 Section, CCB, 4th

Armored Division, 1944); (Stauber, 1945, 3); (G-4 Section, 4th Armored Division, 1944); (Hunt, After Action Report, Combat Command B, 4th Armored Division for the Period of 1 to 31 December 1944, 3); (Hunt, Combat Command "B" History, December 1–31, 1944, 4th Armored Division, 1944, 4); (G-2 Section, 4th Armored Division, 1944); (Ellis, January 29, 1945, 13); (Interrogation, Prisoner of War Team, III Corps, December 26, 1944, 2–3, 7); (Interrogation, Prisoner of War Team #60, 134th Infantry Regiment, 1944); (G-2 Section, 4th Armored Division, 1944); (G-2 Section, 4th Armored Division, 1944); (Martin, 1984, 51, 122–23); See maps in back of Heilmann, 5th Parachute Division (December 1, 1944–January 12, 1945), MS B-023 between 1945–1954); (H. E. Brown, Periodic Report No. 116, G-2, 4th Armored Division, December 23, 1944, 1); (H. E. Brown, Periodic Report No. 117, G–2, 4th Armored Division, December 24, 1944, 1); for the German OOB for Fallschirmjäger Division see (War Department, 1945); for a great deal of information pertaining directly to the battle of Chaumont, see Steenkiste, Chaumont, Ardennes, 2005; (Interrogation, Prisoner of War Team, III Corps, December 24, 1944, 4); (Interrogation, Prisoner of War Team, III Corps, December 23, 1944, 1); For *panzerschreck* information, see Bull, 2005, 45–46; (S-2 Section, Headquarters, CCB, 4th Armored Division, 1944); (H. E. Brown, Periodic Report No. 117, G-2, 4th Armored Division, December 24, 1944, 2); (H. E. Brown, Periodic Report No. 116, G-2, 4th Armored Division, December 23, 1944, 2); (Horner, G-2 Periodic Report Number 14, from: 212000 December to: 222000 December, III Corps, 1944, 1); (Interrogation, Prisoner of War Team, December 25, 1944, 4); (Riedel, Battle in the Ardennes, December 16, 1944–January 25, 1945); the activity of the artillery of the 7. Army Supplement to the report of General Major Freiherr von Gersdorff, at the time Chief of Staff of the 7. Army, MS B-467 between 1945 and 1954, 14); to find more information on the 408th Volks Artillery Corps, see Altenburger, Artillerie-Korps (tbew. Mot), 408 Volks-Artillerie-Korps (tbew. Mot), 408, 2012); for information on the Sturmgeschütz III, see Doyle, Sturmgeschütz III and IV, 1942–1945, 2001, 21; for great information on the Sherman tank and how it matches up with German tanks, see Zaloga, Sherman Medium Tank, 1942–1945, 1993; (Hoy, 2011). See Fox, 2003, 383–84); for Bennett's Silver Star, see Connolly, General Orders Number 23, Headquarters, 4th Armored Division, February 3, 1945; for Patton's Silver Star, see Connolly, General Orders Number 11, Headquarters, 4th Armored Division, January 18, 1945; For Gniot's Distinguished Service Cross, see Department of the Army, 1945; for individual actions of the 10th AIB, see Headquarters, 10th Armored Infantry Battalion, 1944–1945; (Connolly, General Order Number 25, Headquarters, 4th Armored Division, February 6, 1945).

CHAPTER 5 | FLATZBOURHOF

1   (Spires, October 19, 1945); (Churchill, January 18, 1945, 2); (Headquarters, Reserve Command, 4th Armored Division, 1944); (S-2 Section, Combat Command Reserve, 4th Armored Division, 1944); (Bush, 1944, 4); (R. Parker, 1945); (Johnson, After Action Report, December 1944, 53rd Armored Infantry Battalion, 1945, 8); (Johnson, Unit Diary, 53rd Armored Infantry Battalion, December 1, 1944–December 31, 1944, 52); (G. L. Jaques, January 8, 1945, 1); (H. C. Jaques, 1945, 82); (Moon, 37th Tank Battalion Diary, 1945, 6); (Whitehill, 1997); (King, 2004); (Department of the Army, 1945); (Bautz, 1999); (J. H. Leach, Twenty Days in December 1944, 1998, 9–10); (Hermes, 2009); (Department of the Army, 1945); (Creighton W. Abrams, 1945); (Headquarters, 37th Tank Battalion, 4th Armored Division, 1944); (Sorley, 1992, 13–67); (W. A. Dwight, 1979); (Department of the Army, 1944); (American Battle Monuments Commission, 2013); For strength rolls, see (G-4 Section, 4th Armored Division, 1944, 3, December 22); (Cowles, 1948, 1–3); (R. Dwight, 2013); (Grand Rapids Officer Leads Tanks into Bastogne, Wins Star, 1945); (Local Man Led Rescue Thrust, 1945).

2   (Klemment, Unpublished Manuscript: The 9th Company, III Battalion of the Parachute Regiment 15 During the Ardennes Offensive until 25 December 1944, Unknown); (Lange, 2010).

3   (Headquarters, 37th Tank Battalion, 4th Armored Division, 1944); (Johnson, After Action Report, December 1944, 53rd Armored Infantry Battalion, 1945, 8); (Johnson, Unit Diary, 53rd Armored Infantry Battalion, 1 December 1944 to 31 December 1944, 52); (G. L. Jaques, January 8, 1945, 1); (H. C. Jaques, 1945, 82).

4   See account of Singling in History Section, European Theater of Operations, 1945; (Headquarters, 37th Tank Battalion, 4th Armored Division, 1944); (Johnson, After Action Report, December 1944, 53rd Armored Infantry Battalion, 1945, 8); (Johnson, Unit Diary, 53rd Armored Infantry Battalion, 1 De-

cember 1944 to 31 December 1944, 52); (J. H. Leach, Greatest Tank Battles: Race to Bastogne, 2010); for a great interview, see (J. H. Leach, Interview with Jimmie Leach (Unedited), 2009); there is some discrepancy with Leach's account. Park was killed that day, but according to the roster on December 12, 1944, his tank was in 2nd Platoon—not 1st. However, the reports claim the losses were in 1st Platoon. It is possible that, due to reorganizing, Park's tank was shifted to 1st Platoon prior to the Bulge operation; see also Warnock, 2010, 43–45.

5   (Klemment, Unpublished Manuscript: The 9th Company, III Battalion of the Parachute Regiment 15 During the Ardennes Offensive until 25 December 1944, Unknown); (Lange, 2010).

6   See account of Singling in History Section, European Theater of Operations, 1945; (Headquarters, 37th Tank Battalion, 4th Armored Division, 1944); (Johnson, After Action Report, December 1944, 53rd Armored Infantry Battalion, 1945, 8); (Johnson, Unit Diary, 53rd Armored Infantry Battalion, 1 December 1944 to 31 December 1944, 52); (R. Parker, 1945).

7   (Thomas, 2010); (Molitor, 2010); (Kettel, 2010); (Lutgen, 2010).

8   (Klemment, Unpublished Manuscript: The 9th Company, III Battalion of the Parachute Regiment 15 During the Ardennes Offensive until 25 December 1944, Unknown).

9   (Headquarters, 37th Tank Battalion, 4th Armored Division, 1944); For more information on tactical radio communication in World War II, see Rottman, 2010, 20–29, 46–47; (G. L. Jaques, January 8, 1945, 1); (H. C. Jaques, 1945, 82).

10   (Klemment, Unpublished Manuscript: The 9th Company, III Battalion of the Parachute Regiment 15 During the Ardennes Offensive until 25 December 1944, Unknown).

11   (Whitehill, 1997); (Headquarters, 37th Tank Battalion, 4th Armored Division, 1944); (Connolly, General Orders Number 16, Headquarters, 4th Armored Division, January 27, 1945); (Fox, 2003, 363).

12   (Klemment, Unpublished Manuscript: The 9th Company, III Battalion of the Parachute Regiment 15 During the Ardennes Offensive until 25 December 1944, Unknown); (Kulinich, 2001).

13   (Headquarters, 37th Tank Battalion, 4th Armored Division, 1944); (G–2 Section, 4th Armored Division, 1944); (Whitehill, 1997); (Headquarters, Reserve Command, 4th Armored Division, December 23, 1944); (G-4 Section, 4th Armored Division, 1944); (J. H. Leach, Twenty Days in December 1944, 1998, 9–10).

14   (Klemment, Unpublished Manuscript: The 9th Company, III Battalion of the Parachute Regiment 15 During the Ardennes Offensive until 25 December 1944, Unknown); (Klemment, Diary of the 9th Company, III Battalion, 15th Fallschirmjager Regiment, 5th Fallschirmjager Division, n.d.).

15   (Holmes, n.d.).

16   (Burdett, 2010).

CHAPTER 6 | WARNACH

1   (Seay, 1945, 3–4); (Clark, Narrative Summary of Operations of 4th Armored Division in the Relief of Bastogne, 22–29 December, Combat Interview 279, 1945, 2); (G-2 Section, 4th Armored Division, 1944); (G-2 Section, 4th Armored Division, 1944); (Pattison, 1945, 17–18); (Earnest, Combat Command A, After Action Report, December 1944, 1945, 4); (Headquarters, Combat Command "A", 4th Armored Division, January 18, 1945, 5); (Bastnagel, February 6, 1945, 12); (Kimsey, 1944, 4–5 (24–25)).

2   (Interrogation, Prisoner of War Team, December 25, 1944, 3–5, 8); For updated unit locations and capture times, see Horner, G–2 Periodic Report Number 18, from: 252000 December to: 262000 December, III Corps, 1944; (Interrogation, Prisoner of War Team, III Corps, December 26, 1944, 2–4, 7); for more captured PW locations, see Horner, G–2 Periodic Report Number 19, from: 262000 December to: 272000 December, III Corps, 1944, 1–2; (Interrogation, Prisoner of War Team #60, 134th Infantry Regiment, 1944); (S-2 Section, 51st Armored Infantry Battalion, 4th Armored Division, 1944, 11 (70)).

3   (Crane, December 1944, 5 (33)); (Dayton, December 19, 1944–January 10, 1945); (H. Peterson, 1993); (Oden, 1945, 2–4); (Oden, 1946–1947, 2–3); (H. B. Lay, After Action Report, 35th Tank Battalion, December 1944, January 3, 1945, 2–3); (Rapp, 1990, 19–21); (Pound, 1990, 21); (Gaydos, Headquarters

Battery, 66th Armored Field Artillery Battalion, 4th Armored Division, 1990); (Mettlen, December 17, 2001, 15–17); for more on Robert Riley, see Wall-Reddy, May 2003; (Donaldson, 1993, 43–45); (Calvert, 2010, 66–68).

4   (Crane, December 1944, 5 (33)); (Dayton, December 19, 1944–January 10, 1945); (H. Peterson, 1993); (Oden, 1945, 2–4); (Oden, 1946–1947, 2–3); (H. B. Lay, After Action Report, 35th Tank Battalion, December 1944, January 3, 1945, 2–3); (Rapp, 1990, 19–21); (Pound, 1990); (Gaydos, Headquarters Battery, 66th Armored Field Artillery Battalion, 4th Armored Division, 1990); (Mettlen, December 17, 2001, 15–17); for more on Robert Riley, see Wall-Reddy, May 2003; (Donaldson, 1993, 43–45); (Calvert, 2010, 66–68); (Connolly, General Orders Number 3, Headquarters, 4th Armored Division, January 9, 1945).

5   (Crane, December 1944, 5 (33)); (Dayton, December 19, 1944–January 10, 1945); (H. Peterson, 1993); (Oden, 1945, 2–4); (Oden, 1946–1947, 2–3); (H. B. Lay, After Action Report, 35th Tank Battalion, December 1944, January 3, 1945, 2–3); (Rapp, 1990, 19–21); (Pound, 1900[Au: stet date?], 21); (Gaydos, Headquarters Battery, 66th Armored Field Artillery Battalion, 4th Armored Division, 1990); (Mettlen, December 17, 2001, 15–17); for more on Robert Riley, see Wall-Reddy May 2003; (Donaldson, 1993, 43–45); (Calvert, 2010, 66–68); (Connolly, General Orders Number 3, Headquarters, 4th Armored Division, January 9, 1945).

6   (Crane, December 1944, 5 (33)); (Dayton, December 19, 1944–January 10, 1945); (H. Peterson, 1993); (Oden, 1945, 2–4); (Oden, 1946–1947, 2–3); (H. B. Lay, After Action Report, 35th Tank Battalion, December 1944, January 3, 1945, 2–3); (Rapp, 1990, 19–21); (Pound, 1900, 21); (Gaydos, Headquarters Battery, 66th Armored Field Artillery Battalion, 4th Armored Division, 1990); (Mettlen, December 17, 2001, 15–17); for more on Robert Riley, see Wall-Reddy, May 2003; (Donaldson, 1993, 43–45); (Calvert, 2010, 66–68); (Connolly, General Orders Number 3, Headquarters, 4th Armored Division, January 9, 1945).

7   (Harrison, Message #66 to Major Harrison, Century 3, from Captain Seay, Olympic 3, December 24, 1944); (Harrison, Message #44 G–3, Century, from Lucky 3, December 23, 1944); (T. J. Sharpe, December 23, 1944); (Hower, December 23, 1944); (Harrison, Message #6 to Commanding General, III Corps,

from Olympic 3, December 23, 1944); (Harrison, Message #38 to Captain Hower, G-3, from Captain Seay, Olympic 3, December 23, 1944); (Harrison, Message #64 to Major Harrison, G-3 Operations, from Captain Seay, Olympic 3, December 24, 1944); (Harrison, Message #63 to Major Harrison, Century 3, from Captain Seay, Olympic 3, December 24, 1944); (Mewshaw, G-3 Situation Report No. 63: Period 240001A to 240600A, December 1944, Headquarters III Corps, 1944).

8   (Mettlen, December 17, 2001, 5, 15–17); for more on Robert Riley, see Wall-Reddy, May 2003; (Doyle, Sturmgeschütz III and IV, 1942–1945, 2001, 4); for Foster's Purple Heart, see Connolly, General Orders Number 3, Headquarters, 4th Armored Division, January 9, 1945.

9   (Crane, December 1944, 5 (33)); (Dayton, December 19, 1944–January 10, 1945); (H. Peterson, 1993); (Oden, 1945, 2–4); (Oden, 1946–1947, 2–3); (H. B. Lay, After Action Report, 35th Tank Battalion, December 1944, January 3, 1945, 2–3); (Rapp, 1990, 19–21); (Pound, 1900, 21); (Gaydos, Headquarters Battery, 66th Armored Field Artillery Battalion, 4th Armored Division, 1990); (Mettlen, December 17, 2001, 15–17); for more on Robert Riley, see Wall-Reddy, May 2003; (Donaldson, 1993, 43–45); (Calvert, 2010, 66–68); (Connolly, General Orders Number 3, Headquarters, 4th Armored Division, January 9, 1945); (Connolly, General Order Number 9, Headquarters, 4th Armored Division, January 16, 1945).

10   (G–2 Section, 4th Armored Division, 1944); (S-2 Section, 51st Armored Infantry Battalion, 4th Armored Division, 1944, 11–12, 70–71); (Oden, 1945, 3–4); (Interrogation, Prisoner of War Team, III Corps, December 24, 1944, 5); (Interrogation, Prisoner of War Team 25, December 1944, 7); (Kimsey, 1944, 5 (25)); (Earnest, Combat Command A, After Action Report, December 1944, 1945, 4); (Dayton, December 19, 1944–January 10, 1945, 3); (G-4 Section, 4th Armored Division 1944); (Bernstein, OPREP A, No. D–24A, first of three, for twenty-four hours ending sunset, December 24, 1944. Ninth Fighter Command Field Order No. 146, 1944).

CHAPTER 7 | BIGONVILLE

1   (Seay, 1945, 4); (Clark, Narrative Summary of Operations of 4th Armored Division in the Relief of Bastogne, December 22–29, Combat Interview 279,

1945, 3); (Headquarters, Reserve Command, 4th Armored Division, 1944); (Creighton W. Abrams, 1945, 3); (Moon, 37th Tank Battalion Diary, 1945, 6); (R. Parker, 1945, 2(88)); (H. C. Jaques, 1945, 82) (G. L. Jaques, January 8, 1945, 1) (Headquarters, III Corps, Artillery, 1944, 1) (Whitehill, 1997); (W. A. Dwight, 1979, 1); For Charles Boggess's background, see World War II Enlistment Records, 2013.

2   (Interrogation, Prisoner of War Team 25, December 1944, 3–5, 8); (G-2 Section, 4th Armored Division, 1944); (G-2 Section, 4th Armored Division, 1944); (S-2 Section, Combat Command Reserve, 4th Armored Division, 1944); (S-2 Section, Combat Command Reserve, 4th Armored Division, 1944); (Petrikat, Unknown); (H. E. Brown, Periodic Report No. 121, G-2, 4th Armored Division, December 27, 1944, 3).

3   (Klemment, Unpublished Manuscript: The 9th Company, III Battalion of the Parachute Regiment 15 During the Ardennes Offensive until 25 December 1944, Unknown); (Thompson, January 10, 1950, 26).

4   (Whitehill, 1997); (W. A. Dwight, 1979, 1); (H. C. Jaques, 1945, 82); (G. L. Jaques, January 8, 1945, 1); (H. C. Jaques, 1945, 1–2, 82); (Creighton W. Abrams, 1945, 3–4, 50–51); (Moon, 37th Tank Battalion After Action Report, 1945, 5); (Moon, 37th Tank Battalion Diary, 1945, 6–7); (Johnson, After Action Report, December 1944, 53rd Armored Infantry Battalion, 1945, 9); (G. L. Jaques, January 8, 1945, 1–2); (Johnson, Unit Diary, 53rd Armored Infantry Battalion, December 1, 1944–December 31, 1944, 53); (Bush, 1944, 4 (22)); (Whitehill, 1997); (Department of the Army, 1945); (Department of the Army, 1945); (J. H. Leach, Twenty Days in December, 1944 1998, 10); (Headquarters, 37th Tank Battalion, 4th Armored Division, 1944); (Lutgen, 2010); (Thomas, 2010); (Mantz, 2010); (Ries, 2010); (Schroder, 2010); (Lange, 2010); for McMahon's award, see Connolly, General Order Number 20, Headquarters, 4th Armored Division, August 28, 1944.

5   (Whitehill, 1997); (W. A. Dwight, 1979, 1); (H. C. Jaques, 1945, 82); (G. L. Jaques, January 8, 1945, 1); (H. C. Jaques, 1945, 1–2, 82); (Creighton W. Abrams, 1945, 3–4, 50–51); (Moon, 37th Tank Battalion After Action Report, 1945, 5); (Moon, 37th Tank Battalion Diary, 1945, 6–7); (Johnson, After Action Report, December 1944, 53rd Armored Infantry Battalion, 1945, 9); (G. L. Jaques, January 8, 1945, 1–2); (Johnson, Unit Diary, 53rd Armored

Infantry Battalion, December 1, 1944–December 31, 1944, 53); (Bush, 1944, 4 (22)); (Whitehill, 1997); (Department of the Army, 1945); (Department of the Army, 1945); (J. H. Leach, Twenty Days in December, 1944 1998, 10); (Headquarters, 37th Tank Battalion, 4th Armored Division, 1944); (Lutgen, 2010); (Thomas, 2010); (Mantz, 2010); (Ries, 2010); (Schroder, 2010); (Lange, 2010); for McMahon's award, see Connolly, General Order Number 20, Headquarters, 4th Armored Division, August 28, 1944.

6   (Whitehill, 1997); (W. A. Dwight, 1979, 1); (H. C. Jaques, 1945, 82); (G. L. Jaques, January 8, 1945, 1); (H. C. Jaques, 1945, 1–2, 82); (Creighton W. Abrams, 1945, 3–4, 50–51); (Moon, 37th Tank Battalion After Action Report, 1945, 5); (Moon, 37th Tank Battalion Diary, 1945, 6–7); (Johnson, After Action Report, December 1944, 53rd Armored Infantry Battalion, 1945, 9); (G. L. Jaques, January 8, 1945, 1–2); (Johnson, Unit Diary, 53rd Armored Infantry Battalion, December 1, 1944–December 31, 1944, 53); (Bush, 1944, 4 (22)); (Whitehill, 1997); (Department of the Army, 1945); (Department of the Army, 1945); (J. H. Leach, Twenty Days in December, 1944 1998, 10); (Headquarters, 37th Tank Battalion, 4th Armored Division, 1944); (Lutgen, 2010); (Thomas, 2010); (Mantz, 2010); (Ries, 2010); (Schroder, 2010); (Lange, 2010); for McMahon's award, see Connolly, General Order Number 20, Headquarters, 4th Armored Division, August 28, 1944.

7   (Whitehill, 1997); (W. A. Dwight, 1979, 1); (H. C. Jaques, 1945, 82); (G. L. Jaques, January 8, 1945, 1); (H. C. Jaques, 1945, 1–2, 82); (Creighton W. Abrams, 1945, 3–4, 50–51); (Moon, 37th Tank Battalion After Action Report, 1945, 5); (Moon, 37th Tank Battalion Diary, 1945, 6–7); (Johnson, After Action Report, December 1944, 53rd Armored Infantry Battalion, 1945, 9); (G. L. Jaques, January 8, 1945, 1–2); (Johnson, Unit Diary, 53rd Armored Infantry Battalion, December 1, 1944–December 31, 1944, 53); (Bush, 1944, 4 (22)); (Whitehill, 1997); (Department of the Army, 1945); (Department of the Army, 1945); (J. H. Leach, Twenty Days in December, 1944 1998, 10); (Headquarters, 37th Tank Battalion, 4th Armored Division, 1944); (Lutgen, 2010); (Thomas, 2010); (Mantz, 2010); (Ries, 2010); (Schroder, 2010); (Lange, 2010); for McMahon's award, see Connolly, General Order Number 20, Headquarters, 4th Armored Division, August 28, 1944) (J. H. Leach, Greatest Tank Battles: Race to Bastogne, 2010); There is some discrepancy in Leach's account. Leach claimed Petrikat was the 6th Company Commander. However,

all other records, including an interview with Petrikat, claim he was the commander of 7th Company. (J. H. Leach, Interview with Jimmie Leach (Unedited), 2009).

8   (Bernstein, OPREP A, No. D–24A, first of three, for twenty-four hours ending sunset, December 24, 1944. Ninth Fighter Command Field Order No. 146, 1944).

9   (Whitehill, 1997); (W. A. Dwight, 1979, 1); (H. C. Jaques, 1945, 82); (G. L. Jaques, January 8, 1945, 1); (H. C. Jaques, 1945, 1–2, 82); (Creighton W. Abrams, 1945, 3–4, 50–51); (Moon, 37th Tank Battalion After Action Report, 1945, 5); (Moon, 37th Tank Battalion Diary, 1945, 6–7); (Johnson, After Action Report, December 1944, 53rd Armored Infantry Battalion, 1945, 9); (G. L. Jaques, January 8, 1945, 1–2); (Johnson, Unit Diary, 53rd Armored Infantry Battalion, December 1, 1944–December 31, 1944, 53); (Bush, 1944, 4 (22)); (Whitehill, 1997); (Department of the Army, 1945); (Department of the Army, 1945); (J. H. Leach, Twenty Days in December, 1944 1998, 10); (Headquarters, 37th Tank Battalion, 4th Armored Division, 1944); (Lutgen, 2010); (Thomas, 2010); (Mantz, 2010); (Ries, 2010);" (Schroder, 2010); (Lange, 2010); (J. H. Leach, Greatest Tank Battles: Race to Bastogne, 2010); (Headquarters, 362nd Fighter Group, 1986, 130); (J. H. Leach, Interview with Jimmie Leach (Unedited), 2009).

10   (Whitehill, 1997); (W. A. Dwight 1979, 1); (H. C. Jaques 1945, 82); (G. L. Jaques 8 January, 1945, 1); (H. C. Jaques 1945, 1–2 (82–82)); (Creighton W. Abrams 1945, 3–4 (50–51)); (Moon, 37th Tank Battalion After Action Report 1945, 5); (Moon, 37th Tank Battalion Diary 1945, 6–7); (Johnson, After Action Report, December 1944, 53rd Armored Infantry Battalion 1945, 9); (G. L. Jaques 8 January, 1945, 1–2); (Johnson, Unit Diary, 53rd Armored Infantry Battalion, 1 December 1944 to 31 December 1944 1944, 53); (Bush 1944, 4 (22)); (Whitehill 1997); (Department of the Army 1945); (Department of the Army 1945); (J. H. Leach, Twenty Days in December 1944 1998, 10); (Headquarters, 37th Tank Battalion, 4th Armored Division 1944); (Lutgen 2010); (Thomas 2010); (Mantz 2010); (Ries 2010); (Schroder 2010); (Lange 2010); (J. H. Leach, Greatest Tank Battles: Race to Bastogne 2010); (Headquarters, 362nd Fighter Group 1986, 130); (J. H. Leach, Interview with Jimmie Leach (Unedited) 2009).

11 (Whitehill 1997); (W. A. Dwight 1979, 1); (H. C. Jaques 1945, 82); (G. L. Jaques 8 January, 1945, 1); (H. C. Jaques 1945, 1–2 (82–82)); (Creighton W. Abrams 1945, 3–4 (50–51)); (Moon, 37th Tank Battalion After Action Report 1945, 5); (Moon, 37th Tank Battalion Diary 1945, 6–7); (Johnson, After Action Report, December 1944, 53rd Armored Infantry Battalion 1945, 9); (G. L. Jaques 8 January, 1945, 1–2); (Johnson, Unit Diary, 53rd Armored Infantry Battalion, 1 December 1944 to 31 December 1944 1944, 53); (Bush 1944, 4 (22)); (Whitehill 1997); (Department of the Army 1945); (Department of the Army 1945); (J. H. Leach, Twenty Days in December 1944 1998, 10); (Headquarters, 37th Tank Battalion, 4th Armored Division 1944); (Lutgen 2010); (Thomas 2010); (Mantz 2010); (Ries 2010); (Schroder 2010); (Lange 2010); (J. H. Leach, Greatest Tank Battles: Race to Bastogne 2010); (Headquarters, 362nd Fighter Group 1986, 130); (J. H. Leach, Interview with Jimmie Leach (Unedited) 2009).

12 (Whitehill 1997); (W. A. Dwight 1979, 1); (H. C. Jaques 1945, 82); (G. L. Jaques 8 January, 1945, 1); (H. C. Jaques 1945, 1–2 (82–82)); (Creighton W. Abrams 1945, 3–4 (50–51)); (Moon, 37th Tank Battalion After Action Report 1945, 5); (Moon, 37th Tank Battalion Diary 1945, 6–7); (Johnson, After Action Report, December 1944, 53rd Armored Infantry Battalion 1945, 9); (G. L. Jaques 8 January, 1945, 1–2); (Johnson, Unit Diary, 53rd Armored Infantry Battalion, 1 December 1944 to 31 December 1944 1944, 53); (Bush 1944, 4 (22)); (Whitehill 1997); (Department of the Army 1945); (Department of the Army 1945); (J. H. Leach, Twenty Days in December 1944 1998, 10); (Headquarters, 37th Tank Battalion, 4th Armored Division 1944); (Lutgen 2010); (Thomas 2010); (Mantz 2010); (Ries 2010); (Schroder 2010); (Lange 2010); (J. H. Leach, Greatest Tank Battles: Race to Bastogne 2010); (Headquarters, 362nd Fighter Group 1986, 130); (J. H. Leach, Interview with Jimmie Leach (Unedited) 2009).

13 (Whitehill 1997); (W. A. Dwight 1979, 1); (H. C. Jaques 1945, 82); (G. L. Jaques 8 January, 1945, 1); (H. C. Jaques 1945, 1–2 (82–82)); (Creighton W. Abrams 1945, 3–4 (50–51)); (Moon, 37th Tank Battalion After Action Report 1945, 5); (Moon, 37th Tank Battalion Diary 1945, 6–7); (Johnson, After Action Report, December 1944, 53rd Armored Infantry Battalion 1945, 9); (G. L. Jaques 8 January, 1945, 1–2); (Johnson, Unit Diary, 53rd Armored Infantry Battalion, 1 December 1944 to 31 December 1944 1944, 53); (Bush

1944, 4 (22)); (Whitehill 1997); (Department of the Army 1945); (Department of the Army 1945); (J. H. Leach, Twenty Days in December 1944 1998, 10); (Headquarters, 37th Tank Battalion, 4th Armored Division 1944); (Lutgen 2010); (Thomas 2010); (Mantz 2010); (Ries 2010); (Schroder 2010); (Lange 2010); (J. H. Leach, Greatest Tank Battles: Race to Bastogne 2010); (Headquarters, 362nd Fighter Group 1986, 130); (J. H. Leach, Interview with Jimmie Leach (Unedited) 2009).

14 (Whitehill 1997); (W. A. Dwight 1979, 1); (H. C. Jaques 1945, 82); (G. L. Jaques 8 January, 1945, 1); (H. C. Jaques 1945, 1–2 (82–82)); (Creighton W. Abrams 1945, 3–4 (50–51)); (Moon, 37th Tank Battalion After Action Report 1945, 5); (Moon, 37th Tank Battalion Diary 1945, 6–7); (Johnson, After Action Report, December 1944, 53rd Armored Infantry Battalion 1945, 9); (G. L. Jaques 8 January, 1945, 1–2); (Johnson, Unit Diary, 53rd Armored Infantry Battalion, 1 December 1944 to 31 December 1944 1944, 53); (Bush 1944, 4 (22)); (Whitehill 1997); (Department of the Army 1945); (Department of the Army 1945); (J. H. Leach, Twenty Days in December 1944 1998, 10); (Headquarters, 37th Tank Battalion, 4th Armored Division 1944); (Lutgen 2010); (Thomas 2010); (Mantz 2010); (Ries 2010); (Schroder 2010); (Lange 2010); (J. H. Leach, Greatest Tank Battles: Race to Bastogne 2010); (Headquarters, 362nd Fighter Group 1986, 130); (J. H. Leach, Interview with Jimmie Leach (Unedited) 2009).

15 (Bernstein, OPREP A, No. D–24B, second of three, for twenty-four hours ending sunset, December 24, 1944. Ninth Fighter Command Field Order No. 146, 1944); (Stoddard, 1944, 1–3).

16 (Phillips, Memorandum for Record, December 24, 1944); (Mewshaw, December 24, 1944); (Mewshaw, Message #3 to Hercules 6, from Century 6, December 24, 1944); (Mewshaw, Message #5 to Olympic 6, from Century 5, December 24, 1944); (Phillips, Telephone Conversation between Colonel Phillips, chief of staff this Headquarters [III Corps], and Olympic 6, at 1115, December 24, 1944); (McAlister, Message #25 to CG, III Corps, from CG, 4th Armored Division, December 24, 1944); (Mewshaw, Operations Directive No. 2 (Confirmation of Fragmentary Orders), Reference FO #1, December 21, 1944, III Corps, December 24, 1944, 1); (Headquarters, 25th Cavalry Reconnaissance Squadron (Mechanized), 1944, 9–10); (Bastnagel, February 6, 1945, 12–13); (Battista, 2002); For a history of the 318th, see Murrell, 1968, 42–43;

(Headquarters, 37th Tank Battalion, 4th Armored Division, 1944); (Phillips, Memorandum for Record—Phone Conversation between Colonel Phillips and General Gaffey at 2145, December 24, 1944); (S-3 Section, CCB, 4th Armored Division, 1944); (Sullivan, Operations Instructions No. 13, Headquarters, 4th Armored Division, 242300, December 1944, 1).

17   (Martin, 1984, 147–48).

18   (G-2 Section, 4th Armored Division, 1944); (J. S. Eisenhower, 1995, 328).

CHAPTER 8 | TINTANGE

1   (Worch, 2007); (Interrogation, Prisoner of War Team, III Corps, December 26, 1944, 2–4, 7); (Zaloga, U.S. Armored Divisions: European Theater of Operations, 1944–1945, 2004, 18–19); (Sayen, 2007, 14–15); (War Department, 1945).

2   (Interrogation, Prisoner of War Team, III Corps, December 26, 1944, 2–4, 7); (Klemment, Unpublished Manuscript: The 9th Company, III Battalion of the Parachute Regiment 15 During the Ardennes Offensive until 25 December 1944, Unknown); (Klemment, Diary of the 9th Company, III Battalion, 15th Fallschirmjäger Regiment, 5th Fallschirmjäger Division, n.d.); (Martin, 1984, 51–52, 146–51); (R. C. Gersdorff, 1946, 68–71); Rudolf Berneike was born in Berlin in 1909 and joined the army in 1935. He received the Knight's Cross on March 15, 1945. See Ritterkreuzträger Rudolf Berneike, 2013; (G-2 Section, 4th Armored Division, 1944); (G-2 Section, 4th Armored Division, 1944); (S–2 Section, 51st Armored Infantry Battalion, 4th Armored Division, 1944, 12–13, 71–72).

3   (Seay, 1945, 5); (Headquarters, Combat Command "A," 4th Armored Division, January 18, 1945, 6); (Earnest, Field Order #2, Combat Command A, 4th Armored Division, December 24, 1944); (Pattison, 1945, 18); (Dayton, December 19, 1944–January 10, 1945, 3–4); (Kimsey, 1944, 5 (25)); (Crane, December 1944, 5–6 (33–34)); (Crane, December 1944, 3 (53)); (S-2 Section, 51st Armored Infantry Battalion, 4th Armored Division, 1944, 12–13 (71–72)); (Dan Alanis, 1945); (Charles F. Geking, 1945); (Edward E. Rueske, 1945, 3–4); (Headquarters, 1st Battalion, 318th Infantry Regiment, 1945): (Connaughton, 1945, 1–4, 7); (Bredbenner, 1998); (H. B. Lay, After Action Report,

35th Tank Battalion, December 1944, January 3, 1945, 3); (Oden, 1945, 4–5 (41–42)); (L. R. Lay, 1945, 3–4 (35–36)); (Williams, 2002);

4   (Seay, 1945, 5); (Headquarters, Combat Command "A," 4th Armored Division, January 18, 1945, 6); (Earnest, Field Order #2, Combat Command A, 4th Armored Division, December 24, 1944); (Pattison, 1945, 18); (Dayton, December 19, 1944–January 10, 1945, 3–4); (Kimsey, 1944, 5 (25)); (Crane, December 1944, 5–6 (33–34)); (Crane, December 1944, 3 (53)); (S-2 Section, 51st Armored Infantry Battalion, 4th Armored Division, 1944, 12–13 (71–72)); (Dan Alanis, 1945); (Charles F. Geking, 1945); (Edward E. Rueske, 1945, 3–4); (Headquarters, 1st Battalion, 318th Infantry Regiment, 1945); (Connaughton, 1945, 1–4, 7); (Bredbenner, 1998); (H. B. Lay, After Action Report, 35th Tank Battalion, December 1944, January 3, 1945, 3); (Oden, 1945, 4–5 (41–42)); (L. R. Lay, 1945, 3–4 (35–36)); (Williams, 2002); (Maxsted, 1945).

5   (Seay, 1945, 5); (Headquarters, Combat Command "A,", 4th Armored Division, January 18, 1945, 6); (Earnest, Field Order #2, Combat Command A, 4th Armored Division, December 24, 1944); (Pattison, 1945, 18); (Dayton, December 19, 1944–January 10, 1945, 3–4); (Kimsey, 1944, 5 (25)); (Crane, December 1944, 5–6 (33–34)); (Crane, December 1944, 3 (53)); (S-2 Section, 51st Armored Infantry Battalion, 4th Armored Division, 1944, 12–13 (71–72)); (Dan Alanis, 1945); (Charles F. Geking, 1945); (Edward E. Rueske, 1945, 3–4); (Headquarters, 1st Battalion, 318th Infantry Regiment, 1945); (Connaughton, 1945, 1–4, 7); (Bredbenner, 1998); (H. B. Lay, After Action Report, 35th Tank Battalion, December 1944, January 3, 1945, 3); (Oden, 1945, 4–5, 41–42); (L. R. Lay, 1945, 3–4 (35–36)); (Williams, 2002); (Maxsted, 1945).

6   (Interrogation, Prisoner of War Team, III Corps, December 26, 1944, 2–4, 7); (Klemment, Unpublished Manuscript: The 9th Company, III Battalion of the Parachute Regiment 15 During the Ardennes Offensive until 25 December 1944, Unknown); (Klemment, Diary of the 9th Company, III Battalion, 15th Fallschirmjäger Regiment, 5th Fallschirmjäger Division, n.d.); (Martin, 1984, 51–52, 146–51); (R. C. Gersdorff, 1946, 68–71); Rudolf Berneike was born in Berlin in 1909 and joined the army in 1935. He received the Knight's Cross on March 15, 1945. See Ritterkreuzträger, Rudolf Berneike, 2013; (G-2 Section, 4th Armored Division, 1944); (G-2 Section, 4th Armored Division, 1944); (S-2 Section, 51st Armored Infantry Battalion, 4th Armored Division, 1944, 12–13 (71–72)).

7   (Seay, 1945, 5); (Headquarters, Combat Command "A," 4th Armored Division, January 18, 1945, 6); (Earnest, Field Order #2, Combat Command A, 4th Armored Division, December 24, 1944); (Pattison, 1945, 18); (Dayton, December 19, 1944–January 10, 1945, 3–4); (Kimsey, 1944, 5 (25)); (Crane, December 1944, 5–6 (33–34)); (Crane, December 1944, 3 (53)); (S-2 Section, 51st Armored Infantry Battalion, 4th Armored Division, 1944, 12–13 (71–72)); (Dan Alanis, 1945); (Charles F. Geking, 1945); (Edward E. Rueske, 1945, 3–4); (Headquarters, 1st Battalion, 318th Infantry Regiment, 1945); (Connaughton, 1945, 1–4, 7); (Bredbenner, 1998); (H. B. Lay, After Action Report, 35th Tank Battalion, December 1944, January 3, 1945, 3); (Oden, 1945, 4–5 (41–42)); (L. R. Lay, 1945, 3–4 (35–36)); (Williams, 2002); (Maxsted, 1945); (J.W. Trone, January 13, 1945, 1); (J. W. Trone, January 25, 1945, 4).

8   (Seay, 1945, 5); (Headquarters, Combat Command "A", 4th Armored Division 18 January, 1945, 6); (Earnest, Field Order #2, Combat Command A, 4th Armored Division 24 December 1944); (Pattison 1945, 18); (Dayton 19 December 1944 to 10 January 1945, 3–4); (Kimsey 1944, 5 (25)); (Crane December 1944, 5–6 (33–34)); (Crane December 1944, 3 (53)); (S–2 Section, 51st Armored Infantry Battalion, 4th Armored Division 1944, 12–13 (71–72)); (Dan Alanis 1945); (Charles F. Geking 1945); (Edward E. Rueske 1945, 3–4); (Headquarters, 1st Battalion, 318th Infantry Regiment 1945); (Connaughton 1945, 1–4, 7); (Bredbenner 1998); (H. B. Lay, After Action Report, 35th Tank Battalion, December 1944 3 January 1945, 3); (Delk M. Oden 1945, 4–5 (41–42)); (L. R. Lay 1945, 3–4 (35–36)); (Williams 2002); (Maxsted 1945); (J.W. Trone 13 January 1945, 1); (J.W. Trone 25 January 1945, 4).

9   (Seay 1945, 5); (Headquarters, Combat Command "A", 4th Armored Division 18 January, 1945, 6); (Earnest, Field Order #2, Combat Command A, 4th Armored Division 24 December 1944); (Pattison 1945, 18); (Dayton 19 December 1944 to 10 January 1945, 3–4); (Kimsey 1944, 5 (25)); (Crane December 1944, 5–6 (33–34)); (Crane December 1944, 3 (53)); (S–2 Section, 51st Armored Infantry Battalion, 4th Armored Division 1944, 12–13 (71–72)); (Dan Alanis 1945); (Charles F. Geking 1945); (Edward E. Rueske 1945, 3–4); (Headquarters, 1st Battalion, 318th Infantry Regiment 1945); (Connaughton 1945, 1–4, 7); (Bredbenner 1998); (H. B. Lay, After Action Report, 35th Tank Battalion, December 1944 3 January 1945, 3); (Delk M. Oden 1945, 4–5 (41–42)); (L. R. Lay 1945, 3–4 (35–36)); (Williams 2002); (Maxsted 1945);

(J.W. Trone 13 January 1945, 1); (J. W. Trone 25 January 1945, 4); (J. W. Trone 16 January 1945, 3).

10 (G–2 Section, 4th Armored Division, 1944); (Harley, 1993, 73); (Third Army Headquarters, 1993, 197); (War Diary (Kriegstagebuch), Armee Korps LIII, December 1944 to March 1945, T–314, Roll 1335, 1st Frame 415, 76106, 1944–1945, 1076).

11 (Bernstein, OPREP A, No. D–25A, first of three, for twenty-four hours ending sunset, December 25, 1944. Ninth Fighter Command Field Order No. 147, 1944, 1); (Bernstein, OPREP A, No. D–25B, second of three, for twenty-four hours ending sunset, December 25, 1944. Ninth Fighter Command Field Order No. 147, 1944, 2); (Bernstein, OPREP A, No. D–25C, last of three, for twenty-four hours ending sunset, December 25, 1944. Ninth Fighter Command Field Order No. 147, 1944, 2).

12 (Klemment, Unpublished Manuscript: The 9th Company, III Battalion of the Parachute Regiment 15 During the Ardennes Offensive until 25 December 1944, Unknown); (Crane, December 1944, 5–6 (33–34)).

13 (Worch, 2007); (J. W. Trone, January 16, 1945, 3) (Headquarters, 1st Battalion, 318th Infantry Regiment, 1945).

14 (Kimsey, 1944, 5 (25)); (Crane, December 1944, 5–6 (33–34)); (Crane, December 1944, 3 (53)); (G-2 Section, 4th Armored Division, 1944); (Headquarters, Third U.S. Army, 1945, 180); (Headquarters, Combat Command "A", 4th Armored Division, January 18, 1945, 6); (E. L. Peterson, 2003).

CHAPTER 9 | CHAUMONT II

1 (G-2 Section, 4th Armored Division, 1944); (G-2 Section, 4th Armored Division, 1944); (John B. Ellis, 1944); (Interrogation, Prisoner of War Team, III Corps, December 26, 1944, 2–3, 7); (Interrogation, Prisoner of War Team #60, 134th Infantry Regiment, 1944); (G-2 Section, 4th Armored Division, 1944); (S-2 Section, Headquarters, CCB, 4th Armored Division, 1944); (Walter Noller, Interrogation, Prisoner of War Team #68, 1945); (S-3 Section, CCB, 4th Armored Division, 1944); (Hunt, After Action Report, Combat Command B, 4th Armored Division for the Period of 1 to 31 December 1944, 1944, 3); (Ellis, January 29, 1945, 16); (S-2 Section, 1945, 2); (Irzyk, 8th Tank Battalion History,

October 19, 1944–February 10, 1945, 18); (Stauber, 1945, 3–4 (30–31));
(Fenchel, 2001); (Irzyk, *He Rode Up Front for Patton*, 1996, 258–60); (Head-
quarters, 10th Armored Infantry Battalion, 1944); (Donnelly, 1945, 3 (12))
Map (Donnelly, 1945, Incl 6); (Baum, 1945, 4–5 (70–71)); (Headquarters, 10th
Armored Infantry Battalion, 1944–1945); (Glenn H. Gardner, 1945, 1–2); (Peter
J. Stanchak, 1945, 21, 25–29); (Slotnik, 2011); (Shapiro, 2011); (Department of
the Army, 1945); For interview on YouTube, see Paul Wiedorfer, Medal of
Honor, WWII, 2011); (J. W. Trone, January 19, 1945); (J. W. Trone, February
2, 1945); (J. W. Trone, February 6, 1945); (Pearson, 1957, 120–21, 353–55).

2   (Fenchel, 2001); (Cercle d'Histoire de Bastogne, 1994, 269–70).

3   (G-2 Section, 4th Armored Division 1944); (G-2 Section, 4th Armored Di-
vision 1944); (John B. Ellis 1944); (Interrogation Prisoner of War Team, III
Corps 26 December, 1944, 2–3, 7); (Interrogation Prisoner of War Team #60,
134th Infantry Regiment 1944); (G-2 Section, 4th Armored Division 1944);
(S-2 Section, Headquarters, CCB, 4th Armored Division 1944); (Walter
Noller, Interrogation Prisoner of War Tean #68 1945); (S-3 Section, CCB, 4th
Armored Division 1944); (Hunt, After Action Report, Combat Command B,
4th Armored Division for the Period of 1 to 31 December 1944 1944, 3); (Ellis
29 January 1945, 16); (S-2 Section 1945, 2); (Irzyk, 8th Tank Battalion
History—19 October 1944 to 10 February 1945 1945, 18); (Stauber 1945, 3–4
(30–31)); (Fenchel 2001); (Irzyk, He Rode Up Front for Patton 1996, 258–
260); (Headquarters, 10th Armored Infantry Battalion 1944); (Donnelly 1945,
3 (12)) Map (Donnelly 1945, Incl 6); (Baum 1945, 4–5 (70–71)); (Headquarters, 10th Armored Infantry Battalion 1944–1945); (Glenn H. Gardner
1945, 1–2); (Peter J. Stanchak 1945, 21, 25–29); (Slotnik 2011); (Shapiro 2011);
(Department of the Army 1945); For interview on YouTube, see (Paul Wiedorfer, Medal of Honor, WWII 2011); (J. W. Trone 19 January 1945);" (J. W.
Trone 2 February 1945); (J. W. Trone 6 February 1945); (Pearson 1957, 120–
121, 353–355).

4   (G–2 Section, 4th Armored Division, 1944); (G–2 Section, 4th Armored Division, 1944); (John B. Ellis, 1944); (Interrogation, Prisoner of War Team, III
Corps, December 26, 1944, 2–3, 7); (Interrogation, Prisoner of War Team #60,
134th Infantry Regiment, 1944); (G-2 Section, 4th Armored Division, 1944);
(S-2 Section, Headquarters, CCB, 4th Armored Division, 1944); (Walter

Noller, Interrogation, Prisoner of War Team #68, 1945); (S-3 Section, CCB, 4th Armored Division, 1944); (Hunt, After Action Report, Combat Command B, 4th Armored Division for the Period of December 1–31, 1944, 3); (Ellis, January 29, 1945, 16); (S-2 Section, 1945, 2); (Irzyk, 8th Tank Battalion History, October 19, 1944–February 10, 1945, 18); (Stauber, 1945, 3–4 (30–31)); (Fenchel, 2001); (Irzyk, *He Rode Up Front for Patton*, 1996, 258–60); (Headquarters, 8th Tank Battalion, 4th Armored Division, 1944); (Headquarters, 10th Armored Infantry Battalion, 1944); (Donnelly, 1945, 3 (12)) Map (Donnelly, 1945, Incl 6); (Baum, 1945, 4–5 (70–71)) (Headquarters, 10th Armored Infantry Battalion, 1944–1945); (Glenn H. Gardner, 1945, 1–2); (Peter J. Stanchak, 1945, 21, 25–29); (Slotnik, 2011); (Shapiro, 2011); (Department of the Army, 1945); For interview on YouTube, see Paul Wiedorfer, Medal of Honor, WWII, 2011; (J. W. Trone, January 19, 1945); (J. W. Trone, February 2, 1945); (J. W. Trone, February 6, 1945); (Pearson, 1957, 120–21, 353–55); (Connor, 2011).

5   (G–2 Section, 4th Armored Division 1944); (G–2 Section, 4th Armored Division 1944); (John B. Ellis 1944); (Interrogation Prisoner of War Team, III Corps 26 December, 1944, 2–3, 7); (Interrogation Prisoner of War Team #60, 134th Infantry Regiment 1944); (G–2 Section, 4th Armored Division 1944); (S–2 Section, Headquarters, CCB, 4th Armored Division 1944); (Walter Noller, Interrogation Prisoner of War Team #68 1945); (S–3 Section, CCB, 4th Armored Division 1944); (Hunt, After Action Report, Combat Command B, 4th Armored Division for the Period of 1 to 31 December 1944 1944, 3); (Ellis 29 January 1945, 16); (S–2 Section 1945, 2); (Irzyk, 8th Tank Battalion History—19 October 1944 to 10 February 1945 1945, 18); (Stauber 1945, 3–4 (30–31)); (Fenchel 2001); (Irzyk, He Rode Up Front for Patton 1996, 258–260); (Headquarters, 8th Tank Battalion, 4th Armored Division 1944); (Headquarters, 10th Armored Infantry Battalion 1944); (Donnelly 1945, 3 (12)) Map (Donnelly 1945, Incl 6); (Baum 1945, 4–5 (70–71)) (Headquarters, 10th Armored Infantry Battalion 1944–1945); (Glenn H. Gardner 1945, 1–2); (Peter J. Stanchak 1945, 21, 25–29); (Slotnik 2011); (Shapiro 2011); (Department of the Army 1945); For interview on YouTube, see (Paul Wiedorfer, Medal of Honor, WWII 2011); (J. W. Trone 19 January 1945); (J. W. Trone 2 February 1945); (J. W. Trone 6 February 1945); (Pearson 1957, 120–121, 353–355); (Connor 2011).

6   (G–2 Section, 4th Armored Division 1944); (G–2 Section, 4th Armored Division 1944); (John B. Ellis 1944); (Interrogation Prisoner of War Team, III Corps 26 December, 1944, 2–3, 7); (Interrogation Prisoner of War Team #60, 134th Infantry Regiment 1944); (G–2 Section, 4th Armored Division 1944); (S–2 Section, Headquarters, CCB, 4th Armored Division 1944); (Walter Noller, Interrogation Prisoner of War Team #68 1945); (S–3 Section, CCB, 4th Armored Division 1944); (Hunt, After Action Report, Combat Command B, 4th Armored Division for the Period of 1 to 31 December 1944 1944, 3); (Ellis 29 January 1945, 16); (S–2 Section 1945, 2); (Irzyk, 8th Tank Battalion History—19 October 1944 to 10 February 1945 1945, 18); (Stauber 1945, 3–4 (30–31)); (Fenchel 2001); (Irzyk, He Rode Up Front for Patton 1996, 258–260); (Headquarters, 8th Tank Battalion, 4th Armored Division 1944); (Headquarters, 10th Armored Infantry Battalion 1944); (Donnelly 1945, 3 (12)) Map (Donnelly 1945, Incl 6); (Baum 1945, 4–5 (70–71)) (Headquarters, 10th Armored Infantry Battalion 1944–1945); (Glenn H. Gardner 1945, 1–2); (Peter J. Stanchak 1945, 21, 25–29); (Slotnik 2011); (Shapiro 2011); (Department of the Army 1945); For interview on YouTube, see Paul Wiedorfer, Medal of Honor, WWII 2011; (J. W. Trone 19 January 1945); (J. W. Trone 2 February 1945); (J. W. Trone 6 February 1945); (Pearson 1957, 120–121, 353–355); (Connor 2011).

7   (G–2 Section, 4th Armored Division 1944); (G–2 Section, 4th Armored Division 1944); (John B. Ellis 1944); (Interrogation Prisoner of War Team, III Corps 26 December, 1944, 2–3, 7); (Interrogation Prisoner of War Team #60, 134th Infantry Regiment 1944); (G–2 Section, 4th Armored Division 1944); (S–2 Section, Headquarters, CCB, 4th Armored Division 1944); (Walter Noller, Interrogation Prisoner of War Tean #68 1945); (S–3 Section, CCB, 4th Armored Division 1944); (Hunt, After Action Report, Combat Command B, 4th Armored Division for the Period of 1 to 31 December 1944 1944, 3); (Ellis 29 January 1945, 16); (S–2 Section 1945, 2); (Irzyk, 8th Tank Battalion History—19 October 1944 to 10 February 1945 1945, 18); (Stauber 1945, 3–4 (30–31)); (Fenchel 2001); (Irzyk, He Rode Up Front for Patton 1996, 258–260); (Headquarters, 8th Tank Battalion, 4th Armored Division 1944); (Headquarters, 10th Armored Infantry Battalion 1944); (Donnelly 1945, 3 (12)) Map (Donnelly 1945, Incl 6); (Baum 1945, 4–5 (70–71)) (Headquarters, 10th Armored Infantry Battalion 1944–1945); (Glenn H. Gardner 1945, 1–2); (Peter J. Stanchak 1945, 21, 25–29); (Slotnik 2011); (Shapiro 2011); (Department of the

Army 1945); For interview on YouTube, see (Paul Wiedorfer, Medal of Honor, WWII 2011); (J. W. Trone 19 January 1945); (J. W. Trone 2 February 1945); (J. W. Trone 6 February 1945); (Pearson 1957, 120–121, 353–355); (Connor 2011); (Rust, 1990, 55–59); (G-2 Section, Headquarters, 4th Armored Division, December 26, 1944, 5).

8   (Fenchel, 2001).

9   (G–2 Section, 4th Armored Division 1944); (G–2 Section, 4th Armored Division 1944); (John B. Ellis 1944); (Interrogation Prisoner of War Team, III Corps 26 December, 1944, 2–3, 7); (Interrogation Prisoner of War Team #60, 134th Infantry Regiment 1944); (G–2 Section, 4th Armored Division 1944); (S–2 Section, Headquarters, CCB, 4th Armored Division 1944); (Walter Noller, Interrogation Prisoner of War Team #68 1945); (S–3 Section, CCB, 4th Armored Division 1944); (Hunt, After Action Report, Combat Command B, 4th Armored Division for the Period of 1 to 31 December 1944 1944, 3); (Ellis 29 January 1945, 16); (S–2 Section 1945, 2); (Irzyk, 8th Tank Battalion History—19 October 1944 to 10 February 1945 1945, 18); (Stauber 1945, 3–4 (30–31)); (Fenchel 2001); (Irzyk, He Rode Up Front for Patton 1996, 258–260); (Headquarters, 8th Tank Battalion, 4th Armored Division 1944); (Headquarters, 10th Armored Infantry Battalion 1944); (Donnelly 1945, 3 (12)) Map (Donnelly 1945, Incl 6); (Baum 1945, 4–5 (70–71)) (Headquarters, 10th Armored Infantry Battalion 1944–1945); (Glenn H. Gardner 1945, 1–2); (Peter J. Stanchak 1945, 21, 25–29); (Slotnik 2011); (Shapiro 2011); (Department of the Army 1945); For interview on YouTube, see (Paul Wiedorfer, Medal of Honor, WWII 2011); (J. W. Trone 19 January 1945); (J. W. Trone 2 February 1945); (J. W. Trone 6 February 1945); (Pearson 1957, 120–121, 353–355); (Connor 2011); (Rust 1990, 55–59); (G–2 Section, Headquarters, 4th Armored Division 26 December 1944, 5).

CHAPTER 10 | ASSENOIS

1   (Seay, 1945, 4–7); (Meyer, 1945, 12–14); (Churchill, January 18, 1945, 2–3 (6–7)); (Blanchard, 1945, 26–27); (Headquarters, 37th Tank Battalion, 4th Armored Division, 1944); (Moon, 37th Tank Battalion Diary, 1945, 7–9); (Headquarters, 37th Tank Battalion, 4th Armored Division, 1944); (Creighton W. Abrams, 1945, 4–11 (51–58)); (J. Leach, 2007); (Bautz, 1999); (Holmes, n.d.);

(Boggess, 1984, 1–8); (W. A. Dwight, 1979, 2–3); (C. W. Abrams, January 8, 1945); (Headquarters, Third Army, February 9, 1945); (Moora, 1945); (Goldstein, 2002); For Hendrix interview, see James Hendrix, Medal of Honor, WWII, 2011; (Department of the Army, 1945); (Johnson, Unit Diary, 53rd Armored Infantry Battalion, December 1, 1944–December 31, 1944, 53); (Johnson, After Action Report, December 1944, 53rd Armored Infantry Battalion, 1945, 9–10); (G. L. Jaques, January 8, 1945, 2–3); (Mulvey, 2013); (H. C. Jaques, 1945, 83–85); (Lipscomb, 2013); (Bush, 1944, 4); (Cooke, May 6, 1948, 10–15); (R. Parker, 1945, 2–5 (88–91)); (Bastnagel, February 6, 1945, 13–14 (45–46)); (Bernstein, OPREP A, No. D–26A, first of three, for twenty-four hours ending sunset, December 26, 1944. Ninth Fighter Command Field Order No. 148, 1944); (Bernstein, OPREP A, No. D–26B, second of three, for twenty-four hours ending sunset, December 26, 1944. Ninth Fighter Command Field Order No. 148, 1944); (Bernstein, OPREP A, No. D–26C, last of three, for twenty-four hours ending sunset, December 26, 1944. Ninth Fighter Command Field Order No. 148, 1944); (Headquarters Section, 379th Fighter Squadron, 1986, 493). For Major Chandler's KIA story, see Headquarters, 362nd Fighter Group, 1986, 152; (Taylor, 1944); (Zimmer, 2000, 8); (Leaphart, 2013); (Turbiville, March 10, 1945, 6); (S-2 Section, 327th Glider Infantry Regiment, 1944, 11); (S-3 Section, 327th Glider Infantry Regiment, 1944, 5).

2   (Interrogation, Prisoner of War Team, III Corps, December 26, 1944, 2–3, 7); (Interrogation, Prisoner of War Team #60, 134th Infantry Regiment, 1944); (S-2 Section, Headquarters, CCB, 4th Armored Division, 1944); (Interrogation, Prisoner of War Team, III Corps, December 26, 1944, 2–4, 7); (S-2 Section, Headquarters, CCB, 4th Armored Division, 1944); (G-2 Section, 4th Armored Division, 1944); (G-2 Section, 4th Armored Division, 1944); (G-2 Section, 4th Armored Division, 1944); (Interrogation, Prisoner of War Team, III Corps, December 27, 1944); (Interrogation, Prisoner of War Team, III Corps, December 28, 1944); (Kokott, Ardennes Offensive—Battle of Bastogne MS #B–040, 1950, 142–50); (Kokott, Employment of the 26th Volksgrenadier Division from 16 to 31 Dec 1944, January 5, 1945); For information on the 39th Fusilier Regiment, see Moll 1968, 331–33; (Rust, 1990, 55–59); (Lüttwitz, 1950, 15–17); (H. E. Brown, Periodic Report No. 122, G-2, 4th Armored Division, December 28, 1944, 3); (War Department, 1945).

3   (Interrogation Prisoner of War Team, III Corps 26 December, 1944, 2–3, 7); (Interrogation Prisoner of War Team #60, 134th Infantry Regiment 1944); (S–2 Section, Headquarters, CCB, 4th Armored Division 1944); (Interrogation Prisoner of War Team, III Corps 26 December, 1944, 2–4, 7); (S–2 Section, Headquarters, CCB, 4th Armored Division 1944); (G–2 Section, 4th Armored Division 1944); (G–2 Section, 4th Armored Division 1944); (G–2 Section, 4th Armored Division 1944); (Interrogation Prisoner of War Team, III Corps 27 December 1944); (Interrogation Prisoner of War Team, III Corps 28 December 1944); (Kokott, Ardennes Offensive—Battle of Bastogne MS # B–040 1950, 142–150); (Kokott, Employment of the 26th Volksgrenadier Division from 16 to 31 Dec 1944 5 January 1945); For information on the 39th Fusilier Regiment, see (Moll 1968, 331–333); (Rust 1990, 55–59); (Lüttwitz 1950, 15–17); (H. E. Brown, Periodic Report No. 122, G–2, 4th Armored Division 28 December 1944, 3); (War Department 1945).

4   (Interrogation Prisoner of War Team, III Corps 26 December, 1944, 2–3, 7); (Interrogation Prisoner of War Team #60, 134th Infantry Regiment 1944); (S–2 Section, Headquarters, CCB, 4th Armored Division 1944); (Interrogation Prisoner of War Team, III Corps 26 December, 1944, 2–4, 7); (S–2 Section, Headquarters, CCB, 4th Armored Division 1944); (G–2 Section, 4th Armored Division 1944); (G–2 Section, 4th Armored Division 1944); (G–2 Section, 4th Armored Division 1944); (Interrogation Prisoner of War Team, III Corps 27 December 1944); (Interrogation Prisoner of War Team, III Corps 28 December 1944); (Kokott, Ardennes Offensive—Battle of Bastogne MS # B–040 1950, 142–150); (Kokott, Employment of the 26th Volksgrenadier Division from 16 to 31 Dec 1944 5 January 1945); For information on the 39th Fusilier Regiment, see (Moll 1968, 331–333); (Rust 1990, 55–59); (Lüttwitz 1950, 15–17); (H. E. Brown, Periodic Report No. 122, G–2, 4th Armored Division 28 December 1944, 3); (War Department 1945).

5   (Seay, 1945, 4–7); (Meyer 1945, 12–14); (Churchill 18 January, 1945, 2–3 (6–7)); (Blanchard 1945, 26–27); (Headquarters, 37th Tank Battalion, 4th Armored Division 1944); (Moon, 37th Tank Battalion Diary 1945, 7–9); (Headquarters, 37th Tank Battalion, 4th Armored Division 1944); (Creighton W. Abrams 1945, 4–11 (51–58)); (J. Leach 2007); (Bautz 1999); (Holmes n.d.); (Boggess 1984, 1–8); (W. A. Dwight 1979, 2–3); (C. W. Abrams 8 January,

1945); (Headquarters, Third Army 9 February 1945); (Moora 1945); (Goldstein 2002); For Hendrix interview, see (James Hendrix, Medal of Honor, WWII 2011); (Department of the Army 1945); (Johnson, Unit Diary, 53rd Armored Infantry Battalion, 1 December 1944 to 31 December 1944 1944, 53); (Johnson, After Action Report, December 1944, 53rd Armored Infantry Battalion 1945, 9–10); (G. L. Jaques 8 January, 1945, 2–3); (Mulvey 2013); (H. C. Jaques 1945, 83–85); (Lipscomb 2013); (Bush 1944, 4); (Cooke 6 May 1948, 10–15); (R. Parker 1945, 2–5 (88–91)); (Bastnagel 6 February 1945, 13–14 (45–46)); (Bernstein, OPREP A, No. D–26A, first of 3, for 24 hours ending sunset, December 26, 1944. Ninth Fighter Command Field Order No. 148 1944); (Bernstein, OPREP A, No. D–26B, second of 3, for 24 hours ending sunset, December 26, 1944. Ninth Fighter Command Field Order No. 148 1944); (Bernstein, OPREP A, No. D–26C, last of 3, for 24 hours ending sunset, December 26, 1944. Ninth Fighter Command Field Order No. 148 1944); (Headquarters Section, 379th Fighter Squadron 1986, 493) For Major Chandler's KIA story, see (Headquarters, 362nd Fighter Group 1986, 152); (Taylor 1944); (Zimmer 2000, 8); (Leaphart 2013); (Turbiville 10 March 1945, 6); (S–2 Section, 327th Glider Infantry Regiment 1944, 11); (S–3 Section, 327th Glider Infantry Regiment 1944, 5).

6   (Lüttwitz, 1950, 14–15).

7   (Kinnard, 1944); (MacKenzie, 1968, 233); (B. Wright, n.d.); (G-3 Section, III Corps Headquarters, 1944); (Commanding General, Third U.S. Army, TAC, 1944); (Commanding General, Third U.S. Army, TAC, 1944); (Commanding General, Third U.S. Army, TAC, 1944).

8   (Seay, 1945, 4–7); (Meyer, 1945, 12–14); (Churchill, January 18, 1945, 2–3 (6–7)); (Blanchard, 1945, 26–27); (Headquarters, 37th Tank Battalion, 4th Armored Division, 1944); (Moon, 37th Tank Battalion Diary, 1945, 7–9); (Headquarters, 37th Tank Battalion, 4th Armored Division, 1944); (Creighton W. Abrams, 1945, 4–11 (51–58)); (J. Leach, 2007); (Bautz, 1999); (Holmes, n.d.); (Boggess, 1984, 1–8); (W. A. Dwight, 1979, 2–3); (C. W. Abrams, January 8, 1945); (Headquarters, Third Army, February 9, 1945); (Moora, 1945); (Goldstein, 2002); For Hendrix interview, see James Hendrix, Medal of Honor, WWII, 2011); (Department of the Army, 1945); (Johnson, Unit Diary, 53rd Armored Infantry Battalion, December 1, 1944–December 31, 1944, 53); (Johnson, After Action Report, December, 1944, 53rd Armored Infantry Bat-

talion, 1945, 9–10); (G. L. Jaques, January, 8 1945, 2–3); (Mulvey, 2013); (H. C. Jaques, 1945, 83–85); (Lipscomb, 2013); (Bush, 1944, 4); (Cooke, May 6, 1948, 10–15); (R. Parker, 1945, 2–5 (88–91)); (Bastnagel, February 6, 1945, 13–14 (45–46)); (Bernstein, OPREP A, No. D–26A, first of three, for twenty-four hours ending sunset, December 26, 1944. Ninth Fighter Command Field Order No. 148, 1944); (Bernstein, OPREP A, No. D–26B, second of three, for twenty-four hours ending sunset, December 26, 1944. Ninth Fighter Command Field Order No. 148, 1944); (Bernstein, OPREP A, No. D–26C, last of three, for twenty-four hours ending sunset, December 26, 1944. Ninth Fighter Command Field Order No. 148, 1944); (Headquarters Section, 379th Fighter Squadron, 1986, 493); for Major Chandler's KIA story, see Headquarters, 362nd Fighter Group, 1986, 152); (Taylor, 1944); (Zimmer, 2000, 8); (Leaphart, 2013); (Turbiville, March 10, 1945, 6); (S-2 Section, 327th Glider Infantry Regiment, 1944, 11); (S-3 Section, 327th Glider Infantry Regiment, 1944, 5).

9   (Interrogation Prisoner of War Team, III Corps, December 26, 1944, 2–3, 7); (Interrogation, Prisoner of War Team #60, 134th Infantry Regiment, 1944); (S-2 Section, Headquarters, CCB, 4th Armored Division, 1944); (Interrogation, Prisoner of War Team, III Corps, December 26, 1944, 2–4, 7); (S-2 Section, Headquarters, CCB, 4th Armored Division, 1944); (G-2 Section, 4th Armored Division, 1944); (G-2 Section, 4th Armored Division, 1944); (G-2 Section, 4th Armored Division, 1944); (Interrogation, Prisoner of War Team, III Corps, December 27, 1944); (Interrogation, Prisoner of War Team, III Corps, December 28, 1944); (Kokott, Ardennes Offensive—Battle of Bastogne MS #B–040, 1950, 142–50); (Kokott, Employment of the 26th Volksgrenadier Division from 16 to 31 Dec 1944, January 5, 1945); for information on the 39th Fusilier Regiment, see (Moll 1968, 331–33); (Rust, 1990, 55–59); (Lüttwitz, 1950, 15–17); (H. E. Brown, Periodic Report No. 122, G-2, 4th Armored Division, December 28, 1944, 3); (War Department, 1945).

10   (Interrogation Prisoner of War Team, III Corps 26 December, 1944, 2–3, 7); (Interrogation Prisoner of War Team #60, 134th Infantry Regiment 1944); (S–2 Section, Headquarters, CCB, 4th Armored Division 1944); (Interrogation Prisoner of War Team, III Corps 26 December, 1944, 2–4, 7); (S–2 Section, Headquarters, CCB, 4th Armored Division 1944); (G–2 Section, 4th Armored Division 1944); (G–2 Section, 4th Armored Division 1944); (G–2 Section, 4th Armored Division 1944); (Interrogation Prisoner of War Team, III Corps 27

December 1944); (Interrogation Prisoner of War Team, III Corps 28 December 1944); (Kokott, Ardennes Offensive—Battle of Bastogne MS #B–040 1950, 142–150); (Kokott, Employment of the 26th Volksgrenadier Division from 16 to 31 Dec 1944 5 January 1945); For information on the 39th Fusilier Regiment, see (Moll 1968, 331–333); (Rust 1990, 55–59); (Lüttwitz 1950, 15–17); (H. E. Brown, Periodic Report No. 122, G–2, 4th Armored Division 28 December 1944, 3); (War Department 1945).

11   (Seay 1945, 4–7); (Meyer 1945, 12–14); (Churchill 18 January, 1945, 2–3 (6–7)); (Blanchard 1945, 26–27); (Headquarters, 37th Tank Battalion, 4th Armored Division 1944); (Moon, 37th Tank Battalion Diary 1945, 7–9); (Headquarters, 37th Tank Battalion, 4th Armored Division 1944); (Creighton W. Abrams 1945, 4–11 (51–58)); (J. Leach 2007); (Bautz 1999); (Holmes n.d.); (Boggess 1984, 1–8); (W. A. Dwight 1979, 2–3); (C. W. Abrams 8 January, 1945); (Headquarters, Third Army 9 February 1945); (Moora 1945); (Goldstein 2002); For Hendrix interview, see (James Hendrix, Medal of Honor, WWII 2011); (Department of the Army 1945); (Johnson, Unit Diary, 53rd Armored Infantry Battalion, 1 December 1944 to 31 December 1944 1944, 53); (Johnson, After Action Report, December 1944, 53rd Armored Infantry Battalion 1945, 9–10); (G. L. Jaques 8 January, 1945, 2–3); (Mulvey 2013); (H. C. Jaques 1945, 83–85); (Lipscomb 2013); (Bush 1944, 4); (Cooke 6 May 1948, 10–15); (R. Parker 1945, 2–5 (88–91)); (Bastnagel 6 February 1945, 13–14 (45–46)); (Bernstein, OPREP A, No. D–26A, first of 3, for 24 hours ending sunset, December 26, 1944. Ninth Fighter Command Field Order No. 148 1944); (Bernstein, OPREP A, No. D–26B, second of 3, for 24 hours ending sunset, December 26, 1944. Ninth Fighter Command Field Order No. 148 1944); (Bernstein, OPREP A, No. D–26C, last of 3, for 24 hours ending sunset, December 26, 1944. Ninth Fighter Command Field Order No. 148 1944); (Headquarters Section, 379th Fighter Squadron 1986, 493) For Major Chandler's KIA story, see (Headquarters, 362nd Fighter Group 1986, 152); (Taylor 1944); (Zimmer 2000, 8); (Leaphart 2013); (Turbiville 10 March 1945, 6); (S–2 Section, 327th Glider Infantry Regiment 1944, 11); (S–3 Section, 327th Glider Infantry Regiment 1944, 5).

12   (Seay 1945, 4–7); (Meyer 1945, 12–14); (Churchill 18 January, 1945, 2–3 (6–7)); (Blanchard 1945, 26–27); (Headquarters, 37th Tank Battalion, 4th Armored Division 1944); (Moon, 37th Tank Battalion Diary 1945, 7–9);

(Headquarters, 37th Tank Battalion, 4th Armored Division 1944); (Creighton W. Abrams 1945, 4–11 (51–58)); (J. Leach 2007); (Bautz 1999); (Holmes n.d.); (Boggess 1984, 1–8); (W. A. Dwight 1979, 2–3); (C. W. Abrams 8 January, 1945); (Headquarters, Third Army 9 February 1945); (Moora 1945); (Goldstein 2002); For Hendrix interview, see (James Hendrix, Medal of Honor, WWII 2011); (Department of the Army 1945); (Johnson, Unit Diary, 53rd Armored Infantry Battalion, 1 December 1944 to 31 December 1944 1944, 53); (Johnson, After Action Report, December 1944, 53rd Armored Infantry Battalion 1945, 9–10); (G. L. Jaques 8 January, 1945, 2–3); (Mulvey 2013); (H. C. Jaques 1945, 83–85); (Lipscomb 2013); (Bush 1944, 4); (Cooke 6 May 1948, 10–15); (R. Parker 1945, 2–5 (88–91)); (Bastnagel 6 February 1945, 13–14 (45–46)); (Bernstein, OPREP A, No. D–26A, first of 3, for 24 hours ending sunset, December 26, 1944. Ninth Fighter Command Field Order No. 148 1944); (Bernstein, OPREP A, No. D–26B, second of 3, for 24 hours ending sunset, December 26, 1944. Ninth Fighter Command Field Order No. 148 1944); (Bernstein, OPREP A, No. D–26C, last of 3, for 24 hours ending sunset, December 26, 1944. Ninth Fighter Command Field Order No. 148 1944); (Headquarters Section, 379th Fighter Squadron 1986, 493) For Major Chandler's KIA story, see (Headquarters, 362nd Fighter Group 1986, 152); (Taylor 1944); (Zimmer 2000, 8); (Leaphart 2013); (Turbiville 10 March 1945, 6); (S–2 Section, 327th Glider Infantry Regiment 1944, 11); (S–3 Section, 327th Glider Infantry Regiment 1944, 5).

13   (E. Wright, 2013); (Young, 2013); (Robbins, January 11, 1945, 3); for Heath's account, see Heath, 2013.

14   (Seay 1945, 4–7); (Meyer 1945, 12–14); (Churchill 18 January, 1945, 2–3 (6–7)); (Blanchard 1945, 26–27); (Headquarters, 37th Tank Battalion, 4th Armored Division 1944); (Moon, 37th Tank Battalion Diary 1945, 7–9); (Headquarters, 37th Tank Battalion, 4th Armored Division 1944); (Creighton W. Abrams 1945, 4–11 (51–58)); (J. Leach 2007); (Bautz 1999); (Holmes n.d.); (Boggess 1984, 1–8); (W. A. Dwight 1979, 2–3); (C. W. Abrams 8 January, 1945); (Headquarters, Third Army 9 February 1945); (Moora 1945); (Goldstein 2002); For Hendrix interview, see (James Hendrix, Medal of Honor, WWII 2011); (Department of the Army 1945); (Johnson, Unit Diary, 53rd Armored Infantry Battalion, 1 December 1944 to 31 December 1944 1944, 53); (Johnson, After Action Report, December 1944, 53rd Armored Infantry

Battalion 1945, 9–10); (G. L. Jaques 8 January, 1945, 2–3); (Mulvey 2013); (H. C. Jaques 1945, 83–85); (Lipscomb 2013); (Bush 1944, 4); (Cooke 6 May 1948, 10–15); (R. Parker 1945, 2–5 (88–91)); (Bastnagel 6 February 1945, 13–14 (45–46)); (Bernstein, OPREP A, No. D–26A, first of 3, for 24 hours ending sunset, December 26, 1944. Ninth Fighter Command Field Order No. 148 1944); (Bernstein, OPREP A, No. D–26B, second of 3, for 24 hours ending sunset, December 26, 1944. Ninth Fighter Command Field Order No. 148 1944); (Bernstein, OPREP A, No. D–26C, last of 3, for 24 hours ending sunset, December 26, 1944. Ninth Fighter Command Field Order No. 148 1944); (Headquarters Section, 379th Fighter Squadron 1986, 493) For Major Chandler's KIA story, see (Headquarters, 362nd Fighter Group 1986, 152); (Taylor 1944); (Zimmer 2000, 8); (Leaphart 2013); (Turbiville 10 March 1945, 6); (S–2 Section, 327th Glider Infantry Regiment 1944, 11); (S–3 Section, 327th Glider Infantry Regiment 1944, 5); (Zaloga, Sherman Medium Tank, 1942–1945 1993, 17).

15   (Seay 1945, 4–7); (Meyer 1945, 12–14); (Churchill 18 January, 1945, 2–3 (6–7)); (Blanchard 1945, 26–27); (Headquarters, 37th Tank Battalion, 4th Armored Division 1944); (Moon, 37th Tank Battalion Diary 1945, 7–9); (Headquarters, 37th Tank Battalion, 4th Armored Division 1944); (Creighton W. Abrams 1945, 4–11 (51–58)); (J. Leach 2007); (Bautz 1999); (Holmes n.d.); (Boggess 1984, 1–8); (W. A. Dwight 1979, 2–3); (C. W. Abrams 8 January, 1945); (Headquarters, Third Army 9 February 1945); (Moora 1945); (Goldstein 2002); For Hendrix interview, see (James Hendrix, Medal of Honor, WWII 2011); (Department of the Army 1945); (Johnson, Unit Diary, 53rd Armored Infantry Battalion, 1 December 1944 to 31 December 1944 1944, 53); (Johnson, After Action Report, December 1944, 53rd Armored Infantry Battalion 1945, 9–10); (G. L. Jaques 8 January, 1945, 2–3); (Mulvey 2013); (H. C. Jaques 1945, 83–85); (Lipscomb 2013); (Bush 1944, 4); (Cooke 6 May 1948, 10–15); (R. Parker 1945, 2–5 (88–91)); (Bastnagel 6 February 1945, 13–14 (45–46)); (Bernstein, OPREP A, No. D–26A, first of 3, for 24 hours ending sunset, December 26, 1944. Ninth Fighter Command Field Order No. 148 1944); (Bernstein, OPREP A, No. D–26B, second of 3, for 24 hours ending sunset, December 26, 1944. Ninth Fighter Command Field Order No. 148 1944); (Bernstein, OPREP A, No. D–26C, last of 3, for 24 hours ending sunset, December 26, 1944. Ninth Fighter Command Field Order No. 148 1944); (Headquarters Section, 379th Fighter Squadron 1986, 493) For Major

Chandler's KIA story, see (Headquarters, 362nd Fighter Group 1986, 152); (Taylor 1944); (Zimmer 2000, 8); (Leaphart 2013); (Turbiville 10 March 1945, 6); (S–2 Section, 327th Glider Infantry Regiment 1944, 11); (S–3 Section, 327th Glider Infantry Regiment 1944, 5); (Zaloga, Sherman Medium Tank, 1942–1945 1993, 17).

16   (Seay 1945, 4–7); (Meyer 1945, 12–14); (Churchill 18 January, 1945, 2–3 (6–7)); (Blanchard 1945, 26–27); (Headquarters, 37th Tank Battalion, 4th Armored Division 1944); (Moon, 37th Tank Battalion Diary 1945, 7–9); (Headquarters, 37th Tank Battalion, 4th Armored Division 1944); (Creighton W. Abrams 1945, 4–11 (51–58)); (J. Leach 2007); (Bautz 1999); (Holmes n.d.); (Boggess 1984, 1–8); (W. A. Dwight 1979, 2–3); (C. W. Abrams 8 January, 1945); (Headquarters, Third Army 9 February 1945); (Moora 1945); (Goldstein 2002); For Hendrix interview, see (James Hendrix, Medal of Honor, WWII 2011); (Department of the Army 1945); (Johnson, Unit Diary, 53rd Armored Infantry Battalion, 1 December 1944 to 31 December 1944 1944, 53); (Johnson, After Action Report, December 1944, 53rd Armored Infantry Battalion 1945, 9–10); (G. L. Jaques 8 January, 1945, 2–3); (Mulvey 2013); (H. C. Jaques 1945, 83–85); (Lipscomb 2013); (Bush 1944, 4); (Cooke 6 May 1948, 10–15); (R. Parker 1945, 2–5 (88–91)); (Bastnagel 6 February 1945, 13–14 (45–46)); (Bernstein, OPREP A, No. D–26A, first of 3, for 24 hours ending sunset, December 26, 1944. Ninth Fighter Command Field Order No. 148 1944); (Bernstein, OPREP A, No. D–26B, second of 3, for 24 hours ending sunset, December 26, 1944. Ninth Fighter Command Field Order No. 148 1944); (Bernstein, OPREP A, No. D–26C, last of 3, for 24 hours ending sunset, December 26, 1944. Ninth Fighter Command Field Order No. 148 1944); (Headquarters Section, 379th Fighter Squadron 1986, 493) For Major Chandler's KIA story, see (Headquarters, 362nd Fighter Group 1986, 152); (Taylor 1944); (Zimmer 2000, 8); (Leaphart 2013); (Turbiville 10 March 1945, 6); (S–2 Section, 327th Glider Infantry Regiment 1944, 11); (S–3 Section, 327th Glider Infantry Regiment 1944, 5); (Zaloga, Sherman Medium Tank, 1942–1945 1993, 17).

17   (Seay 1945, 4–7); (Meyer 1945, 12–14); (Churchill 18 January, 1945, 2–3 (6–7)); (Blanchard 1945, 26–27); (Headquarters, 37th Tank Battalion, 4th Armored Division 1944); (Moon, 37th Tank Battalion Diary 1945, 7–9); (Headquarters, 37th Tank Battalion, 4th Armored Division 1944); (Creighton W. Abrams 1945, 4–11 (51–58)); (J. Leach 2007); (Bautz 1999); (Holmes n.d.);

(Boggess 1984, 1–8); (W. A. Dwight 1979, 2–3); (C. W. Abrams 8 January, 1945); (Headquarters, Third Army 9 February 1945); (Moora 1945); (Goldstein 2002); For Hendrix interview, see (James Hendrix, Medal of Honor, WWII 2011); (Department of the Army 1945); (Johnson, Unit Diary, 53rd Armored Infantry Battalion, 1 December 1944 to 31 December 1944 1944, 53); (Johnson, After Action Report, December 1944, 53rd Armored Infantry Battalion 1945, 9–10); (G. L. Jaques 8 January, 1945, 2–3); (Mulvey 2013); (H. C. Jaques 1945, 83–85); (Lipscomb 2013); (Bush 1944, 4); (Cooke 6 May 1948, 10–15); (R. Parker 1945, 2–5 (88–91)); (Bastnagel 6 February 1945, 13–14 (45–46)); (Bernstein, OPREP A, No. D–26A, first of 3, for 24 hours ending sunset, December 26, 1944. Ninth Fighter Command Field Order No. 148 1944); (Bernstein, OPREP A, No. D–26B, second of 3, for 24 hours ending sunset, December 26, 1944. Ninth Fighter Command Field Order No. 148 1944); (Bernstein, OPREP A, No. D–26C, last of 3, for 24 hours ending sunset, December 26, 1944. Ninth Fighter Command Field Order No. 148 1944); (Headquarters Section, 379th Fighter Squadron 1986, 493) For Major Chandler's KIA story, see (Headquarters, 362nd Fighter Group 1986, 152); (Taylor 1944); (Zimmer 2000, 8); (Leaphart 2013); (Turbiville 10 March 1945, 6); (S–2 Section, 327th Glider Infantry Regiment 1944, 11); (S–3 Section, 327th Glider Infantry Regiment 1944, 5); (Zaloga, Sherman Medium Tank, 1942–1945 1993, 17).

18   (Seay 1945, 4–7); (Meyer 1945, 12–14); (Churchill 18 January, 1945, 2–3 (6–7)); (Blanchard 1945, 26–27); (Headquarters, 37th Tank Battalion, 4th Armored Division 1944); (Moon, 37th Tank Battalion Diary 1945, 7–9); (Headquarters, 37th Tank Battalion, 4th Armored Division 1944); (Creighton W. Abrams 1945, 4–11 (51–58)); (J. Leach 2007); (Bautz 1999); (Holmes n.d.); (Boggess 1984, 1–8); (W. A. Dwight 1979, 2–3); (C. W. Abrams 8 January, 1945); (Headquarters, Third Army 9 February 1945); (Moora 1945); (Goldstein 2002); For Hendrix interview, see (James Hendrix, Medal of Honor, WWII 2011); (Department of the Army 1945); (Johnson, Unit Diary, 53rd Armored Infantry Battalion, 1 December 1944 to 31 December 1944 1944, 53); (Johnson, After Action Report, December 1944, 53rd Armored Infantry Battalion 1945, 9–10); (G. L. Jaques 8 January, 1945, 2–3); (Mulvey 2013); (H. C. Jaques 1945, 83–85); (Lipscomb 2013); (Bush 1944, 4); (Cooke 6 May 1948, 10–15); (R. Parker 1945, 2–5 (88–91)); (Bastnagel 6 February 1945, 13–14 (45–46)); (Bernstein, OPREP A, No. D–26A, first of 3, for 24 hours

ending sunset, December 26, 1944. Ninth Fighter Command Field Order No. 148 1944); (Bernstein, OPREP A, No. D–26B, second of 3, for 24 hours ending sunset, December 26, 1944. Ninth Fighter Command Field Order No. 148 1944); (Bernstein, OPREP A, No. D–26C, last of 3, for 24 hours ending sunset, December 26, 1944. Ninth Fighter Command Field Order No. 148 1944); (Headquarters Section, 379th Fighter Squadron 1986, 493) For Major Chandler's KIA story, see (Headquarters, 362nd Fighter Group 1986, 152); (Taylor 1944); (Zimmer 2000, 8); (Leaphart 2013); (Turbiville 10 March 1945, 6); (S–2 Section, 327th Glider Infantry Regiment 1944, 11); (S–3 Section, 327th Glider Infantry Regiment 1944, 5); (Zaloga, Sherman Medium Tank, 1942–1945 1993, 17).

EPILOGUE

1   (G-2 Section, 4th Armored Division, 1944); (G-2 Section, 4th Armored Division, 1944); (John B. Ellis, 1944); (Interrogation, Prisoner of War Team, III Corps, December 26, 1944, 2–3, 7); (Interrogation, Prisoner of War Team #60, 134th Infantry Regiment, 1944); (G-2 Section, 4th Armored Division, 1944); (S-2 Section, Headquarters, CCB, 4th Armored Division, 1944); (Walter Noller, Interrogation, Prisoner of War Team #68, 1945); (S-3 Section, CCB, 4th Armored Division, 1944); (Hunt, After Action Report, Combat Command B, 4th Armored Division for the Period of December 1–31, 1944, 3); (Ellis, January 29, 1945, 16); (S-2 Section, 1945, 2); (Irzyk, 8th Tank Battalion History, October 19, 1944–February 10, 1945, 18); (Stauber, 1945, 3–4 (30–31)); (Fenchel, 2001); (Irzyk, *He Rode Up Front for Patton*, 1996, 258–60); (Headquarters, 8th Tank Battalion, 4th Armored Division, 1944); (Headquarters, 10th Armored Infantry Battalion, 1944); (Donnelly, 1945, 3 (12)) Map (Donnelly, 1945, Incl 6); (Baum, 1945, 4–5 (70–71)); (Headquarters, 10th Armored Infantry Battalion, 1944–1945); (Glenn H. Gardner, 1945, 1–2); (Peter J. Stanchak, 1945, 21, 25–29); (Slotnik, 2011); (Shapiro, 2011); (Department of the Army, 1945); For interview on YouTube, see Paul Wiedorfer, Medal of Honor, WWII, 2011); (J. W. Trone, January 19, 1945); (J. W. Trone, February 2, 1945); (J. W. Trone, February 11, 1945); (J. W. Trone, February 6, 1945); (J. W. Trone, January 25, 1945, 1–2); (Pearson, 1957, 120–21, 353–55).

2   (Damiano, 2013); (R. E. Green, 2013); (Rottman, 2010, 20–29); (Zaloga, U.S. Field Artillery of World War II, 2007, 3); (Sayen, 2007, 7); (War Department, 1945); (Heilmann, 5th Parachute Division (December 1, 1944–January 12, 1945), MS B–023, between 1945–1954, 3); (Zaloga, Panther vs. Sherman: Battle of the Bulge 1944, 2008, 31–32); (Creighton W. Abrams, 1945, 3); (Bozzuto, 1970); (Battiselli, 2009, 21); (Williams, 2002); (Heath, 2013); (Hunt, Combat Command "B" History, December 1–31, 1944, 4th Armored Division, 1944, 5); (Headquarters, Combat Command "A," 4th Armored Division, January 18, 1945, 6–7).

INDEX

★ ★ ★ ★ ★

Page numbers in **bold** indicate organizational charts; those in *italics* indicate maps.

Abrams, Creighton W., **5,** 105, 329, 330
  Assenois, 278–79, 281, 295–96, 297–98, 299, 307–9, 310, 311–12, 313, 314, 317, 318–19, 323
  Bigonville, 203–4, 206, 209, 211, 212, 213–14, 215, 216, 217, 232, 278
  Flatzbourhof, 143–44, 146, 147, 148, 149, 150, 152, 153, 154, 155, 162, 163, 164, 165, 168–69, 172
Abrams, Morris, 73
Air Medal recipients, 304
airpower advantage (U.S.), viii, 70, 120–21, 123–24, 127, 128, 132, 133, 135–36, 149, 150, 161, 180, 209, 216, 228, 239, 253–54, 255–56, 257, 268, 288, 296, 305–7, 327
Alanis, Dan, **5,** 72, 74, 75, 82, 85, 89, 90, 242, 243
Albertson, Roscoe V., 100
Allen, Leven Cooper, 56
American army, 326. *See also* Battle of the Bulge; III Corps; Patton, George S., III; Siege of Bastogne; Third Army
  airpower advantage, viii, 70, 120–21, 123–24, 127, 128, 132, 133, 135–36, 149, 150, 161, 180, 209, 216, 228, 239, 253–54, 255–56, 257, 268, 288, 296, 305–7, 327
  armored divisions, 229
  artillery advantage, 46, 116, 157, 160, 180, 268, 295, 314, 315, 326
  assumptions about German army, 35, 38
  casualties, vii, 4, 93, 118, 119, 128, 138–39, 141, 151, 152, 168, 169, 175, 180, 188, 204, 206, 212, 228, 232, 235, 244, 248, 251, 252, 263, 265, 272, 276, 285, 306, 314–15, 322, 323
  command and control superiority of, 326
  commanders superiority, 62–63, 72, 95–96, 101, 105, 144, 146, 147, 330
  communication system advantage, 157, 158, 307, 326
  Fire Direction Center (FDC), 100, 120–21, 126–27, 269, 310–11, 326
  fratricide, viii, 216–17, 291, 313–14, 314–15
  infantry divisions, 2, 229
  intelligence advantage, 23, 28, 35–36, 38, 107–8, 112, 114–15, 116, 162–63, 252, 302, 327
  long-range firepower advantage, 99–100, 116, 209, 233, 240, 310, 311
  mobility advantage, 41, 88, 117, 326, 327, 328, 329
  morale of, 259–60, 294, 327
  radio communications, 157, 158, 307, 326
  readiness rate of tank battalions, 328
  reconnaissance units, 86–87, 147
  tank battalions, 144, 242, 328
  tank destroyer battalions, 72, 74, 103, 106, 132, 141, 193, 229, 235, 240, 243, 262, 279, 289, 294, 329
  training advantage, 95–96, 101, 105, 329
American response (December 16-21, 1944), 42–75, *44, 69*
Ardennes, 16, 18, 30, 34, 39, 56, 115, 124, 127, 131. *See also* Battle of the Bulge
Arlon, 57, 58, 61, 73, 74, 75, 77, 79, 81, 84, 85, 94, 101, 107, 111, 121, 192, 229, 257, 301
armored divisions (U.S.), 229. *See also specific armored divisions*
Army Group A (German), 325
Army Group B (German), 9–10, 12–17, 21, 22
Army Group G (German), 15, 21, 22
Army Group North/South (German), 131

artillery advantage (U.S.), 46, 116, 157, 160, 180, 268, 295, 314, 315, 326

Assenois (December 25–26, 1944), 268, 278–323, *280*

Astaire, Fred, 19

Ayer, Beatrice (Patton's wife), 52

Barron, Leo, vii–viii

Bastogne, 294. *See also* Siege of Bastogne

battle fatigue, 53–54

Battle of the Bulge (December 16, 1944–January 25, 1945), vii–viii. *See also* American army; German army; Siege of Bastogne

American response (December 16–21, 1944), 42–75, *44, 69*

German plan (November 6–December 15, 1944), 9–41, *11*

terrain impact on, 14, 19, 24, 27, 28, 31, 56, 58

weather impact on, 14, 23, 27, 51, 63, 70, 71

Baukowitz (German), 238

Bautz, Edward, 146, 147, 148, 149, 154–55, 158, 159–60, 162, 163, 317–18, 319, 330

Bennett, Charles W., 138

Bennett, James E., 117, 119

Berky, Eugene, 245, 249

Berneike, Rudolf, 238, 239

Bertram (German), 46, 47, 161, 167, 168, 170, 172, 209, 210, 246, 255

Beyer, Franz, 18

Bigonville, 66, 67, 79, 92, 93, 94, 104, 105, 144, 149, 155–56, 162, 164, 166, 168–69, 170, 171, 172, 173, 174

Bigonville (December 24, 1944), 203–35, *205,* 239, 278, 282, 329

Blackmer, William K., 141

Blanchard, Wendell, **5,** 63, 104, 105, 147, 230, 232, 278–79, 281, 288, 289, 295, 307, 312, 317, 318, 319

Boggess, Charles, 204, 289–90, 291, 296, 297, 308–10, 312–13, 314, 315–16, 317, 318

Boller, Vincent J., 82, 84, 85, 89, 90, 189

Bradley, Omar N., 39, 51, 54, 55–56, 56–57, 58, 59–60, 231

Brandenberger, Erich, 13, 17–18, 21–22, 27, 29, 30, 31, 77, 239, 327

bravery of 4th Armored Division, 94, 100, 125, 130, 138–39, 146, 147, 184, 187, 188, 212, 248, 249, 273, 274, 316, 330–31

Bredbenner, Edward, 251

Bronze Star recipients, 125, 138, 147, 274

Brown, Harry E., 61

Buhl, Günther, 234

Burdett, Bruce, 173–75

Burnon, 94, 96, 97, 98, 100, 103, 106, 108, 114, 116, 120, 126, 128, 135, 262, 263

C-47 Skytrains (U.S.), 133, 303, 304, 306, 307, 308

Caldwell, Gaynor, 184, 185

Calvert, Robert, 188–89

Campbell, Leven, 209–10

Carey, James M., 138–39

casualties

American army, vii, 4, 93, 118, 119, 128, 138–39, 141, 151, 152, 168, 169, 175, 180, 188, 204, 206, 212, 228, 232, 235, 244, 248, 251, 252, 263, 265, 272, 276, 285, 306, 314–15, 322, 323

German army, 48, 49, 55, 93, 152, 153, 155, 160, 167, 169, 171, 172, 173, 201, 210, 233–34, 238, 254, 261, 292, 296, 321, 323

Chamberlin, Ellsworth B., 312, 314

Chaumont I (December 23, 1944), 1–4, 109–42, *113,* 228, 229, 231, 263, 329

Chaumont II (December 25, 1944), 261, 262–77, *264,* 294, 295, 313

Churchill, Thomas G., 96, 105–6

Churchill, Winston, 10

civilians, vii, viii, 66–67, 87–88, 109–10, 155, 156, 203, 218–19, 225–28, 234, 235, 266–67

Clark, Edward H., 152

"Cobra King," 309, 310, 312, 313, 315

Coffy, Herman, 151–52

Cohen, Harold, **5,** 94, 95, 125, 137, 138, 142, 242, 263, 265

Combat Command A (CCA), 324, 330

American response, 62, 63–64, 72–75

Assenois, 294, 295, 307

Bigonville, 230, 233

Chaumont, 142, 265

first contact, 79–82, 84–85, 88–91, 92, 94, 102, 103, 104, 106

Tintange, 240, 242–43, 245, 248, 249–51, 252, 253, 257, 259–61, 295
  Warnach, 176–77, 189, 190–92, 193–202, 208, 231
Combat Command B (CCB), 324
  American response, 56, 63, 64–66, 73, 74
  Assenois, 281, 294, 295, 296, 313–14
  Bastogne, Belgium, 235
  Bigonville, 232
  Chaumont I, 2, 111–12, 117, 120–22, 126–27, 128, 136
  Chaumont II, 231, 261, 263, 268–76, 277, 295, 296
  first contact, 94–98, 99, 103, 106–7, 108, 109
  Warnach, 176, 177
Combat Command Reserve (CCR), 329, 330
  American response, 63, 73, 74
  Assenois, 278–79, 281, 283, 288–92, 293, 294, 295–98, 304, 307–23, 313–14
  Bigonville, 203, 208, 211, 217, 231, 232–33, 239
  first contact, 96, 104–6
  Flatzbourhof, 142, 143–44, 146–48, 149–50, 153–55, 157–60, 168–69, 172, 173, 174, 175, 329–30
  Warnach, 176, 177
command and control superiority (U.S.), 326
commanders superiority (U.S.), 62–63, 72, 95–96, 101, 105, 144, 146, 147, 330
communication system advantage (U.S.), 157, 158, 307, 326
Connaughton, George W., 5, 231, 243–44, 244–45, 247, 251, 260
Connor, Robert, 262, 270–72, 275
Conrardy, Nicholas, 227
Cook, Rob, 221
Cooke, Thomas J., 150, 203–4, 310–11, 314
Cummings, Robert S., 71
Cygan, Don, vii–viii

Dager, Holmes E., 5, 63, 64, 65, 73, 94–95, 96, 142, 262, 263, 276, 330
Damiano, Matteo, 126, 130, 138, 327–28
Danahy, Paul A., 294
Day, Robert H., 119
Dayton, Dello G., 242
D-day, 12, 70
Devers, Jacob L., 57, 58, 60

DiBattista, John J., 96–97, 97–98, 106, 107
Dickerman, Milton, 310, 315
Dickson, Benjamin "Monk," 38–39
Distinguished Service Cross recipient, 139
Distinguished Service Medal recipient, 52
Donahue, Richard, 297
Donaldson, James R., 82, 84, 85, 90–91, 189
"doughboys," 154
Dwight, William, 146, 147, 149–50, 150–51, 152, 153–55, 157–60, 162–63, 163–64, 203, 212, 214–15, 216, 222, 223, 297, 307, 308, 309, 311, 312, 313, 315, 316–17, 318, 319, 330

EAGLE MAIN, 57, 58–61
EAGLE TAC, 51, 56, 57
Earnest, Herbert L., 5, 62, 64, 72, 73–77, 81, 104, 176, 177, 182, 184, 230, 233, 240, 242, 243, 244, 259, 260–61, 330
Ebel, Ferdinand, 6, 114, 115, 267, 281–82, 292, 293
Eddy, Manton, 7, 63
Ehrich (German), 6, 282
Ehrig (German), 287–88
Eighth Air Force (U.S.), 70, 327
8th Tank Battalion "Eight Ballers" (U.S.), 328, 330
  American response, 64, 73
  Bigonville, 232
  Chaumont I, 1–4, 5, 111–12, 118–19, 120, 124–26, 128–30, 134, 137–42
  Chaumont II, 262–63, 265–66, 268–70, 269, 272–73, 275–76
  first contact, 94, 96, 98, 106, 108–9
80th Infantry Division (U.S.), 7, 58, 60, 68, 73, 231, 244, 327
Eisenhower, Dwight D., 1, 53, 54, 56, 57, 58–61, 68, 231, 328
11th Fallschirmjäger Sturmgeschütz Brigade, 25, 26, 32, 137–38
English, Samuel K., 138
Erdmann, Roy G., 141, 263, 269, 271
Ezell, Bert P., 65, 66

fallschirmjägers, 23, 30, 74, 85, 114, 115, 206–7, 236–37, 238, 274, 283, 285, 326, 327. See also specific fallschirmjäger divisions and regiments
Fegan, Forrest H., 305

Fenchel, Bruce, 1–2, 3, 4, 117, 118–19, 266–67, 277
Fire Direction Center (FDC), U.S., 100, 120–21, 126–27, 269, 310–11, 326
5th Fallschirmjäger Division, viii, **6**, 61. *See also* Battle of the Bulge; Siege of Bastogne; *specific fallschirmjäger regiments*
American response, 42–45, *44*, 48–50
Assenois, 288, 301
Chaumont I, 112, 114–16, 122–24, 127–28, 129, 133, 134–35, 137–38, 139, 140–41, 142
first contact, 76–79, 82
Flatzbourhof, 151, 173
4th Armored Division (U.S.) vs., 3–4, 75, 122, 134–35, 176, 206, 208
German plan, 23, 29–35
inexperience of, 24, 25, 26, 27, 49–50, 329
mobility problems, 26, 27, 77, 326, 327
profiteering scheme, 26
Tintange, 236–40, 257–58, 261, 282
veteran officers of, 26, 30, 31, 50, 329–30
5th Fallschirmjäger Pioneer Battalion, **6**, 26, 31, 32, 79, 116, 233–34, 238, 260
Fifth Panzer Army, 13, 14, 20, 27, 32, 34, 35, 62, 77, 135, 293
15th Fallschirmjäger Regiment, **6**, 329–30
American response, 43, 45–48, 50
Assenois, 301–2
Bigonville, 207, 208, 209–11, 219–20, 223–26, 282
Chaumont I, 122, 123
first contact, 77, 85–86, 91–94
Flatzbourhof, 148–49, 153, 156–57, 160–62, 165–68, 170–72
German plan, 26, 30, 31, 32, 34, 40–41
Tintange, 238, 239–40, 246–47, 252–53, 254–57
Warnach, 177, 179–80, 302
15th Panzergrenadier Division, 277, 283–85, 288, 292, 299–300
51st Armored Infantry Battalion (U.S.), 72, 85, 88–89, 90, 94, 176–77, 181, 182–89, 190–91, 193–94, 198–202, 240, 242–43, 259, 260, 324
53rd Armored Infantry Battalion (U.S.), 105, 106, 144, 147, 150, 158, 204, 213, 278,

279, 289, 290–92, 295, 296, 298, 308, 312, 317–18, 319–23
First Army (U.S.), 15, 37, 38, 39, 40, 54, 56, 57, 58
first contact (December 22, 1944), 76–110, *83*
First World War, 12, 18, 24, 36, 39, 52, 101
Fishler, Bennet, 125, 129, 141
Fitzpatrick, John, 151, 212
Flatzbourhof, 66, 79, 81, 82, 85, 86–88, 91, 105
Flatzbourhof (December 23, 1944), 143–75, *145*, 206, 329–30
Foreman, Prentiss, 265
Fortney, Guy, 121
Foster, William B. "Street Cleaner," 136
4th Armored Division "Patton's Best," **5, 7**. *See also* Battle of the Bulge; Siege of Bastogne; *specific armored field artillery battalions, armored infantry battalions, cavalry squadrons, combat commands, engineer battalions, infantry regiments, and tank battalions*
American response, 58, 60, 61–63, 65, 73
Assenois, 294–95, 306–7
bravery of, 94, 100, 125, 130, 138–39, 146, 147, 184, 187, 188, 212, 248, 249, 273, 274, 316, 330–31
Chaumont, 1–4, 134–35, 136, 329
5th Fallschirmjäger Division vs., 3–4, 75, 122, 134–35, 176, 206, 208
reputation of, 62
14th Fallschirmjäger Regiment, **6**, 25, 32, 33, 43, 49–50, 74, 77, 108, 112, 114–16, 267–68, 276, 281–83, 288, 289, 292, 297, 330
408th Volks Artillery Corps, 93, 116, 208, 268, 282, 297
Fox, Don M., 63
France/French, 12, 15, 16, 18, 24, 26, 31, 39, 54–55, 57, 58, 62, 64, 131
Franzke (German), 48, 170
fratricide, viii, 216–17, 291, 313–14, 314–15
Fredendall, Lloyd, 53
Friebe (German), 282
Friedel, Erwin, 234
Führer-Begleit-Brigade, 78–79, 240, 302
FW-190s (German), 127, 304, 305, 306

Gaffey, Hugh J., **5, 7,** 325
  American response, 63, 65, 72–73, 75
  Bigonville, 204, 229–31, 231–32,
    232–33, 235
  Chaumont, 122, 261, 281
  first contact, 101, 102, 103, 104, 105
  Flatzbourhof, 146, 148
Gardner, Glenn, **5,** 262, 263, 265, 269,
    273, 276
Gause, Alfred, 13
Gay, Hobart R., 61
Gaydos, Albert, 79–80, 80–81, 182, 183
Gaydos, Paul, 80
Geneva Convention, 168, 179
German army, 326. *See also* Battle of the
    Bulge; Siege of Bastogne; *specific*
    fallschirmjäger divisions and regiments,
    fusilier regiments, panzergrenadier
    divisions and regiments, and
    volksgrenadier divisions
  advance detachment, 33
  artillery lacking, 116, 326
  assumptions about U.S., 16–17, 20, 21–22
  blitzkrieg, 326
  brutality of soldiers, viii, 88, 227
  casualties, 48, 49, 55, 93, 152, 153, 155, 160,
    167, 169, 171, 172, 173, 201, 210, 233–34,
    238, 254, 261, 292, 296, 321, 323
  Chaumont, 111–12, 117, 130–35
  command and control capabilities
    lacking in, 326
  first contact, 80
  German plan, 9–41, *11*
  inexperience, 15, 22, 24, 25–26, 27, 38,
    49–50, 78, 115, 157, 206, 207, 236,
    286, 329–30
  kindness of, viii, 48, 68, 88, 225–26,
    234, 235
  "last chance in a Game of Hazard," 9, 30
  massing vs. spreading combat power,
    34–35
  mobility problems, 26, 27, 41, 77, 123,
    134, 135, 207, 239, 326, 327, 329
  morale of, 38, 85, 114, 179, 207, 252, 268,
    292, 327
  night assaults, 28–29, 184, 231
  Patton as most pressing issue, 21–22, 34
  readiness rate of tank battalions, 328
  resistance, bypassing, 29, 34, 45

  surprise importance for, 14, 16, 23, 35
  tank destroyer battalions, 20, 329
  wounded soldiers, left behind, 41, 48
  X-day (day of attack), 33, 37, 40, 42
Giallanza, Tony, 129
Gilson, Robert, 165
Girls' Normal School, 101, 107, 121,
    192, 229
Glenn, Lumpkin, 129
Gniot, Charles C., **5,** 139
Goble, William F., 151
Goering, Hermann, 124
Goerke, Gordon D., **5,** 244, 245
Grady, Joseph F., 244
Granatwerfer 12cm mortars, 115, 121, 157,
    207, 236, 237, 238, 249–50, 258, 284,
    286, 292
Grant, Richard K., 228–29
Great Britain, 10, 14, 16, 58
Green, Raymond E., 108–9, 328
Green, Walter E., **5,** 182, 183, 259,
    260–61
Greif, Rolf, 233, 234
Gröschke, Kurt, **6,** 26, 30–31, 32, 50, 77,
    78, 86, 93, 122, 177, 179, 238, 330
Gross, Ludwig, 283, 284–85, 299, 300
Groten (German), **6,** 112, 114
Guild, Donald E., 164, 166
Gurrell, Ford, 184, 186, 188
Gustin, Lozet-Maria, 109–10, 267

Hafner, Harold, 310
Harmon (American), 174, 175
Harvey, Julia Berthe (Abrams's wife), 144
Heath, Irving M., 306–7, 328
Heide (German), **6,** 79
Heilmann, Ludwig, **6,** 9, 23–25, 26–27,
    28–30, 31–35, 43, 49–50, 76, 78–79,
    112, 115–16, 122–24, 173, 177, 206,
    208, 261, 326
Hendrix, James R. "Red," 320–21,
    322–23, 331
Hitler, Adolf, 9–10, 12, 13–14, 16, 30, 54,
    84, 124, 134, 293, 324. *See also* German
    army
Hodges, Courtney, 39
Holland, Russell, 151, 152
Höllander (German), 32
Holmes, Jack, 172–73

Hueske, Edward E., 244
Hyden, Eugene, 185–86, 188

III Corps (U.S.), 7, 102, 327. *See also*
    American army; 80th Infantry Division;
    4th Armored Division; 26th Infantry
    Division
    American response, 57, 58, 60, 65, 66,
        68, 70
    Bigonville, 216, 228, 229–33
    Chaumont, 121–22, 263
    first contact, 101–4, 107–8
    Tintange, 244, 254
    Warnach, 192–93
inexperience (German), 15, 22, 24, 25–26,
    27, 38, 49–50, 78, 115, 157, 206, 207,
    236, 286, 329–30
infantry divisions (U.S.), 2, 229. *See also*
    specific divisions
intelligence advantage (U.S.), 23, 28, 35–36,
    38, 107–8, 112, 114–15, 116, 162–63,
    252, 302, 327
Iron Cross recipients, 18, 19, 234
Irzyk, Albin F., 5, 329, 330
    American response, 64, 65, 66
    Chaumont I, 2, 3, 4, 111, 114, 117, 118,
        120, 124–26, 128–29, 130, 134, 137,
        139–42
    Chaumont II, 262–63, 265–66, 268,
        269–70, 272, 273, 275–76
    first contact, 94, 95–96, 98, 100,
        106–7, 108
    Tintange, 242

"jabos," 124, 132, 133, 254, 255, 300
Japanese bombing of Pearl Harbor, 53, 95
Jaques, George L., 5, 105, 147, 150, 155, 160,
    169, 204, 206, 213, 278, 295, 307,
    308, 317
Jeffries, Kenneth B., 152
Jodl, Alfred, 27

Kane, George W., 248–49
Kaplin, Walter P., 212
Kaufmann, Walter, 135, 285, 286, 301
Kettel, Paul, 86–88, 156
Kieley, Leonard H., 125, 139, 263, 271
Kingsley, John "Buck," 189
Kirkman, Rex O., 5, 265, 276

Kitze, Alfred, 6, 179, 180, 301–2
Klemment, Conrad, 330
    American response, 43, 45–46, 47–48
    Bigonville, 209, 210–11
    first contact, 85–86, 91–92, 93
    Flatzbourhof, 148–49, 153, 155, 156–57,
        160, 161–62, 165–68, 170, 171, 172
    German plan, 40–41
    Tintange, 236, 239, 246, 247, 254–57
Klouker, Wilhelm, 284, 292, 299, 300
Knabe (German), 287
Knestrick, Bernard C., 72
Knieß, Baptist, 18, 19–21, 30, 43, 50, 77, 78
Knight's Cross recipients, 12, 13, 18, 24,
    31, 131
Koch, Adolf, 6, 206
Koch, Oscar, 35–36, 36–38, 39–40, 51,
    57–58, 327
Kokott, Heinz, 130–35, 287, 293, 294, 301,
    302, 303
Konev, Ivan, 325
Kosiek, Stanley M., 138
Kraemer, Fritz, 13
Krebs, Hans, 13, 14, 15
Kunkel, Rolf, 132
Kutak, Frank R., 5, 291, 308

L-4 Piper Cubs (U.S.), 116, 120, 149, 150,
    161, 162–63, 171, 294
Lambay-Chênet Woods, 4, 119, 263,
    265–66, 267, 268, 271, 272, 273,
    275, 276
Lange, Horst, 6, 92, 149, 208, 219–20
Laughlin, Joe, 127
Law, Richard D., 135–36
Leach, James H., 330
    Assenois, 296, 298, 308, 313
    Bigonville, 204, 208, 212–13, 214, 215,
        216–17, 221
    Flatzbourhof, 147, 150, 151, 152–53, 154,
        155, 157–58, 159, 160, 162, 168,
        169, 174
Lead Platoon, Dog Company, 8th Tank
    Battalion, 1–4, 118–19, 144
Leaphart, Bill, 303, 304
LIII Corps (German), 19, 20, 77, 78–79,
    239, 240
Lipscomb, Howard V., 319–20
Listl, Johann, 234, 235

Long Tom howitzers (U.S.), 99–100, 116, 209, 233, 240, 310, 311

Lucas, William, 184, 186, 188

Lucero, Celestino E., 273, 274

Luftwaffe, 15, 23, 24, 25, 31, 37, 206, 235, 236, 288, 304, 305, 306, 327, 329

Lutgen, Sophie-Lion, 66–68, 203, 218–19, 226–27

LXXX Corps (German), 18, 19, 20

LXXXV Corps (German), 18, 19, 20, 33, 42, 43, 48, 49, 50, 77, 239

LXXXVII Corps (German), 12, 15

M1A2 tanks (U.S.), 330

M1 Garands (U.S.), 89, 200, 273, 274, 320, 322

M2 machine guns (U.S.), 89, 198, 305, 328

M3 half-tracks (U.S.), 88, 126, 182. *See also specific battles*

M4 Sherman tanks (U.S.). *See also specific battles*

  advantages of, 328, 329

  M4A3E2 Sherman tanks, 141, 309, 310

  M5 Stuart tanks (U.S.) vs., 3, 80, 117, 184, 185, 186

  StuGs vs., 116

  Tiger I tanks (German) vs., 134, 138, 139, 140–41, 142

M7 Howitzer Motor Carriage (U.S.), 99, 183

M8 Greyhounds (U.S.), 86–87

M18 Hellcat Tank Destroyers (U.S.), 74, 141, 279, 329

MacKenzie, Fred, 295

Madison, Harold, 250

Magoffin, Morton, 127

Marshall (American), 111–12, 117

Martelange, 14, 20, 31, 32, 34, 73, 74, 77, 78, 79, 81, 82, *83*, 84, 85, 88–91, 92, 102, 103, 104, 122, 147, 176, 177, 179, 180, 183, 239, 244, 329

Martin, Gerhard, 26, 31, 79, 116, 238

Mayforth (American), 107

McAllister, Reid, **5**, 244, 245, 250, 257

McAuliffe, Anthony C., 235, 294, 295

McBride, Horace L., **7**, 231, 244

McGlamery, Thornton B., 125

McMahon, John T., 212, 213, 214, 215, 216, 217, 218, 221, 222, 223, 289

McNair, Lesley J., 102, 229

McNiff, John J., 271, 273, 274

McVickar, Lansing, 244

Medal of Honor recipients, 330–31

Meier (German), 239

Metzler, Walter, **6**, 206, 207, 208, 209

Meyer, R. H., 310

MG 42s (U.S.), 46, 112, 114, 161, 207, 256, 274, 275, 326

Middleton, Troy, **7**, 37, 56, 64–65, 70, 294–95

Millikin, John, **7**, 57, 58, 60, 68, 101–2, 102–3, 104, 121, 231. *See also* III Corps

mines, 9–10, 33, 34, 106, 116, 163–64, 166, 169, 173, 174, 175, 239, 240, 259, 287, 315, 316, 319

Mitchell, Hal C., 258

mobility

  American army, 41, 88, 117, 326, 327, 328, 329

  German army, 26, 27, 41, 77, 123, 134, 135, 207, 239, 326, 327, 329

Model, Walter, 17, 21

Molitor, Nicholas, 155–56

morale

  American army, 259–60, 294, 327

  German army, 38, 85, 114, 179, 207, 252, 268, 292, 327

Morphew, Max V., 215

"move all night" (December 23, 1944), 1–4

Mulvey, Roscoe M., 320, 322

Murphy, James G., 310

Murphy, Joseph R., 305

Murphy, William J., 248, 249

NICKEL Operation, 61

night assaults (German), 28–29, 184, 231

Ninth Air Force (U.S.), 70, 303–6, 327

94th Armored Field Artillery Battalion (U.S.), 144, 150, 154, 159, 164, 203–4, 211, 278, 290, 310, 311

Nives, 65, 66, 130, 279, 282, 289, 317, 318

Noll, Marcelle, 186, 187–88

Nolte, Eberhard, 283, 284

Normandy, 12, 31, 54, 179, 206, 292–93, 320

No Silent Night: The Christmas Battle for Bastogne (Barron and Cygan), vii–viii

Oden, Delk M., **5,** 72, 74, 75, 91, 92, 180, 181, 182, 183, 184, 189, 242, 330
OKW (German), 15, 16–17, 22, 78–79
Olbon, Clay, 73
101st Airborne Division "Screaming Eagles" (U.S.), viii, 2, 4, 56, 62, 64–65, 70, 84, 97, 131, 133, 231, 235, 260, 263, 278, 281, 284, 288, 294–95, 302, 303, 308, 309, 315–16, 318, 324
104th Panzergrenadier Regiment, 277, 283–85, 288, 292, 299–300
177th Field Artillery Battalion (U.S.), 106, 159, 210, 233, 290, 311
188th Engineers (U.S.), 173–75, 176, 230
O'Neill, James H., 70, 71
Our River, 19, 20, 22–23, 27, 28, 31, 32, 33, 34, 39, 42, 45, 50, 58, 70, 73, 123, 131, 179, 206, 238, 286, 287

P-47 Thunderbolts "Jugs" (U.S.), 127, 132, 133, 135, 136, 209, 216, 217, 228, 234, 238–39, 245, 253, 296, 300, 305–6, 307, 327
Palmer, Bruce, Sr., 105
Palmer, Marcella, 105
panzerfausts, 3, 27, 85, 86, 89, 115, 119, 149, 157, 160, 166, 170, 172, 180, 207, 212, 217, 221, 222, 238, 246, 255, 256, 268, 269, 282, 291, 309, 322
Panzer Lehr Division, 37, 61, 122, 132
panzerschrecks, 26, 115, 157, 180, 181, 184, 197, 207, 238, 253, 258, 267–68, 269, 282, 286, 309
Park, John H., 151, 152, 153
Parker, Robert, **5,** 278, 279, 311
Pattison, Hal C., 176, 177, 307–8
Patton, George S., III "Old Blood and Guts," **7.** *See also* American army; Battle of the Bulge; 4th Armored Division; Siege of Bastogne; Third Army
Abrams and, 105
background of, 51–55
Beatrice Ayer (Patton's wife), 52
Bradley and, 51, 55–56, 56–57, 58, 59–60
Bulge planning meeting, 57, 58–60, 61
"But what the hell, we'll still be killing Krauts.", 42, 57
Christmas greeting for the troops, 259
confidence in staff, 36, 38, 327

Eisenhower and, 1, 53, 54, 57, 58, 59, 60, 328
first contact, 101, 102–4
France combat experience, 36, 94, 293
Germans, Patton as concern, 21–22, 34
"In this operation we must be the utmost ruthless.", 76
"I want Bastogne by 1350.", 111, 121
Koch (Oscar) and, 36, 37–38, 39
Lucky 6 (Patton's radio call sign), 121
micromanaging commanders by, 102–3, 121
morale of troops boosted by, 259–60
POZIT (proximity-fused artillery shell), 209–10
promise kept by, 324
religious belief of, 70–71
slapping soldiers incidents, 53–54
soldiers' respect and trust of, 101, 327–28
tank advocate, 52–53, 55, 59
villages to be avoided, 229
"Xmas Eve present coming up, Hold on.", 235
Patton, George S., Jr. (Patton's father), 52
Patton, William P., 139
Paul, Willard, **7,** 230
Pearl Harbor bombing by Japanese, 53, 95
Pearson, Drew, 54
Pearson, Robert E., 120
Peischer (German), 79
Pershing, John J. "Black Jack," 36, 52
Peterson, Eric L., 259–60
Peterson, Howard, 190
Petrikat, Rudolf, **6,** 25, 207, 215
Phase Line "Red" at H-hour, 73, 74–75
Phillips, James, 102, 121–22, 230–31, 231–32, 233
Piper Cubs "Lame Ducks" (U.S.), 116, 120, 149, 150, 161, 162–63, 171, 294
Pound, W. King, 185–86, 188
POZIT (proximity-fused artillery shell), 209–10
Price, Paul F., 130–31
Prigge, Hans, 238–39
Purple Heart recipients, 188
Putnam, Roscoe S., 274

Rabe (German), 287
radio communications (U.S.), 157, 158, 307, 326

Rapp, Edward, 183–84, 185, 186–87, 187–88
Raube (German), 115
readiness rate of tank battalions, 328
reconnaissance units (U.S.), 86–87, 147
Red Cross, 167
Remichampagne, 134, 279, 282, 284, 288, 295–98, 299, 301
Remoiville, 114, 130, 267, 279, 282, 283, 288, 290, 291, 310
Richter, Heinz, **6**, 239
Ridley, John S., 80, 181, 182, 183, 184, 260
Riedel, Paul, 26
Ries, Guy, 227
Robert, William, 65
Romig, Raymond L., 80, 182, 183
Rommel, Erwin, 53
"Roosevelt's Highest Paid Butchers," 62. *See also* 4th Armored Division
Rothkirch und Trach, Edwin Graf, 18–19, 20
Rowland, Ralph, 165, 212
Royal Air Force (RAF), 10, 58, 327
Rudder, James E., 43, 45, 48–49
Russia/Russians (Soviet Union), 16, 31, 34, 40, 48, 93, 131, 283, 285, 325

Saint-Hubert Woods, 20, 27, 31, 32, 127, 129, 263, 265
Sallee, Ralph L., 305
Santner, John S., **5**, 244, 245
Sauer River, 19, 20, 58, 70, 73–74, 78, 84, 90, 96, 97, 98, 103, 106, 176, 177, 210, 211, 245, 246
Saxe (German), **6**, 207
Scanlon, John Henry, 244
Schimmel, Arno, **6**, 25, 32, 49–50, 77, 78, 112, 114, 116, 267
Schmidt (German), 114
Scholz, Günther, 282
Schroder, Josef, 223–26
Schultz, Otto, **6**, 244
Schwarz, Max, **6**, 282
Schweda (German), 287
Sears, Hayden A., 96
Seay, Stedman, 281
Second World War. *See* World War II
Seventh Army (German), 10, 12, 14, 15, 17–22, 26, 27, 29, 30, 42, 43, 77, 78, 123, 239, 292, 293, 326, 327

Seventh Army (U.S.), 53, 54, 70
776th Field Artillery Battalion (U.S.), 99, 100, 126–27, 262, 310, 311
Sharpe, T. J., 103
Shermans. *See* M4 Sherman tanks (U.S.)
Sibert, Edwin, 35, 36
Sibret, 31, 32, 34, 133, 238, 284, 295, 298, 300, 301, 306, 308, 313
Siege of Bastogne, vii–viii. *See also* American army; Battle of the Bulge; German army
    Assenois (December 25-26, 1944), 268, 278–323, *280*
    Bigonville (December 24, 1944), 203–35, *205*, 239, 278, 282, 329
    Chaumont I (December 23, 1944), 1–4, 109–42, *113*, 228, 229, 231, 263, 329
    Chaumont II (December 25, 1944), 261, 262–77, *264*, 294, 295, 313
    end of, 315–16, 323
    first contact (December 22, 1944), 76–110, *83*
    Flatzbourhof (December 23, 1944), 143–75, *145*, 206, 329–30
    "move all night" (December 23, 1944), 1–4
    101st Airborne Division "Screaming Eagles," viii, 2, 4, 56, 62, 64–65, 70, 84, 97, 131, 133, 231, 235, 260, 263, 278, 281, 284, 288, 294–95, 302, 303, 308, 309, 315–16, 318, 324
    terrain impact on, 84, 88–89, 112, 139, 147, 179, 215, 244, 247, 263, 291, 309
    Tintange (December 24-25, 1944), 123, 233, 236–61, *241*, 282, 295, 329
    Warnach, Belgium (December 23-24, 1944), 176–202, *178*, 208, 229, 231, 233, 239, 240, 242, 243, 246–47, 261, 302, 329
    weather impact on, 79, 123, 135–36, 147, 181, 184, 228
Siegfried Line, 12, 70, 229, 325
Silver Star recipients, 94, 100, 138, 139, 146, 212, 248, 249, 273, 274, 316
Singleton, John R., **5**, 265, 268
Sixth Army Group (U.S.), 58, 60
Sixth Panzer Army, 13, 14, 34, 59
66th Armored Field Artillery Battalion (U.S.), 72, 80, 183, 245

Sklar, Fred, 97, 141, 232
slapping soldiers incidents (Patton), 53–54
Sloan, Howard M., 305
Smith, DeWitt C., **5,** 312, 314–15, 319, 320
Smith, Hubert J. J., 310, 312
South, William H., 274
Soviet Union. *See* Russia/Russians
Speer, Albert, 30
Stalin, Joseph, 325
Stalling, Ernest, **5,** 265, 268, 270, 271
Stephenson, Paul H., 125, 129
StG44s (German), 285, 286
Stimson, Henry L., 54
Stoddard, Donald, 228, 229
Strong, Kenneth, 59
Stuart tanks (U.S.), 3, 80, 117, 184, 185, 186
StuGs (German), 4, 26, 86, 116, 119, 120,
    129, 137, 149, 151, 152, 153, 154,
    155, 156, 157, 162, 163, 169, 185,
    208, 268

Talfel (German), 282
tank advocate, Patton, 52–53, 55, 59
tank battalions (U.S.), 144, 242, 328. *See also*
    specific battalions
tank destroyer battalions (U.S.), 72, 74, 103,
    106, 132, 141, 193, 229, 235, 240, 243,
    262, 279, 289, 294, 329
Task Force Alanis, 74–75, 79, 81, 82, 84–85,
    88–91, 243, 259, 260
Task Force Oden, 74, 75, 79–81, 82, 85, 91,
    177, 180–81
Tedder, Arthur, 58
Teller, Karl Heinz, 284
10th Armored Infantry Battalion (U.S.),
    56, 65, 94, 95, 100, 106, 108, 121, 125,
    126, 128–30, 137–42, 262, 263, 265,
    276, 327
terrain impact, 14, 19, 24, 27, 28, 31, 56, 58,
    84, 88–89, 112, 139, 147, 179, 215, 244,
    247, 263, 291, 309
Third Army (U.S.), **7,** 327, 329. *See also*
    American army; Patton, George S., III
    American response, 51, 54, 57–58, 60, 62,
        68, 70–71
    Assenois, 293, 294
    Chaumont I, 121
    first contact, 101, 102, 103
    German plan, 15, 22, 35–40

13th Fallschirmjäger Regiment, **6,** 25–26,
    34, 50, 122, 123, 206–9, 219, 221, 239,
    329, 330
35th Tank Battalion (U.S.), 72, 79–81, 82,
    85, 89, 90, 93, 180–89, 191–92,
    195–98, 242, 243, 245, 249–50, 257,
    259, 260, 328, 330
39th Fusilier Regiment, 135, 285–88, 301, 302
37th Tank Battalion (U.S.), 330
    America response, 73
    Assenois, 279, 289–90, 291, 295–98, 300,
        306–7, 308, 311–12, 312–17, 318–19
    Bigonville, 203–4, 206, 211–18, 220–23
    first contact, 105, 106
    Flatzbourhof, 143, 144, 146, 147, 149,
        150–53, 162–65, 168–69, 169, 172
Thomas (German), 267–68
Thomas, Joseph, 155
318th Infantry Regiment (U.S.), 231, 240,
    243–45, 244, 247–49, 250–51, 252,
    257, 262, 263, 265, 269, 270–72,
    273–75, 276, 327
352nd Volksgrenadier Division, 22–29, 40,
    43, 50, 78, 231
377th Fighter Squadron (U.S.), 296, 305–6
379th Fighter Squadron (U.S.), 127, 297,
    304, 305
362nd Fighter Group "Mogin's Maulers"
    (U.S.), 127, 135–36, 209, 216, 228–29,
    253–54, 305, 306
326th Airborne Engineers (U.S.), 285, 316
327th Glider Infantry Regiment (U.S.),
    235, 294
"Thunderbolt," 168–69, 295, 298, 318–19
Tiger I tanks (German), 134, 137, 138, 139,
    140–41, 142, 328, 329
Tintange (December 24–25, 1944), 123,
    233, 236–61, *241,* 282, 295, 329
Tosi, Albert S., 231, 243–44
training advantage (U.S.), 95–96, 101,
    105, 329, 330
Trover, Charles U., 147, 159, 163, 165, 166,
    168, 169, 204
Truman, Harry S., 331
Twelfth Army (U.S.), 15–16, 35, 38, 39, 51,
    54, 56, 58–61
22nd Armored Field Artillery Battalion
    (U.S.), 99–100, 120–22, 126–27, 128,
    141, 262, 270, 310, 311

24th Engineers (U.S.), 72, 98, 106, 279

25th Cavalry Reconnaissance Squadron (U.S.), 86–87, 147

25th Cavalry Squadron (U.S.), 3, 74, 81–82, 85, 91–92, 94, 96–98, 99, 106–7, 130, 155, 180, 232, 233, 262, 290

26th Infantry Division (U.S.), 7, 56–57, 58, 60, 68, 73, 104, 230, 232, 239, 242

26th Volksgrenadier Division, 40, 61, 130–35, 235, 283, 285–88, 293, 300, 301–2

28th Infantry Division (U.S.), 19–20, 28, 38–39, 43, 70, 77

253rd Armored Field Artillery Battalion (U.S.), 99, 100, 127–28, 262, 270, 310, 311

Urth, Nicholas, 227

U.S. Army Air Force, 51, 123–24, 132, 305. *See also specific air forces*

Vaux-lez-Rosières, 31, 32, 34, 64, 267, 279, 282, 289, 299, 300

Vianden, 19, 27–28, 31, 32, 34, 43, 49, 50, 66, 238

VIII Corps (U.S.), 7, 37, 38, 40, 60, 61, 64, 65, 70, 235, 252, 294, 295

Villa, Pancho, 52

Virginia Military Institute (VMI), 51, 52

Voigt-Ruscheweyh, Werner, 17, 21

volksgrenadier divisions, 25, 285–86, 326. *See also specific divisions*

von Gersdorff, Rudolph-Christoph Freiherr, 9–10, 12–15, 16, 17–18, 22, 27

von Lüttwitz, Heinrich Freiherr, 292–93

von Manteuffel, Hasso, 135, 293

von Rothkirch, Edwin Graf, 76, 77, 78

von Rundstedt, Gerhard, 38, 51, 56

von Stauffenberg, Claus, 10

von Tresckow, Henning, 12

Wahl, Goswin, **6,** 25, 206, 207, 208

Walker, Walton, **7,** 70

Walling, Herman, 163, 164, 166

Warnach (December 23-24, 1944), 176–202, *178,* 208, 229, 231, 233, 239, 240, 242, 243, 246–47, 261, 302, 329

weather impact, 14, 23, 27, 51, 63, 70, 71, 79, 123, 135–36, 147, 181, 184, 228

Webster, Duane, 278, 316

Wehrmacht, 22, 24–25, 37, 38, 82, 122, 123, 131, 137, 229, 234, 246, 254, 255, 287, 293, 300, 305, 324, 325, 326, 327

Wellinghoff, Edmund A., 276

Wenden (German), 268

West, Art, 95

Westmoreland, William, 330

West Point, 52, 58, 101, 105

West Wall, 15, 16, 23, 31, 33, 62

Whitehill, John A., 147, 159, 162, 163, 164–65, 166, 168, 204, 212, 213–14, 216, 217–18, 220, 221, 222, 298, 308, 311–12, 313

Wiedorfer, Paul J., 275, 331

Williams, Barton T., 305

Williams, Orie, 249–50, 328

Willie Pete (WP), 120, 121

Wilson, Ruth (Patton's mother), 52

Wilson, Woodrow, 52

Wiltz, 31, 32, 34, 50, 61, 77, 86, 90, 179, 233, 238

Wintzer, Bernd, 33

Winzker, Kurt, 284, 299–300

Withers, William P., 62, 63

Wood, John S., 63, 96

Woods, F., 212, 216, 222

Worch, Alfred, 236, 237, 257, 258

World War I, 12, 18, 24, 36, 39, 52, 101

World War II, 3, 18, 19, 36, 53, 325. *See also* American army; Battle of the Bulge; German army; Siege of Bastogne

Wright, Ben, 294

Wright, Eugene, 306

Wrolson, Walter, 309, 310

X-day (day of attack by Germany), 33, 37, 40, 42

XII Corps (U.S.), **7,** 36, 68, 70, 73

XIX Tactical Air Command (U.S.), 70

XX Corps (U.S.), **7,** 70

XXIII/XXIX Corps (German), 18

XXXXVII Panzer Corps (German), 70, 130–31, 131–32, 292–93, 300, 301

Yaremchuk, John, 152–53

Young, John P., 313

Zhukov, Georgy, 325

ABOUT THE AUTHOR

Leo Barron works for General Dynamics as an instructor of military intelligence officers for the U.S. Army. He holds undergraduate and graduate degrees in history and has served with the 101st Airborne. Barron has seen two tours of active duty in Iraq as an infantry and intelligence officer. His articles about Bastogne and other WWII-related military topics have appeared in *Infantry Magazine*, *Military Intelligence Professional Bulletin*, *WWII History Magazine*, and *WWII Magazine*. He has used some of his research on Bastogne and the Christmas battle to teach his students about intelligence preparation of the battlefield.

CONNECT ONLINE

nosilentnight.com
cobraking1944.com